QMC 338095 b

a30213 003380956b

DATE DUE FOR RETURN

D0311907

EDUCATION
AND
ECONOMIC
DEVELOPMENT

EDUCATION
AND
ECONOMIC
DEVELOPMENT

EDITED BY

C. ARNOLD ANDERSON and MARY JEAN BOWMAN

ALDINE Publishing Company / *Chicago*

156314
HD 82

This volume is the outgrowth of a conference on
The Role of Education in the Early Stages of Development
Chicago, April 4-6, 1963
sponsored by

THE COMMITTEE ON ECONOMIC GROWTH
Social Science Research Council

and

THE COMPARATIVE EDUCATION CENTER
University of Chicago

Copyright © 1965 by Aldine Publishing Company
All rights reserved

First published 1965 by
ALDINE Publishing Company
529 South Wabash Avenue
Chicago, Illinois 60605

Library of Congress Catalog Card Number 65-12453
Designed by David Miller
Printed in the United States of America

Third Printing 1971

QUEEN MARY
COLLEGE
LIBRARY

Initial versions of the papers in this volume were presented at the conference on The Role of Education in the Early Stages of Development, held in Chicago on April 4-6, 1963. The conference was sponsored jointly by the Committee on Economic Growth of the Social Science Research Council and the Comparative Education Center of the University of Chicago.

PARTICIPATING MEMBERS OF THE COMMITTEE ON ECONOMIC GROWTH OF THE
SOCIAL SCIENCE RESEARCH COUNCIL

Simon Kuznets, *Chairman*
Harvard University
Richard Hartshorne
University of Wisconsin
Bert T. Hoselitz
University of Chicago
    Paul Webbink

Wilbert E. Moore
Princeton University
Neil J. Smelser
University of California
Joseph J. Spengler
Duke University
Social Science Research Council

PARTICIPANTS FROM THE COMPARATIVE EDUCATION CENTER

C. Arnold Anderson, *Director*
University of Chicago
Philip J. Foster
University of Chicago

Mary Jean Bowman
University of Chicago
Robert J. Havighurst
University of Chicago

OTHER CONTRIBUTORS AND PARTICIPANTS

W. H. G. Armytage
Sheffield University, England
Gary S. Becker
Columbia University
Rudolph C. Blitz
Vanderbilt University
Robert I. Crane
Duke University
Tom E. Davis
Cornell University
Nicholas DeWitt
Indiana University
Otis Dudley Duncan
University of Michigan
Richard A. Easterlin
University of Pennsylvania
Richard S. Eckaus
Massachusetts Institute of Technology
Torsten Hägerstrand
Lund University, Sweden
W. Lee Hansen
University of California, Los Angeles
Arnold C. Harberger
University of Chicago
Frederick Harbison
Princeton University
Arcadius Kahan
University of Chicago

Harvey Leibenstein
University of California, Berkeley
Jacob Mincer
Columbia University
Arthur T. Mosher
Agricultural Development Council
Kenneth L. Neff
United States Office of Education
Douglass C. North
University of Washington
Harbert Passin
Columbia University
William J. Platt
Stanford Research Institute
Albert J. Reiss
University of Michigan
Simon Rottenberg
University of Buffalo
Irwin T. Sanders
Ford Foundation
Theodore W. Schultz
University of Chicago
George J. Stigler
University of Chicago
Richard J. Storr
University of Chicago
Clifton R. Wharton, Jr.
Agricultural Development Council

PREFACE

The task of editing and reorganizing the chapters that make up this volume has proven both difficult and challenging. The conference itself was exploratory on many fronts. Contributors include historians, economists, sociologists, educators and geographers. Moreover, there are marked differences in approaches even within some of these disciplines. In the end we decided upon a reorganization that included breaking up our own contributions and that of Kahan into several parts, and we thank Kahan for permission to do this. While such a procedure may conceal some of the threads that bound the parts of a particular article together, we hope that it has the more than compensating advantage of making more visible some of the links among contributions of different authors. It is with the same intent that we opted in favor of editorial introductions to each of the main parts of the volume rather than a longer editorial preface; these introductions include remarks on the tenor of discussions at the conference.

Each of the four main groupings of chapters in this volume might be viewed as a clustering around a vector in the web of interrelationships whose center is in the intersections of "education" and "economic development." In Part I the emphasis is upon market pricing and market processes as the framework for analysis of investment in human resource formation and its contributions to the economy. The conventional neoclassical economics that characterizes most of the discussions in this cluster recurs in later papers also, but moving through the volume, emphasis becomes progressively more sociological, more historical, and more "dynamic." Part II brings all disciplines to bear upon the analysis of processes and loci of the formation of human competencies. The common theme of the diverse contributions grouped in Part III is the analysis of patterns and processes in the diffusion of schooling, technologies, and educational opportunity. Finally, the last part of the book points the most directly of all to the evidence of history as it illuminates questions concerning human factor preconditions of development and the pace of change. Easterlin's note adds some interesting data and contributes an economic historian's reaction to the conference as a whole.

One of the major purposes in planning this conference was the stimulation and encouragement of inquiry and analysis of relations between education and development in more historical perspective than is usually the case. A twin purpose was to further interchange between economists and sociologists and between historians and social scientists generally in the analysis of problems that indisputably lie at neglected points of intersection of the areas of concern of these various disciplines. Such an undertaking always runs into obstacles in our minds, for we all wear one or another set of blinders, and often we approach each other's disciplines with some degree of prejudice. Some readers will undoubtedly go through this volume looking for contributions of core interest within their own disciplinary frameworks only; we believe they will find such contributions. However, a volume of contributions so diverse in approach should encourage at least some readers to make the effort that is necessary to seek out challenges that colleagues with other ways of thinking and kinds of evidence may bring to bear upon problems of common interest. These will not necessarily be the same as the challenges that we see. Since it was quite impossible for us to avoid imposing our own orientations and interpretations, we decided we might as well do so deliberately and knowingly. The editorial prefaces and even the organization of the various chapters as they are located in this book inevitably incorporate our ways of looking at it.

Each and all of the members of the Committee on Economic Growth of the Social Science Research Council played an active part in planning the conference that gave rise to this volume. Though none is to be blamed for our editorial biases or defects, we owe all a debt. Particular thanks for their help throughout are due to Simon Kuznets and Wilbert Moore, and also to that unassuming but indispensable and judicious counselor of many such undertakings, Paul Webbink.

Finally, a very special acknowledgement is due to Bert Hoselitz, who was our full partner in every aspect of the planning and conduct of the conference from start to finish.

C. Arnold Anderson
Mary Jean Bowman

CONTENTS

EDUCATION
AND
ECONOMIC
DEVELOPMENT

PART I
The Investment View of Human Resources and the Matter of "Shortages"

The four contributions included in Part I exemplify one of the main approaches of modern economists to the analysis of education's place in the economy. All of them use analytical models in which market pricing or market processes are central, though the contribution by Hansen takes the form of a criticism of other approaches that are less analytical. All are concerned with the allocation of resources among alternative investments. This does *not* mean, as some of the non-economists at the conference seemed to believe, that these contributions are "merely normative," or that they are concerned with policy and hence "non-scientific." All have policy relevance, to be sure; and all can be interpreted from a normative point of view. But each is equally relevant in the context of positive economics, independently of any policy or normative connotations.

Kahan's paper (Chapter 1) introduces us to work by Russian statisticians and economists of the late nineteenth and early twentieth centuries in which empirical assessments of contributions of education to economic productivity were attempted. This chapter is several things: It is a brief historical essay on relationships between socioeconomic development and economic thought; it is an example of a rudimentary application of a method that has since been refined; and it provides some rough clues as to the economic significance of education among Russian urban blue-collar and white-collar workers during the period from 1880 to 1925. The Russian Strumilin and his Czarist predecessors (like Harberger in his daring effort for India) assessed the economic productivity effects of schooling on the basis of market income differentials associated with differential schooling attainments of the labor force in a particular time and place.

Harberger's paper (Chapter 2) is path-breaking in that it is the first systematic attempt to estimate and compare, for a country other than the United States, "internal rates of return"

1

to investment in education (human capital) with analogous assessments of returns to investment in physical capital. Despite the very severe limitations of his sample data, Harberger's empirical findings are suggestive and should challenge sociologists and economists alike. However, most readers will probably find the main interest of this chapter to be methodological.

Although Harberger takes into account some deviations from competitive conditions in his empirical estimates of rates of return to investment, the market structure is not his main concern. Leibenstein's contribution (Chapter 3), on the other hand, centers attention on types of deviations from competitive adjustments and on the nature and extent of biases due to ignorance and uncertainty, as they affect allocations of resources to investment in human resource development and to the utilization of human skills in developing countries. This is to focus upon market structure, but even Leibenstein gives no explicit attention to how market structures may change.

Hansen's paper (Chapter 4), unlike the others in Part I, is concerned with shifts of demands and supplies (for teachers) over time. Nevertheless, his approach is essentially similar. Neoclassical market analysis is the main tool he uses in his critique of teacher shortage projections. His analysis indirectly questions many of the simplified projections of manpower "requirements" and supplies that have become internationally popular in the past few years.

Together the chapters in Part I illustrate one of the major vectors that must be understood in an analysis of relationships between education and development. "Process" in this type of analysis is abstracted in a market model that is nonhistorical and timeless; yet it is a critical dimension of what happens throughout time. Structure is partially assumed and partially examined, but the process of change in structure is largely ignored. This methodology becomes partially "dynamized" by repetition of studies like Harberger's, which enable us to compare certain aspects of market structures and their adjustments (and maladjustments) at successive points in time.

That this kind of methodology can deal with only one of the abstracted vectors in the education-development web should be obvious. Paradoxically, the very clarity and lack of ambiguity in the abstractions to which the empirical observations are linked is one reason why the economists who use it and those who start along other vectors often fail to communicate. This conference was no exception. Although there was a fine discussion of the technical aspects of Harberger's paper within the "rate of return" camp, there was little discussion of the substantive implications of his findings or of their degree of reasonableness in the light of what other participants, with other backgrounds, might contribute. Instead, application of the concept of rate-of-return analysis to development problems was vigorously challenged, and as vigorously defended, in a shadow swordplay among protagonists who never made contact. Nevertheless, important links between the vector represented by Part I and others were forged in several of the papers that followed—especially some of those in Part II.

CHAPTER 1

RUSSIAN SCHOLARS AND STATESMEN ON EDUCATION AS AN INVESTMENT

Arcadius Kahan[*]

Awareness of the role of education in national economic progress can be traced in Russia at least back to the eighteenth century. The efforts of Peter the Great to train and educate the Russians, so that commerce and industry would contribute to the military-political strength of the nation, are well known. It may be interesting to note that the main clause in all the contracts with "imported" foreign specialists during the Petrine period was the obligation to train a certain number of Russian nationals in the particular skill or occupation.[1] In addition, education and skill became an important criterion in the formation of, and admittance into, the ruling elite. Thus a general criterion of usefulness and personal merit moderated the considerations of ancestry and class, encouraging increased upward social mobility through education and skill acquisition.

Members of the group of Petrine administrators tried also in the post-Petrine period to exert pressure on the government and private entrepreneurs to continue in a more organized and systematic manner the policies of skill training and education.[2] However, while special skill training was understood by merchants and industrialists to be beneficial, they still refused during the first half of the eighteenth century to accept formal education as a component of an economic development program.[3]

It was in the second half of the eighteenth century that the requirement of education as a vehicle for successful business for the individual, as well

---

[*]*Editor's note:* This part of Kahan's discussion should be considered in relation to other parts of his contribution included elsewhere in this volume. See Part III, Chapters 14 and 15; Part IV, Chapter 19.

1. In fact, the clause was sufficient to relieve the Russians from their obligations under the terms of the contract even when the production performance of the foreigner was satisfactory. This would indicate that the government placed the future value of skill acquisition and substitution of domestic production for imports above the value of the current output.

2. An interesting example of such an attempt is furnished by the proposal of Tatishchev (1734) to the owners of the iron works that they should establish and maintain schools for the children of their skilled employees. This proposal was rejected on the grounds of prohibitive costs and the economic advantage of child labor.

3. In effect, in 1721, various urban communities petitioned the Tsar to exempt merchant children from the obligation to attend the newly established *tsifirnye* schools, explaining that the training for commerce and the direct assistance in family business would suffer as a result of their school attendance. Their request was granted, although probably on other than the above grounds.

as for the state, was recognized. During the 1760's merchants started to petition the government for the establishment of elementary and secondary schools to provide education that would meet the needs of the business community. Although this clamor for education by the merchant class could conceivably be attributed in part to the demonstration effect of "westernization" among the gentry, the arguments used were phrased primarily in terms of economic needs for and advantages from education in the area of commerce.[4]

But the progress of education and skill training was slow during the next hundred years in Russia. The country not only failed to catch up industrially with the West, but, in fact, was falling considerably behind the countries that first went through the various phases of the industrial revolution. It was only after the resounding defeat in the Crimean War and the liberation of the serfs in 1861 that the government embarked upon an active program to provide the overhead capital for subsequent industrialization. It then began to regard industrial development as being of high priority among the national goals. It is therefore no wonder that the spokesman for the governmental industrialization policy, Finance Minister I. A. Vyshnegradskii, became concerned during the 1880's with the level of skill and education of the industrial labor force. He felt that the low levels of skill and education were the chief shortcomings of Russian industry and called for remedial action.[5]

> At the present, the large majority of workers in our industrial establishments do not receive a general education. The on-the-job training is of the most narrow, practical type. They are specifically trained in the industrial plant exclusively for the work to be performed at the particular plant. The lack of general education prevents the workers in most cases from elevating themselves to the level of a conscious and clear understanding of the operations that they perform in their work and thereby downgrades the dignity of the work performed. A barrier to the necessary improvement of industry is therefore erected. . . . Our industry, regardless of all protective tariffs, is involved in a bitter struggle against foreign production in which our competitors can rely upon an element of workers with a relatively high general education and special training. Those workers considerably exceed, both in

4. The most interesting petition was submitted by the head of the urban community in Archangel, Ivan Druzhinin, in 1764. He pointed to the losses suffered by merchants as a result of ignorance: (1) low level of literacy leads to orthographic errors in commercial correspondence which result in incorrect interpretation of orders, directives, etc.; (2) lack of knowledge or arithmetic leads to inability to deal with foreign exchange or foreign weights and measures; (3) lack of knowledge of bookkeeping leads to ignorance about the solvency of the firm or enterprise; (4) lack of knowledge of geography leads to confusion in the area of transportation costs, freight charges, insurance, etc.; (5) the inability to use foreign languages leads to excessive use of Amsterdam firms as middlemen; (6) ignorance of foreign and domestic laws and trade regulations opens many avenues for abuse on the part of government officials to the detriment of the merchants. Only education, the author concluded, could remedy the existing ills. That establishment of schools would provide for "teaching of attitudes that will produce a good merchant and a good citizen" was maintained by Vasilii Krestinin, another contemporary author. See A. A. Kizewetter, "Shkol'nye Voprosy v Dokumentakh XVIII v.," *Istoricheskie Ocherki* (Moscow, 1915), pp. 91ff.

5. "Trudy Vserossiiskogo Torgovo — Promyshlennogo S'ezda 1896 g, v.," *Nizhnem Novgorode*, Vol. VI, vyp. IX (St. Petersburg, 1897), pp. 122-123.

terms of the quality of their products and speed of production, the performance of the uneducated people who constitute the majority of the work force
in our industrial plants, so that our industry has to conduct its struggle against
foreign competition equipped with inferior weapons, and this of course leads
to economic defeats. Because of all these circumstances, both the areas of
general education and of special training of Russian workers call for the most
energetic and urgent measures on the part of the government.

Finance Minister Vyshnegradskii's concern with the level of skill and
education of the Russian industrial labor force in the 1880's both expressed
and stimulated a concern with education as an economic investment of the
society. His pronouncement was soon reflected in a large number of studies,
both empirical and normative, or policy oriented.

An early and probably representative example of the latter is an interesting collection of essays published in 1896 under the general title of *Economic Evaluation of Popular Education*. It contains contributions by I. I.
Yanzhul', A. I. Chuprov and I. N. Yanzhul'.[6] That by I. I. Yanzhul' (which is
still of considerable historical interest) is based upon the assumption that
various "external" stimuli of economic growth (tariffs, subsidies, government
regulations) are less effective than education and training. He invokes the
authority of J. S. Mill, Thomas Brassey, and Alfred Marshall, and provides
empirical data from American experience to argue that the level of productivity of labor in various countries is positively correlated with per capita
expenditures on education and with rates of literacy.[7] The general conclusion of the essays is summarized by the authors as follows: "There are, of
course, many factors impeding the development of the Russian economy, but
the foremost among them is the general illiteracy which distinguishes our
country from all other civilized countries. . . . An increase of labor productivity is the only means to erase poverty in Russia and the best policy to
achieve it is through the spread of education and knowledge."

It was now left for the statisticians and economists to provide the empirical proof for the "normative" judgment, expressed in various pamphlets,
books and articles, that the phenomenon observed in the United States and
other countries was also valid for Russia.

The first study, by L. L. Gavrishchev, dealt with two sample groups of
1,506 and 1,934 workers in Nikolaev, during 1895 and 1896 respectively,
under the title "On the Impact of General Education of Workers upon the
Productivity of Their Labor."[8] Gavrishchev established two facts. First, the
average literacy rate among the skilled workers was 75 per cent, while among

6. *Ekonomicheskaia Otsenka Narodnogo Obrazovania. Ocherki* I. I. Yanzhula, A. I. Chuprova,
I. N. Yanzhuli' (St. Petersburg, 1896). I. I. Yanzhul' was a member of the Russian Academy of
Sciences; Chuprov was a noted statistician.

7. Circular of Information of the Bureau of Education No. 3 (Washington, 1879), and Eighth
Annual Report of the Commissioner of Labor, 1892, *Industrial Education* (Washington, 1893).

8. L. L. Gavrishchev, "O Vlianii Obshchego Obrazovania Rabochikh na Produktivnost' ikh
Truda," Reported in *Ekonomicheskaia Otsenka Narodnogo Obrazovania* (St. Petersburg, 1896),
cit. in footnote, and in *Vtoroi Siezd Russkikh Deiatelei po Tekhnicheskomu i Professional'nomu
Obrazovaniu V. Rossii, 1895–1896 g.* (Moscow, 1898).

TABLE 1

Ranking of Selected Occupations by Rate of Literacy and
Average Daily Wage, 1895–1896

Occupation	Rate of Literacy	Average Daily Wage
Locksmiths and metal workers	1	2
Carpenters	2	1
Battleship construction workers	3	3
Boilermakers	4	5
Blacksmiths	5	4

TABLE 2

Level of Average Daily Wage by Occupation
and Years of Education, 1895–1896
(Illiterate = 100)

	Years of Education								
Occupation	1	2	Home°	3	4	5	6	7	8
Locksmiths	104	101	106	112	116	118	117	119	114
Carpenters	104	107	108	108	109	125	119	103	95
Battleship construction workers	99	105	106	121	123	—	—	—	—
Boilermakers	94	109	106	106	116	103	—	—	—
Blacksmiths	106	108	116	114	113	128	—	—	—
Total, first sample	102	105	107	114	116	119	120	112	110
Total, second sample	102	105	107	114	116	118	120	—	—

°Literacy acquired outside of school. The original ratios were rounded.

the unskilled it was only 49 per cent. Second, he also concluded that for all
age groups the literacy rate of employed skilled workers was above that of
their social environment.[9] From his data, by ranking the main occupations
according the the rate of literacy and average daily wage, we get the relationship shown in Table 1.

A rank correlation is evident, though we cannot assume that literacy is
the major determinant of the wage level. The correlation would have been
improved had yearly instead of daily wages been used, since both carpenters
and boilermakers were most subject to seasonal unemployment. Of even
greater interest is the relationship between the level of education and the
average daily wage within the major occupations represented in Gavrishchev's
sample. Table 2 provides the information in terms of the ratio of wages of
workers with successively more schooling to the average wage of illiterate
workers within each occupation.

9. The comparison was made by surveying the neighborhoods inhabited by the workers.

The usefulness of the data would be considerably increased if the sample could be standardized by age or years of job experience within the broad occupations. Nevertheless, they are suggestive as they stand. Gavrishchev himself concluded on the basis of his studies that the interest of industry demands from the workers an average formal education of about five or six years. He claimed that industrialists prefer expensive (educated) workers over cheap (illiterate) ones because the increment in labor productivity exceeds the increment in wages.

The example given by Gavrishchev's study was followed in two directions: first, the trend to test the wage differential between literate and illiterate workers continued, with standardization for age and sex; second, scholars started to compare the economic effects of education with the effects of job experience and also attempted to calculate the private and social returns to education. Exemplifying the first category of research, S. S. Kolokol'tsov's study of 2,912 weavers in Tver district yielded wage differentials

TABLE 3

Yearly Wages and Percentage of Literacy of Weavers
(Tver District, 1902)

Age (Years)	Wages of Literates as Percentage of Wages of Illiterates		Percentage of Literacy	
	Male Weavers	Female Weavers	Males	Females
18–22	108	107	87	33
23–27	114	121	80	16
28–32	106	106	79	14
33–37	110	—	72	—
38–42	114	—	70	—
43–47	114	—	54	—
48–52	107	—	46	—

TABLE 4

Wage of Literate Textile Workers as Percentage of the Wages
of the Illiterate, 1912

Age Group (Years)	Wage (%)	Age Group	Wage (%)
20–25	115	41–45	132
26–30	122	46–50	135
31–35	129	50 and over	135
36–40	126		

Source: K. M. Kozminikh-Lanin, *Gramotnost' i Zarabotki Fabrichno-Zavodskikh Rabochikh Moskovskoi Gubernii* (Moscow, 1912).

between literate and illiterate workers within particular age groups, as shown in Table 3.[10]

The data and evidence of Gavrishchev and Kolokol'tsov, who both used small samples, were reinforced in a survey by K. M. Kozminikh-Lanin of 69,000 textile workers in the Moscow district in 1912 (Table 4). The data in this survey also showed the change in wage rates between successive age groups for both literate and illiterate workers (Table 5). While for the age group 15-20, wages were approximately equal for literate and illiterate workers (the literate ones received a lower wage in the age group below 15), the rise in wages until the age of 35 was much more rapid for the literate workers, indicating the impact of literacy (or education). The rise in wages for the illiterates virtually ceased at the age of 40, while for the literate workers it continued until the age of 50. The somewhat smaller decrease in wages for the illiterate group after the age of 50 was insufficient to offset the relative "losses" suffered earlier. Although this survey supported some of the general conclusions reached by other authors, the data suffered not only from limitations in the use to which they could be put but also from the concentration in a few industries, determined by their location in Moscow district.

TABLE 5

Percentage Change of Monthly Wage between Successive
Age Groups for Literate and Illiterate Workers, 1912

| Age Group (Years) | Percentage Change | |
	Literate	Illiterate
Under 15	——	——
15 – 20	76.3	47.3
20 – 25	50.9	29.6
25 – 30	18.3	11.9
30 – 35	10.7	4.2
35 – 40	2.1	4.7
40 – 45	4.8	.04
45 – 50	1.6	−.2
50 – 55	−1.5	−1.2
55 – 60	−5.8	−4.8
Over 60	−13.0	−12.3

The relationship between duration of formal education and the level of skill as measured by wage rates is confounded by associated on-the-job learning of skills. It is therefore necessary to distinguish the impact of formal education separately from skill acquisition on the job. The first attempt in the Russian literature to cope with this problem was made by the economists

10. S. S. Kolokol'tsov, *Sviaz Promyslov s Gramotnostiu i Ekonomicheskimi Priznakami, po Dannym Tverskoi Gubernii* (Chernigov, 1912). Cited from Akademia Nauk SSSR, *Ocherki po Istorii Statistiki SSSR* (Moscow, 1960).

TABLE 6

Years of School and Skill Levels in Strumilin's Samples

Physical Workers		White-collar Workers	
Years of School	Skill Level	Years of School	Skill Level
1	115	1−2	100
2	126.5	3−4	120
3	134	5−7	148
4	139.5	8−9	180
5	144	10−12	208
6	147.5	13−18	220

TABLE 7

Wage Level of Various Educational Groups,
Physical Workers in Strumilin's Sample
(No education = 100)

Years of School	Level of Wages	Years of School	Level of Wages
Under 2	124	4	143
2	129	5	148
3	137	6	152

S. G. Strumilin and B. H. Babynin in the early 1920's.[11] In articles that now possess mostly historical interest, Strumilin attempted to calculate the total returns to education, private as well as social. Although his goal was to advocate an investment program in educational facilities, ". . . a more profitable 'capital' investment would be difficult to think of even in a country of such immense possibilities as our Soviet Russia," he argued on the basis of empirical data. He analyzed two samples, one of 2,602 lathe operators (from the year 1919) and the other of 2,307 white-collar workers. Since he was mostly interested in the effect of education, he tried to establish the functional relation between age, job experience, years of formal education, and skills.

Strumilin had for his physical workers sample the following equation coefficients:

$$K = 2.53648 - .002719 (t - 37) - .0008644 (t - 37)^2 + .1247 (e - 2.36) + .04937 (s - 11.06)$$

where K = skill level; t = age; s = years of job experience; e = years of education. The increment of skill (in assumed units) as a result of education, ex-

11. The studies referred to are S. G. Strumilin, "Kvalifikatsia Truda i Vyuchka Rabochikh" in *Materialy po Statistike Truda* v. 6 (Petrograd, 1919), and "Khoziaistvennoe Znachenie Narodnogo Obrazovania" in *Planovoe Khoziaistvo*, No. 9-10 (1924). See also B. N. Babynin, "K Analizu Faktorov Kvalifikatsii Trudiashchikhsia" in *Vestnik Statistiki*, Vol. 15 (July-Dec. 1923) and Vol. 17 (April-June 1924).

pressed in per cent to uneducated as a base, is shown in Table 6. Strumilin found also for his sample of physical laborers the increments of wages related to education shown in Table 7.

Each year of school attendance contributed, by a large margin, a larger increment to the increase of manual wages than a year of factory job experience.[12] Also, in the existing wage structure, the increment of skill attributable to education in comparison with job experience was relatively higher for white-collar workers than for manual workers. This difference tended to increase with the number of school years, which indicates the relatively higher return from advanced education for white-collar workers as compared with manual workers. Another observation by Strumilin concerns "the law of diminishing productivity of formal education analogous to the decreasing productivity of each additional year of job experience for the increment of skills." In other words, he found diminishing returns from education for each segment of the labor force, but setting in at different levels of education.[13] Nevertheless, Strumilin's data pointed to the fact that under the conditions of the pre-revolutionary period there was a clear incentive to invest in education at almost all levels, and that the incentive persisted during the early period after the revolution.

I pass over the interesting way in which Strumilin combined his empirical observations with the labor theory of value to arrive at his claims of social returns to education, since this goes outside even the broad range of this conference. It is worth noting, however, that a more successful attempt to use mass data in order to derive the relative contributions of formal education to increases in skill was made in 1930 by the Soviet economist E. Liustikh.[14] He standardized the data for age and job experience and found education to be the major factor determining wage differentials in his sample, thus basically supporting Strumilin's findings.

The subsequent direction and findings of economic research in Russia and the Soviet Union have justified Strumilin's claim: "A long time ago we had already arrived at the conclusion, that the expenditures of the state budget to raise the cultural level of the country ought to be considered along with the expenditures on technical reconstruction of production as capital expenditures, and as equal in terms of their importance to our economy.[15]

12. Strumilin assumed a skill scale consisting of "work-units" (*trudovye edinitsy*) using the existing 12 skill categories (reflecting in turn wage differentials) and a conversion coefficient in the equation $x = 1 + .2\ (n - 1)$, where x = number of "work units"; n = number of skill category of the 12-category scale.

13. So, for example, a negative return occurs in Strumilin's sample of white-collar workers at the twelfth year of formal education at the existing wage rates of this period.

14. E. Liustikh, "Vlianie Obrazovania i Stazha na Effectivnost' Truda," *Planovoe Khoziaistvo,* No. 7-8 (1930). Liustikh used a survey of 72,596 workers in the metal and machine-building industries from the 1929 factory census. His basic equation is the following: $X = 327.4 + 11.18\ e + 4.81\ s + 37t$, where X = wage; e = years of education; s = job experience and t = age. From the relationship of the coefficient one can approximately derive the relative contribution of each of the factors.

15. *Planovoe Khoziaistvo,* No. 7 (1929).

CHAPTER 2

INVESTMENT IN MEN VERSUS INVESTMENT IN MACHINES: THE CASE OF INDIA

Arnold C. Harberger°

This chapter attempts to evaluate the economic rate of return to society as a whole of investment in physical capital, on one hand, and of investment in secondary and higher education, on the other. The chapter deals exclusively with data from India. It goes into considerable methodological detail in an effort to indicate ways of making as good use as possible of data that are far from ideal. Poor data are characteristic of underdeveloped countries — indeed, the Indian data are probably better than those for the overwhelming bulk of poor countries. Part of my purpose in presenting this study is to help "break the ice" by suggesting a variety of ways of overcoming potential inadequacies in the data. The other part of my purpose is to draw some inferences about the Indian situation.

Part I of the chapter is devoted to measuring the rate of return to physical capital investment in the private sector of Indian industry. Part II attempts to measure the rate of return to investment in education. The measures of the rate of return to investment in physical capital were consciously biased downward in the choice of procedures; the measures of the rate of return to investment in education were consciously biased upward. In spite of these biases, the "best" estimates resulting from the computations suggest that the economic rate of return to investment in physical capital is higher (and may be substantially higher) than the economic rate of return to investment in secondary and higher education. This does not, of course, say that investment in education is a bad idea, for it has other than purely economic advantages. Part III of the paper attempts to interpret the results of Parts I and II, and to mention some qualifications that seem appropriate.

I. THE RATE OF RETURN TO CAPITAL IN INDIAN INDUSTRY

It is almost tautological to say that the contribution of a given investment

°*Author's note:* The bulk of the research underlying Part I of this chapter was done while I was a member of the MIT Center for International Studies at New Delhi. I am indebted to Gary S. Becker, Mary Jean Bowman, and H. Gregg Lewis for helpful discussions during the preparation of Part II, but no share of such deficiencies as remain should be imputed to them.

to economic development is measured by the annual net increment of national output attributable to that investment. If this year's net investment amounts to 10 per cent of the national income, and it yields a rate of return of 15 per cent, next year's national income should on this account be 1.5 per cent greater than this year's income. Obviously, the rate of return is likely to differ from sector to sector, and among individual projects within sectors. Undoubtedly it would be better to know the rate of return to be expected from each individual project than to have estimates of the rate of return to investment in rather broad sectors of the economy. But we have to start somewhere, and broad sectoral averages seem to be as good a starting place as any, particularly when the issue under discussion is itself as broad as "investment in men versus investment in machines." We begin, then, with an attempt to estimate the rate of return to physical capital in private industry in India.

I shall devote a good deal of space to measuring the return to physical capital because (a) it is on this half of the "men *vs.* machines" issues that the greater amount of relevant and reliable data are available, and (b) this is an area in which very little work has been done relating to underdeveloped countries. I feel that investigators have been reluctant to work in this field — with data from underdeveloped countries — because of uncertainty as to the size and importance of a number of possible biases. In the first place, it is well known that in any country with substantial taxes on company income there is a strong incentive for firms to claim as rapid depreciation as possible on their assets. In this way they postpone the taxation of the income accruing from any given set of assets, obtaining, in effect, an interest-free loan from the government. Under these circumstances the rate of return measured on the basis of net income and net assets appearing on the books of a company may be quite different from the rate of return that we would get if we calculated net income and net assets using the "true economic depreciation" of existing assets in each year. In the second place, companies usually keep their accounts in current prices; changes in the price level may lead to a situation in which the accounts give a false picture of the "real rate of return" on capital assets. In the third place, company accounts measure the private and not the social return to capital, and it is the latter which is of greatest interest to those concerned with promoting economic development.

I propose to show that these potential biases are probably not as serious as one might at first suppose. However, first I should like to discuss a device for dealing with the data that is probably more important than any other single device in coping with problems of this type. In brief, a good underestimate or overestimate is likely to be more useful than a bad estimate. As we move from "raw" to "corrected" estimates, many rather arbitrary decisions have to be taken. If, at each crossroad, we consciously take a course which will bias our final result in a given direction (say, downward), we know where we stand at the end. If we do not try to overcorrect in this way, we will probably come out with an objectively better result, but one which will be less convincing to others.

In this study, I have tried to obtain a good underestimate of the rate of return to physical capital in private sector industry in India. The data are based on a survey conducted by the Reserve Bank of India, covering 1001 companies in virtually all branches of industry. The great bulk of "modern" large enterprises are directly represented in the sample. The Reserve Bank of India presents each year a consolidated balance sheet and a consolidated income statement for the 1001 companies as a group, and for subgroups of the 1001 broken down by industrial classification. We shall here be dealing with the consolidated data for the 1001 companies taken together.

We are interested here in measuring the social net productivity of physical capital. Because it is net productivity with which we are concerned, we want to exclude from the companies' income a provision for depreciation. But because it is the social rather than the private rate of return to capital which interests us, we must define "net income" to be inclusive of corporation income tax payments. Thus we are at the outset taking into account one of the most important sources of divergence between the social and the private productivity of capital.

Being suspicious of the data in a number of ways, I decided to explore a number of alternative methods of measuring the rate of return to capital. Five essentially different methods were followed:

Method I takes as its starting point the ratio of "net income," as defined above, to the net book value of physical assets as shown on the companies' records.

Method II doubts the validity of net book value as representative of the current replacement cost of assets. It uses instead an estimate consisting of the current market value of the firms' shares plus the (book) value of the firms' borrowings minus the (book) value of the firms' net financial assets. This method thus uses the stock market's estimate of the value of the firm as the basis on which to derive the estimated current value of physical assets. The "net income" figures used in Method II are the same as those used in Method I.

Method III doubts the accuracy of the firms' depreciation accounting procedures. It uses the ratio of gross income to gross assets as a device for estimating the ratio of the firms' "true net income" to their "true net assets." This method will be explained in detail at the appropriate place; suffice it to say here that the method consciously aims at understating the ratio of true net income to true net assets.

Method IV also doubts the depreciation accounting procedures, and instead uses the "cash flow" method of modern capital budgeting to estimate the net rate of return to physical capital. For each of a series of years, the expenditures of the firms on physical capital are deducted from the gross income from this form of capital, yielding a net cash inflow (or outflow) for each year. In Method IV the intial cash outflow is taken to be the net book value of the physical assets carried into the first year for which flows are measured, and the final cash inflow is taken to be the net book value of the physical assets carried out of the last year for which flows are measured. The estimated net rate of return is that which yields a zero present value for the pattern of flows thus generated.

Method V recognizes that depreciation accounting procedures still have some influence in Method IV because they affect the net book values used to estimate the initial outflow and the final inflow. Under Method V the extreme assumption is made that all depreciation charges are fictitious; therefore gross book values are taken as the measures of the initial outflow and the final inflow. The net rate of return is then calculated as in Method IV.

Under each method, an estimate based on the raw data (estimate A) was first made; this estimate was then subjected to three successive adjustments (B, C, and D).

Adjustment B takes into account the fact that some of the observed income of the firms may have been due to financial rather than physical assets. Under this adjustment the net financial assets of the firms are estimated, and a rate of return of 10 per cent is arbitrarily imputed to these assets. The resulting imputed income from financial assets is then deducted from the raw income figures to obtain the adjusted income series. As the actual rate of return on net financial assets is likely to be less than 10 per cent, this adjustment probably yields an understatement of the income attributable to physical assets.

Adjustment C begins with the figures emerging from Adjustment B, and modifies them to take account of price level changes.

Adjustment D begins with the figures emerging from Adjustment C, and modifies them to take account of excise taxes. This adjustment recognizes that in cases where excise taxes apply, the value to consumers of the product of a taxed industry is measured by the price of the product gross of tax. Under Adjustment D a fraction (equal to capital's share in value added) of the excise taxes paid by the firms was imputed as part of the marginal product of capital.

The estimated rates of return to capital obtained under these alternative methods and adjustments are summarized in Table 1. (The computations are presented in detail in the appendix to this paper.)

TABLE 1

Estimated Rate of Return to Capital in Indian Industry, 1955–59

(In percentages)

| | | Adjustment | | |
Method	A	B	C	D
I	12.8	11.7	11.4	14.4
II°	15.5	14.7	---†	19.3
III	12.1	11.3	11.1	13.1
IV	13.4	12.4	10.0	13.6
V	12.6	11.4	10.4	13.0

° Method II measures the rate of return for 1959 only, as this was the only year for which an adequate estimate of the market value of the firms' shares could be obtained.

† Since the market value of the assets of the firms is measured for the same year as the corresponding income, there is no need for a price-level correction when Method II is used.

An Adjustment for Market Imperfections

So far we have implicitly assumed that the wages paid to labor by the 1001 companies in the Reserve Bank survey accurately reflect the alternative productivity of the workers employed. There are, however, some grounds for doubting the validity of this assumption. Large companies in many countries appear to pay higher wages to similar labor than do small companies:even more striking are the disparities between the earnings of comparable labor in big companies, on the one hand, and agricultural employment, on the other. In 1956-57 the average annual *wages* paid *per worker* in factory establishments in India was more than Rs. 1200,[1] while the average annual *income per household* was only Rs. 385[2] for agricultural laboring households. Even within urban areas, the factory worker appears to have a substantially better-than-average economic position. More than half of all urban households in India had, in 1957-58, monthly per capita expenditures of less than 24 rupees[3] — and it should be borne in mind that many Indian households have more than one earner.

The idea that factory workers probably receive more than they could get elsewhere is also borne out by the fact that most factories have long lists of applicants who are ready and willing to work at the prevailing wage, but for whom posts are not available. This is not the place to explore the possible reasons why factory wages do not fall. Both union pressure and special wage legislation applicable to factory employment must certainly play an important role, and there may be other additional explanatory factors.

Some economists are prone to assume, when dealing with countries like India, that the alternative productivity of labor is zero. This means that the social marginal product of capital is not what capital gets, but the entire value added of the operation in question. The wages paid to labor in this case are, from the economic point of view, not a necessary cost but simply a sort of transfer payment out of the marginal product of the really scarce factor, capital.

I am not a member of the "zero alternative productivity" school. There is a large and growing body of evidence, and an increasing degree of consensus among Indian economists, against this extreme position. But this does not say that the Indian labor market is a perfectly functioning mechanism, with the value of the marginal product of equivalent labor exactly the same in all employments. Granted that modern industry is recognized to be a high-wage sector, some allowance should be made for this fact in estimating the social marginal productivity of capital. I believe it is reasonable to assume that the wage bill paid by modern industry in India exceeds the alternative earnings of the workers involved by some 25 per cent. That is, the same

1. *Statistical Abstract, India, 1957-58* (Delhi, 1961), p. 570

2. Government of India, Cabinet Secretariat, *National Sample Survey,* No. 33 (Eleventh and Twelfth Rounds, August, 1956 — August, 1957) (Delhi, 1961), p. 61.

3. *National Sample Survey,* No. 80 (Thirteenth Round, September, 1957 — May, 1958) (Delhi, 1961), p. 115.

physical investments that in 1959 produced a return to capital of 2.0 billion rupees, while paying a wage bill of 3.4 rupees, could have yielded a return of 2.68 billion rupees while operating in exactly the same way, simply by paying the same workers 20 per cent less. Once it is assumed that the alternative productivity of the labor employed in a given operation is less than the wages actually paid to that labor, it follows automatically that the accounting profits of that enterprise understate the true social benefit attributable to the capital investment involved.

In the accompanying diagram *OCDH* represents the wages bill actually paid by a given enterprise, while *OFEH* represents the alternative productivity, or "social cost," of the labor employed by that enterprise. Our procedure takes as the social return to the capital involved in the enterprise its accounting profits *BCD*, plus *CDEF*, the excess of the wages actually paid to the labor employed in the enterprise over the alternative productivity of that same labor. Obviously, this measure understates what would be the social return to the capital already invested in the project if its managers faced a market wage equal to the alternative product of labor. In this last case, *OJ* of labor could be employed, and profits of *BFG* would be produced.

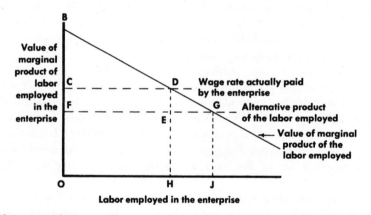

Thus, in making an adjustment for market imperfections, we augment the accounting figures on income from capital by an amount equal to 20 per cent of the wage bill paid by the companies in question in each respective year. Unfortunately, I do not have the data to support the particular numerical value (20 per cent) chosen for this exercise, and as a consequence I fully expect that some readers will not place much weight upon the calculations that follow. But I am certain that the majority of professional observers of the Indian scene would consider my assumption as reasonable or even conservative, and I shall proceed on that basis, anticipating disagreement on the part of some readers and hoping that most will be prepared to go along with my assumption.[4]

4. The data needed to test this assumption are fantastically hard to come by. What is needed are not only the earnings of narrowly defined classes of workers, classified by occupation, industry, size of establishment, and probably region, but also a determination of what classes of workers in

Table 2 shows estimates of the rate of marginal productivity of capital in Indian industry, obtained using the same methods and adjustments that were discussed in detail above. The only difference is that, before these computations were begun, the income from capital used in the previous calculations was augmented by an amount equal to 20 per cent of the wage bill of the 1001 companies.

Whereas our earlier analysis yielded results between 13.0 and 19.3 per

TABLE 2

Estimated Rate of Marginal Productivity of
Capital in Indian Industry, 1955–59
(In percentages)
(Assuming that 20 per cent of wage bill represents the
excess of actual wages over alternative marginal
productivity of labor)

| Method | Adjustment | | | |
	A	B	C	D
I	17.5	16.4	16.0	20.1
II	20.4	20.0	----	26.1
III	15.5	14.7	14.3	17.2
IV	19.6	18.5	15.7	21.3
V	16.9	15.7	14.3	18.3

cent for adjustment D (the most "refined" adjustment), we here get figures between 17.2 and 26.1 per cent under the same adjustment. Bearing in mind that the procedures used to obtain these figures create a presumption of downward bias in the final results, I certainly think that it is fair to conclude that physical capital is highly productive in the industrial sector of the Indian economy.

II. THE RATE OF RETURN TO INVESTMENT IN EDUCATION IN INDIA

For a long time I looked without success for a body of data from which it would be possible to estimate the rate of return to investment in education in India. I had about given up the search when I came across a table in C. Arnold Anderson's paper for this conference. (see Table 3). This is certainly not the best set of data that one could imagine for estimating the rate of

---

industry Y, region II, firm size B are "equivalent" in capacity to the workers in occupation 23, industry X, firm size A, and region I. The first efforts to do anything at all of this kind on a substantial scale are now just getting under way, and even these efforts are concerned only with the labor markets of a particular metropolitan area. I refer to a study of the Chicago labor market, directed by Professors Albert Rees and George P. Shultz of the University of Chicago, and to a study of the Santiago (Chile) labor market directed by Professor Sergio de Castro of the Catholic University of Chile (Santiago).

TABLE 3

Distribution of Monthly Male Earnings by Schooling, Hyderabad[°]

Earnings (Rupees)	Illiterate	Primary	Secondary	Lower Professional & Technical
−25	658	264	220	14
26−	912	541	308	15
51−	376	407	510	44
101−	68	190	417	66
201−	6	15	158	55
501−		3	21	18
1001−			8	3
2501−			3	1
5000+			1	2
Total	2020	1420	1646	218

Earnings (Rupees)	Under-graduate	Graduate-Postgraduate	Higher Professional & Technical	Total
−25	4	2	2	1164
26−	18	1	4	1799
51−	59	22	25	1443
101−	51	56	42	890
201−	49	117	54	454
501−	8	36	9	95
1001−	4	5	11	31
2501−		2		6
5000+				3
Total	193	241	147	5885

[°]Indian Institute of Economics, *A Socio-Economic Survey of Hyderabad* (Hyderabad: Government Press, 1957).

return to investment in education, but it is, to my knowledge, the best that is presently available for India. The rest of this section will be devoted to an attempt to squeeze as much juice as possible out of this "lemon."

The first problem was to decide what to measure. I had some difficulty in interpreting the results for "lower professional and technical" and "higher professional and technical" education, and accordingly decided to leave them out of consideration. In the case of primary education, there was not much difficulty in interpretation, but I felt hard put to estimate the foregone earnings of students at this early a stage. Since foregone earnings are the most important "cost" of education at higher levels, and since I found it easier to estimate foregone earnings than the associated direct costs of education, I decided not to estimate the rate of return to primary education. Within higher

TABLE 4

Estimated Average Earnings and Years of Schooling by Education Class

Level of Education	(1) Est. Average Earnings from Hyderabad Sample (Rupees per month)	(2) Est. Total Years of Schooling to Completion	(3) Est. Average Years Completed	(4) Percentage Rate of Increase of Average Earnings from Prior Educational Class
Illiterate	43.72	—	—	—
Primary	65.04	8	4	10.5
Secondary	132.57	12	10	12.4
Undergraduate	222.74	16	15	11.0
Graduate and postgraduate	391.40	18	17	32.6

education there were two categories—undergraduate and graduate-post-graduate. I decided not to split higher education into two pieces, and instead to measure the rate of return involved in higher education all the way up to the graduate-postgraduate stage.

Three types of "investments" will be dealt with here:

1. An investment in four years of secondary schooling, as compared with a person's entering the labor force after completing primary schooling.
2. An investment in six years of college and university training, as compared with a person's entering the labor force after completing secondary schooling.
3. An investment in ten years of secondary plus college and university training, as compared with a person's entering the labor force after completing primary schooling.

In all these cases we are comparing the situation of a person who completes a later stage of schooling with one who completes an earlier stage. Unfortunately, the data of the sample survey refer to people who have had "some" primary, "some" secondary, "some" undergraduate training, etc. They do not refer to those who have completed the stage in question. We must therefore first estimate the average incomes of "completers" of the various stages.

This was done by the following procedure. First, the mean income in each educational class was estimated from the Hyderabad survey table (Table 3). These are shown in column 1 of Table 4. Second, on the basis of consultation with Indian colleagues, an effort was made to establish the probable duration of each successive stage of the educational process. Since educational practices vary among places and institutions in India, we cannot be certain about these figures. I present the results in the hope that these assumptions are accurate; in the event that readers want to explore some modification of these assumptions, the general method presented and de-completed for the primary category; average earnings of Rs. 132.57 are associated with an estimated average of ten years of schooling completed for the secondary category. The compound rate of increase that will make 65.04 grow to 132.57 in six years is 12.4 per cent.

At this early stage I had to decide whether I would aim for an underestimate or an overestimate of the rate of return to education, and I opted for an overestimate. There are two ways in which the estimates in Table 4 reflect this decision. The first is the estimate that the average of the sample group at each stage was halfway to completing that stage; the second is the decision to treat the undergraduate stage as occupying the fifteenth and sixteenth years of total education. How these assumptions work to produce an overestimate of the rate of return will be indicated presently. First, however, I shall present estimates of the average incomes of "completers" of each stage.

Estimated Average Incomes of Completers:

	Rs./Month	
Primary	100.49	$[= 65.04 \times (1.115)^4]$
Secondary	160.49	$[= 132.57 \times (1.11)^2]$
Graduate and postgraduate	519.00	$[= 391.40 \times (1.326)]$

Rs. 65.04 is the estimated average monthly earnings of a person with four years of primary education. How do we estimate the average earnings of someone with eight years? We observe that the average rate of increase of earnings associated with the first four years of education was 10.5 per cent per year, and the average rate of increase associated with the next six years was 12.4 per cent. I was in doubt as to which of these rates to apply to the last four years of primary education, and settled on a rough average of the two — 11.5 per cent. In the case of secondary education, the rate of increase from the secondary to the undergraduate stage (11.0 per cent) was used to project the earnings of secondary completers from the average earnings of the secondary category. In the case of graduate and postgraduate education, the earnings of completers were projected from the average earnings of the class on the basis of the rate of increase (32.6 per cent) from the undergraduate to the graduate-postgraduate stage.

Turning now to why these assumptions are likely to produce overestimates of the rate of return to education, consider first the assumption that the average years of education in each stage represent half-completion of that stage. This assumption is likely to overstate the average, probably particularly so in the primary category. If Rs. 65.04 represents only three years of average education, we would end up projecting higher average earnings than Rs. 100.49 for primary completers. Since the earnings of primary completers are the foregone earnings of people at higher educational stages, and represent a large part of the total costs of investment in education, our

Turning now to why these assumptions are likely to produce over-estimates of the rate of return to education, consider first the assumption that the average years of education in each stage represent half-completion of that stage. This assumption is likely to overstate the average, probably particularly so in the primary category. If Rs. 65.04 represents only three years of average education, we would end up projecting higher average earnings than Rs. 100.49 for primary completers. Since the earnings of primary completers are the foregone earnings of people at higher educational stages, and represent a large part of the total costs of investment in education, our procedure, by tending to understate foregone earnings, tends to overestimate the rate of return. Since the later educational stages are much shorter than the primary stage, a tendency for the average years completed to be somewhat less than half-completion of the stage would have far less impact than in the primary stage.

My informants were not sure how to treat the undergraduate stage. Apparently some undergraduates begin with two years of prior training at the lower professional and technical level, and spend only two years as undergraduates; others may enter undergraduate school direct from secondary school and spend four years as undergraduates. If the former group dominate in the sample, the average years completed for the undergraduate group is likely to be close to 15; if the latter group predominate, the average years completed is likely to be close to 14. Probably the truth lies in between, and, if this is so, my decision to use the 15-year figure as the average for the group operates to magnify the estimated rate of return to investment in education through the graduate-postgraduate level. If I had set the average years completed of undergraduates at 14 years, the percentage rate of increase between the undergraduate average and the graduate-postgraduate average would have been 20.9 per cent rather than 32.6 per cent; and the average earnings of graduate-postgraduate completers would have been projected at Rs. 473 rather than Rs. 519 per month. The choice of the procedure leading to the latter figure is thus likely to introduce an upward bias in the estimated rate of return to higher education.

The next step in my procedure was to recognize that the sample was heavily weighted with younger people. We do not have data on the age distribution of the people included in the earnings-by-schooling table, but the Hyderabad survey does present a breakdown by age and education of a larger group of which the earnings-by-education sample was a subset. I assumed that the earnings-by-education group had essentially the same age distribution as the broader group for which data were available.

The age-by-education data were classified by very broad age groups, and I thought that further refinement would be desirable so as to reflect the three main forces that determined the age distribution of each educational class. For the very old, mortality and retirement are the principal reasons why older cohorts have fewer earners than younger ones. For the middle age groups, the relationship between adjacent cohorts would tend to reflect the pace at

which the output of given educational levels had been expanding in the
period before Indian independence. For the very young, this relationship
will reflect the postwar rate of growth of the output of the relevant class of
educational institutions. Table 5 presents some relevant statistics.

In estimating the age distributions in Table 6, I tried to bear in mind the
data given above, as well as the information about the broad age distribution
of the Hyderabad survey itself. In the graduate-postgraduate class, I assumed
a recent rate of increase of completers considerably lower than the 10.4 per
cent figure in Table 5, because of the substantial lag between entry into
higher education and completion of this final stage and also because, even
apart from the lag, I would anticipate a slower rate of growth of this "final
product" than of the population of university students as a whole. Table 6
presents a comparison between the percentage distributions of males by age
and education as shown by the Hyderabad survey, on the one hand, and my
allocation, on the other.

Table 7 presents the detailed age distribution resulting from my allocation. The next step in my procedure was to assume age-earnings profiles for
the different educational groups. I assumed that these had the form of a steady

TABLE 5

Average Annual Rates of Growth of Number of Male Students
(In percentages)

Years	Primary	Secondary	University
1916–39°	2.6	3.3	3.7
1950–57†	4.9	7.0	10.4

°Source: *Statistical Abstracts, British India.*
†Source: *Statistical Abstracts, India.*

TABLE 6

Distribution of Males by Age and Education
(In percentages)

Age		Primary°	Secondary†	Graduate and Postgraduate†
13–21	Hyderabad sample	36.4	—	—
	My allocation	36.5	—	—
22–40	Hyderabad sample	43.5	69.0	70.7
	My allocation	43.5	68.5	70.4
41–55	Hyderabad sample	15.5	23.2	23.2
	My allocation	15.4	24.0	23.5
56–70	Hyderabad sample	4.6	7.8	6.1
	My allocation	4.6	7.7	6.1

°As percentages of total from age 13 through age 70.
†As percentages of total from age 22 through age 70.

upward rise of income with age, until a peak (or, better, plateau) was reached, with income staying at this peak level all the way to age 65. The following requirements were borne in mind in estimating these profiles:

1. The average earnings of each education class, weighted by its assumed age distribution, had to be approximately equal to the average earnings estimated above for completers of that stage of education.
2. The peak in earnings had to be reached at a later age for each successively higher educational stage.
3. The peak earnings had to be a higher fraction of average earnings at each successively higher educational stage. This was to be true both when the average was weighted by the assumed age distribution of each class, and when the average was an unweighted one covering all the years from entry into the labor force to retirement at 65.

Table 8 presents some of the key features of the assumed age-earnings profiles. Here, once again, I have consciously tried to bias my assumptions in

TABLE 7

Assumed Age Distribution by Education Class

(Each figure shows assumed number of males of the given age for every 10 males aged 65 in the specified education class)

Age	Primary	Secondary	Graduate & Postgraduate	Age	Primary	Secondary	Graduate & Postgraduate
13	215	—	—	40	68	60	80
14	205	—	—	41	65	58	76
15	196	—	—	42	62	56	73
16	187	—	—	43	59	54	70
17	179	—	—	44	56	52	67
18	171	200	—	45	53	50	64
19	164	187	—	46	50	48	61
20	157	175	—	47	47	46	59
21	151	164	—	48	44	44	56
22	145	154	201	49	42	42	53
23	139	145	190	50	40	40	50
24	133	137	180	51	38	38	47
25	127	130	171	52	36	36	44
26	122	123	162	53	34	34	41
27	117	117	154	54	32	32	38
28	112	111	146	55	30	30	35
29	108	105	139	56	28	28	32
30	104	100	132	57	26	26	29
31	100	95	126	58	24	24	26
32	96	90	120	59	22	22	23
33	92	85	114	60	20	20	20
34	88	81	108	61	18	18	18
35	84	77	103	62	16	16	16
36	80	73	98	63	14	14	14
37	77	69	93	64	12	12	12
38	74	66	88	65	10	10	10
39	71	63	84	66-70	16	16	16

the direction that will produce high estimated rates of return to investment in education. The steeper the age-earnings profile of a given mean earnings, the greater the fraction of total income received late in life, and hence the smaller the present value of a given total income. Now it is universally recognized that age-earnings profiles are steeper with higher educational levels. But I made them only slightly steeper. The ratio of peak earnings to average earnings was 1.11 for primary completers, 1.14 for secondary com-

TABLE 8

Characteristics of Assumed Age-Earnings Profiles

	Primary	Secondary	Graduate & Postgraduate
Age at which peak earnings reached	30	35	40
Ratio of peak earnings to earnings at age 21	1.55	2.11	——
Ratio of peak earnings to earnings at age 26	1.19	1.51	3.00
Ratio of peak earnings to average over lifetime	1.11	1.14	1.20
Ratio of peak earnings to weighted average earnings	1.27	1.33	1.42
	(Rupees per month)		
Average earnings over lifetime	113.92	187.50	611.90
Weighted average earnings	100.15	160.68	519.30
Weighted average earnings computed from sample	100.49	160.41	519.00

TABLE 9

Assumed Age-Earnings Profiles

Age	Earnings (Rupees per month)			Age	Earnings (Rupees per month)		
	Primary	Secondary	Graduate & Postgraduate		Primary	Secondary	Graduate & Postgraduate
14	47	—	—	28	117	157	315
15	52	—	—	29	122	165	350
16	57	—	—	30	127	173	385
17	62	—	—	31	127	181	420
18	67	77	—	32	127	189	455
19	72	85	—	33	127	197	490
20	77	93	—	34	127	205	525
21	82	101	—	35	127	213	560
22	87	109	—	36	127	213	595
23	92	117	—	37	127	213	630
24	97	125	175	38	127	213	665
25	102	133	210	39	127	213	700
26	107	141	245				
27	112	149	280	40-65	127	213	735

pleters, and 1.20 for graduate-postgraduate completers; I am sure that these figures understate the relative steepening of the profile as one moves up the educational ladder. By the same token, they tend to produce an overstatement of the rate of return to investment in education.

TABLE 10

Assumed Schooling Costs by Age

(Rupees per month)

| | Assumption I | | Assumption II | |
Age	Secondary	Higher	Secondary	Higher
14	6	—	23	—
15	8	—	26	—
16	11	—	28	—
17	15	—	31	—
18	—	23	—	33
19	—	30	—	42
20	—	37	—	46
21	—	45	—	50
22	—	54	—	54
23	—	58	—	58

The profiles given in Table 9 permit us to estimate part of the cost of education – the earnings that a person would have been making if he had stopped on completion of primary schooling or, alternatively, on completion of secondary schooling. But they do not include any part of the direct costs of schooling, whether these are borne by the individual or his family, by the institution he attends, or by the government. These direct costs are surely part of the social "investment" in education, and should be incorporated in our analysis. Unfortunately, I had not encountered adequate estimates of them at the time this paper was prepared. The Indian government does publish data labeled "direct costs of education" by educational category. These were, in 1956–57, Rs. 440 per year per student at the university level, Rs. 61 per student at the secondary level, and Rs. 24 per student at the primary level.[5] I find it difficult, however, to believe that these represent total outlays. Rs. 24 represents about $5.00 a year per student at the primary level, and Rs. 61 about $18.00 a year per student at the secondary level. These seem very low indeed as estimates of total direct costs.

For the United States, Becker estimates that university students bear about two-thirds of the total cost of their education.[6] Since what they bear includes fairly substantial outlays for tuition, etc., in addition to foregone earnings, it may well be that total costs are something like twice foregone earnings. In the light of this figure, it seems conservative to assume that in India the direct costs of education amount to 50 per cent of foregone earnings. I make this assumption as Assumption II of Table 10. Assumption I is even

5. Ministry of Information and Broadcasting, *India, 1961* (Delhi, 1961), pp. 93, 94, 98.

6. Gary S. Becker, "Underinvestment in College Education?" *American Economic Review*, L (May, 1961), p. 348.

more conservative. It takes direct costs of the first year of secondary school to be 12 per cent of the earnings of a primary school graduate aged 14; of the second year of secondary school, to be 16 per cent of the earnings of a primary

TABLE 11

An Illustrative Calculation of the Rate of
Return to Investment in Education
(Graduate-Postgraduate Compared with Secondary)

(1) Age	(2) Earnings of Secondary School Product (Rs/month)	(3) Earnings of Graduate-Postgraduate Product (Rs/month)	(4) Schooling Costs of Graduate-Post graduate Product (Rs/month) Assumption II	(5) Net Excess of Income (+) or Net Cost (−) of Graduate as Compared with Secondary Product [(3)−(2)−(4)]	(6) Last Year's Capital at Charge Accumulated at 16.3%° [(7)_{-1} × 1.163]	(7) Capital at Charge at Given Age ÷(−12)° [(5)+(6)]
18	77	—	33	−110	—	− 110
19	85	—	42	−127	− 128	− 255
20	93	—	46	−139	− 297	− 436
21	101	—	50	−151	− 507	− 658
22	109	—	54	−163	− 765	− 928
23	117	—	58	−175	−1079	−1254
24	125	175	—	50	−1458	−1408
25	133	210	—	77	−1638	−1561
26	141	245	—	104	−1815	−1711
27	149	280	—	131	−1990	−1859
28	157	315	—	158	−2162	−2004
29	165	350	—	185	−2331	−2146
30	173	385	—	212	−2496	−2284
31	181	420	—	239	−2656	−2417
32	189	455	—	266	−2811	−2545
33	197	490	—	293	−2960	−2667
34	205	525	—	320	−3102	−2782
35	213	560	—	347	−3235	−2888
36	213	595	—	382	−3359	−2977
37	213	630	—	417	−3462	−3045
38	213	665	—	452	−3541	−3089
39	213	700	—	487	−3593	−3106
40−65	213	735	—	522		

Present value at age 39 of 522 per year at 16.3 per cent per annum =

$$\frac{522}{.163}\left[1 - \frac{1}{(1.163)^{26}}\right] = 3138$$

Net present value at age 39 = 3138 − 3106 = + 32
(Net present value at age 39 obtained using a 16.4 per cent rate is − 142.)

°Columns 6 and 7 represent one-twelfth of the actual capital at charge. If all columns were multiplied by 12, we would have annual earnings, annual costs, and actual capital at charge in the respective columns. I carry capital at charge as a negative figure for convenience of reference. This figure represents what the graduate-postgraduate has yet to recover (in terms of present value) before the investment in his education will have paid off at 16.3 per cent.

school graduate aged 15; of the third year, to be 20 per cent of the earnings of a primary school graduate aged 16; and of the fourth year, to be 24 per cent of the earnings of a primary school graduate aged 17. For the successive years of higher education, the direct costs are taken to be 30, 35, 40, 45, 50, and 50 per cent of the earnings of a secondary school graduate aged 18, 19, 20, 21, 22, and 23, respectively. This latter assumption produces an estimate of direct costs at the university level which is very close to the government figure of Rs. 440 per student per year, if we assume that each higher cohort at the university level contains 10-12 per cent fewer students than the immediately preceding cohort.

Table 11 presents an illustration of the way in which the rate of return to education was calculated. An iterative procedure had to be followed, the iteration being carried to the point where there was a negligible difference between the present value of the capital-at-charge at age 39, and the present value at the same age of the extra income which the better-educated individual in the comparison would earn during the remainder of his working lifetime (to age 65). In the case illustrated, a rate of 16.3 per cent per annum led to such a negligible difference.

Calculations similar to those in Table 11 were carried out for five other comparisons. The final results are given in Table 12.

TABLE 12

Estimated Rates of Return to Investment
in Education in India

	Assumption I	Assumption II
Graduate-postgraduate compared with primary	15.0	14.1
Secondary compared with primary	11.9	10.0
Graduate-postgraduate compared with secondary	16.9	16.3

After the foregoing estimates were prepared, I had the benefit of numerous comments and suggestions, many of which came from Jacob Mincer's excellent critique of my paper at the conference. Moreover, my attention was called to an unpublished paper by G. S. Sahota, "Returns on Education in India" (University of Chicago, Asian Workshop, Paper No. 61-11 [1962]), in which he developed independent estimates of the direct costs of education per pupil at various educational stages. These costs, according to Sahota, ranged from approximately Rs. 20 per student per month in the ninth and tenth years of education, to roughly Rs. 70 per student per month at the university level.

I have accordingly re-estimated the rate of return to secondary and university education combined, taking into account both the suggestions made by readers and Sahota's direct cost figures. The principal changes made were:

a) The earnings figure of Rs. 391.40 per month, given in the Hyderabad sample as the average earnings of persons with graduate and postgraduate education, was taken in this exercise to reflect the average earnings of those with 16 total years of education. This assumption obviously will lead toward an overstatement of the rate of return to higher education. The earnings profile of persons with 16 years of education was then estimated so as to produce an age-weighted average income of Rs. 391.40 for this group and so as to have other reasonable properties. The estimated pattern begins with earnings of Rs. 180 per month at age 22, and proceeds by annual steps of Rs. 20 per month to a maximum of Rs. 540 per month at age 40. The ratio of peak earnings to earnings at age 26 for this group was thus estimated at 2.08; and the ratio of peak earnings to weighted average earnings at 1.38. As in the example previously cited, this allocation of observed earnings by age groups probably tends to overstate the rate of return to education, as the "true" allocation is likely to be steeper than the one assumed.

b) Secondary students were assumed to earn, while in school, average incomes equal to one-third of the estimated incomes of primary school graduates of the same age working full time. Likewise, university students were assumed to earn, while in school, average incomes equal to one-third of the estimated incomes of secondary school graduates of the same age working full time. Thus an ample allowance was made for the possibility of part-time earnings of students.

c) It was assumed that mortality and ill health caused the withdrawal from the labor force, annually, of a certain fraction of workers at ages from 40 onward. This fraction averaged approximately 2 per cent for primary school graduates and approximately 1 per cent for university graduates. The result of this assumption is that only some 60 per cent of primary school graduates are taken to be still working at age 65, while some 80 per cent of university graduates are taken to be in the labor force at age 65. I believe that this assumption allows for a substantial difference in the health and mortality experience of the two groups.

d) It was assumed that 6 per cent of the primary school graduates in each age bracket were unemployed, while there was no unemployment among the university graduates. The 6 per cent figure should really be interpreted as the assumed differential between the unemployment rates of the two groups. The fact that 0 per cent unemployment was assumed for the university group operates once again to bias the results in favor of a high estimated rate of return to education at the secondary and university level; for the estimated net gain to secondary and higher education would be lower if we had assumed, say, 6 per cent unemployment of university graduates and 12 per cent unemployment of primary graduates, rather than the 0 and 6 per cent figures used.

In calculating the implied rate of return to investment in sixteen years as against eight years of education, the age-income profiles were thus modified to take account of reduced labor-force participation, mortality, and unemployment, in all cases using assumptions that would tend to overestimate the rate of return. Moreover, ample provisions was made for possible part-time earnings of secondary and university students; and the income that persons with sixteen years of education were assumed to earn was overstated by imputing to this group the average income observed in the Hyderabad sample for a group with seventeen, or possibly even more, average years of education. The net result of this exercise was an estimated rate of return to university education (sixteen years) compared with primary education (eight years), that was just barely 16 per cent.

III. INTERPRETATION OF THE RESULTS AND SOME QUALIFICATIONS

With all adjustments (including an imputation of 20 per cent of the wage bill to capital), the marginal productivity of physical capital equipment was estimated to be between 17.2 per cent and 26.1 per cent. These figures should be compared with our original estimates of 10−12 per cent for investment in secondary education, of 16−17 per cent for higher education, of 14−15 per cent for ten years of secondary and higher education taken together, and with our more refined estimate of 16 per cent for eight years of secondary and higher education. When it is recognized that the estimates for physical capital were "designed" to be underestimates, while those for investment in education were "designed" to be overestimates, a very strong presumption is created that the economic productivity of investment in physical capital exceeds the economic productivity of investment in education in India. This presumption is reinforced by the fact that differences in natural abilities certainly explain part of the extra earnings of more highly educated groups. That is to say, the foregone earnings of those in secondary school are likely to be higher than the average earnings of those who stop upon completion of primary school, and the foregone earnings of college and university students are likely to be higher than the average earnings of secondary school completers of the same age, purely because of differences in natural ability. If we could take this into account, we would come out with still lower estimates of the economic rate of return to investment in education.

There remain some questions, however, concerning the range of applicability of the results obtained, and it is to questions of this nature that we turn in this section. We consider first the representativeness of the Hyderabad sample. We have really measured the rate of return to investment in education as reflected in that sample; it is by no means clear that this rate of return would apply to all India. In Table 13 certain key features of the distribution of persons by monthly per capita expenditure classes are compared for Andhra Pradesh (the state in which Hyderabad is situated) and India as a whole.

On the whole, I would interpret the figures in Table 13 as showing

TABLE 13

Distribution of Persons by Monthly Per Capita Expenditure Classes
(Rupees per month)

| | Urban | | Rural | |
	Andhra Pradesh	*All India*	*Andhra Pradesh*	*All India*
First quartile	13.7	13.3	9.5	10.3
Median	21.9	20.1	13.3	15.1
Third quartile	26.8	31.2	21.0	22.4
Top decile	41.4	49.7	29.6	32.6

Source: *National Sample Survey, No. 80* (Thirteenth Round, Sept. 1957 – May 1958), pp. 6 – 7, 117 – 8.

Andhra Pradesh to be reasonably representative of all India. The median expenditure per capita is higher in urban areas in Andhra Pradesh, but lower in rural areas. The distribution is less skewed for Andhra than for all India, but that is to be expected, since Andhra does not contain any of India's great metropolitan centers. Moreover, the sample did not cover Andhra Pradesh as a whole, but only the Hyderabad area; and the distribution of male earnings in the Hyderabad sample (see Table 3) is considerably more skewed than the distribution of per capita expenditures for all urban areas in India, the top decile in the Hyderabad sample being about twice the third quartile, and the third quartile about twice the median. The distribution of male earnings in the Hyderabad sample is also more skewed than the distribution of households by per household expenditure in all India. For this latter distribution, the third quartile is about two-thirds higher than the median, and the top decile about six-sevenths higher than the third quartile.[7] It is likely that, the greater the skewness in the distribution of earnings in the sample, the higher will be the estimated rate of return to investment in education. Hence on this criterion we have no good grounds for suspecting that the sample has led us to underestimate the rate of return to investment in education in India as a whole.

I now inquire into the representativeness of the sample of 1001 companies represented in the Reserve Bank survey. As already indicated, these companies constitute a large part of "modern" industry in India. Their total value amounted to about 4 per cent of the national income, while all mines and factory establishments taken together accounted for less than 10 per cent of the national income during the period surveyed. Moreover, they accounted for more than two-thirds of all gross capital formation in the corporate sector in India (see Table 14).

The 1001 companies clearly do reflect the corporate sector rather well, but this does not mean that they are representative of all investment in physical capital. Total physical capital formation in India has been about ten

7. *India, 1961*, p. 178.

TABLE 14

Gross Capital Formation in India, 1956−59

(Crores of current rupees)

Year	1001 Companies, RBI Survey°	Total Corporate Sector†
1956	238	330
1957	236	327
1958	159	220
1959	130	188

°"Estimated Outlay on Physical Assets," as derived in Section I of this paper, under Method IV.
†Government of India, Central Statistical Organization, *Estimates of Gross Capital Formation in India for 1948−49 to 1960−61* (Delhi, 1962), p. 43.

times corporate capital formation in recent years, the remainder being accounted for by the household sector and the public sector. I believe, however, that the rate of marginal productivity of capital in the corporate sector is something of legitimate interest in its own right, and also one of the elements needed to determine a wise allocation of the community's investable resources.

Some readers may be disturbed by the fact that I included capital's share of the excise duties paid by the 1001 companies in my measure of the marginal product of capital, while I made no similar allowance in estimating the rate of return to investment in education. The main reason behind this procedure is that so long as primary school graduates, secondary school graduates, and university graduates are similarly distributed among industries, an adjustment for excise taxes would have no effect on our calculations of the rate of return to investment in education, since that adjustment would be proportional across the board. A subsidiary reason is that excise taxes are disproportionately concentrated in the corporate sector, the 1001 companies alone paying between 40 and 50 per cent of all excise duties. Under these circumstances it is quite important to recognize excise taxes explicitly when treating the 1001 companies; while in the case of labor, where only disproportionalities of distribution would affect our calculations, the results would be only slightly affected.

Probably the most serious defect of the measures of the rate of marginal productivity of capital presented in Section I is their failure to take account of some important divergences between actual and "shadow" prices. Such a divergence was taken into account in the case of wages, but there are, in addition, a number of other areas in which actual prices do not reflect the true economic scarcity of the items in question. Without a doubt the most important of these cases is foreign exchange, of which the supply and demand are brought into balance only through a very rigid system of licensing, allocation, import prohibitions, etc. But it is clear also that railway transport and electricity are sold by public enterprises at prices below their current scarcity

values, and also below the levels that would be dictated by the cost of expanding these services.

It is difficult to assess the net effect of these factors on the profitability
of the 1001 companies. Looking at the cost side, it would appear at first glance
that the maintenance of low prices for foreign exchange, electricity, and rail
transport would add to the profitability of the corporate sector as a whole. But
this effect is at least partly offset by the fact that none of the above-named
items is freely available at the prevailing low price. Company profits are not
helped when the firms have to generate their own high-cost electricity to
supplement an inadequate allocation, or when production lines are closed
down while waiting for an allocation of foreign exchange for essential raw
materials; or when very high-cost, domestically produced substitutes are used
in place of imported goods.

Looking at the receipt side, there can be no doubt that a "realistic" price
of foreign exchange would greatly enhance the profitability of the Indian
corporate sector as a whole, even though not all the products of the corporate
sector would experience price increases. I have no way of guessing whether
an appropriate allowance for the effects of existing distortions in the fields of
foreign exchange, electricity, and rail transport on costs and receipts, taken
together, would result in an increase or a decrease in our estimates of the rate
of marginal productivity of capital. As I know of no way to deal with this
problem empirically, with the data that are available, I must leave the question open, as something that might lead to a significant revision of the estimates of Section I.

There are other considerations that may cast some doubt on the validity
of the conclusions suggested by the estimates of the rate of return to physical
capital. First, the 1001 companies in the Reserve Bank of India survey probably include some with significant monopoly power. Even though it is quite
proper to include monopoly profits in the estimated social return to a given
investment, it is likely that there would be a lower incidence of potential
monopoly profits on new investments to be made than on the total of existing
investments in the companies surveyed. For this reason, and possibly for
others as well, the marginal social rate of return to capital (*i.e.*, the rate to be
expected on new investments) may be lower than the average rate of return
estimated in this chapter. Second, the period for which data were available
was a period of rising price levels. We were able to correct for this, in a sense,
by the deflation procedure used in adjustments C and D, but even this procedure does not correct for the tendency for real profits to be higher than
normal in inflationary periods. Finally, there is the fact that the 1001 companies are, in general, large and successful firms, whose profitability is likely
to be greater than that for the average of all firms in the modern industrial
sector of the Indian economy.

These considerations, which were raised by Mincer in his commentary
on my original paper, make somewhat uncertain my assertion that the methodology used operates to understate the social rate of return to capital in-

vested in modern industry in India. I personally believe that they are not sufficiently weighty to counterbalance the many downward biases that were consciously introduced into the estimative procedure. However, I cannot expect that all readers will agree with this judgment.

I do not want to conclude on the note that investment in physical capital appears, from the evidence, to be economically more beneficial to India than investment in education. This is indeed what is suggested by the data that I have examined, but I prefer to regard this study as suggesting future research rather than as indicating particular alterations of existing investment patterns. We have dealt here with very broad aggregates, within each of which there is almost certain to be a great deal of diversity. For individual industries, the Reserve Bank survey data themselves show crude rates of return (Method I A) ranging from less than 10 per cent to more than 25 per cent. I have no doubt that an analysis of the rate of return to different types of education (broken down by subject matter, level, type of school, etc.) would also produce a wide variety of results. It seems to me that a number of detailed surveys, yielding age-income profiles of various types and levels of education, would surely be worth their cost. Their results would be exceedingly useful in the process of educational planning in India, even though it is recognized that the goals and rewards of education are not exclusively economic.

In a similar vein, I would suggest follow-up studies of the graduates of different types of institutions in the same general field. Educational techniques surely differ from institution to institution, and with careful follow-up studies it should be possible to discover some determinants of later economic success about which educators can do something. I suspect that it will turn out that many actions can be taken by educators to raise the economic productivity of their students without in any way detracting from the cultural and other advantages of the educational process. The key, I think, is to recognize that education *is* an investment. When corporations contemplate particular projects, they do the best they can to assess their prospective profitability. Economic considerations influence not only the general nature of investments but also the detailed ways in which they are carried out. I am sure that educators do take economic considerations into account, in a vague way, in planning their programs. But I am also sure that a really serious effort to understand the economic consequences of different detailed types and classes of investment in education would help greatly to improve the contribution that education can make to economic progress.

Appendix

PROCEDURES USED IN MEASURING THE RATE OF RETURN TO PHYSICAL CAPITAL INVESTED IN 1001 COMPANIES IN INDIA

THE INCOME SERIES, WITH ADJUSTMENTS

The Concept of Income from Capital

As a first approximation, I take the net income from capital of the 1001 firms to be:

> Profits before tax
> + Interest paid
> + Managing agents' remuneration.

Profits are taken before tax because the economic productivity of capital includes that part of the proceeds which goes to the government as well as that which is retained by the private owners of the capital instruments. Interest is included because it represents a prior claim on the earnings of capital, even though for accounting purposes it is treated as an expense. I follow common Indian practice in counting managing agents' remuneration as part of the economic return to capital, since this remuneration is largely in the nature of a participation in the profits of the company.

The Basic Series

Net income, as I have defined it above for the purpose of this study, is obtained as follows from the Reserve Bank Survey data.

	1955	1956	1957	1958	1959
	(Crores of rupees)[1]				
Profits before tax	117.7	130.9	107.8	120.9	161.5
Managing agents' remuneration[2]	14.7	11.9	8.4	8.9	11.0
Interest	12.9	16.0	23.4	27.5	29.7
Net income (Y_a)	145.3	158.8	139.6	157.3	202.2

1. A crore of rupees is worth $2,100,000 at the present exchange rate.

2. Managing agents' remuneration arises out of a relationship by which the shareholders of Company A arrange for Company B to manage Company A for them. For tax purposes in India, the remuneration paid by Company A for Company B is deductible in obtaining the taxable income of Company A, but is taxable as part of the income of Company B. Our procedure recognizes that this income was generated by the operations of Company A.

Adjustment for Earnings of Financial Assets

	1955	1956	1957	1958	1959
	(Crores of rupees)				
Receivables	210.4	253.3	273.7	284.7	296.1
Investments	103.6	104.3	105.4	107.6	114.1
Other assets	22.4	23.4	20.5	20.3	19.9
Cash and bank balances	90.0	80.6	71.9	73.8	88.8
Total	436.4	461.6	471.5	486.4	518.9

Before computing the possible return to these financial assets, we deduct certain offsetting financial liabilities.

	1955	1956	1957	1958	1959
	(Crores of rupees)				
Trade dues, etc.	251.3	296.0	336.5	357.9	383.4
Misc. non-current liabilities	13.8	15.8	16.4	17.7	18.2
Total	265.1	311.8	352.9	375.6	401.6

The reason for deducting these liabilities (principally trade dues) is that if we impute a return to receivables, etc., we must impute a corresponding cost to "payables" of the same type.[3]

The "net financial asset" position of the 1001 companies is the differences between the two series just presented.

	1955	1956	1957	1958	1959
	(Crores of rupees)				
Net financial assets	171.3	149.8	118.6	110.8	117.3

In order not to overstate the amount of income to be attributed to physical assets, we impute a fairly high rate of return on net financial assets. This rate is taken to be 10 per cent, which substantially exceeds the rates actually obtainable on the government and industrial securities that comprise the bulk of the "investments" of the 1001 companies and that are the financial assets that can most reasonably be considered "earning assets." We obtain net income adjusted for the earnings of financial assets by deducting these imputed earnings on net financial assets from the basic "net income" series (Y_a).

3. No account is taken of the asset category "Advance of income tax," since it is invariably exceeded by the corresponding liability category "Taxation reserve." I did not choose to consider the excess of taxation reserve over advance of income tax as a liability to be offset against the other financial assets because (a) it is not a liability on which interest should appropriately be imputed; and (b) the size of taxation reserves is in part a matter of arbitrary accounting decisions.

	1955	1956	1957	1958	1959
		(Crores of rupees)			
Net income (Y_a)	145.3	158.8	139.6	157.3	202.2
Imputed income from net financial assets	17.1	15.0	11.9	11.1	11.7
Adjusted net income (Y_b)	128.2	143.8	127.7	146.2	190.5

Adjustment for Price Level Changes

To deflate the net income figures, I have chosen the index of wholesale prices of manufactured goods. This is the index that appears to correspond most closely to the output composition of the 1001 firms in the survey. To deflate the earnings of 1956, I have taken the 1956–57 index, since, in point of fact, the earnings carried in the survey as belonging to 1956 actually correspond to company financial years ending anywhere between June 1956 and June 1957. The index is given below, adjusted to make 1955 = 100.

	1955	1956	1957	1958	1959
		(Index points)			
Price index of manufacturers	100	106	108	108	111
		(Crores of rupees)			
Adjusted net income (Y_b)	128.2	143.8	127.7	146.2	190.5
		(Crores of 1955 rupees)			
Deflated adjusted net income (Y_c)	128.2	135.5	118.3	135.4	171.6

Adjustment for Excise Taxes

The price that consumers pay for a product includes whatever excise taxes apply to that product or its components. In this sense, therefore, one can defend including excise taxes in the "value added" by a process of manufacture or transformation. Naturally, such excise taxes which are included in the value added by any process should be those taxes which become applicable as a result of that process, not those which may have been paid at a much earlier stage (e.g., on raw materials before they entered the process of manufacture). When excise taxes are included in measuring the productivity of a process of transformation or manufacture, the question arises as to how those taxes should be allocated among factors of production. There is no universally valid answer to this question; but a rule that is likely to be appropriate in most cases is to allocate the excise taxes between labor and capital in proportion to their contributions to value added net of excise tax. This method is appropriate when there is a fixed input-output relationship between inputs of materials and the output of the final product, and when there is at the same time some degree of substitutability between capital and labor in the process of elaborating the materials into the final product. The relevant calculations are presented below:

	1955	1956	1957	1958	1959
	(Crores of current rupees)				
Net income of capital (Y_a)	145.3	158.8	139.6	157.3	202.2
Salaries, wages, welfare expenses	250.0	280.6	300.5	315.1	342.0
Value added net of excise tax (V)	395.3	439.4	440.1	472.4	544.2
Ratio Y_a/V	.37	.36	.32	.32	.37
Excise taxes (Rs. crores)	67.2	84.4	120.4	149.2	159.1
Capital's share of excise taxes (Rs. crores)	24.9	30.4	38.5	49.2	58.9
Price index	100	106	108	108	111
	(Crores of 1955 rupees)				
Capital's share deflated	24.9	28.7	35.6	45.5	53.0
Net income, adjusted and deflated (Y_c)	128.2	135.5	118.3	135.4	171.6
Net income, adjusted, deflated, and including capital's share of excise tax (Y_d)	153.1	164.2	153.9	180.9	224.6

The series on gross income can be obtained by adding the income figures. The gross-income counterparts to the two first net-income series (Y_a and Y_b) are obtained by adding the "depreciation provision" figures in current rupees to Y_a and Y_b. The gross-income counterparts to the last net-income series (Y_c and Y_d) are obtained by adding to these series the "depreciation provision" expressed in 1955 rupees.

	1955	1956	1957	1958	1959
	(Crores of rupees)				
Depreciation provision (D_a)	42.6	46.8	52.8	56.8	65.4
(G_a) = ($Y_a + D_a$)	187.9	205.6	192.4	214.1	267.6
Adjusted gross income ($G_b = Y_b + D_a$)	170.8	190.6	180.5	203.0	255.9
	(Index points)				
Price index of manufactures	100	106	108	108	111
	(Crores of 1955 rupees)				
Deflated depreciation provision (D_c)	42.6	44.2	48.9	52.6	58.9
Deflated, adjusted gross income (G_c) = ($Y_c + D_c$)	170.8	179.7	167.2	188.0	230.5
Gross income, adjusted, deflated, and including capital's share of excise tax (G_d) = ($Y_d + D_c$)	195.7	208.4	202.8	233.5	283.5

ESTIMATES OF CAPITAL STOCK AND OF THE
RATE OF RETURN

The basis and derivation of the data used for capital stock are presented below, in conjunction with the calculations of estimated rates of return.

Method I: Using Ratio of Net Income to Net Fixed Assets
plus Stocks and Stores[4]

Under this method, we use either the value (K_1) of net fixed assets plus stocks and stores as it appears on the combined balance sheet of the 1001 firms (adjustments A and B); or this value (K_2) expressed in 1955 prices (adjustments C and D). There is no difficulty in obtaining the figures for the K_1 series. In obtaining K_2, the deflation of the figure for stocks and stores is not troublesome, but difficulties arise in the deflation of net fixed assets. The net fixed assets figure represents a cumulation of gross asset acquisitions, less an accumulated depreciation figure. A "correct" procedure for deflating net assets would entail isolating each year's acquisition of gross assets (starting substantially earlier than 1955), deflating this figure by an appropriate price index, accumulating a fixed asset series expressed in constant prices, and applying in each year an appropriate rate of depreciation to the "real" fixed assets at the beginning of that year.

The difficulties of applying this procedure are (a) the gross annual acquisitions of assets in the years prior to 1955 cannot be calculated from the data of the Reserve Bank survey, and (b) available price indices do not appear to be very suitable for the purpose of deflating asset acquisitions. I have chosen not to deflate the net fixed asset figures shown on the combined balance sheet of the 1001 companies. My defense for this choice is that it almost certainly leads to an overstatement of the "real" capital stock and hence to an understatement of the rate of return.

To elaborate on the reasons why this procedure overstates the value of fixed assets in 1955 prices, let me consider first the situation in 1959, the end of the period being considered. The gross acquisitions of fixed assets between 1955 and 1959 exceeded the total of net fixed assets held in 1955; as virtually all prices in India were rising somewhat in the 1955—59 period, this large component of 1959 fixed assets should be deflated by price indices greater than 100 in order to convert it to 1955 prices. Consider now the fixed assets in existence in 1955. It is likely that more than half of these represent assets acquired between 1950 and 1955; and for these it is likely that the book values as of 1955 overstate value in 1955 prices. This is so because the principal price indices that come closest to being relevant for the deflation of expenditures on fixed capital goods were falling during the 1950–55 period. Thus we have:

4. "Stocks and Stores" is the term used in the Reserve Bank survey to represent "Inventories."

	1950	1951	1952	1953	1954	1955
Import prices	97	199	130	129	114	116
Wholesale prices (general)	110	120	102	104	100	92
Manufactures	100	119	104	99	100	99
Intermediate products	106	125	104	98	98	98
Raw materials	124	147	106	107	104	97

Only for assets that were more (and perhaps substantially more) than five years old in 1955 can one presume that acquisition prices were less than 1955 prices; such assets would be represented by no more than half of the book value of fixed assets at the beginning of the period surveyed, and by no more than 20 per cent or so of the book value of fixed assets at the end of this period. With the remaining 50−80 per cent of assets having acquisition prices almost certainly in excess of 1955 prices, there seems little doubt that book values overstate the values that would be produced by an appropriate deflation procedure.

In the derivation of the K_2 series, the stocks and stores figures are deflated by the simple average of the price index for manufactured goods (which includes intermediate products) and the price index of industrial raw materials. The details of the computation are given below:

	1955	1956	1957	1958	1959
		(Crores of rupees)			
Stocks and stores	421.1	512.4	564.7	569.8	585.2
		(Index points)			
Deflating index	100	110.4	111.6	111.3	117.0
		(Crores of 1955 rupees)			
Stocks and stores, deflated	421.1	464.1	506.0	512.0	500.2
Net fixed assets	534.5	634.7	765.8	862.5	911.6
Net assets deflated (K_2)	955.6	1098.8	1271.8	1374.5	1411.8
		(Crores of rupees)			
Net assets undeflated (K_1)	955.6	1147.1	1330.4	1432.2	1496.8

We can now proceed to derive the estimated rates of return to capital, based on Method I, with the four successive adjustments indicated earlier.

RATES OF RETURN ON CAPITAL (METHOD I)

	1955	1956	1957	1958	1959	Average
I A (Y_a/K_1)	15.2	13.8	10.5	11.0	13.5	12.8
I B (Y_b/K_1)	13.4	12.5	9.6	10.2	12.7	11.7
I C (Y_c/K_2)	13.4	12.3	9.3	9.9	12.1	11.4
I D (Y_d/K_2)	16.0	14.9	12.1	13.2	15.9	14.4

*Method II: Using Ratio of Net Income to 'Market Value
of the Enterprise'*

The market value of the enterprise — the total market value of its shares
plus its borrowings — is taken in this method as an alternative measure of net
fixed assets plus stocks and stores. This measure has the advantage of tending
to reflect price level changes more or less automatically. Also, it is not likely
to be as strongly influenced by arbitrary accounting procedures as the "book
values" of assets. While the "market" is not perfectly informed about the
procedures adopted and decisions taken within a company, it is likely to be
aware of situations in which the true economic value of a company's assets
differs substantially from their book value, and to price the shares of the
enterprise somewhat closer to "true" value than to book value. While probably being superior to book value as far as price level errors or accounting
procedure errors are concerned, the market value of the enterprise has its own
flaws and peculiarities. It is sensitive to waves of optimism and pessimism in
the market for shares; one can hardly hold that all movements in share prices
neatly reflect variations in the true economic value of a company's assets.
Second, some of the value that the market places on a company may stem from
its management and know-how rather than simply its assets. This second
type of error is more likely to lead to an overstatement than to an understatement of the true economic value of a company's assets; the first (expectational)
type of error can easily work in either direction.

To measure the market value of the shares of the 1001 companies in the
Reserve Bank survey, we start with the tax-free yields on industrial securities.
These are measured by the Reserve Bank of India on the basis of a different
sample of companies, but one broadly similar in industrial coverage to the
1001-companies survey. For the financial year 1959−60, the tax-free yield
of preference shares was 5.44 per cent, and that of variable dividend industrial securities was 5.27 per cent. These tax-free yields are obtained after
deducting a 30 per cent income tax-*cum*-surcharge from the dividends paid
by the respective companies. The ratios of dividends to stock prices without
deduction for personal income tax were accordingly 7.77 and 7.53 per cent,
for preference and regular shares respectively. Actual dividends paid in 1959
by the 1001 companies in the Reserve Bank survey were Rs. 64.06 crores.
We do not have a breakdown as to what fraction of this total was paid on
preference and what fraction was paid on ordinary shares, but we roughly
estimate that 14 per cent (or Rs. 8.97 crores) was paid on preference shares
and 86 per cent (or Rs 55.09 crores) was paid on ordinary shares.[5] Dividing
these amounts by the respective rates of return, we estimate the total market
value of the shares (ordinary and preference) of the 1001 companies to have
been Rs. 847 crores in 1959. To this we add borrowing of Rs. 563 crores.

5. Preference share capital is 17.6 per cent of the total paid-up capital of the 1001 companies,
and 10.5 per cent of total paid-up capital plus free reserves and surpluses. The 14 per cent figure
chosen lies midway between these two limits. I did not consider that a more refined weighting
procedure was worthwhile attempting, in view of the near-equality of the dividend rates on the
two classes of shares.

These are taken at the values shown on the combined balance sheet.[6] Thus the "Market value of the enterprise" is estimated to have been Rs. 1,410 crores in 1959 for the 1001 companies. Since these companies had a Rs. 117.3 crores excess of financial assets over short-term financial liabilities in this year, we reduce the Rs. 1,410 crores figure by this amount, obtaining an estimate of Rs. 1,292.7 crores as the value which the market placed on the firms' physical assets in 1959. This is the value (K_3) of capital stock, used in calculating rates of return under Method II.

Estimated rates of return using K_3 are presented below:

$$\text{II A } (Y_a/K_3) \ldots \ldots 15.5 \text{ per cent}$$
$$\text{II B } (Y_b/K_3) \ldots \ldots 14.7 \text{ per cent}$$

Both these estimates are implicitly corrected for price level movements, as they refer to the ratio of 1959 income to the market value of the companies' assets in 1959. There is thus no need for an adjustment corresponding to I C above. In making an adjustment for excise taxes, we simply add capital's share of these tax payments in 1959 (Rs. 58.9 crores) to the adjusted net income Y_b (Rs. 190.5 crores) for 1959, without attempting to convert the result to 1955 prices. In this way we estimate II D $249.4/K_3 = 19.3$ per cent.

Method III: Using the Ratio of Gross Income to Gross Fixed Assets Plus Stocks and Stores as a Device for Estimating the Rate of Net Return on Net Assets

It is important to realize that the ratio of gross income to gross assets is not being measured for its own sake, but as a device to enable us to say something about the economically much more meaningful ratio of net income to net assets. The method here presented is important because it provides a way of correcting for possible errors and biases in the depreciation accounting procedures used. Let me begin with two identities:

Gross income = True net income + true depreciation allowance
Gross assets = True net assets + true accumulated depreciation

By "true depreciation allowance" I mean that (unknown) amount which truly reflects the fall in economic value of existing assets during an accounting year. I mean by "true accumulated depreciation" that amount which would appear on the books of the companies if "true depreciation allowances" had been made in past years. Now, using the obvious initials for notation, we have:

$$\text{TNI} = \text{GI} - \text{TDA}$$

6. Most of the borrowings of these companies were not marketed, and those which were marketed did not, in this period, sell at prices far from their par values.

$$TNI = \frac{GI}{GA} [TNA + TAD] - TDA$$

$$\frac{TNI}{TNA} = \frac{GI}{GA} + \left[\frac{GI}{GA} \cdot \frac{TAD}{TNA} - \frac{TDA}{TNA}\right]$$

$$\frac{TNI}{TNA} = \frac{GI}{GA} + \frac{TAD}{TNA} \left[\frac{GI}{GA} - \frac{TDA}{TAD}\right]$$

Thus the ratio of true net income to the true net assets can be expressed as the ratio of gross income to gross assets, plus an adjustment factor. The sign of this adjustment factor will be determined by whether the ratio of gross income to gross assets is greater or less than the ratio of true depreciation allowance to true accumulated depreciation.

Now we do not know the ratio of true depreciation allowance to true accumulated depreciation, but—and this is the "trick" of the method here discussed—the ratio of book depreciation allowance to book accumulated depreciation is likely to be a relatively good estimate of the "true" ratio. If a company's depreciation procedures always charge an allowance which is 20 per cent too great, then book accumulated depreciation will also tend to exceed true accumulated depreciation by something like 20 per cent.

We may now turn to the actual procedure of estimating the ratio of true net income to true net assets under Method III. The ratio of gross income to gross assets is taken as the first approximation. Then, taking the book ratio of annual to accumulated depreciation as an estimate of the true ratio, we inquire whether this first approximation should be adjusted upward or downward. If the indicated adjustment is upward we do *not* make it, once again following the principle of biasing our estimates downward. Where the indicated adjustment is downward, however, we *do* make it, and we use a procedure likely to exaggerate the magnitude of the required adjustment. The procedure tends to exaggerate the downward adjustment because the ratio of book accumulated depreciation to book net assets is almost certain to be greater than the corresponding "true" ratio. Accepting that company taxes create a clear incentive toward overdepreciation, we presume that book accumulated depreciation will be larger than the true figure. This in turn implies that book net assets will be smaller than the true figure, their values having been written down at an excessive rate. So our use of the book ratio of accumulated depreciation to net assets, in cases where a downward adjustment is necessary, operates to overstate the magnitude of the adjustment and to underestimate the true ratio of net income to net assets:

Table 1 illustrates the calculations under Method III. To obtain estimates III B, the same procedure is followed, but income series G_b is used in place of G_a. Results are shown in Table 2.

To obtain estimates III C and III D we require a series on gross fixed

TABLE 1

Line		1955	1956	1957	1958	1959
(1)	Income gross of depreciation (G_a)	187.9	205.6	192.4	214.1	267.4
(2)	Gross fixed assets plus stocks and stores (W_1)	1360	1587	1817	1970	2091
(3)	Ratio (G_a/W_1)	13.8	12.9	10.6	10.8	12.7
(4)	Annual depreciation allowance (D_1)	42.6	46.8	52.8	56.8	65.4
(5)	Accumulated depreciation (F_1)	404.4	441.1	487.2	538.2	593.8
(6)	Ratio (D_1/F_1)	10.5	10.6	10.8	10.4	11.0
(7)	Difference $[(3)-(6)]$	3.3	2.3	−0.2	0.4	1.7
(8)	Accumulated depreciation/net fixed assets plus stocks and stores (F_1/K_1)	——	——	.37	——	——
(9)	Adjustment $[(7) \times (8),$ if (7) is negative]	——	——	−0.1	——	——
(10)	Estimated net rate of return to capital $[(3)+(9)]$ III A	13.8	12.9	10.5	10.8	12.7

TABLE 2

Line		1955	1956	1957	1958	1959
(1)	Ratio of gross income to gross fixed assets plus stocks and stores (G_b/W_1)	12.6	12.0	9.9	10.3	12.2
(2)	Ratio of annual depreciation allowance to accumulated depreciation (D_1/F_1)	10.5	10.6	10.8	10.4	11.0
(3)	Difference $[(1)-(2)]$	2.1	1.4	−0.9	−0.1	1.2
(4)	Accumulated depreciation/net fixed assets plus stocks and stores (F_1/K_1)	——	——	.37	.38	——
(5)	Adjustment $[(4) \times (3),$ if (3) is negative]	——	——	−.3	−.00	——
(6)	Estimated net rate of return to capital $[(1)+(5)]$ III B	12.6	12.0	9.6	10.3	12.2

assets plus stocks and stores, expressed in 1955 prices. Here, for similar reasons, I adopt the same procedure used in deriving the K_2 series for "net fixed assets plus stocks and stores." That is, the figures for stocks and stores are deflated by an index covering manufactured products and industrial raw materials, while the book figures on gross fixed assets are left undeflated, on the ground that this procedure is likely if anything to overstate their value in 1955 prices. Table 3 presents the derivation of estimates III C.

When capital's share of excise tax payments is included in gross income (series G_d), we obtain the estimates (III D), given in line 1 of Table 4. Since line 1 exceeds line 2 for every year, our procedure calls for no adjustment to the figures in line 1.

Table 3

Line		1955	1956	1957	1958	1959
(1)	Gross income, adjusted and deflated (G_c)	170.8	179.7	167.2	188.0	230.5
(2)	Gross fixed assets plus stocks and stores, deflated (W_2)	1360	1540	1759	1913	2006
(3)	Ratio (G_c/W_2)	12.6	12.8	9.5	9.8	11.5
(4)	Rate of annual depreciation allowance to accumulated depreciation (D_1/F_1)	10.5	10.6	10.8	10.4	11.0
(5)	Difference $[(3)-(4)]$	2.1	2.2	−1.3	−0.6	0.5
(6)	Accumulated depreciation/net fixed assets plus stocks and stores	——	——	.37	.38	——
(7)	Adjustment $[(6) \times (5)$, if (5) is negative]	——	——	−0.5	−0.2	——
(8)	Estimated net rate of return to capital $[(3)+(7)]$ III C	12.6	12.8	9.0	9.6	11.5

Table 4

Line		1955	1956	1957	1958	1959
(1)	Ratio of gross income, including capital's share of excise tax to gross fixed assets plus stocks and stores (G_d/W_2) III D	14.4	13.5	11.5	12.2	14.1
(2)	Ratio of annual depreciation allowance to accumulated depreciation (D_1/F_1)	10.5	10.6	10.8	10.4	11.0

Readers will note that in obtaining estimates III C and III D, I used the same figure for the ratio of annual depreciation allowance to accumulated depreciation as was used previously to obtain estimates III A and III B. I made no attempt to deflate the annual and accumulated depreciation figures because (a) the appropriate deflating indexes would be complicated weighted averages of past price levels, for which neither good component indexes nor adequate data on weights were available, and (b) the procedure already adopted of carrying gross fixed assets and net fixed assets at their book value in the deflated capital stock indices W_2 and K_2, seemed to dictate a corresponding treatment of the depreciation associated with these assets.

The following tabulation summarizes the results obtained using Method III, giving averages of the five annual estimates obtained under each successive adjustment.

Estimates of Ratio of Net Income to Net Assets

| III A | 12.1 per cent | III C | 11.1 per cent |
| III B | 11.3 per cent | III D | 13.1 per cent |

III C   11.1 per cent
III D   13.1 per cent

Method IV: *Using Cash Flows plus 1955—59 Changes in Net Fixed Assets plus Stocks and Stores To Obtain an Implict Rate of Return*

Modern techniques of project analysis do not place the same weight of reliance on the depreciation concept, nor on attempts to measure depreciation, as standard accounting procedure does. For determining the worthwhileness of a particular project, it suffices to know the expected time path of outlays and receipts. In the years of a project's gestation, outlays exceed receipts; later on receipts exceed outlays for most of a project's life. If one knows the time pattern of net outlays and/or net receipts, one need not inquire into whether outlays are on current or on capital account, nor what is the appropriate pattern of depreciation. The worth of the project can be determined on the basis of the net-outlays—net-receipts pattern alone. If one knows the rate of return required for acceptance of the project, one simply accumulates and discounts the time pattern of outlays and receipts at this rate to see if it has a positive net present value at a given point in time. If so, the project is worthwhile undertaking. If one does not know the rate of return to be used as a criterion, one may calculate the project's internal rate of return—the rate at which its outlay-receipt pattern has zero present value—and utilize this rate for comparison with those of alternative investments.

While the "internal rate of return" is used mainly for individual projects, it may also be computed for a going concern as a whole, or even for large aggregates of companies. In these cases one must recognize that the entity of which the internal rate of return is being measured does not have a definite expected life span; one must measure the internal rate for some arbitrary period, counting as an "outlay" the value of assets carried into this period and counting as a "receipt" the value of assets carried out of this period. This is precisely what Methods IV and V attempt to do for the 1001 companies in the Reserve Bank survey.

We take as "receipts" for estimate IV A the value of net fixed assets plus stocks and stores (K_1) at the end of 1959, and the gross income G_a for 1956, 1957, 1958, 1959. We take as "outlays" the value of K_1 at the end of 1955, and the amount spent on acquisition of physical assets during 1956, 1957, 1958 and 1959. These last amounts are estimated to a first approximation by the annual increments in book value of gross fixed assets plus stocks and stores. But actual cash outlays on physical assets are likely to exceed the change in gross book value of such assets, because of the retirement of some fixed assets in each year. If gross value of fixed assets goes up in a given year by Rs. 1000, and assets are retired in that year which were carried on the banks at Rs. 200, actual expenditure on new fixed assets would be Rs. 1200, not Rs. 1000.

We can estimate the amount of retirements of assets in any one year with considerable accuracy by looking at the depreciation accounts of a company.

Suppose in a given year depreciation allowance of Rs. 500 was made on the books, but the accumulated depreciation account rose by only Rs. 400. This reveals that Rs. 100 of accumulated depreciation "disappeared" during the year—*i.e.*, was written off, reflecting retirement of assets. Since assets are generally fully depreciated before they are retired, we can estimate that expenditure on new assets exceeded the growth in the book value of gross assets by the same amount (here Rs. 100) by which depreciation allowances exceeded the change in accumulated depreciation during the year. Results for the 1001 companies are shown in Table 5.

Table 5

		1956	1957	1958	1959
		(Crores of rupees)			
(1)	Depreciation allowance	46.8	52.8	56.8	65.4
(2)	Increase in accumulated depreciation	36.7	46.1	51.0	55.6
(3)	Difference [(1)−(2)]	10.1	6.7	5.8	9.8
(4)	Increase in gross fixed assets plus stocks and stores	228.2	229.1	152.8	120.2
(5)	Estimated outlay on physical assets	238.3	236.1	158.6	130.0
(6)	Gross income (G_a)	205.6	192.4	214.1	267.6
(7)	Net cash inflow on account of physical assets [(6)−(5)]	−32.7	−43.7	55.5	137.6

In computing the implicit rate of return, one must be specific about the timing of the respective net inflows. I have arbitrarily "dated" the capital stock at the beginning of the period at December 1955, all annual flows at June of the corresponding year, and the capital stock at the end of the period, December 1959.

To obtain the implicit rate of return, one must use an iterative procedure, trying out alternative rates of return until one is sufficiently close to a rate which yields a present value of inflows and outflows equal to zero. I have not attempted to carry this iteration process to extremes of accuracy; I have instead been content to stop with a rate of return that yielded a relatively small positive present value. As the rate yielding zero present value is higher than rates yielding small positive present values, the procedure adopted again introduces a slight downward bias into my estimates.

The rate of return estimated under Method IV A is 13.4 per cent. I have accumulated net inflows at this rate in Table 6, and the resulting present value (as of December 1959) is Rs. 13.5 crores.

To obtain estimate IV B, we substitute G_b for G_a as the gross income figure. The estimated outlay on physical assets remains the same as before. The estimated rate in this case is 12.4 per cent; it yields a net present value of only Rs. 6.5 crores at the end of the period. (See Table 7.)

TABLE 6

	(1) Net Inflow (Rs. crores)	(2) Accumulated Net Inflow (Rs. crores)	(3) Accumulation Factor	(4) Accumulated Net Inflow Carried into Next Period (Rs. crores)
Dec. 1955	−955.6	−955.6	1.067	−1019.6
June 1956	−32.7	−1052.3	1.134	−1193.3
June 1957	−43.7	−1237.0	1.134	−1402.8
June 1958	55.5	−1347.3	1.134	−1527.8
June 1959	137.6	−1390.2	1.067	−1483.3
Dec. 1959	1496.8	13.5		

TABLE 7

	(1) Net Inflow (Rs. crores)	(2) Accumulated Net Inflow (Rs. crores)	(3) Accumulation Factor	(4) Accumulated Net Inflow Carried into Next Period (Rs. crores)
Dec. 1955	−955.6	−955.6	1.062	−1014.8
June 1956	−47.7	−1062.5	1.124	−1194.3
June 1957	−55.6	−1249.9	1.124	−1404.9
June 1958	44.4	−1360.5	1.124	−1529.2
June 1959	125.9	−1403.3	1.062	−1490.3
Dec. 1959	1496.8	6.5		

We now turn to estimating the implicit rate of return by Methods IV C and IV D. Here I have adopted a different procedure for obtaining the deflated value of the capital stock than was used under Method I C and I D. The procedure adopted in measuring K_2 was designed to overstate the value of capital goods in 1955 prices. Since K_2 appeared in the denominator of the expression for the rate of return, this meant biasing our estimate of the rate of return downward. In the implicit-rate-of-return method, however, the higher the terminal capital stock, the higher the estimated rate of return. Hence, in order to bias our estimate of the rate of return in a downward direction, we must avoid using a method which exaggerates the terminal year's capital stock. I have accordingly chosen an alternative method of measuring capital stock in 1955 prices, which is designed, if anything, to understate the 1959 stock.

The relevant calculations appear in Table 8. In column 1 there appears for each year a figure giving the change in gross fixed assets, plus the amount of retirements estimated earlier. This reflects the expenditures made on acquiring new fixed assets in each year. These expenditures are then deflated so as to express them in 1955 prices. The price index of manufactures, which

Table 8

Net Fixed Assets, 1955   *Rs. 534.5 crores*

	(1) Expenditure on New Fixed Assets (change in gross fixed assets plus estimated retirements) (Rs. crores)	(2) Deflating Index (price index of manufactures) (index points)	(3) Expenditure on New Fixed Assets in 1955 prices [(1) ÷ (2)] (Crores of 1955 rupees)	(4) Depreciation Allowance
1956	147.0	106	138.7	46.8
1957	183.9	108	170.3	52.8
1958	153.5	108	142.1	56.8
1959	114.5	111	103.1	65.4
			554.2 total	221.8 total

I used for deflation, is not ideal for deflating capital goods expenditures, but I have encountered no superior alternative index. The deflated gross additions to assets are then summed for the four years 1956 through 1959; they yield a total of Rs. 554.2 crores, at 1955 prices. To obtain the 1959 level of net fixed assets in 1955 prices, we must add this figure to the 1955 level of net fixed assets, and subtract the depreciation which accrued during the intervening years. I did *not* deflate the depreciation allowances, partly because of the difficulties of obtaining an appropriate index, but mainly because the failure to deflate depreciation allowances leads to an understatement of the 1959 capital stock, and therefore to a downward bias in the estimated implicit rate of return. To the figure for deflated net fixed assets in 1959 (Rs. 866.9 crores, at 1955 prices) we add the estimate (used earlier in the construction of the K_2 figure) for the 1959 level of deflated stocks and stores (Rs. 500.2 crores, at 1955 prices), obtaining Rs. 1367.1 crores as our estimate of the 1959 level of net fixed assets plus stocks and stores, expressed in 1955 prices.

Estimated net fixed assets, 1959,
   in 1955 prices. = 534.5 + 554.2 − 221.8   = 866.9
Stocks and stores, 1959, in 1955 prices.   = 500.2
Net fixed assets plus stocks and stores, 1959, in 1955
   prices.   = 1367.1

In the case of the net inflows in each of the years 1956 through 1959, the deflation procedure is straightforward. The net inflows used in obtaining estimate IV B are simply deflated by the price index of manufactured goods for the corresponding year, as shown in Table 9.

The implicit rate of return based on Method IV C is 10 per cent. The computation verifying this result is given in Table 10.

In order to compute the implicit rate of return by Method IV D, we make no alteration in the initial and final capital stock figures used for the IV C

TABLE 9

	(1) *Net Inflow,* *Undeflated*	*(2)* *Deflating* *Index*	*(3)* *Net Inflows in* *1955 Prices*
1956	−47.7	106	−45.0
1957	−55.6	108	−51.5
1958	44.4	108	41.1
1959	125.9	111	113.4

TABLE 10

	(1) *Net Inflow* *(Rs. crores* *at 1955* *prices)*	*(2)* *Accumulated* *Net Inflow* *(Rs. crores* *at 1955* *prices)*	*(3)* *Accumulation* *Factor*	*(4)* *Accumulated* *Net Inflow* *Carried into* *Next Period* *(Rs. crores* *at 1955 prices)*
Dec. 1955	−955.6	−955.6	1.05	−1003.4
June 1956	−45.0	−1048.4	1.10	−1153.2
June 1957	−51.5	−1204.7	1.10	−1325.2
June 1958	41.1	−1284.1	1.10	−1412.5
June 1959	113.4	−1299.1	1.05	−1364.1
Dec. 1959	1367.1	3.0		

TABLE 11

	(1) *Net Inflow* *including* *Capital's Share* *of Excise Taxes* *(Rs. crores at* *1955 prices)*	*(2)* *Accumulated* *Net Inflow* *(Rs. crores* *at 1955* *prices)*	*(3)* *Accumulation* *Factor*	*(4)* *Accumulated* *Net Inflow* *Carried into* *Next Period* *(Rs. crores at* *1955 prices)*
Dec. 1955	−955.6	−955.6	1.068	−1020.6
June 1956	−16.3	−1036.9	1.136	−1177.9
June 1957	−15.9	−1193.8	1.136	−1356.2
June 1958	86.6	−1269.6	1.136	−1442.3
June 1959	166.4	−1275.9	1.068	−1362.7
Dec. 1959	1367.1	4.4		

estimate. The annual net inflows for 1956 through 1959 do change, however. Here we must add capital's share of excise tax payments (expressed in 1955 prices) to the net inflows used in the IV C computation. These figures were given earlier in the derivation of the Y_d income series. The net inflow series, adjusted for capital's share of excise taxes, is presented in Table 11, together with the computations supporting the estimate of 13.6 per cent as the implicit rate of return under Method IV D.

Method V: Using Cash Flows plus 1955−59 Changes in Gross Fixed Assets plus Stocks and Stores To Obtain an Implicit Rate of Return

Here we recognize that depreciation accounting procedures may have led to a bias in the computations under Method IV, through their influence on the figures used for net assets carried into and out of the period for which the computations were made. In order to allow for this possible bias, we here make the extreme assumption that true depreciation is zero−i.e., that the gross book value of fixed assets plus stocks and stores reflects their true economic value. The gross value of fixed assets plus stocks and stores was Rs. 1,360 crores at the end of 1955, and Rs. 2,090.6 crores at the end of 1959. These are, respectively, the figures for initial "outlay" and final "receipt" under Methods V A and V B. The figures for the intervening annual inflows are the same as those used under Methods IV A and IV B, respectively. The implicit rate of return estimated under Method V A was 12.6 per cent, and that obtained under Method V B was 11.4 per cent.

Methods V C and V D use the deflated 1955 and 1959 values of gross fixed assets plus stocks and stores as the initial "outlay" and final "receipt" figures. The 1959 value here is obtained by a procedure similar to that used in obtaining the 1959 stock figure under Methods IV A and IV B, except that no deduction of depreciation allowance is made. We accordingly estimate the increment in gross fixed assets between 1955 and 1959 to be Rs. 554.2 crores (expressed in 1955 prices). Since the 1955 level of gross fixed assets was Rs. 938.9 crores, we estimate deflated gross fixed assets in 1959 to be Rs. 1493.1 crores. Adding deflated stocks and stores of Rs. 500.2 crores, we have a final 1959 figure of Rs. 1993.3 crores for gross fixed assets plus stocks and stores, expressed in prices of 1955. The inflow figures (apart from initial and terminal values) are the same under Methods V C and V D as they were under Methods IV C and IV D, respectively. The implicit rate of return is calculated to be 10.4 per cent under Method V C, and 13.0 per cent under Method V D.

Chapter 3

SHORTAGES AND SURPLUSES IN EDUCATION IN UNDERDEVELOPED COUNTRIES: A THEORETICAL FORAY

Harvey Leibenstein

It is quite common for underdeveloped countries to have a deficiency of certain types of skills and, at the same time, a surplus of other skills. For example, a country may lack various types of engineers, skilled mechanics, machinery maintenance personnel, entrepreneurs, and people with managerial talents while at the same time having a surplus of individuals with a bachelor of arts degree. It is not uncommon in some underdeveloped countries to find pools of unemployed intellectuals and a shortage of craftsmen and technicians who appear to require roughly about an equal amount of education. Why should this be the case? This chapter examines that problem from a theoretical viewpoint, which naturally leads us to examine the factors that determine the demand and supply of various types of skills and to consider how the market functions with respect to such skills. The word *skills* will be used very broadly to refer to acquired capacities of any kind, including that of, say, the surgeon, the scientist, or the university professor. As visualized here, skills are seen as the consequence of formal and informal education; we include experience as part of informal education.

I. THE MARKET MECHANISM AND THE MEANINGS OF SURPLUSES AND SHORTAGES

Applying ordinary economic analysis to our problem, we can break it down into three categories: What determines the distribution of skills in an economy? What determines the demand for skills in an economy? Does the market operate in such a way as to wipe out shortages and surpluses?

All skills are built on a foundation of informal and formal general education. The informal education takes place in the early years of childhood, normally through the mechanism of the family. General motor skills are learned, and the basic linguistic skills of an individual are established. Formal education usually increases linguistic capacities and adds other types of general knowledge. This point is of significance because anyone who is deprived to some degree in achieving general education will be handicapped in acquiring some types of specific skills. It is therefore important to note that the basis for acquiring some types of skills is likely to be determined largely without regard to the market mechanism or the incentives for improvement in pursuit of higher lifetime income. An individual born into a poor family who acquires limited linguistic skills will be handicapped in comparison with the individual born into an intellectual family.

General education is valued for its own sake, and in part it is recognized as a necessary stepping stone to the acquisition of specific skills. The motivations toward the acquisition of general education are also likely to be mixed. In part such education may be looked upon as a consumption good since it is desired for reasons other than its value in the production process. But in part it is also a production good. The same may also be true of some types of specific skills. For example, in upper class families it may be thought desirable for people to acquire a profession even though they do not practice it. Thus, many people trained in law may not be primarily interested in the practice of law, and many may, indeed, not practice it, but the status of their family may require that they receive a level of education which at some point forces them to make a professional decision.

It is obvious that the acquisition of different types of skills requires gestation periods of various lengths. Indeed, one of the most significant aspects of human investment as distinguished from other types of investment lies precisely in the length of the gestation period. Thus, there are limitations to the extent to which investment in the short run can change the skill distribution of the population. Obviously medical doctors cannot be created in a short period out of people with a low level of literacy. As a consequence, within any year only marginal adjustments could be made to the skill distribution of the population. This is obviously the case if some skills take more than twenty years to acquire. But this in itself does not explain the shortages and surpluses that exist in underdeveloped countries.

Let us turn now to the demand side. According to conventional economic theory, the demand for skills will depend on skill prices and on the nature of the production function of the goods produced. The nature of the production function is crucial in such an analysis. Let us assume that the skill distribution of the population is given. Further, we will assume that there is no change in the skill distribution during the period in question. In addition, assume that the market in which the use of skills is involved operates as perfectly as possible and, further, that there is a high degree of substitutability between some skills and others and between skills and other inputs in the production techniques involved. Under such circumstances we would expect the price of a skill to fall until a point is reached at which the entire amount available of that skill is employed. As the price of the skill falls, it is substituted for more expensive skills, and, as a consequence, its use becomes fully employed at an equilibrium price. As long as the marginal productivity of any skill is greater than zero, there should be a positive price for that skill that will clear the skill market. This means that as long as anybody with a skill can conceivably do something that is productively useful in an economy, there should be a positive price at which he would be employed if markets really functioned effectively.

The above description of how the market might operate to eliminate surpluses also applies to shortages. However, before we go further a semantic note is appropriate. The word *shortage* has been employed here in the sense in which it is used in market theory, implying failure to clear the market. However, there is another sense in which the term is commonly used. A *shortage* of a certain skill is said to exist when there is too little of it to achieve some given end. For example, there might be a desire to increase steel capacity in some country by 500 per cent within a given period, but too few technicians and engineers to achieve this change. However, that way of using the term is not necessarily meaningful. It may be that such desired rates of growth are entirely unrealistic on many counts.

In a third and more subtle sense, *shortage* may refer to factor bottlenecks in what would appear to be otherwise a feasible achievement. For example, suppose there exist the savings necessary in order to increase GNP by 5 per cent. Let us assume that in many industries this can be easily achieved, but some of the cooperating industries require types of technical personnel that are not available in sufficient number to achieve the necessary coordinate expansion. I believe that this is an important sense in which the terms *shortage* and *surplus* could reasonably be used in development economics. While this sense of the term is not exactly the same as that used in the theory of competitive markets, it is very closely related to that usage. Thus, the third as well as the first meaning of *shortage* will be employed here.

II. WHY MARKETS FOR SKILLS MAY NOT BE CLEARED

Under the conventional competitive assumptions we can have a model under which the price system will operate in such a way as to eliminate surpluses and shortages. However, deviations from this model can lead to the existence of surpluses and shortages. I will consider briefly some of the possibilities.

A. *Fixed Factor Proportions*

One possibility is that the skill involved may not readily be substitutable either for other skills or for other factors of production. At the extreme, suppose a situation in which there is one best technique irrespective of price; if the best technique requires a given ratio of inputs, and if the existing quantities of the potential inputs are not in that ratio, then there will be an absolute surplus or shortage of some of them. But, although it may be conceivable that fixed factor proportions in the best or only technique could prevail in particular cases for technical reasons or because of institutional arrangements, absolute rigidity in factor proportions, with substitution elasticities of zero, is unlikely. With substitution elasticities greater than zero, a flexible price mechanism will do the equilibrating, though price adjustments will have to be greater, the lower the factor substitution elasticities. Low substitutabilities thus put a heavy burden on the price mechanism.

B. Institutional Rigidities in the Market

Institutional arrangements may prevent the proper working of the price mechanism to reflect the demand and supply situation; such arrangements will then give rise to surpluses and shortages. For example, the rates of pay in the civil service may be arbitrarily determined on the basis of political considerations, and as a consequence there may be an excess supply. The fact that there is an excess, and that as a consequence only a small proportion of the candidates make it, may even lend unusual prestige to such a service. This in turn may even attract more candidates. The surplus will be further augmented when people overestimate probabilities of receiving an appointment, or when they prefer gambling rather than making their decisions on the basis of mathematical expectations with respect to money incomes.[1]

C. Need to Stay in Market

One major difficulty in the markets for skills is the lack of information. One of the many ramifications of this problem is the need to stay in a particular skill market.

The possessor of a skill may feel that if he takes a job of another kind he will no longer be considered as a potential appointee in his most preferred skill. In addition, the time consumed working elsewhere may make it difficult for him to keep up with market information in his preferred skill. For example, he may find it difficult to make appointments and to take the time off to visit potential employers if he takes a job elsewhere. As a consequence he may prefer to be partially employed or even unemployed in order to pursue opportunities in the field of his choice.

Lack of information on the other side of the market may also operate in the same direction. That is to say, firms may not know who all the potential candidates are who may be employed currently in other fields. The result is that possessors of skills will find themselves in mutually exclusive categories, and in such circumstances there will be surpluses in some areas and shortages in others.

D. Lack of Knowledge of Production Techniques

Conventional economic theory assumes that firms have an accurate knowledge of the production function. That is to say, that they know all the possible techniques of production and the output outcomes associated with each different technique. In fact this is rarely the case. It is quite likely that in a backward economy there is even less knowledge about the range of

---

1. The "gambling effect" idea goes back at least to Adam Smith, and is spelled out in Marshall's *Principles* (8th ed.; London: The Macmillan Co., 1927), p. 554. See especially the discussion by Milton Friedman and Simon Kuznets, *Income From Independent Professional Practice* (New York: National Bureau of Economic Research, 1945), pp. 127 ff.

potential techniques than in an advanced economy. In other words, entrepreneurs may seriously underestimate the degree of substitutability of some
of the factors of production. This is especially likely to be the case with those
factors whose part in the production function is least well understood. That is
to say, this is certainly likely to be true with respect to some types of skills.
Tradition and convention are much more likely to determine the way certain
skills are employed than is the case with non-human factors of production.
As a result, firms may behave as though there are almost fixed factor proportions even if, in fact, this is not the case. The point of this paragraph is
simply that ignorance may lead to a bias in that direction.

E. Skill Gaps and Excess Supply

One element of importance is the fact that most people have a variety of
skills. But there may be discontinuities in the "skill-payoff" relationship for
any specific individual. Let us consider the case in which some individuals
have two skills, say, A and B, and others only one. In Figure 1, the curve S
shows a supply function for skill B. We assume that 400 individuals possess
only skill B, but that there are 500 individuals who possess both skills A and
B. Their reserve price for skill B is $200, given that the salary for skill A is
$200. In other words, unless they can get at least $200 in skill B they will
shift over to skill A. S is the step supply function that combines both types of
suppliers of skill B.

The demand function D crosses the supply function at 500 units. At the
equilibrium wage of $200, 500 workers will be employed, but there will be a
surplus of 400 workers in the market. However, there is no way of telling what
the actual amount of surplus workers will be. This all depends on which
workers are hired in market B. If the workers hired are all those who also

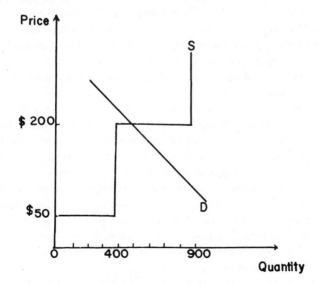

have reserve skill A, then there will be 400 unemployed in the B market who do not have the reserve skill. Let us assume that, of those hired, 200 have reserve skill A. This will mean that only 200 will be unemployed, because the other 200 (with reserve skill A) will obtain a job in the market for A. It may appear at first blush that this, in fact, could not be a general equilibrium solution — that if the ones without the reserve skill are unemployed initially in B, they will force the wage rate to fall, which in turn would induce those with the reserve skill to shift to market A. But this mode of reasoning assumes perfect information, perfect factor mobility, and the non-attrition of skills. If, in fact, those working in market B are not able to get information about opportunities or to appear to be actively available to market A because their work in B does not allow them to be, then a surplus will result.

In time, those who are not employed in B, although they had skill B initially, may gradually cease to be substitutes for those who are employed. Those who are employed gain experience and seniority, and hence become superior to those not currently employed. Also, just as people learn by doing, others *unlearn* by *not doing*. Hence those who have jobs in B become more attached to their jobs, while those who do not have jobs become less potentially attachable to them. This implies, clearly, that some of the surpluses may be due to either lack of information, the high costs of speading market information, or the relative attrition of skills by lack of employment in a specific skill.

F. Knowledge, Skill Labeling and Market Imperfections

It is clear that a great many of the reasons for market imperfections and the existence of surpluses and shortages have to do with the high degree of imperfections in knowledge in the market for human skills. Indeed, it is worthwhile to examine various manifestations of this phenomenon not only from the point of view of understanding specific situations, and from the standpoint of increasing our capacities to diagnose specific situations, but also because it may suggest some policies for underdeveloped countries.

Lack of information about an individual's capacity may result in various means of labeling and categorizing degrees of skill, as manifested in such things as the issuance of diplomas, certificates, professional degrees, and admittance to membership in trade unions, guilds, and professional and semi-professional associations. Nobody really believes that individuals holding the same degree or certificate in fact possess the same amount of skill, but employers very frequently may act as if they believed it. In many situations salary levels have to be set, and setting them in accordance with an externally determined label seems to be a reasonable compromise, given the insuperable difficulty of measuring degrees of skill or, more relevant, of actual productivity. Frequently the more highly trained people are part of overhead cost rather than part of direct cost, and hence in principle it may not be possible to attribute any direct change in output to such an individual's efforts.

For example, while we may speculate about the marginal productivity of a university dean, no one has suggested an actual means of measuring such productivity. An additional piece of evidence is that salaries of American executives appear to be correlated best with some index of size of firm rather than with profit.[2]

One consequence of skill labeling is to introduce an artificial degree of discreteness into an individual's skill capacities. This becomes especially true if the skill label includes more than one dimension. The usual thing would be for two dimensions to be involved: the existence of the certificate and years of experience. Thus, if an individual has a second skill which may be real but for which he has not earned a certificate, and if he has accumulated a number of years of experience in the certificated skill, then it may be exceedingly difficult for him to move from one skill to the other even if market conditions should dictate such a move. Indeed, the reserve skill may become almost worthless as he accumulates more experience. Thus, individuals may gradually move into non-competing groups even though in reality the degree of substitutability is much higher than it appears to be.

Let us summarize some of the causes of discontinuities in the skill patterns of individuals. We have seen that skill labeling as a response to imperfect knowledge will itself cause such discontinuities. Ignorance of the market on the part of skill sellers is another cause. In an important sense, ignorance of the market on the part of sellers is connected with the cost of search for market opportunities. It can readily be seen that there are many cases where the cost of search cannot be borne by the seller and will not be borne by anybody else. If the seller has another job, then he may not be able to take the necessary time off to search for a job in a skill area that he prefers. In part, this is due to another type of imperfection in the market. Labor discipline may require that all workers work the same hours. Certainly this is a highly institutionalized phenomenon. Hours of work is one area in which there is considerable inflexibility in the wage contract. The seller of labor cannot choose his hours of work; as a consequence he cannot choose an arrangement whereby he could pursue other opportunities were he so inclined. In addition, he may be living sufficiently close to the conventional standard in his group so that he may, in fact, feel that he cannot afford to pursue such alternative opportunities.

There is another aspect that is exceedingly important. A man cannot show his capacities apart from conventional labeling procedures. This may involve qualifications that are irrelevant for the job at hand. This is especially likely to be true in supervisory and managerial posts. A man possessing these skills but without experience may have no way of proving to a potential employer that he has the requisite skills. A potential employer in turn may have no way

2. David R. Roberts, "A General Theory of Executive Compensation Based on Statistically Tested Propositions," *Quarterly Journal of Economics*, May 1956, pp. 276ff.

of evaluating anyone's claims on this score. In addition, there may be costs involved in making such evaluations that neither party is in a position or has the inclination to bear.

Not only does the conventional nature of many labeling devices create discontinuities in skill patterns; it also has the effect of greatly increasing costs of training up to a certain standard of performance. Usually the training procedures are the same for all candidates, but it is unlikely that all in fact need the same degree of training. For some candidates the deficiency to be made up may be relatively small, but they may be forced to proceed in the lockstep fashion with the others.

To sum up, I have emphasized four factors stemming from the demand side of the picture to indicate why markets are not cleared where skills are concerned. These are (1) market pathology that distorts actual wages and quantities from their equilibrium values; (2) skill labeling and associated skill discontinuities; (3) ignorance of production functions, especially of factor substitution potentials; and (4) deliberate exaggeration of skill requirements for certain jobs.

III. DETERMINANTS OF THE RATE OF ADJUSTMENT TO SKILL REQUIREMENTS

Much of what has been said already anticipates the question as to why skills may adjust slowly to demand situations, whether the latter are distorted or not. Much of what I have not said already on this topic is common enough knowledge. I can therefore be brief here.

Consider the matter of surpluses. If there is a surplus of some skill, those people who have it will not automatically lose it simply because there is no market for it. In many cases they will possess this skill to some degree for the rest of their lives. While normal mortality patterns may reduce the surplus slightly, we obviously must not expect rapid adjustments through that means. The major solution where there are significant surpluses is for the individuals to develop substitute skills that they believe are equally good or sufficiently good so that they are willing to leave the market of their major skill. Hence, we see that the supply side of the surplus problem is similar to the shortage problem. In both cases new skills have to be created; we have to raise the question of why such skill creation does not respond rapidly to market conditions.

Probably one of the major reasons for lack of adjustment to a new demand situation is a lack of economic resources. In one way or another, potential candidates who might wish to learn new skills do not have the resources to bear the cost of such education. This involves not only the cost of tuition and maintenance but also the necessity to forgo other earnings. As a consequence, the mere creation of educational facilities, and even the existence of free tuition, will not necessarily do the job.

In addition, there may simply not be facilities to learn the necessary skills. Education depends on an appropriate hierarchical distribution of educational skills. For example, there must be some relation between people with university degrees, those with some advanced education, those with secondary school diplomas, and so on. Too few people at the top of a teaching pyramid may make it impossible to teach a sufficient number of teachers at intermediate levels in order to train those at the bottom level. On the other hand, it is possible for there to be a surplus of people at the highest level because facilities at the lower level are so deficient that not enough students are put through the mill to the highest level to employ fully the high-level talent available. These relations, which can easily be worked out mathematically, are of a type familiar to demographers. The main point to be made here is that a gap at some point in the student-teacher pyramid will cause deficiencies and surpluses elsewhere. It is significant to note that such gaps are not easily correctable simply because at some levels there is a very long gestation period involved. The importation of teaching talent may solve the problem at some levels, but there are a host of potential difficulties with this solution. For example, it may be impossible to recruit talent at the local wage level, but institutional or political reasons, as well as economic difficulties, may be involved in either raising the salary scale or having different scales for local people as against outsiders.

The development of some particular skills requires the prerequisite of possessing certain basic linguistic or calculating skills. If such linguistic or calculating skills do not exist, or if they do not exist in sufficient degree in the population, then it becomes difficult or impossible for enough people to acquire the other skills. The use of the word *impossible* in an absolute sense is probably incorrect. From a purely theoretical point of view it may always be possible for a great many individuals to learn basic linguistic and calculating skills at a later age than is normal if the resources are available. But from a practical point of view this may, in fact, be impossible. The specialized skill may be acquired through on-the-job training or by attending specialized evening courses. But there may be no way for an older man to make up linguistic and calculating deficiencies that are due to gaps in his education when he was a child.

A fundamental difficulty that runs through all these problems is the lack of self-knowledge. An individual is unlikely to know his basic deficiencies although he is frequently likely to be aware of a lack of specialized knowledge. This is especially true with linguistic skills. An individual with deficiencies in this area is unlikely to know that it is this deficiency which is the bottleneck preventing the acquisition of better paying skills. Of equal importance is the lack of self-knowledge of aptitudes. Few people really know where their potential alternative skills lie or what potential talents they may possess. As a consequence they have no way of knowing whether investment in a certain skill will pay off because they do not know the extent to which they may become accomplished in a given skill. When we add to this the lack of market knowledge, we can readily see why in many situations the necessary adjustments to changes in demand do not take place.

Other important determinants of adjustment rates relate to personal motivation. Although potential training for a given type of work may be available, many people may not be motivated to acquire it even when monetary rewards appear to be substantial. Lack of motivation probably will not manifest itself in the absolute sense of unwillingness to make an effort, but rather in preferences for alternative activities that have a smaller monetary reward. Men may be drawn toward professions that have a higher degree of prestige but a lower reward. Some will choose a job in a preferred location at considerable sacrifice in income. When we add to these motivations tthe general uncertainty surrounding careers and the lack of market knowledge, we can readily see the possibility that non-economic factors may win out over economic considerations.

Thus far we have considered two types of educational shortages: those related to imperfections in the market place and those related to deficiencies in basic skills, which in turn become bottlenecks to the acquisition of other skills. There is a third type of shortage that could be significant: the level of skill, in an aggregative sense, may not be sufficiently large to produce the rate of growth in skills that is currently desired. That is to say, there may be an over-all educational deficiency in the production of educated individuals at the rate required for a given rate of economic growth — even though the economic growth rate could be achievable on other grounds. In this case the low aggregate level of education becomes a bottleneck to economic growth at the desired rate. Whether or not this is a real problem in underdeveloped areas today is difficult to say. Here too the answer depends on the extent to which other types of resources are substitutes for human knowledge and skill. It is the writer's impression that complete substitutability does not exist and that, in fact, this is a real problem in many areas.

IV. BASIC EDUCATION AND ENTREPRENEURIAL MOTIVATION

It is self-evident that motivation is an important aspect of the development problem. While the motivation toward entrepreneurial activities is probably not a sufficient condition for a high rate of growth, it most likely is a necessary one. In addition to motivation there are minimal educational skills required for successful entrepreneurial activities. As a consequence the problem of education enters. The exact way in which it enters is difficult to determine. What follows are a series of speculations about the relationship between education and entrepreneurial activity. Some of the connections stated may be incorrect. Nevertheless, these speculations are of interest if for no other reason than that they raise interesting questions about the significance of some of the shortages.

Education in its broadest sense creates not only specific skills but also attitudes about the desirability of certain activities and about the value of education itself. It is quite likely that these attitudes are more important in fostering economic development than are the specific skills created directly by the educational process.

In this connection it is of interest to observe that many of the groups that have shown a marked talent for entrepreneurial activities have frequently been those whose culture fosters an attitude of a high degree of reverence for the written word and frequently for specific bodies of literature. For example, this is true of the Chinese in Southeast Asia, of the Japanese in Japan and in other parts of the Far East, of Jews in various parts of Europe, and of non-high-church Protestant groups in Western Europe. In some cases this is clearly connected with religion. Those groups whose religious beliefs and practices emphasize contact with a priesthood that mediates between the people and revered texts are less likely themselves to have as high a reverence for the written word as those groups who receive their inspiration directly from the sacred texts. As a consequence, we would expect Quakers, Congregationalists, and Jews, for instance, to have a greater reverence for the written word than, say, Catholics and Moslems. This generalization is probably too simple in its present form to be correct in all instances. There are obviously other intervening variables, such as the attitudes of people toward the clergy and toward more direct literary sources of knowledge. It is quite likely that reverence for the written word in literature may have been higher in Italy during the Renaissance, when the clergy was believed to be corrupt, than in earlier or later periods when there was greater respect for the interpreting priesthood. These are merely examples; we are not interested at all in stressing the religious element. Whatever the source of reverence for writing and literature, it will create attitudes and capacities that will not exist without such reverence. The reverence attached to literary matters will induce people to acquire at least certain minimum writing and calculating skills. Such skills are necessary in order to carry out trade or manufacturing activities on a scale beyond the level of simple weekly markets and cottage handicraft. Without minimum levels of record-keeping capacities, the notion of trade and entrepreneurial activities beyond an exceedingly small-scale level is out of the question.

In addition, the written word can be a window to the world beyond the village. Trade and entrepreneurship not only imply some knowledge of the "outside world," but also require some degree of mobility. The exact relationships between literacy and mobility of the geographic, social, and economic sorts have not been worked out. Nevertheless, it seems most likely that linguistic and literacy skills are prerequisites for a high degree of mobility. These reflections indicate at the very least that groups with a high degree of reverence for literacy will also be motivated to acquire the minimal skills for trade and entrepreneurial activities. Reflection suggests that what we have worked out are necessary but not sufficient conditions. While the Chinese are significant traders in Southeast Asia, mainland China was decidedly an under-developed country. Clearly, many members of groups are able to engage in activities outside their home environment that they find difficult within their native cultures. We shall not speculate here about why this should be the case. Even if the propensity to truck and barter were the same for all groups, those with greater reverence for the written word would surely be able to develop skills that would yield a greater perceptiveness of entrepreneurial opportunities and a greater capacity to take advantage of such perceptions.

V. CONCLUSIONS

The foregoing speculations suggest certain conclusions about general educational policy in typical underdeveloped areas in which there are sur-pluses and shortages of educated skills.

1. Formal education in backward economies should be designed so as to minimize the time taken to learn specialized skills. This means that the over-all educational mix should be such as to maximize general education within the constraint of minimal specialized training to meet specialized skill needs. Such a policy clearly fits in with the need to maximize mobility between jobs so as to minimize specific skill shortages and surpluses.

2. Economic development requires a high degree of mobility of various types, and general education is a necessary condition for such mobility. This follows, in part, from the fact that mobility requires a high degree of com-municability between different segments of the economy.

3. Economic development and mobility are probably fostered in a society which is culturally well integrated. General education serves these purposes as well.

4. Specific vocations require not only specific vocational skills but also certain social capacities, such as the abilities to get along with fellow workers, to receive and give orders, and to fit in easily into complex productive units. Clearly, certain minimal general education requirements are called for in this connection.

5. Two indirect aspects of general education are also of great importance. To a considerable extent, linguistic skills and attitudes toward literacy and learning are fostered and determined by the whole environment. As a con-sequence the general education of women is of significance in this connec-tion. The education of potential mothers is an indirect investment in the most basic elements of the education of the future work force. While this indirect element cannot readily be measured, it may be more important than the out-put of direct investment.

6. The general education of parents may foster a reverence for the writ-ten word and for literary skills that is connected in the long run with some of the necessary conditions for the creation of an active entrepreneurial class.

CHAPTER 4

HUMAN CAPITAL REQUIREMENTS FOR EDUCATIONAL EXPANSION: TEACHER SHORTAGES AND TEACHER SUPPLY

*W. Lee Hansen**

I. INTRODUCTION

Overcoming current and prospective shortages of teachers looms as one of the biggest hurdles facing countries that are attempting simultaneously to expand rapidly and to improve their educational systems. While reports on various plans for educational expansion abound with expressions of concern about teacher shortages, little effort has been devoted to analyzing the economic dimensions of these shortages.[1] In a sense this is understandable because the complexities of the issue, which cut across several areas within both education and economics, defy any easy formulation; and the task of assembling the relevant data needed to analyze shortages properly is even more difficult. Yet teacher shortages and the determinants of teacher supply are subjects of vital concern in development planning; they deserve far more attention than has been given to them by either educators or economists.

The role of teachers in any educational system is rather obvious — teachers represent a key input of a highly skilled labor resource which, combined with the educational plant and its allied services, produces "educated" or at least "schooled" individuals. Or, if we put this into the context of some of the recent work in the economics of education, teachers represent a stock of highly valued human capital whose input into the educational process is a most significant one. Depending on the quality and quantity of teacher supply, or the stock of available teaching capital, the quantity and quality of educational output will be greater or smaller.

If schooling is thought of as a good that is desirable in its own right, then the question of teacher shortages is usually viewed as one of securing enough "dedicated" and "highly qualified" teachers to facilitate the promotion of

---

Author's Note: Some preliminary ideas on this subject were sketched out in the author's "Educational Plans and Teacher Supply," *Comparative Education Review* (October 1962), pp. 136-41.

1. See United Nations, Economic Commission for Africa-UNESCO, Conference of African States on the Development of Education in Africa, *Final Report* Document No. UNESCO/ED/181, (Paris, 1961), cited as *African Education Report;* and UNESCO, *The Needs of Asia in Primary Education,* Document No. UNESCO/ED/60, XII 41a (Paris, 1960), cited as *Asian Education Report.*

learning among the young. Unfortunately, sufficient numbers of such people are seldom available, thus forcing the hiring of "substandard" people to staff the classrooms and leading, in turn, to claims of teacher shortages. Various proposals for increasing the supply of teachers are often advanced, but they usually lack much substance, being couched in terms of raising the status of teachers, granting them additional fringe benefits, presenting them with special awards, and the like. The very lack of vitality in the suggested remedies may well stem from the belief (among those who bemoan shortages) that because teaching represents a "higher" calling, there should be no shortages.

More recently, however, discussions of shortages have taken on a new twist. In developed countries the emphasis is on preparing projections of teacher requirements that extend over the next decade or so, in the hope that these will be in some way useful to educators, legislators, and the like, who presumably require a relatively long time horizon to develop plans for the expansion of their educational systems. Given expected rates of population growth, estimates of teacher requirements for, say, 1970 look far more impressive—and frightening—than those for, say, 1965.

In the less-developed countries numerous plans for educational expansion are also being prepared. These too involve projecting well into the future both teacher requirements and teacher supplies. The estimates of needs in these plans look still more frightening, since they take into account not only population growth but also large-scale expansion of enrollments across all levels of education. By comparison, even the most optimistic estimates of additions to teacher supply look meager. So on the strength of the apparent discrepancy between teacher requirements and actual or projected supplies, discussions of teacher shortages flourish.

How these vast numbers of new teachers will be recruited is a most perplexing problem and one that is seldom treated directly. In advanced countries, where the output of new teachers is rather sizeable, the situation is less critical because there already exists a large stock of educated people from whom potential teachers can be drawn. But in most of the less-developed countries (there are a few exceptions, as we shall see) the situation appears much more hopeless; not only do such countries have almost no reservoir of educated people but their current rate of teacher output is appallingly low. Moreover, in view of the extreme narrowness of the educational pyramid at all levels above elementary school, it will be some time before greatly increased flows of entrants into teacher training can be expected. Thus, the prospects of quick success in any "crash" teacher-training program look dim indeed. In fact, whether these countries can physically produce the number of teachers they expect to need over the next decade is a question that remains to be investigated.

In view of the apparent magnitude of the present and oncoming teacher shortages, some study of the determinants of teacher supply is warranted. Any number of questions immediately come to mind, such as: Can the length of the teacher-training courses be shortened? Can the student-teacher ratio be varied, that is, raised? To what extent can untrained people be substituted for trained teachers? Are alternative teaching technologies, such as the use of television, available? Can greater numbers of women be attracted into teaching? Are increased levels of pay effective in expanding the numbers of people desiring to become teachers? And so on.

Should the answers to these questions be negative and should the likelihood of physically producing the necessary number of teachers be small, then projected educational programs will undoubtedly have to be scaled down. Such scaling down will be required even assuming that reasonably adequate financial resources somehow become available to underwrite these programs. The prospects of obtaining such financing do not appear to be bright, but questions of finance, crucial as they are, cannot be considered here.

More pertinent to the immediate discussion is an analysis of the labor market for teachers with particular reference to the determinants of teacher supply. Two variables are of central importance in such an analysis: teacher qualifications and remuneration levels. Ideally these variables and their interrelationships should be examined within an analytical framework that defines excess and shortage in the allocation of resources to investments in formation of human versus physical capital, and also in the allocation of resources among types and levels of education. Though data are not available to permit such an examination empirically, I shall begin by sketching that framework. It will set the later discussion in a more adequate perspective.

Although education ordinarily brings a wide and rich variety of benefits to the recipient and to the society in which he functions, much of the recent enthusiasm for increased education stems from faith in the economic benefits that accrue, and is argued on those grounds. While this faith finds some support in recent estimates of the apparent growth-inducing effects of education in many of the now-developed nations,[2] the conclusion that formal education will have similar growth-inducing effects elsewhere, especially in the underdeveloped countries, still seems premature. Yet this view is voiced and acted upon irrespective of any realistic appraisal of the likely returns. Frequently the strong political, social, and cultural pressures for an expanded, broadly based education are misleadingly reinterpreted or set aside in "justifications" on economic grounds alone.

Some larger framework within which to assess education's economic contribution seems essential before we can proceed. Such a framework has already been provided as a consequence of the rapidly expanding research on the economics of education, which reveals that the magnitude of resources devoted to education and the economic returns from it prove to surprisingly large. If expenditures on education are thought of as a kind of invest-

2. T.W. Schultz, "Education and Economic Growth," in *Social Forces Influencing American Education,* ed. H.R. Richey (Chicago: National Society for the Study of Education, 1961); and Edward F. Denison, *The Sources of Economic Growth and the Alternatives before Us* (New York: Committee for Economic Development, 1962).

ment in human capital, then the allocation of resources to education becomes an investment problem, in which rates of return to education must be compared with rates of return to alternative types of investment in guiding the commitment of scarce resources to new investment projects, among them education.[3] Similarly, rates of return to investment in various types of education will also have to be considered in arriving at some "optional" mix of educational investment.[4]

This treatment of education as an investment activity can be applied directly to the subject of teacher supply. We can think of teachers as representing a stock of human capital whose services constitute one of the principal inputs to the production of a nation's intellectual capital. Given the demand for education, as reflected by the rate of return both to education generally and to various types of education, the question arises as to what amount of resources should be invested in increments to the stock of teaching capital. Since such an approach amounts to treating teachers as a kind of capital good, an exploration of rates of return to teacher training as compared to alternative types of training becomes necessary. This approach is likewise gaining greater currency and provides a fresh, and at the same time, more meaningful, approach to the subject of shortages.

If rates of return to educational investment and to teacher investment fall below alternative rates of return, then from an economic point of view scarce resources are clearly being misallocated. Under these circumstances the whole problem of teacher shortages and teacher supply considerations evaporates. On the other hand, if these rates exceed the alternative rate, then people should be clamoring for more education and for entry into the teaching profession.[5] At present, however, we know very little about rates of return to education and teacher-training investment in the United States, and almost nothing about such rates in less developed countries; the prospects of our learning much more in the near future about the latter, especially, are limited by non-availability of the necessary data. Despite its conceptual advantages, applications of the investment approach in empirical analysis of shortages and teacher supply must consequently be deferred.

II. PROJECTED SHORTAGES OF TEACHERS: METHODS OF ESTIMATION

Exactly what are the origins of the recent concern over teacher shortages? Discussions of teacher shortages certainly represent nothing very new or

3. Gary S. Becker, "Underinvestment in Education?" *American Economic Review,* May 1960, pp. 346-54.

4. W. Lee Hansen, "Total and Private Rates of Return to Investment in Schooling," *Journal of Political Economy,* April 1963, pp. 128-40.

5. W. Lee Hansen, "Shortages, Excess Demand, and Underinvestment in Training," (typescript). Some special problems arise in the case of teachers because salaries are usually fixed by governments. Although divergencies arise between the social and private rates of return, these can be handled without any great difficulty.

unique to this age. On the contrary, references to shortages can be found in discussions of the U.S. educational system over the entire course of its history; the same is true of other countries.[6] Implicit in most of these discussions is the idea that sufficient numbers of teachers of the desired quality are not obtainable at salaries currently being paid, thus forcing school authorities to hire less qualified people. The resulting claims of shortages by school officials seek to promote the idea that something should be done to help attract better qualified people into the profession. In other cases, any deviation from some "desired" number of teachers is labeled a shortage, irrespective of the possibilities of securing this number of teachers.[7]

Though it might be argued that educational output is something less than it should be as a result of a teacher shortage, the electorate is often unwilling to pay the higher salaries necessary to attract the better qualified entrants to teaching that it supposedly wants. If there already exists a superabundance of less qualified people not now teaching, they can undoubtedly be hired at prevailing salaries; but quality will clearly fall in this effort to economize. If quality is to be insisted upon, higher salaries will be required to attract people of higher quality. Eventually, this higher salary level will induce additional numbers of people to qualify themselves.

Increasingly, interest focuses on prospective rather than existing shortages in projections that ignore the question of responses to salary expectations. "Prospective shortages" become estimated discrepancies over the next decades between increased requirements for teachers and increased numbers of teachers available. The number of teachers is generally assumed to increase less than requirements. In view of the difficulty of estimating the numbers of teachers that will be available, the usual approach is to indicate the level of requirements only. Under such circumstances the prospective shortage in effect becomes the difference between future requirements and the current number of teachers.

The prospective-shortage approach appears in much of the recent work on educational planning, as exemplified in the plans for the African states, the Asian countries, and the OEEC nations.[8] While purely advisory, these plans do attempt to spell out estimates of the enrollments, teacher requirements, and costs necessary to insure that certain stated educational objec-

6. For example, see Joseph A. Kershaw and Roland N. McKean, *Teacher Shortages and Salary Schedules*, RAND Corporation Research Study (New York: McGraw-Hill, 1962); and World Confederation of Organizations of the Teaching Profession, *Survey on the Status of the Teaching Profession in Africa* (Washington: WCOTP, 1962). For the historical flavor of the "shortage" discussions in the U.S., one is advised to consult random issues of the various state reports on education, particularly in the period 1850-80.

7. See National Education Association, "Class Size in Urban Elementary Schools, 1962" (Washington, 1962), which notes the discrepancy between the number of teachers available and that necessary to reduce elementary school class size to 25 pupils.

8. *African Education Report; Asian Education Report;* and Ingvar Svennilson and others, "Targets for Education in Europe in 1970," *Policy Conference on Economic Growth and Investment in Education* (Paris: O.E.E.C., 1962).

tives are met. Many of the African nations, are already taking measures to implement their plans.[9]

Let us briefly examine the magnitudes of the projected teacher requirements in the various regions for which projections are available; these are as summarized in Table 1. For the advanced countries (lines 1-4), projected increases in teacher requirements to 1970 range from 50 to 60 per cent using the low and high estimates, respectively. By contrast, the projected total number of teachers required by the African states in 1970 is almost double the number available in the base year; for the Asian countries the number required for primary education alone was set at more than double the number available in the base year. When we realize that achievement of these totals requires not only the production of great numbers of new teachers but also

TABLE 1

Projected Teacher Requirements: 1970

(In thousands)

Line	Area	Base Year: 1960°	1970	Percentage Change
(1)	United States†	1,683.7	2,309.8 – 2,630.7	37 – 56
(2)	United Kingdom†	372.4	443.8 – 485.2	19 – 30
(3)	USSR†	1,944.0	2,606.0 – 3,082.0	34 – 59
(4)	OEEC countries†	1,885.9	2,283.1 – 2,682.9	21 – 42
(5)	African states (primary and secondary)	329.5	622.0‡	88
(6)	Asian countries (primary only)	1,838.0	3,879.0	111

° Base year varies, and for lines 1–4 tends to be for late 1950's.

† Requirements are for 5–24 age groups.

‡ Estimated by dividing projected enrollments (primary and secondary) by pupil-teacher ratio for 1965/66.

Sources: Lines 1–4: Ingvar Svennilson and others, "Targets for Education in Europe in 1970," *Policy Conference on Economic Growth and Investment in Education* (OEEC, Paris, 1962), Table 4, p. 110.

Line 5: United Nations, Economic Commission for Africa – UNESCO, Conference of African States on the Development of Education in Africa, *Final Report,* UNESCO Document No. ED/181 (Paris, 1961), Table 1, p. 26, and Table IV, p. 14 (of "Outline of a Plan for African Educational Development").

Line 6: UNESCO, *The Needs of Asia in Primary Education* (ED 60, XII 41A) (Paris, 1961), pp. 13-15.

9. Meeting of Ministers of Education of African Countries Participating in the Implementation of the Addis Ababa Plan, *Final Report,* organized by UNESCO in cooperation with the United Nations Economic Commission for Africa, UNESCO House, March 26–30, 1962, Document No. UNESCO/ED/191 (Paris, 1962). This report gives preliminary information on the development and implementation of plans for individual countries, including information on enrollments, teacher training, budgets, and the like.

the replacement of those teachers who leave teaching, the scope of these plans appears even more ambitious.

Exactly how are these estimates of requirements developed? Usually they are prepared in a rather straightforward fashion.[10] First, the population of school age is projected forward for a period of from 5 to 20 years; second, the proportions of the school age population that will be attending school are also projected forward and then used in conjunction with the figures on school age population to make estimates of the numbers of students enrolled; and third, student-teacher ratios are projected forward for these same years, and the ratios then divided into the number of students enrolled to estimate the required number of teachers. Usually such projections are broken down by the various levels of school, or by convenient age groups, so that the full dimensions of the requirements and their timing can be determined. In some rare cases, alternative estimates based on different sets of assumptions are given, thereby indicating the possible range of error that can be expected. The end results of this type of exercise are shown in Table 1.

The rather wide differences in percentage changes in requirements reflect in large part the position of a country on an educational growth curve. In a country which has universal school enrollment, enrollments and teacher requirements will increase at the same rate as the growth of the school-age population. By contrast, in a country which is rapidly expanding its enrollment rates from very low initial levels, teacher requirements will rise at a much faster rate than the growth of school-age population. Thus, a country's starting point is of great importance in understanding the varying dimensions of teacher requirements, as shown in Table 1. (Varying rates of growth of the school-age population are also important and help to account for some of the differences in lines 1−4 in particular.)

Some of the more subtle timing relationships would appear if the projected requirements were disaggregated by level of schooling. To illustrate this, the African countries cannot greatly expand their secondary school system until they are graduating large numbers of people from their primary schools. Since this may require a decade, the bulk of secondary school expansion might be expected to occur sometime in the late 1960's or early 1970's.

Estimates of teacher supply are ordinarily much less explicit, even when an attempt is made to treat them, something which itself is rare. However, there are two commonly used methods of projecting supply: supply is projected forward on the basis of number of new entrants into teaching, or it is projected forward on the basis of the recent proportion of college or teacher-training graduates entering teaching. These projections are often constrained, especially in the less-developed countries, by the projected availability of

---

10. E.G. Jacoby, *Methods of School Enrollment Projections*, UNESCO Educational Document No. 59, XII 32a (Paris, 1959).

places in teacher training schools. In any case, an attempt is usually made to identify prospective supply by level of school.

A combination of such supply projections is exemplified in the report of the Fund for the Advancement of Education in the United States, which shows that at the high school level the proportion of college graduates needed to staff the classrooms will far exceed the proportion of those graduates who have teacher training; it will exceed by an even greater amount the proportion who usually enter teaching in the fall following college graduation.[11] Much the same picture emerges at the college and university level where, the report indicates, the proportion of Ph.D.'s who can be expected to teach will fall well below the number needed to teach the ever-expanding college enroll- ments. It should be noted that in both these cases the possible increments to teacher supply are assumed to be drawn from a higher quality group than present teaching staffs.

These methods of estimating requirements and supply are almost certain to yield results which indicate teacher shortages. The reasons are simple. First, if a population has been experiencing an increase in the proportions enrolled in school, particularly at the earlier age levels, or if it is planning an increase in the proportions enrolled, then the rate of growth of the school population will almost certainly exceed for some years the rate of growth of that part of the school population from which teachers are drawn, namely, the college and teacher-training school age groups. This tendency will be accentuated if the rate of growth of the school-age population has been in- creasing in the past few years, as it has been in most countries.

Second, and equally important, these projections frequently impose some new and higher quality standard on the supply side, reflecting the hope that the quality of the teaching staff can or will in some way be raised. Conse- quently, shortages of qualified teachers by reference to this new standard look much larger than they might have looked according to the existing standard. If the average quality of the teaching staff were to remain unchanged the numerical "shortage" would be considerably reduced.

Because the projected-shortage approach leaves so much to be desired, it seems hazardous to place any significant weight on the results it generates. Past experience with projections only serves to emphasize this point.

Let us examine some recent experience with teacher requirement pro- jections. First, in 1954 the Fund for the Advancement of Education prepared projections of elementary, secondary, and college teacher requirements for periods up to 1970; on the basis of these projections the report indicated that the U.S. would be hard-pressed to meet these needs.[12] Yet by 1960 the in- crease in the actual number of college teachers considerably exceeded that which had been projected. At the secondary level the actual number of

11. Fund for the Advancement of Education, *Teachers for Tomorrow*, Bulletin No. 2 (New York, 1955).
   12. *Ibid.*

teachers was almost twice that projected, while at the elementary level the actual number of teachers fell short of the projected need by a wide margin (see Table 2). Second, the highly regarded Crowther Report indicated that a serious shortage of teachers was already developing in Great Britain because the current and expected inflow of new teachers was far below projected requirements. Nevertheless, by 1960 and 1961 the number of new entrants into teaching was up sharply from the 1955-58 period, being approximately equal to projected needs.[13] Third (and this is one of the few examples available to the author for one of the less-developed countries), the Beecher Report for Kenya in 1948 indicated that the number of teachers required by 1957 for the African schools would be approximately 10,000.[14] In fact, the number of teachers amounted to 13,095, an increase far exceeding that thought possible eight years earlier[15] (see Table 2).

TABLE 2

Selected Comparisons of Projected Requirements
with Actual Numbers of Teachers

Country	School Level	Base Year Level	Projected Level	Actual Level
		1954	*1960*	*1960*
	Primary	876,000	1,122,000	993,000°
United States	Secondary	288,000	367,000	650,000°
	College	190,000	250,000	284,000
		1949	*1957*	*1957*
Kenya (African)	Primary	6,990	9,860	13,095
	Secondary	226	129	693

° Estimated with help of enrollment ratios.

Sources: *United States:* Cols. 1 and 2, Fund for the Advancement of Education, *Teachers for Tomorrow* (New York, 1955), Tables 6 and 7. Col. 3, *Statistical Abstract of the United States* (1962), p. 124 for public and p. 128 for private. Private teachers were allocated to primary and secondary schools on basis of enrollment ratios.
Kenya: Cols 1 and 2, *Beecher Report,* pp. 87, 92, and 94. Col. 3, *World Survey of Education,* Vol. III (Paris: UNESCO, 1961), pp. 1188-97.

While the number of examples cited is limited, the evidence clearly shows that projections of requirements are unlikely to square with the actual numbers that are or will be forthcoming. In most of these examples, the

13. Ministry of Education, *15 to 18,* (London: HMSO, 1959), Vol. I, pp. 154-55; this is commonly known as the Crowther Report. *Annual Abstract of Statistics 1961* (London: HMSO, 1961), Table 99, p. 89.
14. *African Education in Kenya,* Colony and Protectorate of Kenya (Nairobi, 1949), pp. 87, 92, and 94; this is commonly known as the Beecher Report.
15. UNESCO, *World Survey of Education* (Paris, 1961), Vol. III, pp. 1188-97.

actual numbers exceeded rather than fell short of requirements that were thought to be almost impossible to achieve. This causes one to ask the question: How was it possible to recruit these substantially larger numbers of teachers? We shall pursue this question later in the paper.

III.THE AFRICAN AND ASIAN EDUCATIONAL PLANS

A more detailed examination of several of the educational plans, focusing particularly on their treatment of teacher requirements and teacher supply, may be appropriate at this point. Since the African and Asian countries are slated to experience the greatest relative projective shortages, they seem to be the most appropriate choices for this purpose. Specifically, we will attempt to assess the likelihood that these plans will achieve their objective of supplying the larger outputs of teachers necessary to instruct the growing school enrollments. In making this assessment, we shall take as given the basic elements of these plans, in order to highlight the teacher supply aspects.

The African plan has both short-term and long-term components. Since the time horizon of the long-term plan (to 1980) makes any conclusions about teacher requirements and teacher supply highly tenuous, more can be said about the short-term plan for the period 1960 to 1965. Thus, we shall confine our remarks to the short-term plan.

Because no stock of already-educated people exists from which potential teachers can be drawn, all additions to teacher supply must come from the teacher-training schools.[16] Two principal types of training schools exist: the lower which prepares people for primary school teaching, and the higher which prepares people for secondary school teaching. Both courses of study have been set at three years' duration, the lower to commence after the completion of primary school and the higher after the completion of secondary school.

The short-term plan calls for additional primary and secondary school teachers (both replacement and new demand) in the amounts shown in lines 1 and 2, respectively, of Table 3; these amounts are summed in line 3. The numbers who are expected to be enrolled in training are given in lines 4 and 5. To estimate the annual output of new teachers, the amounts in lines 4 and 5 must be divided by three, since the teacher-training courses are of three years' duration. The estimated numbers of graduates at the two levels appear in lines 6 and 7; these outputs are summed in line 8.

Although the output of primary school teachers exceeds requirements throughout the duration of the plan, the output of secondary school teachers will be 50 per cent short of requirements in the terminal year, 1965. Since primary school teachers cannot readily convert to secondary school teaching, there will be a surplus of one type and a shortage of the other. It seems odd that we would find such an unexplained situation emerging in a development plan of this type. An additional inconsistency may exist: because pri-

16. This is admittedly an oversimplification.

TABLE 3

Prospective Teacher Requirements and Supplies
for African Education

Line	Level or Type of School or Training	School Year				
		60/62	62/63	63/64	64/65	65/66
	Number of additional teachers required					
(1)	Primary	22,600	27,800	32,400	37,200	43,300
(2)	Secondary	4,200	8,700	13,000	15,720	21,300
(3)	Total	26,800	36,500	45,400	52,920	64,600
	Projected enrollment in teacher-training schools					
(4)	Lower	75,300	92,700	108,000	124,000	144,000
(5)	Higher	12,000	17,300	21,300	26,500	35,000
	Estimated graduates of teacher-training schools					
(6)	Lower	25,100	30,900	36,000	41,300	48,000
(7)	Higher	4,000	5,800	7,100	8,800	11,700
(8)	Total	29,100	36,700	43,100	50,100	59,700
	Adjusted estimated graduates of teacher-training schools					
(9)	Lower	12,550	15,450	18,000	20,650	24,000
(10)	Higher	2,000	2,900	3,550	4,400	5,850
(11)	Total	14,550	18,350	21,550	25,050	29,850
	Projected secondary school enrollments					
(12)	Intermediate	135,600	150,200	178,800	212,400	264,000
(13)	Academic	542,200	600,700	715,200	849,700	1,056,100
	Estimated graduates of secondary schools					
(14)	Intermediate	45,200	50,000	59,600	70,800	88,000
(15)	Academic	90,400	100,200	119,200	141,500	176,000
(16)	Total	135,600	150,100	178,800	212,300	264,000
	Gross estimate of potential additional supply of teachers (sum of lines 8 and 16)					
(17)	Total	164,700	186,800	221,900	262,400	323,700
	Adjusted estimate of potential additional supply of teachers					
(18)	Total	82,350	93,400	110,950	131,200	161,850

Source: Lines 1, 2, 3, 4, 5, 12, and 13 from *African Education Report*, pp. 24-28. Line 6: line 4 divided by 3. Line 7: line 5 divided by 3. Line 8: sum of lines 6 and 7. Lines 9-11: lines 6-8 divided by 2. Line 14: line 12 divided by 3. Line 15: line 13 divided by 6. Line 16: sum of lines 14 and 15. Line 17: sum of lines 8 and 16. Line 18: line 17 divided by 2.

mary school teachers must be trained by secondary school teachers, any deficiencies in the number of secondary teachers will undoubtedly restrict the training of primary teachers. So the realized numbers of primary graduates may fall short of those indicated.

In fact, however, the number of additional trained teachers that will be forthcoming is grossly overstated by my crude calculations, for several reasons. First, no allowance has been made for dropouts during the teacher-training course. Second, as calculated here, the number of graduates is too large; when enrollments are rising rapidly, the flow of current graduates is a function of past rather than current enrollment figures. (This means that lines 6 and 7 would have had to be divided by some figure greater than three to allow for the growth factor.) And, third, not all teacher-training school graduates can be expected to actually begin teaching. Hence, actual additions to teacher supply will be substantially below the potential additions which are shown in my calculations. Although it is difficult to make a proper adjustment for some of the factors just mentioned, it does not seem too unrealistic to believe that actual output might be on the order of 50 per cent of potential output. Accordingly, lines 9-11 show the numbers of new teachers that are more likely to be forthcoming. Should this set of numbers materialize rather than those in lines 6-8, the planned provision of "education for all" in the African states will be off to a slow and shaky start.

One way of dealing with the shortages of teachers that emerge under the conditions just set forth involves recourse to educated people not formally trained as teachers. Let us assume that intermediate school graduates and academic secondary school graduates are to be employed in teaching primary and secondary schools, respectively. The projected enrollments for these levels of school appear in lines 12 and 13; the estimated numbers of graduates, assuming an intermediate course of three years and an academic course of six years, appear in lines 14 and 15, respectively, and are summed in line 16. If we then add potential trained teachers and other graduates, the potential supply of teachers (line 17) is roughly six times that which is required. But as before, this figure is on the high side, given the manner in which it was calculated. In addition, it fails to take account of the flows of students into higher education, vocational education, and education administration. After a crude downward reduction of 50 per cent in this figure, a more realistic potential supply figure (line 18) yields a ratio of more than two and one-half to one over requirements. But whether any of these people will be available for teaching (aside from those trained as teachers) seems rather unlikely; undoubtedly the top-level and middle-level manpower experts have already assigned these people to other key positions in the economy. Our conclusion, then, must be a cautious one: additional non-trained but educated people will be required to supplement the trained teacher corps; whether sizeable numbers of them will be available for teaching is not at all clear.

The Asian plan, like the African plan, focuses on the period 1960 to 1980 but with greatest emphasis on the period through 1965.[17] In examining this plan, which is much more sketchy than the African plan, we need only consider its first year to point up inconsistencies on the teacher supply side. The plan calls for an additional 194,000 primary school teachers in 1961. Since total enrollment in teacher-training schools amounted to only 280,000 in 1958, it is difficult to envision how the required 194,000 new teachers can be produced without substantial enrollment increases over the period 1958-61. Assuming a three-year study course, enrollments would have had to rise to approximately 588,000 to sustain this level (194,000) of graduates. Such an increase seems unlikely to have occurred, though no firm evidence is available on training school enrollments in 1961. Thus, it appears that the timing of the Asian plan will be upset from the very beginning; not only will it be impossible to recruit sufficient trained teachers but it will also be impossible to reduce the number of untrained teachers, which now accounts for more than 35 per cent of the teaching force. If we introduce any positive attrition rate in the teacher-training course, and if we further allow for the possibility that not all graduates will teach, the Asian plan cannot even begin to succeed in supplying sufficient numbers of teachers.

As in the case of the African countries, Asian secondary school enrollments are already substantial and might provide the necessary additional flow of graduates to help staff the primary schools. As of 1957-58 secondary enrollments amounted to 11,654,000 which, on the basis of a six year course of study, suggests a maximum output of about 2 million graduates per year. While this estimate is very crude and, among other things, makes no allowance for wastage, there would nonetheless be ample numbers of untrained people to fill the gap. But again, this means competing for these educated people against the demands emanating from other growing sectors of the economy. ,

On the basis of this cursory examination of the teacher supply aspects of the African and Asian plans, it appears that they can succeed only by attracting large numbers of untrained people into teaching. Unfortunately, nowhere is this point made clear. The impression is given that, provided financial resources are available to establish the necessary training schools, all will go well. Yet a closer examination indicates that the quality of the teaching staff must decline if enrollment increases at the projected levels are to be maintained. This decline, which is independent of the rising pupil-teacher ratios already built into the projections, indicates a further decline in the over-all quality of education.

One of the economist's traditional roles has been that of advising others about the consistency of their goals and the means they have for achieving them. To pursue this line, we are forced to conclude that the proposed tech-

17. See "Report on the Regional Meeting of Representatives of Asian Member States on Primary and Compulsory Education," Karachi, 28 December 1959 to 9 January 1960, Document No. UNESCO/ED/173 (Paris, 1960), pp. 32-48.

nology and the available resources will not permit expansions of the educational systems of the indicated magnitudes or at the proposed speeds. Even if these expansions could be achieved, it would be at the cost of a substantially larger decline in educational quality than has been anticipated. In view of the costs to be incurred and the probable rapid decline in quality as the size of the educational system expands, one must seriously question the efficiency with which resources will be allocated if these plans proceed. From all appearances, it seems likely that compromising on quantity and attempting to hold to quality may be a necessary step if educational expansion is to hold any hope for accelerating economic growth.

This bring us to still another point regarding these plans; namely, that they have been drawn up to indicate the kind of educational program these areas would *like* to have rather than the kind they *expect* to have. What we are suggesting is that these plans represent a plea for a greater commitment of resources to education, resources which will have to be obtained from external sources, such as UNESCO, foreign-aid programs, private foundations, and the like. To the extent that these plans indicate desires rather than expectations (and aside from any of their inconsistencies), it is difficult to take them too seriously.

Nonetheless, we must recognize that whether or not we are confronted with "realistic" plans, great political, social, and economic pressures will be exerted on governments to provide more education. As a consequence there will undoubtedly be shortages of teachers just as there will be shortages of numerous other types of people as development occurs. Since the plans tell us nothing about how to cope with shortages, we must turn elsewhere. At this point the experience of other countries that have successfully passed through periods of rapidly expanding demand for education and teachers may have some lessons to offer. To this we now turn.

IV. SHORTAGES AND THE DEMAND FOR EDUCATION

Talk of teacher shortages implicitly assumes that enrollments are given and that all adjustments must occur in the size of the teaching staff. While convenient, this is by no means a satisfactory way of viewing the matter, for we know that teacher shortages will look larger or smaller depending on the magnitude of expected changes in the demand for education and in the technology of education. To the extent that both the demand for education and the technology of education can be affected by policy measures, no discussion of teacher shortages is complete if it is limited to supply considerations alone.

The demand for teachers depends basically on the demand for education, which is affected in turn by a large number of considerations. To the extent that schooling is compulsory and registration is enforced, the demand for

TABLE 4

Comparison of Projected and Actual Enrollments
from Base Year, Selected Countries

Country and Level of School	(1) Base Level	Projected		Actual	
		(2) Level	(3) Index°	(4) Level	(5) Index†
United States†	1954	1960		1960	
Primary	26,265	33,650	128	33,300	126
Secondary	7,203	9,200	128	9,600	133
College	2,478	3,249	131	3,750	152
New Zealand	1950	1957		1957	
Primary	258,000	334,000	129	345,000	133
Secondary	48,000	62,000	129	78,000	163
Kenya	1948	1957		1957	
African Primary	256,000	547,000	215	420,000	163
African Secondary	567	2,400	423	11,265	1900

° All indexes have as their base the year in the "base level" column.
† All U.S. figures are given in thousands.

Sources: *United States:* Cols. 1 and 2: *Teachers for Tomorrow.* Col. 4: U.S. Department of
   Health, Education, and Welfare, *Trends 1961,* p. 39.
   New Zealand: Data read from Figures 2 and 3, E. G. Jacoby, *Methods of School En-
   rollment Projections* (ED. 59, XII. 32.a), pp. 14-15.
   Kenya: Beecher Report and *Education Report, Annual Summary 1960.*

education will be largely a function of the school-age population.[18] Where
schooling is not compulsory, other variables become important: the availability of space in schools, entry examinations and requirements, direct school
fees, opportunity costs of schooling, not to mention various noneconomic
variables. To judge from the work done in projecting enrollments, little effort
has been made to explore the importance of any of these factors.

To make conventional estimates of the demand for education (enrollments), we require school-age population projections and projected school
enrollment ratios for corresponding age groups, by which projected enrollments can be estimated. However, two sources of error crop up in the use of
this crude model. First, the population projections may be in error (this is
not as uncommon as might be thought). Second, and very likely, the projected
enrollment ratios may be incorrect. Ideally we require both a tested theory
of population growth to help improve population projections, and a tested

18. Compulsory schooling, while frequently embodied in law in underdeveloped countries,
is seldom enforced with any rigor.

theory of labor force behavior for school-age people to help improve enrollment ratio projections. Since we possess neither of these, projections will
continue to yield poor predictions except by sheer accident.

A comparison of actual and projected enrollments for several countries
may be helpful in demonstrating how far off the projections invariably are.
(See Table 4.) In reviewing these projections several things stand out. First,
the projections for the United States and New Zealand tend to be better than
those for Kenya, suggesting that projection accuracy is a function of the uni-
versality of the school system. Second, the accuracy of the projections seems
to be inversely related to the level of schooling. Expressing these same observations in another way: the accuracy of the projections is positively related to the proportion of the school-age population enrolled in school. Obviously the impact of other factors in affecting enrollments can be much more
important where differences between maximum potential and actual (or
projected) enrollments are greatest.

In the United States, discrepancies (actual figures over projected ones)
at the primary and secondary levels appear to have been negligible; the wider
discrepancy at the college level can probably be explained by the recent
stress on the gains to be obtained from more education, the increased ability
to pay for education, and the decline in the relative direct price of schooling.
These same factors have probably been instrumental in the Kenya case, with
the greater expected weight falling on the relative decline in the direct costs
of schooling and the realization of the gains to be had from education. Clearly
the evidence needs to be checked more closely, but it does suggest that the
price of education, among other things, is important and hence might be used
more effectively in influencing the level of demand for education.

In practice, average pupil-teacher ratios are used as a rule-of-thumb in
translating projected enrollments into projected teacher requirements. But
relatively little is known about the way in which educational output is
affected by varying pupil-teacher ratios. If these ratios can be higher than
they now are, or if educational output is unaffected by temporary changes in
these ratios, the possibilities of adjusting teacher requirements will be
greatly increased. Until studies of these technological relationships between
educational input and output are undertaken and completed, we really have
no useful estimates of the derived requirements for teachers.

In summary, then, teacher shortages are not independent of actions taken
(or not taken) to affect enrollments and pupil-teacher ratios. Some effort
should be made to study the way in which enrollments change in response to
varying fees, among other things, and to what extent educational quality is
affected by varying pupil-teacher ratios. The findings should make it possible
to deal more effectively with shortage situations.

V. THE SUPPLY OF TEACHERS

In understanding the supply dimensions of teacher shortages, we must begin by exploring the operation of the teacher labor market. I will organize discussion around four topics: (1) recruitment; (2) retention policies; (3) qualification standards; and (4) remuneration. The first two of these relate to the structure of the market; the third and fourth are variables that condition the success of recruitment and retention policies.

Recruitment

Potential additions to teacher supply are, in the short-run, limited by (1) the current output of new teacher-trained graduates of the schools, and (2) the existing stock of teacher-trained people inside or outside the labor force but not now teaching. Of the current output some part will be lost, either because of movement out of the labor force (especially women) or movement into other types of jobs. Of the previous output of teachers, some portion can probably be lured back into teaching, either from other occupations or from home activities, though some retraining may be necessary for this group. In addition, there is (3) the current output of all graduates, whether teacher-trained or not, as well as (4) the existing stock of all graduates. Of the former group, those interested in teaching might be converted into teachers after a short course in teacher training. The same is true of the latter group, though its training would probably have to be more lengthy.

I remarked earlier that already developed nations will undoubtedly have a sizable stock of previously trained teachers from which additional teachers can be drawn. Also, in addition to the current output of teacher graduates, they can draw upon other current graduates to help fill out teaching staff needs. But less-developed countries will possess only a negligible stock of educated people, and their output of new teacher graduates will probably be only a trickle, at least at first. Consequently, they will have to rely primarily upon the flow of other new graduates unless they establish some short adult education-teacher training program. The only exception is those countries where teacher training is a part of the formal curriculum taken by all students.

A major alternative source of supply is expatriates and nationals of other countries, not to mention members of the Peace Corps. Substantial numbers of these people are already in use in many of the African states, but the higher cost per teacher tends to make this option less attractive than it might otherwise be.

One of the major constraints on teacher supply is the virtual absence of any stock of educated women and the failure to provide educational opportunities for women in most of the underdeveloped countries. This failure to educate women stems from a number of considerations, but undoubtedly the low ratio of expected returns for the cost of education outlays plays an important role.[19]

19. See "Access of Women to the Teaching Profession," Commission on the Status of Women, Document No. UNESCO, E/CN 6/375 (Paris: January 1961).

Retention

Rates of attrition in teaching usually tend to be rather high for assorted reasons. In developed countries large numbers of females enter teaching only to leave after several years to marry and raise families. In underdeveloped countries where the bulk of the teachers are male, the lure of other higher-paying and higher-status occupations quickly drains off much of the existent supply. The fact that large proportions of the new political leaders in Africa were formerly teachers testifies to this. Although women can possibly be attracted back into teaching at some later date, it is unlikely that much can be done to delay or prevent their marriages. In this sense it will always be difficult to retain them. Of male leavers (whether in developed or less-developed countries), experience shows that very few are likely to return to teaching.

Qualifications

The qualifications established for teaching have an important bearing on the success of recruitment policies. By the simple expedient of lowering standards, it becomes far easier to recruit additional teachers. However, as a country's educational level rises or is projected to rise, teacher qualifications tend to be raised rather than lowered. This is done apparently in the belief that the quality of education must be raised, though it may be that the educators are also attempting to restrict supply by raising standards.

Undoubtedly, some minimum qualifications for teachers exist in order to insure that given levels of educational quality prevail.[20] One of the real tasks seems to be that of introducing greater flexibility into the qualification standards, which are too often stated in terms of the completion of certain amounts of schooling rather than in terms of the ability to do a good job of teaching. Recent experience has shown that some people can become effective teachers without extensive formal training in pedagogy; it has also been demonstrated that a much-shortened course of teacher training may often be as effective in preparing teachers as the longer, more traditional programs.

By reexamining and, where appropriate, revamping teacher qualifications, the supply-restricting effects of qualification standards can probably be reduced substantially without forcing undue compromises on teacher quality. Some efforts being made along these lines will be mentioned later.

Remuneration

Even though some people desire to teach for the intrinsic satisfactions derived, such people cannot be expected to supply the whole of the teaching staff. For most people the costs of securing the required level of training will act as a deterrent to entry even though the additional income obtained from that training acts as an inducement to entry. The incomes avail-

20. Some of these are outlined in WCOTP, *Survey on the Status of the Teaching Profession in Africa* (cited in fn. 6).

able in alternative endeavors requiring approximately the same amount of training will also be relevant in affecting career decisions between teaching and other occupations.

Teachers' salaries in many of both the advanced and the underdeveloped countries are often judged to be too low relative to those in other occupations requiring comparable amounts of training, with consequent undesirable effects upon recruitment and retention.[21] One of the major difficulties is that teacher salary schedules are not only rigid but are often tied to other salary schedules, so that their usefulness in meeting changed market conditions is greatly limited. Teachers' salaries in the U.S., for example, where the bulk of the teachers are females, may well be tied to the female labor market so that males are virtually precluded from entering the field, at least at the primary and secondary levels. On the other hand, in underdeveloped countries the salary schedules are frequently tied to the civil service schedules (which apply almost exclusively to men) so that there would be a strong, positive incentive for females to enter teaching. In either case, however, these ties to other (and often dissimilar) labor markets limit the possibility of necessary adjustments in teachers' salaries reflecting current market conditions. Furthermore, where salary scales are established on a national basis, they provide no means for facilitating adjustments in the distribution of teachers as, say, between rural and urban areas. Since urban areas are normally preferred, higher salaries in the rural areas might be expected to offset this preference.

While high starting salaries are instrumental in aiding initial recruitment, the rate of salary progression with length of experience is important in retaining already experienced teachers. Too often insignificant attention has been given to this dimension of the salary structure.

Finally, the costs of securing teacher training will also enter the calculus. In a great many countries teacher training is free or nearly so, except for the time of the person undertaking training. Thus, costs do not pose a major deterrent to entry. On the other hand, if salary levels in teaching are not attractive enough, people will undertake teacher training and then move into other occupations. In this sense the expenditure made by society on their training will have been wasted.

All in all, the prospects for improving the success of recruitment and retention policies by rationalization of the salary structure appear to be worth considering. Although the effect of financial incentives is widely appreciated, their applicability to the problem of teacher supply is less generally recognized.[22] Admittedly, a vast network of institutional forces works against alteration of the current salary structure, but it would seem that if the efficacy of a dynamic salary structure could be demonstrated some of this resistance might begin to disappear.

---

21. *Ibid.* A sampling of teacher salary schedules and those of approximately comparable groups is given for a number of the African countries.

22. See Kershaw and McKean, *op. cit.*

VI. CASE STUDIES

In this section I sketch how some countries have managed to cope with rapid increases in the demand for education. The best data available to me are for Kenya and the United States in the 1950's. To summaries of these I will add fragmentary material on Jamaica and Brazil to show other types of adjustments.

Kenya

The experience of the African schools in Kenya offers a challenge to anyone seeking to explain how adjustments occur in response to rapidly increasing requirements for teachers.[23] To summarize briefly, projected teacher requirements over the period 1948-57 called for large relative increases in the numbers of teachers at both primary and secondary levels, but in fact the actual increases far exceeded those projected at both levels (Table 2). In this sense, the plans were more than achieved. Just how was this accomplished?

First, a word about enrollment increases. African primary plus intermediate enrollments jumped from 310,000 in 1949 to about 725,000 by 1960. Meanwhile, secondary enrollments fell off through the mid-1950's, reattaining the 1949 level in the late 1950's; the 1960 total of about 11,000 includes academic secondary, teacher-training, and vocational students not shown separately in 1949. The bulk of the pressure of enrollments has thus been felt at the primary-intermediate level. Undoubtedly, many factors contributed to the increased primary enrollments, one of which was the relative fall in the price of schooling. For example, whereas primary tuition amounted to 10 shillings in 1949, the fee was raised to 20 shillings in 1955 and has remained at that level. After the increase, tuition exemptions undoubtedly increased so as to partially offset the rise in fees. But at the same time all prices far more than doubled, and the wages of unskilled Africans in Nairobi rose by about two and one-half times. At the secondary level, where the net change in enrollments was negligible, total fees (including board) apparently increased at a somewhat faster pace (by about three times), reaching a level 15 times that of primary fees by the year 1960. Surely the rising relative cost of secondary schooling, not to mention the absolute level of the costs, would have acted to deter any large enrollment increases even if place rationing had not been in effect. On the other hand, teacher training is ordinarily provided at a reduced cost or at no cost whatsoever. The impact of free or nearly free teacher-training instruction shows up in the enrollments, which rose from 1100 in 1950 to 3700 in 1960, in the face of virtual stability in the numbers enrolled in secondary schools.

---

23. All data are drawn from the *Beecher Report, Annual Reports of the Education Department,* and *Annual Reports of the Labour Department.*

Second, what was happening to the supply of teachers? As already mentioned, low fees certainly encouraged larger numbers of people to enter teacher training. In addition, however, teachers' salaries slightly more than doubled over the period 1949-60. While this might suggest something of a decline in their relative earnings position, the limited alternatives open to educated Africans may in fact impose some kind of ceiling on their salaries. To the extent that the salaries of teachers are linked to those of civil servants, and there does appear to be such a link, this decline in relative wage position would have occurred for all educated groups. The net effect would have been to increase slightly the attractiveness of teaching, given the decline in costs of training. At the same time, however, female wages remained set at about 80 per cent of male wages, in contrast to substantially wider differentials in other sectors of the economy. Thus, from both a relative and absolute standpoint, the inducements for females to enter teaching would seem to have increased. Similarly, to the extent that teaching has provided an entree for males into other even higher-paying occupations (and earlier provided possibly the only occupation open to educated male Africans), the inducements to enter teaching have also been great for males.

Although increases in the numbers of teachers seem to have been reasonably adequate to meet expanding enrollment needs, what can be said about possible changes in the quality of instruction? There is no easy way to assess fully the quality of instruction, but we can resort to two conventional rules-of-thumb: the pupil-teacher ratio, and the average level of preparation and training of teachers. Pupil-teacher ratios have fallen slightly at the primary level and substantially at the secondary level, suggesting quality improvement.

Assessment of the average level of preparation and training is somewhat more complicated. While the proportion of primary teachers who have completed moré than the second course has steadily decreased (from about 5 per cent in 1951 to less than 1 per cent in 1960), the proportion of the remainder who are trained has steadily risen (from about 55 per cent in 1950 to 70 per cent in 1961). On balance, the increased proportion of trained teachers would seem to have more than offset the small decline in preparation.

As the new intermediate schools expanded (they were established in the early 1950's), the initial quality of their staff in terms of preparation was high. This undoubtedly resulted from drawing the best-educated primary school teachers (many of whom were probably over-educated for their existing jobs) as a cadre for these schools. But as time passed, the proportion of trained people at the higher preparation levels decreased, as did the proportion at each level with less preparation. Thus, the decline in quality observed here is probably a transitional one and should not necessarily be regarded as serious.

At the secondary school level the proportions of untrained teachers have been greatly reduced; average preparation has risen. The same has been true of the post-secondary and teacher-training schools. But it may be premature to rejoice over this development inasmuch as it came in a period of virtually no growth.at the secondary level.

What general conclusions can be drawn from this examination of the Kenya experience? First, even though some of the more highly educated people were drawn out of the primary and intermediate schools, they undoubtedly moved to the higher level schools and helped to increase the quality level there. This movement may indicate that considerable numbers of highly-educated Africans were previously forced to seek appointments where their education was not fully utilized; once the secondary schools opened up on a larger scale these individuals were able to move to preferred positions.

Second, despite the loss of these better educated staff members, the increased proportions of teachers with training probably more than offset this loss, so that it can be concluded that the quality of education rose rather than declined. This occurred even in the face of the tremendous increases in enrollments. At the intermediate level, the decline in quality was probably a transitional one that could be anticipated, given the initial establishment of the intermediate level and the subsequent expansion of the secondary system.

Third, the establishment of five-month teacher-training programs undoubtedly permitted many untrained teachers to receive training. Certainly this training requirement did not create an impossible barrier to the fairly rapid improvement in the quality of teachers. Fourth, the provision of free teacher training made possible a further expansion of teacher supply. Fifth, the sizeable income differentials between trained and untrained teachers of otherwise equivalent educational background undoubtedly made it financially worthwhile for untrained teachers to seek training. And finally, the relative salary level in teaching, especially for women, acted as an additional inducement to entry by large numbers of individuals.

United States

In comparison with the projected expansion of education in the less developed parts of the world, the record of U.S. expansion looks slow; yet it has experienced its most rapid expansion in recent times.[24] This growth has been rather uneven, however, reflecting the interaction of demographic and social-economic changes as they affect enrollments. Somewhat surprisingly, the period of most rapid expansion was the 1950's, followed by the period of the 1870's. Of course, the rate of expansion at the college level has been uniformly high, and that of the secondary schools also rather high, though somewhat erratic. Unfortunately the data for the period prior to 1870, which we had intended to explore, are too fragmentary to permit one to gain an impression of the nature of the adjustments that must have occurred.

From 1950 to 1960, primary enrollments rose by 67 per cent, secondary

---

24. Data are drawn from the *Statistical Abstract, Trends, 1961* and *NEA Research Reports.*

enrollments by 79 per cent, and college enrollments by 40 per cent. (The figure for college would be much greater if the veterans whose education had been delayed by World War II were omitted from the 1950 enrollment figures.) At least some portion of this enrollment increase was clearly fore-seen, as evidenced by the projections mentioned earlier in the paper. But what really happened to the numbers of teachers, their quality, and the qual-ity of education received by students, and how these changes were achieved, are some of the points that will be touched upon here.

First, numbers of teachers increased more rapidly than enrollments at both the elementary and secondary levels, so that pupil-teacher ratios fell. The fact that they did not fall as much as professional educators would have liked is, of course, another issue. The decline in pupil-teacher ratios is further indicated by the rising proportions of bachelor-degree recipients preparing to teach, from 26.6 per cent in 1950 to 32.2 per cent in 1961.

Second, while quality of teachers is an elusive matter, there was appar-ently no real decline if some of the more obvious measures of quality are used. For example, at the elementary school level, the proportion of teachers with 120 or more credit hours rose from 48.8 per cent in 1949−50 to 75.2 per cent in 1960. The proportion of teachers with less than 60 hours of credit fell from 16.7 per cent in 1949−50 to 2.5 per cent in 1959−60. By any stand-ard, this represents a substantial upgrading of the educational preparation of the teaching staff.

A related aspect of teacher quality shows up in the proportions of teachers with substandard certification. From 1954 to 1960 these proportions fell at both primary and secondary levels, indicating that quality of staff had im-proved.

Finally, how was all of this brought about? Clearly there have been many reasons for the observed increases in the quantity and quality of the teaching staff. If nothing else, the constant allegations of teacher shortages may have induced many people to enter teaching who otherwise would not have done so. At the same time, the salaries paid to teachers have risen relative to those of many other groups in the economy, suggesting that the financial rewards to teachers had to be raised to assist efforts to recruit and retain teachers. Whether the increases have been sufficient to fully offset the value of the additional training possessed by teachers is beyond the scope of this discussion, but certainly one could argue that the market for teachers has reflected the supposed "shortage" conditions that so many have decried. Here we use the term *shortage* to indicate a discrepancy not between *require-ments* and actual numbers but rather between *expected* and actual numbers of teachers, a discrepancy that would signal the need for a relative increase in salaries to bring the actual up to the expected or desired number of teachers.

At the college level, much of the same pattern is observed. The numbers of teachers have rapidly increased, quality has remained about constant (though there may have been a slight decline), and salaries have risen relatively more rapidly in order to induce a larger number of entrants into the teaching profession.

Jamaica

Although the data are too fragmentary to permit any extensive analysis of the Jamaican experience, there is clear evidence of the kind of improvisation that must occur if the number of teachers is to be expanded.[25] For example, since the output of 100 trained teachers per year represented less than half of the number 250 "needed" annually, a new teacher training program has been instituted. Under it people who have completed the 3rd Jamaican Local examination (equivalent to the completion of high school) can be taken on as teachers; they then have six years to qualify by exam for a bottom rank teaching position (A3). Those who have not completed the 3rd Jamaican Local examination enter on a probationer basis and must meet the same requirements for the A3 position. For both groups a 20-week teacher-training course has been established to provide rudimentary instruction in pedagogic techniques. Of course, these people are used only in the primary grade levels, but nonetheless this type of program will certainly help speed up the rate of expansion of the teacher supply. In addition, other teacher-training programs of rather short duration have been established to give initial training to already established teachers, at least one-half of whom are presently untrained.

The pinch will eventually be felt in the secondary schools, as swelling primary enrollments begin flooding these schools. At present the qualifications for secondary school teachers appear to be rather rigid, but one can predict with a fair amount of certainty that they will have to be relaxed or at least substantially altered in the face of rising enrollments. Whether Jamaica can continue providing the high quality secondary education it has been providing is a basic issue that must be decided.

Brazil

The case of Brazil shows yet another type of adjustment.[26] By any standard there is no substantial shortage of teachers in Brazil, at least as measured in terms of bodies. Admittedly, the proportion who are fully trained is rather low over the entire country, but in the urban centers of Rio de Janeiro and São Paulo the proportion trained reaches 80 or 90 per cent. Teachers in these latter areas have received regular teacher training; those in the outlying areas have had only very short-duration instruction.

The interesting feature of the Brazil case emerges when we find that almost 80 per cent of the teachers are females. This is accounted for by the fact that virtually all females in secondary and higher levels of education must enroll in teacher-training courses, with the consequence that there is a

25. From Elsa H. Waters, *Teacher Training Colleges in the West Indies* (London: Oxford, 1960).
26. From UNESCO, *The Training of Rural School Teachers* (Paris, 1953).

large annual output of teachers every year. Even though some may drop out of teaching when they marry, a certain proportion of them can be expected to return to teaching later in their careers. Thus, there is a large reserve of educated and trained females in the population that can be drawn upon to supply teachers and other types of educated workers.

Whereas the experience of Jamaica indicates the possibility of increasing teacher supply by speeding up teacher training, the Brazilian example shows the merit of incorporating teacher training directly into the female school curriculum. This policy is justified on the basis of the great need for teachers. However, it prevents females from pursuing study for other occupations where their contribution might be considerable, and it probably results in some wasted investment in teacher training, since not all graduates intend to teach. Despite these shortcomings, it is a method of producing large numbers of trained teachers fairly quickly.

CONCLUSIONS

Our knowledge of the determinants of teacher supply, not to mention teacher demand, remains woefully inadequate, both for advanced countries such as the United States and for the less-developed countries of the world. Despite this state of ignorance, manpower and educational experts proceed with their efforts to map out comprehensive educational development programs. The small amount of evidence accumulated here raises some questions as to the possible impact of these endeavors, for it is conceivable that in the absence of more firmly grounded knowledge, it will be just as easy to make disastrous mistakes as to achieve great successes in such planning.

At the moment there is a great opportunity to learn more about the operation of the teacher labor market, the demand for education, and the production function for both teachers and education itself. Only as we acquire greater insight into these matters will it be possible to develop rational plans for producing more highly educated humans who can both increase the pace and enjoy the benefits of economic development.

PART II
The Formation of Human Competencies

Whereas Part I focused primarily upon the *markets* for human competencies, Part II is concerned primarily with their *formation*. The overlap is considerable, for most of the chapters in Part II also stress economic incentives and motivations as integral parts of analyzing the ways in which competencies associated with development may be and have been formed. Not all of them do this, however, and the theme that holds them together is closer to the crossroads of the disciplines represented at the conference. The first brief essay is directed most broadly, with orientations to Parts II, III and IV.

Harberger (Part I, Chapter 2) estimated that rates of return to secondary schooling in India were considerably lower than those to investment in physical capital in the "modern sector" of the economy. If these findings stand up in studies based upon more adequate data, the question might be raised as to whether the relatively low returns in India might not reflect the absence of complementary opportunities for on-the-job training—perhaps along with persisting historical discriminations in job opportunities and a traditionalist elitism. Both the Crane and the second of Bowman's chapters have something to say to this point. The main themes of Bowman's "From Guilds to Modern Infant Training Industries" (Chapter 6) might be recast as two questions out of which other questions follow: (1) What are the characteristics of what might be termed "production functions" in the formation of the various kinds and levels of human competencies that underly development? (2) How do socioeconomic institutions and policies structure the incidence of costs and benefits of job-linked training and learning, and hence the development and diffusion of on-the-job training opportunities? Among the subquestions, we may then ask, for example, whether there is a vicious circle with respect to development of such opportunities, where there is a lack of the human skills that would attract the enter-

89

prises that can provide the learning and training. This in turn brings in, among other things, the whole question of "labor commitment," so widely discussed by Moore and other sociologists, and of occupational or urbanization "inheritance" as outlined by Kahan for eighteenth-century Russia (Part III, Chapter 14). It directs attention also to factors that may inhibit or foster extension of on-the-job training and learning opportunities among population subgroups. Crane's historical study (Chapter 9) of technical education in colonial India is rich in both evidence and interpretation along these lines, and is also closely allied to the chapter by Foster (to which we will come shortly). Bowman places special emphasis upon the variety of paths that have been taken in solving the problems of human resource development through participant observation and training in diverse historical settings, the continuities of these developments in each case, and the economics of this aspect of the transmission of technologies and production know-how from one society to another. Like Storr, she distinguishes sharply between the "transplantation" of cultures and technologies, as in the colonization of North America, and the international or inter-societal transmission of know-how.

In its social-historical framework Storr's chapter (Chapter 7) is furthest removed from the strictly economic orientations of the chapters in Part I; nevertheless, it is very close in many ways to Bowman's. It is not merely that both discuss education and apprenticeship in colonial America, though they complement each other neatly on this topic. The careful reader will soon discover that the links are more fundamental. For the very essence of Storr's analysis is in the roles and scope of learning by doing in a pre-industrial society of "undifferentiated Americans," in the ways in which societal institutions and values shaped the making of productive and innovative men, and in the merging of private and public costs and benefits of education. Noneconomists will probably be quicker to appreciate this paper than the economists, with their inclinations to abstract out only those elements that fit most neatly into their models. However, in our joint editorial judgments, information and analysis such as Storr has contributed bring us very close to the heart of economic development. To note that it does this in a particular historical case only is to recognize, with Storr, that the evidence of history is evidence of diversity as well as of commonalities, and the lessons of any one case must be identified with care and caution when applied to another time and society. But this is to say also that we need more such case studies.

Recurrent in Part II, but most sharply focused in Foster's chapter (Chapter 8), was a challenge to the frequently heard arguments that more "vocational" schooling is needed, that in agricultural societies practical agriculture should be taught in the rural elementary and secondary schools, that the curricula are too "academic," and so forth. This was indeed one of the most discussed themes of the conference. Foster starts from his empirical studies in Ghana, demonstrating the nature of the "vocational school fallacy" for that as for other countries of Africa south of the Sahara. He stresses the economic rationality of African schooling preferences and perceptions of job oppor-

tunities, showing that in these settings the preference for "academic" schooling was a rational economic choice. In view of the fact that India is so often
cited as an example of quite the opposite situation, Crane's chapter then takes
on special interest as a test of the degree of generality of Foster's findings and
the effects of a very different socioeconomic structure and cultural inheritance.
Wharton (Chapter 10) points out that vocational training in agriculture as it is
typically given in elementary and secondary schools is of little value, and that
students of agriculture do not typically return to the farm, especially in the
earliest stages of development. He goes on to advocate a variety of approaches
to education for agricultural development, both in schools and outside of
them: among farmers, those who serve farmers, and the leaders who make
farm policy. Wharton emphasizes in particular the importance of education
for the decision-making process, a point that receives explicit attention by
Harbison (Chapter 11) also. Harbison emphasizes the problem of creating
managers and supervisors in an environment in which opportunities for
effective learning of these skills in conjunction with work experience are
lacking.

It would be a mistake to push the "vocational school fallacy" too far,
however. Crane, for example, considered the lack of genuine technical
education in schools as a damper on Indian economic development even as
he was explaining reasons for the lack. Foster himself, like other members
of the conference, included some caveats. Wharton's chapter is not entirely
unambiguous on this point. And Platt, in discussing Foster's contribution,
injected a number of warnings and reservations. It may be fair, nevertheless,
to sum up a consensus somewhat as follows:

(1) Almost any sort of curriculum can be vocational; it will be vocational
to the extent that it prepares men for the job opportunities that emerge.

(2) Schooling in particular technical skills does not in itself create the
demands for those skills.

(3) The degree of efficiency of schools as agencies for technical or vocational training at the secondary level is a function of the degree of generality
of the competencies taught, of the rate of their subsequent obsolescence, and
of the scale of demand for a particular proficiency. Skills commonly regarded
as "specialized," such as carpentry, may nevertheless be in wide demand in
many sectors of the economy; whether they are "specialized but in wide
demand" or, in another sense, "nonspecialized" (to any particular sector)
is then a matter of definition.

(4) The effectiveness of technical teaching in secondary schools depends
upon the nature of the training and the motivations of the students; the latter
depend upon preceptions of subsequent opportunities, which perceptions
are in turn derived from the realities of the socioeconomic environment.

(5) There are many things that people learn most efficiently when the
learning or teaching is linked to work experience, and some that they can
learn in no other way.

(6) It follows that ultimate job opportunities associated with any given

sort of schooling, technical or other, depend upon opportunities for on-the-job learning. In brief, schooling, on-the-job learning, and other components of education are in large part complementary rather than substitutive.

CHAPTER 5

"BY ART AS WELL AS BY NATURE"

Mary Jean Bowman

The felicitous theme of "education and development" offers a peculiarly favorable entry point to interdisciplinary study of development. This is not to acclaim the current fashion that finds in education or schooling the magic key to development. There is already sufficient empirical evidence to qualify this crude assumption, deductive reasoning aside. We may justifiably assert that the key to economic development is man, but we will not get anywhere by including in education all influences on men's conduct. Neither, however, can we stop at schooling. Here we need not so much a definition as a topographic map that will locate both the "educational center" of our discourse and the rough distance gradients of surrounding territory. The attempt to delineate even the center was frustrating until E. A. J. Johnson led me to Shakespeare, for "Now art thou what thou art by Art as well as by Nature."[1]

This quotation was doubly suggestive. First, it points sharply to a distinction that is obvious but little considered among writers on development: inter-societal universalities in the nature of man versus the cultural molding of man. Some decades ago economists joined issue with sociologists and psychologists concerning the nature of man, and economists were forced to sharpen their tools; they jettisoned many superfluous psychological assumptions and proceeded happily in their purified state.[2] No acute reader today would accuse economists of basing resource-allocation and income-distribution theory on a mythical economic man, or suggest that they fail to take preferences, attitudes, and motivations into account. However, the beautiful theories that permitted economists to have man *in toto* and yet at the same time purified, cannot be carried over bodily into the study of economic development, for development analysts must study how men are changed and what leads them to produce change. So the nature-of-man argument is joined once again; there are real issues here, apart from misinterpretations by non-economists of economists.

1. E. A. J. Johnson, *The Predecessors of Adam Smith.* (New York: Prentice Hall, 1937), p. 260.
2. They ran into severe problems in dealing with certain problems, however — most notably risk and uncertainty. It is no accident that this linkage point with development theory should have been one of those at which a slight depurification of indifference analysis was most necessary.

Second, and more interesting, in Shakespeare's use of "art" we find both a synthesis of what it had meant before him and of the many future meanings that were to be associated with the words *art, artifice, artificer, artifact,* and *artificial.* These words encompass many of the human qualities that have been stressed in theories of economic development, along with some traits (notably trickery and cunning) that have usually been ignored but may play important parts. I cannot do better than to quote Johnson's first paragraph on "Art and Ingenious Labor."[3]

> "Almost every important English writer on economic subjects during the seventeenth and eighteenth centuries made use of the word "art" in explaining the production of wealth. Mun used the term in developing his theory of "artificial wealth"; Coke considered the products of nature as useless to man unless "prepared by human art"; Evelyn proposed that Flemish artisans be permitted to settle in England so that they might "joyn their art to our nature." Many other writers made use of this odd term; Petty believed that "one man by art may do as much work as many without it"; Cary thought laborers were useful in production but "not without the help of art"; Defoe spoke of the "several productions of art and labour"; while Postlethwayt was of the opinion that the introduction of "art" should give rise to new occupations."

For a fascinating exposition of the diverse meanings of *art* and related words as they developed over time, readers should go directly to Johnson's book. Here it must suffice to draw upon him selectively.

The oldest meaning, and the one with most obvious relevance, comes from medieval times: "skill and its application," or "human workmanship as an agent." In another meaning the English word came to refer not to the skill itself but to "anything wherein skill may be attained or displayed," and then to certain branches of learning, to the "practical application of any science," and from this to any skilled pursuit ("a craft, business or profession"), and to the ability to do something "wherein skill is attainable by study and practice." By yet another metamorphosis the word came to mean also covert action or "cunning," one of the senses in which it is often used by Shakespeare. *Artifice* became not only the product of art but also an "ingenious piece of cunning and trickery." An *artificer* became one who makes by skill, a constructor and manufacturer and, via the idea of contrivance, an inventor. And so to technological innovation. In the words of Postlethwayt, nothing could be "more obvious than that the commerce and navigation of this island principally depends on the daily improvement made by our artificers, in the infinite and amazing variety of our mechanic and manufacturing arts."

In some cases the word *art* as used by the early economists merged into the meaning of "artificial wealth," or physical capital. However, in both the derivation of the word and the way in which they wrote about it the idea of ingenuity and innovation were also continuously present. Art, ingenuity, invention, and its application (*i.e.,* innovation) were the foundation of national

3. *Op. cit.,* p. 259.

wealth in the days of pre-Smithian economics, and this called for public action to encourage the development of the arts. "Only by generous encouragement could 'different species of mechanics, artificers and manufacturers' be developed, and with increasing population, unless this is done, 'all the old ways of gain become overstocked.'"[4]

"Art" in pre-Smithian political arithmetic is closely related to the "human factor" or "organization" or "technique" in some recent aggregative studies of production functions and productivity. But this gives us too broad a definition of education. Taking a different route, we might arrive at a definition of education in terms of the functions of creating skills and the capacities for the exercise of ingenuity and invention. Innovation is another matter; education could be defined to include creation of the readiness to innovate, and by a slight extension of this, to take chances.[5] However, innovations depend not only upon such readiness but also upon the likelihoods of rewards and losses. Perhaps the most interesting thing about mercantilist "art" is the clear perception of the oneness of skill and ingenuity; the mercantilists were not sophisticated enough to become tangled in that conglomeration of attitude, behavior, and concealed objective opportunities called "propensities." They were interested in attitudes and, emphatically, in "character."

Unimpeded by either theoretical models or democratic self-consciousness, the early writers stressed the puritan virtues. These were visualized as associated with "art" rather than "nature." Thus Blewitt spoke of the "artificial advantages" derived from "the skill, industry, and frugality of the inhabitants."[6] Many words were written to deplore idleness and luxury and to praise thrift and industry. Here we have part of the Protestant ethic and one of the variants of "labor commitment," identification with an industrious economic order. It was industrious, not industrial — which could lead to another dip into etymology. In any case there can be no doubt that from the Elizabethan poor laws onward, attempts to inculcate industrious and frugal behavior in the lower orders extend to our day. This is not after all so remote from many current specifications of the characteristics required of the populace and of the somewhat different traits needed in the elite if development is to be assured. The salient oversight of the early economists was the countervalue of nonfrugality. The question arises, then, as to what part "educational" institutions might play in encouraging these assorted qualities.

What, if anything of importance, did these ancestors of ours omit from "development-man"? Comparing their stipulations with a list composed from current writings, the chief differences seem to be four. (1) As was already noted, the earlier writers put far more stress on ingenuity as an inseparable part of skill, whereas we more often think of invention as a separate thing,

4. *Op. cit.*, pp. 268-69. (One could pick this up to arrive at chronic unemployment in the absence of technological advance, modern style.)

5. Or to *not* take them. It should be noted, in any case, that readiness to take chances is probably a very heterogeneous thing, that does not exist in a general sense, but only with respect to certain aspects or phases of life.

6. Quoted in E. A. J. Johnson, *op. cit.*, p. 265.

organized in bigger ways at higher levels. They may have the edge on us; with great shrewdness they anticipated the thesis that development may stem from the institutionalizing of activities and attitudes that yield a continuing and comparatively sustained process of technological change. (2) We talk more about readiness to take chances and less about frugality. (3) While seventeenth- and eighteenth-century writing about the working classes touched on something akin to "achievement motivation," it was achievement of perfection of work and skill within a more limited context. They put less emphasis upon direct overt competitiveness and spoke little about open-end social mobility; they saw mobility within more constrained bounds. (4) They gave no consideration at all to managerial skills at the upper or supervisory levels, and correspondingly no attention to ability to work in teams. Adaptability as distinct from ingenuity found no place, to my knowledge. Nor would you find suggestions that society needed leaders fired with the desire and ability to initiate social change.

None of these contrasts should be particularly surprising, but we would be unduly vain if we attributed them primarily to the progress of the social sciences. A comparison of the attributes they stressed with those we now stress points to the background each of us reflects—and thus to some of the salient differences between the context within which new nations are seeking to bring development and the one from which English economic development emerged.

The creation of human resources for economic development has many facets,[7] and valuable as the economist's construct of "human capital" may be, it could lead us into a mechanistic viewpoint that exaggerates the similarities with physical capital. Moore is clearly right in taking the position that appropriate attitudes and even aspirations must be included as a critical component in the "human factor." On the other hand, to be deplored is the tendency of many writers to treat attitudes, and especially aspirations, as aspects of human-factor supply functions or inputs that can be assessed independently of the demands or the objectively justified opportunity perceptions that condition them.

This sortie into Art and so forth offers no ready escape from the dilemma of defining education as "what creates all attributes of man that affect development," thereby explaining almost everything in development or stagnation. However, it does suggest that we locate a central focus in the area of maximum convergence between the functions with which we may be concerned and the activities and agencies that would most universally be regarded as "educational." The function vector carries us back to theories of development and their hypotheses. The agency-activity vector sorts out for initial attention the manifest, as against the latent, "educational" functions. Priorities for attention would range out from this center according to their nearness to it.

7. I have discussed some of these in "The Land-Grant Colleges and Universities in Human-Resource Development," *Journal of Economic History,* XXII, No. 4 (December 1962).

Here the concept of "art and ingenuity" gives us a first foothold in the area of maximum convergence. Enough has been said to underline that this does not mean that only art and ingenuity should be considered. Neither does it mean that attention should be confined to "schools." For one thing, what is done by schools here is done by other agencies there. More important, the variety of agencies of education is just as great as the range of human attributes, preferences, and perceptions that claim our attention. There is on-the-job training. There are also newspapers, lyceums, migration of embodied human capabilities, peddlers, advertisements, and bankruptcy. Then, somewhere along the line, we must turn around to ask just what part one or another manifest agency of education plays in the totality of processes that form development-men.[8] How do men learn what, under what circumstances? To answer this question requires both an identification of the "whats" that make up development-man and a new sort of learning theory. That theory, which we might christen as "macro-learning" theory, would have to include as one of its most important elements the processes of diffusion—not only *of* education but *as* education in a broad and fundamental sense.

The past decade has brought economists back to man and to long-term growth as high priority foci of research; and attempts to apply modern tools of theoretical and econometric analysis to problems with these foci have begun. In the elaboration and refinement of those tools and the range of theoretical models available to us we have an advantage over our mercantilist and classicist predecessors. But we have a disadvantage too. The progress of social science has narrowed the training of each of us, and we go forth ill-equipped to see what orientation to man and growth implies, if once our blinders are shed. Even when an economist moves into sociology (or vice versa), all too often he "crosses over" in a schizoid fashion, standing astride a mental chasm. I am sometimes reminded of a trick some children played on a small dog. They placed a mirror on the floor in a doorway and called the dog from across it. The poor animal was eager to come, but terrified by the great hole in the floor. Finally he took a shivering leap.

Between most economists and history, the distance of ignorance has been too great for leaping, imaginary chasms aside. I am at least as guilty as most of my brother economists. However, the more I strive to look into the problems of economic development the greater becomes my conviction that *even as economic theorists* we must become students of history, and that this means study of man and his institutions in a very human sense—incentives, opportunities, and how men as economic agents come to be made. We have to do this walking, reforging the links with our home base as we move back and forth; it will not do to leap over mirror chasms placed where the linkages should be.

8. Including what the manifest agencies do to block his formation (or to build his opposite).

CHAPTER 6

FROM GUILDS TO INFANT TRAINING INDUSTRIES

Mary Jean Bowman

The contrast between the success of Marshall Plan aid to Europe and the frustrations that have followed assistance efforts to the less developed parts of the world has been pointed out many times. Something besides physical capital is obviously missing in the latter cases. However, schooling is not the only "something" that the less developed countries lack. This conclusion becomes increasingly evident as we watch the rising tides of unemployed school leavers in many parts of Asia and Africa. It is not enough to reply that the school pyramid has the wrong shape or that the curricula are out of line with needs. There are many other deficiencies of complementary factors. Indeed, such gaps are at the heart of the development problem, whether they be labeled "the factor proportions problem," "external economies," or just plain "bottlenecks."

An especially critical gap is in the skill and know-how that comes only with on-the-job experience. This obstruction can be peculiarly awkward when the creation of the opportunities to acquire a skill depends upon the establishment of enterprises that in turn look for available supplies of skills when making their location decisions. Nevertheless, economies have developed, both with and without a long period in which artisan skills dominated secondary industry. What shapes has the problem taken in one societal setting versus another, and with changes in the technological world environment? In what ways has it been overcome? What part have restrictions on mobility, removal of restrictions, public subsidy, and public enterprise played in this? How far are schools and on-the-job training potential substitutes, and for the acquisition of what kinds of competencies? How far are they instead essentially complementary? Looking behind the more descriptive recounting of history (old and new), what are the contrasts and common elements that we can find in economic history to give us greater analytical power for understanding contemporary development problems and processes? Questions such as these have stimulated the quite immodest effort represented by this chapter.

Given my purposes, it is evidently necessary to begin by presenting the essential concepts and analytical framework that constitutes a point of de-

98

parture. This I do in section I. The middle section discusses apprenticeship and schooling in pre-industrial England and colonial America, along with a few suggestions as to how these early histories extended their shadows into an industrialized future. The last section deals with the problems of transfer and development of skills among nations appearing later on the development scene; this focuses up into the "infant training industry" problem and the story of how it has been resolved or circumvented.[1]

I. SOME KEY CONCEPTS AND SIMPLE PROPOSITIONS

A few concepts and very general assumptions form the essential analytical framework of this chapter. I am laying them out at the start so that readers may be alerted to their later applications. Such applications are made only as they are needed. In this way I hope to facilitate interdisciplinary communication and to retain a fuller flavor in the presentation of illustrative materials than would be possible if I attempted to hang these illustrations more obtrusively upon refined theoretical constructs. The concepts themselves derive from more than one disciplinary base, though most of my discussion will nevertheless remain firmly rooted in economics. This part of the chapter divides into three subsections, concerned respectively with (1) four perspectives in the classification of attributes of development-men; (2) substitution elasticities and complementarities in the learning process; (3) an assumption (treated also as an hypothesis) of economic rationality in private decisions to invest in education and training.

Development-Men: Attributes and Classificatory Perspectives

It was only after much struggling with the pros and cons of widely debated issues in the literatures of economic development, the economics of education, and educational and manpower planning—together with a light seasoning from readings of history and the sociologists on "commitment"—that I became aware of how contrasting perspectives on human resources might be focused as mutually supportive contributions to the understanding of problems that were central to this conference. Classifications of relevant human competencies fall conveniently into four perspectives: (1) technological categorization; (2) economic, market-structural classifications; (3) distinctions between competencies that do and do not involve social-interaction skills, and (4) a no-man's land that is also everyman's land—innovative "propensities." Having dealt with this last perspective in another paper, I shall touch on it here only incidentally.[2]

1) Technological Categorizations. The most obvious and rigid of the technocratic views of human resources is exemplified by the most extreme versions of a detailed "manpower approach," which assumes essential-

1. My use of the term "infant training industries" will become clearer in the last section of this paper.

2. "Schools For and Against Innovation" (mimeo).

ly fixed one-to-one relations between training and occupation. This may be a convenient simplification for some purposes, but it is unrealistic and has little analytical interest. Much more interesting is the technological distinction between general and specialized skills and capacities. This distinction is one of degree, not merely a dichotomy; it has two major dimensions that are closely interrelated. First, generalized capacities are the foundations of readiness to learn any of a wide variety of more specialized skills. Such generalized capacities are sequentially prior to specialization, and provide the adaptability that can help counter recurrent skill obsolescence in a dynamic environment. Second, generalized capacities have a wide variety of potential applications in varied jobs whatever their positions may be in a learning sequence.

It is important that two likely confusions be avoided. (a) The degree of technological generality of a skill must not be confused with the scale of the demand for it. Scale of demand is a function of the scale of the economy and its level as well as of the skill itself. Moreover, though the most general skills will almost necessarily be in relatively wide demand, some occupationally specialized skills may also be demanded in large quantities and in several industries; carpentry is an example. (b) More important, technical generality of a skill is not to be tested by whether a man acquiring it in a particular firm or agency will have equal opportunity to use it in other enterprises.

2) *Economic Skill Mobility and Immobility.* The most fundamental economic base for categorization of skills is their degree of mobility, not merely among kinds of jobs but also among firms or employing units. Capacities that have even potential applicability in only one firm will usually be technologically specialized to a particular kind of job, to be sure. However, technologically specialized skills are not necessarily immobile as among firms; and technologically general skills may nevertheless be immobilized in certain institutional settings. Putting this the other way around, some of Becker's "specific" skills can be technologically general and his "general skills" can be technologically specialized.[3] Technological generality fosters skill mobility, as do labor market fluidity and a large-scale economy, but the mobility classification is not to be identified with the technological. The distinction between mobile and immobile skills relates fundamentally to labor market structures despite the fact that technological constraints condition the operation of those markets. This economic perspective underlies analysis of how the incidence of costs and rewards conditions the loci of human resource development, the kinds of human resource bottlenecks that may prevail, and the paths by which such bottlenecks may come to be broken or may be circumvented.

---

3. Technologically general and specialized skills are not the same as "general" and "specific" skills in Gary Becker's analysis. See his "Investment in Human Capital" (and also Jacob Mincer, "On-the-job Training") in the *Journal of Political Economy* Supplement on *Investment in Human Beings,* Vol. LXX, No. 5, Part 2, (October 1962), pp. 9-49 and 50-79.

3) Social-interaction Skills. Many sociologists and a few economists have stressed labor "commitment" and/or shortages of supervisory skills as hindrances to development. This leads to a classification of human competencies in terms of those skills that pertain to human interaction and those that do not. However, both economists and educational manpower planners commonly slur this distinction, which is especially relevant in comparing the potentials of training in schools with training and learning on-the-job. I would argue further that the toughest aspects of the "factor proportions problem" or the "technological dualism" dilemma lie in the social-interaction dimensions of human competencies.

Substitution and Complementarity in the Learning Process

Myint wrote: "the educational effect of apprenticeship and promotion to skilled grades in ordinary economic life is more far-reaching than huge sums of money spent on educational institutions."[4] Harbison, looking at somewhat higher levels in the manpower complex, would probably agree.[5] However, such dicta, like their opposites, must always be interpreted in a context that sets forth the nature of the relevant decision margins for both private action and public policy. What is deemed "most important" *next* depends on what one already has—in this case the schooling and on-the-job mix of training opportunities as of the reference base, and the kinds of human competencies that are desired.

A few factors determine the relation of learning any given competency in school and at work, assuming the absence of institutionally restricted labor mobility. They are (a) the nature of the human raw material that determines how men most readily learn different things (and the competencies already attained); (b) the costs of providing equipment and procedures for simulation of work situations within schools; (c) the alternative direct costs, if any, of developing the same competencies on the job—*i.e.*, direct outlays on instruction and on training equipment within operating production units, as well as the disruptive effects upon production organization and productivity; (d) the foregone working time entailed for the student in school versus foregone working time of in-service trainees.

Evidently the balance with respect to any of these factors will depend upon the kinds of competencies under consideration. For specialized skills that are quickly learned but require practice equipment that is expensive and becomes rapidly obsolescent, schools are expensive substitutes for training on the job; yet on-the-job learning is no substitute for the basic literacy and knowledgeability that facilitate specialized learning and adaptation. Where

4. H. Myint, "An Interpretation of Economic Backwardness," in A. N. Agarwala and S. P. Singh (ed.), *The Economics of Underdevelopment* (Bombay: Oxford Press, 1958), p. 124. (This is a reprint of the original, which appeared in *Oxford Economic Papers*, June 1954.)

5. In many publications, including his contribution to this conference. Especially interesting in this context is his study, with I. A. Ibrahim, of *Human Resources for Egyptian Enterprise* (New York: McGraw Hill, 1958).

the competencies sought have major attitude components that are non-traditional and nonacademic, and where supervisory skills are entailed, there may in fact be no adequate simulation substitute for learning by participation.[6]

Comparison of alternative agencies and methods of training and learning is complicated by the facts that individuals virtually always acquire attitudes along with skills, and that this context of associations and motivations can foster or impede learning. Also, there is more than one possible sequence and combination of learning at school and at work; for example, "sandwich" courses can be given in schools as part of a program of in-service training.[7] Finally, it must be noted that much "learning by doing" is costless, and the pace of this learning is influenced by the extent of exposure to fresh experiences. Arrow has underlined this last point, arguing that learning is a function of the rate of gross investment in ever-improving forms of physical capital.[8]

Neither the range of potentially efficient substitution between schools and other loci of training nor the constraints on substitution have received sufficient attention from economists or manpower planners — or even from educational planners. Though technically the potential substitutabilities between learning in school and learning at work extend over a wide range, these are not and cannot be perfect substitutes short of the absorption of the school or the production organization into an undifferentiated structure that fully encompasses both.[9] I would contend that some of the kinds of competencies that are most critical for development can rarely if ever be learned in schools, and that the costs of effective in-school teaching and learning of some others are prohibitively high, even though in-service learning may require prior education of kinds best provided in schools. Transformation functions between inputs of schooling and inputs of on-the-job training in the development of such competencies are characterized by very low marginal elasticities of substitution. This is a critical consideration in assessing actual and potential human resource formation in the less advanced economies.

None of my comments thus far specifies anything about over-all proportions in combinations of schooling and other training; the scalar locations of the transformation functions and their curvatures are two quite different matters. However, there is enough historical and contemporary empirical

6. Note, however, that a speed-up of quasi-experience is accomplished by simulation techniques and the use of computers in teaching business administration. But this sort of equipment is expensive. Case studies are the nearest approximation for less developed countries, and suitable cases are only beginning to be collected.

7. Treatment of sequence in analysis of relations between schooling and on-the-job learning and training is discussed in my "Costing of Human Resource Development," forthcoming in the proceedings of the conference of the International Economics Association on the economics of education (at Menthon St. Bernard, France, Aug. 29-Sept. 7, 1963).

8. Kenneth Arrow, "Learning by Doing," *Review of Economic Studies*, Vol. 29 (June 1962), pp 155-173.

9. One of the reasons often given for boarding schools in African countries is the advantages of controlling the total environment where a supportive culture is lacking in students' homes. However, the social relationships experienced in such an environment have only tenuous links to the adult world of work; this is not at all a substitute for on-the-job experience.

evidence to enable us to say at least three things about these locations with reasonable assurance:

First, the more rapid the pace of economic change, the higher the levels of generalized schooling that are needed to provide adaptability in subsequent occupational positions.

Second, a prescription of higher levels of generalized schooling does not imply a reduction in on-the-job training and learning, even though such a prescription may involve substitution of schooling in a particular case. History suggests that typically both types of human resource development must, and in fact do, rise together if economic growth is to be rapid and sustained.

Third, in any given society, institutionalized constraints and opportunities condition how men will combine learning in school and at work, and their choices can be of major importance for the subsequent path of development. They affect the kinds of human competencies that come to be most fully developed, and hence also the ways in which human factors are combined with each other and with other factors in production.

A Strictly Economic Proposition

Despite occasional use of the terms "efficiency" and "costs," the above discussion of substitution and complementarity in the learning process is more technological than economic; in fact I specifically excluded market immobility in discussing substitution potentials. However, what people do or what they can be expected to do is not determined solely by the range of choices that might be open to them in the absence of institutional constraints upon opportunities. With all deference to non-economists, I assert that strictly economic considerations have major value in explaining the extent, the forms, and the agencies of human resource development that come into existence, expand, and become elaborated in any given historical setting, past or present. In other words, I assume that expected economic returns and perceived costs in alternatives foregone are key factors in private decisions to invest in education and training. This applies whether the decision-maker in question is an individual (or parent) or an employer. It becomes empirically testable if we add the assumption that there is a significant positive correlation between these expectations and perceptions and the empirically observable contemporary average experience of similarly situated decision-makers.

Even taken together these assumptions are weak. I do not assume rigorously maximizing or optimizing calculations and behavior, or anything approximating perfect knowledge. No stipulation is made with respect to economic structure and competition or the extent of central government controls. However, I am differentiating between private and public decision-making; the twin assumptions refer to the former only. They do not say that education must be or ever is viewed solely as an economic investment; they merely relegate the noneconomic components of private decisions to a role that will not dominate the course of educational expansion. I should be very much surprised if anyone were to challenge the applicability of economic considerations insofar as provision of training on-the-job by private employers is concerned, and this is the chief use to which I shall put it in the present paper. However, I am prepared to argue that the economic incentive model holds for the mass expansion of schooling over a wide range of historical and contemporary situations – to the degree that the individual has to bear the cost himself. I would not argue that the model has general applicability to decisions of small elite minorities.

Private decisions were separated from public ones for two reasons. First, I am distinguishing public from private hierarchies of goals in decisions to put resources into education. Political ends of many kinds, including militaristic nationalism and democratic equalitarianism, can be and have been decisive incentives to collective efforts for human resource development in schools and in other locales. However, even in societies characterized by a large measure of central direction, human beings must be motivated to conform to plans. Schools have remained empty where people saw no purpose in attending them; even where education is provided by the state, individual balancing of economic costs and rewards affects the pace of educational development. Foregone earnings of potential students can be critical here.

The second important public-private distinction pertains to the relations between costs and benefits even within the context of narrowly economic accounting. In particular, collective bodies may have economic incentives to undertake investments yielding returns that could not be recovered by a private investor. The greater the emphasis in public policy upon economic development, the more important it is to identify discrepancies between private and total economic costs and returns as a basis for decisions in the strategy of collective action.

II. APPRENTICESHIP AND THE THREE R'S IN
PRE-INDUSTRIAL BRITAIN AND
COLONIAL AMERICA

No one would claim that the preludes to development and the early stages of transition to a "modern" economy in Britain and the American colonies must be the pattern for nations that are emerging on the development scene today. Among the salient differences, the most important is probably the role of the artisan. Nevertheless, that early history had some fundamental features that throw light on contemporary situations – a fact that is all the more interesting precisely because the contrasts are also so great. Early histories are interesting also for the long shadows that these past events cast into futures that have now become history. I shall begin by a digression on the latter, before turning to the main topics of this section.

Considerably Later: Some Shadows of Past Events

In British parliamentary hearings conducted in 1840, several manufacturers were queried about the relationship between educational backgrounds and competence of their workers. The responses were remarkably consistent and it suffices to quote a single reply.[10]

"You are an engineer residing at Zurich?" "Yes, I am one of the partners of the firm . . ."

"What opportunities have you had of observing the moral and intellectual condition of working men, the natives of different countries, differently educated?" "We employ from six to eight hundred men in our machine-making establishment at Zurich; we also employ about two hundred men in our cotton mills there; about five hundred men in our cotton manufactories in the Tyrol and in Italy. I have occasionally had the control of from five to six hundred men engaged in engineering operations as builders, masons, etc., and men of the class called navigators in England."

"Are the working people whom you employ, or have employed, in Switzerland natives of that country?" "No; partly Swiss, partly Germans of all the different states . . . partly French, some few Danes, some Norwegians, some Polanders, some Bohemians, some Hungarians, some English and Scotch, and some Dutch. . . ."

"What do you find to be the differences of acquirements imparted by specific training and education?" "As workmen *only,* the preference is undoubtedly due to the English; because as we find them they are all trained to special branches, on which they have had comparatively superior training and have concentrated all their thoughts. As men of business or of general usefulness, and as men with whom an employer would best like to be surrounded, I should, however, decidedly prefer the Saxons and Swiss, but more especially the Saxons, because they have had a very careful general education, which has extended their capacities beyond any special employment, and rendered them fit to take up, after a short preparation, any employment to which they may be called. If I have an English workman engaged in the erection of a steam-engine, he will understand that and nothing else; he will understand only his steam-engine, and for other circumstances or other branches of mechanics, however closely allied, he will be comparatively helpless to adapt himself to all the circumstances that may arise, to make arrangements for them, and give sound advice or write clear statements and letters on his works in the various related branches of mechanics."

"Will the workman with the better general education, or the Saxons with the same special opportunities as the English workman, get before him?" "In general, he will. The Saxon or the educated workman will under the same circumstances much sooner advance and become a foreman or manager. In other words, he will be found by his employer more generally useful."

Perhaps it is more than chance that the eighteenth century, Massachusetts cotton mills were displacing skilled British workers with semiskilled

---

10. "Evidence of Employers of Labourers on the Influence of Training and Education on the Value of Workmen, and on the Comparative Eligibility of Educated and Uneducated Workmen for Employment." Printed by W. Clowes and Sons for Her Majesty's Stationery Office (London, 1840).

Americans who were more adaptable.[11] And then, in the middle of the twentieth century, we have Frankel comparing Britain and the United States as follows:[12]

> Evidence of the greater extent to which the specialization factor has operated in the United States is found in two areas. The first concerns the quality of the skills among production workers in the two countries. This quality seems always to have differed, with United States factories employing a smaller proportion than United Kingdom factories of craftsmen who have undergone lengthy apprenticeships. American reliance upon semi-skilled and unskilled labor implies specialization of function, just as British reliance upon skilled labor implies its opposite. . . . This type of specialization obviously is closely related to the degree of mechanization, since it is mechanization which greatly reduces skill requirements. The second area where labor specialization manifests itself is in administrative, consultative, and supervisory ranks. American industry employs production and design engineers . . . and other specialists in larger proportion than British industry. Such specialists are, on the whole, quite skilled. Their employment compensates for the lack of all-round, artisan-type skills available on the shop floor. It is also tied in with the degree of mechanization in that capital intensive methods are dependent on such skills for their efficient functioning.

The relationships among characteristics of educational systems and the structuring of industry, including choices of technology, are evidenced in these quotations. So are the distinctive long threads of continuity that run through the histories of dynamic change among the cousins on either side of the Atlantic.

The Evolving Economics of Pre-Industrial Apprenticeship[13]

Under serfdom the labor of children was "contracted out" between villein and lord, and the sons of the villeins were placed to work in "manufactures." This practice grew, especially in the towns. It was common among the London guilds by 1300, it prevailed in most towns by the mid-fifteenth century, and was made national by statute in 1562. Contractual apprenticeship had developed from a private custom to a public institution. Initially only one of the ways of gaining entry to a guild or obtaining the freedom of a borough, by the mid-sixteenth century it had become the usual way to both. Meanwhile, entry was becoming more restricted; the poor and the servile were largely excluded from the preferred occupations. Thus apprenticeship became both a pervasive training agency and a device for rationing access to

11. See M. D. Morris, "The Recruitment of an Industrial Labor Force in India, with British and American Comparisons," *Comparative Studies in Society and History*, vol. II, No. 3 (April 1960), pp. 315-20.

12. Marvin Frankel. "Anglo-American Productivity Differences: Their Magnitude and Some Causes," *American Economic Review*, vol. 45 (May 1955), p. 111.

13. For its historical evidence this section relies wholly upon O. J. Dunlop, *English Apprenticeship and Child Labor: A History* (London: Unwin, 1912). Since what is included here is telescoped from an entire book and is the mere bones of what recurs on many pages, no specific citations are given. Except as explicitly attributed to Dunlop, the interpretations are mine.

preferred occupations and to rights of fuller civic participation.[14] The training included personal habits and morality as well as skills, and the system was even regarded as a strategy of birth control.

This complexity of functions shows up clearly in the 1562 act and the 1601 poor law. The statute required a term of seven years training and forbade practice before the age of 24; the restriction on marriage and various other London guild rules were adopted nationally. A special clause reserved the wealthiest trades to sons of propertied persons. Farmers with half a tilled ploughland might take apprentices and compel service from artisans and laborers during harvests, and writs could be required of servants before moving. (Note the numerous parallels to Soviet policies of a few years ago.) The poor law of 1601 reaffirmed earlier statutes permitting compulsory apprenticing of pauper children, and stipulated long terms; most of these were only pseudo-apprenticeships in which little skill was learned. Their aim was to insure that poor children contributed to their own support, to restrict vagrancy, and to improve the morals of the "degraded" classes. In an age when education was not yet a mass aspiration and there were few free schools, there was undoubtedly an essentially moral basis for these provisions, in addition to their convenience as a method of poor relief, but the outcome was extensive exploitation of child labor.

To assess adequately how far early apprenticeship contributed to social and economic mobility and how far it restrained mobility would require a better historian. The age believed in status, but it was not monolithic on this issue. Beginning as early as 1437, a series of acts tried to bring guild rules under scrutiny and approval in order to prevent monopoly. The steady stream of complaints about evasions suggests that mobility exceeded what the sponsors of the regulations anticipated. Meanwhile, restrictions were coming to be "justified" on grounds of raising and controlling quality; in this the guilds received support from a government that believed expansion of sales depended upon raising quality rather than reducing prices. This was not inconsistent with sumptuary legislation, since policy focused on foreign sales. Dunlop cites five methods used in the sixteenth century to preserve and promote industrial skills: (1) specialization, enforced by prohibiting intrusion into other crafts; (2) detailed stipulations of standards; (3) requirement of apprenticeship for practice of a craft; (4) use of marks on work done, and (5) powers of search for guild masters within cities and for Crown officers elsewhere.[15]

The stirrings that had been reflected in the mixture of mobility and restriction in apprenticeship were but part of the broader currents that led to the Civil War (1660); the war brought disorganization and weakened the guilds. There had earlier been attrition of many regulations, accompanied by weakening belief in minute regulation of trade. Then in 1669 the courts ruled that the apprenticeship act applied only in the towns. But for some years the

---

14. Note the relation of these functions to Anderson's contributions to this volume.
15. Dunlop, *op. cit.*, Ch. 3.

guilds became increasingly exclusive; consequently evasions multiplied and the courts progressively withdrew their support. Practice and training in crafts grew outside the towns, free of guild rules; the hold of masters over apprentices weakened. Apprenticeship was inching toward the freedom and flexibility of modern times. When, in 1756, a guild sued a man for trading without having been an apprentice, the court ruled that every man had a natural and legal right to exercise whatever trade he pleased. Before the end of the eighteenth century the guild system had largely broken down, less because of factories themselves than because of the growing spirit of capitalist commercialism and the pre-factory victory of freedom over regulation. Picking up the thread at this point, Smelser demonstrates how factories completed the transformation—almost.[16] But this is a later time, to be referred to below.

Apprenticeship was an institution for the formation of skills, and we may gain considerable insight by viewing it as "investment in human capital." This view is obviously appropriate for the era in which apprenticeship entailed onerous servitude, albeit for only a seven-year term. Apprentices were indeed treated as property from the early sixteenth century, and their services could be sold by the master (though this came to be subject to a tax and approval of the guild). At an early date the guilds found it necessary to introduce regulations to prevent pirating.

The seven-year contract enabled the master to reap a rich reward from the outlays for maintenance and training he made during the earlier part of the term, but he wanted to protect this investment. So long as he could do so, apprentices were in demand, and the boy did not have to pay directly for his training; rather he sold himself into indenture. As this firm grip on the apprentice weakened, the market changed. By the early seventeenth century a complex system of premium payments had emerged. These were scaled according to both the father's trade and status and the standing of the trade to which a boy was apprenticed. (It should be remembered that apprenticeship was not restricted to manual occupations.) Lower-status fathers paid premiums to get their sons into better occupations. This practice of paying premiums continued to spread, though it was never part of formal guild policy. By the end of the seventeenth century it was common in London and Manchester, and the sums required were growing. By the eighteenth century, premiums might run to several hundred pounds, and now better (or more alert) families paid higher fees to place their sons with the better masters. Meanwhile, the amount of genuine training under apprenticeship had increased, the more extreme forms of exploitation by masters were curbed, and the security of the master's investment had sharply declined. Accordingly there was a change in the way in which the apprentice paid, for he had always paid.

My reading of this chapter in economic history suggests several points

---

16. Neil J. Smelser. *Social Change in the Industrial Revolution* (Chicago: University of Chicago Press, 1959).

that may be relevant for less developed countries today. But let me first summarize. The groundwork for English economic development was laid not by a free, wide-open system but by one embracing rigid controls, including compulsory training and consequent compulsion in choice of vocation. The system fostered limited mobility from rural areas to towns, but only when a stable, job-training place was available. (Others escaped the meshes in the legal net and drifted townward, though in moderate numbers.) Geographic and occupational mobility expanded with the widening market economy. Apprenticeship was not only training in manual skills; it provided participant education on a broad front. This no doubt fostered ingenuity. It also gave apprentices from lower levels of society an introduction to the ways of living of their betters.[17] Meanwhile, the whole system provided the capital for investment in training by contracts based upon private returns, but—and this is important—these arrangements were enforced first by monopolistic groups and then also by the state.

Today developing countries face a very different world. Usually human freedoms are supposed to be respected and no one may sell himself into indenture. (However, indenture is used for some rare skills, such as teaching. And there was a legitimatized alternative for doing this more broadly inherent in Stalinist patterns of industrialization, which in practice amounted to widespread slavery to the state.) In the less industrialized economies there is still a large subsistence sector, but migration to towns is largely uncontrolled. In contrast to sixteenth- and seventeenth-century England, training does not follow in the wake of the demand for skills. Instead many countries today are trying to create skills in a massive way in the hope that these supplies will generate their own demand. They are trying to do this with little in the way of participant observation, either at home or with a master. Add the greater speed of change today, and the facts that many countries are in a hurry and would jump several centuries, that the artisan is likely to have a small place in these new economies, that an immense cultural leap must be made by the masses, and we begin to appreciate the task the schools are being asked to shoulder.

To "Read and Wright and Siffer"

So far as I am aware, there was not usually training in literacy in British apprenticeship, though some guilds and some masters were exceptions and literacy was a prerequisite for some apprenticeships. New England adopted a different course, as Seybolt points out.[18]

---

17. We might draw parallels here with the "apprenticeships" of the household domestics in contrast to the field hands in the American ante-bellum South, as with the learning of the African "boy" in the colonies and ex-colonies of that continent. Further from this, and yet related, is part of the rationale of the secondary boarding school in Africa, as a total environment.

18. R. F. Seybolt, *Apprenticeship and Apprentice Education in Colonial New England and New York* (New York: Teachers' College, 1917), pp. 30-39.

Our Puritan forefathers were familiar with the English practice as established by the laws of 1562 and 1601, and recognized its shortcomings. The Statute of Artificers provided for the industrial training of youth, but did not take into consideration the need of even the rudiments of education for the lower classes. The Poor Law of 1601 made no pretense of providing anything but a home for those bound out, and as a natural consequence thousands of Poor Law apprentices were exploited in "blind alley" occupations. To protect their new commonwealth from the evils arising from such imperfect legislation, the Massachusetts Bay colonists insisted (1) that masters must teach, or "cause to be taught," their apprentices to read; and (2) that apprentices must be trained in "employments which may be profitable to the Commonwealth." No useless occupations, such as minding cattle, were to be tolerated; apprenticeship was not a scheme of exploitation, but was essentially an educational institution.

Before 1642 the English law obtained in the matter of regulating apprenticeship, but now apprenticeship was seen to possess new and broader possibilities of use. Not only was it viewed as a mode of poor-relief, and of keeping up with the supply of skilled labor, but it was also considered a means of compelling the education of all youth. To include this added feature new legislation was necessary, the type of which is represented by the Massachusetts Bay Order of 1642 and the New Plymouth measure of 1671. In these Orders the obligation was laid upon all parents, rich and poor, as well as masters, to teach their children to read.

There was a strong religious and moral tone in these orders, though they were also highly practical; the Massachusetts Bay ordinance of 1642 comments on the neglect by parents and masters in "training up their children in labor and learning," and goes on to emphasize "especially their ability to read and understand the principles of religion and the capital laws of the country." The Plymouth law of 1671 runs in the same vein, also linking ability to read with skill in an honest calling.

It would be unwarranted to assume that all masters could read; the ordinance therefore implied that apprentices would often be sent to school. A few schools had already been established and new ones now began to appear. Commonly a teacher would be appointed by the town selectmen, his wages to be paid by masters, parents, and inhabitants in general, by whatever arrangements they might evolve. Payments were frequently in kind. In binding out poor children the town sometimes paid the master to take an apprentice and provide his subsistence and education. Sometimes the town paid the tuition for poor children with private teachers. Gradually free town schools were established. Thus apprenticeship and the schools evolved together.

But reading came to be considered insufficient, and we find a 1651 agreement between a Dorchester master and the selectmen to teach his apprentice "to read and wright." A York (Maine) indenture of 1674 specified that the master must teach his apprentice "to write and siffer." Though these cases multiplied, amidst much backing and filling, many masters furnished only the reading specified by law. So a Massachusetts law of 1703 required that boys be taught to write; this was not insisted upon for girls. A 1741 law insisted upon the three-R's for boys but only reading for girls; in 1771 writing was added for girls. Seybolt reports he found no single instance in which a girl was taught to cipher or "cast accounts."[19]

The informal and diverse ways in which economic support for elementary teaching developed have been indicated. But paying the teacher in kind or in scarce coin was not the whole problem. There was also the cost of sparing apprentices from their labors. This problem was recognized in agreements with masters by adapting school hours and seasons.[20] Often this entailed evening school, usually in the winter; agreements often specified three month's winter evening school. (Girls who went to school usually seem to have done so in the daytime.) This pattern reflects the greater reliance upon juvenile labor in those days. (This emphasis is seen now at a very different educational level in some Latin American countries; in Panama, for example, university students typically go to school at night.)

It is common knowledge that Puritanism as a religion fostered widespread reading, of sorts, among the populations of the early colonies. To me one of the interesting aspects of this history is how soon for boys reading appears to be not enough. Writing and ciphering were desired also, for quite utilitarian reasons. Old England seems to have lagged a century in obtaining schooling for those in the lower stations of life. The wider establishment of this ethical outlook in the northern American colonies, together with their more universalistic orientations, was bolstered by pioneer conditions enhancing the value of men and loosening the bonds of status.

At this point I should turn to Smelser to recount how in England Sunday schools operated as "virtually the only education for the working classes during the first two generations of the industrial revolution"[21] — though Anderson tempers that generalization.[22] In the manufacturing districts attendence at nonconformist Sunday schools rapidly outstripped the Anglican.

Smelser has many important things to say about the late eighteenth century that I must disregard. But I do want to underline his account of how the early English factories followed the still extant apprenticeship system.[23] He points out that efficient factory operations were hindered by diffuse responsibilities for the welfare of the apprentice, by lack of freedom to lay him off in slack times, and so on. At first, there was much family hiring in the factories; children worked and learned beside their parents. Education in a generalized sense continued to be fused with other family functions.

But changing technology and organization rapidly altered this pattern. Smelser dates the differentiation of education from diffuse family functions from around 1825, as longer mules and the power loom broke up a "pseudo-apprenticeship" based on kinship.[24] Children less often worked beside their

19. *Ibid.*, p. 47.
20. See, for example, the contracts cited in Seybolt, *op. cit.*, p. 94 ff.
21. Smelser, *op. cit.*, p. 76.
22. See Anderson's data on literacy in Britain.
23. Smelser, *op. cit.*, pp. 103-05, 185-88.
24. *Ibid.*, pp. 198-200.

mothers. Meanwhile, agitation for the Factory Act of 1833 was accompanied by agitation for schooling. That act barred employment of children under nine years; those under thirteen were not to work over eight hours and must spend two hours in school. Thus differentiated schools came rapidly to emerge out of prior job training and poor laws, to teach reading and writing to ordinary boys and girls.

In the New England colonies and New York, schools emerged as part of an integrated program for the proper rearing of youth, in which preparation for a useful calling was the larger part of education in practice. The belated English schools, where apprenticeship had been more abused, tended to be more rapidly divorced from work precisely because the spread of schools accompanied the shift from mainly artisan work to factory manufacture. But the commonalities of English and American experience are equally impressive. In both countries the school for ordinary people came as a part of a broad movement of emancipation; it was both child and father of rising democracy and fluidity in all aspects of life. This common element must not be forgotten, even though the differences conditioned the educational systems and the characteristics of business enterprises for generations.

Out of the American scene evolved the more rapid expansion of mass schooling and eventually the land-grant system, with an education that was remarkably undifferentiated within the schools.[25] Stratification and differentiation of schools persisted much longer in Britain. For better or worse the old apprenticeship system cast its shadow even into twentieth-century England, as recent comparisons attest.[26] If time permitted, one could trace yet other and even more striking contrasts from Russia or, especially, Japan. Educational choices in the now-developing countries may similarly condition their future.

Earlier, in contrasting British history with conditions today in underdeveloped lands, I emphasized the fact that in England demands for vocational skills had taken priority over supplies. This could have been said of literacy and classical education as well, had we traced training for clergy and bureaucracy. In colonial New England there was unquestionably an economic rationale behind the early concern with schooling which may be too easily ignored because of the frequent references to reading the Bible. It is more difficult to trace out these leads and lags in nineteenth-century Britain. I am convinced, however, that as we probe more deeply into the connections between education and development in the West we will decide that England continued near one extreme, with deficient mass education retarding advance right up to recent years. I say this despite Anderson's figure for English literacy being higher than has been generally assumed. Education feeds upon itself through the economy, as the pace of economic life alternately soaks up educational advances and in turn demands more. But we will see also, I

25. See my "The Land Grant Colleges and Universities in Human Resource Development," *Journal of Economic History* (December, 1962).
    26. *Ibid.*, pp. 12-13.

strongly suspect, that populations who have paid their own school costs have not gone forth en masse to learn when no return on the expenditure and effort was visible.[27] Elitist education as a status and consumption good and as a road to sinecure occupations is one thing. Mass education is another. I doubt that there are any historical examples of mass schooling that long anticipated the appearance of coordinate economic opportunities, or vice versa. Contemporary Africa may be unique in this, as in some other respects, precisely because formal schooling is such a lonely institution there, lacking supportive roots and branches in families and jobs.

It is important in thus looking at the less developed countries that we distinguish quite sharply among them. Where education is a great faith, bolstered by images of the former colonial powers (and by their exchequers) schooling may take a very long lead ahead of the complementary human factors that can bring development. The contrast between Africa and the open spaces of North America and Australia that were colonized and filled up with men who brought European culture with them is a very significant one. Some Latin American countries have displayed a still different pattern. There faith in education has often been lacking, and we should therefore look at both the ignorance that in itself breeds this continuing disinterest and the social and political institutions that may make schooling for the ordinary man both costly and economically unrewarding.

III. MODERNIZATION AND INFANT TRAINING INDUSTRIES

The term "infant industry" has a long and somewhat ambiguous history in the politics of restrictions on international trade, and alleged infants have sometimes been remarkably big and lusty fellows. Nevertheless, there is a sound economic interpretation of the concept, which is always a relative one. A brand new industry will not be an "infant industry" if it has never existed anywhere before; the industry must have already established bigger brothers in other countries, *and* conditions must be such that the newcomer would encounter difficulties in becoming established and growing to adulthood in the face of competition from those big brothers. Some industries could never grow to adult efficiency, to stand on their own, in some locations, however much they were protected and force-fed through the initial stages. Setting these aside, what makes a potentially productive industry an infant is then one or both of two things: gaps in human competencies and know-how, and gaps in complementary industries and physical infrastructure (external economies). I use the term "infant training industries" to direct attention to the role that the industry itself may play in developing new kinds of human re-

27. Foster stresses this in his Ghanaian observations. It is a theme that runs through a number of discussions of early land-grant history and pre-land-grant history. See especially Frederick Rudolph, on the theme of "buying students." *(The American College and University,* New York: Knopf, 1962.)

sources and know-how. All "infant industries" are at least potentially in greater or lesser degree "infant training industries." (I do not intend to distinguish in this definition between "training" and opportunities to learn that are not formalized training programs.)

All successful economic development entails both innovative initiative at home and borrowing from abroad. Even the British borrowed many things from the continent. However, if latecomers have the advantage that is sometimes alleged—that they can imitate and select from a much wider range of technological models—this in itself must mean also that the relative importance of infant industries in the total industry mix is increased. To some extent schooling may substitute for on-the-job learning, but there are limitations to the pace at which the level of schooling in the adult labor force can be raised. Moreover, given substitution inelasticities between learning in schools and on the job, even extraordinary success in the spread of schooling cannot meet all the requirements. Under these circumstances we face a circular problem: the potential learning opportunities that infant industries provide depend upon their technologies, and the technologies chosen depend in significant degree upon the human resource mixes that are available. The determinants are not altogether technological, however. Social-economic institutions and public policies may encourage or impede a mutually supportive evolution of economic activities and human resource development. In attempting to cut into this tangle I shall organize my discussion under three heads: (1) The Factor Proportions Problem and Scale Bias; (2) The "Raw Group" Problem and the Tasks of Management; (3) The Making and Circumventing of "Infant Training Industries."

The Factor Proportions Problem and Scale Bias

In an elegant paper, Eckaus sought to explain the "persistence of unemployment and underemployment, the coexistence of modern capital—intensive techniques and methods using a great deal of labor and little capital, and large differentials in factor returns in different sectors."[28] He showed that these conditions could result from "factor market imperfections, and limited technical substitutability of factors, with divergences between the proportions in which goods are demanded and in which they can be supplied with full use of available factors." He went on to note that "these possibilities are again more important for the underdeveloped areas whose resource endowments are often not suited to the factor proportions dictated by the technological leadership of advanced countries. Differences in income distribution and the range of products may also make limited technical substitutability a more pressing problem in underdeveloped than in advanced areas."

Many other writers have deplored alleged tendencies to high capital-

28. R. S. Eckaus, "Factor Proportions in Underdeveloped Areas," *American Economic Review* (Sept. 1955), Vol. 45, pp. 539-65.

intensity investments because they provide few jobs at any skill level. A few have gone on to bemoan the absence of learning opportunities and on-the-job skill ladders under these conditions. What Marcus has said of Gabon has been repeated in substance for other countries.[29]

> ... it is necessary to draw a distinction between large aggregates of equipment and large employers of labor. Both, of course, require significant amounts of financial support, but the former has a much higher ratio of capital to labor and is generally characterized by a high degree of mechanization— perhaps even automation. These highly mechanized units may become only small pockets in an otherwise backward economy, often not even sparking any further stimulus to local development. In a sense, therefore, the host country is wasting its assets, drawing on the available supplies of capital, which then produce only a limited contribution to any further evolving of the area.

Later Marcus points to a critical contrast between the educational effects of capital-intensity and large-employment projects.[30]

> In the firm employing a relatively large labor force, there is need for an entire hierarchy of skills and trades. While at first the raw native labor can be used only for the very crudest of tasks, leaving the skilled jobs to expatriates, the latter's high cost necessitates the gradual training and upgrading of the native. In contrast, the highly mechanized plant presents so great a gulf between the present level of the native employee and the minimum essential to operate the intricate equipment that it is all but impossible to establish a schedule of skills that would permit the gradual adaptation of the raw recruit to the demand of the machines. A smooth progression is virtually impossible in such an environment.

A number of important questions are raised by these and related discussions of the problem of factor proportions or the alleged "technological dualism" in less developed countries: Why are capital-intensive installations adopted in countries short of capital and overflowing with labor, and by private enterprises as well as prestige-conscious politicians? Is this primarily due to technocratic enthusiasm or has it a more rational basis? How far do such tendencies go in fact? In what sense, if at all, are factor proportions "dictated by the technological leadership of advanced countries?" And following upon these themes, do the countries that begin development later have in fact a real advantage with respect to choice of technologies? Coming more specifically to the quotations from Marcus, is there any reason to suppose that large-scale labor-intensive projects undertaken in relatively backward countries will in fact be characterized by a wide spectrum of skills? For that matter would large enterprises, each with a wide skill spectrum, offer the best opportunities for in-service learning and training among populations of less developed countries?

29. Edward Marcus, "Large-Scale Investment and Development—The Dilemma of the Gabon Republic," *Economic Development and Cultural Change*, IX, No. 1, Part 1 (October 1960), p. 64.

30. *Op. cit.*, pp. 66-67.

Let me start at the end. There are many enterprises in the United States in which skill spectra range through all levels and along multiple dimensions; but even under the most advantageous conditions, in this most fluid of societies, the notion that an individual can move from the bottom to the top of the ladder in a large modern enterprise is clearly pretty much of a myth. On-the-job learning for advancement among semiskilled operatives who genuinely start at that level is likely to hit a ceiling at the foreman or junior overseer's job. Few sub-professional technicians become full-fledged engineers. For the higher jobs, prior formal schooling has become increasingly essential, along with other educationally supportive non-job experiences (far more difficult to arrange in underdeveloped countries). Such schooling becomes a condition of entry to on-the-job ladders to the higher skill and managerial ranks, and its continuation in one form or another (reading, "sandwich" courses, etc.) is likely to be equally essential to the attainment of qualifications needed for effective performance in the more responsible positions of decision and control. Does this mean that on-the-job training recedes into unimportance in modern enterprises even where skill spectra are multidimensional with many gradients as well as parallel streams? Clearly the answer is No. However, today's ladders differ from the earlier ones in that they are more often broken into segments with differing schooling-qualification entry levels. Such a change is virtually inevitable given the great distances in human capital formation encompassed by the full extent of the skill and qualification ladders laid one upon another.

How far all this has relevance to potentials for in-service training (both on and off the job) in less developed countries could be debated, primarily because the skill spectra take a different form there. However, as long as we assume a big enterprise to start with, discontinuities in the ladders of genuine on-the-job learning can hardly be less in the underdeveloped countries. Indeed, the greater the training that workers need to attain efficiency at the semiskilled level, the more likely it must be that the enterprise will be organized to simplify their jobs, and the wider will be the gap remaining between the semiskilled men and the foremen. The ladders from the lowest rungs are more likely to be inter-generational, via diffusion of changed perceptions of economic life and opportunities combined with more pre-employment general education. On the other hand, at higher levels promotions may be more rapid and quality gradients blurred—at least so long as highly trained and experienced men are rare and the pressures to "localization" are strong.

Is there any reason to suppose, as the quotation from Marcus might suggest, that large-scale labor-intensive projects in relatively backward countries will in fact be characterized by wide spectra of skills? If a "wide spectrum of skills" is interpreted to mean a wide range in types and/or levels of non-supervisory skills that includes a continuum of in-between skill levels, the answer is demonstrably No. History gives us plenty of examples of skill dichotomization in large labor-intensive undertakings, especially in the construction industries. On the other hand, where many men are employed there must be some sort of supervisory hierarchy, and there must be at least something of a spectrum of supervisory jobs. When Nigeria, for example, bogs down on a labor-intensive road project because of too few supervisors, this fact is brought home to us. But the same illustration should serve also as a warning against tendencies to generalize from sub-Saharan Africa (or, if it happens to be more familiar territory, from quite different situations in Latin America). The contrast in scale is indeed one of the crucial differences between artisan manufacture and the factory system, old or new. But large-scale organization of teams of workers has not been confined to industrial undertakings. China built her wall and Egypt her pyramids many centuries ago, and what about the comparatively youthful cathedrals of medieval Europe, or the armies of Czarist Russia and early Meiji Japan? How, for that matter, did history make organized industry out of the individualists of American frontier civilization?

Kuznets, among others, has played down the advantage arising from the opportunity to imitate and to choose from many technologies. Most development has involved successive imitations, but these have always been highly selective; hosts of available technologies have been ignored. Though a large range of technologies may be in use somewhere in the world, many are so distant from the needs and circumstances of a particular country as to require fundamental innovation and invention before they can be adopted. Moreover, no economy has yet developed over an extended period until it has assimilated and digested enough to become itself a participant in technological advance. Japan's agricultural modernization took few innovations from the West except in methods of research and basic agronomic science; this kind of transfer and the ensuing application presupposes a developed educational system in the broadest sense — in schools and homes, in places of work and even of entertainment. To accomplish the transfer is in fact to have already reached a relatively high level of development.

Scientific and innovative capacities do not spring into being, they evolve, and they are fed by smaller imitations along the way. But innovation is essential; mere imitation can play only a modest part in transferring technologies. If this is the heart of the transfer problem, what becomes of Eckaus' notion of "factor proportions dictated by the technological leadership of advanced countries"? If there is such "dictation," why does it occur, what is its rationale, and in what ways does it affect the mix in demands for human skills and in the creation of on-the-job opportunities for their development?

The proposition that advanced technologies force developing countries to practice technological dualism is easiest to dispose of with respect to export industries, where the theme of "dictation" is most often evoked. There are certainly problems of quality control and economies of scale in producing such crops as tea or sugar; these involve organizational modernization but do not support the capital-intensity bias. The shift of textiles from cottage to town has been the hallmark of early industrialization; there is some increase in capital intensity, but this demonstrates only that there are many steps on the labor-capital intensity continuum.

The Ivory Coast, for example, should illustrate technological dualism for us as well as any other country. But we are shown, among other things, a textile firm that employs 2,000 workers along with smaller knitting mills, a mechanical repair work that employs 200, and an automobile assembly plant employing 100. India, which is much further developed, presents a wide spectrum of capital intensities and degrees of "modernity" in manufactures. Even in Japan today there are modern and traditional factories in the same industry sitting across the street from one another. To point to the location of an aluminum plant in Gabon is irrelevent so far as this argument is concerned; the aluminum industry is oriented to natural resources (including power); like mining, it knows comparatively few locational constraints otherwise. It is also a new product that can be turned out only with capital-intensive processes, which are indeed "dictated" — but there is nothing to dictate that industries such as this must be built up in countries at a low stage of development if those countries are to advance. Thre are other sides to this story however.

Eckaus did push back to explain his divergent factor proportions, but this is a problem to which many writers have given attention. Those who take as fact the tendency to a dichotomous technology (whatever their assumptions about substitutability) come again and again to problems of skill shortage or labor commitment. Gerschenkron has been especially emphatic about these problems, which he weaves into his theory of the "big push" and the relation between degree of initial backwardness and the explosiveness of propulsion into development.[31] Leibenstein notes "an incentive in backward economies, whenever technologically feasible, for the entrepreneur to employ skill-displacing rather than skill-using capital."[32] Kafka makes a related point: "If human and physical capital are admitted to be close substitutes over a very wide range (rather than complementary), we can explain in part the propensity of underdeveloped countries for large-scale ultramodern projects: since there so much organization is, as it were, built into the machinery and can be imported along with it, to replace a lack of organizing ability which reflects deficient human capital."[33] In other words, a deficiency in human

31. He states, for example: "Under these conditions the statement may be hazarded that, to the extent that industrialization took place, it was largely by application to the most modern and efficient techniques that backward countries could hope to achieve success, particularly if their industrialization proceeded in the face of competition from the advanced country. The advantages inherent in the use of technologically superior equipment were not counteracted but reinforced by its labor-saving effect. This seems to explain the tendency on the part of backward countries to concentrate at a relatively early point their industrialization on promotion of such branches of industrial activities in which recent technological progress had been particularly rapid."

(A. Gerschenkron, "Economic Backwardness in Historial Perspective," in B. F. Hoselitz (ed.), *The Progress of Underdeveloped Areas* (Chicago: University of Chicago Press, 1952), p. 7.

32. Harvey Leibenstein, *Economic Backwardness and Economic Growth* (New York: Wiley, 1957), p. 141.

33. Alexandre Kafka, "Discussion," *American Economic Review* (May 1959), p. 172. W. Brand

factors that are complementary to the less-than-modern technique evokes substitution of techniques that do not require these skills. This is where foreign aid programs and manpower planning are most likely to go astray, though it is also where they may be most needed. It is also where the "factories quick" school of thought might find its major justification — provided the factories are of a kind to train as well as produce.

Unfortunately, despite my remarks about alternatives along a capital-intensity continuum, most local government-sponsored and foreign investments that are most likely in the most backward countries (and that may take up a sizeable proportion of the maneuverable investment resources) tend not to be of the kind that supply training. Moreover, given the nature of both private and public bureaucracies, I must concede a considerable measure of validity even to the technological dualism thesis, at least in the African context. (Technical assistance to agriculture may be almost the sole saving grace.) Given the limitations of simple imitation, the difficulties of more subtle transfer, the existing human-factor gaps, and the nature of modern world politics, there is undoubtedly a tendency toward an unfortunate sequence of investments in industry where there is virtually nothing at the start.

These unfortunate biases stem from at least four main sources:

1) It is much easier to transfer a technology intact (plant, staff, know-how and all) than to innovate in line with the best interests of the new locale. And it is easier to transfer a package that includes much physical capital and small numbers of highly trained staff than a package requiring less physical capital but many semiskilled workers and foremen.

2) The process of search for promising investment opportunities is an expensive one, justified only for those undertakings that will entail large total capital outlays. International agencies and governments evaluating alternative aid projects need not be so constrained by this second consideration, but in practice their behavior is much the same. They are not organized to explore scores of smaller possibilities that might add up to a greater economic push in the long run.

3) Looking at each possible new type of enterprise by itself works against the smaller ones, for each one alone is likely to be highly risky. Only a large investor can spread this risk.

4) Finally, we come back to the heart of the human-factor dilemma. The serious disjunction between social and private returns inhibits initiation of ventures requiring large programs for labor-force training. This is where the complementarity problem is most recalcitrant unless public policies are deliberately designed to overcome it; education in the widest, and at the same

---

pointed out that the lower education of Indonesian workers put greater demands on supervisory staff; the training of foremen was consequently a greater problem. *The Struggle for a Higher Standard of Living*, (Glencoe, Illinois: Free Press, 1958), p. 111. Brozen argues that by introducing industries with low skill requirements the skill level of a labor force may be raised in the process of learning the small skills needed. "Technological change in underdeveloped areas," *Explorations in Entrepreneurial History*, 3:149-50, (1951).

time most crucial, sense has some laws of its own, and these imperatives of the learning process have built into them their own logic of internal complementarities.

Notice, however, that the second and third biases are simply statements of bankers' and foreign investors' biases of scale. Moreover, the first takes its coloration from the scale-of-investment bias; it may have quite different training implications when the producing units are more modest ones. The fourth bias directs us to kinds of public policy that can circumvent it, and historically often have done so. Only the first and fourth are relevant to local enterprising behavior. Finally, the force of all of these points depends upon the level and patterns of development already existing in any particular case; they are applicable in full force only to the situation I specified initially "where there is virtually nothing at the start." And this is where international programs of technical assistance to agriculture, a growing interest in "soft loans," and a host of small endeavors that are too often dismissed as "peanuts" come into the picture.

The "Raw Group" Problem and the Tasks of Management

Seven years ago I was engaged in interviewing manufacturers who had located or considered locating plants in eastern Kentucky (almost none) or central Kentucky (a sizeable number) over the previous decade. No one was drawn to Kentucky by the wealth of local skills; there was no such wealth. Few were attracted by the large surplus of raw labor, though this was one among several factors influencing manufacturers of cheap standardized apparel. Nevertheless, those who had gone to Kentucky had plenty to say, both favorable and unfavorable, about local labor, the training and learning process for semiskilled jobs, and the effect of workers' attitudes on productivity. Most of those workers were men out of the hills of southern and eastern Kentucky. Few were ex-coal miners; most came from back-country subsistence farms. All were acquiring the first elements of industrial skills as learners in the factories.

Five of my findings are relevant here. (1) Even with imported supervisors and skilled workers, it is far easier to train raw men a few at a time to enter a going operation than to train a semiskilled force all of whom start together; this is hardly surprising, but the difference was sometimes of a magnitude I would never have dreamed. (2) Even when there was more of a mix in the labor force, the mountain recruits often took more time to learn than young managers fresh from the north had anticipated. (3) Again and again the better managers would say: "The mountain men are fine workers, but you have to understand them. We get along fine because I know how they think and how to work with them. They work hard; absenteeism and turnover are low, but you have to give them a sense of freedom, to let them work things out with you in their own way." (4) Those managers who complained most about mountain labor were themselves ignorant and inefficient, especially in the apparel firms. They had high turnovers and poor production records.

Had they known the lingo they would undoubtedly have attributed all this to lack of "commitment" by the mountain people. (5) It was commonly reported that Kentucky workers were still individualists and believed in work. (This was not a question of unionization, for all the firms were organized.) The managers felt that Kentuckians had not yet learned the culture of slowdown and other annoyance tactics experienced in northern plants. The first two points and this fifth one help underline a generalization that can be supported on other grounds as well: Premature injection of "advanced" behavior and welfare institutions into less developed areas can block development. Minimum wage laws, social security, and unionization may be very costly when they preclude on-the-job training opportunities (quite aside from the fact that they never protect or support more than a small minority, who are thereby privileged to live at levels above the average for the society as a whole).

The raw recruits out of the Kentucky hills knew and believed in the "Protestant ethic," better perhaps than many of their northern fellows. They accepted universalistic-achievement as against particularistic-ascriptive criteria for selection and advancement; they fitted readily into a specific (as against a diffuse) pattern in the differentiation of functions. In fact, one of the things managers had to learn was the men's insistence upon this specificity, but in their own way. In these fundamental respects, then, they were committed from the start. Nevertheless there were training problems closely resembling those reported from many developing countries.

My first observation has many ramifications, but it must suffice here to note that even within the United States the raw group problem can run into extremely heavy cost disadvantages; it may take as long as two years to bring such a group up to the efficiency of an experienced force where new workers are added a few at a time. Even where experienced shop supervisors (foremen) are available or can be imported, labor costs may often be prohibitive unless the enterprise is insulated from competition by import quotas (or prohibitions), tariffs, or subsidies. Moreover, if foremen must be imported there is the problem of cultural distance and misunderstandings between supervisors and workers; this retards the development of effective interaction patterns at work.

My second point was that the Kentucky hill people had to spend much time climbing to northern efficiency even in a mixed work group that included some experienced workers. But the eastern Kentuckians had tinkered with autos. The technical naiveté of natives in truly underdeveloped countries have been sufficiently described; teaching often has to begin at the child level, not because individuals are unintelligent but because they lack relevent experience. It was for this reason that Anderson recommended construction and manipulative toys as basic primary school equipment in Kenya.[34] Vakil has demonstrated the importance of complementary learning

34. In his report for the World Bank Mission to Kenya (Fall 1961).

experience for the productivity even of semiskilled workers in the textile factories of Bombay and Calcutta.[35] He found that men approached their first factory jobs with excitement and favorable expectations, and the workers were malleable; they were already in a significant degree "committed" to factory work. Some were literate, some illiterate, but the productivity differences among the workers were less associated with literacy or formal schooling as such than with any one of several other attributes — changes in religious ideas, knowledge concerning the mills, active use of leisure time, newspaper reading. Similar factors undoubtedly lie back of Kahan's evidence for the "hereditary worker" hypothesis in eighteenth-century Russia (Part III, Chapter 14).

Slowness of learning raises labor costs, but does the "raw group" problem make special demands upon managers and supervisors that add to the problems of finding and training people for such posts? How important are managers for the pace of learning? My third and fourth Kentucky observations (about tactful mutual adjustment between workers and management and the question of managerial efficiency generally) touch upon these matters. But I can now no longer evade more direct consideration of "commitment" and its meaning.

As I read the literature on commitment there seems to be a seesawing back and forth among several distinct meanings of the term.[36] These hinge on what it is to which there must be commitment; everyone is committed to something, and clearly the problem is in the transformation of these commitments. One variant would be commitment to a particular occupation or career line, which may or may not incorporate perceptions and aspirations with respect to progressive advance up one or another ladder, and may or may not be linked to a particular industry. Its importance for development would evidently depend upon the extent of commitment to non-traditional occupations and career patterns. Another variant is commitment to a particular firm, which may be transfer from commitment to a kinship group, as in Japan; in advanced economies this becomes "loyalty to the corporation." However, this kind of commitment can easily become "overcommitment," and is especially likely to become so when alternative opportunities are few and attachment to a particular enterprise is seen primarily as security, as in Tata Steel and some of the Bombay mills.[37] Overcommitment, as I interpret it, can be allied with particularistic and ascriptive (and even diffuse) patterns that are contrary to yet another and more fundamental interpretation of com-

35. C. N. Vakil, *Report on Social and Cultural Factors Affecting Productivity of Industrial Labour*, v. I, ch. 5; v. II, pp. 6, 7, 44f, 86, 97 (1958).

36. See Wilbert E. Moore and Arnold S. Feldman (ed.), *Labor Commitment and Social Change in Developing Areas* (Social Science Research Council, 1960).

37. M. D. Morris points out also the ease of establishing commitment in a limited sense. "Where the discipline is more demanding, the advantages in terms of money, opportunity, and prestige have eased adjustment to discipline. Indian industry from its earliest stages had had little difficulty in keeping skilled groups attached permanently to the discipline of the factory." (p. 188 of his "The Labor Market in India" in Moore and Feldman, *op. cit.*)

mitment—attachment to a universalistic and achievement-oriented way of life and system of values. The latter seems to be Moore and Feldman's interpretation and is certainly the one Singer relied upon in criticizing them.[38].

The extent, kinds, and advancement potentials of learning on-the-job are evidently closely associated with these various dimensions of commitment. But on the simplest and lowest level of learning in the factory it may not matter much which definition of "commitment" we use; all of them require as a first step that workers become sufficiently identified with a kind of job and even a particular job to stay at it fairly steadily. The first educational task of management is to bring this about.[39] The means may include many policies that have no direct relation to training in a skill (though good teaching will certainly contribute to an enterprise's holding power). Evidently, until commitment at this level has emerged, there can be little learning, and only as identification with a job grows can learning grow.

It is around this level (Kerr's first two "stages"?[40]) that many of the arguments between anthropologists and economists seem to revolve (and to which in large measure my Kentucky respondents were directing their attention). To attract and hold workers you have to take account of the ways they look at things. Mutual adaptation will favor steadiness on the job and progressively rising efficiency. This is why forced recruitment delays commitment, though it may get some jobs done at fearful human and economic costs.[41] Nash's Guatemalan textile enterprise impresses me as a case of good business decision-making;[42] Hammond's Niger Irrigation Project is equally convincing as an example of blind managerial decisions.[43] Nash was stressing the importance of adaptation to an indigenous culture, while Hammond was castigating managers for failing to move into the twentieth century as rapidly as their Mossi workers. These sound like polar points of view, and yet they are really very much the same as a good business economist would look at them. Perhaps most interdisciplinary arguments about adapting to traditional culture versus remaking the workers turn into barking at butterflies.

Being an economist, I see sensible economic calculation in the timing of wage payments to take account of the motives of target workers; ultimately

38. Milton Singer, "Changing Craft Traditions in India," (in Moore and Feldman, *op. cit.*, pp. 258-276).

39. Feldman and Moore remarked, insightfully: "Meaningful involvement of employees in a labor market is frequently and paradoxically a consequence of their initial employment rather than antecedent to it." (in Moore and Feldman, *op. cit.*, p. 41.)

40. See Clark Kerr in Moore and Feldman, *op. cit.*, pp. 352-54.

41. Feldman and Moore refer to "the failure to appraise correctly the motivational resistence to manipulation on the part of the 'managed,' the cynical view that only minimal, bribed cooperation can be expected in any event." (Moore and Feldman, *op. cit.*, p. 45.)

42. M. Nash, "The recruitment of wage labor and development of new skills," *Annals* (May 1956), pp. 23-31. Also "Introducing industry in peasant societies," *Science* 130:1456-62 (1959). He emphasizes the possibilities and advantages of adapting enterprise to indigenous life patterns.

43. P. B. Hammond, "Management in Economic Transition," in Moore and Feldman, *op. cit.*, pp. 109-22.

this sort of adaptation is a step in wedding workers to a more conventionally western sort of commitment. And again, as an economist I am impressed by Kilby's Nigerian study:[44] he compares enterprises with respect to wage rates, conditions of work, and physical surroundings, and shows that absenteeism and turnover were more a measure of managerial policies than of worker acculturation. Unfortunately, the economic common sense that I see in the analyses by Nash and Hammond may require very subtle insights in practice, at least where managers and supervisors come out of societies very different from those in which their workers have lived.

Nash and Hammond studied undertakings initiated and managed by outsiders. Moreover, there are other things besides mutual adaptation involved in training workers and especially in providing conditions that permit learning for advancement on the job, whatever the supplementary and supportive educational activities. This is where perceptions of authority and mobility enter. Unfortunately, I know too little about how the local manufacturers emerging out of Lebanese commerce, or the new engineer-enterpriser of India, or the Mexican entrepreneurs stimulated by Sears have functioned in such matters. But even when a local supervisor knows his workers, there are relatively few pre-industrial societies in which he will have a model for behaving as a supervisor of disciplined team endeavors. There are virtually none in which he can observe established models of supervision where machine-geared reliability and accuracy are required of the worker. He is equally unlikely to know how to teach these skills in a setting that bears little resemblence to native apprenticeship. The local manager may be more constrained by familiar role patterns that would be less binding on a foreigner, patterns that both condition the operation of the authority structure within the enterprise and delay the transition from nepotistic to rationalistic selective processes in promotion. I suspect that it is not merely, and often not even primarily, the difficulty of bringing large sums of capital together that makes most native private enterprises in less developed countries comparatively small. It is also that smaller units facilitate the transition from one world into quite another.

It would be a mistake to overdraw this picture, however. There is all too great a tendency toward ethnocentrism of two opposite kinds. One of these is to assume that the only kind of management that can be viable and efficient must be a close imitation of the structures of relationships of Western societies or even more narrowly of a particular Western stereotype; this is the economist's and often the sociologist's ethnocentrism. Equally fallacious is the anthropologist's ethnocentrism, which takes as its model one or another favorite case from one of the economically most undeveloped societies, typically a society that has had no pre-industrial large-scale undertakings and no elaborate bureaucratic tradition (as the Indian societies of Central America or most African societies south of the Sahara).

44. P. Kilby, "African Labour Productivity Reconsidered," *Economic Journal* 71:273-91 (1961).

Japanese history provides what is probably the most dramatic demonstration of the dangers of such generalizations and stereotypes—which have often led to a sort of mystification at the alleged "paradoxes" of that country's system. The paradoxes are constructs of our minds, and they quickly resolve when we take a more careful look at the facts. Home-grown Japanese factory organizations combined traditions of teamwork, the institution of adoption of able sons, diffuse as against particularistic ties within the firm, strong achieve-' ment orientations, an ethic of hard work, and a deeply ingrained respect for hierarchical authority. Under Japanese bosses and policy-makers these merged to produce a new social structuring of industrialism that was truly "Japanese spirit and Western technology." This combination of Japanese genius and good fortune may deserve more attention, and more credit for economic and human-resource development in that land, than has heretofore been recognized. It is part and parcel of the fact that Japan went deliberately about the task of creating infant *training* industries, and of the ways in which this was done.

The Making and Circumventing of Infant Training Industries

Throughout the centuries men have moved over the earth carrying with them the cumulated learning from their experiences in work and in the total round of life. This is far more than schooling, and not so easily transmitted from one society to another, for it is not as amenable to abstractions from context. In a pre-industrial era, when the scale of production in the fabricating industries was small, migration of a skilled artisan was almost the equivalent of migration of the essential elements of an entire working establishment as an operating entity. Colonization was the mass migration of such entities, involving transplantations of entire socio-economic sub-cultures from one place to another. There were always metamorphoses in the transplanting, but this was not in itself an *international* transfer. The industries that migrated with the colonizers were not "infants" in their new locales, and there was no question of the making of infant training industries. However, we begin to edge up to the problems that are our concern here when we come to mass migrations in which the settlers became centers for diffusion of skills among native populations, instead of liquidating those populations or remaining totally separate. Even in South Africa many of the European immigrant skills are filtering through the various racial and ethnic barriers. Where such diffusion becomes substantial and the indigenous population takes over the controls, we could conceive the transmission of the settlers' skills as an "international" transfer of know-how; in retrospect this sort of skill diffusion could then be viewed as a circumvention of the infant training industry problem.

Once manufacturing shifts to a factory system it becomes more important to distinguish migration of individuals (however numerous they may be) from migrations of establishments as operating entities. True enough, if enough people with skills and experience in a particular industry migrate to the same new locale, it would not be difficult to reassemble them; but this is not likely to occur by totally spontaneous and individually independent decisions. The more meaningful model is the enterprise that is set up as a planned "package deal" in which supervisors, workers and equipment are moved together. Morris describes a striking example:[45] entire clusters of experienced workers were imported from England along with the machinery for the early Bombay textile mills, and for a long period these mills remained insulated from Indian society and labor markets. Prejudice and exclusivism maintained and reinforced stereotypes of Indian workers that deferred the day when the mills would become loci of training for a new indigenous industrial labor force.[46] Rigid attitudes undoubtedly blocked adaptations of organization and technology to local labor conditions; the contrast with colonial Massachusetts, where such modifications were made, is an interesting one. However, even in India the balance of economic forces progressively shifted, stereotypes of Indian workers were modified, and the mills began to form local skills incidental to the profitable production of cloth. The "package deal" in the establishment of these mills was based upon simple economic calculations of the original investors; the long duration of the policy was also a prolonged circumvention of the infant training industry problem. Whether or not the mill owners were correct in their profit-loss calculations, the delay in training Indian workers presents an image that gives both validity and emotional intensity to the arguments of former colonials who attack the whole "package deal" notion. The Bombay mills, like early colonizations generally, were little more (or less) than transplantations from one part of the world to another.

Establishment of a foreign-owned firm in a less developed country (or at any rate in one to which the industry is new) is also in part a transplantation, but with a difference. The Indian mills were established by nationals of the colonizing metropole who were subject solely or almost solely to its laws and controls; only later, with Indian independence, did the British mills of Bombay and Calcutta cease to be extensions of Britain. By contrast, "foreign" establishments are in another independent country by the official courtesy or sufferance of the latter. This difference can be economically as well as politically important, as is strikingly manifested in the contrast between modern bargaining between Arab governments and foreign oil companies, and the exploitation of gold or diamond mines in the Africa of a generation ago. Of special relevance are contractual agreements that require foreign concerns to engage in active programs for the training and upgrading of local people to fill ever more of the higher skilled and supervisory posts. Some industries that offered little in local training prior to such requirements have become training industries even when most of the local trainees are carried in supernumerary posts.

Obviously such a policy can be enforced by host governments only when

45. In the article cited in footnote 11.
46. See the contribution by R. I. Crane in this volume.

they have leverage to hold the foreign concern despite training costs – or when the host government pays outright for training services. It is no accident that oil companies are often required to engage in training and localization policies that are not required of firms in other industries, or that oil companies have done this voluntarily, as political insurance; valuable oil resources tie these firms to particular locations. Where local markets are sufficiently strong, policies requiring training and localization may be enforceable on foreign concerns selling in those markets (usually under tariff protections). There have been more indirect inducements to educational endeavor by foreign enterprises as well. The Mexican government's requirement that Sears buy more local products led to the development of a cluster of supplying establishments: these provided both training and learning in factory entrepreneurship and on-the-job development of semiskilled cohorts of workers and low-level supervisors.

Back in the eighteenth century, long before anyone had dreamed of a Soviet state, the Russians were encouraging the in-migration of German workers along with German equipment and supervisory-technical personnel for the early iron industry. This, like the Bombay mills, was a package deal and in this sense a transplantation. However, the whole relationship was very different. Coming at least in part by invitation, encouraged by deliberate Czarist policies, the Germans settled in a nation of which they became a part. It was with the hope and intent of merging them and their skills into Russian society that efforts had been made to attract them.[47] Moreover, French technicians were employed by the Russian military from the 18th century. By providing military on-the-job learning opportunities, they contributed ultimately to a transfer of know-how by diffusion back into other spheres of Russian life; and an in-migration of French skills in the production of luxury consumer goods was fostered under the aegis of the Court. The French in-migrations were more directly and closely tied to the government and its cliques, whereas the Germans came both as enterprisers in their own right and to work for the Czars; however, there was never any doubt as to who remained politically in control. This was an importation of skills and know-how, not a transplantation by a colonial power.

If I assess this history correctly, the initial package importations of German equipment and workers in the early iron industry can be interpreted as a process of circumventing the problems of training in an infant industry. The importation was further encouraged and protected by government buying of its hardware, paralleling the protected market the Court provided for the French luxury good manufacturers. Development of the military partially as an infant training industry for the transmission of foreign skills was of course directly and unambiguously at public expense.

Under the Meiji, Japan subsidized infant training industries on an extra-

47. It was no accident that men with German surnames came to occupy key positions in the Russian military and have continued to do so.

ordinary scale from the start. The men responsible knew exactly what they wanted most to accomplish: to build the industry and skills required as the foundation of military strength for national survival. They went about this task unhampered by either economic theologies or insecurities of self-esteem. Like the Russian Czars, but in contrast to the Russian Soviets, the early Meiji left the coordination of the major part of economic life to the markets and in private hands, while the central government concentrated its efforts on the priority sectors of industry. The extent to which these sectors were taken over by the Japanese government or manipulated under semi-private or private control varied with the time and the industry; priorities came quickly to include not only such obvious candidates as shipbuilding, but also export industries needed to maintain balance of payments. The strategy aimed at the transfer of skills and know-how was multipronged, including expatriate teachers of western subjects in the schools, overseas scholarships, and the importation of foreign experts to accompany the equipment for a new factory.

The foreign technicians were paid by the government at whatever world price was needed to attract them, regardless of Japanese pay levels.[48] But their authority was confined to the exercise of only their technical expertise. Japanese controlled the factories and their human organization, which was adapted to the requirements of technology in a Japanese way. The foreigners were required to train Japanese counterparts and assistants, and they were retained so long as they were needed to fulfill this task. During the early Meiji decades, labor mobility among enterprises was high at all skill levels, and the training that was subsidized by the government became diffused into other parts of the economy as newly trained Japanese technicians moved to set up or assist in the operation of new enterprises. But none of these Japanese received or expected expatriate rates of pay. The foreigners remained cultural inferiors even if their incomes were several times those of both the Japanese who were over them and those who took their place as trained technicians and engineers. Probably never before or since in history (and I do not exclude Russia) has so rational a human resource development program for industrialization been conceived and executed.

The structure of the Japanese labor market has changed substantially since the early Meiji period. Today there is less mobility of skilled and supervisory personnel from one employer to another. But one thing persists; on-the-job training is a key aspect of Japanese life. Both custom and law insure that discrepancies between private and social costs and benefits will not cramp the range of learning opportunities. With on-the-job training programs so pervasive and with wide room for mobility within the purview of single employers, the limitations on inter-firm movement become relatively unimportant so far as concerns the spread of skills among the population.

48. Interesting evidence on this early Japanese policy is provided by Yasuichi Emi in a study that will appear in English translation in UNESCO's *Readings on Education and Economic Development* (1965).

In his conclusion to an M.I.T. symposium on "Investment Criteria and Economic Growth," Fellner emphasized that two sets of hurdles must be overcome if rapid development is to be launched and sustained.[49] Both involve complementaries in the broadest sense. The first set he labeled the "infant industry problem," hinging it upon delayed returns, the problem of time horizons, and the uncertainties that these entail — including the uncertainty that the complementary developments that alone can insure profitability will infact emerge. He notes that this problem appears on a greatly aggravated scale in the least developed countries. His second set of hurdles exists where societal returns diverge in major degree from private returns, and would continue to do so indefinitely. Fellner gave no explicit attention to human resources, however; when we focus attention upon the circular implications of technical inelasticities of substitution between schooling and on-the-job learning, the sharpness of Fellner's distinction between his two categories of hurdles becomes blurred. It is still less clear when we consider how potentially maneuverable institutional factors may condition the incidence of costs and returns, and hence the extent and nature of the discrepancies between private and social costs and benefits.

All of this brings us back to the conditions that may produce or reduce the biases that lend plausibility to the technological dualism thesis. I suggest that we will gain much more penetrating and also more useful insights into these and other problems of economic development when we come to give more attention to how human capacities of various kinds are formed, to the place of job-linked training and experience in these processes, and to the commonalities and diversities of the solutions that can be read from history.

49. W. Fellner, "Individual Investment Projects in Growing Economics," in *Investment Criteria and Economic Growth* (Bombay, 1961), pp. 121-55.

Chapter 7

THE GROWTH OF
AMERICAN EDUCATION

Richard J. Storr

The American advising with respect to education and development overseas almost inevitably draws upon the experience of the United States, however unwittingly; the man who scorns history may be influenced by inherited prejudice that he is not equipped to identify. Needless to say, it would be foolish not to use American history where it has some application abroad, either as a model or a warning; but it would be intellectually irresponsible to do so without first examining the past critically. If we are to avoid exporting untested myth, we must ask if our thinking is historically sound. I shall comment on some fundamental patterns in American education from the time of colonization to about the middle of the nineteenth century, when the United States had arrived at economic adolescence.

American education stems from family life much as the economy comes (even etymologically) from household management. At the beginning of British settlement in North America, the family was the dominant institution in education, partly of course because the young were moved in families but also because traditionally English education centered there. The colonists were just that, and not a *colonial people* in the modern sense of the term — a fact we must bear ever in mind when we apply American experience abroad. They did not adopt but rather transplanted the institutions of the mother country. The word "system" hardly applies to English education in the seventeenth century; but an ordering of education resulted from the hierarchical arrangement of families, each one preparing its young for life in the class to which the family belonged or (in religious terms) for the work to which God called his several creatures. Rearing a son meant more than teaching him a way to get a livelihood, but it *was* a mode of occupational training, the practice of which had the support of fundamental morality. Blackstone summed up the tradition I speak of when he wrote that one of the duties of parents to their children was "that of giving them an *education* suitable to their station in life. . . ." Blackstone added, be it noticed, that "the municipal laws of most countries seem to be defective at this point, by not constraining the parent to bestow a proper education upon his children."[1] Such parental responsibility was established, apparently without question, in

1. William Blackstone, *Commentaries on the Laws of England*, Vol. I (American edition, Philadelphia: 1771), pp. 450-451.

America. Indeed, in the nineteenth century Chancellor James Kent echoed Blackstone almost word for word: "The education of children in a manner suitable to their station and calling is . . . [a] branch of parental duty, of imperfect obligation generally in the eye of the municipal law, but of very great importance to the welfare of the state."[2]

In early Virginia, the heart of the statutory law on education consisted of provision for orphans, *i.e.*, for children who had no natural families. The first Massachusetts statute on education specifically obligated parents to educate their children and enabled town officers to bind out the children of parents who failed to do their duty—a real penalty in a land where labor was dear. The problem of education, as the Puritans of New England originally saw it, was one of adult delinquency. Of a Connecticut law to the same effect, another commentator, Tapping Reeve wrote in 1816: "This law has, by some, been branded as tyrannical, and as an infringement of parental rights . . . but I have no doubt that this law has produced very astonishing effects; and to this is to be attributed that general knowledge of reading and writing so observable among the people of this state."[3] During 27 years of legal practice, Reeve added, he had found but one person who could not write and was obliged to make his mark. Incidentally Reeve remarked that the laws of England did not reach farther than the binding out of the children of the poor; if England had not also developed industrially with impressive speed, one might be inclined to attribute Connecticut's economic development to the nearly total literacy produced by its deeper penetration into the old realm of family rights.

In wealthy families the private tutor appeared, presumably after the model of English practice, and conceivably in response to John Locke's description of the proper education of a gentleman. The seriousness with which education was taken in one great Virginia house, that of Robert Carter of Nomini Hall, its tutor, Philip Fithian, fully attests.[4] Yet here the humble instance of Benjamin Franklin's learning to read at home is more to the point. "House-education"—a phrase used casually in Robinson Crusoe as if it required no explanation—must often have been very informal, but it was not wholly accidental. Indeed, in Professor Bernard Bailyn's view, the disruptive effect of life in America upon the family made Americans acutely aware of its worth: the legislation that they passed expressed "a heightened consciousness of what the family had meant in education, of how much of the burden of imparting civilization to the young it had borne, and of what its loss might mean. . . ."[5] What in England was the special problem of the

2. James Kent, *Commentaries on American Law,* Vol. II (second edition, New York: 1932), p. 195.

3. Tapping Reeve, *The Law of Baron and Femme; of Parent and Child* . . . (New Haven: 1816), pp. 286-287.

4. See Hunter D. Farish, ed., *Journal and Letters of Philip Vickers Fithian, 1773-1774: A Plantation Tutor of the Old Dominion* (Williamsburg: Colonial Williamsburg, Inc., 1943).

5. Bernard Bailyn, *Education in the Forming of American Society* (Chapel Hill: University of North Carolina Press, 1960), p. 26.

children of the poor was becoming a general problem in America as (about the middle of the seventeenth century) the original immigrants came to fear a falling-away of their children from the old ways. That first crisis of American youth moved the leaders of the older generation to enforce explicitly what had previously been implicit in the very structure of society.[6]

The family may be thought of as society's primordial element; the guild was a fundamental unit of the particular kind of society that seventeenth-century England inherited from the middle ages. The provision for the young in the guild, *i.e.*, the binding of a boy to a master, resembled membership in a family. The master was a surrogate parent, possessed of a right to the boy's labor and obliged to provide him education to a calling. The boy was at once a worker and a learner. The method of his education was indeed learning by doing—a method practiced traditionally long before its theory became "progressive." (John Dewey looked backward explicitly to the education of the self-sufficient household, the decline of which he considered a reason for the reformation of schooling.) Like the family, apprenticeship was introduced into America, as it were, on its own momentum, and became the usual form of vocational education.

In America, however, apprenticeship was confronted by conditions different from those in the old world, perhaps most notably by a shortage of labor. Entry into apprenticeship was less expensive than in England, terms of service were harder to enforce, and the privileges to be acquired only through completion of apprenticeship were not always so valuable, nor so grand. Workmanship and those parts of the economy dependent upon the higher skills may have suffered because of some decline in the rigor of training and in the protection of master-craftsmen from the competition of uncertified practitioners of the manual arts, but versatility and enterprise were encouraged. In Professor Daniel Boorstin's phrase, "the undifferentiated man" flourished in the Colonies.[7] The boy of some talent could try his hand at many things, perhaps to become a jack-of-all-trades—a once characteristically American type that may have had more importance in the development of the country than its somewhat pejorative label immediately suggests. The boy of genius, with some good luck, could go far.

After having had some schooling, Benjamin Thompson was indentured at the age of thirteen to a dry-goods merchant in Salem, where the scholarly minister of the First Church instructed him informally in mathematics. Later Thompson served as an apprentice in a dry-goods shop in Boston and then as an apprentice to a physician in Woburn. At that time, he was guided into

6. For accounts of family life in colonial America, see Edmund S. Morgan, *The Puritan Family: Essays on Religion and Domestic Relations in Seventeenth-Century New England* (Boston: Trustees of the Public Library, 1944) and Morgan, *Virginians at Home: Family Life in the Eighteenth Century* (Williamsburg: Colonial Williamsburg, Inc., 1952).

7. Daniel J. Boorstin, *The Americans: The Colonial Experience* (New York: Random House, 1958), pp. 185-188.

natural philosophy (physics) by an older boy, Loammi Baldwin, later a prominent civil engineer. The two boys organized a scientific society and exchanged problems for a number of years. Thompson also attended some of Professor John Winthrop's lectures in natural philosophy at Harvard but did not matriculate there. So armed, Thompson pursued his enquiries until he reached a place of eminence in science and technology. Unfortunately for America, Thompson simultaneously conducted a pursuit of the main chance that carried him out of his native country. But it had educated Count Rumford.[8]

By statutory injunction as well as by contractual stipulation, masters were obliged to see that their charges became literate. Presumably many apprentices picked up reading and writing in odd moments, and others constituted the clientele of proprietary evening schools. Such schools became quite numerous in cities during the eighteenth century, and offered more than rudimentary instruction. Isaac Greenwood, sometime Hollis Professor at Harvard, taught in such a school after his dismissal for drunkenness and may, one imagines, have given excellent or even brilliant, if irregular, instruction to young mechanics. (While still holding the Hollis chair, he had given popular lectures.) One must not romanticize the life of colonial cities such as Boston and Philadelphia to create a paradoxical vision of an urban Arcadia, but neither should one write off altogether the culture available to apprentices with lively minds. Benjamin Franklin's early life was atypical more in the exceptional quality of the man than in deviation from the pattern of experience open to an urban boy of his class—a pattern of modest but legally protected opportunity to master letters, on-the-job technical training, and miscellaneous but not necessarily random education outside of a trade.[9]

Opportunity for acquiring "useful knowledge" became somewhat institutionalized in the course of time as libraries and other agencies of popular education were organized. Thus, the successor to Hogarth's industrious apprentice was the enlightened mechanic. In 1833, Allen and Ticknor of Boston published *Scenes of American Wealth and Industry . . . for the Instruction and Amusement of Children and Youth,* a panorama in words and woodcuts of a developing America. Popular education also appeared in the countryside at least as early as 1807, when Elkanah Watson exhibited a pair of Merino sheep under an elm in the public square of Pittsfield.[10] Shortly thereafter the Berkshire Agricultural Society received a charter and held a fair, perhaps the first in the American sense of the word.

Some apprentices were thirsty for information about the nature of

8. Sanborn C. Brown, *Count Rumford: Physicist Extraordinary* ("Science Study Series"; Garden City, New York: Anchor Books, Doubleday & Company, 1962), pp. 1-22.

9. See Carl Bridenbaugh, *The Colonial Craftsman* (New York: New York University Press, 1950); *Cities in the Wilderness: The First Century of Urban Life in America, 1625-1742* (New York: Ronald Press, 1938); and *Cities in Revolt: Urban Life in America, 1743-1776* (New York: Alfred A. Knopf, 1955), *passim.*

10. Elkanah Watson, *Men and Times of the Revolution; or, Memoirs of Elkanah Watson,* ed. by Winslow C. Watson (New York: 1856), pp. 419-439.

things; but perhaps most were moved far less by curiosity than by those forces, sweeping in upon them from their environment, that a French traveler, Michael Chevalier, observed in 1833-1835:

> Almost everywhere in the North all children go to the primary schools. Elementary education is there more practical than with us; it is our primary instruction with less emphasis on literature and ideality and the addition of some instruction in commercial and economic affairs. But there is no practical industrial education here except by apprenticeship. There are no mechanical or agricultural seminaries. It is useless here to shut up the young in such institutions to inspire them with a taste for commerce, agriculture, or the mechanical arts; they suck it in with their mother's milk; they breathe the air of industry under the paternal roof, in public meetings, everywhere, at all times and in every act of life. When an American wishes to learn a trade, he goes into the workshop, the counting-house, the manufactory, as an apprentice. By seeing others act, he learns how to act himself; he becomes an artisan, a manufacturer, a merchant; all the faculties of his firm and watchful mind, all the energies of his ambitious spirit are centered in his workshop or warehouse. . . . The American learns by example merely; we must learn by general principles; we stand more in need of them and we have a greater aptitude for mastering them than they.[11]

Chevalier's reference to primary schooling would not have been wholly inaccurate even if he had been reporting a visit to America before the Revolution. Quantitatively, the provision for schooling then was less different from our own than may be sometimes supposed; but qualitatively, colonial schooling was less like our own than the mythology of educational reform used to suggest. In particular, the town school of New England was not Mark I of public education in the modern sense. Until the nineteenth century, the words "public" and "private" did not have the meaning in the context of education that they now have. The older American usage was close to English, according to which Eton may logically be called a "public school," *i.e.*, an established institution drawing boys away from the privacy of their homes. In England, writers on education saw the issue of private vs. public education in precisely that light: should the boy be kept at home or sent away to school? In American usage at least, one detects the shadow of a distinction between that education (private) which touched personal interests or pleasures and that education (public) which prepared the young to render service to society. Our sharp distinction between public and private support of education was not observed. A school tapped what resources it could: tuition fees, legislative grants, local tax money, and the gifts or bequest of philanthropists. In England, the school was the child of philanthropy; the magnitude of such philanthropy in 16th and 17th centuries has recently been demonstrated by Professor W. K. Jordan.[12] He argues, from a mass of evidence, that philanthropy provided the realm with new or resuscitated schools

11. Michael Chevalier, *Society, Manners, and Politics in the United States* (Garden City: Anchor Books, 1961), pp. 334-335.
12. See Wilbur K. Jordan, *Philanthropy in England, 1480-1660: A Study of the Changing Pattern of English Social Aspirations* (New York: Russell Sage Foundation, 1959).

(and other good works) so copiously and upon such principles that philanthropy itself must be thought of not as a palliative of inevitable privation or distress—mere charity—but rather as an aliment of the whole society— the stuff of growing tissue. In a different metaphor, philanthropy and the state were harnessed in tandem to the same purpose by a statute that gave protection to philanthropy. The state did not conduct schools by its own act, but did encourage schooling by other means.

It is in the light of the brilliant success of that precedent that we must, I believe, view the founding of schools in the colonies, southern as well as northern, and in particular the sequence of school laws beginning with the "Old Deluder" statute of 1647. It was the work of the original (immigrant) generation of Massachusetts Puritans, men who loved learning and who belonged to the middle class from which philanthropic wealth flowed, and so could have been expected to be familiar with the rise of the school. Passed five years after the law requiring parents to do their duty to their children, the statute ordered each town of Massachusetts Bay to maintain an elementary teacher and, if the town was of a certain size, a grammar master as well. The colony would thus acquire by legal compulsion what the mother-country already possessed, thanks to private wealth called out by a moral imperative and permissive legislation.

The General Court was more aggressive than Parliament but did not go so far in the advancement of schooling as the state legislatures of a later era. But to say that is to flirt with anachronism: when the Court passed the statute of 1647, it was legislating, not a fragment of our (then remote) present, but the full image of England's immediate past. The door was left open to the philanthropist, for what the law required was the maintenance of schools somehow, not by taxation in particular. Inferentially, the taxpayer's obligation was contingent: he had to support the schools if nobody else did. (It can be argued that English policy was based upon the assumption that somebody else would.) Also, the Court did not make attendance at school compulsory. Retaining his ultimate responsibility for the education of his child, the parent could decide whether or not he would discharge that responsibility by sending the child to school. If he did opt for the school, he might have to pay fees or declare his poverty. Thus, the intention of the statute (as I interpret it) was conservative; but in a raw land that was a colony of England, to be boldly conservative was to be constructive.[13]

Looking backwards in time past Adam Smith, we may see a resemblance between the broad pattern of English education and economic laissez faire. As Book V of *The Wealth of Nations* indicates, Smith himself disapproved heartily of endowed education and would presumably have been wary of a policy influenced by its example; but he might have recognized the respon-

---

13. Early legislation on education is discussed in Marcus W. Jernegan, *Laboring and Dependent Classes in Colonial America, 1607-1783: Studies of the Economic, Educational, and Social Significance of Slaves, Servants, Apprentices, and Poor Folk* (Chicago: University of Chicago Press, 1931), *passim*.

sible parent as the counterpart in education of the independent entrepreneur in business. Neither in the law of education nor in his economy did the state directly control the current of affairs. Notably, the invisible hand of competition guided education in the province of the proprietary school and the itinerant teacher of dancing, for instance. And who can say how many ambitious parents pointed their children towards something like a market for talent? Yet custom did not release its hold on the organization of education overnight; and custom meant discrimination in respect to social class.

As the hierarchically ordered society evolved into a new genus of its species, however, schooling became increasingly important to the life of that society. When America was first settled, both society and education were finding a new balance, which was neither that of the middle ages nor that of democracy. Society became more open without being egalitarian, and the school more accessible—and more attractive to men of secular ambition—without being free in our sense. The multiplication of schools was a product of the shift in the equilibrium of society, but schooling was one of the mechanisms that made evolution within the existing structure of society possible. (The American faith in formal education as an alternative to revolution might be traced back this far.) The new genus of the body politic may conveniently be called the *commonwealth*, and the mode of education associated with its rise, *commonwealth schooling*.

The two segments of English society did not evolve in adaptation to identical environments. In America, however, the conditions of frontier life produced fear of both spiritual and civil degeneration; that fear intensified concern over education while a shortage of capital undermined confidence in philanthropy as a sufficient foundation of the school. The combination of anxiety and relative poverty moved the leaders of New England to exert the power of the state directly, not to create democratic education (which lay far outside their universe of thought), not to build a public school system, but rather to force the growth of commonwealth schooling.

In the decades just after the Revolution, the positive interest of the state in education was frequently affirmed by word; but it was not confirmed very impressively by act. A number of Americans engaged in the educational counterpart of constitution-making; *i.e.*, they framed projects for education under public auspices.[14] "The revolution is not over," wrote Dr. Benjamin Rush as he proposed the founding of a national university in the year (and the city) in which the federal Constitution was drafted. A republic had been created but its principles had yet to be secured, which could best be done, Rush argued, "by promoting such institutions as have a tendency to remove local views and habits, and beget mutual confidence, esteem, and good fel-

14. See Allen O. Hansen, *Liberalism and American Education in the Eighteenth Century* (New York: Macmillan Company, 1926), *passim*; and Frank C. Abbott, *Government Policy and Higher Education: A Study of the Regents of the University of the State of New York, 1784-1949* (Ithaca: Cornell University Press, 1958), p. 8 ff.

lowship between those who are embarked in the same bottom, and must rise or fall together. . . ."[15] That sense of a new nation and its dependence upon education (or a sense of the individual states in the same connection) was keenly felt by prominent men; but the principle of systematic public support of education was not well-received by the people. So the first dawning of the idea was largely false. The dream of a national university; land grants, which cost the taxpayer nothing in cash on hand; the creation of school literary funds; the founding of the first state universities; the enabling act of the New York Regents — these things did not work a profound change in the polity of formal education.

But schooling did develop strikingly in another quarter, indicated (as it happens) by an early revision of the University of the State of New York. The removal of Columbia College from the jurisdiction of the Regents symbolizes the disintegration of effort at public control in the face of conditions favoring the independent school. From about the middle of the eighteenth century, colleges and academies, each with its own board of governors or proprietor, had multiplied at an accelerating rate as the religious denominations, the philanthropists, and the legislatures became patrons of particular institutions. (Perhaps the most significant encouragement given education by the legislatures was the generous bestowal of charters. Even before the Revolution there were more degree-granting institutions in America than in the mother country.)

The force of private enterprise must not be forgotten either: keeping a school was a genteel business and could support a scholar's family. The independent school, chartered or not, was conspicuously viable and dynamic. As it advanced just behind the frontier itself, the country became dotted with colleges and academies, to the benefit of communities far removed from the old centers of formal education, although still not to the ultimate advancement of the higher learning. The multiplication of institutions meant the dispersion of talent.

Expansion also occurred in the curriculum, especially at the academies but also at the colleges, partly because of competition from the academies. Science and technological subjects appeared in distinct, non-classical curricula and in specialized departments or schools; *e.g.*, Rensselaer Polytechnic Institute and the scientific schools at Harvard and Yale. (West Point, of course a federal institution, offered an introduction to engineering, which may have been more important at the time than the strictly military portion of the program at the Academy. Notice that it was a discrete institution rather than a part of a national system of service schools.) In 1819, the formal independence of the philanthropic (or "eleemosynary") school was established in the Supreme Court as Chief Justice John Marshall handed down his famous

15. Benjamin Rush, "Address to the People of the United States," (sic) *American Museum,* I (1787; 3rd ed., 1790), p. 11; and "Plan of a Federal University," *American Museum,* IV (1788), p. 444.

opinion in the Dartmouth College case: the State of New Hampshire must not interfere in the government of the college.[16]

In 1845, Edward Hitchcock, clergyman, scientist, and educational administrator, offered an argument for the academy that may be read as a general theory of voluntarism in education. Accepting the general premise that Creation is but a series of harmonies produced by adaptation, he found that the "academical plan of education" was peculiarly well-adapted to the genius, character, and government of the country. The plan afforded "an opportunity for youth of both sexes, from every class in the community, to enjoy an elevated course of instruction on almost every elementary branch of science or literature to which they may choose to attend, and for a longer or shorter period as they shall wish . . ." and also enabled the young to pursue classical studies in preparation for admission to the "higher seminaries." That mode of education differed, Hitchcock pointed out, from practice in most European countries where education was almost entirely controlled by the government and where studies were rigidly prescribed: ". . . in this country the government presumes that every parent is intelligent and judicious enough to judge what sort of education it is best to give his children; and, therefore, it (the government) leaves the community to establish such seminaries as it pleases; extending to them only its protection and occasional pecuniary aid. It never enquires where or how a man was educated in order to judge whether he is eligible to a post of honor or profit; but only whether he *is* educated." Whether considering or ignoring the early state universities and West Point, Hitchcock remarked that he knew of no case where a "literary" institution started and controlled by the government of a state, or the United States, had had anything more than ephemeral success: ". . . if we wish to have an institution fail, let the government start it and attempt to support it."[17] The words have a familiar ring, and for good reason. In 1845, Hitchcock was defending an old order in education against such intervention by government as we have observed today in the spheres of welfare, housing, and medicine.

Paradoxically, the argument used to justify constitutional protection of chartered colleges undermined the customary conception of the school's relation to the commonwealth (and perhaps of the commonwealth itself) by establishing the distinction between public and private institutions of education in its modern and now commonplace sense. As if aware that the dichotomy upon which the Dartmouth decision was based might not be understood, Joseph Story intimated in his opinion in the Bowdoin College case (1833) that an eleemosynary institution might be "public" in common usage

16. Daniel Webster's famous argument in the Dartmouth College case and John Marshall's opinion are available in Richard Hofstadter and Wilson Smith, *American Higher Education: A Documentary History*, Vol. I (Chicago: University of Chicago Press, 1961), pp. 202-219.

17. Edward Hitchcock, *The American Academic System Defended* (Amherst: 1845), pp. 1-9.

and yet not be a public corporation in the eyes of the law.[18] Under the terms of the Dartmouth and Bowdoin decisions, philanthropy and the state would be harnessed not in tandem but abreast of each other. The commonwealth would be served by two kinds of formal education.

The advocates of public education were shortly to argue their case with the greatest possible vigor and with a moral force that obviously still has powerful momentum. The attack upon privilege and the corresponding demand for equality of opportunity that we associate with Jacksonian democracy; fear of uneducated majorities, coming to power under the same dispensation; anxiety over social cleavage, produced by industrialism and immigration; an awakening to the presence of the city and of a threat to traditional family life; observation of reform abroad; the decline of the Calvinistic and the rise of the romantic view of the child; and (in New England) a sharpened sense of past glory—these things generated a zeal surpassed only by that of abolitionism in an age of zealous reform. In one aspect, the movement was an amplification of an existing tendency to conceive of education as schooling, the reformers enjoying some of their most spectacular successes in states (perhaps most notably Massachusetts) where the schoolhouse was a familiar part of the landscape. Enthusiasm for the common school was partly an old anxiety reminted: a threatened society had deliberately to impress a sense of its identity upon the young, lest it otherwise lose its very life. As the commonwealth became egalitarian, disunity had taken the place of barbarism as the enemy. The weapon of defense was a common culture, imparted—according to the pure ideology of the reformers—in a school attended by all children, whose common experience would be the cement of society. Education would be established somewhat as religion had been. In Massachusetts, disestablishment of the church was followed shortly by the first great victory of the common school. Education so thought of appears in a changed aspect, emerging as a challenge to the old order. The common school movement worked towards general school taxation and tuition-free instruction for all, and so against miscellaneous and discriminatory financing of education. In particular, the common-school principle implied rejection of philanthropy as a foundation-stone of public policy. (In New York City, reform meant transfer of responsibility for schooling from a philanthropic society to a public agency.)

The logic of the movement also carried through to compulsory school attendance; but law did not follow logic until after the middle of the century. Again, Massachusetts led by requiring attendance in 1852; but other states did not fall in line until some years later. Thus, the idea of parental responsibility for the decision that a child should or should not be educated at school

18. *Allen v. McKeen, Reports of Cases Argued and Determined by the Circuit Court of the United States for the First Circuit,* ed. by Charles Sumner (Boston: Hilliard, Gray, and Company, 1836), I, pp. 296-297.

survived the first impact of reform. In language often used, the "struggle"
for public education was prolonged and did not end (or perhaps I should say
has not yet ended) in complete victory for reform, if by that one means the
establishment of a common experience for all of the young throughout the
course of formal education. Political and legal action produced a virtual compromise, which allowed private education room for immense growth, with
the nourishment of a philanthropy beyond the conception of Americans in
1850. (It is perhaps ironic that in Massachusetts itself the colleges so
flourished under private auspices that public higher education was long
overshadowed.)[19]

But the consequence of the common school movement must not be
measured by its reverses. Plainly, greatly increased intervention on the part
of the state brought about a new balance of educational institutions in the
United States, and prepared the way for a transformation of American society
as well. (Be it noted that education was moving into public hands and internal
improvements out of them simultaneously: what inferences are we to draw
about the attitude of the American people towards the place of the state in
society?) The common school movement wrought a change not only in the
pattern of education but also in the mechanism of its growth. I refer to the
institution of state superintendencies, *i.e.*, to the commissioning of public
officers to oversee formal education. During the incumbency of a vigorous
superintendent (or "secretary"), a single intelligence was brought to bear
unwaveringly upon the development of public policy in regard to education.
Localism remained the ruling principle of school government, but the governors served under the eye of an officer representing the whole people of
the commonwealth. He might indeed preside over the awakening of the
people to the value of educated human beings—or the people enlightened—
as an asset of the commonwealth. Thus Horace Mann preached that the mines
of Massachusetts were the limitless resources of the human intellect.[20] As
an increasingly large commitment of material wealth, in public and private
hands, to the realization of human potentiality has followed the sharpening
of such awareness, the advancement of schooling and the development of
the economy have become one movement.

How are we then to conceive of American experience as we seek to apply
it in the transformation of other nations? Are we to export the apparatus of
an educational revolution or the fruit of evolution? Probably something of
each; but I submit that we should employ the category of revolution in the
sphere of education with the same caution that we have been taught to exercise when we think of the economic history of the West. If American experience is drawn upon, the diagnosis of educational need and the prognosis

19. See Lawrence A. Cremin, *The American Common School: An Historic Conception* (New
York: Bureau of Publication, Teachers College, Columbia University, 1951).
20. Horace Mann, *Annual Reports of the Secretary of the Board of Education of Massachusetts for the Years 1845-1848* (Report for 1846) (Boston: Lee and Shepard Publishers, 1891), p. 136.

of investment in education elsewhere must be based upon a calculation (1) of the degree to which the fundamental institutions of other nations resemble those of the United States, and (2) of the degree to which conditions in other nations approximate those in which growth has occurred here. For growth through several centuries has been of the essence in this not so new nation of commonwealths.

For further bibliographical information on American education during the period reviewed here, see Bernard Bailyn, *Education in the Forming of American Society* and R. Freeman Butts and Lawrence A. Cremin, *A History of Education in American Culture* (New York: Henry Holt and Company, 1959).

CHAPTER 8

THE VOCATIONAL SCHOOL FALLACY IN DEVELOPMENT PLANNING

Philip J. Foster

In current controversies regarding the relationship between the provision of formal education and the economic growth of underdeveloped areas, few issues have been debated with more vehemence than the question of the desirability of providing technical, vocational, and agricultural instruction within the schools. So far as Africa is concerned, the controversy has been sharpened by the recent publication of a series of observations by the British economist, Thomas Balogh, on the conclusions of the 1961 Conference of African Ministers of Education at Addis Ababa.[1]

Briefly put, Balogh's views may be stated in the following manner: Since between 80 and 95 per cent of Africans are dependent upon agriculture, the essential need in African education is the development of large scale technical and agricultural programs within the schools at all levels: "The school must provide the nucleus of modern agriculture within the villages" and play a central role in the general raising of standards of living within the subsistence sector. Present educational facilities constitute an obstacle to rural progress because people are not trained for agriculture, and academic systems of formal education are the chief determinant of attitudes hostile to the practice of rural agriculture. Schools are regarded as primarily responsible for the flight from the rural areas to the towns. Balogh's views, stated in perhaps more measured terms, are paralleled in a recent United Nations publication in which it is observed that one of the chief educational priorities in economically developing areas is "the creation of a fully integrated system of agricultural education within the general framework of technical and vocational education."[2]

Although only two examples of this trend of thought are given here, it is possible to indicate numerous current publications dealing with education and economic development that accord high priority to schemes for agricul-

1. UNESCO, United National Economic Commission for Africa, *Conference of African States on the Development of Education in Africa*, UNESCO/ED/181 (Addis Ababa, 1961). Balogh's observations are to be found in "Catastrophe in Africa," *Times Educational Supplement*, Jan. 5th, 1962, p. 8; and Feb. 9, 1962, p. 241. Also in "What Schools for Africa?", *New Statesman and Nation* (March 23, 1962), p. 412.

2. United Nations, Committee on Information from Non-Self Governing Territories, *Special Study on Educational Conditions in Non-Self Governing Territories* (New York, 1960), p. 8.

142

tural, vocational, and technical education as against the provision of substantially more "academic" types of instruction. In the following pages I hope to show that these views are generally fallacious and ignore a series of crucial variables that must be taken into account if any realistic proposals for stimulating economic growth are to emerge. In developing the discussion I shall use examples from Ghana, which is not altogether unique among African territories in spite of the relatively high level of per capita income that it enjoys.

It should be said at the outset that there is no disagreement with two of Balogh's contentions. First, it seems clear that agricultural development and a rapid rise in rural incomes must definitely be accorded priority in all development schemes. Apart from the probability that such growth must precede even limited industrial development, there is the immediate question of raising the bare subsistence basis upon which many African cultivators are obliged to exist. Second, it is likely that such programs must depend in part upon the provision of technical and agricultural education as a necessary but by no means sufficient condition of growth.

However, in spite of vague general agreement on the desirability of such programs, there is a virtual absence of explicit dicta regarding their nature. For example, what would an educational scheme adjusted to developmental needs look like? What role would the schools themselves play in such a program? At what stage in formal education should specifically vocational subjects be begun, and how would technical and agricultural schools be integrated with the general system? Then there is the problem of the content of studies; frequently vocational curricula are ill designed to serve the needs of developing economies. Agreeing on the need for agricultural development does not lead us directly to any particular specifications for educational content or organization. Even assuming that well-validated prescriptions existed, it is equally apparent that these would vary considerably with the degree of effective centralized control exerted by governments. This latter factor seems to be rarely considered by educational planners, yet it is probably the single most crucial variable in determining the effectiveness of an agricultural or a technical program.

Having entered these caveats, our major disagreement with Balogh lies in the "strategy" that he proposes and the degree to which he places reliance upon *formal* educational institutions in instituting change. Secondly, Balogh tends to view vocational and general education as substitutes for each other rather than to see them as essentially complementary and hardly substitutable.

There is, perhaps, a general tendency to accord to the schools a "central" position in strategies designed to facilitate economic development. To some extent this reflects an appreciation of the relative lack of alternative institutions that can be utilized, but it stems partially from the notion that schools are particularly manipulable institutions. It is widely believed that schools can readily be modified to meet new economic needs and, more particularly, to accord with the intentions of social and economic planners. I shall argue, on the contrary, that schools are remarkably clumsy instruments for inducing prompt large-scale changes in underdeveloped areas. To be sure, formal education has had immense impact in Africa, but its consequences have rarely been those anticipated, and the schools have not often functioned in the manner intended by educational planners.

I. THE COLONIAL EXPERIENCE IN GHANA

If there is anything surprising in Balogh's views it lies not in their originality but in the degree to which they reproduce with virtually no modification a series of arguments that were first stated in equally cogent fashion by the Education Committee of the Privy Council in 1847.[3] So far as Ghana, in particular, is concerned, the viewpoint was forcefully advanced in the Appendix to the Report of the Commission on the West Coast of Africa in 1842 and by a succession of colonial governors and educators thereafter.[4] Indeed, stress on the provision of vocational and agricultural education was included *without exception* in every major document related to educational development in the Gold Coast up till the grant of independence in 1957.

In spite of this, by 1959 the structure of the Ghanaian educational system was essentially that prevailing in most of British Africa: an expanding base of primary and middle school education of a predominantly academic variety capped by a group of highly selective grammar schools and a university college modeled closely upon British prototypes.[5] In that year only about 1 per cent of all persons enrolled in formal educational institutions were receiving instruction in vocational, technical, or agricultural subjects. The paradox in Ghanaian education has been the emphasis placed on vocational and agricultural training in all documentary sources and the relative absence of it within the actual system of education.[6]

A priori, it might be suspected that no serious attempt was ever made to implement schemes for agricultural and vocational training in the schools or

3. The text of this early document is to be found in H. S. Scott, "The Development of the Education of the African in Relation to Western Contact," *The Yearbook of Education* (London: Evans Bros., 1938), pp. 693-739.

4. There is considerable literature on this point but a few major examples may be cited. See the report of the Commissioner in the Appendix to the "Report of the Committee on the West Coast of Africa," *Parliamentary Papers*, Vol. XI, 1852. Also Gold Coast, *Report of the Committee of Educationalists* (Accra: Government Printer, 1920); Jesse Jones, *Education in Africa: A Study of West, South and Equatorial Africa by the African Education Commission* (New York: Phelps Stokes Fund, 1922); Gold Coast, *Report of the Education Committee, 1937-1941* (Accra: Government Printer, 1942). This list cannot present numerous additional statements of this nature and there should be no need to refer the reader to the famous policy statements of the Advisory Committee on Education in the Colonies. However, in Appendix I to this paper we have included a selection of statements from these earlier documents.

5. Ghana, Statistical Reports Series I, No. 6, *Education Statistics 1959* (Accra: Office of the Government Statistician, 1959).

6. The Ghanaian Ministry of Education, like most African Ministries, does not include in its reports technical and vocational training being undertaken in special schools connected with Railways and Harbors, the Public Works Department, etc.

that such proposals remained stillborn as the result of disinterest in them by the colonial rulers. In the case of Ghana this argument can be totally dismissed. There is ample documentary evidence throughout the latter half of the nineteenth century and the early twentieth that strenuous efforts were being made by both government and missions to establish agricultural schools, devise special agricultural curricula, and provide technical and vocational education. The development of academic secondary schools upon the British model was regarded with disfavor, as being inappropriate for the economic needs of the Gold Coast. Agricultural education was regarded as the key to economic development in that area. Particularly in the case of the activities of the Basel Mission, a system of schools based on agricultural and technical education was attempted which was probably unrivaled in any other territory in Africa.[7] Yet all of these earlier experiments were unsuccessful, and the educational history of the Gold Coast is strewn with the wreckage of schemes corresponding to Balogh's proposals.

In practice, the demand by Africans for western education was and is predominantly oriented towards the provision of more academic-type schools. This preference springs, I contend, from a remarkably realistic appraisal of occupational opportunities generated within the exchange sector of the economy as a result of European overrule. So far as the clientele of the schools was concerned, the primary function of formal education was to enable individuals to move from subsistence activities to occupations within the European-dominated sector. An examination of opportunities within that sector throughout the colonial period reveals that *relatively* there was a greater demand for clerical and commercial employees than for technically trained individuals. Opportunities certainly existed in technical fields and in agriculture, but they were inferior to the other alternatives. Access to most of the highly paid occupations was, therefore, achieved through academic-type institutions. Those who criticize the "irrational" nature of African demand for "academic" as opposed to "vocational" education fail to recognize that the strength of academic education has lain precisely in the fact that it is preeminently a *vocational* education providing access to those occupations with the most prestige and, most important, the highest pay within the Ghanaian economy. The financial rewards and the employment opportunities for technically trained individuals were never commensurate with opportunities in the clerical field. Since the graduates of the academic school were manifestly more advantageously placed,[8] the pressure for "academic" education reflected fairly accurately the demands for alternative types of skill within the exchange sector of the economy. One of the major ironies of the situation is that while proponents of technical education were criti-

7. For a succinct account of the activities of the Basel Mission see W. J. Rottman, "The Educational Work of the Basel Mission," Appendix A.I to *Special Reports on Educational Subjects,* Vol. XIII, Part II. (London: H.M.S.O., 1905), pp. 307-318.

8. See also I. M. Wallerstein, *The Emergence of Two West African Nations: Ghana and the Ivory Coast* (New York: Columbia University Press, 1959), p. 241.

cizing the neglect of technical provision in the schools, the products of such technical institutions as existed were often experiencing difficulties in obtaining employment. Frequently those persons entered occupations unrelated to the training they had undergone.[9]

This form of "wastage" among trained manpower is endemic in underdeveloped countries.

1. Initially, trained individuals may be produced for whom there is no actual demand so far as the market is concerned. There may be a considerable "surplus" of these trained men where "new nations," in their desire to emulate more economically developed areas, invest considerable sums in the training of technicians before they can be utilized in the existing economy.

2. Second, a real demand may exist for trained personnel, but at the same time scarce personnel are not utilized and skilled workers are involved in tasks not directly relevant to their professional accomplishments. This would appear to occur more commonly in government service and we shall draw attention to it specifically in later pages.

3. Third, skilled personnel may not enter the type of job for which they have been trained because opportunities seem so much greater in alternative occupations. Thus, for example, many graduates of the Basel Mission schools who received agricultural and industrial training entered clerical employment. Here the most saleable component of their education experience was literacy, not trade training, and the former was thus utilized in the job market.[10] Wastage of skills must always be considered in assessing programs of vocational training.

To be sure, such wastage has also been characteristic of developed countries, but in the case of many of the "new nations" such a phenomenon is particularly undesirable in view of the limited resources available.

We do not intend here to underestimate non-economic factors that contributed to African demand for academic schools though these, in fact, reinforced the pattern we have described above. The European colonial elite itself acted as a reference group for African aspirations; emulation of that elite led to a pressure for "parity" between metropolitan and colonial institutions. Since the colonial elite provided only a partial image of western society and was composed overwhelmingly of administrators and government servants educated primarily in academic institutions, African demand for education was understandably oriented to the acquisition of that kind of education that was perceived to be the key to European-type occupational roles. In this the Africans were acting astutely. One of the striking features of most post-colonial economies is the domination by government agencies of well-paid and high-status employment opportunities. Since such institutions, through recruiting primarily upon the basis of "universalistic" criteria, stress the possession of an academic formal education, a higher premium is

9. See Gold Coast, *Report of the Education Department,* 1935, para. 332; also Gold Coast, *Legislative Council Debates,* 1933, pp. 5, 94; and 1935, p. 5.
10. Rottman, *op. cit.,* p. 300.

placed upon such schooling than occurred in early stages of development in most western societies.

In this context, one of the most striking differences between many of the new nations and the western world at earlier periods of its development is their lack of mobility opportunities lying outside the formal educational structure. Systems of apprenticeship, opportunities to open small enterprises, etc., all provided institutionalized modes of social and economic ascent in western society. The relative absence of those sorts of alternatives to formal education in many new nations sometimes produces the paradoxical result, as in Ghana, that educational requirements for obtaining employment are now as high, if not higher, than in the former metropole itself, notwithstanding a very low level of diffusion of formal education in the population as a whole.

Thus when colonial peoples were involved in unequal competition with resident Europeans for a limited number of high-status jobs, it was considered imperative to obtain qualifications virtually identical to those prevalent in the metropole. This was a perfectly rational estimate of the relative advantages of alternative types of education; in the competition for scarce job opportunities nonmetropolitan curricula were by definition inferior.

It is important to note, however, that the termination of colonial overrule has made virtually no difference to the over-all structure of occupational opportunities within the exchange sector. To be sure, Ghanaians are less involved in direct competition with Europeans for high-ranking posts within the administration. However, in the nongovernmental sector there has been little change in the premium placed on academic training; indeed, there has been an intensification of certain features apparent in the colonial period. At present, out of a total employed labor force of 2.56 million not more than 13.7 per cent (or 350,000) are employed full-time in the "modern" sector of the economy. It has been calculated that the rate of growth in wage employment opportunities amounts to just over 4 per cent per annum; though this estimate is probably too low, a rather generous estimate of employment growth would be 20 to 25 thousand per annum.[11] On the other hand, the annual output of the middle schools alone has now risen to over 30 thousand per annum.

Parallel with this, however, has been the fact that government employment has absorbed an increasing proportion of the labor force: 42 per cent in 1951 and 51 per cent in 1957. The progressive enlargement of existing government agencies and the creation of new public corporations has, if anything, tended to favor employment for clerical and administrative workers. Since, relatively speaking, the balance of job opportunities has shifted even more in favor of clerical employment, there is a mounting demand for the academic secondary school education that provides access to such positions.[12]

11. These estimates have been computed from the 1960 *Population Census of Ghana,* Advance Report of Vols. III and IV; Ghana, *Quarterly Digest of Statistics* (Accra: Office of the Government Statistician, 1959); and Ghana, *Economic Surveys,* 1955-1958 (Accra: Government Printer, 1959).

12. This trend in demand for academic secondary is, of course, indicated most sharply by the

What is implied here is that although considerable attention has always been paid to the so-called problem of "white-collar" unemployment in West Africa, there has been little realization that opportunities for technical employment have been even more limited and certainly more poorly paid. In virtually every African territory there appears to be a current stress upon the need for the provision of technical education upon a massive scale to meet the "needs" of the economy. Sometimes such demands are based upon the conclusions of manpower surveys, the source of whose projections may not be too clear. Yet a sober inspection of the actual structure of job opportunities within an economy such as that of Ghana gives no reason to suppose that the products of technical schools can be absorbed soon on a large scale.[13] In actuality, we are not faced by the problem of white-collar unemployment at all but by a far more serious form of generalized unemployment.

II. THE "WHITE-COLLAR" MYTH
AND VOCATIONAL ASPIRATIONS

There is no doubt that unemployment among school-leavers has reached alarming proportions in West Africa. Investigations by Callaway in Nigeria and by the present writer in Ghana confirm its extent and incidence and give no reason to suppose that it is likely to diminish in the near future.[14] However, the crucial question is not the amount of such unemployment but the delineation of significant factors determining its incidence. It has been frequently asserted that the problem has its source in the reluctance of literate individuals and school graduates to enter manual occupations and in their unrealistic search for white-collar employment, which they believe to be commensurate with their status as "educated men."[15] In this interpretation unemployment is conceived to be "frictional" in nature, and the schools are perceived to be the villains of the piece; it is inferred that the type of education to which students are exposed (specifically, the curriculum of the schools) largely determines their vocational aspirations and operates as an independent variable in setting the level of vocational choice. This has been a favorite theme for well nigh a century. Balogh, for example, specifically attributes the present employment crisis in Nigeria to the provision of a particular form of academic elementary education that has generated unrealistic employment expectations for clerical work, caused a flight from the rural areas, and fostered a disdain for manual occupations.[16] If this diagnosis

growth of private and proprietary secondary schools in Ghana which by 1961 numbered no less than 52 schools.

13. No data exist on the occupational destinations of the products of technical institutes, but in 1961 there was some concern that the products of Junior Technical Institutes, in particular, were experiencing difficulty in finding adequate employment.

14. Arch C. Callaway, "School Leavers in Nigeria: 1," *West Africa*, No. 2286 (March 25, 1961), p. 325.

15. This view is to be found throughout the literature. For a recent example see Ghana, *Economic Survey 1958*, p. 24.

16. Balogh, *op. cit.*, *Times Educational Supplement*, Feb. 9, 1962, p. 241.

of the problem were correct, the solution would be simple: change the curricula to provide instruction based upon agriculture and technical subjects, and the aspirations of young people will, in consequence, be directed towards agricultural activities; the flight from the land will be checked and the volume of "frictional" unemployment will correspondingly diminish.

This reasoning is largely fallacious.[17] It has already been pointed out by others that the idea that children's vocational aspirations can be altered by massive changes in curriculum is no more than a piece of folklore with little empirical justification.[18] In Nigeria and Ghana the graduates of the graduates of the primary and middle schools do work with their hands and they often seek employment as general laborers. Conversely, it is possible to show that even where students have been educated in agricultural or technical schools, a high proportion of them have never entered those occupations for which they were trained but have gravitated to alternative employments offering greater opportunities. These observations would tend to throw some doubt on programs whose efficacy depends on the notion that the schools exercise a decisive influence upon vocational aspirations of students. However, more definite empirical evidence is available to suggest that in Ghana, at least, the disdain for manual labor believed to be so typical of the products of formal education is not at all in accord with fact.

In December 1959 the author drew a sample of 210 boys from the fourth forms of nine academic-type middle schools in Accra. These students were in their final month of studies preparatory to seeking employment or, in a few cases, continuing their education in other schools. They were asked, first, what kind of employment they would most like to obtain if they were *completely free* to choose. This enabled children to fantasy as much as they wished regarding their careers. Then they were asked what type of employment they actually *expected* to be able to obtain.

The findings in no sense indicate a predisposition to favor professional and white-collar employment (Table 1). Even where children were free to respond as they wished, no fewer than 62 per cent favored artisan employment or farming (even in an urban center such as Accra). Only 30 per cent favored employment in varying levels of white-collar activity (categories I-III). The most instructive section of the table, however, concerns job expectations. The pupils displayed a remarkable level of realism. Although 51 per cent expressed the hope of ultimately becoming skilled artisans, only 22 per cent *expected* to be able to do so, and 35 per cent were fully reconciled to entering semiskilled or unskilled occupations. These observations

17. We do not wish to imply here that the problem of the "unemployed intellectual" who refuses to accept a type of employment "below his status" is a myth in all areas. There is little doubt that this phenomenon was clear enough in India. However, this is a very different thing from saying that such attitudes were a result of the kind of formal western schooling undergone by students. They probably stemmed from a much older tradition of Brahmanic intellectualism. However, in the case of West Africa, this would not appear to be the case, and there is a very high correlation between perceived prestige and perceived income variables.

18. Callaway, "School Leavers in Nigeria: 3," *West Africa*, Vol. 2288, (April 8, 1962), p. 371.

Table 1

Occupational Choices of Form IV Children in Ghana Middle Schools
(N = 210)

Occupational Category°	(1) Free Choices		(2) Job Expectations		Difference Between (1) and (2)	
	Percentage	Number	Percentage	Number	Percentage	Number
I Higher professional	11.0	23	5.2	11	−5.8	−12
II Lower professional	10.0	21	1.9	4	−8.1	−17
III Teacher	0.9	2	3.8	8	+2.9	+6
IV Clerical and allied	8.1	17	10.0	21	+1.9	+4
V Artisans and skilled workers	51.0	107	22.4	47	−27.6	−60
VI Commercial	1.9	4	9.5	20	+7.6	+16
VII Semiskilled and unskilled	3.3	7	35.2	74	+31.9	+67
VIII Uniformed services	2.4	5	4.8	10	+2.4	+5
IX Fishermen and farmers	10.5	22	6.7	14	−3.8	−8
X Miscellaneous and unclassified	0.9	2	0.0	0	−0.9	−2
No Answer	0.0	0	0.5	1	+0.5	+1
Total	100.0	210	100.0	210	− −	− −

° The occupational categories were:

Higher professional: Doctor, lawyer, minister of religion, etc.

Lower professional: Nurse, dispenser, draughtsman, journalist, agricultural officer, surveyor, etc.

Teacher: All teaching roles within the primary, middle, secondary or technical institutions.

Clerical and allied: Clerk (unspecified), cashier, bookkeeper, typist, bank clerk, librarian, letter writer, etc.

Artisans and skilled workers: Electrician, motor mechanic, plumber, carpenter, mason, printer, painter, shoemaker, locomotive engineer, tailor, etc.

Commercial: Petty trades and small-scale shopkeepers.

Semiskilled or unskilled workers: Laborer (various), messenger, bus conductor, watchman, steward, quarryman, miner, cook, etc.

Uniformed services: Police, army, Builders Brigade.

Fishermen and farmers
Miscellaneous and unclassifiable: Musician, boxer, artist, jockey, etc.

(which confirm an earlier study by Barnard) would seem to indicate that there is little foundation to theories attributing to the curriculum a major influence on vocational aspirations.[19]

It seems clear that mass unemployment among school-leavers in many new African nations is due to dysfunctions existing between the gross rate of school output and the slow expansion of occupational opportunities of all types within the exchange sector. It may be easy enough to increase the output of the schools but it is far more difficult to expand employment opportunities. The operative fact here is not that graduates will not accept certain types of employment but rather that the schools (irrespective of what they teach) have been shrewdly used as the gateway into the "emergent" sector

19. G. L. Barnard, "Gold Coast Children out of School," *Oversea Education*, Vol. XXIII, No. 4 (January 1957), pp. 163-172.

of the economy. The schools themselves can do little about this. So long as parents and students perceive the function of education in this manner, agricultural education and vocational instruction *in the schools* is not likely to have a determinative influence on the occupational aspirations and destinations of students. Aspirations are determined largely by the individual's perception of opportunities within the exchange sector of the economy, destinations by the *actual* structure of opportunities in that sector. The nature of educational instruction has little to do with the process, and the schools are unfairly criticized for creating a condition for which they have not been responsible — except insofar as they turn out too many graduates.

The reasons why graduates do not return to subsistence or quasi-subsistence agriculture has, of course, little to do with a disdain for farming that is created by an academic education. In 1961, a questionnaire was administered by the present writer to more than 700 Ghanaian male students in 20 highly selective academic secondary schools. The students were asked to rate 25 diverse occupations in terms of two criteria, occupational prestige and perceived income (Table 2). In practice, farming was rated 16th in prestige rankings (above middle and primary school teaching and office work, for example) and 10th in perceived income. Even among these advanced students farming is still rated moderately high. However, only one per cent of the students wished to become farmers in spite of the fact that it was rated higher in terms of both prestige and income than was primary or middle school teaching, which no less than 34 per cent of the students expected to enter.

It would seem that the factors inhibiting the "return to the land" lie primarily in the institutional milieu of farming. Initially, of course, in certain areas of Ghana (such as Ewe territory) acute population pressure and land fragmentation pose the problem of getting people away from the villages and into alternative employment, or at least into areas where land is available. In other localities suitable cash crops that might provide the basis for reasonable cash incomes to supplement subsistence activities have not yet been discovered. However, even in areas where cash crop farming can be moderately profitable, it takes place within a neotraditional framework. The farmer is not only obliged to reside in areas whose amenities are demonstrably inferior to those of the urban areas, but he is necessarily involved in the obligations and constraints of traditional rural structure. The demands of kin and the constrictions of traditional land tenure with its usual concomitant of endless litigation combine to make "progressive" farming a hazardous endeavour. In effect, if we are to really appreciate the factors that militate against individuals entering agriculture, we must examine the neotraditional institutional complex in which agricultural activities take place. It is probably in this complex and in the structure of accompanying incentives that the primary variables lie — not in the deficiencies of agricultural instruction in the schools nor in the "academically" oriented values of students. Young people do not object to farming *per se* or to the desirability of enter-

TABLE 2

Secondary Student Perceptions of the Occupational Hierarchy
(N = 775)

Occupation	(1) Prestige Rankings			(2) Income Rankings		
	Mean Score	S.D.	Rank	Mean Score	S.D.	Rank
Medical doctor	1.12	0.31	1	1.24	0.47	1
University teacher	1.16	0.38	2	1.28	0.51	2
Lawyer	1.45	0.64	3	1.40	0.55	3
Chief	1.89	0.78	4	2.47	0.80	8.5
Author	1.97	0.80	5	2.25	0.86	6
Secondary school teacher	2.05	0.51	6	2.23	0.58	5
Clergyman	2.96	0.84	7	3.10	0.95	15
Merchant or businessman	2.50	0.73	8	1.92	0.79	4
Nurse	2.60	0.64	9	3.01	0.57	13
Political party worker	2.70	0.93	10	2.38	0.9C	7
Government clerk	2.71	0.59	11	2.78	0.58	11
Soldier	2.78	0.81	12	3.00	0.64	12
Actor	2.81	0.90	13	2.47	0.94	8.5
Chief's counsellor	2.82	0.74	14	3.21	0.79	17
Policeman	2.94	0.73	15	3.21	0.55	17
Farmer	2.95	0.96	16	2.75	1.06	10
Office worker	2.96	0.60	17	3.03	0.56	14
Middle school teacher	3.00	0.50	18	3.21	0.51	17
Primary school teacher	3.25	0.67	19	3.53	0.65	21
Motorcar fitter	3.59	0.73	20	3.35	0.77	19
Petty trader	3.62	0.75	21	3.36	0.82	20
Shop assistant	3.80	0.66	22	3.84	0.64	23
Carpenter	3.84	0.73	23	3.73	0.75	22
Farm laborer	4.47	0.70	24	4.51	0.63	24
Streetcleaner	4.74	0.56	25	4.73	0.53	25

ing "modern" farming.[20] They are perfectly aware, however, that this is precisely what the institutional framework does not offer. Vocational instruction in agriculture by itself cannot induce youth to take up farming until an institutional complex exists which makes the utilization of new techniques profitable and meaningful. This reluctance would still prevail even if it were evident that such instruction was the principal mode of raising agricultural production. A high priority for research is indeed the delineation of those disincentives which spring from the neotraditional complex of institutions surrounding agriculture.

We have argued so far that the vocational aspirations of children and the occupations which they enter are almost exclusively determined by factors which lie outside the schools. Indeed, in terms of the actual opportunities

20. See also Callaway, *loc. cit.*

open to them, the students' perceptions are remarkably realistic. It follows, therefore, that no amount of formal technical, vocational or agricultural instruction alone is going to check the movement from the rural areas, reduce the volume of unemployment, or indeed necessarily have any effect on the rate of economic development. Those factors which really give the impetus to early economic growth are far more subtle than the proponents of vocational education suppose. We would suggest that the crucial variables lie, instead, in the structure of incentives within the economic system and in the degree to which the institutional milieu is supportive of entrepreneurial activity. Without such a milieu no amount of vocational instruction can be effective since the skills acquired will not be utilized. To put the issue more colloquially, in the initial stages technical and vocational instruction is the cart rather than the horse in economic growth, and its development depends upon real and perceived opportunities in the economy. The provision of vocational education must be directly related to those points at which some development is already apparent and where demand for skills is beginning to manifest itself.

III. DIFFICULTIES OF MANPOWER PLANNING

In this respect, there may be some dangers attached to large-scale high-level manpower estimates which have recently been derived in some African areas. The bases upon which these projections are made are sometimes not clear and some of the assumptions about the rate of growth in the exchange sector of the economy seem to be questionable. In one instance such estimates have formed the basis for a large-scale system of general and vocational schools to meet these hypothetical manpower needs.[21] There is a tendency to talk of the "needs" for development as if they were quite independent of the actual structure of job opportunities in the economy. This is daring planning, but it need hardly be said that if the rate of growth of the economy is not sufficient to absorb the products of a vastly expanded educational system, then the unemployment situation will become even worse. The production of large numbers of specifically trained individuals does not, at the same time, create employment opportunities for them.

Furthermore, the calculation of varying shortfalls for different types of specific skill is a hazardous endeavor, particularly in areas where there is an absence of any really satisfactory or meaningful data to make such projections realistic. Cumulative errors in the projection of a whole range of manpower needs can ultimately add up to an alarming misallocation of scarce resources, particularly when these are invested in the establishment of highly expensive vocational institutions. In certain sectors dysfunctional

21. Nigeria, Federal Ministry of Education, *Investment in Education* (the Ashby Report), (Lagos, 1960).

shortfalls will exist, while in other sectors surpluses will be produced; even accurate estimates may go awry when occupational wastage occurs.[22]

Perhaps the most disturbing feature of the manpower approach lies in the accent upon large-scale planning independent of the market. Large-scale planning involves large-scale miscalculations, which can be disastrous in economies with such limited resources. Major miscalculations, which are inevitable, then force either wasteful adjustments to conceal the magnitude of the errors or major reversals of policy, or both. At best, large-scale planning in the output of specific skills may induce subsequent extensive imposition of controls upon the trained men by something approximating to forced labor allocation. Certainly this writer can lay no claim to being an expert on manpower, but these dangers are not easily dismissed.

It might be more fruitful to encourage small-scale vocational training schemes closely associated with actual ongoing developments and quite divorced from the formal educational system. This implies a strategy that relates specific vocational training to other necessary changes in the institutional framework.[23] Maximum effort can be undertaken with individuals already involved in specific forms of economic activity. The chances of gross aggregate distortions are minimized while the moderate size of a large number of specific projects permits continuous feed-back correction of errors. Failure in a number of small activities is counterbalanced by small successes that point the way to broader programs. There is an important place for planning, but planning to provide the institutional framework for small-scale operative decision-making, not the wholesale making of such decisions. Perhaps we can examine the application of this approach first with respect to technical and commercial training, and second in the context of agriculture.

IV. TRAINING TECHNICAL MANPOWER

Initially, the production of really high-level technical manpower is perhaps the easiest problem. There is no question here that formal educational institutions at the university level (locally or overseas) must take the general responsibility for training professional workers, though there is a need to make sure that curricula are suitably modified to meet the needs and actualities of the local environment. There is no doubt that certain portions of prevailing instruction can be adapted more closely to actual work situations. There is perhaps also a need to ensure that study, even at this level, is combined with periods of field-experience for the high-level specialists concerned. Nonetheless, we contend that, at present, African needs for the

22. For a discussion of similar problems in planning outputs of skilled personnel in another area, see Arcadius Kahan, "The Economics of Vocational Training in the U.S.S.R.," *Comparative Education Review*, Vol. 4, No. 2 (October 1960), pp. 75-83.

23. For a specific application of this approach see discussion of education, pages 210-237 in The World Bank Survey Mission on Kenya, and the much fuller analysis in the initial report prepared by C. A. Anderson for the Mission (mimeo). The Mission's report, entitled *The Economic Development of Kenya,* was published in 1963 (Johns Hopkins Press, Baltimore).

uppermost levels in trained manpower are not so great as supposed. The issue here is to see that limited numbers of individuals possessing high-level skills are used effectively and economically. It is frequently evident, for example, that highly trained engineers in some areas are heavily involved in routine administration and paperwork which could be effectively performed by individuals possessing no professional skills.

It should also be noted that at this level there may be no shortage of numbers of applicants for high-level training but an acute shortage of applicants who have had the basic education that is essential if they are either to complete a regular schooling sequence or to qualify for technical post-secondary training programs at high levels within industry. This points to the need for more adequate general education at the secondary level and a more thorough preparation in basic subjects on the part of aspirants. Indeed, we suggest that this is the really effective thing that the schools can do at every level. Rather than attempting to load them with vocational subjects, providing a sound general education with a bias towards general science and English or French, essential at all levels, can provide the basis for later effective specialist training. Here, indeed, is the area in which imaginative and constructive curriculum work can be undertaken.

However, it is at the intermediate levels of technical and vocational training that the greatest difficulties arise. Many observers acquainted with the development of intermediate technical institutes and vocational schools in underdeveloped areas are only too aware that many institutions built at considerable cost remain partially empty or are filled with students who are for the most part composed of "rejects" from selective academic-type institutions. This is a situation that the technical schools are likely to face for some time. In itself, this is not disastrous since it implies that intermediate technical schools must reconcile themselves to being unable to choose freely the most able students. But there is also a subtle pressure developed which tends to transform these schools progressively into academic institutions. Students at entry frequently do not regard their courses as terminal, leading directly to artisan work; instead they regard them as "stepping stones" to enable them to enter professional-type courses. In some areas disturbances have resulted when students were not allowed to take pre-university examinations. It must be recognized that wherever technical education is given largely in institutions which are part of the formal educational structure, the expectations of the students may pervert the intentions of the planners.

Furthermore, there is a need to examine most carefully the actual courses given in such institutions. To a considerable degree in colonial and former colonial territories the pressure to emulate the standards of the metropole has led to a remarkably generous investment in institutions that provide lengthy and elaborate instruction. In practice, certain specific forms of vocational education may in consequence become quite dysfunctional in terms of the later work experience of trainees. To be sure, skilled artisans are produced, but in some cases they may be trained on technical equipment that simply cannot be matched outside the schools. Training which is closely related to work situations is very desirable; yet it is strange that although marked criticisms are often made of the "deadwood" and inappropriate content of academic curricula, there is little realization that technical curricula may also be ossified and irrelevant. This argues not only for a careful examination of what the schools teach, but also for the provision of "sandwich" courses in technical schools alternating with on-the-job experience. Such an approach narrows the gap between formal vocational instruction and actual work situations. Some African territories must be commended for initiating developments in this direction.

When all is said and done, however, vocational and technical training must be carried on mainly outside formal institutions. There is ample precedent for this in the West, whose early expansion was facilitated by a host of informal educational and training programs outside the schools. Some readers may rejoin that such alternative institutions as apprenticeship do not exist in Africa and that this necessarily throws the burden of training on the schools. This is not altogether true. For example, a considerable amount of road transport in West Africa is serviced and maintained not by highly trained operators but by "bush mechanics" who themselves have very little formal instruction. Upon this basis has developed a burgeoning system of informal apprenticeship; though most of the instruction is extremely rudimentary, here is an expanding base which can be built upon. The provision of short courses and up-grading instruction for this sector of workers would provide an opportunity to develop on the basis of a going concern. The plain fact of the matter is that there are more opportunities for this kind of training than most of the large-scale planners are prepared to admit.

Second, there is opportunity to capitalize upon the labor needs of existing industrial and commercial firms. It is not infrequent to hear the schools criticized by some of the larger concerns for not producing the kind of people needed in their activities. Most of these complaints rest upon a totally unrealistic notion of what schools can do. What these complaints do show, rather, is the need for stimulating these employers to undertake their own training programs, since they have a clearer definition of their requirements. It is heartening to observe that some of the larger companies are moving in this direction. Such activities are clearly advantageous to both employer and government, and there is no reason why training of this type should not be aided through tax remissions or partial government subsidy. It is important for the governments of these areas to appreciate that the best kind of vocational education is that which is partially paid for by those who participate in the market for the skills to which the training is directed.

Furthermore, the direct role of government as the largest single employer of skilled labor cannot be ignored. In most areas the public service has been obliged to develop its own vocational training schemes connected with railways and harbors, roads, and a number of other activities. These training schemes are not directly part of the formal educational system, but they have the great advantage of being adjusted closely to the quantitative and qualitative requirements of employment. Interestingly enough, these programs are often not included in official enumerations of students undergoing vocational training. Such activities constitute another existing base upon which vocational training can be developed and expanded without complicating the task of already overloaded schools. The expansion of ongoing programs is likely to be more economical and the wastage of trainees is almost certainly likely to be less than it has been from vocational training schools which are part of the formal educational system.

Particular importance must be attached, in the context of the new African nations, to one group who are of immense strategic importance for the growth of local economies—the local small-scale entrepreneurs who are to be found in increasing numbers in trade, commerce, transport, and small-scale manufacturing. To a great extent these are the "forgotten men" in development plans. Yet it may be suggested that the quickening in the rate of economic growth will be largely dependent upon their activities. However, the majority of these businessmen possess limited education and lack knowledge of elementary business procedures that would enable them to survive and expand their activities. There is no shortage of business acumen in many parts of Africa, but there is a deficient mastery of routine procedures of stock-taking, simple accounting, and management; many small-scale enterprises fail for lack of these skills. There is a good case to be made for providing instruction in simple business procedures to this class of person through the development of extension courses, both residential and nonresidential. This aspect of adult education is particularly valuable in the urban areas, and it has the advantage that there is no lack of direct incentive to acquire useful techniques on the part of businessmen themselves. In this context it should be noted that the provision of short courses for small-scale traders has met with some success in some parts of East Africa, an area in which development is at a far lower level than in West Africa.

Finally, it should be noted that one of the major failures of colonialism was not an over-all lack of development. The primary shortcoming lay in the fact that colonial personnel did not perceive that a large part of their activities should have been directed towards the training of African artisans and technicians as part of ongoing projects—that these should have been in part "educational" projects. There was an understandable conflict between the need to complete particular developments as rapidly and economically as possible and a competing requirement to create a reservoir of trained individuals. It was assumed that the schools should undertake this latter function. As a result, the completion of individual enterprises produced too few Africans who had benefited from specific on-the-job training. It would seem desirable in the future that a large number of enterprises (public and private) have built into them some provision for training of middle-range personnel, often in association with alternate short courses in technical institutions. It must be admitted that this requirement may slacken the speed with which enterprises are completed and it may initially increase costs. But these disadvantages would seem to be outweighed by the possibility of creating an additional force of skilled and semiskilled workers; thereby the costs of future projects would be reduced and the potentials of both private and public enterprises for the future would be increased.

This policy would seem especially appropriate where large-scale projects are undertaken on contract by overseas companies or agencies; governments might well insist that provision for on-the-job training of Africans be made part of any contractual agreement with an overseas enterprise. It may be necessary to give additional financial inducements to such agencies in order to enlist their cooperation but it should be clear that it presents another chance to shift the responsibility for particular types of vocational training onto the shoulders of those particularly qualified to undertake it. It seems especially crucial here that such training have specific reference to maintenance and upkeep of newly developed physical capital; in the past, lack of specific training of this nature has frequently resulted in the rapid deterioration of plant and facilities because of a lack of adequate personnel with the "know-how" that can be learned only in close association with ongoing projects.

In summary, these limited examples drawn from various fields of activity point to the possibility of inaugurating various types of vocational training without, at the same time, forcing vocational education into the formal school structure or providing massive developments in the forms of specific technical and vocational schools for full-time pupils. To be sure, such institutions must play a role in development but their number should be expanded carefully; they should be associated closely with actual developments in the economy through the provision of "sandwich" and short courses, and their clientele should be largely individuals who are actually employed. So far as possible, the burdens of vocational training should be shifted to those groups who are actually demanding skilled labor of various types.

In this context, the role of the formal schools becomes clearer. At present, their most marked inadequacy at the lower and intermediate levels is that they perform relatively ineffectively the basic functions of general education upon which further vocational training can be given with profit. At present a number of vocational schemes are hamstrung by trainees' lack of basic skills in literacy, English, computation, and general background. If at present the schools perform these basic functions ineffectively, it is patently absurd to expect them to incorporate a range of auxiliary vocational activities – quite apart from the relative absence of staff either competent or willing to undertake such activities. Given more limited objectives the schools can make a significant contribution to development of technical competence by turning out pupils able to absorb and utilize effectively specific forms of vocational training. Lack of auxiliary vocational training does not support the argument that the schools should or can provide a good substitute; the main problem is to stimulate the growth of informal ancillaries without which no self-reinforcing economic growth is likely to emerge.

V. PROBLEMS OF AGRICULTURAL TRAINING AND DEVELOPMENT

Agriculture remains, however, the most crucial area for development; here also it seems that the most intractable problems of resistance to change exist. We have asserted that scientific training in agriculture by itself is unlikely to have any marked impact on agricultural output. Any attempt at vocational training in agriculture presupposes that a meaningful structure of incentives exists for the individual farmer to increase his output, improve his techniques, and expand his range of activities. Without such incentives and opportunities, agricultural education can have little impact. Instruction must go hand in hand with changes in those institutional factors that militate against innovation. Clearly, an important area for investigation is the functional impact of traditional systems of land tenure in retarding development. It might be argued that the emergence of the concept of land as an individually owned resource, freed from traditional restrictions upon alienation and transfer, could do more than anything else to facilitate the emergence of progressive farming.

It must not be supposed that African farmers are uniformly apathetic to innovation and change when new opportunities present themselves. No one acquainted with the spread of cocoa farming in West Africa, largely the result of African initiative and enterprise, could assume that all traditional cultivators are inherently "conservative." Furthermore, in Ghana, in particular, there are encouraging signs of innovation: the development of commercial poultry farming, the production of foodstuffs for sale to the larger urban centers, and the gradual utilization of new techniques such as crop spraying in the cocoa areas.

Agricultural education of farmers must include not only instruction in new techniques but also information on new and profitable cash crops and potential local markets. Such agricultural education must be directed towards the farmer himself and not towards school pupils. No one acquainted with agricultural teaching in West African schools can fail to be impressed by the apathy of the students, which is matched only by that of the teacher. Indeed, the cynic can observe with some truth that the best way to ensure that students acquire a lifelong distaste for anything savoring of agricultural activity is to see that they are obliged to have courses in agriculture during their school careers. So long as one of the primary motivations for entering school remains the desire to escape from traditional agriculture, no amount of exhortation to remain on the land and take up farming is likely to have any effect.

Returning to some of our opening remarks, we may now ask what effective role *can* formal educational institutions perform in agricultural change? In this paper their task has been conceived to be two-fold in nature. First, higher institutions, whether university departments or specialist agricultural institutes, can undertake significant research in the development of new agricultural techniques and new crops suited to particular environments. It has already been pointed out that the absence of suitable crops in some areas holds back agricultural growth; in such a region as the Accra Plain, for example, much experimental research is necessary before agriculture can become profitable. There is need also for veterinary and livestock research and investigation into the nature and extent of plant and animal diseases.

The second function of higher institutions lies in the effective dissemination of research findings. Here, indeed, the example of the American land-grant colleges can be utilized, although their primary contribution was not to train farmers.[24] These institutions failed their early founders in this respect; relatively few graduates became practicing farmers although many became agricultural specialists. But the land-grant colleges have made unique contributions in the field of research; they developed effective extension work in rural communities to disseminate information for farmers and their wives. This kind of activity needs to be expanded in Africa.

No doubt the objection will be raised that much of the agricultural extension work undertaken in Africa, particularly by the agricultural departments of governments, has not been very striking in its results. There is substance to this contention, indicating the need to examine carefully the content and nature of many existing techniques of extension work and to integrate instruction with other much needed change in order to promote conditions in which new techniques can be utilized. Thus there is evidence from Kenya that such efforts are effective when accompanied by programs of land consolidation and land tenure change. In the last resort, extension work will be utilized where farmers perceive it to be to their advantage to change. Recent developments in both West and East Africa show that agriculturalists can effectively utilize new techniques of agricultural production when given meaningful incentives to do so. Even the emergence of a relatively small group of "progressive" farmers can operate as a catalyst for the agricultural sector as a whole.

The lower schools, however, must be given a more limited role in these developments. Reciting rote formulas about new curricula which will not detach children from the rural environment is merely an excuse for lack of reflection. The schools will detach children from the rural environment largely irrespective of what they teach. Middle and especially secondary schools can produce individuals with a sound general education and some knowledge of science, some of whom can undertake further training to become either rural agricultural technicians advising farmers or research

24. See Mary Jean Bowman, "The Land Grant Colleges and Universities in Human Resource Development," *Journal of Economic History* (December 1962), Vol. 22, pp. 523-546.

workers on agricultural problems. It is not likely that the schools will ever be able to do much more than this, but this could be quite a lot.

In the last resort, it must be confessed that we know very little about the factors that really promote large-scale agricultural development among peasant farmers in Africa. There is no doubt that agricultural education outside the schools is a necessary if not a sufficient factor in growth, but at present there is no simple formula for application. After 30 years of agricultural experiment and a vast technological revolution in agricultural methods, the Soviet Union is still faced with a chronic problem of raising agricultural output. It is therefore not likely that overnight growth will be achieved in Africa by the naive application of new technology. The farmer himself remains the greatest unknown variable in the equations of large-scale agricultural planning.

VI. EDUCATIONAL STRATEGIES FOR DEVELOPMENT

Throughout the previous pages I have argued against total mobilization of the formal educational system in the direction of specific vocational training. Schools, in general, tend to be rather monolithic institutions not easily susceptible to manipulation; no amount of curriculum juggling is likely to produce the kinds of mass results anticipated by the proponents of technical, vocational, and agricultural education. I have advanced the thesis that a great deal of training must be developed outside the schools through the use of auxiliary institutions, with special vocational institutes being created in particular cases where their endeavors can be closely meshed with on-the-job training and with the actual manpower requirements indicated by the market for skills. Rather than massive reforms in the whole educational system I have suggested a multiplicity of small-scale experiments which may meet with some success and enable development to proceed from the roots of the economy. The alternative is to involve the schools in broad development schemes only to discover that results fall far short of objectives. Those who favor such broad schemes expect far too much from the schools, and certainly anticipate far more from them than has ever been possible in even the most economically advanced nations. Indeed, it may well be that future research will indicate that the most marked impact of education on economic development in these areas will come not from the vocational implications of formal education at all, but rather through the indirect effect that schooling has on consumption aspirations. Formal education of whatever type is likely to lead to personal dissatisfaction with current living standards and opportunities. If such dissatisfaction provides personal incentives and if at the same time institutionalized means exist to meet new aspirations, then the schools will have contributed indirectly to economic growth.

In this sense, formal schooling is valuable in terms of its "detachment" effect from the traditional environment as well as in terms of the specific skills it inculcates. However, anthropologists have not been slow to point

out that anomic phenomena may frequently be the consequence of levels of
aspiration that cannot be met by the occupational structure. This is precisely
the kind of risk that must be offset against the apparent advantages stemming
from formal education.[25]

Some of the observations made here are not likely to commend themselves to those who automatically assume that over-all massive economic
planning into which the schools must be fitted is the *sine qua non* for African
development.[26] There are, of course, multiple strategies that can be employed
in economic development programs. These range from compulsion and
forced labor to making existing opportunities more visible to individuals
or manipulating salary differentials to stimulate variations in the supply of
different types of labor. Such methods, whether effective or not, do not necessarily involve the direct mobilization of the schools in the planning process
but rather influence them through indirect pressures.

"Thinking big" is, of course, sometimes an excuse for not thinking at all.
Paradoxically enough, it is one of the legacies of "capitalist" colonialism,
where it was generally assumed that most economic advance was necessarily
the result of governmental planning and centralized direction. The real
problem is not the issue of planning versus non-planning. Rather, it is (1)
to ascertain where government activity in the field of education can make a
contribution and where it cannot; (2) to identify potential situations in
which other agencies can with adequate inducements take over a large number of educational functions; and (3) above all, to indicate what are the comparative advantages and limitations of various types of educational programs,
in the schools and outside of them, in economic growth.

Appendix

It is an interesting exercise to examine successive pronouncements regarding technical and vocational education in colonial areas in general and
the Gold Coast in particular. It will be noted that in a span of over a hundred
years the same formulas occur. Though this list is very truncated it serves to
indicate that most contemporary pronouncements have a hoary ancestry.

1.   It will be necessary to establish a model farm in each settlement and . . . in
      the towns, to afford the masters the facilities of having every child taught
      some trade or calling at the same time that he is sent to school to read or write.
      (Great Britain, Parliamentary Papers, "Appendix to the Report of the Com-
      mittee on the West Coast of Africa, 1842," p. 94.)

25. See M. G. Smith, "Educational and Occupational Choice in Rural Jamaica," *Social and
Economic Studies* (University College of the West Indies, Jamaica, 1960), Vol. 9, pp. 353-354.
      26. It is not entirely unjust to suggest that the mediocre success of large scale economic plan-
ning in Britain itself has led certain individuals to consider it worth while trying in far less developed areas. How this can be possible in regions which lack even the rudimentary data essential
for large scale decision making is not very clear.

2. Connected with the general branches of education, model schools for the instruction and training of boys in the knowledge of various useful mechanical arts are most important desiderata; at present there is no employment for educated boys, except as teachers in schools, and clerks in government and mercantile establishments and hence the results of education, pleasing as they may be, are not so healthy, vigorous, and permanent as they would be if they were associated with various branches of useful mechanical knowledge. These desiderata are greatly worthy of the attention of an enlightened government.

   (An early policy statement by Governor Winniett [1847] cited in J.J. Crooks, *Records Relative to the Gold Coast of Africa* [Dublin: Browne and Nolan Ltd., 1923], p. 308.)

3. The masses will require elementary training both moral and intellectual, and some measure of agricultural training, in order to develop fully the agricultural wealth for which the country possesses such natural advantages. To this end the establishment of agricultural schools is not only one means, it is by far the greatest means.

   (*Report of the Inspector of Schools,* Lagos, Colonial Office, Nigeria Pamphlets, Vol. II, No. 40.)

4. The following are salient points drawn from the 1847 *Report of the Education Committee of the Privy Council* (Great Britain, Colonial Office Library, Miscellaneous Pamphlets, Vol. I, No. 1). Some of the aims of education were perceived as follows:

   1) To make the school the means of improving the condition of the peasantry by teaching them how health may be preserved by a proper diet, cleanliness, ventilation and clothing, and by the structure of their dwellings.
   2) To give practical training in household economy and in the cultivation of the cottage garden as well as in those common handicrafts by which a laborer may improve his domestic comfort.
   3) To communicate such a knowledge of writing and arithmetic and of their application to his wants and duties as may enable a peasant to economize his means, and give the small farmer the power to enter into calculations and agreements.
   4) Improved agriculture is required to replace the system of exhausting the virgin soils, and then leaving to natural influences alone the work of reparation. The education of the colored races would, therefore, not be complete for the children of small farmers, unless it included this object.

   Note also that the Committee then proceeded to develop plans for an educational structure based largely on agricultural and technical training. These included "day schools of industry," model farms and teacher training institutions with agricultural and technical curricula.

5. At Beulah, near Cape Coast, the mission undertook in 1850 its first agricultural experiment, instruction being given on the land as well as in the school.

   (A. W. Cardinall, *The Gold Coast 1931* [Accra: Government Printer, 1932], p. 182.)

   It should be noted that this and similar projects at Dominassie and Ahassa were complete failures.

6. In 1887 the Gold Coast Government initiated a class of Industrial Schools in
    which a proportion of pupils . . . devote not less than ten hours a week to
    manual labour on a regular and approved plan . . . . Manual labour shall be
    understood to mean any kind of handicraft, manufacturing process, or agri-
    cultural work, and, in the case of females, household work.
    (Gold Coast, *The Education Ordinance 1887,*No. 14 of 1887, Para. 12.)

    This stipulation also included the provision of extra grants-in-aid
    to stimulate such activities.

7. Most of the schools in the interior have connected with them small planta-
    tions where coffee, cocoa, sisal, hemp or other suitable products are culti-
    vated by scholars.
    (F. Wright, "The System of Education in the Gold Coast Colony," *Special
    Reports on Educational Subjects* [London: H.M.S.O., 1905] Vol. XIII,
    Part II, p. 9.)

8. How far this manual work will have a lasting influence upon the character
    of the scholars is difficult to say. The hope which one of the School Inspectors
    had in proposing technical instruction would induce scholars who had passed
    Standard V to apprentice themselves for a period of three years at least, in
    order to become workmen in the Public Works Department will, we are afraid,
    meet with sad disappointment. There is a distaste for anything savouring of
    labour among upper standard boys who think that to be a scholar is to be a
    gentleman, and to be a gentleman precludes the possibility of gaining a liveli-
    hood except by the pen. Therefore it is and will be always an exception to the
    rule when a boy who has passed Standard V makes up his mind to learn a
    handicraft, as smith or carpenter.
    (W. J. Rottman, "The Educational Work of the Basel Mission," Appendix
    A.I to Special Reports on Educational Subjects, XIII, Part II [London:
    H.M.S.O., 1905], p. 300.)

9. The terms of appointment of "Governor Rodger's Education Committee"
    of 1908 specifically referred to the desirability of establishing industrial
    and agricultural training in all schools. The resulting Rules of 1909, in
    fact, made industrial or agricultural training *compulsory*.
    (See "Education in Africa," *Report of the Phelps-Stokes Commission*
    [New York: Phelps Stokes Fund, 1922].)

10. In spite of this, the proposals were reiterated in the *Report of the Com-
    mittee of Educationists,* 1920.

    From an educational point of view, however, the Committee equally strongly
    advocates plenty of manual work to overcome the mere "bookishness" of
    most of our school instruction.
    (Gold Coast, *Report of the Committee of Educationists* 1920 [Accra:
    Government Printer, 1920], p. 54.)

11. Education should be largely industrial and agricultural so that the people
    may be trained to make the best use of the natural resources of the Country.
    (*Report of the Director of Education on his Visit to Educational Institu-
    tions in the United States* [Accra: Government Printer, 1922], p. 22.)

12. The African Natives are relatively far more dependent on agriculture than any people in the world. Agricultural education should correspondingly receive large consideration in the schools plans.

    (Phelps-Stokes *Report,* 1922, p. 36.)

13. Government has probably paid more attention to the development of technical and trade training than to any other form of education.

    (Sir Gordon Guggisberg, "A Review of the Events of 1920-26 and the Prospects of 1927-28" [Accra: Government Printer, 1927], p. 204.)

14. The educational system should, from an early date, provide ample opportunities for technical training in the various vocations incidental to the development of the land, industries, and health of the country. This will entail the formation of special schools for mechanics, carpenters, engine drivers, and other artisans; for nurses, dispensers, midwives, and sanitary inspectors; for electricians and telegraphists; for agriculturalists, foresters, and surveyors; and ultimately for engineers and doctors.

    (Sir Gordon Guggisberg and A. A. Fraser, *The Future of the Negro* [London: Student Christian Movement, 1929], p. 82.)

But compare this with Fraser's comment:

We are often told that the solution of all African educational problems is to be found in vocational education, and that that has hitherto been neglected. But the reason why there has been so much disappointment in the past is that the system has been overwhelmingly vocational, and that the real work of education has been sacrificed to narrow vocational ends.

(Ibid., p. 104.)

15. The basis of African life is, and is likely to remain agricultural. If this is so, one of the primary tasks of African education must be to assist in the growth of rural communities securely established on the land.

    (Advisory Committee on Education in the Colonies, *Memorandum on the Education of African Communities,* Colonial No. 103 [London: H.M.S.O., 1935], p..6.)

16. The whole life of the Gold Coast demands that agricultural and biological subjects should be given a principal place in the secondary school curriculum.

    (Report of the Education Committee of 1937-1941 [Accra: Government Printer], p. 12.)

The Committee proceeds to recommend precisely the principal proposals of Governor Rodger's Committee of 1908.

17. Since for a long time to come large numbers of primary school leavers will be unable to attend secondary schools it seems imperative that some sound and effective agricultural education be imparted to those who will be returning to the land.

    (Nigeria, The Report of the Commission on Post-School Certificate and Higher Education in Nigeria, *Investment in Education* (the Ashby Report) [Lagos: Federal Ministry of Education, 1960], p. 103.)

The Commission recommends *compulsory* agricultural education in primary schools (p. 18) and stresses the need for vocational agricultural education in secondary schools (p. 103).

18. More than a hundred years of controversy have, in fact, produced virtually no effect. Perhaps the sharpest comment on this kind of proposal made by an African is as follows:

> It is a sheer waste of time to go to a class room or to go to a secondary school and say to the children: 'Go back to the land.' It is sheer dishonesty. You have brought up these young boys; they know electricity, they know cinemas, they know concrete buildings, they know all these things. And you want them seriously, knowing all these social amenities, to go back to the farms.
>
> (E. Ofori-Atta, Gold Coast Legislative Assembly Debates, Session 1953, Issue Number I, Vol. II, p. 667.)

CHAPTER 9

TECHNICAL EDUCATION AND ECONOMIC DEVELOPMENT IN INDIA BEFORE WORLD WAR I

Robert I. Crane

Prior to World War I there was little technical, industrial, or scientific education in India, and the little that was provided was limited in scope, in quality, and in effectiveness. Voluminous reports were published and many memoranda written, but most of the proposals proved abortive. During the same decades the Indian economy remained substantially underdeveloped and undiversified. Insofar as economic growth took place it was primarily in the production of agricultural raw materials. Industry had some promising beginnings in a few lines, but only a tiny element of the population came to depend on factory labor for their livelihood. Even more significant, perhaps, was the fact that a large proportion of technical, engineering, and supervisory posts remained in European hands.

After World War I the situation changed, albeit rather slowly. Technical and industrial education improved and was more widely spread, and the industrial sector of the economy increased in size and in diversity. It is clear, in a general way, that developments in technical education were concomitant with the modernization and industrialization of the Indian economy. It is not so clear that technical education was a primary condition of industrialization. Put another way, the evidence is largely circumstantial.

The attempt is made in this chapter to describe and evaluate the degree and character of the technical and industrial education which was provided in India, with special emphasis on the period prior to World War I. Attention is also paid to the causes of the shortcomings in the efforts at technical education. The chapter also essays an examination of the more obvious ways in which the deficiencies of the educational system limited, or helped to limit, the growth of a modern economy and of industry.

It must, however, be made clear that the retarded rate of growth of the modern sector of the Indian economy reflected a variety of causes. It is very difficult to assess the importance of the lack of technical education when so many other factors played a part. This chapter does not attempt to concern itself with the other factors which affected the rate of modernization; it can give no final answer to the question of the extent to which deficiencies in education influenced economic retardation. Nor has it been possible to arrive at a satisfactory answer to a subsidiary question which arises whenever the role of technical education in economic growth is discussed; *i.e.*, whether technical education breeds industry, or industry calls forth technical education. This question cannot be dealt with in this essay, as the information available is not adequate. Perhaps no more can be said than that the two must go together, each proving the necessity of the other.

1. Nineteenth-Century Indian Higher Education, Primarily a Training Ground for Civil Service.

For our purposes here, the first really significant development in western education in India was the creation of the universities of Calcutta, Bombay, and Madras in 1857, by governmental action. Prior to that the decision had already been made for a higher education in the English language; the establishment of the universities, on the model of the University of London, as examining and degree-granting agencies, set the distinctive seal upon upper secondary and collegiate education.[1] The need to pass the matriculation examination prescribed by the universities determined the content of upper secondary education, and the need to pass the first arts and B.A. examinations decided the content of collegiate training. The distinctive bias in this system of education was its literary and humanistic content. In character it was largely official, being closely supported and dominated by the Government of India through the agency of grants and of the provincial offices of education. The administration of the universities had a substantial official element and capped the system. There remained little scope for individual Indian initiative in decision-making. This situation did not change until the end of World War I. Meanwhile, the bulk of college graduates tried for a position in the civil service or in the subordinate government services.[2]

In the early discussions and controversies over the aims and characteristics of the education to be imparted, the needs of science were not overlooked. After Thomas Babington Macaulay wrote the famous *Minute* of February 2, 1835, which decided in favor of western learning, Lord William Bentinck, Governor-General of India, ordered that "the object of the British Government should be the promotion of English literature and science."[3] This position had the general liberalizing objective typical of Utilitarians. However, as will be seen, science received less than a reasonable share of attention for a long time to come. However, even before Macaulay's *Minute*

1. For a discussion of the origins and nature of western education in India up through the founding of the universities, see the following titles: Arthur Mayhew, *The Education of India, A Study of British Educational Policy in India, 1835–1920* (London: Faber & Gwyer, 1926), p. 18 and *passim*. Also L.S.S. O'Malley (ed.), *Modern India and the West* (London: Oxford University Press, 1941), p. 658.

2. The pronounced bent toward government white-collar service is frequently stressed in the literature. See, S.N. Mukerji, *History of Education in India (Modern Period)* (Baroda: Acharya Book Depot, 1961), p. 95; Mayhew, *op. cit.*, p. 149.

3. E. Thompson and G. Garratt, *Rise and Fulfilment of British Rule in India* (London; Macmillan, 1934), p. 314.

had cleared the air, the government had taken its initial steps toward scientific and technical training.

As early as 1822, the East India Company opened a Native Medical School in Calcutta for the preparation of Indian medical assistants, and in 1826 medical classes were attached to the Sanskrit College.[4] In 1835 the Calcutta Medical College was established to teach medical science on European lines and in 1845 Grant Medical College was opened in Bombay. A medical school for training apprentices and native medical pupils had also been opened in Madras in 1835.[5] The chief aim of opening these medical schools and colleges seems to have been the training of doctors and medical assistants for government medical service, although some of the graduates went into private practice. The general tendency of the system to train Indians for posts in the Administrative bureaucracy affected both medical and engineering training substantially.

Engineering schools represented the other significant effort at scientific and technical training in India prior to the last years of the nineteenth century. On the origins of engineering education, Nurullah & Naik say

> . . . the Court of Directors sanctioned the establishment of an Engineering College which was opened in Calcutta in 1856.
> "As early as 1824, an Engineering class was organized by the Bombay Native Education Society . . . In 1854, an Engineering class and mechanical school were opened at Poona for training subordinate officers of the Public Works Department (of Government). There was no institution for imparting instruction in Civil Engineering in Madras prior to 1857. There was, however, a Survey School, under the Board of Revenue, established as early as 1793.[6]

There was also an Engineering College at Roorkee, in Upper India, which was opened in 1847 in connection with the workshops and headquarters of the Public Works department office responsible for building the Ganges Canal. The aim of the college was to provide engineers (British and Indian) for the works in progress. From this time forward there was a slow but steady growth in the number of Indians who received civil engineering training. Years later, the Indian Industrial Commission remarked as follows on engineering education:

> In the past, the education of engineers has been too much influenced by the immediate requirements of the Public Works Department, without regard to the future or to those other interests in India which can be handled only by engineers. The higher branches of the engineering services in this country absorb but a very small proportion of the engineering students who pass through the colleges, and the rest enter the upper subordinate ranks or find private employment of a not very remunerative character. The greater

---

4. H. Sharp (ed.), *Selections from Educational Records, Part I, 1781-1839* (Calcutta: Government Printing, 1920), p. 184.
5. Mukerji, *op. cit.*, p. 294.
6. S. Nurullah and J.P. Naik, *History of Education in India, During the British Period* (Bombay: Macmillan & Co., 1943), pp. 556-57.

part of the work done in each college is the training of upper subordinates, lower subordinates, surveyors and draftsmen.[7]

2. Early "Industrial". Education: Opinions and Occasional Practice

There were in the early years a few stray instances of attempts at technical or "industrial" education other than medical or engineering. For example, a school for training ordnance artificers was opened in Madras in 1840. In the early years, at least, its clientele consisted largely of European boys whose fathers were in the Indian Army. A School of Industrial Arts was opened in Madras in 1850; it was taken over by Government in 1855. The next year, in 1856, the Bombay government started the J.J. School of Art and Industry with the aid of Sir Jamshedjee Jeejeebhoy Tata, who provided a substantial endowment. These schools had small enrollments and limited curricula. Drawing and mensuration were stressed in the course of study, along with what we would call craft training. Carpentry, blacksmithing, and allied callings were taught.[8] Educational opinion of the time seems to have stressed the idea that drawing was a fundamental subject for elementary education in industrial arts. In fact, the evidence is that many of those who received instruction in drawing were attracted because they hoped to find employment as primary school teachers who could instruct others in drawing; actually a disproportionate share of the time spent in drawing classes went to freehand drawing rather than mechanical drawing. A charming comment was made in one of the government studies of technical education on the previous efforts at drawing instruction. Sir E.C. Buck, author of the report, said:

> The present system throughout India is to teach freehand drawing of a somewhat high standard. Local Governments may perhaps be advised that . . . this seems to be unnecessary.[9]

The heavy nineteenth-century emphasis on craft training in skills such as carpentry seems to have reflected several factors. To begin with, many officers of the educational establishment seem to have had a most limited view of what was meant by technical and industrial education. Government reports and proposals abound with conflicting opinions as to what should be done. Perhaps the easiest thing to do was to open a smithy shop at the local school and hope that there would be a fruitful result. In addition, government efforts were influenced by missionary enterprise in lower education. The missionaries faced a special problem, for the children of Christian converts often faced real difficulties in securing gainful employment because conversion

7. Indian Industrial Commission, *Report, 1916-18* (Calcutta: Superintendent of Government Printing, 1918), p. 121.

8. Nurullah & Naik, *op. cit.*, p. 559-60. See also *Papers Relating to Technical Education in India, 1886-1904* (Calcutta: Superintendent of Government Printing, 1906), pp. 83-85.

9. Sir E.C. Buck, *Report on Practical and Technical Education* (Calcutta: Superintendent of Government Printing, 1901), p. 10.

from Hinduism had removed their families from the ancient caste system of occupational apprenticeships. The missionaries opened simple craft schools to equip their converts for humble but honest lives, and government educational officers tended to follow suit in public schools.

Moreover, the provision of basic craft training was a relatively inexpensive venture for the educational service. Education always lacked funds, and those who were inclined to see the system as providing literacy for white-collar employment tended to deprecate the diversion of money to technical training. Craft schools met the demand for technical training at a modest cost. Since it appeared that the Indians who went to school were most interested in literacy, the modesty of the sums set aside for craft training could be defended on the ground that Indian preferences were for literary skills. It was also a fact that the bulk of those who continued in school past the primary level came from the upper castes of Hindus. Traditionally these castes had favored intellectual, literary, and administrative callings, not those occupations which required manual labor.

Still, it is clear from the literature that educational officers were apprehensive lest industrial training create a population with skills for which there might be no openings or employment. This apprehension served to justify timidity in experimenting with technical education. This position became, however, increasingly irrational because the characteristic literary education to which so much attention was given was in the process of producing its own unemployment problem.[10]

3. Elementary and Secondary School Curricula in the 1880's

Meanwhile, attempts were made, at least in a tentative fashion, to give elementary education a more practical flavor. The regular curriculum was modified so as to make a place for the rudiments of science. Before the end of the century changes in the curriculum had sufficiently matured, despite

---

10. In *Papers Relating to Technical Education in India, 1886-1904, op.cit.*, pp. 118-19, we find the following representative observations.

". . .the circumstances of India, it is obvious, are very unlike those of England. India is essentially an agricultural country . . . and under these circumstances it is not surprising that the scientific and manufacturing developments of the community are backward. It thus happens that, except in Bombay, where certain industries are considerably developed, the experience obtained from Europe is not altogether applicable . . . technical education cannot create manufactures; it merely forms the adjunct of good general education for the supply of skilled labour. . . . Technical schools create a directive power but the power must find at hand a sphere in which it is to be exercised.

"The prudent way of proceeding seems to be by careful enquiry . . . to ascertain local and special wants, and to provide for these wants practically, as they arise. This can best be done by developing the scientific element in existing institutions . . . which will be thoroughly in harmony with Indian Society as it now exists, which will keep in touch with native managers, foremen and artisans of all kinds as they are; improving them gradually, increasing their number and developing their ingenuity and their taste."

Other government reports on technical education laid due stress on the fact that supply must not be allowed to outpace demand and, in fact, more than one survey was mounted to enquire of management the extent to which they were prepared to give employment to Indians with technical training of a somewhat more advanced character if the educational system were to be changed so as to quicken the production of students with such skills.

172   ROBERT I. CRANE

argument over what ought to be done, so that the 1883 *Report of the Indian Education Commission* included the following kinds of courses in the lower and upper primary standards (classes) and in the secondary schools.

Lower Primary Standard:[11]

Madras	*Bombay*	*Bengal*
Arithmetic—the first four rules, simple and compound, with easy miscellaneous questions founded on them.	Arithmetic—the first four simple rules. Mental Arithmetic on the Native Method. Geography— Boundaries, mountains, rivers of the collecorate (district)	Arithmetic—the first four rules, simple and compound. Mental arithmetic on the native method. Bazaar and zamindary accounts and simple mensuration. Cunningham's Sanitary Primer.

Upper Primary Standard:

Madras	*Bombay*	*Bengal*
Arithmetic—Reduction, Compound Rules & Vulgar Fractions. Mental Arithmetic applied to bazaar transactions. Geography of Asia. *Optional Subjects:* Cunningham's Sanitary Primer. Robertson's Agricultural Class Book	Arithmetic—Vulgar fractions. Simple Rule of 3; Simple Interest. Mental Arithmetic and bazaar accounts. Geography of India. *Optional Subjects:* Model & Object Drawing. Practical Geometry. Field Instruction in Agriculture. Printing; carpentry; joinery; smithery.	Arithmetic—Vulgar and Decimal fractions & Simple Proportion. Native accounts. Euclid, Bk. I. Elements of Physics Cunningham's Sanitary Primer.

Initial Standards of Instruction in Secondary Schools (science subjects):[12]

Madras	*Bombay*	*Bengal*
Arithmetic—To compound rules & vulgar fractions; easy decimals	To decimals, compound proportion, and discount	To decimal and vulgar fractions, and proportion; native arithmetic
Geography—Europe	Geography—Asia and India in detail; elementary knowledge of the world	Asia and India in detail; general knowledge of the world.
Additional subjects— none	Optional subjects: free hand drawing; model & object drawing; practical geometry	Euclid to I. 26. Mensuration of lines and native methods of mensuration. The Sanitary Primer with an additional textbook.

Speaking of the final standards in high school curriculum, the Report had the following comments:

11. *Report of the Indian Education Commission* (Calcutta: Superintendent of Government Printing, 1883), p. 121

12. *Ibid.*, pp. 206-07.

With high schools, however, this divergence [in curricula] comes practically to an end. The course in every high school is determined by the matriculation standard of one or another of the Indian Universities. . . . [In Madras the following is included:]
Mathematics—(a) Arithmetic, including proportion, decimals, and interest, (b) Algebra, to simple equations, (c) Euclid, Books I—III, with easy deductions. General Knowledge . . . (b) General geography and India in detail, (c) Roscoe's Primer of Chemistry, (d) Balfour Stewart's Primer of Physics.
Bombay: Mathematics—(a) Arithmetic, the whole from first principles, not merely by rules, (b) Algebra, to simple equations, (c) Euclid, Books I—IV, with easy deduction. General Knowledge—(b)Elementary geography, physical, political and mathematical, (c) Elementary knowledge of the mechanical powers, (d) elementary chemistry, (e) Outline of the Solar System.
Calcutta: Mathematics—(a) Arithmetic, including proportion, decimals and interest, (b) Algebra, to simple equations, (c) Euclid, Books I—IV, with easy deductions, (d) The mensuration of plane surfaces, including the theory of surveying with the chain. History and Geography—(b) General geography, (c) Physical geography.[13]

From these quotations one can gather the character of the science instruction which was given to pupils at the various levels in primary and secondary schools. On the face of it, the quantity of science instruction imparted does not seem unimpressive. The observations of a number of reporters, however, suggest that the situation was not quite so unambiguous. For instance, the same Report which offers the information on curriculum just given goes on to say:

Throughout India high schools have hitherto been regarded . . . it may almost be said exclusively—as preparatory schools for those who are to become students of the University . . . the attention of students is too exclusively directed to University studies, and no opportunity is offered for the development of what corresponds to the 'modern side' of schools in Europe. It is believed that there is a real need in India for some corresponding course which shall fit boys for industrial or commercial pursuits. . . .
We therefore recommend that in the upper classes of high schools there be two divisions, one leading to the Entrance examination of the Universities, the other of a more practical character, intended to fit youths for commercial or non-literary pursuits. . . .[14]

The tone of these and similar remarks in other official reports is such as to suggest that the science component in the secondary school program was anything but practical. That this was the case seems likely from another kind of "evidence" to be discerned running through many a report. Only a small percentage of the population went to school beyond the elementary level (in India the drop-out rate after completion of four or five years was pronounced). Of those who continued beyond primary grades a fairly large proportion aimed at college entrance, *i.e.*, a decidedly literary program. Another substantial proportion continued into high school in order to enter government

13. *Ibid.*, pp. 217-18.
14. *Ibid.*, pp. 219-20.

Table 1*
Results of University Examinations, 1885-86.

Number of those who passed the final examinations.

Province	Medicine	Engineering
Madras	26	3
Bombay	39	13
Bengal	32	3
Northwest Provinces	—	4
Punjab	7	—
Total	104	23
Total for 1884-85	59	17

*Tables 1-4: *Review of Education in India in 1886* (Calcutta: Central Printing Office, 1888), pp. 41, 82, 250, 254.

service as primary and secondary school teachers. This would suggest that science instruction tended to serve ends other than those of stimulating the growth of modern industry.

4. The Situation of Technical Education in the 1880's

That this conclusion is not ill-founded seems apparent from the 1886 official report on the progress of education in India. It said:

> It is obvious from what has preceded that, apart from the higher instruction in law, medicine and engineering, required for the attainment of University degrees, there is not as yet in India anything like a general or systematic provision of technical instruction . . . The provision that exists is partial and fragmentary, directed by no guiding principle. . . . The cry has gone up for more technical instruction. . . . The Department (of Education) has been anxious to respond . . . but has not known how. In default of setting up a system of industrial education of its own, it has been prompt to aid schools established by private effort even when their utility was questionable. . . . But the problem was an obscure one; all the conditions were strange; the social and industrial circumstances of India were so different from those of European countries that the experience of the latter seemed likely to throw but little light on the question. . . .[15]

These comments were accompanied by a survey of existing scientific and technical education in India, which is summarized in Tables 1-4 to indicate how much had been accomplished. In reading the figures to be given it should be kept in mind that the total population of British India in 1881 (the last census prior to the date of the educational statistics given) was estimated to be 257,380,000.[16]

15. *Review of Education in India in 1886* (Calcutta: Central Printing Office, 1888), p. 261.
16. Kingsley Davis, *Population of India and Pakistan* (Princeton: Princeton University Press, 1951), Table 7, p. 27.

TABLE 2
Professional Colleges
(1881-82, 1884-85, 1885-86)

Province	1881-82 Medicine		1881-82 Engineering		1884-85 Medicine		1884-85 Engineering		1885-86 Medicine		1885-86 Engineering	
	Schools	Students	Schools	Students	Schools	Students	Schools	Students	Schools	Students	Schools	Students
Madras	1	76	1	9	1	116	1	19	1	136	1	18
Bombay	1	283	1	151	1	370	1	184	1	296	1	116
Bengal	1	117	1	170	1	132	1	149	1	152	1	156°
N. W. Prov.	-	—	-	—	-	—	1	155	-	—	1	154†
Punjab	-	—	-	—	1	188	-	—	1	183	-	—
Total	3	476	3	330	4	806	4	507	4	767	4	444

°Includes 104 non-University students.
†Includes 154 non-University students.

TABLE 3

Technical and Other Special Schools

(1881-82)

	Art		Medicine		Survey or Engineering		Industrial	
	Schools	Students	Schools	Students	Schools	Students	Schools	Students
Madras	1	84	2	200	1	42	3	138
Bombay	1	177	3	143	1	10	7	509
Bengal	1	77	4	310	4	161	3	113
N. W. Prov.	–	——	1	39	–	——	2	152
Punjab	1	43	1	138	–	——	4	128
Central Province	–	——	–	——	–	——	23	440
Burma	1	58	–	——	2	37	1	17
Assam	–	——	–	——	1	60	1	12
Total	5	439	11	830	9	310	44	1,509

TABLE 4

Technical and Other Schools

(1884-85)

Province	Art		Medicine		Survey of Engineering		Industrial	
	Schools	Students	Schools	Students	Schools	Students	Schools	Students
Madras	1	162	5	197	1	106	5	179
Bombay	1	251	3	164	1	21	7	522
Bengal	1	157	6	672	4	171	5	172
N. W. Prov.	–	——	1	89	—	——	2	186
Punjab	1	85	—	——	—	——	4	93
Central Province	–	——	—	——	—	——	19	316
Burma	–	——	—	——	5	110	1	38
Assam	–	——	—	——	7	163	1	18
Total	4	655	15	1,122	18	571	44	1,524

In the next year, 1886, the totals had grown slightly in the category of Industrial Schools, from 44 schools with 1,524 pupils to 50 schools with 2,024 pupils. In the other categories, however, there had been a slight decline in enrollments.[17] Thus, by 1886, with a population of more than 257 million, India had fewer than 4,300 students enrolled in secondary schools providing training in art, medicine, engineering or surveying and industrial pursuits. At this time there were approximately 220,000 students enrolled in secondary schools in British India. Evidence in the reports makes it clear that the teachers in these schools were often poorly prepared; that some of the training was less than practical; and that many of those recorded as being in

17. *Review of Education, op. cit.,* p. 256.

industrial schools were, in fact, being trained in a craft such as carpentry. In many of these cases, the school staff consisted of *mistries* (skilled craftsmen) who had been employed to show boys how to handle the tools of the trade, in what amounted to an organized apprenticeship system.

The viewpoint of Government at that time was nicely expressed in the *Review*, which argued regarding technical education as follows:

> . . . any scheme of technical instruction, to be successful, must be governed by the extent of the demand. All has not been done when we have opened classes. . . . We must satisfy ourselves . . . the men so educated will find useful and lucrative employment.
>
> At present the difficulty is two-fold: capital waits for skilled labour; skilled labour waits for capital. There is no demand for technical instruction because the industries in which it could be utilized do not exist. The industries do not exist because in the absence of skilled labour, capital cannot be employed. . . . India already has an enormous advantage in the low rate of wages for factory hands; that advantage would be greatly increased if the skilled labour of a native manager could be substituted for the more costly agency of a foreman imported from Europe . . . but it will probably be found that capital will not risk itself . . . without the aid of European supervision.
>
> It seems unlikely, therefore, that the establishment of a central technological college will, of itself, go far to create or introduce new industries. . . .
>
> The final, if not very satisfactory, conclusion seems to be that technical education can only advance rapidly in a country where the industries and manufactures are highly developed; that India is not such a country; and that it is a fallacy to suppose that any scheme of technical instruction will open out a royal road to industrial prosperity, the attainment of which depends upon far different conditions.[18]

5. The Abortive "Note on Technical Education in India"

However, at the time when this pessimistic report was being published, external circumstances were forcing a change in attitude in Government. Indian public opinion, now mobilized by the newly established Indian National Congress, was vocal in its demand for technical education and other aids to the growth of industry. This demand harped on the theme that Britain was intentionally keeping India's economy backward so as to provide full scope for the importation of English goods. Whether the nationalist argument was valid or not, it had an effect.

Moreover, government was increasingly concerned over the evidence that its schools and colleges were producing an oversupply of educated white-collar men. These men were finding it difficult to secure employment and were swelling the ranks of political agitation. Furthermore, in the same years, considerable steps were being taken to push technical education in Britain and in Ireland. These circumstances combined to draw the attention of Government to the plight of technical education in India.[19] In July 1886,

18. *Ibid.*, pp. 276-77.
19. Indian Industrial Commission, *Report, 1916-18* (pp. 104-05) comments pointedly on the effects of the literary bias in Indian education in creating an unemployed intelligentsia and the

the Government of India issued a *Note on Technical Education in India*
which drew sharp attention to the existing deficiencies and provided a series
of recommendations upon which the local governments (of the provinces
such as Bombay, Madras and the Punjab) were supposed to act. This Note
made some valid suggestions, a few of which were acted upon in some of the
provinces of British India. It is clear from the record, however, that the
response of the provincial departments of education was uneven and rather
lethargic. Speaking of the years after the publication of the Note, Sir E.C.
Buck commented:

> In 1888, at the instance of the Conference held in that year, the Home
> Department included in its Quinquennial Resolution on educational progress
> a request that the Departments of Education and Agriculture . . . work out in
> concert a scheme of primary education 'which would render the agricultural
> population capable of assimilating new ideas. . . .' The subject was again
> discussed at the Imperial Conferences in 1890 and 1893. It was then ascer-
> tained that, although some reforms had been affected in primary education,
> the definite action suggested in 1888 (based upon the *Note* of 1886) had not
> been taken, and the Home Department was again in 1893 moved to issue
> further instructions. . . . No concerted schemes were, however, worked out. . . .
>   . . . [a] Resolution issued . . . in 1897 . . . summarized the defects dis-
> covered . . . [and] . . . reforms . . . were advocated. . . .
>   The Resolution of 1897 was issued by the Department of Revenue and
> Agriculture with the concurrence of, but not by, the Home Department. This
> circumstance may partly account for the fact that it has not in some provinces
> even yet, after four years (1901), been brought under the formal consideration
> of the Local Governments . . . however . . . there is a general tendency in all
> provinces to introduce practical methods.
>   The conclusion drawn from my examination of the position . . . is that the
> general intention of all the Educational departments is in sound accordance
> with the principles of the Imperial Resolutions (1886 and 1888) . . . but that
> the measures taken or to be taken for the application of the principles are not
> always clearly defined. . . . It is . . . unsatisfactory to find that in some provinces
> no definite scheme has yet been drawn up . . . no final consideration has been
> given to those Resolutions, no modification yet made in the curricula; that
> progress effected in the teaching of teachers is slow; and that some of the
> school books still offend more or less against leading principles.
>   The main and to some extent valid excuses are that funds are not avail-
> able for more rapid progress; that education already absorbs a large portion
> of State expenditure; that famine and plague have reduced such grants as
> been accorded for education; and have generally interfered with the con-
> sideration of educational subjects.[20]

---

inadequacy of the efforts which had been made for technical and industrial training during the
19th century.

   20. Sir E.C. Buck, *op. cit.*, pp. 2-8. Sir Edward included in his fascinating report a wry comment
regarding the limitations of some of the officers of the educational system as an aspect of the failure
of efforts at technical education. "It is admitted by all the Directors . . . that education is a science
in which educators must themselves be educated; that those who come out to India to direct the
educational scheme have rarely received any professional training; and that measures should
certainly be taken to remedy this defect." (p. 15). Unfortunately for many years the well-paid posts
of provincial directors of education were the political patronage of the Secretary of State for India.
Amiable, well-intentioned, and intelligent young men of good family, normally Oxford graduates

Efforts at industrial education suffered in another respect which must be mentioned. A number of the industrial schools and most of the art schools were influenced by a desire to help revive India's antique art handicrafts (such as fine embroidery and delicate handwork in brass). It is evident that these schools did, in fact, resuscitate dying art industries which had been prominent in medieval India. It is equally apparent that this emphasis contributed in no way to the modernization of the Indian economy or to its industrial growth. In one instance a lovely journal was published in support of Indian art industries (I have had the privilege of seeing several issues) by the Government of India. But the journal was printed and, apparently, largely distributed in England. Today is is a collectors' item of fine color reproductions of the best Indian jewelery, embroidery, and handwork of high skill in metals and ornaments.

6. Apprentice Schools for Europeans and Eurasians

Finally, it may be mentioned that a number of the schools for industrial training catered primarily to Europeans domiciled in India and to the Anglo-Indian community. In 1875 a committee surveyed schemes for training apprentices in industrial pursuits in the existing establishments. There were, at the time, seven such institutions: the Ordnance Department, Madras; the Futtegarh Gun Carriage Agency; the Calcutta Dockyard; the Bombay Dockyard; the Workshops of the East Indian Railway; the Workshops of the Oudh and Rohilcund Railway; and the Scinde, Punjab and Delhi Railway. At Futtegarh there were no provisions for industrial training. The Bombay Dockyard was prepared to accept European boys and Anglo-Indians but Government had not sanctioned the scheme. The East Indian Railway took "European and East Indian apprentices of fifteen years of age."[21] The Calcutta Dockyard had abolished its apprentice school in 1862. The Oudh and Rohilcund Railway trained apprentices as mechanists for the jobs of firemen and fitters. The Scinde, Punjab and Delhi Railway trained European, Eurasian (Anglo-Indian) and Portuguese boys. The Madras Ordnance Department had normally recruited from among the sons of European soldiers, and the trainees were treated as if in the military service. In 1875 there were 22 applicants for admission. Fourteen were the sons of military men, five were the orphans of "civilians" (civil servants), and three were described as the sons of "poor civilians." The Report adds:

> The formation of a training school at Dehree, Sone Circle, Public Works Irrigation Department, Bengal, was finally sanctioned . . . in 1872. The order was:

---

in humane letters, frequently secured these political appointments. One report on technical education carefully pointed out that though these were fine young men they knew nothing whatsoever about technical or industrial education and had rarely had any training as educators. It is to this phenomenon that Sir E. C. Buck refers in the quotation just given.

21. *Report of the Committee . . . for Establishment of a School of Apprentices in Calcutta* (Calcutta: Superintendent of Government Printing, 1875), p. 2.

To give Christian lads subsistence allowance at Rs. 20 each per mensem . . .
To give the Native lads Rs. 5 per month . . . The boys are to be bound by
indenture to serve from four to six years. . . . The lads who, at the end of this
period possess the required qualifications, to be drafted into the Department
as upper subordinates. . . . This school has been a great success as regards
English and Eurasian boys, but not as regards Natives.[22]

The committee then recommended creation of an apprentice school in
Calcutta, open to boys of respectable European or Eurasian extraction, with
preference to be given to the orphans of government employees. In some
sense, of course, the creation of skills among European orphans living in
India could be said to be a potential contribution to the economic development and modernization of India. But the training of an Indian industrial
population tended to be overlooked. Meanwhile, the question of technical
education continued to exercise the minds of government officers at various
levels. In a volume on technical education in India, published by Government in 1906, the following remark was made:

Proposals for the institution of a new examination with a technical side . . .
were submitted by the Director of Public Instruction in 1887. . . . The opinion
of the University on this scheme . . . is now before Government. . . . In these
circumstances it will be convenient to postpone any reference to these questions until a decision is come to on the High School examination scheme.[23]

It will be noted that more than fifteen years had elapsed since the 1887 proposal had been submitted and no decision had yet been taken. Worse than
that, the response to official prodding after the turn of the century was met by
reference to the unfinished matter of a decision on a new type of high school
examination; this in turn rested with the machinery of the universities, since
the latter decided courses through the examinations they administered.

7. Concerning Indian Interests, Alleged Aptitudes, and the Vocational Rationality of Student Demands

There is another aspect to the matter of technical attention which must
be noted. Through the literature there runs a recurrent theme of official
European comment on Indian school boys' alleged lack of interest in or
aptitude for any form of technical or manual training. In all candor, this is a
difficult subject to evaluate. The official view may have been, at least in part,
a cliché which fed upon itself. In the opinion of the writer it was at best a half
truth. The point is that, whether truth or not, it played a role in dampening
official zeal for the extension of technical or industrial training. Official
opinion on the matter was backed by some kinds of "evidence," including
some expression of educated Indian opinion which agreed with the view.
More important was the fact that a large proportion of school and college
students opted for literary training.

22. *Ibid.*, p. 7.
23. *Papers Relating to Technical Education in India, 1886-1904* (Calcutta: Superintendent
Government Printing, 1906), pp. 84-85.

However, careful study of all of the evidence entombed in official reports leads one to feel that some of the evidence was spurious. For example, it is very clear that most of those who went to high school or to college had severely practical aims. Education was not a luxury but a means to employment. Students pursued those courses which were supposed to be most likely to result in decent posts. If a majority entered the literary course it seems to have been because what little "empirical" evidence they had taught them that the literary course was most likely to gain them respectable employment. Whenever Government announced that posts would be reserved for those who passed a given course, enrollments in that course would go up.

This is not, of course, the whole story. It is true, as has been noted here and in many other studies, that a high proportion of those who went to high school and to college, at least prior to World War I, were from the upper castes of Hindu society. Brahmins were clearly overrepresented in higher education, which was predominantly literary or legal education. Now, it is certainly a fact that the traditions of the higher castes were not traditions which favored manual labor or "field work." This is still obvious today in educated circles in India, though it is a decreasing phenomenon. So there was a basis of fact to support the widely held view that Indians did not have any aptitude for technical or industrial training. Those classes of Indians most likely to go to high school or college were also the classes least likely to have a tradition of manual, technical or craft occupation.

At the same time, as is made clear in numerous official reports, those classes which did have a tradition of artisanship or of labor were least likely to go to high school or to college; this was perhaps in part because the typical training given was literary, and literary achievement was not part of their tradition. When industrial schools were opened they often lacked for students: higher castes did not enroll because of their "bias" against such work, while the lower castes stayed home and learned their simple skills in the ancient fashion from their parents or caste members.

Nonetheless, it seems apparent that the cliché tended to stifle zeal for experiments in technical training. It is also quite apparent, as will be shown, that the cliché operated to bias English entrepreneurs against risking the employment of Indians who had technical training—with the often reported result that English foremen and technicians were imported to fill the slots in industry which required trained personnel. Thus a vicious circle was created. Government hesitated to give technical training on the ground that an unemployed technical class would be the outcome. Employers reported that trained Indians were not available and that Indians had no aptitude for such posts. Therefore, they argued, they had to rely upon English-imported technicians. In the end, there was no demand for trained Indians.

8. The Gap between Technical Schooling and Jobs, and European Bias Against Indian Technicians

Because of the years of incomplete and indifferent results achieved in the provision of technical and industrial training in India up to the turn of the century,[24] the early years of the 20th century witnessed a renewed effort for solid accomplishment. This included a number of "re-surveys" to find out what had gone wrong. Many technical and pedagogical arguments were advanced both to account for what had been wrong with previous efforts (as in the *Report* by Sir E.C. Buck already cited), and to attempt to find a way out of what seemed to be an impasse.

One such effort by Government sheds specific light on the matter just discussed — the alleged lack of aptitude of Indians for technical or industrial training and employment. In 1912 the Government of Bengal published the report of a committee it had appointed to study the matter of a technical institute for Calcutta. In the course of its proceedings, the committee touched on a number of matters, and in particular on the question of employment for Indians who might be trained by the proposed technical institute. The committee also heard from two Government of India experts who had been detached to study and report on the problem of technical education in India. The proceedings of the committe contain interesting remarks and expressions of opinion — including some difference of opinion — on the subject.

> . . . The President (of the Committee) then proposed that Lt. Col. Atkinson, Principal of Rurki College, and Mr. T. Dawson of Bombay, who had been placed on special duty . . . should be requested to favour the Committee with their attendance. . . .
>
> He (Lt. Col. Atkinson) stated . . . they thought that the present colleges in India more than met the demand . . . the Bachelor of Engineering students are educated far above the requirements of most of them, as many have to accept Overseerships . . . owing to the paucity of higher grade appointments.
>
> The Hon'ble Mr. Finnimore pointed out that men are imported from England, and asked why the training at Sibpur (College) cannot be improved so as to meet this demand. . . .
>
> Col. Atkinson stated he had been informed that . . . Indian students are at a disadvantage owing to racial defects.
>
> The Hon'ble Mr. Kuchler said that if Indian students are fit to become mechanical or electrical engineers they are *a fortiori* fit to become Civil Engineers.
>
> The Hon'ble Mr. Finnimore referred to the want of initiative and of power of observation of Bengalis. . . .
>
> Mr. Dawson said he did not agree with the prevalent idea that Bengalis as a race are unfit for practical work. . . . In Bombay he has had fifteen or twenty Bengali students and they have done well. On the western side of India there is much more Indian enterprise and hence Indians obtain employment easily. About Calcutta, on the other hand, where the foremen are generally English, Indians are not so readily accepted.
>
> Mr. Danby explained the course at Lillooah. . . . Some Indians have done well, but those recruited now seem to be 50% inferior . . . they lack interest and stamina. . . . After completing the course they are taken on as mechanics,

24. Tabular data in Appendix I will summarize the extent of technical training given to Indians up to the beginning of the present century. Appendix II will present summary data on the progress of technical and industrial training in the early years of the present century, and Appendix III will summarize data on such training after World War I.

on an initial pay of Rs. 80 for Europeans and Rs. 50 to 60 for Indians. The former may finally rise to Rs. 400 and the latter to Rs. 200, but few Indians rise much above Rs. 60.

Mr. Everett and Mr. Hoogewerf have . . . interviewed representatives of the following firms, to ascertain . . . as to whether there is an opening for students who have been technically trained. . . .

Firm	General Opinion
A. E. Henderson & Co.	Adverse
A. A. Yule & Co.	Adverse
Birkmyre Bros.	Favourable
A. Ernsthausen	Favourable
Jardine Skinner & Co.	Favourable

(However) Jardine Skinner said it 'was now trying three Anglo-Indian youths. They would prefer these to Indians'. . . . Mr. Birkmyre says: – 'There will probably be some prejudice against the employment of local technically trained men to begin with. . . .'[25]

In the same year another Government body dealt with problems of technical instruction in India and criticized severely what had so far been done. In the course of their report, they too adverted to the deficiencies of Indians for technical and industrial callings. They said, in part:

They [employers] state that in most cases students from technical institutions will not work with their hands, will not observe factory hours, ask too high wages for learning their practical work and generally think they know everything. . . . The reasons that technically trained Indians have so far partially failed to meet the demands of employers seem to be: –

(a) Certain races in India are more fitted by nature for this class of work than others . . . certain races are not, on the average, naturally fitted for technical work. . . .

(b) Most technical institutions, up to date, have . . . endeavoured to get posts for their students . . . and in most cases have thereby damned technical education in the eyes of employers (because the students were not suitably equipped for the posts).

It is the universal opinion of employers . . . that a man however carefully prepared in a technical institution is utterly useless . . . till he has had practical experience. . . .

The idea which is prevalent in the minds of most technically trained Indians that the successful completion of their college course fits them for one of the higher . . . posts must be removed. The authorities . . . must make it clear to their students that they are totally unfit for any position of authority . . . that they must first of all be subjected to discipline and learn under practical conditions . . . the authorities . . . [must] insist upon a satisfactory apprenticeship of at least two years. . . .

Mr. Strain drew special attention to the difficulty of employing Indians in positions of trust in mills in Calcutta, where chiefly Europeans were employed. These men were very clannish, and it would be difficult for an Indian to retain his position, if appointed. . . .

Their opinion was that no openings yet existed for the highly trained

25. *Proceedings and Report of the Committee Appointed to Advise on the Creation of a Technical Institute for Calcutta* (Calcutta: Bengal Secretariat Book Depot, 1912), pp. 3-11.

Indian and they would not employ such a man, the reason given being that he could not, as a rule, be trusted in times of emergency or danger.

They (another European firm) had many openings occurring, and would be glad to give any technically-trained Indian a splendid opportunity, if he was of the right sort. The men they had had from Sibpur (College of Engigeering) proved quite unfit, and they did not want any more of them. . . . Their opinion was that at present no openings were available for the highly educated man.[26]

To go on in this vein would be to gild the lily. The point is that technical or industrial education in India was materially hampered by the existing bias among the major European employers against hiring Indian technicians. Given this fact, Government did not feel impelled to push the provision of this kind of training.

9. Report of 1916–18 Concerning the Paucity of Technical-Industrial Training

When the World War I broke out, the result of the absence of industrial training, combined with all other causes which had served to keep India industrially backward, was soon apparent to all. The war effort demanded a rapid increase in India's industrial and productive capacity, but such increase was not at all easy to achieve. Meanwhile, the preoccupation of England with her own domestic and military supply problems led to a sharp diminution of imports into India of many manufactured goods; as critical shortages developed, this produced severe strains in the wartime Indian economy. This situation led to the appointment of the Indian Industrial Commission. The Report of the commission reached a number of hard-hitting conclusions about various factors which had limited the growth and diversification of the Indian economy, and it featured the paucity of technical education as one of the significant causes. Some of its most incisive comments on the lack of industrial training are quoted below.

Generally speaking, the industries based on technical science have been disregarded, because profits in other ways have been easy. . . . The neglect of applied science is perhaps the most conspicuous among our administrative deficiencies. (p. 51)

. . . it is obvious that the great obstacles are the lack of even vernacular education and the low standard of comfort. The higher grade of worker, the mechanical artisan, in the absence of an adequate education, has also been prevented from obtaining a greater degree of skill. . . . There is at present only very inadequate provision for any form of technical training. . . .

The effect of the purely literary type of education which was the only one generally provided, has been . . . frequently discussed . . . it is, however, necessary to realize its importance as a factor which has militated against industrial development, and to emphasize the necessity for a system of education which will impart a practical bias to the minds of Indian youths. (p. 71-72)

26. *Report on the Enquiry to bring Technical Institutions into closer touch . . . with the Employers of Labour in India* (Calcutta: Government Printing, 1912), pp. 8-10, 21, 24.

The success which attended their initial industrial endeavour led the Government of Madras in 1899 to . . . [appoint] a whole-time officer to supervise and stimulate technical and industrial education. . . . These . . . activities aroused the opposition of the local European commercial community, who interpreted them as a serious menace to private enterprise and an unwarranted intervention on the part of the State.

In Madras, the Industrial Department was broken up, after the receipt of the Secretary of State's order of 1910 . . . The Industrial Department was reconstituted with effect from 21 March 1914, but owing to various causes little progress has been made. . . . (p. 81)

At the beginning of the present century, it was realized that measures taken in the Education Department during the previous fifteen years had been totally inadequate . . . Lord Curzon accordingly summoned . . . in 1901 an Educational Conference which reviewed the situation and recommended drastic reforms. . . .

The Simla Education Conference also dealt with technical and industrial education; but its recommendations were of little practical value owing to the dominating idea that it was outside the province of Government to take any part in the industrial development of the country. . . . Almost immediately after the Conference, the Government of India appointed a Commission to report on industrial education; but the report . . . was never published. (p. 106)

When we come to discuss the various forms of technical training required in this country, we are faced with the fact that there are very few industries which can . . . supply from the ranks of the workmen or of the educated classes connected with the industry the recruits wanted (as supervisors) for the control of existing or future undertakings. The former are at present too uneducated to rise; the latter are to a large extent non-Indians and are in any case too few in numbers. We shall, therefore, require special arrangements to supply candidates for supervisory posts. . . . (p. 113)

Above the skilled workman is the . . . foreman, and the provision for training such men is hopelessly insufficient. . . . We were forcibly struck . . . with the almost complete absence of Indians from the ranks of foremen. . . . The continuance of conditions which force the industrialists of the country to import so many of their subordinate supervising staff is clearly most undesirable. (p. 118)

The arrangements made for Indian apprentices are at present inadequate; and the stipends paid them during the period of training and the salaries offered on its completion are very much lower than the corresponding amounts in the case of Europeans and Anglo-Indians, a fact which is largely responsible for the failure of the better educated Indians to take advantage of these courses. . . . (p. 119-20)

Our enquiries force us to the conclusion that the crying need of industrial India at the present time is the provision of much greater facilities for the education of the artisan population . . . [therefore] we have recommended the establishment of an efficient system of industrial education in special industrial schools under the control of Departments of Industries. (p. 196)

We have shown . . . that the economic development of India has been very incomplete, and that its numerous deficiencies have left her exposed to disadvantages and dangers from which a proper organization of her resources and workers would make her free. This end cannot be achieved . . .

without the adoption of a national policy. . . . We have drawn attention to the necessity of technical and industrial education and we have recommended a comprehensive scheme. (p. 223)[27]

In its Report, the commission also noted that, in 1916-17, there were the following numbers of Indians securing education which could be described as technical or industrial.[28] The Report remarked, however, that "only a few of these institutions are under competent superintendents with a trained staff of teachers. . . ."[29]

Type of Institution	Number of Students
Engineering colleges	1,319
Schools of art	1,695
Engineering and surveying schools	874
Technical and industrial schools	10,037

By this time the total population of India had risen to some 306 million. Of these millions less than 14,000 were enrolled in institutions which could be described as technical or industrial. There were in this period 165 recognized Arts colleges in India with a total enrollment of upwards of 45,000 students. The proportion undergoing industrial or technical training was small not only in absolute numbers but also in relation to the numbers pursuing a liberal arts education. Just a very few years later, in 1921, there were reported to be 1,100,000 students in high schools in India, with the bulk of such students enrolled in the literary course. At that date it was reported that the attempt to develop the non-literary curriculum in high schools was virtually a failure. The reason given for this view was that so small a proportion of students took the practical courses.[30]

10. Lack of Agricultural Education

Given the agricultural character of the Indian economy, it might be assumed that agricultural education of a practical variety might have been developed even though, as has been seen, industrial education had not. Unfortunately, agricultural education was in as bad condition as technical education. Speaking of the weakness of agricultural education in India, a Government report said:

> . . . it will be seen that, although much anxious consideration had been given to the subject and although there were in the year 1901 five institutions in India at which theoretical and practical instruction in Agriculture was imparted, the results which up to that time had been achieved were incommensurate with the time, labour, and money which had been devoted to the subject; and it was considered that this result was chiefly due to the fact that the Agricultural colleges and schools were regarded primarily as an avenue to Government service (white collar), and the training afforded at them had not

27. Indian Industrial Commission, *Report, 1916-18*, pp. 51-223.
28. *Ibid.*, p. 258.
29. *Ibid.*, p. 261.
30. L. S. S. O'Malley, *op. cit.*, pp. 164-65. Also Mayhew, *op. cit.*, p. 154.

been taken advantage of to any material extent by those who would turn their instruction to practical account. . . .[31]

Shortly after this date, steps were taken to improve and extend advanced agricultural research in India, but this had no material effect upon the provision of training for the rural population. Agricultural training institutions were all too few in number, enrollments remained very small, and the bulk of the students continued to seek employment in government in the Land Revenue or Agriculture departments. Posts in the Agriculture Department were rarely of the type which involved any idea of an extension service or of field work.

11. Provincial Responsibility and Technical Education Following World War I

At the end of World War I, education was made a provincial subject under ministries responsible to majorities in the legislative assemblies. From that time forward there was a slow but steady growth of technical and industrial training.[32] The qualitative implications of this growth must, however, be examined critically. The evidence available indicates that many of the factors which had hampered healthy development in earlier years continued to exert their influence. This is made clear by the *Interim Report* of the Indian Statutory Commission, published in 1929. This Report makes rather disheartening reading; many of its leading observations could easily have been lifted from the pages of reports published several decades earlier. The commission said:

> In fact, the present type of high and middle English school has established itself so strongly that other forms of education are opposed or mistrusted. . . . There is nothing corresponding to the exodus from any English secondary schools either into practical life or into a vocational institution.
> . . . the figures . . . are disturbing in that they point to the lack of other and more practical forms of training than those given in the high schools.
> The reason for the uniformity of the course in the middle English and high schools is not far to seek; it is the influence of the matriculation [exam] and all that this means to the Indian boy, both as an immediate qualification for [government] service and as a gate to a university course. . . .
> In some provinces a School Final examination has been set up, distinct from the matriculation examination, with the double object of providing an alternative qualification for . . . government service and of widening the secondary curriculum by permitting the inclusion of vocational and pre-vocational subjects. But this innovation has been to a great extent a failure. . . . We cannot say how far this may be due . . . to the continued insistence of government on the matriculation as a minimum qualification for almost every form of public employment. But it is this practice which maintains and strengthens the belief in matriculation as the only goal. . . .[33]

31. *Progress of Education in India, 1902-1907*, 2 vols. (Calcutta: Government Printing, 1909), I, pp. 175-76.

32. Data on the growth of technical education are to be found in the Appendices.

33. Indian Statutory Commission, *Interim Report . . . Review of the Growth of Education in British India* (London: H.M.S.O., 1929), pp. 104-05.

The Report argued that much of the failure of vocational and technical training efforts in India could be ascribed to confusion over the appropriate role of practical as opposed to general education and to a failure to comprehend the appropriate relationship between the two.[34] In some provinces, the Report pointed out, technical training was regarded as a form of manual training; while in other cases industrial education was given in the higher classes of secondary schools to students who were, in most cases, bound for college and who had no interest in practical skills.

The Report also took exception to the position which had been adopted by the Indian Industrial Commission in favor of control of technical education by the departments of industry. In seeking to reverse the previous decision, the Report argued that technical education ought to be under the education department.[35] As had its predecessors, the Report expressed concern over the danger of creating an unemployed population of technicians; thus continuing the argument, which served to inhibit technical training, over the causal relationship between the growth of industry and the provision of industrial education. In view of the sharp remarks which had been published in the report of the Indian Industrial Commission 11 years before on the failure of government to sponsor and create minimal necessary technical education, the revival of the theme of caution over the prospects of employment for hypothetical trainees seems rather irrelevant.

The same Report provided data on the numbers of students enrolled in technical and industrial schools and colleges in India in 1927, which may be compared with figures given above for earlier years. These figures show that by 1927 there were 1,911 students enrolled in colleges of engineering and an additional 1,136 enrolled in engineering schools. These enrollments compare favorably with the numbers in similar institutions ten years earlier. By 1927 there were 854 students in agricultural colleges and 363 in agricultural schools; veterinary colleges enrolled 344 students and the Forest School had 123 students.[36] Table 5 displays the progress which had been made in technical and industrial training. Unfortunately the existing reports do not make it possible to evaluate the quality of the education being given, but there is reason to believe that it continued to suffer from defects which had been noted by the earlier commentators. The world depression hit education in India rather harshly, as revenues declined and expenditures were retrenched. Despite problems of finance, however, the number of science and technical schools and the enrollments in them continued to grow.

34. *Ibid.*, pp. 111-12.
35. This is a good example of the uncertainty and vacillation which governed views on technical education in India. This was by no means the first time that one report had strongly criticised the position adopted by a previous report. Each time this happened officials responsible for administering the educational program grew more wary of accepting any decision as final. The tendency, therefore, was to wait and see, with obvious effects for implementation of any recommendations which might be made.
36. *Ibid.*, pp. 395-97.

TABLE 5

Technical and Industrial Schools by Province

Province	1917		1922		1927	
	Schools	Students	Schools	Students	Schools	Students
Madras	40	1,961	41	2,039	63	4,307
Bombay	26	1,798	31	1,829	33	2,878
Bengal	59	2,035	86	3,631	153	6,234
United Provinces	28	1,478	37	1,780	111	3,941
Punjab	33	2,991	25	2,399	24	3,535
Bihar & Orissa	38	1,316	32	1,543	43	2,462
Central Provinces	9	350	7	298	2	101
Assam	7	71	12	170	15	476
Total	240	12,000	271	13,689	444	23,934

Source: Indian Statutory Commission, *Interim Report* . . . (London: H.M.S.O., 1929), pp. 395-97.

The number of medical colleges in British India rose from four with 1,466 students in 1901-02, to eleven with 4,936 students in 1936-37. . . . Similarly, the number of medical schools . . . rose from 22 with 2,727 students in 1901-02 to 30 with 6,999 students in 1936-37. . . . An All-India Institute of Hygiene and Public Health was established in Calcutta by the Rockefeller Foundation in 1932. In 1936-37, there were ten universities with Faculties in Medicine as against four in 1901-02.

Engineering education also expanded considerably. The number of engineering colleges in British India rose from four with 865 students in 1901-02 to eight with 2,199 students in 1936-37. Certain institutions that were regarded as 'engineering schools' in 1901-02 were classed as 'technical schools' in 1936-37, hence it is not possible to compare (the numbers of engineering schools).

In 1936-37 there were fourteen schools of Art in British India, with 2,106 students. When it is remembered that some of these schools of Art were really craft schools . . . it is obvious that the expansion of art education cannot be said to be satisfactory.

Commercial education made considerable progress. . . . In 1936-37, eight commercial colleges were working . . . as against *nil* in 1901-02. . . . The total number of students reading in these institutions in 1936-37 was 1,336. Besides these colleges there were 357 commercial schools with 12,586 pupils in British India in 1936-37.

The second step in the new policy was to create an agricultural college in each imperial province. . . . Unfortunately, this policy has not been carried out in full. Even in 1936-37 there were . . . only six colleges of agriculture (as against three in 1901-02). . . . Of the six . . . five were conducted by Government. . . .

. . . no satisfactory provision of agricultural instruction was made at the secondary stage. Consequently the agricultural colleges had to recruit their students from amongst those who had undergone a purely literary education and who did not often have even an aptitude for manual labour. . . . The agricultural colleges of this period, therefore, did not succeed in giving practical training. . . . Their students still continued to seek employment under Government. . . .

... in 1936-37, the total number of 'technical, craft and industrial schools' was 535, with an enrollment of 30,509. Of these 140 were conducted by government, 31 by [local] Boards, and 364 by private agencies. . . .[37]

An important development of the period after World War I was the creation in India of a few advanced institutes for technological training, and research. In these institutions an effort was made to provide the highest type of technical and technological training. These institutions included the Indian School of Mines, the Harcourt Butler Technological Institute, and the School of Chemical Technology. Despite these innovations on the Indian educational scene, in 1937 most Indians who wanted higher technological training had to go abroad to study.

CONCLUSIONS

In this chapter, I have attempted a description of the quantitative and qualitative development of technical and industrial education in India. The several appendices attached show these developments in summary form. It is now necessary to attempt an estimate of the ways in which the deficiencies of the system of technical education inhibited the growth of a modern industrial economy in India. The concern now is with that complex of factors, each of which, in its own way, contributed to the failure of Indian education to develop anything like a sufficient number of men with the technical qualifications for modernization.

A major problem for the system was its lack of clear-cut, consistent, and effective aims. There was much vacillation, uncertainty, and aimless compromise, both in the making of policy and in its execution. Decisions made one year were often canceled a very few years later; policy lines were frequently so ambiguous as to leave great latitude for local "interpretation"; local interpretation frequently vitiated the effects of whatever policy decisions had been reached. This was especially true because technical education tended to get caught between various branches of government, each of which had its own preoccupations and objectives. Technical education was often a "problem child," bandied from one department to another.

In part this situation reflected an allied problem. The education service was all too frequently staffed and administered by men with purely literary training. When "technicians" taught in the system they were often less than competent. In addition, their opinions tended to be overlooked by the dominant groups within the system. This situation was compounded by the fact that pay scales for teachers were hardly adequate, even at the college level. Liberal arts teachers could be secured at poor salaries, competent technicians could not. This meant that the Indian education service was not geared or staffed to provide first-rate technical or industrial education; the effects upon the students who enrolled should be obvious.

37. Nurullah and Naik, *op. cit.*, pp. 584, 588-89, 597.

Technical and industrial education suffered from an allied handicap. Funds were normally scarce for education, and existing interests resisted the diversion of resources to new kinds of pedagogy. Effective scientific, technical, and industrial education requires an expensive input of laboratory equipment and demonstration machinery. With limited budgets, it was not deemed possible to equip Indian technical courses or schools with adequate hardware. The result was an "industrial" education which relied upon textbooks and pictures. Employers were naturally suspicious of lads who had never had the opportunity to touch a machine before they sought employment.

Without adequate practical training, the graduate of a technical course had little to display but his diploma. This put him at a disadvantage compared to imported technicians. It meant difficulty in finding employment which would in any way utilize his training, and it meant low pay scales. This being the case, there was very little inventive to enroll in technical courses. Evidence of lack of interest in technical studies reinforced the disinclination to spend money on it, though such expenditure could have broken the vicious circle.

This situation was exacerbated by a related problem. Even the best technical training normally has to be followed by apprenticeship in which one's training is put to the test of practice. In India, for many reasons, few graduates of technical courses could find employment as apprentices. Since they lacked on-the-job experience, employers looked askance at their credentials. As a result, technically trained Indians were frequently employed at jobs well below the level for which they had been trained. This problem was most acute, it seems, among those who were trained to be civil engineers —a large proportion of whom ended up in relatively low-level "supervisory" posts.

In part this reflected another defect of the system. Despite some efforts made by the Government, in general the directors and policy-makers of the educational system—usually able bureaucrats—had little effective contact with the leaders of business and industry. As a result, the system of technical and industrial education was at best only loosely related to the industries whose needs were to have been served. When efforts were made to put education in touch with employers, too much attention was focused on employment prospects and too little on the changes which the system would have to undergo if its graduates were to be suitable.

This defect had another aspect which tended to limit the influence of technical training in India. If Indian technical education was underdeveloped, even more underdeveloped was the network of scientific agencies, learned journals, and associations which has had so much to do with the growth of technological skill and instruction—or scientific knowledge—in the West. India has had almost no such organizations or journals. As a result, research and training efforts were isolated from the consuming public and from the economy. Government-dominated and service-oriented, the technical education and research system, insofar as it existed, was largely devoted to its own ends.

The factors just mentioned operated in a context which was not entirely hospitable to the growth of technical training. The technical and craft schools, being part of the educational system, included general education along with specific craft training. On the surface this would be taken as a wise decision, and in certain respects it was so. But it interacted with the motivational system of those Indian classes whose children went beyond primary school to create a difficulty which has not been "solved" to this day—the tendency of the Indian with literacy to seek a white-collar post. Government reports often complained that literacy meant removing the student from any further contact with technical skills or manual labor.[38]

It is obvious that government service held great attraction for Indians with education beyond the primary grades. A prime result was that students passed the required examination as soon as possible and immediately sought government jobs. In a bureaucratic setting, government jobs were not characteristically jobs which required manual, technical, or industrial skills. The character of the prized government service affected the education imparted and the psychological orientation of those who were educated. These effects were negative for an interest in technical and industrial callings.

Similarly, the high emphasis placed on the passing of examinations, in order to secure posts, led to what has often been described as a "diploma mentality." Although this was by no means unique to India, it was clearly important here. The "diploma mentality" looks upon formal qualification—such as the passing of an examination and the achievement of a certificate—as proof of preparation. But it does not create the kinds of attitudes which make the bearer of the certificate an effective part of an industrial undertaking.

The interaction of the complex of circumstances just discussed operated within the context of a system of technical training which had its own internal limitations. To begin with, an outstanding feature of technical education in India in the period under review was its absolute paucity. There were too few schools and they had small enrollments. It is hard to believe that the needs of a growing industrial establishment could have been met, even under ideal conditions, by the turnout of India's technical schools. The recurrent importation of technicians from abroad makes it clear that local talent was not, in fact, available in sufficient quantity or quality. The Government of India had the major responsibility for education in India, but in regard to technical education and industrial training it did not meet its responsibility. Reasons have been suggested above for this failure.

Apart from serious deficiencies in the amount of technical education

38. This matter of literacy removing people from interest in the application of technical training to industry can, of course, be pushed too far. Literacy is a valuable element of any education, including technical and industrial training. Of that there can be no question. The issue is how to avoid a divorce from practical pursuits among the literate.

available, there were important defects in the kind of education provided. This hampered the growth of modern industry. One of these was the existence of a system which was inherently theoretical and nonpractical. Indian education, throughout the period under discussion, was noted for its reliance on textbooks, memory, and passing written examinations. Although such a system might work for literary education, it could hardly provide technical and industrial training. The evidence points to a lack of reality surrounding training in science and technology.

At the same time, the system tended to jump directly from the textbook to a native craft instruction. In an unreflective effort to achieve practicality, the system trained schoolboys in carpentry and similar crafts. Many times local bazaar craftsmen were employed to give this training in the schools. Carpenters and shoemakers may have been produced but that could hardly be called a contribution to the modernization of the Indian economy. The students who went to these simple craft schools did not become integral parts of a developing, modern economic system.

At the same time, there was an undue emphasis on the revival of ancient Indian art handicrafts, such as fine brasswork or silver inlay. These efforts had their own merit, but they were not contributory to the modernization of the Indian economy. They reflected the aimless and vacillating character of technical education policy, which wanted to do *something* but hardly knew what to do. Meanwhile, in those areas of industrial training which were developed, such as the preparation of mechanics at the railway workshops, a large proportion of the trainees were Europeans who could be expected to return to England if given a chance.

Finally, it may be mentioned that until after World War I, the system of technical and industrial training received almost no attention or recognition from the universities of India. The matriculation examination remained virtually unaffected by the intrusion of any "practical" knowledge, and the universities ignored those aspects of the secondary school curriculum which did not conform to their own liberal education objectives. The only exception to this, for the universities, was in respect of medical and engineering degrees. This meant that for a long time, technical education could not mature beyond the public school level. It also meant that evidences of accomplishment in a technical field (certificates or diplomas) did not carry the prestige which they would have had if they had been associated with the universities. In both ways technical education suffered from neglect at the hands of the institutions of higher learning.

With all of these defects, it is not surprising that there was very little technical education in India, and that the little which was given had only a slight effect on the course of economic growth. As was made clear in a number of the government reports cited herein, it is a matter of some surprise that anything contributory to economic modernization was accomplished. The obvious result was, of course, that the Indian economy remained singularly undeveloped and that its modernization was severely retarded. Though a number of different factors played upon the economy to keep it backward, the absence of anything like an effective system of technical, scientific, and industrial education was surely a considerable element of the causal complex. Perhaps equally regrettable, technical training in India did little or nothing to create a set of values—diffused among the population—which could have been the basis for a rapid modernization of the economy when the system of technical education eventually underwent transformation and improvement.

Appendix I

PROGRESS OF TECHNICAL EDUCATION IN INDIA
DURING THE NINETEENTH CENTURY

A. Numbers of Students Who Passed Technical and Scientific Degree Examinations, 1857-1871

Degree Examination	Calcutta University	Madras University	Bombay University
License in Medicine and Surgery	439	1	77
Bachelor of Medicine	26	2	0
Doctor of Medicine	4	2	0
License in Civil Engineering	42	0	41
Bachelor of Civil Engineering	1	8	0

Source: *Selections from Educational Records of the Government of India, Vol. I, 1859-71,* foreword by Prem Kirpal (Delhi: Manager of Publications, 1960), pp. 490-91.

B. Growth of Education in British India, 1855-1882

Year	Arts Colleges		Professional Colleges		Secondary Schools		Primary Schools	
	Schools	Students	Schools	Students	Schools	Students	Schools	Students
1855	21	3,246	13	919	281	33,801	2,810	96,923
1871	45	3,894	26	2,894	3,070	128,708	18,924	686,287
1882	70	7,205	52°	527°	3,916	214,077	84,740	2,154,311

°In 1882 there were also 62 "unattached professional and technical institutions" which enrolled an additional 4,163 students. It is not clear whether these were colleges or not, though it seem unlikely. One must assume that these were unrecognized institutions and that the figures for 1871 had included such institutions.

Source: *Report of the Indian Education Commission* (Calcutta: Superintendent of Government Printing, 1883), Appendices, p. v.

C. Technical and Other Schools in India, 1881-82

Province	Art		Medicine		Engineering & Surveying		Industrial		Other	
	Schools	Students	Schools	Students	Schools	Students	Schools	Students	Schools	Students
Madras	1	84	2	200	1	42	3	138	2	106
Bombay	1	177	3	143	1	10	7	509	27	1,029
Bengal	1	77	4	310	4	161	3	113	14	1,476
N.W.P.	–	—	1	39	–	—	2	152	—	—
Punjab	1	43	1	138	–	—	4	128	—	—
C. P.	–	—	—	—	–	—	23	440	13	369
Burma	1	58	—	—	2	37	1	17	—	—
Assam	–	—	—	—	1	60	1	12	—	—
Total	5	439	11	830	9	310	44	1,509	56	2,980

Source: *Review of Education in India in 1886* (Calcutta: Central Printing Office, 1888), p. 82.

D. Technical Education in India, 1891-92

Province	Engineering Colleges		Schools of Art		Engineering & Survey Schools		Industrial Schools		Agricultural Schools and Colleges	
	Schools	Students	Schools	Students	Schools	Students	Schools	Students	Schools	Students
Madras	1	10	1	426	1	185	18°	997	1	45
Bombay	1	50	1	286	1	14	16	1,220	–	—
Bengal	1	244	1	181	3	417	18	672	–	—
N.W.P.	1	180	–	—	–	—	3	148	–	—
Punjab	–	—	1	134	–	—	3	443	–	—
C. P.	–	—	2	21	1	11	8	332	–	—
Burma	–	—	–	—	17	411	1	18	–	—
Assam	–	—	–	—	1	4	1	6	–	—
Other	–	—	–	—	—	—	1	24	–	—
Total	4	484	6	1,048	24	1,042	69	3,860	1	45

°Of these, four were schools for girls, with 82 female pupils.

Source: *Progress of Education in India, 1887-88 to 1891-92*, p. 275.
    It should be noted that statistics were relatively unreliable in British India, especially in the earlier years. The figures given in the above tables cannot be considered to be precise. Changes in area and changes in definition hampered the collection and compilation of accurate data. Furthermore, there were often more than one reporting agency for the same kinds of data, each one of which followed its own precedents in definition and in method of collection. Data reproduced in the tables in this paper have been selected to be as accurate and as comparable as possible; nonetheless they must be used with some caution and should be considered to be guides to conditions rather than accurate representations of conditions.

Appendix II

PROGRESS OF TECHNICAL EDUCATION IN INDIA, 1901-1921.

A. Technical and Industrial Schools and Students in India, 1896-1907

Province	1896-97		1901-02		1906-07	
	Schools	Students	Schools	Students	Schools	Students
Madras	4	137	12	406	14	290
Bombay	16	1,223	19	1,829	31	2,030
Bengal	23	623	26	756	52	1,275
U. P.	2	296	9	736	11	782
Punjab	7	759	7	962	19	1,639
Burma	—	—	4	83	3	193
E. Bengal & Assam	2	16	1	1	12	475
C. P.	3	47	6	204	5	136
Total	57	3,101	84	4,977	147	6,820

Source: *Progress of Education in India, 1902-07*, 2 Vols. (Calcutta: Government Printing, 1909), Vol. II, p. 127.

B. Pupils Enrolled in Schools of Art (including Industrial Art) in India, 1896-1907

School	1896-97	1901-02	1906-07
Madras	633	321	455
Bombay	228	423	366
Calcutta	261	228	252
Lahore	179	248	301
Total	1,301	1,220	1,374

Source: *Progress of Education in India, 1902-07*, Vol. II, p. 128

C. Government Medical Colleges, Enrollments, 1902-07

School	1902	1907
Madras	121	195
Bombay	569	679
Calcutta	595	425
Lahore	181	243
Total	1,466	1,542

Source: *Progress of Education in India, 1902-07*, Vol. II, p. 125

D. Government Engineering Colleges, Enrollments, 1906-07

Madras	263
Poona	143
Sibpur	342
Thomason	495
Total	1,243

Source: *Progress of Education in India, 1902-07*, Vol. II, p. 126.

E. Engineering and Survey Schools, Enrollments

Province	1897	1902	1907
Madras	21	20	—
Bombay	20	14	16
Bengal	194	128	171
Punjab	17	54	198
Burma	16	27	63
E. Bengal & Assam	—	140	304
Central Prov.	30	33	24
Total	298	416	776

Source: *Progress of Education in India, 1902-07* Vol. I, pp. 173.

F. Veterinary Education, British India, 1902-07

Province	Total Number of Graduates, 1902-07	Number of Students Enrolled, 1906-07
Punjab	209	259
Bombay	59	111
Bengal	65	104
Madras°	29	90

°The School in Madras was opened in 1905.
Source: *Progress of Education in India, 1902-07*, Vol. I, p. 188.

G. Results of Examinations for University Degrees, 1912-13

Degree	Number of Examinees	Number Passed
B. A.	5,160	2,954
B. S.	601	368
M. B.	45	25
B. C. E.	34	16
L. C. E.	115	86
Lic. Agric.	78	54

Source: East India. *Statement Exhibiting the Moral & Material Progress and Condition of India, 1913-14* (London: H.M.S.O., 1915), p. 95.

H. *Enrollments in Schools and Colleges, 1908-09 and 1912-13*

Category	1908-09	1912-13
Arts Colleges		
English language	18,418	32,112
Oriental studies	868	1,419
Professional Colleges:		
Medicine	1,498	1,461
Engineering	1,177	1,216
Agriculture	255	284
Veterinary	——	181
Public high schools	329,559	448,682

Source: *Moral & Material Progress . . . of India, 1913-14*, p. 95.

I. *Technical and Industrial Education in India, 1916-17*

Type of School	Number of Students
Engineering colleges	1,319
Schools of art	1,695
Engineering & survey schools	874
Technical and industrial schools	10,037
Total	13,925

Source: Indian Industrial Commission, *Report, 1916-18*, p. 258.

J. *Enrollments in Government Medical Colleges*

Institution*	1916-17	1921-22
Madras	278	426
Bombay	727	1,161
Calcutta	906	1,030
Lucknow	136	174
Lahore	232	439
Total	2,279	3,230

*In addition there were three aided colleges. Belgachia in Calcutta had 554 students in 1921-22; Tibbia College, Delhi, had 199, and Lady Hardinge in Delhi had 82.

Source: *Progress of Education in India, 1917-1922*, Vol. II (Calcutta: Government Printing Office, 1924), p. 143.

K. Technical and Industrial Schools in British India

Province	1901-02		1906-07		1911-12		1916-17		1921-22	
	Schools	Students	Schools	Students	Schools	Students	Schools	Students	Schools	Students
Madras	12	406	14	290	44	2,121	40	1,961	41	2,039
Bombay	19	1,829	31	2,030	31	2,267	26	1,798	31	1,829
Bengal	26	756	52	1,275	50	1,862	59	2,035	86	3,631
U. P.	9	736	11	782	35	1,671	28	1,478	37	1,780
Burma	4	83	3	193	3	231	4	252	3	116
Punjab	7	962	19	1,639	30	2,614	33	2,991	25	2,399
Bihar	—	—	—	—	37	966	38	1,316	32	1,543
C. P.	6	204	5	136	7	289	9	350	7	298
Assam	1	1	12	475	5	43	7	71	12	170
Other	—	—	—	—	—	—	7	454	2	277
Total	84	4,977	147	6,820	242	12,064	251	12,706	276	14,082

Source: *Progress of Education . . . 1917-22*, II, 147.

L. Enrollment in Government Agricultural Colleges°

Province	1916-17	1921-22
Madras	77	100
Bombay	108	200
U. P.	88	103
Punjab	113	150
Bihar	—	53
C. P.	59	52
Total	445	658

°One other Government research institute and college did not report its enrollments in the above table.

Source: *Progress of Education . . . 1917-22*, II, 146.

M. Enrollment in Government Engineering Colleges and Schools

Institution	1916-17	1921-22
Madras Engineering College	511	449
School of Engineering, Madras	—	146
Poona Engineering College	220	194
Bengal Engineering College	284	356
School of Engineering, Bengal	118	375
Rurki Engineering College	304	237
Punjab School of Engineering	99	103
Burma School of Engineering	74	59
Bihar School of Engineering	166	153
Nagpur School of Engineering	39	82
Total	1,815	2,154

Source: *Progress of Education . . . 1917-22*, II, 145.

Appendix III
PROGRESS OF TECHNICAL AND SCIENTIFIC EDUCATION
IN INDIA, 1921 AND AFTER

A. Enrollment in Medical Colleges, 1926-27

Institution*	Number of Students
Madras	586
Bombay	518
Calcutta	939
School of Tropical Medicine	79
Lucknow	(closed)
Lahore	488
Bihar	154
Total	2,764

*This report gives no data on the aided-institutions such as Lady Hardinge College in Delhi.
Source: *Progress of Education in India, 1922-27*, Vol. II (Calcutta: Government of India, 1929).

B. Technical and Industrial Schools, 1926-27

Province	Institutions	Students
Madras	63	4,307
Bombay	33	2,878
Bengal	153	6,234
United Provinces	111	3,941
Punjab	24	3,535
Burma	2	167
Bihar & Orissa	43	2,462
Central Provinces	2	101
Assam	15	476
Coorg	1	10
Other	3	426
All India	450	24,537

Source: *Progress of Education . . . 1922-27*, II, 198.

C. Enrollment in Agricultural Colleges, 1926-27

Province	Students
Madras	82
Bombay	201
United Provinces	147
Punjab	186
Burma	46
Bihar	(closed)
Central Provinces	109
Total	771

Source: *Progress of Education . . . 1922-27*, II, 197.

D. Students in Engineering Colleges, 1926-27

Institution	Students	Institution	Students
Madras Engineering College	183	Roorki Engineering College	198
Madras Engineering Schools	162	Punjab Engineering School	129
Poona Engineering College	184	Burma Engineering School	251
Bengal Engineering College	291	Bihar Engineering School	167
Engineering School, Bengal	518	Nagpur Engineering School	160
		Total	2,713

Source: *Progress of Education . . . 1922-27,* II, 196.

E. Medical Schools, 1926-27

Province	Institutions	Students	Province	Institutions	Students
Madras	7	881	Burma	1	96
Bombay	4	441	Bihar	2	387
Bengal	10	2,282	C. P.	1	247
U. P.	2	351	Other	1	296
Punjab	4	772	Total	32	5,753

Source: *Progress of Education . . . 1922-27,* II, 195.

F. Schools of Art, 1891-1922

Year	Number of Schools	Number of Pupils
1891-92	6	1,048
1896-97	6	1,398
1901-02	7	1,399
1906-07	10	1,664
1911-12	8	1,602
1916-17	9	1,695
1921-22	8	1,332

Source: *Progress of Education . . . 1917-22,* II, 150.

G. Enrollments in Recognized Institutions, 1933-1936

Type of Institution	1933°	1934†	1935‡	1936§
Universities	10,041	10,762	11,003	11,311
Arts colleges	75,329	78,669	81,307	83,864
Professional colleges°°	18,391	18,917	19,498	20,049
High schools	978,702	1,007,544	1,043,897	1,081,791

°*Education in India in 1932-33,* p. 5.
†*Education in India in 1933-34,* p. 5.
‡*Education in India in 1934-35,* p. 6.
§*Education in India in 1935-36,* p. 6.
°°Enrollments under this category were in law schools, medical colleges, and engineering colleges. The largest single number of students was enrolled in the law schools.

CHAPTER 10

EDUCATION AND AGRICULTURAL GROWTH: The Role of Education in Early-Stage Agriculture

Clifton R. Wharton, Jr. *

I. INTRODUCTION

The basic questions to be discussed in this chapter are:

1. What is the role of education in agricultural growth? That is, does education play a positive role in bringing about agricultural growth in the early stages of development?

2. If education does have a role, in what fashion is the role performed? That is, how does education make a contribution to agricultural growth?

At the outset, certain definitions are necessary. I shall use the term *education* in its broadest sense as a perceived experience which leads to a change in future behavior patterns — both external behavior patterns such as physical action, and internal behavior patterns such as cognition, reflection, and other mental processes. Education is a process whereby new knowledge is transmitted or acquired by man. (For simplicity of exposition I will omit "invention.") But the new knowledge must be perceived and it must alter future behavior patterns. Economic growth depends to a large extent upon alterations in human behavior patterns because man is the primary catalyst in the productive process through his managerial ability, and he is also a key factor of production through his physical labor. Education or the learning process involves a change in human behavior and is therefore crucial to economic growth, both from the individual and the aggregate standpoint. This is especially true in the case of agriculture.

Some of the knowledge which man acquires through the educational process is useful only to the individual in a personal sense; *e.g.*, learning how to play golf or how to use chopsticks or how to prepare curry. The kind of knowledge with which we are concerned in the present paper is that knowledge which has special significance for the process of economic growth and economic development. One might perhaps call this "economically-useful-knowledge." I will call it *developmental knowledge* and the process

Author's Note: My greatest intellectual debts are to Professor T. W. Schultz and Dr. A. T. Mosher whose thinking preceded and stimulated me, but they are in no way responsible for any failures in the present effort because I did not learn sufficiently from them.

developmental education, to emphasize the role which such knowledge and education play in the development process. Thus, *developmental education* is one sub-set of *general education.* Making a clear and valid distinction between developmental education and non-developmental education is extremely difficult.

Another subset of general education might best be termed *basic education.* Certain kinds of knowledge, when transmitted and acquired, facilitate or improve the transmission of further knowledge. The traditional three R's — reading, writing, and arithmetic — readily come to mind. Since education inevitably involves a communicational process of either seeing or hearing, any new knowledge or skill which increases the efficiency of transmission is an indirect but important contributor to subsequent education. These skills are somewhat like the economist's category of social overhead capital (roads, bridges, dams, etc.); they are the individual's social overhead capital or infrastructure which make their greatest contribution to increased output or productivity in an indirect fashion. As a rule most of the education given at the primary level can be considered "basic" in the infrastructure sense. Literacy (or effective literacy) is the first important unit in the development of infrastructure.

I must emphasize that while the basic or infrastructure skills up to some specified level are sufficient conditions for developmental education, there is no *a priori* reason to think them necessary conditions. Developmental education can take place even though the recipients of the new knowledge are illiterate; this is true despite the fact that it is undoubtedly easier to teach a literate person. Intuition would also indicate that at any stage of development there is some point of diminishing marginal returns to the increased acquisition of these skills — again, as viewed from the standpoint of developmental education and the goal of economic growth. At any particular stage of development, increased acquisition of these skills cannot be indefinitely extended without running into zero marginal returns. The level at which this occurs is itself a function of development.

There are differing time horizons involved in the contribution of respective kinds of human knowledge. Some developmental knowledge makes its contribution in a rather immediate fashion. For example, knowledge of a better planting depth for rice which will increase yields per acre by 5 per cent has an immediate, visible impact, once it is adopted by the farmers. Other developmental knowledge has a slower impact. For example, it is much more difficult to convince a semi-subsistence farmer of the virtues of a new soil conservation program because its effect is frequently distributed gradually through time, with its greatest benefits for future yields, and it is always measured against a hypothetical standard of "what might have been." Similarly, knowledge of a new plant variety may be readily diffused throughout a group but adoption may lag considerably.[1]

1. For an excellent example, see the studies of Zvi Griliches on hybrid corn in *Science*, 132 (July 1960) and *Econometrica*, 25 (October 1957).

The fundamental question to be explored here is whether certain kinds of education contribute most appropriately to agricultural growth in the early stages of economic development. The importance of this question arises from the fact that it seems unlikely that many low-income countries will be able to meet their stated goal of universal free primary education in the near future. The relationship between the cost of providing free primary education for all and the other competitive developmental goals has recently been subjected to critical review in connection with the "Karachi Plan."[2] Given the undiminished population upsurge in such countries, the pressure upon governmental resources to meet the needs of education assumes alarming proportions.

Types and Levels of Education Relevant for Agriculture

There are two major types of education—formal or deliberate and informal or nondeliberate. Each of these in turn has its major subdivisions grouped according to institutional medium, level or content of instruction, method of instruction, and characteristics of recipients. Formal or deliberate education includes primary and secondary schooling (plus vocational or technical training); college and university (diploma, undergraduate, graduate); adult education, and extension education, community development, etc. Informal or nondeliberate includes personal experience, social contacts and family, neighbors, business firms (salesmen, advertising), radio, movies, newspapers, and other communication/diffusion media.

The category with which I am concerned in the present paper is the formal or deliberate. I am particularly concerned with that component of education which I have called developmental education, the transmission of knowledge which is useful in the process of economic growth and development.

There are four levels or areas in which general education and developmental education can be considered to affect agricultural progress.

First, the education of *farmers.* By farmers I mean those persons who work the land to grow crops, including owner-operators, tenants, laborers, and unpaid family workers.

Second, the education of *those serving farmers directly:* such people as extension agents, district agricultural officers, community development experts, and so forth.

Third, the education of *those serving farmers indirectly:* businessmen who buy and sell goods produced or used by farmers, manufacturers who produce items used by farmers in production, etc.

Fourth, the education of *those who are leading the farmers and/or who are making policies which affect farmers.* In the latter category of course, there are times when those who are the leaders of farmers are not necessarily those who are making the policies affecting the farmers.

2. UNESCO, *Report of Meeting of Ministers of Education of Asian Member States Participating in the Karachi Plan,* Tokyo, April 2-11, 1962 (Bangkok: UNESCO, 1962), especially Annex IIIA.

Throughout the following discussion my primary focus will be on the ultimate effect of developmental education upon farmers, the producers of the agricultural commodities. The farmers are the starting point in the productive process. In the case of the second, third, and fourth categories, the emphasis will not concern the role of education in improving them or their personal lot, but rather how education through them affects the farmer.

Education and Man as the Catalyst in Agricultural Production

Man is the central catalyst in the process of agricultural production, perhaps more than in any other type of economic activity. It is man who manipulates plants and animals to provide the food and fibres which he requires. It is man who is the decision-maker in the productive process: what and when to plant, how to plant, in what kind of soil to plant, how to cultivate the growing plant and how to protect it against pests and diseases, and when to harvest. It is man who is the operator in the process; he provides the labor to carry out the decisions by tilling the soil, planting, weeding, etc. Hence, man and his economic behavior are the central starting points in any discussion of agricultural growth.

Attitudes toward wealth, work, thrift, or profits will affect human economic behavior. The political, social, and economic institutions created by man also affect human economic behavior. Other forces and factors are the givens of nature and the limits imposed by current technical knowledge. But man is the prime actor. Consequently, the crucial role of education for agricultural growth is the effect it ultimately has upon the *economizing behavior* of the farmer and upon the *economizing setting* in which he operates. It is the economizing behavior of the large aggregate of farmers which in the final analysis makes for economic growth or stagnation of agriculture; and it is the economizing setting (institutional and cultural) in which he operates that controls the limits of his economizing behavior.

The term *economizing* involves a deliberate distinction between economics as a substantive activity and economics as a logic or system of rules. I would stress that the *substance* of economics concerns the actual ways in which man acts, organizes, and undertakes economic activity in pursuit of his economic goals; whereas the *logic* of economics provides the rules or techniques by which man can most efficiently act, organize, and undertake economic activity in the pursuit of an economizing objective. The rules of economization apply regardless of size or form of organization; they apply whether or not the economic activity is undertaken by an individual alone, by a family group, or by some larger social grouping.

Perfect execution of the logic of economics could be termed optimum economization, but the pattern of actual economic activity in the real world and the degree to which economization approaches the optimum vary considerably. Various economies or sub-sectors of economies in the real world display varying degrees of divergence from this optimum. The causes of divergence are many. The most important one of course is differing levels of technological knowledge. When dealing with agriculture, especially agriculture of the family-farm type, one is faced with the fact that the managerial skill of each farmer constitutes his "state of the arts" or his technology. His level of knowledge in a very fundamental sense determines the production function. Two farmers given identical resources in all respects but endowed with differing levels of technological knowledge will operate along different production functions. There are a number of other causes which might be mentioned: different social values and preferences regarding forms of social and economic organization; different attitudes regarding life on earth, such as the rule of man vs. the rule of God; different degrees of rationality, a-rationality, and irrationality; and different degrees of closeness to minimum levels of subsistence living. All of these can lead to different actual levels of economization even though the rules still apply. Adherence to values which conflict with the economization rules for growth leads to a loss of agricultural output. This judgment of "loss" is viewed solely from the standpoint of optimizing rules of behavior against the goal of economic growth.

Thus, the divergence between the actual levels of economization and the optimum levels, as determined by the logic of economics, provides a crude measure of the exploitable gap for achieving more rapid rates of growth. Given the goal of economic growth, the major role of education is its ultimate effect upon the economizing behavior of individual farmers and their economizing setting, because actual and potential levels of aggregate economization in turn affect rates of economic growth.

II. THE FARMER

General Education

Education pushes back cultural limits or prohibitions; it widens the scope for decision-making, because it broadens the individual's notions of the "possible"; it adds new tastes and stimulates motivation; it very often induces frustration which usually leads to heightened personal and political activity with important economic consequences; it enables the individual to engage in the general process of improved rationality, or thinking through the problems which he faces and no merely accepting them as unchangeable "givens."

Education increases the farmer's inquisitiveness, which heightens the likelihood of self-discovery of new knowledge concerning the operation of his own farm with its unique bundle of resources. It is no accident that in agriculture in the early stages, the majority of new inventions and innovations have come from farmers themselves. Given the physical and climatic heterogeneity which is so characteristic of agriculture, self-discovery is an important ingredient necessary for agricultural growth.

Education in its broadest sense influences the choice of values or the goals which the individual has, and thereby the activities which he carries out toward those goals. If education is not exclusively an ethnocentric propagation of inherited values within a given culture stream, then to that extent the individual has been exposed to other value systems. My basic point is that the man or farmer who is exposed to value systems other than his own is more likely to question certain aspects of his own value system which are in conflict with his desired goal of economic growth, provided he has one. Although his particular culture system may not have a strong work ethic or materialistic goal of accumulation of personal wealth and capital, if he is exposed to one which does, this may cause a change in his adherence to his inherited value system.[3]

Perhaps most important, education provides a wider boundary of freedom; that is, a knowledge of alternatives has been made a conscious ingredient in the farmer's thought processes. To be sure, a farmer who has only one way, or who knows only one way, to grow corn (which has been followed for generation after generation) can be provided via extension education with a possible alternative crop, so that his freedom of choice regarding method or technique will be widened. Education is even more broadening in the sense of individual freedom; it provides a greater awareness of a wider scope for individual decision-making in all aspects of one's life.

One of the difficulties connected with evaluating the economic growth impact of general education upon farmers is the difficulty of measurement. Number of years of school completed is an extremely imperfect measure when one is working at the low end of the scale with very few years of schooling completed.[4] The same general comments apply to the distinction between literate and illiterate. Two countries or regions may have the same percentage of literacy, but the average number of years of schooling completed or the level of functional literacy may be substantially different. Where education is via extension, measurement of the impact upon agricultural growth is somewhat easier, especially where the information or technical knowledge being imparted is limited to a few recommended practices. In such cases, it is pos-

3. I do not mean that a materialistic value system is a *sine qua non* for growth and development, or that perfect duplication (or transplanting) of another culture's values will result—or is good.

4. A number of years ago I conducted a study which typifies the problem of using any measure of years of schooling completed. In a detailed study of two farming areas in Minas Gerais, Brazil, I attempted to find some relationship between level of education and changes in output and technological efficiency over a five year period. The average number of years of formal schooling completed was 1.9 years in one area and 2.4 years in the other, with about half the farmers reporting. But there was no relationship between agricultural performance and education as measured by years of schooling completed.

See C. R. Wharton, Jr., "A Case Study of the Economic Impact of Technical Assistance" (unpublished Ph.D. dissertation, Department of Economics, University of Chicago, 1958), pp. 63-76.

A similar finding was made in an interesting study by G. K. Pierson. Pierson attempted to use Cobb-Douglas production functions to estimate the returns to education using data from 51 countries cross-sectionally. He used seven different measures of education ranging from number of literates in the labor force to number of school years in the labor force and calculated over 140 multiple regressions. His analysis failed to develop meaningful coefficients for education. However, expressing labor force school years in monetary terms in the United States studies on a state basis, did provide reasonable estimates.

See Gordon K. Pierson, "An Investigation of the Contribution of Education to Economic Growth" (unpublished Ph.D. dissertation, University of Washington, 1962).

sible to utilize measures of adoption in relation to indexes of performance and thereby secure some crude measure of the impact of new knowledge. (My Brazilian study referred to below used this approach.)

Although all the above broad virtues of general education for the developmental process are undoubtedly valid, their greatest weakness is that their effect is long-run in character. "Value exposure" can alter farmer's attitudes towards goals, but the changes are gradual.[5]

Although we have avoided the obvious distinction until now, one must necessarily distinguish between general education that is directed at the youth who will eventually become farmers and the general education that is directed at adult farmers.[6] Even if general education affects the values, attitudes, motivations, or decision-making of rural youth, there is a time lag before they become farmers capable of implementing these changes. Moreover, such new entrants into production will continue to be a small fraction of all farmers for some time; even though a "new breed" of farmers result from exposure to the effects of general education, the "old-style" farmers will continue in the majority for a considerable time. Even with adult education, there is a lag in farmer change. General education may very well enhance receptivity to new ideas or practices disseminated via extension, but greater receptivity does not take place overnight. A wider sense of individual freedom and greater control over one's own destiny may be an important seed planted by general education, but the plant takes a long time to germinate, reach maturity, and bear fruit. Hence, the developmental contribution from general education is at best a long-run one. The more important contribution of short-run immediate relevance is basic education, the transmission of what I have termed "infrastructure skills."

Basic Education and Literacy

Basic education given at the level of either the primary school or as adult education provides the individual farmer's infrastructure, as I pointed out above. The three major infrastructure skills (reading, writing, and arithmetic) make two contributions to agricultural growth. First, they facilitate or improve the transmission of further knowledge. Although in most countries primary education is not usually geared to the acquisition of skills which would be of themselves directly useful in the conduct of an individual farm enterprise, it does carry with it the elements which facilitate the process. For example, the illiterate farmer must be in his home or the community

5. Moreover, McClelland has pointed out that when only partial new value exposure occurs, achievement motivation is rarely affected, since "school experience is very minor as contrasted with the major shaping influences of the family" and general culture. McClelland's empirical data deals with Arab Children in Israel and Indian youth. David McClelland, *The Achieving Society* (New York: Van Nostrand, 1961), p. 415.

6. The content of "adult education" is therefore different from "extension education" even though both involve adults. This conceptual distinction is traditional. In low-income countries, "adult education" and "primary education" essentially transmit the same body of general knowledge and skill but to different age groups, since "adult education" in such countries rarely includes secondary school materials.

center at the specified time to hear the radio broadcast on how to apply fertilizer or when to sell his crop; but the time of the broadcast may not always coincide with his free time. The farmer who is able to read can learn these facts at his own convenience; he can read the bulletin or pamphlet when he chooses and re-read it as many times as he likes.

Second, these infrastructure skills are also directly useful in production. For example, the ability to keep records of one's farm operations and to make simple calculations in order to perform simple kinds of budgeting are extremely useful devices enabling a farmer to determine optimum factor combinations, to reduce costs, and to increase output.

Those who argue against the value of literacy as a contributor to economic and agricultural growth seem to do so on the following grounds. (a) Literacy is rarely relevant to the everyday life and needs of the people and is usually lost through disuse. (b) There are cheaper but equally efficient ways of transmitting useful developmental knowledge – posters, radio, movies, slides, demonstrations, etc. – which do not require the ability to read and write. The farmer can learn by hearing and by seeing just as well. (c) Reducing or eliminating illiteracy is an expensive proposition, even for the instruction of the most elementary skills, skills which all too often are lost by disuse. Why teach a man to read, to write, and to calculate when his village has no newspaper, his family all live in the same village, and he never writes letters and has no paper and pencil for doing sums?

I readily agree that eliminating illiteracy probably has a long-run effect upon economic growth. The cost issue is serious especially when treating a nation or region in the early stages of growth.[7] If one is dealing with a nation in the early stages of economic growth, then one is automatically also dealing with a country where literacy rates are low and where primary education facilities are very limited (see Table 1).

The cost problem of closing the gap between existing and required facilities for universal primary education is particularly acute in the case of the rural sector. Rural educational services invariably are behind those in urban areas; since rural peoples predominate in those nations in the early stages of economic growth, the handicap is especially acute. Nationwide averages tend to hide this internal imbalance in educational facilities.

Once the cost issue is overcome, there are additional rebuttals which can be made. (1) One of the greatest problems with literacy and limited primary schools years is loss of the basic skills through disuse. I have often wondered how much of this recidivism is due to the inappropriate nature of the teaching materials used with rural peoples. Although I have never under-

7. The fifteen Asian nations subscribing to the "Karachi Plan" estimated that in 1959 there were 87 million children in the region who did not enjoy any education facilities whatsoever, and that to a large fraction of the 65 million children going to school only a very limited amount of education was available. In order to meet the 1980 target of having 20 per cent of the total population in primary school, total primary school enrollment will have to rise from 62 million in 1960 to 237 in 1980. The estimated total cost of bringing this about is US$ 56.2 billion. See UNESCO, *The Needs of Asia in Primary Education* (Paris: UNESCO, 1961), Table 11, pp. 24-25.

TABLE 1

Number of Persons in Total Population Per Student in
Selected Countries of Southeast Asia°

Country	Type of School		
	Primary Schools	Secondary Schools	Vocational Schools
Cambodia	9	184	5,647
Indonesia	117	313	634
Laos	12	545	545
Malaya	6	54	626
Philippines	6	42	231
Thailand	6	45	242
Vietnam	11	86	1,643
Burma	13	62	12,127

° Computed from data in UNESCO, *International Yearbook of Education 1960*, Vol. XXII (Geneva: International Bureau of Education, Publication No. 224).

taken a systematic study of texts and materials used in primary schools in the rural areas of low-income, early-stage countries, the few texts which I have seen were sadly deficient in examples which reflect everyday rural life.[8] Dr. F. F. Hill has advanced a suggestion[9] to emulate the ideas of Dr. Liberty Hyde Bailey, who was responsible for introducing nature study in the primary schools of New York state as a device to encourage the useful habit of direct observation by rural youth. I would go a step further and say that while agriculture as an applied science cannot be taught at the primary level, the examples chosen for such things as simple sums and "worded problems" can be accurately presented in terms of the typical problems which rural youth and their fathers face in their everyday production and consumption.[10]

8. I am reminded of a recent survey of Sarawak school by the Education Adviser to the British High Commissioner for Southeast Asia. Not only did he find rural primary and secondary schools deficient in materials dealing with agriculture and rural life, he even found that none of the existing history texts made any reference to Sarawak and only brief mention of Southeast Asia.

9. F. F. Hill, "Key Issues for Policy Makers," *International Development Review*, Vol. IV, No. 4 (December 1962).

10. I will use two actual examples from a country which for obvious reasons I will not identify:

Example 1: "A milkman sold 28 gallons, 1 quart, 1 pint of milk in all. He sold 104 half pint bottles and all the rest in pint bottles. How many pint bottles did he sell?"

This problem comes from an actual textbook in a country where the rural people do not drink milk and where quarts and pints are not the conventional units of measure.

Example 2: "A nautical mile is 6080 feet. By how many feet is 9 nautical miles longer than 10 miles?"

You guessed it; the students asked to work this problem have never seen the ocean and probably do not know what a *mile*, much less a *nautical mile*, is.

How much better would it be for the examples to reflect the problems which they are likely to face and thereby show the students (whether youths or adults) the usefulness of such calculations for their everyday practical problems.

Example 1: Ismail charges M$3.50 a day to harvest rice. He harvests two acres a day. Rah-

I would argue for literacy programs on two other scores. (2) Provided that the skills required are sustained, literacy is the first step on the most important voyage of self-education or discovery. (3) One should not discount the effect which achieving literacy has on the individual. The typical peasant knows that he is illiterate, and it is a source of personal shame. The accomplishment of achieving literacy brings more than prestige or status. It brings with it a sense of personal accomplishment—the idea that he too is capable of perfecting himself through his own efforts and that he is not merely a lump of humanity spending a few tortured years of suffering on earth without hope of improving his lot and that of his children.

Developmental Education

There are two major avenues for formal developmental education of farmers: secondary vocational education (including diploma courses in agriculture) and extension education.

In low-income countries in the early stages, it will be some time before secondary vocational education becomes important for providing farmers with new skills and useful knowledge. The same is true for diploma courses in technical agriculture which provide instruction between the secondary and university level. Persons trained at these levels often serve the farmer and thereby contribute indirectly to agricultural growth (see below) but only a small number become actual farmers. The only exceptions are those who join large commercial farms—plantations, estates, land settlement schemes, etc. Very few graduates of a vocational or technical course at these levels return to farming on their own account; this phenomenon comes at a later stage in development.[11] Hence my remarks will be limited to extension education.

Extension education, community development, and related programs will continue for quite some time to bear the brunt of transmitting new developmental knowledge to farmers in low-income countries. Dr. A. T. Mosher's definition of extension education is the one with which I agree:

> The essence of . . . extension is that it is an out-of-school educational process:
> 1. working with rural people along those lines of their current interest and need which are closely related to gaining a livelihood, improving the physical level of living, and fostering community welfare; 2. utilizing particular teach-

---

man charges $2.80 a day to harvest rice, but only does 1½ acres a day. Which worker would you hire?

Example 2: To transport a load of wheat to market Town A five miles away cost $.10 per basket, and the price in the town is $2.20 per basket. To market it ten miles away in Town B is $.13 and the price is $2.25.

If a cart load of wheat holds 35 baskets, then how much is the cost of transporting the wheat to Town A? Town B?

How much would the load sell for in Town A? Town B?

In which one would you sell the load?

11. Thus, the percentages of 1959 graduates from secondary schools of agriculture entering farming in five Asian countries were: Burma 1 , Thailand 13, Ceylon 36, Taiwan 31, Japan 46.

See C. W. Chang, *The Present Status of Agricultural Education Development in Asia and the Far East* (Rome: F.A.O., 1961), p. 18.

ing techniques; 3. conducted with the aid of certain supporting activities; and 4. carried on within a distinctive spirit of cooperation and mutual respect.[12]

The present section will concentrate attention on the kinds of developmental knowledge that should be transmitted via extension education and that will contribute to agricultural growth in the early stages rather than discuss techniques of extension education.[13]

The two issues to be faced here are (a) what kind of developmental knowledge is most required during the early stages of agricultural growth? and (b) how much developmental knowledge is required by early-stage farmers?

Let us assume that there are no serious cultural, institutional, or technical impediments to individual short-run decision-making by farmers in low-income countries. Then, a farmer who wishes to change requires three major kinds of new developmental knowledge:

(1) *knowledge about new inputs* which are available and which will in fact produce favorable results: new seeds, varieties, breeds of animals, animal feeds, fertilizers, pesticides, sprays, farm implements and equipment (mobile and immobile). These are usually purchased inputs but need not be: some require only a single purchase with subsequent development left up to the farmer; others require sustained purchase in the future. In view of the high labor component in low-income agriculture, I would also include new knowledge about food inputs which will improve the nutritional level of the farm family and family labor force, as a preventive health measure; also health measures. These items may or may not, but usually do, involve new production techniques; they may or may not, but usually do, involve some cost.

(2) *knowledge about new techniques of production:* time and technique of planting (depth, elevation, watering; if irrigated, drainage and spacing); maturation and protection of crop or animal (weeding, spraying, fertilizing plus timing and rate of application); harvesting; culling, weaning, feeding and fattening, inoculation, general medication (spraying, dipping, vaccinating, pills); and crop rotation, cover, forage, soil conservation. These techniques may or may not involve purchase of new factor inputs and may or may not be costless.

(3) *knowledge about how to economize in production and marketing* (*i.e.*, the farmer's net return or maximum output for minimum cost).

12. A. T. Mosher, *Varieties of Extension Education and Community Development,* Comparative Extension Publication No. 2 (Ithaca: Cornell University, December 1958), p. 12. I agree completely with Dr. Mosher that, although there are admitted differences between extension education and community development (and within each), the fundamental essence of each is one of education. "Any discussion of this topic easily falls into a largely verbal wrangle because of the ambiguity of the term *extension* and the several common meanings of *community development.*"

13. The major techniques are: farm and home visits, method demonstrations, result demonstrations, local participation in program planning, tours, meetings, and exhibits. Mosher, *op. cit.,* pp. 14-15. To this I would add youth clubs since I firmly believe them to be an excellent technique to introduce new farming methods among rural youth.

In *production* he requires knowledge about how best to combine factor inputs, *i.e.*, the optimal combinations of factor input and, if a multi-product farm, the optimal combination of output mix. Of course, this is essentially a choice of level of output (one point on production surface) at which he has equated substitution in production with substitution in the market.

In *marketing*, the farmer needs knowledge about new or improved techniques of marketing such as when to sell, how to prepare for market (grading, quality control, processing, packing, storing, transporting), and how to secure accurate price information.

The farmer also needs knowledge of how to live with uncertainty in the short-run and long-run. In the short-run, for example, developments during the crop or animal maturation period may require numerous readjustments of factor inputs to protect his eventual net return. In the long-run, the farmer must secure a capital structure and asset distribution which enable him to insulate himself against risk and uncertainty: fluctuating yields due to weather or natural calamities, changing institutional settings, unexpected shifts in government policies, etc.

The first two are the technical aspects of farming; the third largely involve the economic aspects of farming. We often fail to realize that the successful farmer must be both a good technician and a good businessman. Developmental education involves the provision of knowledge involving both the technical and the economic. But by far the most difficult task facing the individual farmer is the last, the economic.

As soon as the farmer steps outside of the autarchic state of self-sufficiency, he is immediately faced with the very difficult task of economic decisions involving two comparisons:[14] (a) a comparison of costs and returns for any enterprise or combination of enterprises; and (b) an economic comparison among possible enterprises or combinations of enterprises. The rational calculus involved in both comparisons is far more difficult than is usually appreciated. The farmer must know the expected physical return (production) from a variety of alternative choices of product and techniques of production. He must know the expected costs of producing these various levels of output under these various technological conditions. He must be able to estimate with reasonable accuracy the future price which he is likely to obtain for each of the possibilities which he is considering.[15] Proficiency

14. Actually, even in a pure subsistence production unit economic decisions are involved even though market or exchange prices are not used.

See C. R. Wharton, Jr., "A Note on the Economic Meaning of Subsistence," *Malayan Economic Review*, Vol. VIII, No. 2 (October 1963).

15. I readily recognize that the above analysis only obtains where the farmer is able to exercise free choice; *i.e.*, that there are no cultural or institutional or technical obstacles to carrying out his decisions. An institutional imperfection such as repressive landlordism or compulsory sales leading to monopsony would of course prevent this. Similarly a perennial agriculture would impede rapid product mix changes.

See C. R. Wharton, Jr., "Marketing, Merchandizing, and Moneylending: A Note on Middleman Monopsony in Malaya," *Malayan Economic Review*, Vol. VII, No. 2 (October 1962) and my "The Inelasticity of Southeast Asian Agriculture: Problems of Monocultural Perennial Export

in manipulating these variables to arrive at a reasonably successful decision is no small accomplishment. It is one thing to raise a crop or an animal technically; it is another to do so economically.[16]

One of the current difficulties faced by extension education programs in low-income countries is that greatest attention has been given to the first two areas and the least to the third. Diffusing knowledge about new inputs is basically quite easy. Providing information about new techniques via demonstrations, exhibits, model farms, etc., is only slightly more difficult. Developmental education in the third area is a much more difficult process. Farm management research, provided it is successfully extended to farmers, plays a vital role in this area. As an element in extension, farm management is an attempt to provide the individual farmer with a generalized answer to the economic problems of decision-making which he faces concerning the choice of output level, output mix, inputs, etc. But it is a substitute, and the critical difficulty is that the individual farmer still needs to individualize even this summary information to meet his unique situation. Farms, their resources, their physical environment and their manager-operators are extremely heterogeneous. And the task of sound economic decision-making is a difficult one which rests on each farmer's skill at individualizing the information to meet his unique needs. The farmer must be able to determine (a) whether or not the new knowledge in the form presented is applicable to his situation (*i.e.*, can he make use of the new knowledge and will its introduction constitute an improvement over his present situation); and (b) if it is not applicable in its present form but requires modification, how can he alter, adapt, or change the new knowledge to suit his particular needs.

The two-fold individualization process is complex and difficult, one requiring a high level of competence of each farmer. This point is where I believe extension education has been deficient and where the educational process for agriculture in the early stages of growth has a stronger role to play. The skill and competence required for "individualization" is not one capable of simple transmission or diffusion but one which rests upon self-discovery, practice, and personal experience. Mastery of the ability to think through the economic calculus is, I believe, most closely linked to the level of education of the farmer using our original broad definition of education as a perceived experience. Economic efficiency in the individual sense and in the aggregate sense requires that the farmer be able to work the economic calculus of his farm himself. Providing the farmer with new inputs or new techniques may result in adoption but they need not result in economic utilization of resources. And it is the degree of economic efficiency in the

Dominance," presented to Agricultural Economics Society of Thailand, November 1, 1962 (mimeographed, December 15, 1962).

16. Many U.S. city dwellers grew "victory gardens" during World War II, but I wonder how many urbanites could grow such crops *economically* and have their family subsistence depend upon the success of their decisions.

utilization of resources which leads to sustained growth toward a modern, prosperous, and progressive agriculture.

III. THOSE SERVING THE FARMER —
DIRECTLY AND INDIRECTLY

There are two categories of persons serving farmers, those serving farmers directly and those serving farmers indirectly (the second and third of the areas named above). The former include extension agents, district agricultural officers, community development workers, multi-purpose village agents, etc. These persons will be called "direct servers." I would also include persons involved in the conduct of research at experiment stations, crop-testing stations, etc. (There is some question as to the category in which the rural teacher falls.) The second group are the business men who buy and sell the goods produced or used by farmers, the manufacturers who produce the tools, fertilizers, seeds, etc., used by farmers in production. This group will be called "indirect servers." Of the two categories, the group which is most likely to be affected by education and in turn affect the farmer's rate of growth is the "direct server" group.

The level of training and education required by direct servers is basically determined by the level of technical competence and economic skill of the farmers being served. If the average level of the farmers is low, the technician does not require as much subject-matter technical training as if the average level of the farmers is high. Although this statement sounds trite, it too frequently is forgotten. This proposition is true through time and cross-sectionally. For example, compare the level of technical and economic competence required by an extension agent in New York state in 1900 and today. It is not merely that we know more about agriculture today; some of the change is because the farmers know more,[17] and if the agent is to give useful assistance he needs to know more, though not necessarily on every subject. To the extent that each extension agent is successful in imparting new knowledge to the farmer, his successor must have a higher level of technical and economic knowledge to continue to serve the farmer. Cross-sectionally, one can observe this same phenomenon of agents' levels being closely linked with the farmers' levels. A rubber advisor visiting a five-acre smallholding certainly does not require the same technical and economic competence as one visiting a 10,000-acre estate; the same would be true for a county agent in Breathitt County in Kentucky compared with one in Salinas Valley, California. Let me stress that the issue is not one of the over-all competency and incompetency of direct servers. In fact, there are certain other important areas of competence required of direct servers in low-income countries which are higher than in an economically advanced nation; I am

---

17. Competitiveness for academic distinction among educational institutions and the need for certain uniform minimum standards have also caused the upgrading of levels through time.

thinking here of the problems of establishing rapport with the farm family and the very difficult task of winning their trust and confidence. But fundamentally the technical and economic training of direct servers is determined by the level of the farmers being served.[18]

During the early stages of agricultural growth, direct servers will come primarily from some type of secondary educational level. For example in the ECAFE region, most governmental field agents who are in direct contact with farmers have received at least secondary education, either vocational education with special reference to agriculture or a general secondary education supplemented by a special diploma course in agriculture.[19] The pattern of course varies from country to country.

Despite the variation in required levels or skills among countries in the early stages of economic growth, some general remarks are in order concerning the content of secondary education in rural areas and vocational education in agriculture.

Secondary Rural Schools

Secondary schools in rural areas in the early stages are not likely to educate many persons who will return to farming. (As development proceeds, of course, more and more rural youth with secondary education will enter farming.) The occupations which they enter after graduation may or may not be connected with agriculture. A few go on to higher education at a university. Some secure urban or commercial occupations with no direct relationship to agriculture or rural life as clerks, semiskilled industrial laborers, policemen, firemen, etc. Some remain in rural areas with occupations in the indirect server category as merchants, tradesmen, salesmen, etc. Others, however, do enter the direct server category.

A crucial problem facing rural secondary schools in the early stages of economic growth is the rate of rural-urban migration. The rural pool of labor which is a source of unskilled labor for the urban sector has had considerable discussion. The traditional view of rural-urban wage differentials which induce farm to city movement as an equilibrating mechanism has many versions. What sometimes tends to be forgotten is that rural-urban migration is also a selective process; rural youth with higher levels of education and skill join the migration. For the typical rural youth, educational success and the opportunity to secure higher education appear as an opportunity to escape from the farm, not an opportunity to secure knowledge which can be put to use on a farm.

Two questions arise out of this problem: (1) Are the low-income countries now in the early stages of economic growth likely to experience a similar pattern of rural-urban migration as was the case with the industri-

18. As I point out below, the biggest weakness with direct servers in low-income countries in the early stages of development is not necessarily the nature of the training which they are given but may be personal backgrounds which are non-agricultural.

19. C. W. Chang, *The Present Status of Agricultural Extension and Development in Asia and the Far East* (Rome: F.A.O., 1961), *passim*.

alized nations? (2) To what extent should the content of rural secondary education cater to the needs of rural youth who move to non-farm jobs in the cities (and correspondingly, to what extent should the education be geared to farming and rural occupations)?

There are good *a priori* reasons for questioning the validity of any historical analogy about rural-urban migration for certain countries in the early stages of economic growth. Migration to urban areas depends on the availability of employment opportunities fully as much as on rural-urban wage differentials. Most early-stage nations which are engaged in attempts at industrialization naturally wish to establish industries which make use of the latest, most advanced techniques. Since these techniques are very often capital intensive, industrialization tends to result in far fewer job opportunities than is expected. Moreover, the unskilled labor requirement of such capital intensive industries is low; this prevents the unskilled rural labor pool from affecting the general level of wages in urban areas, except in the unskilled categories. Skilled labor opportunities exist but can only serve marginally as a source of attraction for the unskilled rural labor which may be suffering from lack of full employment or low levels of income. Thus, while the average level of urban wages is higher than the average level of returns to farm labor, the impact of this differential in the urban areas is initially felt only in the unskilled labor categories. Given such a pattern of industrialization, increased employment opportunities for unskilled rural labor will rarely proceed as rapidly as would be expected nor would the related rates of rural-urban migration.[20]

In view of the probability in today's early-stage nations of somewhat slower rates of rural-urban migration, I would argue in favor of a higher content of agricultural or rural subjects in the curriculum of secondary schools in rural areas. The best students will naturally continue on to higher levels of education or migrate to urban areas to enter semiskilled occupations. But the vast majority of students in rural secondary schools will return to occupations either directly or indirectly related to agriculture. For these persons likely to enter occupations directly or indirectly involving agriculture, vocational agricultural schools will play an important part.

Vocational Agricultural Education[21]

Vocational agricultural schools are the major training institutions for direct servers. Graduates from these schools provide the bulk of farm experts

20. There is an obvious question: why are capital-intensive industries established in the face of the apparent labor-cost/capital-cost comparisons which would favor fewer capital-intensive industries. The equally obvious answer is: governmental policies regarding the pattern of industrialization rarely take account of this economic issue but are more readily based upon noneconomic considerations of prestige, status, etc. (The latter is especially true if the industry is government owned or operated by a semi-governmental agency.)

21. Years of schooling and admission requirements vary so much that nomenclature may be very misleading. For example, in some countries vocational schools come after only four to six years of schooling; in others, after ten years. In some the course lasts two years; in others, three to four years. Diploma courses in agriculture in some countries are given in "colleges of agricul-

who are in direct contact with farm people. Such schools are usually of secondary level with a trade, craft, or applied orientation. To a certain extent
they are a modern replacement for the old guild apprenticeship system
whereby youth "learned a trade."

Such vocational schools should not be considered as a device to train
better farmers, but to train those who will work with or serve farmers. There
is little question of the need for direct servers. For example, in 1959, the
number of rural people per extension agent in selected Southeast Asian
countries was a follows:[22]

	Number of Rural People per Extension Worker
Vietnam	115,800
Thailand	56,200
Malaya	13,000
Burma	12,500
Philippines	9,000

These ratios of farmers to direct servers have little meaning until one knows
how the farmers live (i.e., in nuclear villages or scattered with homesteads
on their respective farms), how far are the distances between the farmers
and/or villages, and how much work time direct servers spend in the office.
Each of these factors affects very substantially the actual amount of farmer
contact. Although any criterion such as one direct server per 5000 or 10,000
farm people is exceedingly arbitrary and highly misleading, there is little
question that present ratios should be much lower if more frequent contact
and growth stimulus are required.

There seem to be two problems plaguing vocational agricultural education of direct servers in countries in the early stage of economic growth.

First, the content of education is too frequently a pale carbon copy of a
university course in agriculture rather than a course to meet the unique and
legitimate needs of "direct-servers."

> The field of sub-university level training and education in agriculture
> presents unique opportunities, especially as regards courses of study and
> methods of teaching. In this area, problems of progressive agriculture and
> the farm job constitute the materials of instruction. The systematic scien-
> tific disciplines such as biology, chemistry, and physics become related
> information useful in illuminating the nature of farm operations and per-
> mitting the learner to generalize. Moves which will orient such courses

ture" but these may be a level above the secondary and below the university; or these diploma
courses in one country may actually be equivalent to a vocational school in another country. Therefore, I will use the term *vocational* to cover all such schools below the university level where
the primary focus is upon learning agriculture as an applied field.

22. These figures were computed by using population estimates for 1959 and 1960 from the
United Nations, *Demographic Yearbook;* the percentage of total population estimated to be rural
from the U.S. Department of Agriculture, *Notes on the Agricultural Economies of the Far East,*
"III Southeast Asia," (Washington: FAS, August 1960); and the total number of extension agents
estimated by C.W. Chang, *op. cit.,* Table II, "Status of Agricultural Extension."

in this direction are to be encouraged as an alternative to courses which train field workers merely by using 'watered-down' degree courses.[23]

In other words, the emphasis should be on farming; the scientific disciplines should come in as supplements to aid in understanding certain basic farming problems, rather than be required as separate studies in all their fullness. In the early stages of economic growth, such study would appear to be an unnecessary luxury. It would be preferable to begin with the more basic, restricted approach and use the latter, broader content as a goal toward which to move as development proceeds.

Second, the number of years considered desirable for vocational education may be greater than is realistically necessary for those working as direct servers in early stage agriculture. That is, vocational agricultural schools which imitate the current Western pattern may be requiring more years than are actually necessary, and the number of years could be reduced without reducing the effectiveness of the direct server's efficiency in working with farmers. As in the case of content, the number of requisite years can be increased as development proceeds.[24]

The general field of vocational agricultural education has been a particularly neglected field for low-income, early-stage agriculture and would profit considerably from research and experimentation.[25]

IV. THE LEADERS AND POLICY MAKERS

The leaders and policymakers for agriculture, the fourth area of concern, include not only the members of political parties involved in the legislative process (in a democratic nation) but also the top stratum of the government ministries, agencies, bureaus, etc. These persons affect farmers and agricultural growth in the early stages largely through the policies and programs which they formulate for agriculture. In fact, I have argued that political considerations, such as economic nationalism, will probably be the most important factors affecting the rates of agricultural growth in Southeast Asia in the immediate future.[26]

A serious factor is the nonagricultural background and training of the agricultural leadership. Very few of the leaders involved in agricultural policy making are specifically trained in agriculture, even though most do

23. Ralph H. Allee and C. R. Wharton, Jr., "Observations on Methods to Intensify Malayan Agricultural Diversification," memorandum submitted to National Development Planning Committee, Federation of Malaya, March 12, 1962, p. 7.

24. In both cases the early graduates who are still serving agriculture could easily return for refresher and in-service training to bring them up to date with the latest graduates.

25. The same point is valid for the development of vocational schools oriented toward rural handicrafts and certain semi-skilled manual and engineering skills required by small-scale rural industries.

26. C. R. Wharton, Jr., "Economic and Non-Economic Factors in the Agricultural Development of Southeast Asia: Some Research Priorities," *CECA Paper* (New York: Council on Economic and Cultural Affairs, 1962), p. 11. The name of this council has recently been changed; it is now the Agricultural Development Council.

have some form of advanced university education. Moreover, very few of them come from rural or agricultural backgrounds.

> Those countries with the most restricted educational base, *i.e.*, systems primarily serving urban areas, are exactly those countries whose greatest need is professionals with a thorough knowledge of national agriculture and its problems, and with a sincere understanding and appreciation of rural people. Yet these are exactly the countries where one is least likely to find a person with such qualities . . . Students from urban areas and without farm backgrounds are *not* automatically or inherently unsympathetic towards rural people and problems. Nor is an interest in these problems and a desire to be of service a universal characteristic or monopoly of farm youth. However, it must be recognized that finding urban youth who are interested and capable, and who also seek a career in agriculture is extremely difficult.[27]

University graduates are the persons primarily responsible for the formulation, implementation, and evaluation of five-year plans, development schemes, and national policies. They play both an advisory and an active role. The nonagricultural background and training of such experts can seriously affect the success of programs designed to foster more rapid agricultural growth. It has often hampered understanding, sympathy, and communication between the nonagricultural makers of agricultural policies and the rural people. Moreover, policies and programs formulated in capital cities are often based on misconceptions or inadequate information due to lack of familiarity with the basic facts of agriculture. The lack of agricultural training among agricultural leaders and policymakers is of course a temporary phenomenon until graduates from colleges and faculties of agriculture move into these key positions.

Faculties and Colleges of Agriculture

Persons specifically trained in agriculture at faculties and colleges of agriculture are most likely to secure occupations involving agriculture. Therefore, the nature of the instruction given in faculties of agriculture is of special importance for early-stage development. A number of difficulties beset the undergraduate training of agriculturists in early-stage agriculture.

First, if the country is small or poor, either there are no faculties or colleges of agriculture or those which do exist are deficient in equipment, staff, etc. Foreign training under those circumstances is therefore unavoidable, with all the added problems which this creates. There are a number of problems connected with the study of agriculture and related disciplines overseas. Since I have covered a number of these elsewhere,[28] I will restrict my remarks to a few which are especially applicable for early-stage agriculture

27. Wharton, *The U.S. Graduate Training of Asian Agricultural Economists* (New York: Council on Economic and Cultural Affairs, 1959), p. 34.

28. *Ibid.* Among the problems mentioned are: screening and selection, ignorance of problems to be faced, financing, choice of school, language, philosophy and motivation, orientation, adjustment to teaching methods and courses, field contacts, dissertation, employment and professional adjustment upon return.

and for the problem of maximizing the economic efficiency of early-stage farmers. Foreign training is frequently in temperate zones and involves temperate-zone agriculture, whereas the majority of the nations in early stages of agricultural growth are in tropical or subtropical regions. Therefore, much of what is learned has little if any applicability to conditions at home. The costs of foreign training are very high and, unless an individual can receive outside support, only the more affluent can afford to go. The foreign student abroad is usually in the minority compared with other students, and professors must give first priority to their own nationals. Moreover, there is the perennial problem of what I have termed the "underdeveloped Master's" and the "oriental Ph.D." Fortunately foreign training is recognized as a temporary arrangement until local facilities are sufficiently developed to meet local requirements. Even after local requirements are met, however, foreign training will continue to be necessary, especially for university lecturers, teachers, professors—if only to widen their contacts and perspectives.[29]

Second, even where local facilities for training exist, numerous problems plague the training of agriculturists. Once again the most serious difficulty is that the students come from predominantly urban backgrounds.[30] In fact, many have not chosen agriculture deliberately but by default, because they were unsuccessful in attempting to enter medicine, law, etc. Agriculture is a low-prestige field and therefore rarely attracts the best; the derogatory stereotype of the peasant farmer can too easily rub off on the agricultural graduate. The nonagricultural background of the agriculture students presents a unique challenge. The successful role of graduates from agricultural colleges in the United States, England, Australia, New Zealand, etc., in serving agriculture and promoting agricultural growth has often been ascribed to the agricultural college. At the risk of overstressing my case, I would argue that we too often forget that a large measure of the success of our American "cow colleges" was due to the fact that its students were farm boys. When they entered as freshmen they already brought with them to the land-grant colleges a wealth of experience in practical agriculture. What the agricultural college did was to teach them to "think about farming."[31]

29. Despite the great urge for foreign advanced training in many early-stage countries, there is an interesting paradox in this respect when *senior* professionals are involved. It is not unusual to find a strong reluctance on the part of senior academicians in early-stage nations to visit or to study in more advanced nations. The reasons given are couched in terms of the biased "Western" views of foreign educational institutions and the inapplicability of their approaches to the problems of low-income early-stage nations, whereas the real reason is very frequently fears of their own inadequacies and deficient training. This phenomenon is particularly noticeable where there are only a few trained professionals in the country, and it promptly disappears after several foreign-trained local persons return.

30. For example, Kasetsart University, which is the major agricultural university in Thailand, in a study of 51 third year students found that 36 of them (71 per cent) had never engaged in agriculture in any way. Arb Nakajud, *A Study of Students' Backgrounds in Relation to Their Agricultural Experience*, (Bangkok: Department of Agricultural Economics, Kasetsart University, 1961), p. 8.

31. "The proper role of the agricultural college is to help men to learn to *think* about farming.

Current builders of agricultural colleges in low-income countries or early-stage countries seem to have forgotten this important fact and have therefore blindly re-created institutions with only token adaptations and adjustments.

I firmly believe that such crude imitation fails to realize the important differences in the "product" passing through the classrooms. Agricultural undergraduates in advanced nations usually come from farms. Providing them with knowledge about the sciences dealing with soils, plant life, and animal life is useful because they can relate the knowledge to their own farming experience. Scientific education about the chemical, biological, and physical aspects of farming can be assimilated because such knowledge can be related to personal, practical experience of farming. Agricultural undergraduates in low-income, early-stage nations do not have the same agricultural backgrounds and experience upon which to build. Providing them with the separate scientific parts of agriculture does not necessarily give them the tools or the capacity to understand the relationship of such knowledge to practical farming. The implication is obvious: far more attention and time should be given to the practical aspects of farming for the nonagricultural undergraduates in colleges and faculties of agriculture in early-stage countries. Once the general educational system has become sufficiently broadened to channel talented farm youth up into colleges of agriculture, the problem should disappear. Meanwhile, techniques must be developed to handle much more effectively the non-farm agricultural undergraduates.

Third, another serious issue arising from unadaptive imitativeness of foreign institutions is related to the financial resources of such countries. Very few countries in the early stages of development can afford the large staff and facilities which are characteristic of similar faculties in advanced nations; yet these nations are determined to have the very best and to "do it up" in similar style. Academicians who go abroad and study in a faculty of agriculture of 100 persons and then return to a faculty of agriculture of 20 or 25 and try to imitate the 100-man faculty face a number of obvious problems. The most serious difficulty in the present context is that the local syllabus frequently tends to be an imitation of the one in an advanced nation, and the number of courses and course hours tend to be the same but without the same size staff. The returnee tends to be specialized and wishes to teach only one or two courses in the fields in which he concentrated and in which he feels specifically qualified; but given the limited resources of the home institution it might be necessary for him to teach five or seven courses. Or, for example, instead of teaching an introduction to agricultural economics, it may be necessary to teach an introduction to the rural social sciences, yet

This involves helping them to *understand* the physical, social, economic, and spiritual realities on which the lives of farmers and their families are based. It involves helping them learn to *analyze* farming and rural life . . . It involves helping them *master the known techniques whereby unsolved problems may be tackled* while awakening them to the need for the creation of new techniques which are necessary if we are to think more deeply about certain phases of farming." A. T. Mosher, *Learning To Think About Farming*, CECA Reprint (New York: Council on Economic and Cultural Affairs, 1961), p. 1.

he does not feel qualified or justified in violating the existing order which imitates the "mother" country or university. The only alternative is to reorganize the syllabus or curriculum.[32]

There are a number of other problems which have been slighted: limited size of well-trained staff; the ever-increasing demands for more and more graduates and the consequent strain on standards; professional isolation of the teaching staff from their international colleagues (sometimes even their local colleagues); inadequate finances, especially for research; the subtle, and sometimes not so subtle, strictures imposed upon academicians who engage in research dealing with sensitive subjects; lack of teaching materials suitable for local conditions and problems; low salary levels which sometimes cause *de facto* part-time work and multiple job-holding by academicians. The most important omission is teacher training and teacher education. Any one of these topics would require a separate paper.

Post-Graduate or Graduate Training[33]

The personnel requirements for agricultural growth also include the more highly trained technicians and professionals with master's and doctor's degrees. Even in the early stages, such persons are needed because of their important role in research, planning, and policy.

One issue is numbers: how many are needed? Several persons in the past have disagreed with my estimate of the numbers needed. However, I must confess that my views are biased by the number of "foreign experts" who are demanded by such countries and are serving in them. Many of these experts have graduate training and they are sent by the well-known alphabet soup of international, governmental, and private agencies. In a typical Southeast Asian country, one can find experts from UNTAB, FAO, ILO, UNESCO, WHO, USAID, USIS, Asia Foundation, Colombo Plan, SEATO, Ford Foundation, Rockefeller Foundation, ADC, and so on. A large proportion of these experts have advanced degrees (plus experience), yet the myth persists that an early-stage country does not need to develop its own graduate professionals. If the early-stage nations are able to call upon and make use of so many foreigners with graduate training and skills, then why is it that similarly trained local persons are not required?

There is an interesting conceptual difference between American and British notions of graduate studies which is relevant in this context. The British, and I daresay the French, view the graduate degree-holder as essentially an academician (possibly an ivory-tower theoretician) and as a member of a very exclusive elite. The American, however, views advanced degrees

32. For an excellent example of a proposed revision specifically for agricultural economics, see A. T. Mosher, "Education, Research, and Extension in Agricultural Economics in Asia and Latin America Today," *10th International Conference of Agricultural Economists*, August 1958 (London: Oxford University Press, 1960).

33. Terminology differs between countries with respect to education beyond the BA and BS degrees. Some refer to advanced training as "postgraduate" and others as "graduate"; I will use the latter terminology.

both as an academician's and a "working-man's" degree, meaning merely that the person has achieved a higher level of proficiency in the tools of his profession, not that he has entered a very elite circle of initiates. This attitude may well account for the different views in low-income, early-stage nations concerning the role which such persons can play in the development process.[34]

In the early stages, graduate training is usually secured abroad. Foreign graduate study is subject to the same difficulties as foreign undergraduate study: high cost, inapplicable and unfamiliar subject matter, differing problems and emphases, etc. During the early stages a nation does not require a very large number of graduate level professionals, yet an adequate local graduate program requires a certain minimum student body and faculty. Given the probable delay before early-stage countries will be able to develop full-scale graduate programs, some attention should be given to the possibility of developing a few regional, international centers where adequate facilities can be developed. Regional centers are also required to reduce the strain upon the educational facilities in the more advanced nations, which will be unable to meet the full needs of low-income nations with existing resources. Such a proposal faces a number of obstacles, but the sooner that graduate instruction is provided within early-stage countries, the more rapidly will these nations benefit from research conducted by their own nations, whose intuitive insights often lead to new knowledge beyond the scope of the best trained foreign expert.

V. SOME PARTING REMARKS

Agricultural growth is the result of individual changes on millions and millions of farms. Farming is a economic activity which involves knowledge on the part of the farmer, skill in applying his knowledge, the physical ability to execute this knowledge, and the will to apply the knowledge and carry on the activity. Growth occurs as the result of changes in each of these areas, changes which come largely through education or a "perceived experience which leads to a change in future behavior patterns." Thus, the fundamental problem of agricultural growth is an educational problem.

Although most of the empirical evidence which can be brought forward on the impact of education is for periods after take-off, limited evidence for early-stage agriculture indicates that education does play a role. The major contribution of education comes in its effect upon the economizing behavior and the economizing setting of farmers.

General education affects agricultural growth by changing values, atti-

34. For an interesting debate on this point see my article and the reply of Professor T. H. Silcock, "The Teaching of Economics in Southeast Asia," *Malayan Economic Review,* Vol. IV, No. 2, (October, 1959). Unfortunately, several persons viewed Professor Silcock's remarks as a perfect example of a colonialist's apologia for refusing to encourage or to allow local persons to secure advanced degrees.

tudes, and decision-making, but such effects are long run because of slowness in human change and the even slower changing composition of farmers. Basic education and literacy, with emphasis upon primary and adult education, have more immediate effect insofar as they add to a farmer's "infrastructure skills," because these improve the transmission of new knowledge and are often directly useful in production. Developmental education with primary focus upon extension education methods probably has the greatest role to play in the early stages. Three kinds of developmental knowledge are required: about new inputs, about new techniques of production, and about how to economize in production and marketing. Extension education should particularly concentrate on the third area because of the great need of farmers to "individualize" the developmental knowledge provided. The difficulties of individualizing the new knowledge of inputs and techniques is probably greatest in the economic realm, and extension materials should reflect a greater awareness of the farmer's lack of previous experience in using the economic calculus. Inability to apply the economic calculus is responsible in large measure for the gap between the logic of economics and the substance of economics as seen in actual agricultural performance. The gap is particularly noticeable among early-stage farmers who are just entering or are marginal to commercial agriculture. The knowledge deficiencies of farmers regarding the economic tasks of farming are as great impediments to rapid agricultural and economic growth as cultural and institutional factors are.

In closing, I wish to comment briefly on two broad questions of balance: the balance between human and non-human capital within agriculture, and the balance between rural and urban development in economic growth. Space limitations preclude discussion of the difficult problem of allocation decisions among the types of education for agriculture except as a few judgements on these matters have been introduced implicitly in the preceding pages.

Capital Balance: Human and Non-Human

The provision of new "developmental knowledge" to farmers must always be mindful of the general need to balance the introduction of human and non-human capital, especially in early-stage agriculture.

One of the most intriguing propositions advanced by Schultz is that of the implied limits to substitutability between human and non-human capital. Schultz' notion of balance and imbalance between human and non-human capital which can lead to growth or stagnation deserves fuller attention. A broadened formulation of the Schultz proposition might be as follows: Human capital and non-human capital are more complements than substitutes in production; there is undoubtedly some range of substitution between the two but the range is limited. In fact, I would argue that the range of substitution is itself a function of economic growth and widens as development proceeds. As development proceeds, non-human capital inputs, with and without technology included in them, become available. Similarly, human capital formation provides a wider range of choice of technologies given any non-human capital mix available. In a low-income country, which almost by definition means low human and non-human capital, the elasticity of substitution between human capital and non-human capital is close to zero. Thus, any additional input of non-human capital which is not accompanied by corresponding increases in human capital results in zero increase in output. That is, the marginal product of non-human capital is zero or close to zero as long as the level of human capital input is fixed.

This formulation helps to explain why providing new inputs and additional capital to semisubsistence and subsistence farmers rarely produces dramatic results. It also explains why a well-conceived and executed program of supervised credit does. The supervised credit formulation not only provides additional capital inputs, but also encourages the introduction of new practices (technology) plus planning in the use of the credit funds and in the total farm and home operation. Where such planning is done jointly by the farmer (or farm wife) and the technician, its effect is to raise the farmer's level of human capital (skill). Some have even gone so far as to say that the managerial skill of the technician is substituted for that of the farmer; however, I would prefer to view it as a joint process involving educating the farmer and giving him the opportunity to acquire a higher level of skill with a reduced degree of risk and uncertainty. Raising the level of human capital while simultaneously increasing the available factor inputs allows a higher

TABLE 2

Cost and Returns of Supervised Credit (Capital plus Technology) Program Curvelo, Minas Gerais, Brazil *

Proportion of Change in Output:	
Accounted for by change in input	44%
Not accounted for by change in input	56%
Value of total change in annual output per farm *not* accounted for by change in inputs	Cr$ 7,800
Average annual costs of assistance program per family	Cr$ 1,200
Return in increased output per Cr$ 1 of investment in new knowledge	Cr$ 6.5

Source: From Wharton, "A Case Study of Economic Impact," *op. cit.*, Appendix C. Tables C. 2, C. 3, C. 4, C. 5. All costs and returns are deflated and output/input figures are corrected ones.

* (a) Curvelo is a semisubsistence frontier area. (b) Loan funds for the program resulted in purchases of new factor inputs and are reflected by changes in the level of the input index. Changes in output not accounted for by changes in inputs have been ascribed to the new knowledge or practices (technology) which was introduced simultaneously with the loan via farm and home planning and extension education (farm visits) received by farmers during participation in the program.

level of output; viewed in a different fashion, the farmer is shifted to a higher production function.

Empirical evidence on this point is not lacking. A few years ago I conducted a five-year study of selected farmers in Brazil who participated in a supervised credit program.[35] The purpose of the study was to measure rigorously the economic impact of a technical assistance program. The study covered 126 selected farmers who received a combination of credit (capital to purchase farm requisites) and extension education (technology). Seventy-seven of the farm families were semi-subsistence type farmers. The average annual change in output during participation in the program was 21 per cent! After the first year of participation in the program, the increase in inputs accounted for only 44 per cent of the total change in output in real terms. A subsidy of $1 to pay for the full costs of technological introduction (excluding al output over and above his inputs. (See Table 2.)

The findings given above and Schultz' hypothesis have a number of useful implications for "developmental education." Earlier in the paper I pointed out that the level of training required for direct servers was in part determined by the level of technical and economic skills of the farmers being served. The direct servers need to be ahead but not very far ahead of the farmer. A somewhat similar situation prevails in the present case. Provision of new knowledge about inputs may well be limited not so much by the lack of capital as by the lack of human capital to go with it. Moreover, providing the farmer with new knowledge about techniques of production may facilitate the utilization of the new physical inputs. But even this combination faces obstacles unless the farmer is able to individualize these techniques and include them within his economic calculus. (Of course, one could define human capital to include the capacity to individualize and apply the economic calculus; nevertheless, the restrictions imposed by imbalance between human and non-human capital would still be valid.) Thus the level of developmental education must always take account of the need to balance human and non-human capital, especially in early-stage agriculture when the rate of substitution between them is probably very limited.

The Rural-Urban Gap

We have mentioned earlier the difference in educational services between the urban and rural areas. This problem can often be found even in the most advanced nation, but it is particularly acute and important in an early-stage country. The rural-urban imbalance in levels of literacy, years of schooling, etc., which results from the lower level of facilities in rural areas, is hidden by national averages.

Another aspect of the rural-urban imbalance is of special relevance to national economic growth. If we accept the proposition that certain kinds of

35. C. R. Wharton, Jr., "The Economic Impact of Technical Assistance: A Brazilian Case Study." *Journal of Farm Economics,* vol XLII, No. 2 (May, 1960).

education contribute to agricultural growth, then failure to utilize educational measures to the fullest will result in a slower rate of agricultural growth. But the penalty of a slower rate of agricultural growth does not fall solely on the rural or agricultural sector; it also affects over-all national rates of economic growth. Agriculture plays a critical role in the process of over-all growth and development. Events in the agricultural sector are key determinants of the rapidity with which over-all economic growth takes place.[36] Both the agricultural and the nonagricultural sectors make separate contributions to national economic growth. As Professor Simon Kuznets has ably pointed out, what is equally important is the fact that their separate contributions are interrelated. Failure of the agriculture sector to do its share in early-stage, agriculture-dominant nations will delay considerably the date of take-off. Given the importance of agriculture as the income base upon which a majority of people depend in the early stages, agriculture can not be ignored. Since events in the agricultural sector are of paramount importance in any discussion of economic growth, any imbalance or gap in the level of educational services between rural and urban areas merely aggravates the drag upon general growth and development. Consequently, considerable attention should be given not only to the content and type of education which is required for faster agricultural growth in the early stages, but also to the level and quality of resources and facilities devoted to the rural sector compared with the urban sector.

36. This point has been discussed at length by a number of authors: Gustav Ranis and J. C. H. Fei, "A Theory of Economic Development," *American Economic Review,* Vol. LI, No. 4 (September 1961); B. F. Johnston and J. W. Mellor, "The Nature of Agriculture's Contributions to Economic Development," *Food Research Institute Studies,* Vol. I, No. 3 (November, 1960); and their "The Role of Agriculture in Economic Development," *op. cit.,*; S. Kuznets, "Economic Growth and the Contribution of Agriculture: Notes on Measurement," *International Journal of Agrarian Affairs,* Vol. III, No. 2 (April, 1961).

CHAPTER 11

THE PRIME MOVERS OF INNOVATION

*Frederick Harbison**

The slogan of the world-wide revolution of rising aspirations is *development;*
like other revolutionary slogans, however, this has various meanings to different groups. In many countries, development means industrialization. To
some it symbolizes the achievement of political independence. In others it
connotes opportunity for education, the construction of a huge dam, rural
land reform, the building of skyscrapers, steel mills and television networks,
or the achievement of instantaneous worldwide communications and modern
jet airplane travel. The sociologists and political scientists tend to think of
development as the process of modernization, and they concentrate their
analyses primarily on the building of social and political institutions. Economists tend to equate it with economic growth, and they are concerned for the
most part with the accumulation of savings, investment, national income, productivity, and trade balances. But, to everyone, development means change
requiring rapid innovation. A country which fails to adopt and put to work a
broad succession of new ideas will inevitably lag behind in today's march of
progress. In the end successful development depends upon making a society
change-conscious.

Ideas come from people *and* are put to work by people. Thus innovation
has its roots in human-resource development. In this chapter, I propose to
raise for discussion the following questions: Who are the human agents of
innovation — that is, the prime movers of change? What kinds of innovation
are strategic for development? And what measures are best designed to create
the type of innovators needed in the newly modernizing economies?

At the outset, let us be clear about the meaning of *innovation.* It includes
creative new discoveries and inventions; but it is much more than invention,
and it goes beyond the discovery of a new method, machine, or system of
organization. Innovation also includes adaptation of known technologies to
concrete problems, and the securing of recognition and acceptance of new
ideas and new concepts. In analyzing innovation within the context of business enterprise, John Corson has developed a concept which, I think, has
general meaning: "The creative act in innovation," he says, "does not so
much involve conceiving something that has no counterpart or antecedent,

Author's Note: I am grateful to my colleagues at the Center for the Advanced Study of the Be-
havioral Sciences, and particularly to Charles A. Myers, for rigorous criticism and helpful comments.

but recognizing the possibility that a new process or concept can be applied to a particular situation." And he adds that a vital part of innovation is selling the new approach echelon by echelon until it is properly modified, fully tested, and generally accepted.[1] In almost all societies, however, innovation meets resistance. And, in the newly developing countries, this resistance to change is not confined to primitive peoples and traditional tribes. It permeates the so-called modern sector as well. Government bureaucracies, large enterprises and even universities may be the more formidable resistors of change as they become encrusted with conformity. Innovation cannot occur unless resistance to change is overcome, and thus it implies a continuous struggle between the old and the new.

I. THE HUMAN AGENTS OF CHANGE

Who then are the prime movers of innovation? Certainly, the Schumpeterian entrepreneur who perceives and exploits new business ventures belongs in the group. Likewise, the manager or top administrator in large private and public establishments should be included. He may not always have new ideas of his own, but his function is to organize and stimulate the efforts of others. He structures organizations, and either infuses hierarchies with energy and vision or fetters them with chains of conformity. And, as Hoselitz has pointed out, a very important element consists of the owners of many small and medium-sized industrial, commercial and financial enterprises which tend to proliferate in nearly all of the less advanced nations. For the most part, these small owners are "imitative entrepreneurs" who adapt new methods, new products, new sources of supply, or new markets to the conditions prevailing in their countries.[2]

In the newly developing countries, however, other prime movers of change are perhaps even more important. The leaders of the independence movement, who emerge as the new nationalist ruling elite, are perhaps the most spectacular agents of change. Those who are the organizers and manipulators of new movements and political parties should also be included. The agronomist who discovers better methods of cultivation, and the agricultural assistants who teach the farmers to use them, belong to the innovator class, as do public health officers, nurses and medical assistants. Engineers are in essence designers of change, and engineering technicians and supervisors put the changes to work. Last but not least, professors, teachers and administrators of educational institutions in many countries may constitute the largest group of prime movers of innovation; they are the "seed-corn" from which new generations of manpower will grow.

1. See John S. Corson, "Innovation Challenges Conformity," *Harvard Business Review* (May-June 1962), p. 68.
2. Bert F. Hoselitz, "The Entrepreneurial Element in Economic Development," paper presented to the United Nations Conference on Science and Technology, mimeo (Geneva, 1963).

In the newly developing countries, therefore, the prime movers of change are not just the private entrepreneurs. They are creative people in government service, in private activities, and in education. Some of them are "change-designers" who make new discoveries, suggest new methods of organization, and plan broad new strategies. Others are "change-pushers" who are able to persuade, coach and inspire people to put new ideas to work. Some innovators, of course, are at the same time change-designers and change-pushers. But whether they are designers, pushers, or a combination of the two, the prime movers of innovation must have extensive skill and knowledge. Thus, for the most part, they are drawn from the ranks of high-level manpower.[3] But they need more than proven intelligence and thorough technical training. They should have in addition keen curiosity, a capacity for self-discipline, and an unquenchable desire for accomplishment.[4] They should be adept at asking questions. They should have the knack of stimulating others to produce ideas and to activate the ablest minds about them; and they should be able to sell ideas to superiors, subordinates, and associates. As Hoselitz, Hagen, McClelland, and others have pointed out with reference to entrepreneurs, there is a psychological dimension as well. The prime mover of innovation must be convinced that change can occur as a result of individual action, and he must have the drive within him to bring it about. This may stem from a desire to rise in social status, to build up material wealth, to acquire political influence, or to preserve an already established prestige position.[5] Those who have the capacity to innovate thus have rather intangible personal qualities, and their numbers within both the population and the high-level manpower category are limited. Admittedly, many of those in the ranks of high-level manpower are conformists or even obstructors of innovation. The problem facing the newly developing countries, then, is to make the high-level manpower group as innovation-conscious as possible, and to develop within its ranks as many creative innovators as possible.

3. I include the following occupational categories in the definition of high-level manpower:
   1. Entrepreneurial, managerial and administrative personnel in both public and private establishments, including educational institutions.
   2. "Qualified" teachers, defined as those who have had a minimum of 12 years of education themselves.
   3. Professional personnel such as scientists, engineers, architects, agronomists, doctors, veterinarians, economists, lawyers, accountants, journalists, artists, etc.
   4. Sub-professional technical personnel, such as agricultural assistants, nurses, engineering assistants, technicians, senior clerks, and supervisors of skilled workers, the highest level of skilled craftsmen, and skilled clerical workers, such as stenographers.
   5. Top-ranking political leaders, labor leaders, judges, and officers of police and the armed forces.

These are the types of people who, in general, fill the strategic occupations in modern economies. From their ranks are drawn the leadership for social, political, and economic activities. And according to our definition, such persons in the high-level manpower category would normally be expected to have at least a secondary education or its equivalent.

4. Here again indebted to Corson, *op. cit.*
5. See Hoselitz, *op. cit.*, pp. 11 and 12.

II. STRATEGIC AREAS OF INNOVATION

Our analysis may be sharpened if we can identify some of the areas of innovation which are of particular importance to today's underdeveloped countries which now aspire to ride on the bandwagons of progress. Without attempting to present a definitive list, let us take a few examples for the purpose of encouraging discussion.

First, most of these countries need to modernize agriculture and to reorganize rural life. As Arthur Lewis has said, "If agriculture is stagnant, it offers only a stagnant market, and inhibits the growth of the rest of the economy."[6] But more is required than improvement in agricultural production. Rural communities need to be organized to provide new work opportunities for under-utilized rural labor forces and to provide higher standards of living, health and education for the people. The innovating institutions may be community development projects (such as those being tried in India) to enlist the participation of villagers in self-help development and to utilize underemployed manpower constructively. Here the change-designers are the agronomists, soil scientists, agricultural engineers, and community organization planners who suggest new methods and formulate general strategies. The change-pushers are the far more numerous agricultural extension gunctionaries and community development workers who attempt to carry forward the transformation of rural life.

Second, most newly developing countries are committed to rapid industrialization with modern technologies of production. Nasser, for example, exhorts the Egyptians to "march forward as one people who have vowed to work and to proceed on a holy march of industrializing." The processes and machines of industry, however, are not in themselves innovations; they are usually imported from advanced countries, together with the technical personnel required to install them and get them in operation. In a newly developing country, the critical innovating process is the introduction and use of well-known technologies. The change-designers are those who plan the organization of the enterprise and program the hiring and development of the local manpower that may be required. The change-pushers are the technicians, supervisors, and foremen who in effect are responsible for labor forces which may have had little or no previous experience with factory life. Here it would appear that both the change-designers and the change-pushers require particular skill in human relationships as well as knowledge of technical processes. In the end, the really thorny problems requiring creative thought are those connected with training people, building new types of organizations, finding productive ways of using cheap labor, opening up new markets, and developing initiative within the managerial hierarchy.[7] Despite

6. W. Arthur Lewis, "Reflections on the Economic Problem," paper delivered to the Oxford Conference on Tensions in Development, New College, Oxford, mimeo (September 1961).

7. A common complaint of expatriate managers and engineers who direct enterprises in underdeveloped countries is that the local engineers or assistant managers, though competent to handle routine matters, are incapable of handling unusual or new situations. For this and other reasons, it

this rather obvious fact, however, technical training rather than education in interpersonal relations is almost always emphasized in the preparation of high-level manpower for industry.

A third example is the need for encouragement of small industrial, commercial, and financial establishments in the private sector, for these are powerful transmitters of change. There are two ways in which governments can and should create a favorable climate for the small-scale entrepreneurs who are vitally important change-pushers. First, they can provide services such as market information, technical information, credit, and manager-training courses; second, as we shall stress later, it is possible deliberately to encourage a "spillover" of experienced manpower from the larger public and private establishments.

A fourth example is in the area of public health. It is clear that the newly developing countries need doctors and should train them. An even more critical problem, however, and one requiring the greatest innovating skill, is the organization of medical services which are appropriate for the country's stage of development. The change-pushers, such as medical assistants, midwives, and nurses, are invariably in short supply. Doctors, for the most part, are likely to be found primarily in the large urban areas. While it may be impossible to get many doctors to "live in the bush," it might be possible for them to make regular visits to rural areas, to give general guidance to medical technicians based in such areas, and to treat the more serious cases. This idea is being tried in Tanganyika and some other countries. However, there is little in modern medical training, either in the advanced or the underdeveloped countries, which would encourage the design of innovations of this kind. Instead, there is a propensity to build extremely expensive medical schools designed to produce replicas of the physicians and surgeons in the advanced countries.

A fifth example is education, where innovation is probably the most urgently needed in the newly developing countries. For example, in countries which are committed to rapid achievement of universal primary education, it is necessary to utilize teachers with only meager training and to operate schools with very high student-teacher ratios. It makes little sense for the newly developing countries to copy the educational systems of advanced countries. The solution lies in the discovery of new methods, new materials, and new technologies of education. Here inventions by change-designers are fully as important as the training of large numbers of teachers as change-pushers. Indeed, the need for basic research in the technology of education is probably much greater in the underdeveloped countries than in the more advanced nations.

A final example is the planning function of government. Most of the newly modernizing countries are convinced that development plans are pre-

---

is alleged, local members of the managerial hierarchy often refuse to accept greater responsibilities when offered. Whether this is myth or fact, it does emphasize the need for development of initiative.

requisites of accelerated growth—if not also a prerequisite of external aid. Recently, great strides have been made in the design of development plans by innovators in the developing nations themselves as well as in the advanced countries. The techniques of national income accounting, input-output analysis, the use of "shadow prices," and other tools of economic analysis are being developed rapidly. The most needed innovation now is perhaps not in the formulation of plans but in the art of getting them understood, accepted, and implemented. Here the importance of creating more change-pushers is obvious. There is need for persons in government ministries who know how to put a plan to work, and also for persons who are skilled in explaining the plan to the masses and enlisting to some degree their participation in its implementation. Here, as in the case of introduction of modern industries, a great deal of emphasis needs to be placed on the skills of communication and human relations.

III. CREATION OF INNOVATORS

As already suggested, innovators are most likely to spring from the ranks of high-level manpower. The development of high-level manpower is continuous and life-long. It starts with formal education but does not end there; it is a result of employment. It grows in response to incentives, and its development is influenced by organizational, cultural, social, and political environments. Sometimes these critical human agents are imported fully developed from the more advanced countries and used to train local human resources.

A developing country should have a strategy of human resource development—a key element in such a strategy is the generation of high-level manpower in accordance with estimated needs. These needs, of course, are related largely to the nature and extent of expected innovations in government, education, industry, and services, and they may be estimated roughly by means of a manpower survey. On the basis of such assessments in several countries as well as from personal observations, I offer the following tentative generalizations regarding the relationship of high-level manpower requirements and economic development.

First, the proportion of persons in the high-level manpower category and in the high-level occupations is much greater in advanced than in underdeveloped countries. In the most advanced countries, for example, the number of persons with completed secondary education probably exceeds 100 per 1,000 population. (In the United States it is over 288 per thousand.) In the more primitive underdeveloped countries, on the other hand, only one person per thousand may have received this much education. Between the primitive underdeveloped countries and the most advanced countries, one may rank the less advanced developed countries and the more advanced underdeveloped countries. (The same relationships would prevail if one could use a scale of persons in high-level occupations rather than a scale of educational attainment).

Second, the requirements for high-level manpower are determined as much by the pace of change as by the levels of technology employed; it is much more costly in terms of high-level manpower to get a new program moving than to maintain its momentum. For example, it takes more high-level manpower to get a steel works started in a developing country than it does to operate it after the labor forces have been trained. The same is true for introduction of agricultural extension services, public health schemes, and most other activities. Since underdeveloped countries want rapid growth which calls for high rates of innovation, the required ratios of high-level manpower accumulation may be much higher than in more advanced countries.

Third, in the newly developing countries which are introducing new technologies rapidly over a broad range of activities, the desirable rate of increase in high-level manpower is usually many times greater than the rate of increase in the labor force, and also usually between two and three times greater than the rate of the increase in national income.

Fourth, the most critical shortages in the high-level manpower category are likely to be persons with the higher intermediate skills: engineering technicians, agricultural assistants, medical technicians and nurses, and senior foremen and supervisors. This sub-professional group should be about three to five times as numerous as the senior administrative and professional categories.

Fifth, the total number of persons with secondary education is usually insufficient to provide the required flows of persons into intermediate and higher education and into direct employment. With some notable exceptions (such as India and Egypt), the shortage of secondary education (both technical and academic) is a major bottleneck in high-level manpower development.

If a developing country wants to introduce rapid changes in order to spur its economic and political growth, therefore, its educational system should be capable of producing both the quantity and quality of high-level manpower that modernization demands. But, in general, the educational systems of most developing countries are not very well designed to achieve this end. In Africa, as Arthur Lewis has pointed out repeatedly, the newly developing countries put too much emphasis on early diffusion of primary education and spend too much on universities in comparison with secondary education. This lack of emphasis on intermediate post-secondary technical and academic education is today characteristic of practically all underdeveloped countries. The output of universities generally is greater than that of the intermediate institutions, whereas the needs for high-level manpower indicate that the reverse would be desirable. If one assumes that post-primary education fosters the development of innovators, then it would appear that too many potential change-designers are coming from universities, but too few potential change-pushers from the intermediate institutions.

Quantitative analyses of manpower in underdeveloped countries, never-theless, should be used with extreme caution. Particularly with respect to the production of innovators, the qualitative factors may be relatively more im-portant. No one can yet specify just what kind of curriculum and orientation in education at various levels is likely to produce innovators rather than con-formists. Here is an area which calls for imaginative and serious study, and a discussion of the concrete measures which might be taken lies beyond the scope of this paper. The newly developing countries might well ask whether students are learning about the processes of change in the life of their coun-tries or whether they are merely conforming to arbitrary standards of knowl-edge or professional training copied from the more advanced countries. It would be appropriate also to find out whether students view higher education as preparation for productive service or whether it is used as "a permanent escape from the bush" into a privileged class, or as an indispensable down-payment for a secure and comfortable job in the higher ranks of government.

It is a mistake, however, to assume that the system of formal education is the only or even the most important influence in building high-level man-power and creating innovators. Experience and training are also important. And since both training and experience are accumulated in the course of em-ployment, a country's employing organizations usually play a vital role in strategic human-capital formation. Some employing organizations provide a working climate which encourages creativity and experimentation; others tend to stifle initiative and to discourage change. For better or worse, there-fore, the major employing establishments in both the public and the private sectors are producers of experienced high-level manpower as well as con-sumers of talent. The possibility of deliberately using them to produce in-novators should be thoroughly explored by all newly developing countries. Let us press this point further with some examples.

In some of the least developed countries, teachers are the largest single category of high-level manpower. In these countries a large proportion of the politicians, statesmen, government administrators, and managers of the larger firms are former teachers. This is quite plausible, of course, since the pools of experienced high-level manpower for expanding government activities in the early stages are stocked largely by secondary school teachers. To educa-tors, the drawing-off of teachers by government or business is rather deplor-able as it greatly complicates the task of staffing the schools. As a manpower economist, however, I see some advantages in looking upon teaching as an avenue for advancement into other activities. Because of their skills in com-munication and in activating young minds, teachers are potentially good pro-ducers of change in many walks of life. If, as we pointed out, the major prob-lems in introducing modern industries are human rather than technical, then a teaching background may be ideal for many managerial positions and par-ticularly for those engaged in training the labor forces. Furthermore, if there is widespread upward mobility from the teaching profession to other act-ivities, then more and better people will be attracted to teaching. Let me pose, therefore, these questions for discussion and perhaps serious research: In the early stages of development, is it not cheaper and more efficient for a country first to broaden, improve, and expand its teacher-producing institutions than to establish expensive law faculties, business schools, and higher technological institutions? And would it not be good policy in some cases to deliberately emphasize teaching experience rather than an academic degree as a prerequisite for entry into senior posts in government?

Large industrial or commercial enterprises, particularly those managed by expatriates, can be excellent producers of skilled manpower. For example, the oil companies in Saudi Arabia, Iran, and Kuwait, and the mining companies in Liberia and South America have done an impressive job of training craftsmen and supervisors in remarkably short periods of time. To a lesser degree, some have developed persons for middle and top management as well. Many of the persons trained have left the companies to set up machine shops, trucking companies, laundries, trading houses, and other kinds of small business establishments. The newly developing countries have much to gain by requiring foreign companies to produce skilled and high-level manpower beyond their immediate needs. This might be a better policy in the long run than attempting to squeeze the companies too tightly on sharing of profits. The same policies might apply also to the larger locally owned enterprises.

In the typical underdeveloped country, however, the government services are usually the principal consumers of high-level manpower; of necessity, government is the primary initiator or agent of agricultural reform and rural development; it is the moving force in accumulating capital; and it may also be the owner and manager of enterprises. It can be the major supplier of the human agents of change because it is the largest "producer of experience."

In a previous paper I suggested that each major ministry of the government in developing countries should assume responsibility for upgrading its personnel; and that it should maintain a training organization responsible for on-the-job and in-service programs of instruction, for supplementary off-the-job programs of training in cooperation with educational institutions, for periodic examination of accomplishment, and for certification of qualification for promotion, transfer and advancement.[8] In-service training is especially needed in underdeveloped countries because of the relatively meagre pre-employment education and the comparatively short experience of most employees. In African countries, where there is strong pressure to replace expatriates with local personnel, young men with hardly more than a secondary education and little experience hold the top posts in many of the ministries. These men need systematic training and coaching as they assume large responsibilities, even if expatriate personnel must be employed to help shoulder the training responsibility.

8. Frederick H. Harbison, "Human Resource Development Planning in Modernizing Economies," *International Labor Review* (May 1962).

The top officials of these countries are likely to complain, however, that their organizations are too busy and too understaffed to afford the luxury of in-service training. They cling to the misguided notion that the high-level manpower for the future should spring full-blown from universities and technical schools. They fail to recognize the distinction between education and training, or the linkages between them in development of human resources. Education supplies general knowledge and develops basic mental ability, whereas training is concerned more with the development of specific skills to perform concrete tasks. Much of the expenditure on education will be wasted unless it is followed up by intensive and systematic training in the course of employment.

It might be appropriate for governments to allocate a specific proportion of educational funds to in-service training programs in the major ministries. And, if governments did undertake such training and upgrading of personnel, they might be induced to go one step further and try to produce experienced people in excess of their own requirements in order to provide a spillover into the private sectors. Then if their training could select, inspire, and push forward the creative people instead of merely spawning conformists, governments could become producers of the prime movers of innovation which they need so desperately. Certainly, the techniques for organization and development of in-service training programs are available. The task of training the instructors, though difficult, is no greater than that of training teachers for formal education. The greatest problem is to inculcate the idea that a major function of every government ministry is to build people in addition to engaging in routine activities, and that a government agency is successful to the degree that it creates an organizational climate that nourishes innovation in addition to rewarding loyalty.

In the advanced countries, government is expected to create a climate that promotes private initiative and private enterprise. By various means, governments encourage private entrepreneurs to take risks, assisting them by providing information, credit, and technical services. The governments of underdeveloped countries must do this also, but in addition they may have to spawn many of the entrepreneurs whom they may later encourage, for there are relatively few other institutions capable of bringing those men into existence. Admittedly, the task of transforming the poorly staffed and overburdened governments of newly developing countries into institutions for building high-level manpower is formidable. Countries with aspirations for forced-draft modernizations must shoulder formidable tasks. They must try measures which were never dreamed of by the presently advanced nations, whose development proceeded for the most part in a more leisurely and unplanned fashion.

The conclusions from the argument may now be summarized. Accelerated development requires rapid innovation throughout a society, and the prime-movers of innovation are creative individuals who are either "change-designers," "change-pushers," or a combination of the two. These innovators are not merely business entrepreneurs, but include as well political leaders, agricultural experts, engineers and technicians, suppliers of medical services, teachers, and other personnel who fall largely, though not exclusively, within the so-called high-level manpower category in both public and private activities.

Innovators have personal traits and characteristics that may not be widely distributed in the population. Formal education, particularly at the higher levels, should be designed to nourish and promote creative talent, not simply spawn conformists. There is indeed a need for systematic evaluation of the orientation of education in newly developing countries.

In addition to a careful consideration of reforms and needed innovations in a country's educational system, however, the newly developing countries should exploit the possibilities of turning employing institutions into potential producers rather than just omnivorous consumers of high-level manpower. These organizations should deliberately produce experienced manpower and, hopefully, creative innovators beyond the requirements for their own activities, thus providing a spillover of talent for the rest of the economy.

The techniques for making employing organizations producers of talent as well as mere conductors of activities are probably available. The practical difficulties encountered are in reality more conceptual than technical. The idea, however, is worth exploring, and offers a challenging opportunity for innovators of research on the problems of the newly developing nations in the modern world.

The dominant theme that gives focus to the chapters in Part III is the analysis of how schooling and other innovations spread through a population. With the exception of the short contributions by Rottenberg and by Blitz, these processes are examined as sequences in historic time; that is, the time dimension itself is a critical one.

Hägerstrand's study (Chapter 12) can serve very well as an organizing structure for most of the other contributions included in Part III. He is concerned with the spread of innovations, not their initiation. Though his empirical work is geographic, he points out that it could be adapted to treatment of social status or other dimensions of diffusion as well. Hägerstrand presents a theoretical framework, a methodology for testing it, and a series of empirical tests. His formulation of the diffusion process has two major components: "information fields" and what he calls, somewhat misleadingly, "resistances." Among other things, he demonstrates remarkable stability in the spatial sequences of diffusion of technologies and practices of extremely diverse kinds over a period of several generations in Sweden. He links these findings to the incidence of person-to-person contacts, or "tellings." The information field analysis could incorporate also directional assymetries in the impacts of "tellings." "Resistance" enters in to explain the pace of change, and also non-adoption of particular traits. The economist's profitability analysis belongs on the "resistance" side of this analytical framework, though it is of course limited to those types of innovations in behavior or practice that are subject to profit incentives. Much of Rottenberg's abstract discussion (Chapter 13) of the "International Transfer of Knowledge," which is based upon communication theory, might be quite easily recast within something like the Hägerstrand framework, though Rottenberg makes some ingenious applications of economic theory that lie on the periphery of Hägerstrand's analysis. (Readers will quickly see Rottenberg's affinities with the contributions in Part I.)

What has all this to do with education? Evidently this question has several answers. For one thing, diffusion or transfer of knowledge is in itself education, and so, therefore, are Hägerstrand's "tellings" and the flows through Rottenberg's channels. In addition, education is undoubtedly a factor that influences the frequencies of "tellings" of one versus another kind. Education undoubtedly plays an important part on the "resistance" or "receptivity" side, as a factor influencing the ratios of adoptions to tellings. And finally, schooling of various kinds and levels is itself a trait the diffusion of which follows patterns such as those Hägerstrand has delineated, presumably for similar reasons. It is this last fact that joins his analysis with the chapters by Anderson (Chapter 17) on "Patterns and Variabilities in the Distribution and Diffusion of Schooling" and by Kahan on hereditary workers and the incidence of literacy in rural nineteenth-century Russia (Chapters 14 and 15).

Before going on to comment further on some of the chapters in Part III, it may be helpful to take note of a confusion that arose in the discussion, since it might be repeated by some of our readers. Some (not all) of the economists were inclined not only to argue the importance of profitability considerations in determining rates of adoption of innovations, but also to see this as conflicting with Hägerstrand's model. This was clearly a misunderstanding. The economist's studies of profitability differentials as explanations of diffusion patterns (for example in the adoption of hybrid seed corn) are a special subset, albeit an important one, on the "resistance" side of the Hägerstrand construct. This assertion takes on more meaning if we try applying it to speculate concerning the interpretation of a fascinating set of data presented in the discussion by T. W. Schultz. These were rough computations concerning international inequalities in productivity for each of several crops, together with changes in productivity inequalities through time. Schultz pointed out that the greater inequalities, persisting for longer periods, were positively associated with the degree of complexity of the technical changes underlying productivity increases. Putting this another way, the techniques that spread more slowly were those requiring the most intricate complex of mutually supportive factors and conditions. The fact that the societies adopting these more demanding technological innovations were also those in which we would expect a high incidence of "tellings" (the "information field" side of Hägerstrand's model) would not explain the differences among crops in the adoption rates. However, if we replace the term "resistance" by something like a generalized "readiness to assimilate," which is the same thing with a change of sign, we see immediately that for investment decisions the "profitability" measure becomes an index of resistance; it is an index of the extent to which a particular set of complementary or mutually supportive resources and attributes are present. For diffusion of new consumption traits this same generalization with respect to presence of a complex of complementary traits will still apply, but such complementarity cannot be summed up in profitability assessments. Education itself is a complex that to a major degree provides the supportive conditions for adoption of many kinds of innovations, both technological and organizational; in other words, it may be a significant factor on the "resistance" side.

The two short chapters by Kahan are especially interesting in the context of these disputes, for Kahan bridges the disciplinary gulf simply and neatly. Although he could not have had Hägerstrand's work in mind, Kahan's argument concerning the "hereditary workers" hypothesis fits beautifully—a fact Kahan himself noted in revising for publication. Kahan's note on determinants of the incidence of literacy in rural nineteenth-century Russia is equally appropriate. In the evidence he provides us from the work of Russian statisticians we have unambiguous indications of the relations between diffusion of literacy and the incidence of "tellings" on the one hand, the incidence of economic incentives or rewards on the other. The geographic section of the chapter by Anderson provides further illustration and confirmation, especially in the data for France.

Finally, readers will note that stability in diffusion patterns does not imply detailed predictability in individual cases, and it says nothing about the over-all pace of change. In these respects there is indeed great diversity. Important contrasts are evidenced by comparison among the chapters (Blitz, Kahan, and Anderson) dealing with distributions of schooling and also, notably, by comparisons among the historical sequences reported in several chapters, both in Part III and elsewhere in this volume. Indeed, the bits of historical evidence with respect to diffusion of education by social status categories portray both associations that repeat themselves (from one society to another and within one society over time) and also, strikingly, a wide range of variation within the common limits.

CHAPTER 12

QUANTITATIVE TECHNIQUES FOR ANALYSIS OF THE SPREAD OF INFORMATION AND TECHNOLOGY

Torsten Hägerstrand

Many relationships are like two boxes, each containing the key of the other. Education and innovation are cases in point. Demand for education, educational techniques, and organization are at times themselves innovations which have to be introduced in order to open a society for further innovation. Literacy and other new skills eventually transform social communication and resistance into more susceptible patterns. Innovations follow which in their turn will create demand for further educational advances and refinements. Innovation goes on even in preliterate societies, though it may take less sophisticated forms. Since our innovational box has a slight opening, it would seem appropriate to peep into the dark of this box separately, and try to file out some skeleton key to the education box.

In this chapter a flanking movement will be made relative to the main theme of the conference. Certain specific aspects of the spread of innovations will be the focus of attention. Illustrative cases of diffusion of innovations are first described and mapped. The spread of schools is treated like other innovations. Then a technique for analysis is presented, a rather special technique but one which is perhaps suitable to help in engineering induced change. Notice that the theme is the *diffusion*, not the initiation of a new object, trait, or way of doing things.

In recent years innovation has been much studied by focusing attention on the individuals involved: what are the attributes of "innovators," of "early adopters," "late adopters," and of "laggards"?[1] There seems to be a place also for more impersonal interpretations, especially when we are concerned with larger populations. With all respect for the complexities of human behavior, there are a number of external constraints, walls in our labyrinth of action, which have to be brought into the picture. The most indisputable of these walls arises from our imprisonment in time and space.

It is well known that the spread of innovations in society exhibits certain regularities. From statistical publications one can pick out large masses of figures showing the growth in quantity of various phenomena, from railroads

1. The literature is summarized in E. M. Rogers, *Diffusion of Innovations* (New York: Free Press, 1962).

to divorces. Among them one will normally find trends which more or less closely follow an S-shaped curve (see Figure 1). Many attempts have been made to fit mathematical functions to such empirical findings in order to establish a "law of social growth."

A complementary approach, the geographic mapping of culture-element distributions, has long been a standard procedure among anthropologists and cultural geographers. The purpose has been to establish "culture areas" and "cultural boundaries." More stress has been laid on stability and tradition in space than on change over time—and with good reason, for there exists a surprising amount of immobility in the picture. Change has been viewed as a displacement of culture boundaries between two widely separated points in

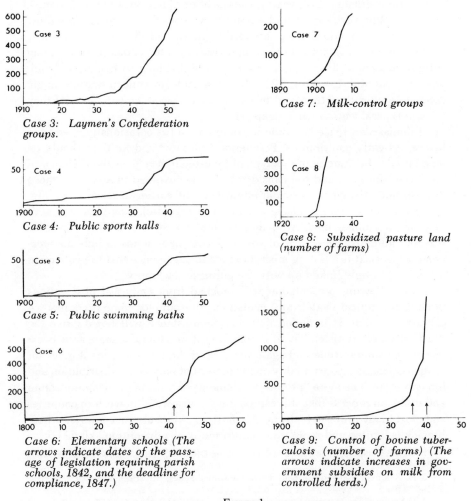

Case 3: Laymen's Confederation groups.

Case 4: Public sports halls

Case 5: Public swimming baths

Case 6: Elementary schools (The arrows indicate dates of the passage of legislation requiring parish schools, 1842, and the deadline for compliance, 1847.)

Case 7: Milk-control groups

Case 8: Subsidized pasture land (number of farms)

Case 9: Control of bovine tuberculosis (number of farms) (The arrows indicate increases in government subsidies on milk from controlled herds.)

FIGURE 1
Timing of the diffusion of new organizations and practices

time. Although the precision is notoriously low, a kind of "law of geographical spread" has been ventured; it is said that innovations spread like ripples on water. It has accordingly also been argued that the geographical extent of a trait could be used as a criterion of its age; this idea can be seriously misleading, however.

An exclusive ordering of data along a time scale presents events in a denatured way; an exclusive ordering in space gives little indication of how changes take place. It seems desirable, therefore, to copy the physical scientist and go to work with a clock and a yardstick in combination. Here the merits of using a space-time framework when considering cultural change will be emphasized. Although "space" will be taken in a simple geographic sense, the door is left open for such transformations of the space concept as might prove suitable (e.g., various measures or dimensions of social status). The discussion revolves around a number of cases for which sources allow continuous observations from the very beginning of the process. But it is hardly possible to grasp all the complexities of interactions in an evolving pattern; to attempt this would be to become lost among particulars and endless reservations. It seems, after all, reasonable to concentrate on single cases, one after the other, and to use them as trace-elements, even if they mark only weak currents in a deep sea.

Emphasis on space and time in combination has occasionally been tried before. As early contributors, Pemberton,[2] McVoy,[3] and Kniffen[4] should be mentioned. The scarcity of this type of investigation reflects the difficulty of finding useful data, and the considerable work involved in arranging those one can find. Always of particular interest are the earlier stages of a development. But census bureaus have a habit of disregarding new elements until they are no longer new. Also, the standard procedure—adding data over irregular administrative areas of very differing size—tends to blur the locational aspects. It is a lasting misfortune for social science that the collection of data is so firmly linked up with the political machinery.

The following presentation will proceed from empirical observations through theoretical models to speculation. All examples come from my own country, Sweden. It is hoped that this circumstance will not deprive the illustrations of all effect. There is some merit in using the same area as experimental ground time and again because of the opportunities it gives for comparing cases against a fairly stable pattern of population distribution and infrastructure. The more "primitive" elements or traits of the communication and diffusion process that still can be clearly discerned in western countries and most likely prove to be by far the most important also in countries where literacy is limited and social communication is of a "neolithic" kind.[5]

2. H. E. Pemberton, "The Spatial Order of Culture Diffusion," *Sociology and Social Research*, 22:246-51 (1938).

3. E. C. McVoy, "Patterns of Diffusion in the United States," *American Sociological Review*, 5:219-27 (1940).

4. F. Kniffen, "The American Covered Bridge," *Geographical Review*, 41:141-53 (1951).

5. M. S. Edmonson, "Neolithic Diffusion Rates," *Current Anthropology*, 2:71-102 (1961).

I. CASE STUDIES

It has proved possible to find various cultural items whose spread is sufficiently well documented for our purpose: certain farming techniques and types of equipment, new crops, social organizations, new occupations and kinds of establishments. The range is from national to local, and the time runs from the middle of the 18th century up to the present. The ten cases are grouped according to diminishing scale of the area studied and within each group in time sequence. Time series for all but the first two and the tenth cases are graphed together in Figure 1; the mapped sequences with their spatial patterns of change follow.

Case 1: Reallotment of Land, Following The Acts of 1749 and 1757 (Figure 2)[6]

In the middle of the 18th century, fragmentation of landholdings began to be considered a major obstacle to agricultural improvements. The first serious reallotment movement was called *stor-skifts*, "reallotment in big pieces." Its aim was to collect the thirty to a hundred scattered fields of every farmer into a small number of consolidated units. The policy was explicitly inspired by the enclosure movement in Great Britain.

Between the first act of 1749 and the revised act of 1757 only a handful of reallotments were carried out in villages north of Stockholm. In nearly all these cases the Crown was part owner in the villages. Reallotment required consent of all shareholders in the village. After 1757, redivision in a village was possible at the request of only one owner, but the surveyor had to satisfy the village as a whole with his proposal. Figure 2 picks up the diffusion of reallotments beginning with the stage reached in 1772.

The spontaneous movement after 1757 started in the vicinity of the first enforced experiments on the plains north of Stockholm. Early adoptions appeared also in scattered localities extending northward and to the southwest. A secondary center arose in the province of Skåne, the southernmost tip of the country. In all, some 10,000 villages were reorganized under these two acts. (White areas on the maps denote localities in which less than 50 per cent of the villages were included in the movement.)

Case 2: Reallotment of Land Following Danish Reform Patterns, 1783 Onward (Figure 3)[7]

A reallotment movement started in Denmark in the 1760's in which the radical step was taken of moving the farmsteads out from the old nucleated settlements to one assembled piece of land; shortly before 1800 this innovation was taken up in Sweden. From 1803 to 1827 a series of acts were passed;

6. The data come from registers and village maps of the Swedish Land Survey Board, those used here being taken from S. Helmfrid, "The Storskifte, Enskifte and Laga Skifte in Sweden: General Features," *Geografiska Annaler*, 43:114-29 (1961).

7. Data from registers and village maps of the Swedish Land Survey Board; and Helmfrid, *op. cit.*

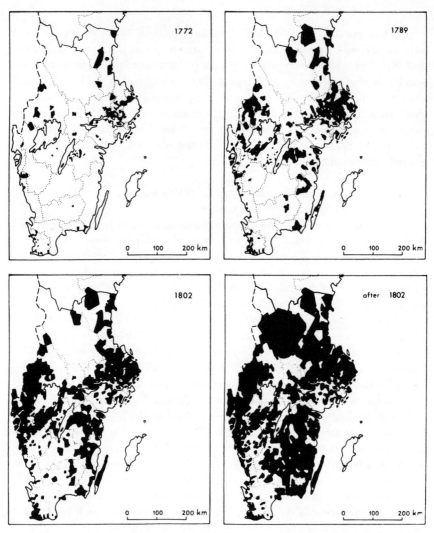

FIGURE 2
Case 1:   Reallotment of land following the 1749 and 1757 acts

the first of these required that every farm comprise only one piece of land,
though later this specification was relaxed to three or four pieces. The main
point was that dwellings had to be moved out from the old village to the
center of the new farm. The government subsidized new buildings to some
minor extent, and neighbors had to give further help insofar as they could
stay in their old houses. The whole village had to accept reallotment if only
one landowner in the village requested it.

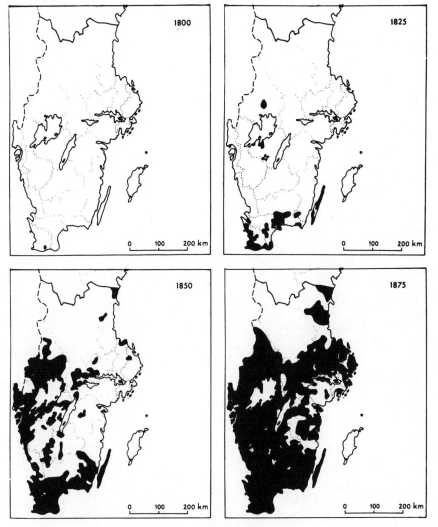

FIGURE 3
Case 2: Reallotment of land following Danish patterns, 1783 onward

The first reform in Sweden along the radical chessboard principle was carried out in the far south by a private estate owner in the years 1783-85. A few other estates in the vicinity followed before the procedure was legalized in 1803. From then on the reform moved with rising momentum along the south and west coasts and from thence inland toward central-east Sweden. The number of dispersed farms was finally of the order of 100,000. As can be inferred from the maps, many villages went through both reforms. The spatial

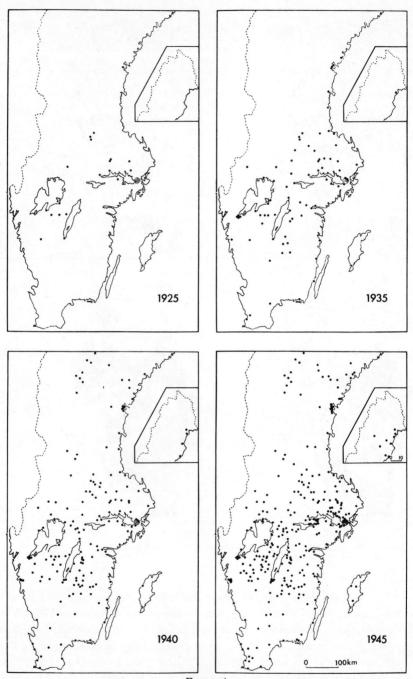

FIGURE 4
Case 3: Laymen's Confederation groups

course of this development appears to be nearly the obverse of the former case.

Case 3: The Layman's Confederation of the Swedish Church
(Figures 1 and 4)[8]

The confederation is a voluntary social organization with a moderate fee. Its purpose is to form local groups for study and practical work in support of the parish church. No government action was needed as the law vindicates the freedom to form such associations. The minister seems very often to be the initiator, but this is certainly not always the case. Usually there is one group in each parish, though at times individuals from neighboring parishes form a common group.

The movement started in 1918 in a small town in central Sweden, immediately west of Stockholm. In 1925 we find two loose clusters of local groups, one in the Stockholm area and the other in the southwestern part of central Sweden. It is important to observe that almost all groups outside the two clusters at that time were situated in urban communities. Still in 1945 the main concentrations were extensions of the same clusters as 20 years earlier. The newly founded groups are regularly situated in cities and towns, while rural parishes are to a large extent included in the movement's high-density areas. Skåne, the southern tip of the country, took part late and hesitantly.

Case 4: Public Sports Halls
(Figures 1 and 5)[9]

The spread of public sports halls indicates roughly how organized sport progressed. (The maps locate only establishments with accommodations for spectators.) Since 1935 the government has contributed to about twenty new halls out of taxes on football betting. The halls were built by the communes or by local sports organizations with communal and private aid, and there are a few communes with more than one hall.

Stockholm and Göteborg, the two largest cities, introduced this kind of establishment. Progress was rather slow to begin with, but by 1919 we find three loose clusters over central Sweden. Fifteen years later the widened cluster has the same general location, but in addition there is a small group of three in Skåne. Then a breakthrough occurred; already at the end of 1939 the density is much higher, particularly along the west coast. Northern Sweden enters the picture. The same tendencies persist through 1952; northern and central Sweden are still much underrepresented in relation to population if the densest clusters are taken as norms. Though the two biggest cities came in early, for the rest there is no clear correlation between size of commune and time of adoption.

8. The data are taken from printed membership lists.
9. Source: Tables in S. Svensson (ed.), *Svensk Idrott* (Stockholm, 1953).

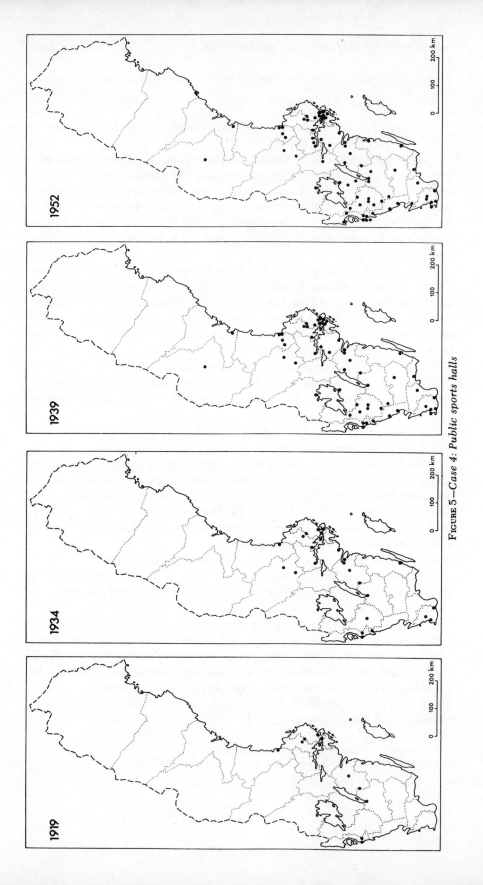

FIGURE 5 — *Case 4: Public sports halls*

Case 5: Public Swimming Baths
(Figure 1)[10]

This is a second indicator of sports development (the data are not mapped). Public aid was given similar to that for sports halls; baths were built either by communes or by private organizations.

Between Cases 4 and 5 there were many similarities, but also differences in the distributional patterns. Swimming baths started somewhat later. In 1919 there was a small cluster in the Stockholm area plus three scattered adoptions: one in each of Sweden's two next largest cities, on the west coast, and one in northern Sweden. In 1934 the establishments were still very much concentrated in the Stockholm region, but with a definite spread along the northern coast that did not appear in the case of sports halls. By 1939 a band over middle Sweden was established, adoptions had appeared inland to the north, and there was a secondary center along the southern west coast. By 1952 baths were found in scattered inland locations far to the north.

Case 6: Elementary Schools
(Figures 1 and 6)[11]

The early parts of the long and complicated history of the introduction of elementary schools into Sweden has to be omitted. As is so often the case, action by the central authorities limped behind measures taken by local leaders in certain areas. At the end of the 18th century the Pietists in particular began to work for the principle of one school in each parish. This idea began gradually to be adopted within the formerly Danish provinces of southern Sweden. (Denmark had already inaugurated compulsory elementary schools in 1814.) By the time that legislation required elementary schools in every parish (the 1842 law required at least one school to be founded by 1847), establishment of schools was already well on its way in the province of Skåne opposite Denmark. The schools were to be organized by parishes under the supervision of the clergy, and villages had representatives on school committees.

The first of these parish schools seems to have been opened in 1777 in the parish where a leading Pietist was dean (one of the twin dots on Figure 8 for 1804). With several years in between, four more schools were founded in the same corner of the province, forming two slightly separated clusters. Ten years later those clusters had grown somewhat, and a secondary center appeared inland. By 1824 we notice some further spread to the southeast, the formation of a fourth small separate cluster in the northwest, and appearance of the first, so far isolated, school in the northeast. The pattern of 1814 stands

10. *Ibid.*

11. Printed tables in reports by school inspectors from 1861-63 give the initial year of every school in the province, except for some areas that are shaded on Figure 6. The data are probably not quite complete within the open areas either, but only a handful of dots are missing. Only communal schools are included.

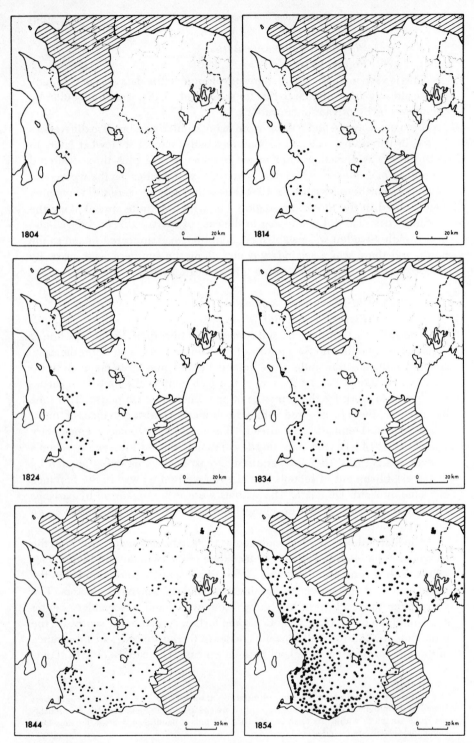

FIGURE 6—Case 6:   Elementary schools

254

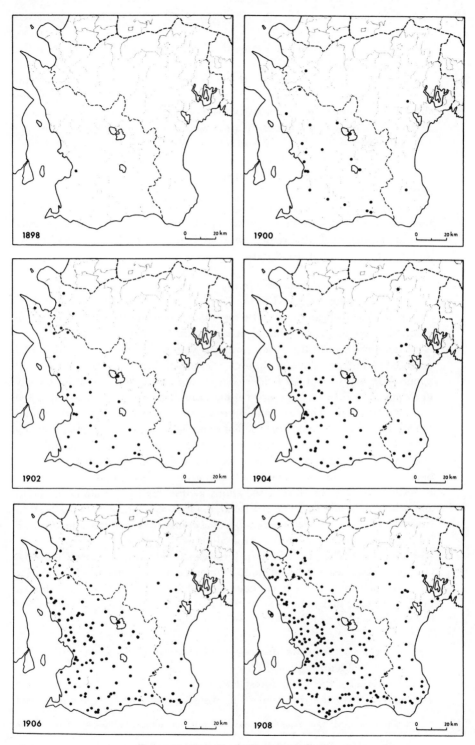

FIGURE 7 – Case 7: Milk-control groups

255

out in 1834, along with some growth of the more isolated clusters in the corners of the province.

In 1844, two years after enactment of the law, the distribution was still uneven and reflects the location of the first centers. The following decades show a strong increase, and many parishes organized more than one school. This latter tendency is strongest in areas where elementary schools were first adopted; since only one school was required by the law, this trend indicates the persisting leadership of this area. Even as late as 1862 (very like 1854), many parishes in the rest of Sweden still had only one school, despite longer distances between settlements. In passing we may notice that inspectors in the beginning complained that parents tended to keep older children at home for work but sent their very young children to school to be taken care of. This is not much different from what is said to happen in many of the underdeveloped countries of today.

Case 7: Milk-control Groups
(Figures 1 and 7)[12]

In 1895 a small group of cattle owners in Denmark started a cooperative enterprise, such as is now found in most parts of the world where dairying is an important industry. Their purpose was to improve the quality and quantity of milk production through regular measurements of output and appropriate adjustments of fodder composition. The idea caught on rapidly in Denmark, and in 1898 the first similar group was organized in Sweden just opposite Denmark. The instigator here was the headmaster of an agricultural school. Most of the farmers in this first group had herds of from ten to twenty cows. A small subsidy was administered by the provincial agricultural societies. Neighboring farmers formed local groups with fifteen to thirty members, though spatial overlapping between groups was common.

After the start in 1898, associations swiftly multiplied along the coast and inland. Already in 1900 two isolated adoptions appeared in the eastern part of the province which later on became centers of secondary clusters. The bigger empty areas gradually shrank along with a growing internal density within clusters. The pace of expansion was slowing around 1910 (Figure 1). Groups in the central areas began to reorganize into bigger and economically more satisfactory units than had been formed in the first enthusiasm. Most of the larger herds had come in early, but there is generally only a weak correlation between size of herd and time of joining.

Case 8: Subsidies for Improved Pasture on Small Farms
(Figures 1 and 8)[13]

Traditionally the open forest between villages was used for summer grazing, but this extensive method held milk production at a low level and

---

12. Source: printed yearly reports from the provincial agricultural societies, which supervised the work.
13. Source: registers of subsidies kept by the provincial agricultural society.

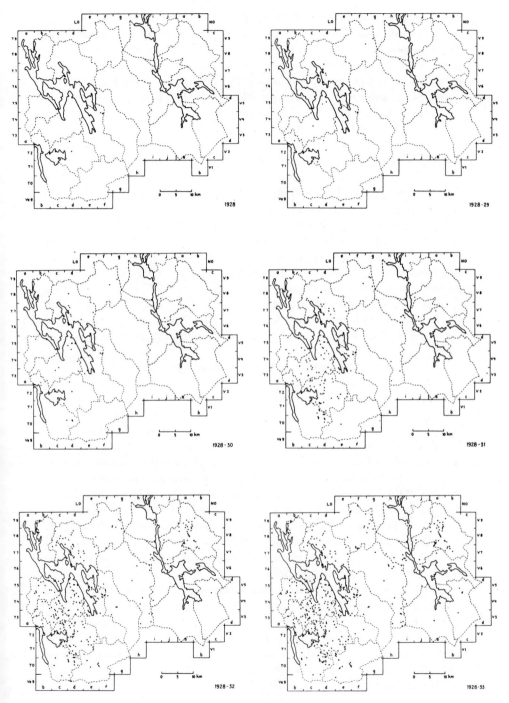

FIGURE 8
Case 8: Subsidies for improved pasture

was detrimental to forestry. Between 1910 and 1920 agronomists began to advocate that pasture be fenced and improved by sown grass and manuring. This new practice spread over the whole country within a couple of decades, particularly on the smallest farms. Its diffusion can be followed through records of subsidies (rather than of adoptions themselves), for from 1928 the government gave on application a grant for improvements to farmers with less than ten hectares of tilled land. The individual farmer applied for the subsidy whether he was owner or tenant. Dots on the maps are located at farmsteads. (It happened that tenants on an estate in the northeastern corner of the sample area applied as a group at one time, 1932; see Figure 8.)

Underlying conditions were relatively uniform in that farms with less than ten hectares of tilled land were quite evenly spread over the area, and suitable land for small pastures was to be found everywhere. The first adopters appeared immediately in 1928 in the western half of the area, and adopters in that area multiplied in the following year. In 1931 about 30 per cent of the farmers in the parent locality had received subsidies although wide areas were still untouched. Although from 1931 on the innovation gained ground also in some eastern parts of the region, by 1933 only isolated spots there had passed an adoption rate of 30 per cent. By this time the adoption rate in the parent locality exceeded 60 per cent. The first adopters did not show any definite distinction as to farm size within the group in question.

Case 9: Systematic Control of Bovine Tuberculosis
(Figures 1 and 9)[14]

The seriousness of bovine tuberculosis had become evident from about 1900. Effective countermeasures were expensive for the farmer, however, and it was possible only slowly to gain acceptance of the fact that control rested on efficient husbandry and social responsibility. The maps indicate the dates when farmers in the sample area first started systematic control. Interest is focused on the start in this example, no attention being given to the date of final success. From 1934 compensation was paid for infected cows that had to be slaughtered. From 1937 a further subsidy was given; a higher price could be paid by dairies for milk from controlled herds, and from 1942 this subsidy was increased. The individual farm was the unit of adoption, and the aim was to reach all herds irrespective of size. Dairy farms are quite evenly spread over the sample area.

The map for 1900-24 portrays the pioneering farms that worked with the problem continuously during the first 25 years. Three clusters can be discerned. Ten years later many more farms were included. The three clusters are still there, the northeastern one by now embracing over 60 per cent of the farms in its center. A trace of a fourth cluster appeared in the southeast. From then on the pace of change increased rapidly. The clusters grew outwards and became at the same time denser. Bridges began to join them—along the

14. Source: registers kept by the provincial agricultural society and the veterinary board.

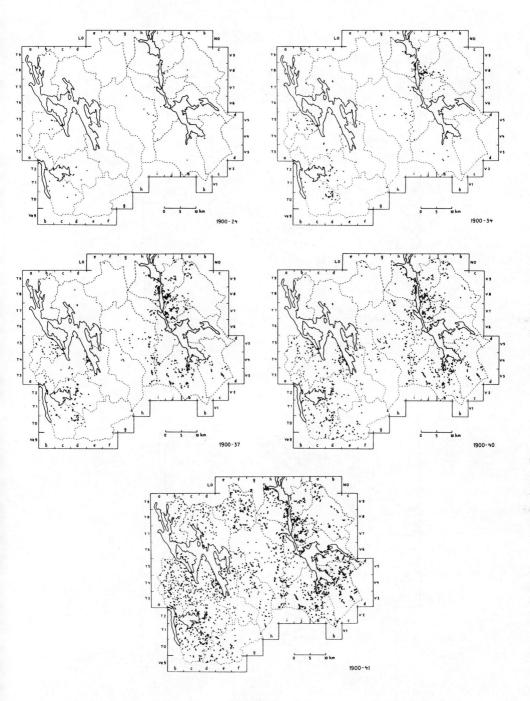

FIGURE 9
Case 9: Control of bovine tuberculosis

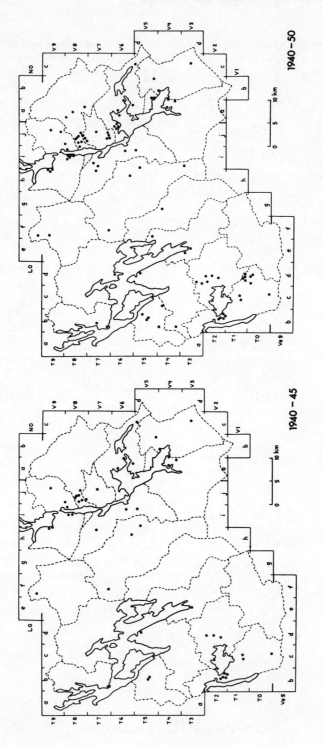

1940-50

1940-45

FIGURE 10—Case 10: Soil mapping

main roads. In 1940 the whole eastern section shows more than 60 per cent of adopters and the western part over 30 per cent; nevertheless, districts in between were still untouched. At the end of 1941 adoption reached on the whole 90 per cent, with the exception of a small zone remaining in the middle. Until about 1930 the bigger farms predominated among adopters, but from then on there is no correlation between farm size and time of adoption until the final stage when the smallest units came to be included.

Case 10: Soil Mapping
(Figure 10)[15]

A map of the soil conditions of the individual farm is a rather new device in Swedish agriculture. The first maps began to appear on ordinary farms at the end of the 1930's. The maps were supplied at a low price; agronomists maintained that a map given to a farmer without his own initiative would not be used efficiently. No particular propaganda and no subsidies existed during the years dealt with here. On Figure 10 each dot is located at the individual farmstead.

In 1945 the clustering of adopters is very similar to that for tuberculosis control in 1924. Five years later adoption is somewhat denser within the main clusters, and some outward expansion has taken place. The 1945 spatial distribution compares well with the diffusion of control of tuberculosis accomplished by 1934. Unfortunately the data cover only the initial stages of the spread of soil mapping.

II. COMPARISON OF OBSERVATIONS

It was first noticed long ago that spatial diffusion of new cultural items tends to occur in a regular space-time order, at least in predominantly rural societies. The miscellaneous data on diffusion of the kind set out for inspection here may help to refine our conceptions of the nature of the underlying regularities, if any exist. Our sample areas differed greatly in size, but for the present let us disregard these different scales and attend only to the space-time behavior of adoptions. First, when and where do later adoptions appear in relation to earlier ones within a series? Second, how do parent localities emerge, when compared between series? Like all historical trains of events, each case has of course its own individuality. Yet in this connection it is more interesting to look for similarities than for differences.

The pace during the initial stage differs widely. In some cases adoptions multiply very quickly, while in others there is a long and hesitating introductory growth. Nevertheless, there is a general tendency to deferred acceleration rather than uniform growth from the very start (Figure 1). Only a few cases have been followed up to the stage of retardation in growth rates.

The main spatial similarity is, briefly, that the probability of a new

15. Source: registers kept by the provincial agricultural society; consultants of the society did the mapping.

adoption is highest in the vicinity of an earlier one and decreases with increasing distance. Later events seem to be dependent on earlier ones according to a principle for which the term "neighborhood effect" would be apt. It is quite clear that there exists a chance mechanism, of which the old phrase "circles on the water" gives a reasonable picture if we interpret the circles as invisible adoption probabilities which extend out from every effected adoption, adding interference patterns of cumulative probabilities "hanging over" the population. After every new adoption one "quantum" is added to this accumulated field of probabilities. That explains acceleration.

When an adoption occurs at some distance from the initial cluster, the neighborhood effect normally manifests itself in the new area and a secondary center arises. Even while adoptions become more scattered away from the parent locality, the density of adoptions continues to increase amidst the earlier ones. This goes on with increasing speed at first and then eventually at a decreasing rate until a local or total state of saturation has been reached. The slowing of growth rates tends to start around the parent locality and around the earliest secondary clusters.

It is noteworthy that the same general traits repeat themselves on different scales, ranging from the whole country down to a small rural locality in which one can distinguish separate farms. The concept of neighborhood effect is applicable in a hierarchy of scales, even on a global scale.

Further comparison of the examples leads to another conclusion. The same parent localities or innovation centers appear time and again in the most differing connections and over the long time our series cover. Considering all of Sweden, east-central Sweden (around Stockholm) is a persistent parent locality; new elements are introduced sometimes in the capital itself and sometimes in a smaller town or rural commune in the vicinity. Examples include such varied items as reallotment of land, 1749 (Figure 2), the church laymen's confederation (Figure 4), sports halls (Figure 5), and swimming baths (not mapped).

A sometimes competing parent locality exists in the southwestern corner of Sweden. Examples are: reallotment of land, 1783 (Figure 3), elementary schools up to 1862 (Figure 6), and milk-control groups, 1898-1909 (Figure 7). This is the best agricultural area of the country; it is particularly important as a gateway for innovations in farming. Impulses often enter from Denmark, to which the area formerly belonged. Urban innovations which enter the country in this corner will usually jump up to the Stockholm area rather quickly and then take the regular paths. South and southwestern Sweden, on the other hand, are often late in adopting items emanating from central-east Sweden (Figure 4).

Within the province of Skåne it is nearly always some part of the western half of the province that acts in the initial stage (Figures 3, 6, 7). The first steps in the spread regularly follow within the southwestern triangle. Soon, also regularly, a jump occurs to a secondary center near the northeastern corner, and gradually areas in between become affected. Finally, if we pay attention to our smallest sample area (Figures 8, 9, 10), we can again trace a pattern of repetitions. A southeastern center is active in all three cases, the northeastern center in only two of them (Figures 9 and 10). Further observations indicate that a spread outward from the two centers at about the same time is most common. (The one-sidedness of Case 8 [Figure 8] will be discussed later.)

There seems then to exist a hierarchy of centers, each one dominating subcenters and surrounding areas of its own and acting in the most varied connections. The stability over time in this pattern is striking.

Looking more closely at the parent localities, we shall find that it is not the same individuals or exactly the same places which act as initiators, even when innovations come close in time. I think this is an important fact which should be kept in mind in further research on the function of innovation centers. In order to trace the secrets of centers of change it is not sufficient to pick out single individuals and test their tendencies to be innovators and/or early adopters. We have to take a closer look at whole populations.

The hierarchical system of rural centers seems to be associated with what is alleged to be the order of prehistoric and early medieval colonization of the country. A wild guess is that status and other social relationships between localities have their roots far back in time and that parent localities once acted as such in the literal sense of the word. Anyhow, it is as if there existed an invisible system of channels and sluices, governing the flows of influence. In this system there are definite upstream and downstream directions. In most countries of the world we can expect to find such a system, reflecting itself in geographic space. Analytically, what we should try to grasp on the micro-scale is the links between individuals exchanging information. I think that the "telling" between people who meet and talk informally is the most important part of the picture. Dissemination through private or group conversation easily outbalances other means of communication. Even today we are very neolithic in that respect, I am sure. In the next sections I shall follow up this line of thought.

III. SPATIAL ASPECTS OF PRIVATE COMMUNICATIONS

In principle it is easy to imagine a huge matrix which, with the aid of probability indices, records the structure of the communication network, knitting together a given population. In practice, however, this population need not become very large before the matrix would be completely intractable for analysis.

Instead of trying to handle all these individual data I am suggesting a simplification taking advantage of the spatial approach. First we can set out to divide our population in subsets according to the distribution over distance of the communication links. We will then find that a certain distance inertia always manifests itself but with differing strength. Some people have links extending far over the national boundaries, more people operate on a regional level, but the majority remain with their links within the local area. From a classification of this kind — which should be much refined, of course — it seems possible to produce a hierarchy of *mean information fields* by the aid of spatial matrices of the type:

$$P_{11} \quad P_{12} \quad P_{13} \quad P_{14} \quad P_{15}$$

$$P_{21} \quad P_{22} \quad P_{23} \quad P_{24} \quad P_{25}$$

$$P_{31} \quad P_{32} \quad P_{33} \quad \ldots \quad \ldots$$

$$\ldots \quad \ldots \quad \ldots \quad \ldots \quad \ldots$$

$$\ldots \quad \ldots \quad \ldots \quad \ldots \quad \ldots \qquad \text{Sum } P_{ij} = 1$$

where P_{11} P_{12} give the probability by which a communication emanting from an individual living in the central cell hits individuals living in different other cells in the surroundings. A matrix of this kind is preferable to an ordinary functional expression because when we finally come down to applications, the matrix has an advantage in the relative ease with which it can be adjusted to approximate the anisotrophic conditions of the real world. So, for example, if the matrix refers to farmers, it may be reasonable to let the P-values extend symmetrically in all directions out from the central cell. But if it refers to, say, a group of university professors in a certain city, then it should perhaps have noteworthy indices only in the central cell and some other scattered ones which contain other universities.

I have tried to estimate the probabilities of the mean information field on the local level for the farm population in the same rural area for which three of our innovational processes were recorded (Figures 8, 9, and 10). The method was indirect rather than direct. One set of data emanated from a census of telephone calls between villages, and another from recordings of local movements between dwellings. The use of telephone data where available is a self-evident procedure. The measurements of population movements may seem a little farfetched at first glance. Yet it is a fact (and can be shown in great detail in Sweden) that gross population movements within rural areas show small variations as to destinations over time. Generation after generation follow the same pattern. Stability persists because most vacancies are made known through private channels. This process maintained over a long time must inevitably have given the frequency of family and friendship relations between places a high degree of stability; and the movements as such reflect these relations.

The telephone-call distribution and the migration field of any rural area turn out to be very similar also in their deviation from the normal rule of decreasing contact with increasing distance. Local migration as a measure of contact gives more detail and is applicable in the Swedish context for two hundred years back in time. That is why these data have been preferred in the

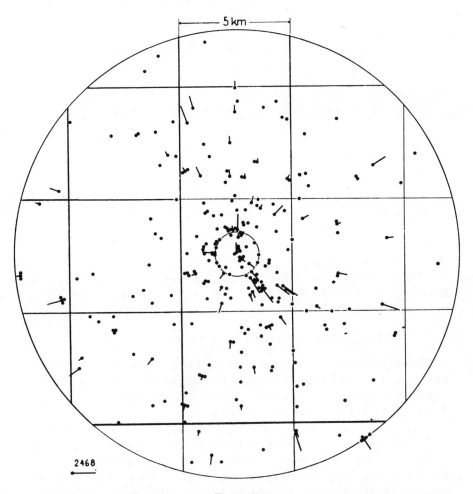

FIGURE 11
Distance distribution of movements between dwellings

following demonstration, although any reasonable estimate of contact probabilities will serve. For groups of people having communication connections
extending to the regional or international ranges we have to resort to estimates from quite different sources.[16]

The distance distribution of movements between dwellings from 1935
through 1939 in a sample area is shown on Figure 11. Each single mover or
family group is represented by a dot giving the length and direction of the
movement. Bars indicate sizes of families. After smoothing we get the following relative figures, collected in a matrix of which the cells are 5 × 5 km.

16. Presently I am trying to find out from newspapers how far away from home and in what
sorts of places such people participate in reported activities.

.0096   .0140   .0168   .0140   .0096

.0301   .0547   .0301

.4431

and so on symmetrically.

Some similar observations have been supplied by Professor Forrest S. Pitts of the University of Oregon in a private letter relating to the Kagawa district in northern Shikoku, Japan. His data give the following associated probabilities for 785 marriage distances in the year 1951.

.0103   .0150   .0181   .0150   .0103

.0279   .0557   .0279

.4319

and so on symmetrically.

The similarity to the earlier Swedish data is so striking that it is almost disturbing. However, it is likely that corresponding figures from other areas would differ considerably.

IV. ON SIMULATION MODELS OF DIFFUSION

The concepts of a mean information field and a hierarchy of such fields provide instruments for making deductions about the diffusion of information in a way that is entirely independent of our innovational data. One way to do this is by the aid of Monte Carlo simulations.

The simulation technique makes it possible to create imagined societies of different structure, to endow individuals with various behavior probabilities and rules of action, and finally to let random numbers infuse life into the system. The course of events can then be observed, starting from different initial situations. It might well be said that simulation lacks the generality and elegance of a strictly mathematical formulation; nevertheless the technique is a very useful one. To work with sets of assumptions on which to run the simulations and to study the outcomes aids both in improving concepts and in ruling out impossible ideas. Also, the simulation may well lead to observations that can be verified later on by actual facts, but would have been left unnoticed without this device.

Some specific examples of simple simulations will be cited, first using material and ideas from a book published in Swedish.[17] To begin with we choose a model-plane with isotropic conditions as to population distribution and transportation. It is made up of square cells, supposed to correspond to the 5 × 5 km. cells which were used as a reference grid in Cases 8-10 above and for the mean information field. The model-plane has an evenly distributed population with 30 inhabitants in each cell, chosen to correspond roughly to

17. T. Hägerstrand, *Innovationsförloppet ur korologisk synpunkt*, (Lund: Gleerupska, 1953).

the density of farmsteads in the area just referred to. Further, the model-plane is considered to form a transportation surface on which movements can proceed in all directions without barriers.

The rules of the game for model I will be chosen as follows:

1. At the outset there is one single adopter of some hypothetical innovation.

2. The innovation is adopted as soon as it is heard of.

3. Information is spread exclusively through private tellings at pairwise meetings.

4. The tellings take place at constant intervals of time (called generation intervals); then every adopter informs another individual, adopter or non-adopter.

5. The destination of every telling is given by the aid of random numbers according to the probabilities of the mean information field.

The second rule is of course very unrealistic, but it is nevertheless convenient to start in this simple way. The fourth rule, involving a constantly pulsating interval of time, is also a simplifying device. To introduce in addition a probability distribution over time would complicate operations without much gain at this experimental stage. A typical run of this simulation is shown in Figure 12.

The growth curve is steeply ascending without an elongated initial stage. Among the given empirical cases it resembles the milk-control groups (Case 7) and the subsidies for pasture-land (Case 8). As could be expected, at first the number of adopters follows the relation $g_n = 2^n$ (where g stands for generation):

g_n	2^n	Number of adopters	g_n	2^n	Number of adopters
g_0	1	1	g_5	32	31
g_1	2	2	g_6	64	60
g_2	4	4	g_7	128	114
g_3	8	8	g_8	256	215
g_4	16	16			

Soon, however, a "blocking effect" manifests itself because of the growing number of tellings from adopter to adopter. This effect makes the first adopters less and less influential in producing further growth.

Looking at Figure 12, isolines and profiles depict percentages of adoption according to the scale 2, 4, 8, 16, 32 per cent; we find that the spatial distribution soon becomes somewhat irregular with secondary centers appearing. We can easily see the neighborhood effect at work. Thus the distribution of the very first adopters is decisive for the location of areas where a high number of adopters appear later on. The horizontal spread is rather swift; in g_8, when central adoption reaches around 50 per cent, the radius of the cluster can be

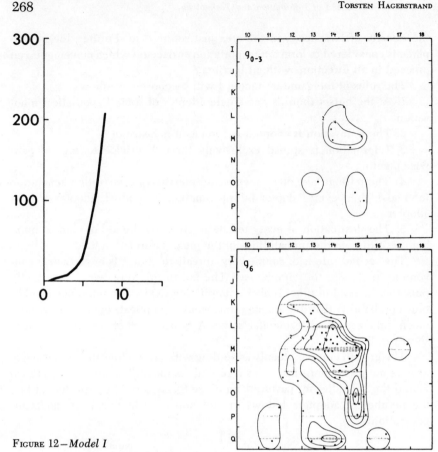

FIGURE 12—*Model I*

estimated at 45 km. All this compares in principle quite well with the space-time course of Case 8, which this model was designed to imitate in the first place.

Comparing the space-time course of Case 9 (Figures 1 and 9) with our simulation, we notice at once two main differences. Case 9 has a long initial development before the breakthrough; this initial phase we miss in model I. Further, the local concentration of adoptions became quite high within centers, in combination with a rather restricted outward extension. In the northeastern center, for example, more than 90 per cent of the farmers had adopted control methods in 1937, before the east-west spread from the center exceeded 20 km. The assumptions made for model I do not imply such an outcome.

When changing the assumptions, it would be preferable to introduce just one new factor which alone could influence both growth-curve and spatial distribution in the direction indicated. We know from everyday experience

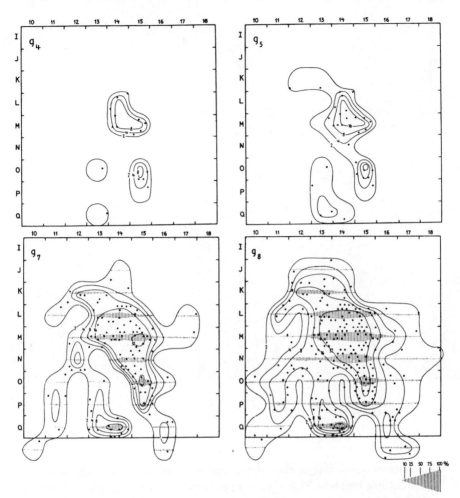

that we do not normally accept a novelty at the first moment we learn about it. One has to get accustomed to new ideas and/or one has to revise existing plans and arrangements, look over economic problems, and so on. There is a wide variety of factors which we may boldly hide under one roof, *resistance*. For a multitude of reasons a population offers a resistance to change. The noble lord of Londonderry opposed the prepaid penny-post in 1840 because he did not want to cut a slit in his mahogany door, and William Wordsworth opposed it because he did not like to answer letters. Of course resistance is variable, and probably we should not assume that individual behavior is always the same from innovation to innovation; a given individual may show a high resistance to one trait, a low resistance to another. In addition to individual variations, or rather governing them, there is also a general level

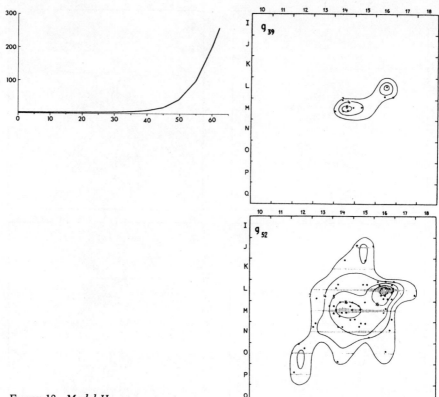

FIGURE 13—*Model II*

of resistance according to the relation between the innovation and the state of the culture it enters. This is all very easy to talk about in a general way but a hard nut to crack empirically.

In the present theoretical context it has seemed simplest to express resistance as a threshold which normally can be overcome by repeated contacts with adopters. We assume that every telling contains one parcel of positive influence towards adoption. We assume further that some people have low resistance thresholds and need only to receive one or a few such stimuli before adopting. Others need many, or have an inpenetrable wall instead of a threshold.

For model II, rules 1, 3, 4, and 5 are the same as in model I, but rule 2 becomes: adoption takes place after a specified number of tellings (the threshold), different for various individuals. We arbitrarily endow the population on the model-plane with a resistance which varies only between 5 and 1. In the absence of empirical evidence, we assume further that most people cluster around the average resistance classes with the following populations: 2, 7, 12,

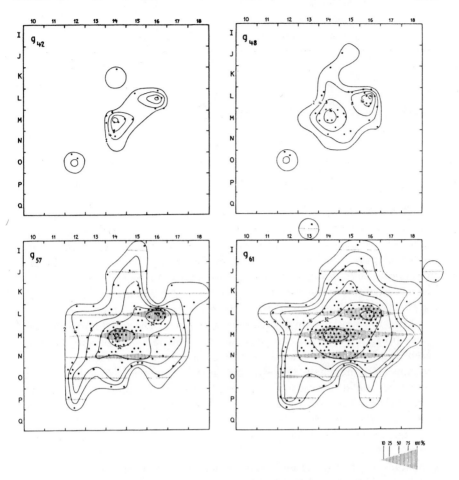

7, 2. Who will be assigned what resistance is decided by random numbers. The cell was used as the unit of stratification in order to maintain a general isotropy on the plane.

When playing this new variant of the game we soon notice — as could readily be expected — that the population will be divided into three categories: (1) non-knowers, (2) knowers but non-adopters, and (3) adopters. Spatially the distribution of knowers is much wider than that of adopters. We will get two growth curves, one for the first information and the other for the adoption. The time-lag is an expression of resistance, which could be ascertained empirically through interviews.

A typical run of this model II simulation is shown in Figure 13, the growth-curve of adoptions has a long initial phase with slow development, like the majority of our empirical cases, but in striking contrast to model I:

g_n	Number of adopters	g_n	Number of adopters
g_0	1	g_{35}	7
g_5	1	g_{40}	11
g_{10}	2	g_{45}	20
g_{15}	2	g_{50}	43
g_{20}	2	g_{55}	90
g_{25}	3	g_{60}	186
g_{30}	4	g_{62}	261

There is a long period of time during which discussions go on but very few adoptions take place, but finally a breakthrough appears. At that time, every new adopter near the parent locality is more effective in influencing further adoptions than was the case in the beginning, because the prolonged discussions have brought so many persons close to adoption. On the other hand, at least where the density is highest, we also find a considerable blocking effect at work (just as in model I), since adopters tell adopters.

Also, the spatial growth differs from model I. The neighborhood effect is still present and so also are secondary centers at some distance from the parent locality, thanks to an early coincidence between a telling and a low resistance. On the whole, however, the cluster is much more regular than was the case in model I; there is also a much higher rate of adoption at the center in relation to outward spread. The graph of model II can in a general way quite well be exemplified by Case 9 (Figures 1 and 9).

Thus without changing the mean information field it is possible simultaneously to adjust both the growth curve and the spatial clustering in a desirable direction using the single device of the resistance concept.[18]

It should be added that finer details implicit in the assumptions can be brought forth only after many repeated runs of the simulation. Such work becomes worthwhile when we specify a model-plane and a model population with properties closer to real areas and populations. One experiment in that direction will be presented as a demonstration. The design was made with Case 8 in mind, which means that we go back to the set of assumptions given for model I. Now a model-plane is used which has at least two attributes in common with the actual sample region. First, the distribution of potential adopters equals the number of farms in each cell entitled to the subsidy in question. Second, some barriers to communications are located along certain cell-boundaries in order to imitate the effect of the lakes and roadless forests that cut up the real area. These barriers on the model-plane prevent communications entirely in some places and diminish their frequency in some

18. The technique was originally worked out for a conference on quantitative techniques in geography held in 1960, "On Monte Carlo Simulation of Diffusion," *Sumposium on Quantitative Methods in Geography.*

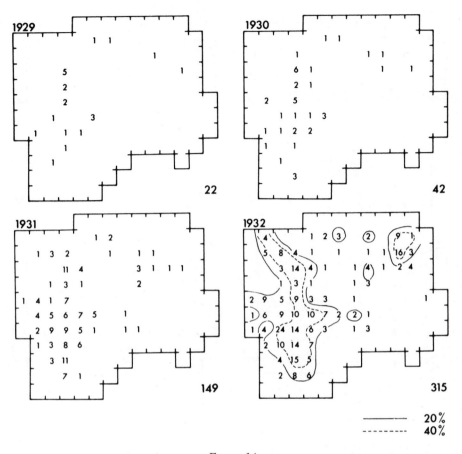

FIGURE 14
Spread of subsidized improvement of pasture (number of farms up to given date)

other places, according to indications given by the census of telephone calls between villages. As hardly any innovation meets with so small an *a priori* resistance as subsidies to farmers, the resistance element is left out altogether. We use the assumptions of model I with the exception that we do not let the process start out from only one initial adopter (as in assumption 1), but use as input the distribution of adopters reached in 1929.

Skipping over all technical details, we arrive at the three simulations given in Figures 15–17. These figures should be compared with actual data as given on Figure 14, which has the same content as Figure 8 but in numerical translation.[19] We have to accept that there is no independent way to connect real time and model time; instead we parallel years and generations that have approximately equal numbers of adopters. Then we ask whether

19. For planning the computer work I am indebted to Professor Carl Erik Fröberg.

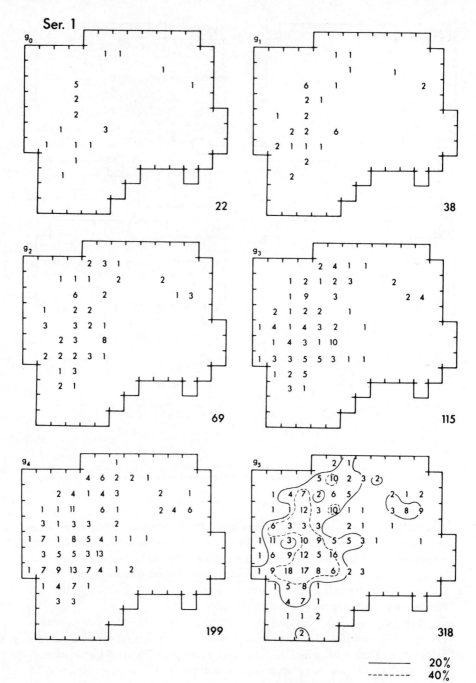

FIGURE 15
Simulation: Series 1

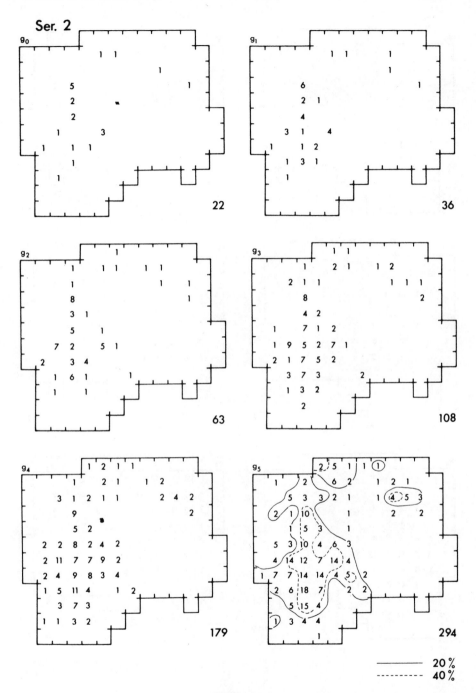

FIGURE 16
Simulation: Series 2

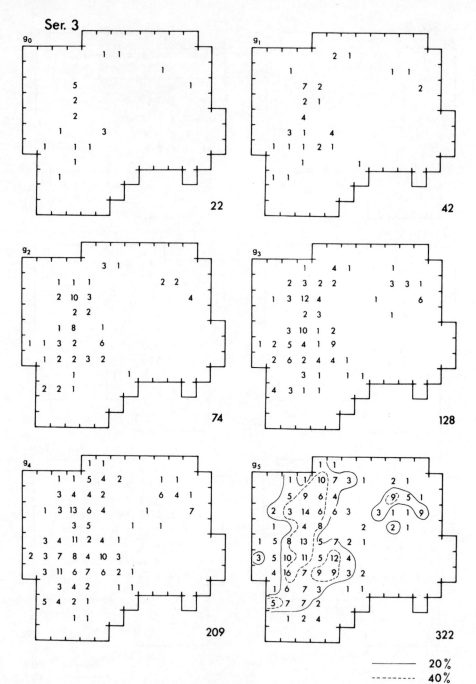

FIGURE 17
Simulation: Series 3

the spatial distributions at the same "times" are approximately similar. In order to facilitate this comparison, isolines have been inserted for adoption rates of 20 and 40 percent. Inspection shows a surprising correspondence. The high ridges and spots and the empty areas come back in every simulation in about the same localities as in the empirical case. The difference between separate runs is of about the same magnitude as that between each run and the observation series. It would seem that simulations of this kind may have interesting and perhaps useful predictive power.

The refining of the structure of the model-plane and the rules of the game introduces difficult test problems that have not been sufficiently studied as yet. In order to simulate the real Case 9 we need to introduce the resistance factor. Empirical evidence suggests that initial resistance should be distributed according to farm size. No experiment has so far been tried since a computer with sufficient memory capacity was not available.

I hope it has been shown that models of this kind are very attractive because they admit a wide variety of elaborations. At the moment there is nothing quite ready for demonstration of such variations, so I have to indicate in a very general way some of the lines along which work is going on parallel with the collection of empirical observations. Two main groups of variations present themselves: those connected with *communication* and those connected with *resistance*.

For the sake of simplicity and because of lack of practicable data, we have assumed so far that one and the same communication field was at work throughout the whole model population. This may be acceptable as long as we work in a restricted area, focusing on only one fairly homogenous social group, as farmers. The next step will be to widen the scope and introduce a hierarchy of information fields of different spatial range, and let them operate all at the same time.[20]

In this connection we have to introduce also some device which makes tellings in one direction within the hierarchy normally more powerful than tellings in the opposite direction. In their present form the models do not illustrate the obvious perseverance of parent localities. On the contrary, they allow the starting-points to be located anywhere with equal effect. Real innovations do not seem to behave that way. One can find new ideas appearing in isolation outside established centers and remaining isolated and unaccepted until eventually a center is activated and the innovation begins to approach from the usual quarter. In all probability there exist rather stable hierarchical systems of normative centers which are very difficult to counteract because they reflect not the accidental status of a few single individuals but a status-order between whole clusters of populations. A good idea in itself, but suggested in some remote spot, may set down the proposer as a

20. As suggested by G. Karlsson in *Social Mechanisms* (Stockholm: Almqvist and Wiksell, 1958), one should also allow for a variation in the frequency of contacts in broad groups.

fool; while the same idea will flow out into the population in good order when it comes from the nearest normative center.

Our present material gives rise to further speculations around the importance of due order of introduction. In the smallest sample area (Figures 8–10) there are, as pointed out earlier, two distinct centers of introduction, one in the northeastern and the other in the southwestern corner. Cases 9 and 10 show both in operation at the same time. Several series of observations not included here indicate that this equilibrium between the particular centers is common.

Case 8 (Figure 8) shows something different. This innovation develops in a one-sided way in the western half of the area and flows eastwards only gradually, in spite of the fact that the density of small farms is about equal throughout. It is worth noting that the Provincial Agricultural Society distributed its information evenly over the whole area, with demonstrations in the field, yet these had little effect on the eastern farmers. Now it so happens that many farms in the southwestern center have less than 10 hectares of tilled land. Their size entitled them to the subsidy in question, and so this area could function in the usual normative way. The leading farms in the northeastern center, on the contrary, have acreages above 20 hectares and were not entitled to subsidies. One may guess that the smaller farms in the latter neighborhood failed to act because they lacked their customary exemplars. This made them enter the picture later on, after there was already wide adoption in the western half of the area. The above discussion is hypothetical and not easy to test so many years after the actual events. But at least it poses a problem which should be looked out for in other situations.

Models I and II treat other forms of communication than pair-wise tellings as non-existent. It would be feasible to take mass media into account by supposing some randomly distributed information poured out over the population and added to the information spread through tellings.[21] It should be kept in mind, however, that if the concept of a status-hierarchy of centers is applicable, then messages from mass media may well find scattered adopters everywhere, but their influence in the next step of interpersonal communications would be limited outside the "proper" centers.

Further modifications of the models should take up the case in which two or more competing centers propagate mutually exclusive messages. First we have to invent adoption and conversation rules which formalize the effect of competing (say, + and −) tellings, and which are reasonably acceptable to psychologists. Then we can set out to study many fascinating problems. One would be the conditions for stable cultural boundaries (= zones where competing influences meet) and for moving boundaries. A second problem would be to study the effect of different locations of propaganda centers. What will happen if a new idea likely to be opposed is introduced in the midst of an

---

21. This would be a simulation approach to the two-step flow hypothesis. Karlsson (op. cit.) discussed the assumptions for a model combining mass media and interpersonal communication, but actual experimental work remains to be done.

established center? What if it is introduced far from such a center? Some data on voting behavior should provide material for testing.

In model II different grades of resistance were evenly distributed over the model area. In order to come closer to real-world conditions we have to study the effects of different regional patterns of high and low resistance and also of different resistance distributions among individual units of adoption in the same area.

V. SOME COMMENTS ON APPLICATIONS

It must remain an open question as to how far findings, ideas, and techniques of the type set forth here may become useful for the engineering of induced innovations. The concepts used in model II form at least a basis for classifying possible practical measures into two broad groups: those referring to *communication* activities and those referring to *resistance*.

To influence the structure of the network of private links in the system of social communication in a desired direction is probably next to impossible. In fact, not even literacy or modern means of transportation and communication seem to change certain basic mechanisms very much. How else can we explain that diffusional patterns persist over two centuries as they obviously have in Sweden? (Reservations must be made for the possible impact of radio and television.) The main effect of education perhaps must be sought in other directions, which have to do with the resistance part of the matter. Obviously, however, education is a necessary prerequisite for gradually more and more complicated innovations. On the whole, when trying to induce innovations, it would seem to be wise to collect what information there is about the existing network and to try to use it as it is.

There seem to exist two schools of action when it comes to tactics in the locating of information activities. One tries to spread out demonstrations, lectures, group-discussions, and individual advice as evenly as possible over an area in order to reach as many people as possible. The other school concentrates its efforts on more or less well-chosen centers, or gives advice upon request; this probably automatically gives a variation of the center principle. The center principle has a long history, and was being used already by the Christian monks when they erected churches at the heathen centers of sacrifice. Our observations suggest that a concentrated effort at existing centers would be more effective than an even spread of effort. However, the possibility must be held open that hierarchies of centers and sub-centers are most neatly evidenced in countries like Sweden or France, which have enjoyed centralized bureaucracies for centuries. In many present-day preindustrial countries, one may well expect to find a cell-structure of areas dominated by provincial centers that are only loosely interconnected and that oppose domination.

Whatever the case may be, it would seem worthwhile to try to get some idea of the communication structure (as defined here) in development areas. One standard procedure then would be to map what new developments have already been successfully spread and to trace the underlying direction of influences for subsequent use. It would be important to know not only the number of adoptions but also their spatial distribution. If, for example, model II is approximately valid, then there is a direct relation between the general level of resistance and geographical spread. A highly concentrated cluster of adoptions should indicate a high level of resistance and vice versa. Today it is an annoying fact that although so much effort and money is spent on development projects, the follow-up side is almost completely neglected.

The resistance factor is probably more within reach of moderately successful manipulations. Even if extremely complicated cultural factors enter the picture, in some cases we may perhaps resort to a conviction that human rationality has some common denominators irrespective of culture. In our sample of cases from Sweden, economic rewards and coercive measures have broken down resistance in several cases. Progressive control of bovine tuberculosis was accompanied by subsidy measures. The raising of milk prices in particular had noticeable effects two times, as can be seen on the growth curve (Figure I, Case 8, vertical arrows); a first small subsidy in 1937 caused some upward bend of the curve, and the bigger subsidy of 1941 had a similar but much stronger effect. It is interesting to look for the spatial outcome of this accelerated adoption. On both occasions we find the first reactions in areas which—according to model II—ought to be next in turn to adopt even without external stimulus; that is, where we had reason to believe that the innovation was already best known and talked about. In 1941 the innovation proceeded at a very high speed without losing its spatial orderliness.[22] If it is politically possible to differentiate when giving aid, it would seem most efficient to·move out step by step from centers of innovation.

More coercive methods to overcome resistance were used in connection with the reallotment of land and the introduction of elementary schools. In the first case one single landowner in a village could get the work started against the will of his fellow farmers. This device must have speeded up adoption a great deal; nevertheless the neighborhood effect was not thrown out of gear. Elementary schools were enforced in 1842 with the stipulation that every parish should have organized a school within five years. In the province of Skåne, which had the biggest cluster of schools already before 1842, we again notice two steps in the growth curve (Figure 1), a smaller one immediately before 1842 and a much larger one just before 1847. Then follows, after some retardation, the introduction of more than one school per parish. Between 1842 and 1847 the spatial spread still follows the neighborhood-effect principle, though with a greater speed than would have been realized without the existence of a deadline. A closer analysis of the reports of school inspectors would give interesting information about quality of schools and parent reactions in remote areas where the "natural" innovational process was forestalled. Unfortunately, no one has yet undertaken this research.

22. Maps for shorter periods of the year are given in Hägerstrand, *op. cit.*

CHAPTER 13

THE INTERNATIONAL EXCHANGE OF KNOWLEDGE

Simon Rottenberg

The idea that the wealth of nations is determined by the rate of formation of human capital has trickled down from the scholarly community to the lay consciousness. It is now not uncommon for the idea to make its appearance in Presidential addresses and in the talks of business tycoons. A study of the diffusion of this idea, of the areas into which it has infiltrated, and of those which have remained impervious to it, would itself be a fascinating object of research and would tell something about the transfer of knowledge.

To form human capital is equivalent to increasing the stock of knowledge. We take as a first premise.that the spatial distribution of income in the world is like the distribution of knowledge: countries in which the stock of it is large are rich; those in which the stock is small are poor. Countries in which the rate of increase of the stock is high become richer faster than those in which these rates are low.

What is the meaning of "knowledge" in this context? If the Burmese were to copy every work in the British Museum and place the reproduction in a depository in Rangoon, it would be possible to value this activity by summing the costs of the productive services employed in the enterprise. There would be an increment to the wealth of the country and to its income in the period in which the enterprise was carried out. But if the productive services engaged in the copying were drawn from other uses, as in principle they must be, it is not clear that the increment will be positive.

Knowledge on paper is not *per se* income-producing, but only that knowledge comanded by men. It is in this sense that it can be said that an increase in the stock of knowledge is the same as the formation of human capital.

The proposition that the spatial distribution of knowledge and income are congruent is not here defended, but offered as an axiom. If evidence is sought, it might be searched for in such data as those on the international distribution of literacy, of teachers, of real resource expenditures for education, or of Nobel prize winners. The latter is of particular interest. Between 1901 and 1960, 209 persons were awarded Nobel Prizes in physics. chemistry, and medicine and physiology. Of these no less than 187 were from the countries of North America and Western and Central Europe. Many of the residual 22 were from the relatively high-income countries of other regions of the world—Russia, Australia, Argentina, South Africa. The coincidence of the geographical concentrations of Nobel prize winners and income is striking, even when adjusted for population, and is here asserted to be not accidental.

A dictionary definition of *knowledge* is "acquaintance with facts; range of information, awareness, or understanding; all that has been perceived and grasped by the mind; learning; enlightenment." The definition is not very helpful in the context of a discussion of the causes of economic growth. There are diverse classes of facts and information. Some have relevance to the production of goods and services and others do not. Of those that do, some have large, and others small, output effects.

Primitive peoples have knowledge of techniques of accommodation to deserts and jungles that are not commonly commanded by the inhabitants of the high-income regions of the world. Their incomes are higher because they possess this knowledge than they would be in its absence; but the hypothesis can be ventured that they are among the low-income-earning people of the world partly because they are confronted by inhospitable environments, but mainly because they do not possess the classes of knowledge the increments of which earn Nobel awards. In other words, it is here ventured that economic growth and high levels of income are correlated with the possession of the kinds of "facts and information" that are produced by what has conventionally come to be called "basic research." A community that commands a large stock of knowledge of this kind finds applied uses for it. Such a community possesses also a large stock of cognate knowledge that complements other resources and cheapens the cost of production.

If the proposition that knowledge and income are highly correlated is true, and if a causal relationship runs from knowledge to income, it follows that the redistribution of income in the world requires, as a prior condition, the redistribution of knowledge. This is the framework within which the international and inter-regional transfer of knowledge has relevance to life.

Knowledge does not move from place to place at zero cost. Real resources must be devoted to both its transmission and its reception. The quantity that will move can be expected to be an inverse function of the unit cost of movement. Whatever diminishes the quantity of resources employed in transferring a unit of knowledge will cause the number of units transferred to be larger. The quantity moved will also be a direct function of the total cost of the movement. The larger the total quantity of resources devoted to the spatial transfer of knowledge, the larger will be the magnitude of movement.

The critical importance of knowledge in the economy can be perceived if all productive inputs are collapsed into two classes: knowledge and energy. Nothing can be said about the relationship of the two classes because each is an aggregate of diverse things; if they were decomposed, some kinds of knowledge would be seen to be substitutable for some kinds of energy, and other pairs would be clearly complementary. It is also likely to be true that, when the class "knowledge" is disaggregated, some of the components will be more or less good substitutes for one another and some will be complements.

A number of observations about the processes of the transfer of knowledge are suggested by analogy from information theory.[1] Imagine signals being emitted by a source, passing through channels, which are media over which signals are transmitted, and being received. The signals may be more or less powerful when emitted; their number may be more or less numerous in some time period; they may be repeated with more or less frequency. The channels through which they move may be more or less "noisy" (there may be more or less resistance to the transmission); they may be narrow or wide; the noise may be equally distributed in the channel or some parts may be relatively noise-free. The number of channels may be many or few; given signals may be transmitted over only one or more than one channel. There may or may not be filters separating signals from signals-*cum*-noise; if there are filters, they may be more or less efficient.

The movement of knowledge simulates the processes postulated by information theory. The relevant variables determining the volume of flow of knowledge from places with large stocks to those with small stocks seem to be the following:

1) the quantity of knowledge emitted at the source;
2) the quantity of resources employed in emission;
3) the frequency of repetitive emission of any given unit of knowledge;
4) the number of channels over which transmission occurs;
5) the dimensions of these channels;
6) the degree of freedom with which emitted knowledge flows through channels; and
7) the quantity of resources employed in reception.

These hypotheses are, however, not helpful until we are able to achieve pragmatic verification of the variables. The "quantity of knowledge" is an empty phrase until units of knowledge can be assigned their appropriate weights. Populations of weights will be variant from place to place; their structures will depend upon the kinds and quantities of resources which knowledge complements in different places.

It is uncertain whether the cost of retransmission falls or rises at the margin, or whether it is constant. Nor is there a certain rate at which knowledge received increases as the number of repetitive transmissions increases; nor again is there a fixed relationship between the rate of increase of received knowledge and diminished durations of intervals between transmissions of a given unit of knowledge. Unless these marginal cost and marginal "revenue" schedules can be at least implicitly constructed, one cannot know the optimal number and frequency of retransmissions.

1. I have found Leon Brillouin, *Science and Information Theory* (New York: Academic Press, Inc., 1956), to be especially helpful in the preparation of this chapter.

What is the meaning of "dimensions" of a channel used for conveying knowledge? The breadth of a channel may be said to be determined by the efficiency with which it carries knowledge from place to place. If we assume a given quantity of resources devoted to emission, transmission, and reception, that channel is broadest which causes the smallest numerical ratio of the quantity of knowledge emitted to the quantity of knowledge received. Channels of communication are myriad. Some that are broad in one cultural context are narrow in another. We cannot yet distinguish clearly the large and small dimension channels in given cases. We do not yet know the principles for the optimal association of characteristics of channels and the characteristics of culture; nor do we even know which cultural characteristics are relevant and which irrelevant to the construction of this association. Of those that are relevant (were we able to make the foregoing distinction), we do not know which are to be heavily weighted and which only lightly.

Similarly "noise" in channels is culturally determined. Noise, in information theory, is whatever causes information received to be different from information emitted. There are such noises in channels over which knowledge is transmitted. In addition, there are "noises" of another kind—those that impede the free flow of knowledge, causing the flow to be viscous and increasing the cost of moving a given quantity of knowledge over a given distance in a given time. Both kinds of "noise" are variant with cultures. The qualities that produce differences of some magnitude between emitted and received knowledge among Basutos are not the same as those producing this difference among Canadians; similarly, the qualities that raise the cost of transmission for the one are not the same as those that do so for the other. We know little about what the respective qualities are.

Resources employed in the reception of knowledge may be of high or low quality. The higher the quality, the less the quantity of resources needed to bring off a given transfer of knowledge. We can distinguish these qualities of different resources *ex post* by examining the cost of some output transferred in different ways. But we do not seem to know how to rank resources qualitatively by some technique that is independent of output.

The burden of the foregoing paragraphs is that the principles of optimization for the knowledge-transferring industry can be spelled out; what is difficult is to apply them. Willy-nilly they would be applied if the whole industry were in the private sector and if there were free entry into it; for, even if every firm in the industry used random processes in choosing knowledge to be emitted, channels of transmission, processes of transmission, recources to be used in reception, etc., only those most closely approximating the optima would survive. But the industry is not wholly in the private sector, and its public sector component, which is not subject to the discipline of the consumption of capital, must resort to non-market criteria for determining optimal performance. If it cannot find them, it will produce waste.

This is not to say that the whole problem comes into existence because there is a public sector component in this industry. If households systematically underestimate the return to investment in the acquisition of knowledge, or if knowledge-producing behavior creates external economics, then action by instruments expressing the aggregated preferences of households is essential. In the absence of such action, the knowledge industry will be too small, and the output of goods and services in general over a sufficiently long run will be less than maximized with given resources. Given postulates that yield underinvestment by households, it is desirable that governments act. But how shall they act? If knowledge is to be redistributed in the world, what are the processes by which it is to be done? Of the whole range of knowledge, which parts are most usefully moved? Shall it be "imported" in wholesale lots — as knowledge of the physical laws of the behavior of gases — or in retail — as knowledge of the techniques of repair of internal combustion engines? Shall new indigenous knowledge-producing industries and firms be created, or shall the output of such industries and firms in other countries be imported? Shall a country that is poor in knowledge manufacture or trade?

The last of these questions raises the problem of the international trade in human capital. Some simple propositions can be made about this. Suppose a country's government desires to increase the stock of knowledge within it. Suppose it is offered human capital at a zero price — as technical assistance personnel made available by the government of another country. Suppose further that the offering country proposes "take it or leave it" terms and permits the receiving country no option with respect to the particular kind of human capital that is offered. Surely the poor country should accept, for by so doing it will increase the resources it commands at no additional cost to it, and, therefore, increase its economic output.

Suppose now that a zero-price offer permits the receiving country to opt among kinds of human capital. It will still be advantaged by accepting, and it should choose that form of capital that will have the highest yield, discounting at an appropriate interest rate the income streams this capital will yield in the future.

Suppose the price is not zero. Here familiar principles of the theory of exchange come into play to distinguish cases in which trade pays from those in which it does not. In private market decisions, the problem of whether to have traded or not does not explicitly arise. On the rational behavior postulate, if the transaction occurred, it should have; if it did not, it should not have. If there are no artificial constraints on movement, human capital resources move from knowledge-rich to knowledge-poor countries, or they do not. If they do, it is because, all things considered, they are advantaged by doing so.

One operational hypothesis is that they are paid more for the services they render in the new country than they would have been paid for those they would have rendered in the old country. Another is that they are paid exactly as much as identical human capital resources native to the country to which they move. A relevant prediction is that if (relative to the quantities of other resources) human capital is scarce in some countries and abundant in others, while the demand for it is equal in all countries, net movement will be from the countries where it is abundant to those where it is scarce, responding to price differentials for the services of these resources in the two places, which make this movement attractive to the owners of the capital. It is also predicted that the volume of movement will, over time, be just sufficient to equalize the proportional quantities of human capital and other resources in the two sets of countries. When this occurs, the prices of human capital in the two places will be equal; the inducement for movement will have been liquidated; the distribution of knowledge in the world will be, if not equal, at least proportional to other resources; and, on the hypothesis offered earlier, income will also have been redistributed so that it is more equal.[2]

The price is said to be positive in the foregoing case because the payments made to in-migrant human capital for its services (even if the migration is permanent) gives its owner a claim on the output of others in the community. Permanent migrants are no different in this respect from temporary ones.

The processes just described tend towards, and finally achieve, equilibrium and optimal solutions. They can work themselves out, however, only if barriers are not put in the way of movement. In the real world, of course, there are such barriers, which are erected to advantage a sub-community of incumbents in, and aspirants to entry into, the professional employments. It is often said that the interests of the whole community are served by policies inhibiting the entry of outsiders, but such policies are really costly.

These barriers take diverse forms. They may be requirements that the practitioners of a profession be graduates of a local university or members of a local association (to which, however, membership is effectively barred). They may prohibit foreigners from practicing specified professions, or may permit this only if some public agency determines that nationals are "not available."

2. Some attention must be given to the qualifications which have been written into the preceeding paragraph. If there are constraints on movement among countries, human capital may be locked out of the countries in which it is relatively scarce. If there are no such constraints, or if they are not powerful enough to defeat the response to differential incentives, it is only *net* movement that will be towards the scarce human capital countries; there will be countercurrents of movement but the current in the one direction will be stronger than that going the other way. And if the demand for human capital is less in one country than in another, even the net movement may appear to be from scarce supply to abundant supply countries, when, in fact, it is the other way around, since scarcity of supply is always relative to demand.

Thus, if in some hypothetical "Nigeria," the demand for the services of medical doctors is very small, because witch doctors are believed to be a good substitute, even a small number of medical doctors would be an abundant supply, and we should perhaps find the net movement of physicians to flow away from "Nigeria" to other countries where the demand for physicians' services is large; therefore, the supply (although absolutely larger) may be relatively more scarce. The demand for some particular form of human capital is determined not only by taste, as in this case, but also by the quantities of complementary resources in different places. The demand for nuclear physicists is, perhaps, determined by the supply of nuclear reactors; absolutely small numbers of physicists in "Nigeria" may be relatively abundant, if there are no reactors there. In both of these cases, therefore, net movement of human capital from hypothetical "Nigeria" to a hypothetical "United Kingdom" is consistent with the conventional predictive propositions about the movement of capital from places where it is abundant to places where it is scarce.

Knowledge is often explicitly transacted internationally.[3] Consulting firms are prepared to render services, most of which "contain" knowledge, for a fee. In addition, firms mainly engaged in the production of goods will sometimes sell services, as will industrial research and testing and analysis laboratories. These services are of enormous variety. Their purchase is an instrument by which small firms can achieve economies of specialization usually associated with scale. Large firms may have sufficient testing to be done to warrant the organization of internal specialized testing laboratories. Small firms may need such services only occasionally; they may acquire specialized knowledge by employing the part-time services of laboratories exclusively devoted to testing and analysis work.

The price of knowledge sold by firms of this kind is difficult to measure because of the great diversity of product that they produce; these range from hydrological surveys to the preparation of building specifications and information on the casting of dental plates.

This private sector market in knowledge can be of great value to the low-income countries because firms in those countries tend to be smaller than those in the richer countries. They are encouraged by cost-minimizing principles to subcontract to others more than larger firms would.

Specialization is, however, a function of the extent of the market. In countries of relatively small populations, there are likely to be few firms in any one industry. Specialized knowledge-producing and selling firms are less likely to be found there. Therefore, small firms in small countries must often resort to the knowledge-selling markets in the richer countries, if they desire to buy these services at all. The pay-off to investment in the purchase of explicit bits and pieces of knowledge in this market will often be high. Nonetheless, there is less purchasing than would be expected because information about the nature of the product sold and about the terms of its sale is not as widely diffused as it should be. More aggressive dissemination of this information would have very great utility.

If the price of knowledge rises in this market more than the price of other things, more intensive use of knowledge can be expected. That is, to the extent that the rule of fixed proportions is not operative, knowledge will be combined in production with larger quantities of other factors. If the relative price change is contra-directional, opposite consequences can be predicted. It would be interesting to examine price trends in this market. As already mentioned, this is extraordinarily difficult because the product is so heterogeneous. Even if this mensuration problem were solved, however, another poses itself.

The market for the sale of knowledge really consists of two markets. In one, inter-firm transactions occur at explicit prices; in the other, transactions are intra-firm at accounting prices. The positions of demand and supply schedules in the former are affected by changes in the quantity of transactions

3. See S. Rottenberg, "How United States Business Firms Promote Technological Progress," *The Sale of Technical Knowledge* (Washington, D.C.: National Planning Association, 1957), pp. 78 ff.

internal to the firm; this is a function of scale and perhaps of other variables. A change in the proportional distribution of the industry's output between the two markets will shift the schedules in the market in which explicit transactions are consummated. Since the shifts may not be of the same magnitude, explicit prices may be affected, even if the schedules are unchanged for the industry as a whole.

One might, of course, look at the labor market as a proxy for the product market. The price trend of knowledge may parallel the price trend of the services of labor in occupations in which the ratio of knowledge to energy is high.

The price of knowledge that is offered in international trade will affect whether a country devotes resources to its re-creation internally or to its acquisition in a trade transaction. Knowledge is a commodity that can be manufactured as well as bought from others, and the principle of relative comparative advantage ought to govern in this respect. Every increment of knowledge is aggregated to the current stock, but, in addition, the production of the increment uses current stock as capital. Thus knowledge has a quality which distinguishes it from almost any other commodity: it is not consumed when used in the productive process. The capital-output ratio for the production of an incremental unit of knowledge seems, however, to be very large, relative to the corresponding ratios for the production of almost any other commodity.

The magnitude of the ratio can be illustrated by reference to the history of the technology of cinematography. Marey, a professor of physiology at the College de France, constructed his *chambre chronophotographique* in 1888 "following the suggestion" of Janssen who, in 1874, had designed the first apparatus for photographing consecutive phases of a single movement. Janssen's work was, in turn, a link in a very long chain that included Alhazen's discussion (in the 11th century) of the persistence of vision. The intermediate inputs that produced Marey's product included the relevant knowledge that had previously been discovered, including Alhazen's work. The sum of all this prior-discovered relevant knowledge must be enormous when compared to Marey's addition. It is in this sense that the capital-output ratio in the knowledge-producing industry is large. On the other hand, it must be observed that, since Janssen's apparatus already contained results of Alhazen's "findings," it was not necessary that Marey be explicitly aware of those findings; if he "knew" Janssen, he "knew" Alhazen, too.

Where the production of knowledge follows a sequential pattern of this kind, with each increment having prior discoveries embedded in it, a community may increase its stock greatly by acquiring only the most recent discovery. This suggests that low-income countries can often acquire knowledge more cheaply by purchasing it from countries that have accumulated a large stock of it than by manufacturing it themselves.

The social cost to the world as a whole of the independent manufacture of knowledge already possessed by others is very large. This is so, given the unique characteristic of knowledge—that it may be given away and still be possessed. But this is true only in a physical, not necessarily a value, sense. If I command the knowledge of writing, I have it still if I teach it to another; but its worth to me is greater, the fewer people who have it. Like other commodities, knowledge has a scarcity value; seen from another viewpoint this is the reason that it carries a price.

Neither a country that imports knowledge nor one that manufactures it wants knowledge without limit, but only enough so that the last increment acquired shall cost a quantity of resources equal in value to that of the product it will yield. Knowledge is capital; it gives up its product over time. The income stream it produces must be at least implicitly capitalized when the decision is made whether or not it will pay to import a unit of it. Other things being equal, the longer the payoff period to any given quantum of resources employed in acquiring knowledge, the more worthwhile it is to put those resources to that rather than some other use. The payoff period ends when the knowledge imported becomes obsolete; obsolescence occurs when "superior" knowledge is discovered. The rate of obsolescence of knowledge of different classes is a partial function of the quantities of resources devoted to discovery in each class. All of this suggests, *caeteris paribus,* that importing countries should expect the costs of purchasing knowledge to be greater in fields in which research investment is small than in fields in which research investment is large. Thirty thousand drachmas spent to learn about the tanning of leather are better spent than thirty thousand to learn about rocket fuel.

It was suggested earlier in this paper that knowledge on paper is not income-producing, but only that knowledge commanded by men. Put somewhat differently, knowledge is income-producing only if it is put to use; this occurs only if it is acted upon by men. A book describing the operations necessary for the production of heat-resistant steel produces nothing until it is taken down from the shelf, its contents assimilated, and the operations performed. In the same way, of course, a man who possesses this knowledge but who does not act upon it produces no steel. Increments of output will occur, there, only if resources are consumed and costs incurred. The knowledge-producing industries do employ other intermediate goods and services (as well as the knowledge they produce for each other)—for instance, laboratory technicians and laboratory equipment—to produce knowledge as a final product, and this adds an increment to the social output. But once produced as a final product of one industry, knowledge becomes an intermediate product in other industries; these industries in turn yield another final product *only if* some other intermediate products are combined with the new knowledge in productive operations. At least one of those complementary inputs must be human time and energy.

In principle, *all* classes of already-existing knowledge can be transferred from one person to another, whether or not both are in the same country, independently of other "assets." All classes of knowledge can be disembodied: they can appear on paper; they need not be carried by men. This is true both of knowledge which says that the sequential performance of operations *a* and *b* will yield consequence C; and of that which says that consequence C will result from the performance of *a* and *b* and not *d* and *e*.

There are some qualities, of course, that are embodied purely in men and cannot be disembodied. Suppose, for example, that a country wanted to increase its stock of thriftiness or responsibility or punctuality or honesty, or to diminish its stock of aversion to risk. In some circumstances the cheapest way to do this might be to import thrifty, responsible, punctual, and honest people —and gamblers. The more a country has of these qualities, *caeteris paribus*, the larger will be its output from given resources or perhaps its growth rate. But these qualities should not be confused with the possession of knowledge.

This chapter has sought to discuss aspects of the international exchange of knowledge in the framework of discourse of the disciplines of economics and information theory. These are vantage points from which this industry is not often seen. Questions have been formulated but almost none have been answered. Defense of this procedure must lie in the claim that the disciplines on which the analysis builds are useful vehicles for the construction of questions appropriate to penetrating understanding of the process through which the exchange of knowledge takes place.

CHAPTER 14

THE "HEREDITARY WORKERS" HYPOTHESIS AND THE DEVELOPMENT OF A FACTORY LABOR FORCE IN EIGHTEENTH- AND NINETEENTH-CENTURY RUSSIA

Arcadius Kahan

Eighteenth-century Russia lacked any developed system of apprenticeship within either crafts or factory system, literacy was low, and there was no extensive network of either general or trade schools. Nevertheless, that century saw the beginnings of a modern factory labor force. That entailed not merely the learning of skills. Indeed, under the conditions of early industrialization or pre-industrialization, the development of work discipline, cooperation within the manufacturing establishment, and other habits that we usually associate with industrial employment (or take for granted in a developed industrial society) is as important and poses at least as great a problem as the formation of skills. The acquisition of the requisite work habits can be painful, costly, and slow.[1]

One of the means by which the acquisition of industrial "habits" and the facilitation of skill transfer from one group of industrial workers to another could be achieved was assuring continuity of industrial employment within a particular occupational or other social group — in other words, the formation of an expanding nucleus of an "hereditary" labor force. It is therefore of interest to trace the development of the hereditary component in the total labor force. The concept "hereditary workers" as used here includes employed second-generation factory workers in general, regardless of whether or not they followed their parents' specific occupation. As I read Professor Hägerstrand's contribution to this conference (Part III, Chapter 12), it appears to me that this note could be viewed as a crude application of his concept of "information fields" in nongeographic (as well as geographic) dimensions. For lack of the measure of "inheritance," I am fundamentally hypothesizing patterns of exposure ("tellings"). Economic choices, given such exposure, are the other half of the story.

1. Factory discipline was instilled in the labor force of the Russian manufacturers of the eighteenth century literally by the whip of overseers, managers, or armed guards. During the nineteenth century, an elaborate system of fines was substituted to enforce discipline and norm fulfillment.

291

Needless to say, the mere percentage of hereditary workers in the total labor force will vary with the pace of industrial change (probably declining relatively in a period of rapidly increasing demand for wage labor), and could therefore not be considered an accurate measure of industrial progress. But over a long period this indicator coupled with some others (urban origin, degree of literacy) might together imply progressive spread of industrial arts. To investigate this problem I began with data for the earliest period of the development of manufacturers in Russia; these eighteenth-century data reflect the situation prior to the general enserfment of the skilled labor force. Data for the period 1897-1913 were then used to provide evidence concerning the period of early Russian industrialization based on modern technology. The first even halfway reliable and indicative data on the social origin and literacy of the labor force in Russian manufactures are those for the second quarter of the eighteenth century. Perhaps their presentation is more of an historical curiosity than an enlightening contribution on this subject. They may be of interest, however, for the similarities or contrasts they present with the formation of an industrial labor force in other countries (see Tables 1 and 2).

A larger sample, covering a broader variety of manufactures during 1737-1740, and therefore more representative than the figures in Tables 1 and 2, provides information with regard to the same general questions, with the results shown in Table 3.

The majority of the manufacturing labor force sampled for the data in Table 3 was of urban origin; for obvious reasons (the newness of the manufactures and the low mobility of the craftsmen) nonindustrial groups supplied the majority of employees. However, additional information from the same

TABLE 1

Urban Origin, Descent, and Literacy Rate among Employees in Linen and Cotton Cloth Manufactures, 1732 and 1737/38°

(In percentages)

	Urban Origin		Worker Descent		Craftsman Descent		Literacy Rate	
	1732	1737/38	1732	1737/38	1732	1737/38	1732	1737/38
Total Workers	42.4	42.8	9.1	13.3	9.7	9.7	6.2	8.6
Males	36.5	39.0	9.2	15.0	7.7	7.7	6.2	8.6
Females	68.3	55.1	8.2	8.2	2.9	2.6	—	—

°The total number of workers in the sample for the two respective years was 1,535 and 1,954, of which males were 1,116 and 1,367 and females 419 and 587 respectively.

Source: The availability of documents that enable us to look into these problems is explained by the orders of January 7 and March 2, 1736, to report the state of the labor force in manufactures following the enserfment of the skilled and semi-skilled workers by the decree of January 7, 1736. (P.S.Z. No. 6858). The data were published in Akademia Ñauk SSSR: *Sotsial'ny Sestav Rabochikh Pervoi Poloviny XVIII veka.* (Moscow-Leningrad, 1934.)

TABLE 2

Social Origin of the Skilled Labor Force in State-Owned Iron and Copper Works, Ural and Siberia (1726, 1745)*

	1726		1745	
	Number	*Percent*	*Number*	*Percent*
Peasant serfs	456	34.5	2,780	78.5
Workers	336	25.5	586	16.5
Raznochintsy†	500	37.7	170	4.8
Foreigners	30	2.3	9	.2
Total Identified	1,322	100.0	3,545	100.0
Unidentified	215	16.3	34	.95

*S. G. Strumilin, *Istoria Chernoi Metallurgii v SSSR* (Moscow, 1954), pp. 286, 321.

†*Raznochintsy* was a description for free members of various service classes.

TABLE 3

Urban Origin, Descent, and Literacy Rate among Employees in Manufactures, 1737-1740*

(in percentages)

	Urban Origin†	*Worker Descent*	*Craftsmen Descent*	*Literacy Rate‡*
Total				
Workers	60.6	10.8	1.1	9.9
Males	64.2	10.9	1.1	9.9
Females	27.6	8.2	.6	(n.a.)

*Number of employees in the sample 6,992, of which 6,405 males and 587 females.

†Percentage of the 6,063 employees who responded.

‡Percentage of the 5,116 employees who responded.

Source: *Sotsial'nyi Sostav Rabochikh Pervoi Poloviny XVIII Veka* (Moscow-Leningrad, 1934).

source suggests that descendants of workers were given preference in the hiring policies of the entrepreneurs.[2] In favor of such a policy the argument

2. The preference given to descendants of employees might be inferred from the age distribution of the various groups of employees at the start of their employment in the establishments.

Percentage Distribution of Employees by Age at the Start of Employment in Manufactures, 1737-1740

	Descendants of Employees	*Total Labor Force*
Less than 11 years	48.6	32.2
12 – 14 years	25.3	22.2
15 – 19 years	17.0	22.8
20 – 24 years	6.1	9.5
25 – 29 years	1.3	5.3
30 and over	1.7	8.0
	100.0	100.0

might be advanced that in numerous cases the skill training for the young workers was provided directly by their employed fathers. In addition, as Table 4 shows, early entrance into manufacturing employment may have spared a number of workers the cruel experience of "vagrancy" and other perhaps similar alternative opportunities open to the early urban laboring class. The impression of relative stability of the worker-descendant group when compared with the other groups suggests that formation of a stable work-force for manufacturing had begun.

TABLE 4

Percentage Distribution of Total Manufacturing Employees and of Manufacturing Employees of Worker Descent According to Their Prior Means of Earning a Living

	Total Employees	Employees of Worker Descent
Stayed with relatives	31.7	67.6
Vagrancy	21.6	9.7
Other wage employment	22.6	8.8
Employment in other manufactures	13.9	8.8
Trade	2.2	1.2
Crafts	1.8	.9
Other odd jobs	6.2	3.0

Source: same as Table 3.

Early entrance into the labor force was more frequent among descendants of factory workers in subsequent periods. Increasing degrees of attitude "commitment" aside, the economic rationality of such behavior has often been remarked; the demand for income by workers' households in which a child was primarily a consumer, not automatically an income earner (as in agriculture), could explain the data almost perfectly. One could probably add that, given the short life expectancy during this period, it was advantageous to begin training as early as possible in order to be able, after the completion of training, to compensate the household for previous outlays.

As long as the income position of workers' households required the early earnings of the rising generation, and as long as technology was more or less stable and general education a prerequisite for few industrial skills, the manufacturers resisted attempts to place upon them the responsibility for educating their young workers. It was plausible for both household and factory to accept a decrease in child labor only after the government had assumed the direct costs of elementary education. Meanwhile, developing technology was coming to require general education as a prerequisite for some kinds of skill training and as a partial substitute for others.

In the eighteenth century, however, early entrance into the labor force provided a visible advantage in skill acquisition in absolute terms (one became a skilled worker at an early age). There is indirect indication also that the early entrants (and the descendants of employees) had the advantage of being able to train for the more highly skilled occupations.

Although skill training was probably the obvious road toward advancement in manufactures, it appears that it was both competing and complementary with more general education (as expressed by literacy). The distribution of literacy among the labor force could almost serve as a proxy for its distribution within the social groups that supplied labor to the manufactures (Table 5). The more detailed data on literacy rates for the sample used in Table 5 indicate that in a substantial number of manufacturing occupations there was a close relation between literacy level and level of skill.[3] Literacy among the more highly skilled workers was substantially above that among the less skilled ones. The data are too fragmentary to argue that literacy was a precondition of higher skills or that the income differential in the past made it profitable to invest in education (although the previous table might provide a hint in this direction). The relationship between skill level and literacy, however, is present.

TABLE 5

Percentage of Literacy by Social Origin of Employees in Manufactures, 1737-1740

Social Group of Parents	Percentage of Literacy
Clergy	31.7
Government officials	18.3
Postal employees	15.0
Non-mercantile urban inhabitants	14.1
Merchants and traders	13.1
Inhabitants of craft and mercantile settlements	10.6
Soldiers	7.4
Workers	6.8
Peasants	6.8

A jump of 150 years, prohibited to historians, can perhaps be pardoned an economist. Thus a factory census of 1897, covering 116,798 workers in the Vladimir district of central Russia provides us with information of the type discussed above. The sample in Table 6 is biased to the extent that it represents heavily the textile industry, which had a very high proportion of women employees.

The information on hereditary workers by age groups points to the fact that the supply of hereditary workers exceeded the rate of increase of the total labor force during the approximately 50 years preceding the census

---

3. The literacy rate among masters in linen and cloth manufactures was 31.8 per cent in 1732 and 33.3 in 1737/38, compared with an average literacy rate for the labor force of 6.2 and 8.6 per cent respectively.

Table 6

Percentage of Hereditary Workers and Literacy Rate of
Various Age Groups of the Factory Labor Force
(Vladimir District, 1897)

Age Group	Percentage of Hereditary Workers[*]			Literacy Rate of Total Labor Force		
	Males	Females	Total	Total	Males	Females
12-15	62.2	80.6	68.0	62.8	72.3	43.7
15-17	54.1	50.1	52.3	55.7	76.8	29.8
17-20	44.0	41.4	42.7	48.0	69.8	22.8
20-25	42.6	39.0	41.0	46.5	57.4	18.5
25-30	37.8	34.4	36.5	40.3	59.3	11.1
30-40	32.9	29.1	31.5	36.7	53.3	6.6
40-50	28.5	24.3	27.3	33.8	45.6	4.0
50-60	25.9	18.4	24.3	31.3	39.8	2.1
Over 60	24.9	15.2	23.7	29.2	33.5	1.4
Average	37.7	36.7	37.2	41.9	59.6	15.5

[*]That is, their fathers worked in factories. Incidentally, this was a district of preponderant out-migration.

Source: I. M. Kozminikh-Lanin, *Fabrichno-Zavodskoi Rabochii Vladimirskoi Gubernii* (1897 g.) (Vladimir, 1912).

Table 7

Percentage of Hereditary Workers by Duration of Work Experience[*]
According to the 1929 Factory Worker Sample

	Duration of Work Experience	
Branch of Industry	More than 24 Years	16-24 Years
Cotton	48.9	52.8
Metalworking	52.0	57.4
Metallurgy	60.0	56.8
Coal mining	35.6	38.6
Oil	30.8	32.5
Total	48.7	51.7

Source: A. G. Rashin, *Sostav Fabrichno-Zavodskogo Proletariatas SSR* (Moscow, 1930).

[*]The first category embraced 54,500 workers, and the second category 43,701. The first category represents workers who entered employment prior to 1905, the second category entrants in employment during 1906-1913. Further information, unfortunately unavailable, concerning the attrition rates for both categories, would make the data more conclusive and valuable. Metallurgy had shifted during the previous generation from the Urals to this district. Coal and oil were young industries. Inheritance in this table refers to factory-work types of occupation in general.

date, and that the last decade witnessed an accelerated growth of the share of hereditary workers within the labor force. That this tendency was continuing can be discerned from the data in Table 7, which are derived from a much later factory-worker sample, covering six industry branches.

My original hypothesis asserted that the "hereditary workers" phenomenon was important during both the preindustrialization phase and the early phases of industrialization, when both rudimentary technical skills and "industrial habits" were rare. The continuation of the industrialization process, accompanied by urbanization, some mechanization of agriculture, increasing levels of education, and the provision of facilities for technical training outside the industrial plants all tended to decrease the importance of the "hereditary workers" for the development of industry. It would be my guess, that if the process of industrialization in Russia had continued uninterruptedly after 1913, "hereditary workers" would have lost their economic and social significance during the next decades. If this phenomenon did in fact persist, the causes ought to be sought primarily outside the economic sphere.

CHAPTER 15

DETERMINANTS OF THE INCIDENCE OF LITERACY IN RURAL NINETEENTH-CENTURY RUSSIA

Arcadius Kahan

In rural Russia in the middle of the nineteenth-century, 1 of every 6 boys and 1 in 14 girls, at the most, were acquiring literacy to a level that enabled them to retain it. This is judging from data concerning literacy rates among men and women over 60 years of age in the 1890's. By the last decade of the century two-fifths of the rural male and one-sixth of the rural female youth between the ages of 10 and 19 were literate.[1] Male literacy rates among army recruits, which reflected predominantly rural rates, rose from one-fifth in 1874 to two-fifths in the mid-1890's and to two-thirds in 1913.[2] Among those recruits the rates of literacy at the low extreme (Ufa district) and the high extreme (Lifland district) were as follows: 7 per cent and 95 per cent for 1874-1883; 13 per cent and 97 per cent for 1894; and 27 per cent and 99 per cent for 1904. Evidently rural literacy was rising rapidly in Russia during the second half of the nineteenth century, but in a pattern of great diversity. The incidence of literacy both among and within geographic areas varied with the characteristics of subpopulations and with the extent of contacts with markets (rural or urban) and with urban life.

About 1900 the relationship between the various degrees of literacy within the rural population and the levels of income or nature of employment of different groups within that population became the subject of study by economists and statisticians in Russia, giving rise to prolonged controversies. The most widely accepted hypothesis concerning the relationship between literacy and income levels or occupational structures of the rural population was that advanced by Vorobiov and Lositskii, and tested and substantiated by Vikhliaev and others.[3]

In essence Vorobiov *et al.* attempted to prove the following propositions: (1) literacy is positively related to income within the broad income and

1. See Table 1 in Part IV, Chapter 19.
2. See Table 2 in Part IV, Chapter 19.
3. K. Ia. Vorobiov, *Gramotnost' Sel'skogo Naselenia V. Sviazi s Glavneishymi Faktorami Krest'-ianskogo Khoziaistva* (St. Petersburg, 1902); A. E. Lositskii, *K. Voprosu ob Izucheniu Gramotnosti Naselenia Rossii* (Chernigov, 1900); P. A. Vikhliaev, *Ekonomicheskie Uslovia Narodnogo Obrazovnia v Moskovskoi Gubernii* (Moscow, 1910).

occupational groups of the rural population; (2) rural residents engaged in nonagricultural activities have a higher literacy rate, regardless of their income position relative to the agricultural population; (3) the relatively higher literacy rate of the nonagricultural rural population varies with the degree of their contact with the market, particularly with urban markets. One should therefore differentiate, within the nonagricultural rural population, among activities connected with the rural markets, activities performed in the rural areas for the urban market, and employment (seasonal and semipermanent) in urban areas. Literacy increased to the degree that the rural population was exposed to contact with urban areas.

In order to prove his first proposition – that literacy is positively related to income within particular groups of the population – Vorobiov cited a number of studies and surveys. Table 1 is illustrative. Taking size of farm as a proxy for income, it indicates a quite systematic association between income and literacy in the farm population. In Table 2 (from the 1920 census in the Russian Socialist Federated Soviet Republic) this relationship is not nearly so neat; literacy actually declined with size of land holding to about the 5-hectare level, stabilized through a middle-size range, and then rose again only for farms above 8 or 10 hectares. However, the explanation is clear enough, and supports Vorobiov's second proposition – namely, that individuals engaged at least part-time in nonagricultural activities have on the average a higher literacy rate than the agricultural population, regardless of the income they may derive from agriculture. An even more striking relationship between the degree of literacy within a particular area and the development of nonagricultural activities is suggested by comparing the percentage of workers in nonagricultural seasonal employment with the literacy rate of draftees into military service from the same locality (Table 3).

Having established the relationship between literacy rates and nonagricultural activities, it was logical to expect that extent of contact with the

TABLE 1

Percentage of Males in Farm Households,
*Literate or in School**

Size of Landholding (in desiatin)	Heads of Livestock			
	Less than one	1-2	2-4	4 and over
Below 3	42	50	55	52
3-4.9	49	53	54	59
5-6.9	50	55	56	58
7-9.9	48	54	57	59
10-14.9	55	57	61	62
15 and over	—	—	69	64

*Farm households that possess livestock. These data are derived from an 1897 survey of a typical county *(uyezd)* in Iaroslavl district in which land and livestock are used as a proxy for income.

TABLE 2

Percent Literacy in Peasant Farms According to the
Agricultural Census of 51 Districts of RSFSR, 1920

Size of Landholding (in hectares)	Percentage of Literacy		Percentage of Farms with Nonagricultural Incomes
	Males	Females	
.1- 1	48.1	24.5	25.0
1.1- 2	46.2	21.4	16.0
2.1- 3	42.8	18.6	12.5
3.1- 4	40.7	16.6	10.5
4.1- 5	39.7	15.5	9.6
5.1- 6	39.1	15.1	9.0
6.1- 8	39.1	14.9	8.8
8.1-10	39.6	15.0	8.7
10.1-13	39.7	16.1	7.9
13.1-16	41.2	17.1	7.2
16.1-19	42.1	18.1	7.5
19.1-22	42.9	19.4	7.5
22.1-25	43.4	20.2	7.7
25.1-over	46.6	23.6	7.6

TABLE 3

Comparison Between the Percentage of Literacy of Draftees
During 1887-89 and the Percentage of Passports* Obtained by
Peasants in 1887 (Some counties of Kostroma District)

Rank by Percent of Passports	Counties	Percentage of Passports per 100 Males in 1887	Percent Literacy among Draftees
1.	Chukhlomsky	29.1	84.0
2.	Soligalichski	22.4	69.8
3.	Galichski	20.8	64.3
4.	Kologrivski	9.2	53.0
5.	Buiski	8.9	49.2
.			
.			
.			
12.	Vetluzhskii	.4	33.3

*Passports were documents indicating the permission of the village authorities for the peasant's absence of more than a few weeks.

Source: Materialy dla Statistiki Kostromskoi Gubernii (1891), Vypusk 8, pp. 208, 332 and 333.

market would be a determining factor in the degree of literacy. The study of
Vorobiov on literacy of peasants engaged in nonagricultural activities points
both to the relation between income and the literacy level, and to the difference in literacy rates between occupations which can be identified in terms
of a degree of contact with rural or urban consumers, middlemen, or employers (Table 4).

TABLE 4

Percentage of Literacy among Peasants Employed in Various Nonagricultural Activities (Vorobiov's Sample)

Potters	36	Distillery workers	90
Herdsmen	46	Restaurant service	91
Stevedores	54	Restaurant cooks	94
Tailors, Carpenters	57	Meat merchants	96
Day laborers	59	Pastry makers	97
Local coachmen	60	Retail merchants	98
Urban coachmen	84	Dairy merchants	98
Sausage makers	85	Fruit merchants	99
Bakers	86	Textile merchants	100

Source: K. Ia Vorobiov, *Gramotnost Sel'skogo Naselenia v Sviazi s Glavneishymi Faktorami Krest'ianskogo Khoziaistva* (St. Petersburg, 1902).

The distinction between village crafts and urban crafts as being important in determining the literacy rate is supported by the evidence from a study of craftsmen. This study, using a sample of 43,575 rural and urban craftsmen, gave for the year 1890 the results shown in Table 5. Clearly the village trades are at the lower end of the literacy scale, while urban crafts are marked by a higher degree of literacy. To the extent that literacy represents education, the relationship between education and higher skills becomes established. The influence of urban areas, as centers of industry and trade, in the spread of education on their peripheries was steadily increasing. Given the slow pace of commercialization of Russian peasant agriculture in the nineteenth century, the contact with the urban community through the commodity market or employment triggered for rural population the process of discovering the value of (or return to) education.

TABLE 5

Percentage of Literacy Among Rural and Urban Craftsmen, 1890

Toymakers	100	Coopers	33.8
Artist-painters	100	Agricultural implement makers	32.4
Artist-stonecutters	80	Shoemakers	31.4
Carders and reeders	75.4	Weavers and embroiderers	31.2
Leather workers and tanners	72.8	Bristle brushmakers	17.4
Turners	63.3	Carpenters	16.0
Nail makers	44.0	Sieve weavers	15.4
Blacksmiths and Locksmiths	42.3	Cart and sledgemakers	5.0
Cabinetmakers	40.2	Wheelwrights	2.4
Basket weavers	39.0	Total sample	39.5

Source: F. A. Danilov, "O Vlianii Gramotnosti, Shkol'nogo Obuchenia i Professional 'nogo Obrazovania na Razvitie Kustarnykh Promyslov," in *Ekonomicheskaia Otsenka Narodnogo Obrazovania* (St. Petersburg, 1896).

Numerous studies and surveys in Russia established the dependency of the literacy rate upon the distance from cities, and the dependency of the frequency of school attendance on the development of rural trades and home industries.

The data assembled in the various surveys seem to suggest that at intermediate levels of income the labor demands of the farm household hindered school attendance. However, even in cases when the increase from small to middle-size landholdings had a detrimental effect upon school attendance of males, this was in part compensated by increased education of females. The process of social and economic differentiation, which weakened subsistence farming and accompanied the commercialization of agriculture, increased the amount of education at both ends of the income scale, and thereby contributed to the rise of the average level of literacy.

The rise in the level of literacy among both the higher income groups of the peasant population and the agricultural laborers becomes the precondition for introduction of machinery and more modern farming methods.[4] The decline of subsistence farming, a type of farming which had not offered visible incentives for education, made it easier to overcome the long-lasting inertia and maintenance of the status quo and to inject an additional impetus to mobility and change in the economy and society.

Against this background one should not overlook the dynamics of the process underway. Two figures might be sufficient to illustrate the relative rapidity of the spread of education despite the various obstacles and shortcomings cited above.

The number of pupils in rural elementary schools increased from 1,754,000 in 1885 to over 7,000,000 in 1914. The number of teachers in rural schools increased from 24,389 in 1880 to 109,370 in 1911. What is significant, however, is that during the same period the number of teachers of peasant descent in those schools increased from 7,369 to 44,607. Thus an indigenous group fostering education in this milieu was growing rapidly, a group committed to the task of progress.

4. In 1895, the Russian Academician Professor Yanzhul' asked the not entirely rhetorical question: "How will the news about an improvement reach our peasant or rural craftsman while the basic means of communication and transfer of ideas—literacy—is lacking?" I. I. Yanzhul', A. I. Chuprov, I. N. Yanzhul', *Ekonomicheskaia Otsenka Narodnogo Obrazovania* (St. Petersburg, 1896), pp. 50-51.

CHAPTER 16

SOME OBSERVATIONS CONCERNING THE CHILEAN EDUCATIONAL SYSTEM AND ITS RELATION TO ECONOMIC GROWTH

Rudolph C. Blitz*

I. INTRODUCTION

This chapter deals specifically and yet broadly with three aspects of Chilean educational structure and history: (1) the performance of universal free education; (2) the feudal tradition; and (3) the role of women in higher education and in the professions. The focus of the discussion will be, of course, on economic development. The conference gave considerable space to the role of education in the earlier history of economically developed countries, and I believe the discussion of the three topics listed above will be useful because the Chilean experience—and probably the experience of most of Latin America—is very different in these matters from the historical experience of the western countries.

Chile has a compulsory primary education law which dates back to 1920. It has had a tradition of free secondary and university education for more than one hundred years. As a matter of fact, its tradition of free education is in some respect much stronger than in most western countries; it extends also to the substantial number of foreign university students from other Latin American countries, which is quite remarkable considering that Chile is a poor country.

Ever since the days of Smith and Malthus, and even earlier, popular instruction has been advocated by many for the purpose of strengthening the fabric of society.

Adam Smith held that

> . . . An instructed and intelligent people are always more decent and orderly than an ignorant and stupid one. . . . They are more disposed to ex-

Author's Note: This discussion is based to a large extent on a more comprehensive study which will appear as a chapter in a forthcoming volume: *Manpower and Education: Country Studies in Economic Development*, Frederick Harbison and Charles A. Myers (ed.), (New York: McGraw-Hill Book Co., 1964). This research was undertaken during the author's stay in Chile in 1961-62 on the Vanderbilt Overseas Faculty Program financed by the Rockefeller Foundation. The author is also indebted for research help to the Escuela de Estudios Económicos Latinoamericanos para Graduados, and to the Instituto de Organización y Administración de Empresas, Universidad de Chile, Santiago.

303

amine, and more capable of seeing through, the interested complaints of factions and sedition, and they are, upon this account, less apt to be misled into any wanton or unnecessary opposition to the measures of the government.[1]

Malthus specifically referred to these views of Smith with approval and elaborated this point considerably. In spite of his extreme opposition to the poor laws, he advocated at the same time generous public support for education:

> We have lavished immense sums on the poor, which we have every reason to think have constantly tended to aggravate their misery. But in their education and in the circulation of those important political truths that most nearly concern them, which are perhaps the only means in our power of really raising their condition and of making them happier men and more peaceable subjects, we have been miserably deficient.[2]

It is Halevy's view that ". . . the radical theory of population instruction is Malthusian in origin"[3] and that Malthus' preoccupation with popular education stemmed largely from his opposition to Godwin's and Condorcet's notions of the inevitability of progress.

Many reformers have also believed that education would be one of the surest and most important means of accelerating economic development, and some, like Horace Mann, have hoped that it would have a strong leveling effect on the income structure. Since the extremes of income inequality are almost always caused more by the unequal distribution of property income than by the peculiar distribution of human skills, it may be difficult to argue or to show empirically that the spread of education in itself could do much to reduce the highest incomes in favor of the low incomes. It is more plausible to argue that the spread of education will raise the income of low income groups at the expense of high-skilled income groups. We know, indeed, that income differentials between high-skilled and low-skilled groups are markedly less in developed countries than in underdeveloped countries.

I hope readers will be generous enough to permit me one conjecture dealing with the historical pattern of social and economic mobility and the school systems in England, the German Empire, and the Austro-Hungarian Empire during the half century before World War I. It is quite conceivable that during this period the latter two countries were in at least one important respect a good deal more democratic than England. Although precise quantitative evidence is lacking, biographies and similar sources have given me the impression that in Germany and Austria, universal free education and less social differentiation among secondary schools and universities provided

1. Adam Smith, *The Wealth of Nations* (New York: The Modern Library, Random House, Inc. 1937), p. 741.

2. T. R. Malthus, *An Essay on the Principle of Population* (London: Reeves & Turner 1888, ninth edition), p. 430; also see pp. 418, 422; *The Principles of Population* (London: J. Johnson 1806, third edition), Vol. II, pp. 420-21; and my paper "Algunos Economistas Clásicos y Sus Opiniones acerca de la Educación," *Economia*, No. 72-73 (Universidad de Chile), pp. 34-61.

3. Elie Halevy, *The Growth of Philosophical Radicalism* (Boston: The Beacon Press, 1955 ed.), pp. 242-244.

greater opportunities for boys of humble origin to rise in the professions, the universities, the bureaucracy, and perhaps even in the military, than was possible in England.[4] If upon closer examination the above observations should turn out to be correct, they would still be compatible with the notion that during the same period such opportunities were much better in the business world in England than in Germany and Austria.

It is possible that countries with a strong tradition of statism (like Hohenzollern Germany and Hapsburg Austria), geared to a large and efficient but low-paid bureaucracy, need to rely for recruitment on a relatively democratic educational system. Some bureaucratic careers, which may look most unrewarding to boys from more affluent families, may appear as glittering prizes to boys of humble background. With this as a background, let us look more closely at the working of compulsory primary and universal free education in Chile.

II. PERFORMANCE OF UNIVERSAL FREE EDUCATION

Some Quantitative Observations

While Chile has had a law of compulsory primary instruction since 1920,[5] and an even older tradition of free secondary and university education, the Chilean educational pyramid is nevertheless extremely narrow. There is a very heavy rate of school desertion on the primary level, in direct violation of the law; in fact, only 28.6 per cent of the school age population completed their primary education between 1950 and 1959.[6] Approximately 9

4. In a personal letter Professor Martin Bronfenbrenner made the following observation about Japan: "Able young men from poor families can rise either by joining forces with their 'betters' or by competing with them. The first process usually involves acceptance by the upper classes. Characteristically this in turn requires a number of upper-class traits, of which education is one. This first process, I will agree, was easier on the Continent (and Japan) than in England until recently. But there is also a second process, whereby the poor boy without much education (and usually without other upper-class traits) fights his way up by competition with established concerns, usually in business. This second process was, I suspect, easier in Britain than on the Continent or Japan, and probably dominated the total picture.

"The main way in which Japan differed from France and Germany, whose educational system she adopted, was, as you may know, in the Japanese institutions of *moraigo* and *yoshi*. A family without a son of its own, or a family whose sons were an unpromising lot, was expected to adopt one or more bright and healthy boys to carry on the family name. These *moraigo* might be from collateral branches of the family, or children of family friends; but quite often they were children of poor families. As for *yoshi*, these were adopted as young men to marry the daughter or daughters of families without 'proper' sons; they were sons-in-law who took the wife's name and entered her family rather than the conventional vice versa. Even more commonly than *moraigo*, they came from poor families and used this method to rise in the world. Potential *yoshi* and *moraigo* were often 'recruited' from boys who stood high in their classes at all levels from grade school to university. A Mitsubishi Bank manager in Fukuoka told me in 1945 that his duties included recruiting potential *moraigo* and *yoshi* (for higher-ranking Mitsubishi families) in his district, somewhat as college alumni recruit potential left halfbacks for Alma Mater. He told me that, in his opinion, this system was more democratic than anything we had in America, and your observations run along the same lines."

5. Modified in 1929.

6. Ministerio de Educación, *Bases Generales para el Planeamiento de la Educación Chilena* (Santiago, 1961), pp. 31, 94.

per cent of the school age population never attended school, and almost 30 per cent of those who entered the first grade abandoned school within the first two years.

Regionally there are great differences in the rate of school desertion. A study by Eduardo Hamuy showed that in Santiago about 40 per cent complete six grades, but in rural areas only 16 per cent go that far.[7] It also has been demonstrated that wastage is much higher among children from low-income than from high-income families. In Santiago, only 28 per cent of the children of low-income families finish the sixth grade, and 14 per cent enter secondary education; but for high-income groups the proportions are 80 per cent and 73 per cent respectively.[8] Obviously, with such a heavy rate of school desertion, especially in the early stages of the educational ladder, the chances for eradicating illiteracy rapidly are not good. One may again cite Hamuy: "With an average rate of fall in illiteracy during the period 1940 to 1952 of 0.62 per cent annually, it would take us 32 years to eliminate illiteracy."[9] This rate of reduction of illiteracy is actually lower than the one which prevailed between 1920 and 1930, when illiteracy was falling at an annual rate of 2.5 per cent. One may also look at the situation slightly differently: the proportion of illiterates in the total population decreased by only 5.8 per cent between 1920 and 1952, or, from 25 per cent to 20 per cent,[10] and this again brings out the stationary character of the situation. During these years illiteracy was reduced at an annual rate of 0.26 per cent, and at this rate it would take *sixty* years to reduce illiteracy to 4 or 5 per cent.

In 1960 only about 20 per cent of a given age cohort which had started its primary education in 1954 entered secondary education.[11] The combined attrition of primary and secondary education comes to 97 per cent of a given age group. In spite of this very heavy previous selection, in the end only one half or fewer of the high school graduates succeed in passing the *bachillerato* —the leaving examination—which clears the way for university study. Two factors, or a combination of these two factors, suggest themselves as an explanation for this phenomenon. First, secondary school preparation may be largely inadequate; and second, intellectual selectivity may be a minor factor in determining attrition. In spite of the fact that only a very small proportion of the youth manage to enter the university, the secondary school system has been criticized in Chile for being unduly "university-oriented." Chilean critics feel that the curricula of most secondary schools shortchange the bulk of terminal secondary students.[12] In any program of extensive educational reform the secondary schools should receive top priority in order to

7. Eduardo Hamuy, *Educación Elemental Analfabetismo y Desarollo Económico* (Santiago: Editorial Universitaria, 1960), pp. 38, 52.

8. *Ibid.*, p. 68.

9. *Ibid.*, p. 31.

10. *Ibid.*, p. 31.

11. *Bases Generales para el Planeamiento de la Educación Chilena*, pp. 35-36.

12. See, for example, Ahumada, C. Jorge, *En Vez de la Miseria* (Santiago: Editorial Del Pacífico, 1960), p. 27.

give a better preparation both to potential university students and to terminal secondary students.

In the present situation, of an original 1000 students entering the first grade only 12 enter the university. Again, of this small group approximately 40 per cent do not finish their studies. Thus only seven of the original thousand complete university education.[13]

Some Qualitative Observations

We have observed that the Chilean educational system pyramid is characterized by an extremely narrow peak. Of course, theoretically any peak — no matter how narrow — could be the result of an intense intellectual selectivity. The antecedent discussion, however, has attempted to show that this selectivity is actually very strongly determined by economic factors. If the peak, which is much narrower than in most Western countries, were largely determined by intellectual selectivity, a school-age population with innate intellectual endowment similar to that of the same age groups in other Western countries should produce at the top of the academic ladder a selected end product, which would have to be superior to the end product of universities in Europe and the United States. This is clearly not the case. It would be quite impossible to evaluate here precisely the quality of the Chilean university student in many different disciplines. But although the end product of this selectivity is not a superior one, it still appears that this product is a good one.

As a very rough indication of the competence of the student, the following observations may serve. For a long time, small but significant numbers of Chilean students on both the undergraduate and graduate levels have gone to the best universities in the United States and Europe, and have performed well. A number of schools of the University of Chile, such as the schools of medicine, of mining, and of architecture, have a tradition of more than one hundred years. The comments of visiting professors as to the level of teaching in the various departments have been favorable.

There exists in Chile a rather strong tradition for the study of foreign languages; this prevails in many middle and upper class families and in the better Chilean secondary schools. In this respect the beginning Chilean university student is probably better prepared than his counterpart in the United States. A survey of the University of Chile has shown that of the first-year students, 41.8 per cent read and 33.6 per cent speak English; 41.8 per cent read and 23.7 per cent speak French; 4.9 per cent read and 1.3 per cent speak German.[14] This favorable situation has undoubtedly made it easier for Chilean students to study abroad.

13. *Boletín Estadístico de la Universidad de Chile*, Vol. III, No. 1 (1945), pp. 25, 33. The proportion of those who finish with diplomas is even smaller. The selectivity is very much class determined: In 1959 only 2.3 per cent of the total student body of the University of Chile were of working class origin (*Boletín de la Universidad de Chile*, Vol III, No. 3 [1959], p. 53) and not a single university student came from families of *campesinos*.

14. *Boletín Estadístico de la Universidad de Chile*, Vol. III, No. 3 (Santiago, 1959), p. 54.

One may ponder for a moment about the system of selection for higher education in Chile and about the limitations it imposes for the expansion of enrollment in engineering and the biological sciences. We observed earlier that, apparently, only 1.2 per cent of a given group of students starting elementary education eventually enter the university. Of this small proportion, once more, almost one-half are eliminated before the end of their studies; in the school of engineering the percentage of failures is much higher. It was also observed that a very large proportion of university entrants are actually unprepared for study in the natural sciences and therefore take their *bachillerato* in *letras*. This matter can also be viewed in another manner: there is most likely a greater proportion of engineering students who could, if they had the inclination, switch to law, than there is of law students who could switch to engineering or the biological sciences. It is argued here, although this cannot be proven rigorously, that the great proportion of university students who pursue law in many of the so-called underdeveloped countries (in Chile about 12 per cent) may be explained by a more fundamental reason than by saying that it is a "matter of tradition." It thus follows that there may be very narrow limits — although we are at present unable to quantify these — for the expansion of enrollment in the engineering and natural sciences.[15]

The statistics cited previously show that the Chilean educational pyramid is not only extremely narrow, but it is also marked by a heavy rate of desertion in direct violation of the law. Thus the question arises why public education, with all it could have meant for Chilean economic development, has turned out to be so much of a failure.

It is conceivable that a very low per capita income is incompatible with an effective system of compulsory education simply because the costs of such a system are too high. Chile, however, has a per capital income which is higher than that of Japan and approximately equal to that of Italy — two countries which have actually exported capital to Chile during recent years. Thus, the level of per capita income is not so low after all.[16] It must be remembered, however, that Chile, like many Latin American countries, is beset with an extremely uneven income distribution and with much rural isolation; with the given level of income, these two factors may go far to explain the poor performance of the Chilean educational system. Moreover, again as in other Latin American countries, the high-income groups save little and are very successful in avoiding the payment of heavy taxes. Secularly the proportion saved out of GNP has been less than 10 per cent, and Chile is one of the few countries in the world which showed a fall in the per capita national income for the period 1955-59. It appears that Chile has reaped from its uneven in-

15. Actually the number of engineering graduates has reached a stationary plateau of about 210, and my projection for the next ten years suggests that the total number of engineers will grow merely at the low rate of 3.1 per cent per annum (see my Chapter in the forthcoming volume of Harbison and Myers, *op. cit.*).

16. David Felix, "Chile," in *Economic Development*, ed. Pepelasis, Mears and Adelman (New York: Harper and Brothers, 1961), p. 288.

come distribution all the disadvantages but none of the advantages which an uneven income distribution may conceivably have for the process of economic growth. Although the uneven income distribution has not resulted in a rapid rate of accumulation of inanimate capital, it has had a decidedly adverse effect on the growth of animate capital.

It is not claimed here that uneven income distribution with a given level of income is a sufficient factor to explain the poor school attendance. For a more complete picture, other factors such as the efficiency of the enforcement apparatus and the motivation of parents and students would have to be considered. Suffice it to say that because of the complete lack of a guild and apprenticeship tradition (a matter yet to be discussed), educational motivation may, indeed, be weak in Chile.

Moreover, a country like Chile, with a high birth rate and a low life expectancy, will find a system of general education a greater burden than will a society with a lower birth rate and higher life expectancy. In the former case, the potential school age population constitutes such a large proportion of the total population that universal school attendance may well constitute a Malthusian problem in a more specific sense. There exists here, of course, a vicious circle; it has been argued plausibly by some that the lack of compulsory school attendance is conducive to a high birth rate. Thus Nassau W. Senior viewed the situation in England in the first half of the 19th century as follows:

> . . . As each child becomes successively capable of profitable employment, it is so employed in many branches of hand loom weaving at the age of six, or even younger.
> . . . Such a state of things produces a rapidly increasing population, confined by ignorance, by habit, and generally by poverty—chains as strong as those of caste in Hindostan—to their own occupation.[17]

Actually, in the case of England the introduction of compulsory education in 1876 was associated with a fall in the birth rate, and a causal relationship between the two has been suggested.[18]

Although a system of universal education may well have a leveling effect on income differentials between skilled and unskilled, and may also have a dampening effect on the birth rate, the Chilean experience suggests that such a development can take place only with an income distribution and/or level of income which would give the school age population freedom from at least the most pressing economic problems.

III. THE FEUDAL TRADITION

I will discuss next the impact of the feudal tradition on education and economic development in Chile. While it is generally recognized that much

17. Nassau W. Senior, *Industrial Efficiency and Social Economy*, Vol. I (New York: Henry Holt and Co., 1928), p. 196.
18. J. R. Hicks and Albert S. Hart, *The Social Framework of the American Economy* (New York: Oxford Press, 1945), pp. 59-60.

of Latin America's agriculture is still beset by a strong feudal tradition and all this implies, it is perhaps not so clearly recognized that the urban counterpart of Western feudalism, namely the guild system, never had a foothold in Latin America. Thus, Latin American feudalism should be viewed as one-sided, agricultural feudalism.[19]

Much has been written about the drag which the old apprenticeship laws had on the industrialization of England, and how these laws were circumvented and eventually set aside in 1814. In spite of all the failures and shortcomings of the apprenticeship system and in spite of the restraints it put on the industrialization processs, it nevertheless provided the industrialization process with a skilled cadre and was undoubtedly largely responsible for a tradition of workmanship.[20]

Not only is the ratio of highly skilled personnel, such as doctors[21] or engineers, to population much lower in Chile than in the United States; but the ratio of nurses and technicians, who may be viewed here as the supporting troops, is also much lower than in the more advanced countries. The total number of engineers in Chile in 1962 was about 4,250, with the rate of growth of engineers drastically decreasing. The best current estimate of the total number of technicians comes to about 7,000.[22] We thus have a ratio of engineers to technicians of merely 1:1.65. A ratio of 1:3 could be considered adequate and a ratio 1:4 or 1:5 would be on the high side. Blank and Stigler have shown that in the United States specific age cohorts of engineers show substantial augmentation over time because practitioners without engineering diplomas are able to elevate themselves to the status of fullfledged engineer by virtue of their practical experience. Although this may be also

19. Scholars have observed repeatedly that the feudal tradition on the land was especially strong during those periods and in the areas of Western and Eastern Europe where the growth of the towns was for one reason or another slow. (See for example F. L. Carsten, *The Origins of Prussia* [Oxford: Clarendon Press, 1954], pp. 115 ff.). Professional historians may take exception to my statement that in Western Europe the guild system constituted the "urban counterpart of feudalism," as many scholars prefer to view the rise of the towns and the guild system as the most important cause of the downfall of feudalism. For our purposes this issue really does not matter. Suffice it to say that the guild system never had a foothold in Chile.

20. The appropriate mix of small- and large-scale enterprise and the proper price-income relationship between such enterprises from the standpoint of efficiency, stability, and equity has been a matter of great concern and dispute; and the path of economic progress is much determined by the manner in which this interrelationship is resolved. Many accounts suggest Japan has been especially successful in dovetailing the operation of small-scale and large-scale industry.

21. In 1957 the ratio of doctors per 10,000 of population was 13 for the United States and 6 for Chile.

22. Data from my previously cited unpublished manuscript.

Since completion of this paper, Professor Jorge Mardones A. of the Centro de Planeamiento, Universidad de Chile, published *Estudio sobre Empleo de Personal Técnico en la Industria Manufacturera*. This monograph explores both the structure of employment of engineers and technicians in manufacturing in 1960 and attempts to make projections to 1970. The method used in these projections consists essentially of assimilating Chile with certain modifications to projections made for the United States by the National Science Foundation in *The Long-Range Demand for Scientific and Technical Personnel*. I have serious reservations about the methodology of these projections and about their significance.

The *Estudio sobre Empleo de Personal Técnico* raises, however, a fundamental question about the supply of technicians in Chile. If technicians are defined rigorously as people with three to

possible in Chile in rare individual cases, because of the prevailing skill structure it is not likely to be of any great numerical significance.

We may next survey briefly what happened historically to the supply of nurses. The study of nurses seems appropriate for three reasons. (1) Although the nursing profession does not come to one's mind when thinking of traditional apprenticeship programs, it is nevertheless a skill largely learned by closely supervised practice, which is really the essence of apprenticeship training. (2) It is a profession of women. Since I want to discuss subsequently the role of women in the professions and in economic development in some detail, some observations about the nursing profession seems relevant from this point of view. (3) A detailed study of the nursing profession and the country's current need for nurses has been completed very recently by the Servicio Nacional de Salud (National Health Service).[23] This study seems to be at present the only completed investigation focusing on the problem of what we may call, for want of a better word, technicians; that is to say, people with technical skills below the highest professional levels. This study shows that despite the fact that Chile has at present five schools of nursing, there are today only slightly more than 1,500 graduate nurses employed. This implies a ratio of two nurses per 10,000 of population or about one third of the doctor – population ratio. In contrast to developed countries, where the number of nurses is a multiple of the number of doctors – in the United States there are about 2 and in Sweden 2.5 nurses for each doctor – we have in Chile a situation where nurses constitute a fraction of the number of doctors. The study suggests that the doctor – nurse ratio has actually worsened during the past fifteen years, and no reversal of this trend appears to be in sight.

This situation cannot be attributed to a generally low participation of women in the labor market; on the contrary, in some related professions the number of women is surprisingly high. There are, for example, approximately 400 women doctors in Chile, who constitute 8.5 per cent of the total doctors. Similarly there are more than 860 women dentists in Chile; they amount to

four years of higher education beyond secondary education, then the estimate of technicians comes to 2,184 for the entire manufacturing sector, and this would yield a ratio of Engineers to Technicians of 1:1.46 for this sector. On the other, if so-called *técnicos prácticos* are included without regard of educational achievements, the number of technicians swells in the manufacturing sector to 10,943 and the ratio of Engineers to Technicians to 1:7.34.

Mardones himself expresses doubt about this last figure and points out that the sample did not yield adequate job description for the *técnicos prácticos*, and that by a more meaningful definition this figure of 10,943 would undoubtedly appear much exaggerated. The difficulty is partly due to the absence of a tradition of apprenticeship and that *maestro* is used in Latin America as common appellation for any worker above the status of common laborer. The figure of 10,943 *técnicos* in manufacturing alone clearly cannot be reconciled with my figure of 7,000 technicians for the entire Chilean economy, based on another source. Manufacturing employed less than 20 per cent of the labor force in 1960, but undoubtedly a greater proportion of the total number of technicians, by any definition, are employed in manufacturing than in the other sections of the economy. While the figure of almost 11,000 technicians in manufacturing appears exaggerated, it nevertheless suggests that my figure of 7,000 technicians for the entire economy is probably subject to a substantial downward bias. Unfortunately, no reconciliation could be attempted at this time.

23. Doris Krebs W., *Necesidades y Recursos de Enfermería en Chile* (January 1962, typed manuscript).

about one-third of all the dentists in Chile. The great scarcity of nurses may be explained in part by the very low salaries paid by the Servicio Nacional de Salud, which employs 80 per cent of all nurses. This, however, is not the whole story, and broader sociological reasons have to be adduced for a more complete explanation. Because of its feudal tradition, nursing appears to many people in Chile as a job similar to one performed by domestic, menial servants; it is looked on quite differently from social work, much of which has been performed traditionally by society ladies. Señorita Krebs, the author of the report on nurses, for example, informed me that a number of former classmates broke all social relations with her when she started upon her nursing career.

IV. THE ROLE OF WOMEN IN EDUCATION AND IN THE PROFESSIONS

In spite of the fact that the educational pyramid of Chile is extremely narrow and class-determined, and that Chilean economic development is probably impeded by various feudal values and traditions, the proportion of women among university students and in the professions is very high.

The proportion of female students in universities was in 1956 about 40 per cent[24] and has been increasing since 1940 at a rate of a little less than one per cent per year. Obviously, this ratio of women's participation in higher education is drastically higher than the one which prevailed in Western European countries when they had a similar educational profile; as a matter of fact, it is higher than the 36 per cent in the United States for the corresponding year.[25]

The proportion of women among university students is not only high in general, but also very high in the various professional schools. For example, in the years 1957 to 1960 the total enrollment of the medical school of the University of Chile ranged between 1,074 and 1,153; during these years the proportion of women varied from 15.5 to 17.0 per cent. For the school of law, the range of enrollment was 1,363 to 1,668; the proportion of women varied from 21.1 to 22.4 per cent. For architecture the corresponding figures were 306 to 526, and 20 to 24 per cent; for dentistry 488 to 540, and 45.7 to 49.0 per cent.[26] Similarly, a survey by the Instituto de Organización y Administración de Empresas (INSORA) has shown that women, as already mentioned, constitute 8.5 per cent of the 4,729 doctors in Chile, and 32 per cent of the total number of dentists.[27]

24. *Boletín Estadístico de la Universidad de Chile,* Vol. III, No. 1 (1959), p. 26, and Vol. III, No. 3 (1959), p. 46.

25. U.S. Bureau of the Census, *Statistical Abstract of the United States* (Washington, 1960), p. 123.

26. *Boletín Estadístico de la Universidad de Chile* for the respective years: 1957, pp. 62 and 63; 1959, p. 36; 1960, p. 32.

27. In the United States women doctors constitute about 6 per cent of the total and for dentists the corresponding number is 2.8 per cent. U. S. Department of Health, Education and Welfare,

It is almost taken as a basic characteristic of so-called underdeveloped countries that women have not achieved a degree of emancipation in these countries comparable to that of more advanced societies. Many of the underdeveloped countries are portrayed as a man's paradise. Yet, at least for professional women, Chile appears to be a world where they can have their cake and eat it too.

It is well known that even though professional incomes may be lower in the underdeveloped countries as compared with the developed countries, nevertheless the ratio of professional incomes to the income of common labor or domestic labor is much higher in the underdeveloped countries. Because of this it may be much easier for women in a country like Chile to have both a professional career and a large family. In other words, there may well be a stage in economic development where women are no longer discriminated against, yet still have the advantage of cheap household help. It is, moreover, a generally recognized fact that in underdeveloped countries with a strong agrarian tradition, family ties are much stronger, with grandparents frequently partaking very actively in the upbringing of the grandchildren.[28]

At present I do not know whether the high proportion of women in higher education and the professions is a peculiar Chilean feature or a more general characteristic of underdeveloped countries. I have suggested a possible explanation for this factual observation. What significance this has for economic development is more difficult to say. On the one hand it means that the base for selection and development of technical personnel is broadened, and equal educational opportunity for women may also be viewed as a social good in itself. On the other hand it may also mean that a substantial part of scarce educational resources is being spent on a group of which a large proportion may subsequently revert to part-time work or retire early from their professional careers.

Health Manpower Source Book, (Washington: Government Printing Office, 1954), Section 5, pp. 74, 137.

A study by this author has shown, among other things, that for four substrata of the labor force of Santiago and Valparaiso the educational differential between males and females is very small. For employers the average number of years of education for men was 11.0; for females, 9.5 years. For self-employed persons the average was the same for both males and females, namely 7 years. For employees, average education was actually higher for females than for males, namely, 9.8 compared with 9.5 for males. For masculine and feminine manual workers there was again no difference in educational average: for both groups is came to 4.8 years. *Algunas Características de Edad, Educación e Ingreso de la Fuerza de Trabajo de Santiago y Valparaiso* (Instituto de Economía de la Universidad de Chile, 1962), Tables IV, A and B.

28. Perhaps much of the grandparents' vigor in these matters is in turn explained by the fact that they have household servants too, but to explore this issue would go beyond the scope of this paper. Our concern is, after all, with the vigorous professional role of the daughters and not the vigorous family role of the grandparents.

Chapter 17

PATTERNS AND VARIABILITY IN THE DISTRIBUTION AND DIFFUSION OF SCHOOLING

C. Arnold Anderson

Wherever schools exist they become linked to the various dimensions of the social status system in intricate ways, raising questions of access to the schools, propensities to utilize educational opportunities, status maintenance, or mobility. Access to schools is usually quite "unequal" until late in the process of economic development. Entry may be limited as a forthright expression of discrimination; alternatively, differences in aspiration or in circumstances of living may create sharp disparities. These generalizations will be illustrated for several societies in this chapter.

Once schools have become recognized as important agencies in a society, the established elites will watch over them jealously. Since there are several elites, they will often become strong rivals for control of education. A rising group may disdain the existing schools or resent the terms on which the latter are available and seek to displace or to remold them. They may build up a separate system of schools, as exemplified in what Kahan tells about Russia (in Part IV, Chapter 19). In the long run, no doubt, every "significant" group gets the schools it wants. This striving is one reason for the recurrent emergence of proprietary schools in western countries, usually opposed by the licensed schoolmasters.

While the shifting access to schools over time largely reflects broad social changes, it is facilitated by the fact that the boundaries of social strata are vague and shifting. Neither a defensive nor a thrusting group is clearly defined even to its own members; outside a core membership, identifications such as "gentry" are abstractions. Would-be dominant elites often assume a tutelary posture, benevolent or hostile, toward the education of other groups that may be dependent or threatening. It is not rare for a ruling group to assume what we may call the "herdsman's viewpoint": the populace must be disciplined, civilized, and trained to play their dutiful and productive roles. During recent centuries, moreover, every western society has possessed pervasive ideologies of social mobility and has institutionalized devices for encouraging ambitious individuals.

Statistics revealing the selectivity of schooling must therefore be interpreted cautiously. The specialist in social stratification may well emphasize the disparities in educational opportunity; but when attention turns to a consideration of how education facilitates mobility specifically or development generally, the exceptions become important. Historical evidence points to marked stabilities in geographic and occupational rankings of literacy and school attendance. But comparisons over time point also to a wide variation both in the magnitude of these differentials and in the pace of the diffusion processes by which they are altered.

I. CULTURE-BEARING GROUPS AND THE SPREAD OF OPPORTUNITY

In the societies out of which the western dynamic economies emerged, the peasants were subordinated to the bearers of the "high culture."[1] Many of the peasants were not free, and most of them were illiterate; until near the end of the medieval period they were only superficially touched by the higher culture or by the new economic forces. Similar situations have prevailed over much of the Middle and Far East and in lesser degree prevail throughout large parts of Latin America today. A similar conformation began to take shape in Africa as Western culture penetrated that continent, but the rapid diffusion of modern technology has prevented distinct cultural strata (in terms of Western traits) from solidifying.[2]

High social status and high culture were closely articulated in the Western past. Writing had been preserved as a functional skill, and in due time the secular use of literacy spread outside the key groups of clergy and lawyers. Recruitment of the clergy from all strata persisted as a norm (if by no means always practiced), keeping alive some ideas of free mobility. The slow coherence of status with schooling stimulated aspiring individuals and groups to seek education. Successive entrants to the literate and increasingly educated elites were moved to strengthen schools for their own ends, including the preservation of their privileges. The various segments of the middle and upper strata were not sharply separated. There was a gradation, not a disjunction, of educational opportunity, a condition that stimulated aspiring groups to emulate their superiors.[3]

The diffusion of schooling down the social pyramid was both gradual and selective. The English nobility and gentry, for example, could monopolize neither the grammar schools nor the universities. Children of workers or yeomen who obtained that esteemed education were only a small fraction of their classes, to be sure, but they constituted a larger part of the classes into which they moved.

1. L. Fallers, "Equality, Modernity, and Democracy in the New States," in C. Geertz (ed.), *Old Societies and New States* (Glencoe: Free Press, 1963), pp. 158-219.
    2. *Ibid.*
    3. Recent studies show that a mixture of achievement notivated middleclass children in schoolrooms of lower-class children raises the attainment of the latter; similar facilitation must have occurred in earlier periods. See N. Rogoff *et al, Social Structure and College Recruitment*, 1962 (unpublished).

Each status group—actually the more alert, vigorous, or more favorably located portions of each—was a nest of particular educational traditions and aspirations. Each had distinctive ideas of how education could be useful or ornamental for people of their kind. Outside the schools, specialized programs of training through guild and apprenticeship were nourished by artisans and by some of the professions. Much of that training gradually became converted into formal schooling, fusing with training for literacy that was in some countries fostered by religious motives. Distinct family heritages of schooling could no doubt be traced within European strata, traditions much like those described in South Africa recently by Wilson.[4]

... Similarly, in the proportion of children who are enrolled at schools there is wide variation from one community to another: in Burnshill village, for example, where school education has been the longest established in the district, the people are relatively sophisticated, and almost all their children are sent to school; in the more remote villages in the northern part of the district, as many as one child in every three may never be sent to school at all. Demarcation between villages, which was originally founded on political allegiance to headmen or leaders of kinship groups, tends to become accentuated when differences exist in earning capacity, culture, values and aspirations, as betokened by different levels of school education achieved in the communities.

Within each village community, too, differing interests based on educational attainments tend to the establishment of status groupings, which cut across the traditional groupings based on sex and age. It has been found, on analysis, that families tend to be illiterate or literate as a whole, that if parents send one child to school they eventually send all their children. On the other hand, the indications are that the present generation of school-going children are considerably more literate than their parents. Thus, interests as developed by school education are not likely to cause cleavage among siblings, but tend to undermine the traditional respect of youth for age and the subservience of children to their parents. It has been found, too, that among the minimally literate, females are more highly educated than males, and this tends to weaken the dominance of men in the patrilineal society.

The illiterate in the community tend to form a group with mutual interests and conservative outlook. As boys, they will have played and fought together while herding stock, at a time when many of their contemporaries were attending school. As youths, they are recruited from the village, in groups, by the Native Recruiting Corporation, for work on the gold mines, and, not having had their awareness developed by education, their experiences while away on tours of work do little to alter their conservatism. In the villages their social interests centre around beer drinks and the festivities of pagan ritual and ceremonies.

On the other hand, the people with some education prefer to seek employment in industries rather than the mines and, having had their perceptibilities sharpened by education, they are usually greatly influenced by the experiences of town life. ... The more highly educated people usually find employment locally or abroad as teachers, nurses, clerks, ministers, agricultural demonstrators or in other relatively highly paid occupations or pro-

4. M. Wilson *et al*, *Keiskammahoek Rural Survey*, Vol. 8 (Pietermaritzburg: Shuter and Shooter, 1952), pp. 155-57.

fessions. They tend to educate their children as well or better than themselves, so that greater wealth, which is one of the main factors maintaining
higher standards of education, thus tends in turn to be perpetuated by it. The
relative wealth and professional occupations of the "progressive" gives them
the status in the community of "important people" (abantu abakhulu), irrespective of their age. They find a community of interest with others in the
village and tend to marry people holding similar status: they attend church
regularly, their main social interests centre around church activities, and
their group usually includes the ministers and other leaders of church activities. For instance, it was found on analysis that half the school teachers in
the district are actively engaged in church activities: nearly 30 per cent assist
with Sunday school, no less than 15 per cent are pastors, and 5 per cent pro-
fess to do church work. Among "progressives" there is usually a greater
acceptance of innovations, such as scientific farming practices, and also a
higher standard of living reflected in better cared for homesteads, greater
cleanliness, a greater abundance of European material goods and furnishings,
and smarter European clothing.

The newly developing countries today display much diversity in the
social location of educational traditions, depending upon their economic
structure and the particular European educational traditions they have inherited. Thus in British Guiana, Bone found that two-thirds of the male
secondary pupils came from families in which neither parent had reached
secondary school.[5] In Dutch Guiana the proportion was slightly larger, but
in French Guiana only a quarter of the boys had parents with so little education. The respective percentages of pupils coming from families in which both
parents had at least some secondary schooling were 14, 10, and 38 per cent.
Recent research in western countries has been uncovering the influence of
social class and family attitudes upon achievement aspirations. One would
expect such relationships to have been even stronger in the past and to be
powerful in many underdeveloped countries.

It is difficult to disentangle the motives that led groups who had already
come to enjoy educational opportunities (in fifteenth-century England, for example) to acquiesce or act in extending those opportunities to new groups.
There were the religious motives so often mentioned, as well as the notions
that education is a good thing, that knowledge is power, and that education
raises incomes. But fear of the rude populace and the search for some means
to reduce the appalling rate of pauperism also played their part.[6]

Amidst the rising concern with education that Jordan has documented
for sixteenth- and seventeenth-century England, the perceptions of different
localities and strata differed, as did their financial capacity. In London and
the nine counties he studied, education received a fourth of the value of
charitable bequests; the gifts for direct help to the poor were largest, but educational bequests exceeded those for religion. Urban residents gave three-
fourths of the total; though London had only one-fifth of the donors it gave

5. L. W. Bone, "Secondary Education in the Guianas," University of Chicago, *Comparative
Education Center Monograph*, 2, 1962, pp. 39.41.
6. W. K. Jordan, *Philanthropy in England 1480-1660* (New York: Russell Sage, 1959), p. 280.

three-fifths of the sum.[7] The gentry were the most generous donors in rural counties, and merchants gave the most among city residents. In London, for example, education differed widely in its salience as an aim of philanthropy, the percentages of each group's bequests stipulated for education varying as follows: Crown 15, nobility 35, upper gentry 28, lower gentry 17, great merchants 28, lesser merchants 8, the professions 52, yeomen 36, upper clergy 67, lower clergy 50, tradesmen 12, artisans 1.

II. SOCIAL STATUS AND EDUCATIONAL OPPORTUNITY

Changes in English Practice

Educational facilities are not used equally by all social strata in any society, even in the absence of formal barriers.[8] Except in affluent societies, a diligent application of the norm of equity would throttle economic development. The following pages supply a rapid and superficial survey of differentials in social class access to schools throughout English history, together with illustrations for a variety of other countries.

The traditional and much-discussed three-tiered school system — schools for the populace, for clerks, and for the elite — was in many ways distinctly functional. For example, by reinforcing status positions and retarding their realignment, the system sustained a viable polity with its subtle connections of status and deference. At the same time, lower groups were incited to aspire to education and were rewarded when they succeeded. Likewise the problem of insuring industrial discipline in a rapidly changing economy was eased. The congruence of strata and school patronized was by no means precise, if only because the several strata were far from homogeneous. Each section of every stratum had ties with groups in the same and bordering strata.[9] The social scale, as it functioned in daily life, was finally graded.

One cannot take snobbish assertions at face value when trying to identify the clientele of schools. Such aggressive expressions were more relevant when large social differences were in view: the "meaner sort" trying to push their way among gentlemen. Most grammar schools appear to have had a diversified clientele, and of course the schools were themselves ranked. By the eighteenth century, if not earlier, dissenters were entering elite schools or opening their own; dissenters were commonly artisans or traders. Chambers says that at least two Nottinghamshire grammar schools were "free to local residents" in the seventeenth century, and boys proceeded to university from "all social classes, except the poorest."[10] Of all Oxford matriculants from 1587 to 1622, nearly half had "plebian" (lower than gentlemen) fathers,

7. *Ibid.*, pp. 241, 384.

8. Actual compulsory education is rarely rigorously applied above the elementary level and is an exception of no present moment.

9. J. H. Hexter, *Reappraisals in History* (Aberdeen: Aberdeen University Press, 1961), Ch. 5, 6.

10. J. D. Chambers, *Nottinghamshire in the Eighteenth Century* (London: King, 1932), pp. 304, 314.

seven per cent came from homes of clergymen, and five per cent were of unknown and presumably modest origin.[11]

Though the favored groups grumbled about social mixing in the schools, both circumstances and ideology combined to keep some channels of mobility open. The offspring of unfree men are known to have attended grammar school now and then in the fourteenth century, and a law of 1406 specifically assured the entry of children of a man "of what state or condition he be."[12] In 1541 Cranmer had retorted to complaints about sons of husbandmen seeking to enter grammar school, "Wherefore, if the gentlemen's son be apt to learning, let him be admitted; if not apt, let the poor man's child that is apt, enter his room."[13] The numerous approximations to tax-supported local schools, already mentioned, helped to keep opportunities open by giving local residence precedence over status.[14] While the guilds progressively tightened their rules to exclude apprentices from outside the controlling families, the central government opposed this tendency in its "pauper and vagabond" policies over many generations.[15] Indeed, much of the protest against extending schooling reflected genuine fears of losing essential laborers to town or clergy, an early appreciation of opportunity costs.[16]

A historical period is not all of a piece. In the later sixteenth century a considerable literature began to appear exhorting apprentices to take pride in their opportunities and to forge ahead.[17] Many of the charitable bequests tabulated by Jordan were designed explicitly to help areas with insufficient schools; the donors he studied multiplied the schools in some counties tenfold.[18] In Buckingham, 44 out of 210 parishes got substantial help, and 40 others lesser help, with their schools. He estimates that in 1660, by virtue of those bequests, there was a grammar school for each 76 square miles in Norfolk and one per 57 square miles in Yorkshire.[19] London men founded 428 local grammar schools between 1480 and 1660; at the end of the period there was one grammar school for each 4400 people in London.[20]

Hans concludes that during the eighteenth century, England had an

11. M. Campbell, *The English Yeoman Under Elizabeth and the Early Stuarts* (New Haven: Yale University Press, 1942), p. 271.

12. J. E. C. DeMontmorency, *State Intervention in English Education* (Cambridge: Cambridge University Press, 1902), pp. 25-32; L. B. Wright, *Middle-Class Culture in Elizabethan England* (Chapel Hill: University of North Carolina Press, 1958), p. 67. Even in the 17th century men complained that the schools turned out too many white-collar workers.

13. A. E. Dobbs, *Education and Social Movements 1700-1850* (London: Longmans Green, 1919), p. 83.

14. Mrs. J. R. Green, *Town Life in the Fifteenth Century* (New York: Macmillan, 1907), pp. 13-14.

15. I. Pinchbeck, "The State and the Child in Sixteenth Century England," *British Journal of Sociology*, 8:64-5, 1957.

16. De Montmorency, *op. cit.*

17. Wright, *op. cit.*, p. 21.

18. W. K. Jordan, *Charities of London* (New York: Russell Sage, 1960), p. 249.

19. W. K. Jordan, *The Charities of Rural England 1480-1660* (New York: Russell Sage, 1961), pp. 23, 301.

20. Jordan, *London, op. cit.*, p. 290.

average of 200 private classical schools (about 300 around 1750 but only about 100 at the end of the century); there were 400 endowed grammar schools in 1700, and 100 were added during the century. There were also 200 private "academies" in which mathematics, technology, and vocational subjects were emphasized; these were more accessible than grammar schools and were used mainly by the lower middle class.[21]

In the sixteenth century, Christ's Hospital School definitely followed a policy of smoothing the road to the university for able children. Indeed, fostering the academic persistence of clever boys was part of the benevolence that came to be clearly expressed in the charity schools, despite many attempts to limit enrollment to middle-class children. The Sunday schools likewise often made a point of identifying talented children in order to move them into regular weekday schools.[22]

However, upward social mobility of individuals in western countries during the past centuries should not be credited solely to wider educational opportunities. Few humble men could reach high positions without schooling, and of course relatively few from the lowest strata did so under the most favorable conditions. But for less eminent positions a little schooling could suffice for the able and ambitious. For the most capable men, even formal education was not needed in a society prossessing as many auxiliary stimuli to ambition and competence as did England.[23] Those who went up the social ladder were by no means a negligible part of the elite, but they represented a tiny fraction of their stratum of origin. Self-made men were more numerous in business, though surely not a large fraction in its higher ranks. The role of formal education in individual mobility should not be exaggerated.[24] It was the aggregate, not individual, mobility effect of education that was crucial for economic development. Surprisingly little mobility between strata is required to implement development; and mobility is no doubt more an effect than a cause of development.

Class-oriented secondary (and higher) education has persisted up to the present day in England, although substantial changes have been underway.

21. N. Hans, *New Trends in Education in the Eighteenth Century* (London: Rutledge, 1951), pp. 63, 69, 119, 120. A sample of 18th-century Oxford graduates teaching in grammar schools had the following assortment of fathers: gentlemen 10, clergy 16, "arm" 6, plebian 18, pauper 7; among Cambridge graduates in similar positions the fathers were: gentlemen 19, clergy 42, merchant 38, artisan 19, farmer 43, poor 20.

22. Pinchbeck, *op. cit.*, 7:279; M. G. Jones, *The Charity School Movement* (Cambridge: Cambridge University Press, 1938), pp. 3, 43-4. In many colonies this scholarly selection by teachers was quite objective and favored social promotion of humble children among those in the schools; this process is a strong counterweight in the controversy over the bookish nature of colonial schools.

23. Hans, *op. cit.*, p. 33. For eminent scientists in seventeenth-eighteenth century England, 24 per cent had no formal secondary education, 33 per cent were educated at home or in the nine great public schools, and 43 per cent had some other secondary education. Of these men, 31 per cent were sons of peers or gentry, 21 per cent sons of farmers or laborers, and 48 per cent sons of middle-class or professional men.

24. C. A. Anderson, "A Sceptical Note on the Relation of Education and Mobility," *American Journal of Sociology*, 66:560-70 (1961).

TABLE 1

Interrelationship Between Occupation and Schooling in Puerto Rico

Occupation	Years of Schooling Completed					Total
	0	1–4	5–8	9–12	13+	
Professional and semiprofessional	0	2	5	11	47	65
Business, owners	11	27	27	22	8	95
Business, managers and salesmen	5	5	5	12	6	32
Farm owners	14	19	19	4	1	53
Secretaries and clerks	2	2	2	43	8	65
Industrial, skilled	13	49	49	15	1	118
Industrial, semiskilled	31	38	38	14	1	118
Service	28	32	32	29	1	129
Agricultural labor	110	93	93	16	0	257
Housewives, etc.	28	21	21	1	1	66
Total	242	228	227	167	74	998

Even well before the 1944 act, the grant-aided secondary schools had a broad clientele. In 1909 children of laborers made up 19 per cent of their enrollment, 19 per cent coming from professional homes and 22 per cent from other white-collar homes; while 40 per cent were children of businessmen and farmers. In 1926 the corresponding percentages were laborers 28, professional 17, white-collar 24, businessmen and farmers 31.[25] A large number, if a small proportion, of children from ordinary families were moving up the educational ladder.

Education, Occupation, and Income

The conventional conclusion that formal schooling and occupation are closely associated (like the parallel correlation of national per capita income with schooling) rests on an exaggeration of the connection that does exist for occupations at the extremes. In developed countries this correlation is actually comparatively loose.[26] Assorting the literate or trained individuals by vocation and sector is one of the basic ways education enters into development, but the correlation does not need to be precise. In turn, of course, parental education combined with occupation strongly affects the advantages of offspring. In India in 1951, for example, the percentage of literacy among occupied males varied as follows:[27]

25. J. G. Legge, *The Rising Tide* (Oxford: Blackwell, 1929), pp. 40f.

26. This looseness is a serious limitation on manpower planning. That it is perhaps an optimum situation for development has been argued in my "The Impact of the Educational System on Technological Change and Modernization," Ch. 13 in B. F. Hoselitz and W. E. Moore (eds.), *Industrialization and Society* (Paris: UNESCO, 1963).

27. India, "Religion and Livelihood Classes by Educational Standards," *Census Paper #1* (1959), p. 16.

TABLE 2
Percentage Distribution of Education of Men in Selected Occupations in Kanpur, India

Occupation	Level of Education						
	Postgraduate	College	Technical	Secondary	Primary	Illiterate	Private, NA, in School
Senior executives & technical officers	44	35	21	—	—	—	—
Junior executives	8	23	15	54	—	—	—
Clerks	6	32	3	55	—	—	—
Carpenters	—	—	6	9	42	40	3
Businessmen	2	13	1	31	34	14	5
Petty traders	—	1	2	17	40	34	6
Shop assistants	—	7	3	30	38	16	6
Skilled°	—	—	4	14	35	42	5
Unskilled	—	—	2	10	33	52	3

° excluding artisans on own account

322

TABLE 3

Relation of Education and Occupation among Africans
in Stanleyville (in Percentages)

Occupations

Years of General Schooling	Unskilled	Skilled, Semiskilled	White-Collar	Self-Employed	Not Employed	Total
		Distribution of Schooling within Occupation				
0	65	43	8	73	48	50
1–3	21	25	8	12	17	21
4–6	12	29	42	11	26	23
6+	2	3	42	4	9	6
Total	100	100	100	100	100	100
		Distribution of Occupation within Schooling				
0	48	37	2	7	6	100
1–3	37	52	3	3	5	100
4–6	20	54	17	2	7	100
6+	11	17	60	3	9	100
Total	37	43	9	5	6	100

All agricultural	20%	*All nonagriculture*	40%
Landlords	48%	Commerce	52%
Owner cultivators	22%	Transport	42%
Tenants	17%	Services	41%
Laborers	10%	"Production"	32%

Tables 1, 2, and 3 display the connection of occupation with schooling for three different societies in widely scattered locations.[28] The men with more schooling tend to be employed in the higher levels of occupation, but there is a wide scatter of occupations within each education category, and vice versa.[29] The association of income with schooling also is relatively tenuous, in both developing and developed countries. It is by no means only the

28. M. M. Tumin and A. S. Feldman, *Social Class and Social Change in Puerto Rico* (Princeton: Princeton University Press, 1961), p. 66; D. N. Majumdar, *et al*, *Social Contours of an Industrial City; Social Survey of Kanpur* (Bombay: Asia Publishing Co., 1960), p. 120; International African Institute, *Social Implications of Industrialization and Urbanization in Africa South of the Sahara* (Paris: UNESCO, 1956), p. 67.

29. The percentage in each Stanleyville occupation whose fathers had worked for Europeans may be an even more significant index of readiness for modern production: white-collar 43, unskilled 16, domestics 23, masons and painters 15, mechanics 31, carpenters 31 (International African Institute, *op. cit.*, p. 642.

Table 4

Interrelationship of Monthly Male Earnings
with Schooling, Hyderabad, India

Level of Education

Earnings (Rupees per month)	Illi- terate	Pri- mary	Secon- dary	Lower Profes- sional, Tech- nical	Under- grad- uate	Grad- uate, Post- grad- uate	Higher Profes- sional, Tech- nical	Total
−25	658	264	220	14	4	2	2	1164
26−	912	541	308	15	18	1	4	1799
51−	376	407	510	44	59	22	25	1443
101−	68	190	417	66	51	56	42	890
201−	6	15	158	55	49	117	54	454
501−		3	21	18	8	36	9	95
1001−			8	3	4	5	11	31
2501−			3	1		2		6
5000+			1	2				3
Total	2020	1420	1646	218	193	241	147	5885

already-schooled families who will find it easy financially to keep their children in school. Table 4 is taken from a study in Hyderabad, India.[30]

Social Selection for Education

It is useful to begin the discussion of this topic by examining the situation among the developed countries. The data in Table 5 portray the composition of university student bodies at dates between the two world wars for sixteen European countries (plus Mexico) and the United States.[31] The countries are grouped by percentages of males employed in primary production. Despite a variation of primary employment from about 70 to about 20 per cent among these countries, there is small variation in the proportion of students coming from homes of manual laborers as against homes of other types. Perhaps most surprising, the proportion coming from homes of urban laborers does not rise with a shift toward secondary or tertiary production, though this proportion is very high in the United States. (American Negroes have the largest representation both from other than white-collar families and from homes of urban laborers.) In fact, the level of university attendance (as a proportion of the age cohort) has more effect upon attendance of farmers' or laborers' children than does the level of the economy; national education traditions are important.

Scrutiny of the selection ratios reveals that the United States pattern is

30. Indian Institute of Economics, *A Socio-Economic Survey of Hyderabad* (New Delhi: The Institute, 1957), p. 81.

31. C. A. Anderson, "The Social Status of University Students," *Third World Congress of Sociology, Transactions* (1956), V:51f.

TABLE 5

Relation of Social Selection of University Attendance
to Economic Level among Developed Countries

	Percentage Distribution of Students by Parental Occupation				Selection Ratios†			
	I°	II	III	U.S.	I	II	III	U.S.
Agriculture and labor	22.6‡	14.4	11.7	37.3	.28	.19	.25	.57
All other (white collar)	77.4	85.6	88.3	62.7	4.6	2.7	2.9	1.8
Agriculture—all	17.1	8.2	6.8	9.8	.26	.30	.34	.62
operators	17.8	6.3	6.4	——	.37	.27	.58	——
Labor—all	9.2	5.0	3.9	——	.26	.10	.07	——
nonagricultural	7.1	6.4	5.8	27.5	.32	.14	.12	.56
Professional					11.9	10.9	13.6	3.4
Entrepreneurs					4.3	2.4	2.0	3.0

°Average percentage in primary production: I 62, II 40, III 23. The United States is excluded from III and given separately because of the ambiguity of "university" in this country; only data for whites are given for the United States.

†Ratio of the percentages in the left of the table to the percentages of males in the labor force.

‡The subtotals below for this stratum do not add to the given percentage because, for example, all labor was given for some countries and non-farm labor for others.

distinctly nonselective compared to other countries. The relative advantages of children from white-collar families (except the professions specifically) diminish appreciably as countries become less confined to primary production; still, workers' children do not uniformly acquire greater opportunities in any marked degree.

Students in four universities from widely separated parts of the less-developed world can be compared with the foregoing Western data. (Usually only the percentage distributions of parental occupations are given, and the rubrics are not strictly comparable.) The percentage distribution of parental occupations for students in the National University of Colombia was as follows:[32] professional 17; white-collar—upper 14, lower 17; farmers—larger 25, smaller 6; laborers 3; others 8—a pattern roughly similar to that of the United States.

Quite a different distribution is found in Gadjah Mada University in Indonesia:[33] professional 7; officials—higher 6, lower 28; privately and self-employed 23; police and military 3; farmers 17; laborers 3.

Students in the University of the Punjab were distinctively recruited from white-collar homes:[34] officials—higher 10, lower 13; clerical 51; labor 19; other 7.

32. R. C. Williamson, *El Studiante Colombiana*, (1962), typescript, p. 14.

33. J. Fischer, "The Student Population of a Southeast Asian University," *International Journal of Comparative Sociology*, 2:232 (1961).

34. J. J. Mangalam, "Study of Student Mass Failure," (1960), typescript, p. 3.

Jahoda's 1953 study of students at the University College of Ghana relates the backgrounds of the students to the distribution of the employed population.[35] The proportion coming from white-collar homes is slightly higher than in the United States but distinctly lower than in most Western countries. Children of peasants, especially laborers' children, have a relatively good opportunity for university education compared with those from similar backgrounds in Europe, judging by the selection ratios.

Occupation	Students' Fathers	Employed Men	Selection Ratio
Agriculture	26	70	.37
Manual labor	8	23	.35
Other	66	7	8.57
	100%	100%	

The situation at the secondary school level is as diverse among countries as was the university level. The pattern in Poona in 1951 was extremely selective:[36] professional 29, business 19, office managers 8, clerical 28, farmers 2, labor 3, other 11. It is, however, possible for schools to be at the same time highly selective for some occupations and nonselective for other occupations: this situation is illustrated by data for Africans in South Africa in 1921.[37] Children of teachers and clergymen comprised a sixth of the African pupils in Standard VI, and their selection ratio was 54. Children of tradesmen and schooled laborers comprised about a tenth of the pupils, with a selection ratio of 24. On the other hand, tenant farmers' children made up a third of the total enrollment, with a selection ratio of only .6; and children of illiterate laborers supplied a seventh of the pupils, but this was 1.3 times their proportion of the working force.

In British Guiana, as Bone ascertained, secondary schools were drawing broadly from the population, nearly half the boys coming from manual workers' homes.[38] Few upper-status parents are available as a source of students. As in virtually all countries, girls come from homes of higher status than do boys (Table 6).

Foster's recent study of Ghana secondary schools reports a larger proportion of "upper class" boys than Bone found.[39] The Ghana girls were from particularly limited social backgrounds. Nevertheless, the majority of boys came from homes headed by men with very modest occupations, more than a third of them in farming. A third of the boys' fathers, but fewer than a tenth of the girls' fathers had never been to school. Despite the very steep gradient

35. G. Jahoda, "Social Background of a West African Student Population," *British Journal of Sociology*, 5:361 (1954), 6:72, (1955).

36. I. P. Desai, "High School Students in Poona," *Bulletin Deccan Collage Research Institute*, 12:94 (1953).

37. Union of South Africa, *Report of the Commission on Native Education*, 1949-51, p. 116.

38. Bone, *op. cit.*, pp. 39-41.

39. P. Foster, Secondary Schooling and Social Mobility in a West African Nation, *Sociology of Education*, 37:159 (1963).

TABLE 6

Percentage Distribution of Paternal Occupations
of British Guiana Secondary Pupils

Paternal Occupation	Boys	Girls
Administrative, professional	5	9
Civil Service (middle)	5	9
Teachers	10	6
Businessmen	16	20
Clerical	7	9
Services	6	5
Artisans	19	18
Unskilled	6	5
Farming	19	7
N. A.	7	12
Total	100	100

TABLE 7

Percentage Distribution of Paternal Occupations
of Ghana Secondary Pupils

Paternal Occupation	Male Labor Force	Students' Fathers		Selectivity Ratio°	
		Boys	Girls	Boys	Girls
Professional, clerical	2	34	66	14.9	28.5
Skilled	10	13	10	1.3	.9
Trader, business	4	11	7	2.5	1.7
Farmers	70	37	12	.5	.2
Unskilled	14	2	1	.1	.1
Others, N.A.	°	3	4	—	—
Total	100	100	100		

°Computed from unrounded numbers.

of the selection ratios, these schools would seem to be promoting mobility
(Table 7).

From my analysis of Kenya secondary schools I would conclude that
there, also, mobility among Africans is being enhanced by secondary education, though enrollment is definitely influenced by home background. About
40 per cent of the boys and 60 per cent of the girls in the twelfth grade had
fathers engaged in non-farming occupations, which include perhaps 20 per
cent of the labor force. More than 30 per cent of the boys but only 6 per cent
of the girls came from homes in which neither parent had any schooling; only
one per cent of boys and 13 per cent of girls were from families in which both
parents had at least entered secondary school. On the other hand, in a country
where about three-fourths of the African adults are illiterate, the fathers of

Table 8

Percentage Representation of Selected Fathers' Occupations
among Poona Businessmen

Father's Occupation	Factory Owners	Respondent's Business Medium Business	Small Business	Skilled
Factory Owner	24	1	—	—
Medium Business	31	40	5	2
Small Business	12	18	40	4
Skilled	4	3	8	46
Unskilled	21	24	34	40

40 per cent of the boys and 67 per cent of the girls had finished primary school, as had 16 and 49 per cent of the mothers.

Until patterns of vertical mobility have been traced out for more societies of different kinds, it behooves us to be cautious in drawing conclusions about the influence of educational opportunity upon economic development. Analysis of data for Western countries indicates that neither parental status nor schooling appears to play a dominant part in determining occupational status; residual factors (presumably ability, luck, drive, and so on) are equally important.[40] It may turn out that in the nations now undergoing the early stages of development, education will have more effect upon mobility than it has had in Western history. It is apparent that a large volume of inter-generational occupational mobility is occurring in the developing countries. Sovani's study of Poona, for example, reveals a steady climbing of the business ladder.[41] In the process, schooling and practical experience are combined in many alternative ways (Table 8).

Parental Interest: an Intervening Variable

Parents' interest in their children's schooling can be expected to vary widely in any given social stratum, or within a given locality, until the incidence of schooling (of a particular level) becomes very widespread. Families hold divergent views about the utility to their offspring of the not-yet-conventionalized sorts of schooling, and this caution in many cases reflects canny comparison of costs and returns.

The model description of parental apathy was written by the editors of the 1851 educational census of Britain, but the same comment might be made over wide areas of the world even today.[42]

The great fact seems to be obtruded on our notice that the children's absence from, or very brief continuance at, school, is mainly owing to the

40. C. A. Anderson, "A Sceptical Note. . . ." op. cit.
41. N. V. Sovani et al, Poona: A Resurvey (Poona: Gadgil, 1956), p. 464.
42. Great Britain, Census, 1851: Education (London: H.M.S.O., 1854), p. xl.

slight esteem which parents have for the education itself which generally they might easily obtain. Beyond all question, much of this indifference results from a perception of the really trifling value of a great proportion of the education offered for their purchase; for the instances are not a few in which the improvement of a school is followed by increased attendance; but perhaps it primarily flows from an idea, prevalent among the labouring classes, that instruction beyond a certain point can never be of any practical utility to those of their condition; for in general a parent, in whatever station, takes himself and his own social status as the standard up to which he purposes to educate his offspring . . . practically, it is to be feared, the length and character of the education given in this country to the young are regulated more by a regard to its material advantage, as connected with their future physical condition, than by any wise appreciation of the benefits of knowledge in itself.

Elsewhere in this book (Part IV, Chapter 18) I have told a little of the long English struggle to find forms of practical training for the hordes of poor and orphan children. The early solutions were copies of apprenticeship or of traditional family training; *i.e.,* working schools. As these programs spread and called for larger collections of charitable funds, much ingenuity was displayed in demonstrating the practicality of that training.[43] The poor had become too numerous to be viewed merely as cheap labor; moreover, their vices and irresponsibility were national economic liabilities. In that context the steady emphasis on teaching religion in the schools was, with some justification, seen as a contribution to economic welfare. There is a curious parallel in the fact that seventeenth-century English reformers, teachers in colonies around the world, and present-day Soviet rulers alike have turned to boarding schools as a means of isolating children from deleterious home influences.

As economic conditions in Britain improved, many writers began to argue that it was superfluous to operate expensive training programs. One suspects, also, that many parents were offering more resistance to loss of their children's labor. People "ridiculed the idea of building expensive houses throughout the country in order to provide the poor with work which was crying out to be done."[44] The balance of work against schooling came to be calculated in more subtle ways. The superior working-class parents, who were benefiting from the slow rise in prosperity, became able to pay a few pennies for "literary" schooling that would fit their offspring for superior work and even for jobs carrying some social dignity. The Sunday schools came to enroll mainly the children of the less fortunate or the less farseeing working-class parents; those schools entailed no loss of labor by the children.

Economic expansion, as always is the case, was accompanied by expansion of nonindustrial and trade activities. The more general sort of education given by the superior charity schools or other elementary schools qualified children for those non-manual jobs. Contemporary educators were quite aware that schools could be ranked in quality. General education triumphed over practical education, as it was to do in many places around the world in

43. Jones, *op. cit.,* pp. 13, 31.
44. *Ibid.,* p. 42.

Table 9

Number of Kenya School Districts with Designated Percentages of
Children Entering Lower Primary and Upper Primary Classes

Percentage Entering	Entering Std. I		Entering Std. V°	
	Boys	Girls	Boys	Girls
80+	16	4	5	4
60-80	8	7	4	2
40-60	7	8	18	12
20-40	—	11	6	15
-20	2	3	—	—
Total Districts	33	33	33	33

°As a percentage of Std. IV completers.

the following centuries. Parents responded to the degree that they perceived
the balance of opportunities and costs in this situation.[45] Repeatedly it has
been found that an educational program flourishes to the degree that it per-
suades parents that their children will benefit tangibly from enrolling. "The
one condition for the success of an educational policy is not what government
or a nationalist party may want, and not merely what the community in general may vaguely want, but what people want, or can be made to want, so
urgently that they will pay for it either individually or as a community to the
extent at least of going to school or sending their children to school.[46]

III. GEOGRAPHIC PATTERNS IN THE
DIFFUSION OF SCHOOLING

Inequalities in educational facilities and in their utilization among the
areas of a country are usual, and these inequalities display great persistence
even in the face of major social changes. Moreover, definite clusters of other
socioeconomic traits associated with relative educational attainments also
recur in different periods and countries. A few illustrative cases are described
here, for both developing and industrialized economies.

In Kenya certain districts have the highest rates of school attendance;
these are the most densely populated districts, with the earliest mission contacts and highest adult literacy, with greatest accessibility to areas of European residence, and the most contact with urban life. The level of attendance is lower for girls than for boys, as Table 9 shows, but the relative enrollment for the two sexes is similar among districts.

The relation of literacy to various economic and social traits of English
counties in the 1840's is shown in Table 10.[47] Literacy was positively associ-

45. Ibid., pp. 149, 160-1.

46. J. S. Furnivall, Educational Progress in Southeast Asia (New York: Institute of Pacific
Relations, 1943), p. 113.

47. J. Fletcher, "Moral and Educational Statistics," Royal Statistical Society Journal, 10:193-
233 (1847).

TABLE 10

Rank Order Correlation of Literacy with Various Social and Economic Factors in England and Wales in the 1840's

Factors		1	2	3	4	5	6	7	8	9	10	11	12
Literacy: percentage of grooms signing marriage register	1	—	53	44	38	38	19	09	-12	-22	-32	-34	-53
Persons of independent means (in ratio to population)	2	53	—	67	-16	37	-18	03	-27	-09	08	-09	-56
Domestic servants (as percentage of population)	3	44	67	—	-29	31	-27	27	-13	-07	02	15	-61
Persons in trade, commerce, and industry (as percentage of population)	4	38	-16	-29	—	-03	61	-24	11	19	-57	-76	08
Savings deposits (per capita)	5	38	37	31	-03	—	-01	10	-08	18	05	09	-30
Density of population	6	19	-18	-27	61	-01	—	-15	-33	54	-37	-68	08
Real property values (per capita)	7	09	03	27	-24	10	-15	—	-09	26	36	41	01
Illegitimacy	8	-12	-27	-13	11	-08	-33	-09	—	-07	09	22	27
Criminal commitments (of males/population)	9	-22	-09	07	19	18	54	26	-07	—	19	-02	20
Outdoor pauper relief (persons/population)	10	-32	08	02	-57	05	-37	36	09	19	—	66	24
Persons in agriculture (as percentage of population)	11	-34	-09	15	-76	09	-68	41	22	-02	66	—	28
Males marrying under age 21 (as percentages of marriages)	12	-53	-56	-61	08	-30	08	01	27	20	24	28	—

331

ated with nonagricultural activities and negatively related to agricultural predominance, as would be expected. The strong correlation with "persons of independent means" points to a separate and partially noneconomic component of educational traditions. Fletcher's discussion emphasizes the importance in particular areas of artisan traditions of schooling and the distinctive effects, favorable or unfavorable, of individual industries upon education. Where literacy was widespread, indices of social disorganization were lower; for example, literacy discouraged early marriage and stimulated savings.

In an exploration of economic diversities within the American South in 1950, I found that farmers' incomes apparently were raised or lowered by different factors in the several states.[48] For explaining the incidence of high incomes, the between-race component outweighed state or tenure; among whites tenure was more important than state, but among Negro farmers the relative influences were reversed. Low incomes, on the other hand, were more associated with state than with race, and within each race, state was more important than tenure.

Indices of race differentiation in schooling for each southern state delineate some of the forces at work in the economy of that region.[49] Broadly speaking, degrees of race discrimination in educational attainments reflect a combination of the stage of general educational progress and the extent to which the two races are members of distinctive subcultures. One can identify three types of situation. (1) Where educational progress is rapid for whites but social distinctions between the races are great, high indices of racial inequality emerge at each attainment level. This extreme is most nearly approximated in Mississippi. (2) Where there has been little emphasis on education, a mass of semiliterate whites share disadvantages with the Negroes, but a white minority completing elementary and high school stands apart from the rest of the whites and from virtually all the Negroes, as in rural Louisiana. (3) Where racial distinctions are moderate, the value placed upon schooling extends to both racial groups, diminishing both the lag of Negro behind white progress, and the inequality indices, as in Tennessee and Virginia.

French data on the incidence of literacy can be traced back over the past two centuries; the figures range widely among departments (Table 11).[50] In the late seventeenth century the range among departments in percentage literate was over 50 points among men (and 40 among women). At the end of the eighteenth century the range was 85 (65); in the early nineteenth century 85 (75); in the mid-nineteenth century 70 (80); and in the 1870's 50 (65). The departments with greatest literacy tended to cluster, as did those departments with relatively low literacy. Moreover, the relative positions of the

48. C. A. Anderson, "Economic Status Differentials in the South," *Rural Sociology*, 19:50-67 (1954).

49. C. A. Anderson, "Inequalities in Schooling in the South," *American Journal of Sociology*, 60:555 (1955).

50. France, *Statistique de l'Enseignement Primaire; Tome Second: Statistique Comparee de l'Enseignement Primaire 1828-77* (Paris: Imprimerie National, 1880).

TABLE 11
Distributions of French Departments by Percentages of Grooms and Brides Writing Their Signatures on the Marriage Register

Percentage Signing	Years				
	1686-1690	1786-1790	1816-1820	1854-1855	1876-1877
Under 5	−(12)°	−(1)	−	−	−
5.0- 9.9	8 (24)	2 (20)	−(5)	−	−
10.0-14.9	13 (18)	4 (18)	1 (18)	−	−
15.0-19.9	14 (9)	6 (8)	3 (11)	−(9)	−
20.0-24.9	8 (8)	12 (7)	3 (12)	−(7)	−
25.0-29.9	7 (4)	8 (5)	7 (5)	2 (7)	−
30.0-34.9	6 (1)	9 (2)	9 (3)	4 (6)	−(5)
35.0-39.9	5	3 (4)	6 (1)	3 (6)	−
40.0-44.9	5	2 (4)	8 (3)	4 (9)	−(3)
45.0-49.9	3	5 (3)	9 (5)	6 (7)	3 (9)
50.0-54.9	4	3 (1)	3 (4)	7 (3)	1 (4)
55.0-59.9	1	3 (1)	5 (1)	3 (4)	5 (9)
60.0-64.9	2	3 (2)	1 (2)	11 —	2 (5)
65.0-69.9	−	5 (3)	6 (3)	8 (6)	6 (6)
70.0-74.9	−	4	3 (1)	7 (2)	9 (10)
75.0-79.9	−	3	3 (2)	8 (7)	10 (6)
80.0-84.9	−	4	3 (2)	4 (5)	14 (7)
85.0-89.9	−	1	4	6 (3)	8 (5)
90.0-94.9	−	2	3	8 (4)	13 (10)
95.0-99.9	−	−	1	5 (1)	16 (8)
Total	76 (76)	79 (79)	78 (78)	86 (86)	87 (87)
Median	21 (11)	33 (15)	46 (23)	67 (44)	83 (71)
Mean	29 (4)	47 (27)	54 (35)	68 (53)	81 (71)

°The first figure is for grooms and the one in parentheses for brides.

different clusters, as of individual departments, persisted over the whole period. The accompanying four maps (Figures 1-4) portray those clusters for literacy at three dates and the level of primary school attendance in the mid-nineteenth century. The spatial patterns manifested in these maps exemplify the diffusion principles discussed by Hägerstrand (Part III, Chapter 12).

The differences between median male and female literacy at the five successive dates were 10, 18, 23, 23, 12. At the end of the seventeenth century the women were largely illiterate, but men in some departments had already begun to push well ahead of those in other departments. A century later the spread had widened for men, and women had begun to advance in some departments, a century behind the men. In another thirty years dispersion among departments for men had widened even more, though the number of seriously lagging departments had diminished; the lag of women behind

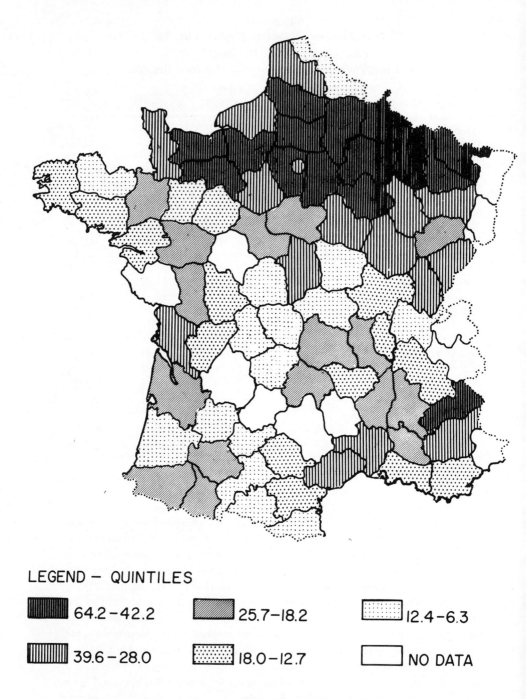

LEGEND — QUINTILES

▓	64.2–42.2	▨	25.7–18.2	⊡	12.4–6.3
‖	39.6–28.0	⋮	18.0–12.7	☐	NO DATA

Figure 1
Percentage of literate grooms in French departments, 1686–90 (in quintiles)

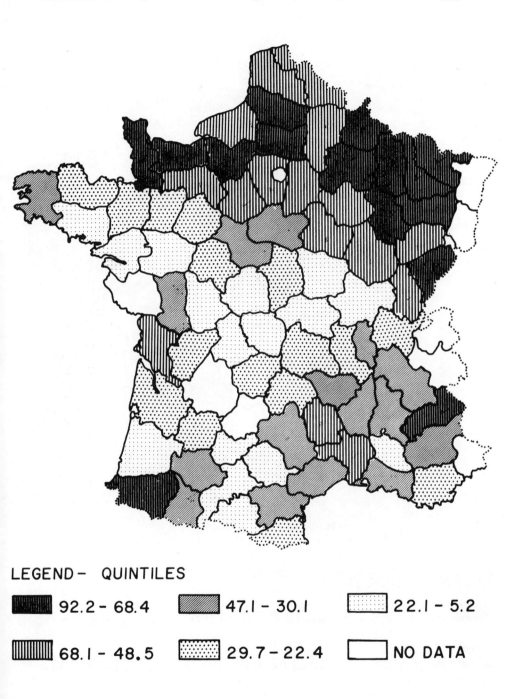

LEGEND – QUINTILES

92.2 - 68.4	47.1 - 30.1	22.1 - 5.2
68.1 - 48.5	29.7 - 22.4	NO DATA

FIGURE 2
Percentage of literate grooms in French departments, 1786–90 (in quintiles)

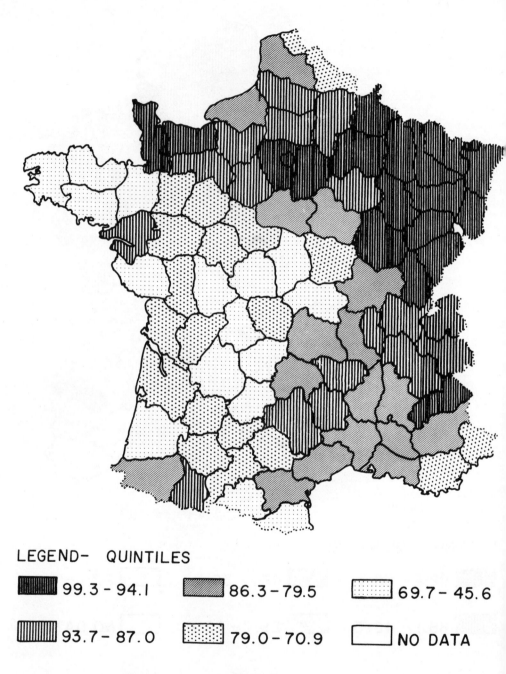

LEGEND- QUINTILES

99.3 - 94.1   86.3 - 79.5   69.7 - 45.6

93.7 - 87.0   79.0 - 70.9   NO DATA

Figure 3
Percentage of literate grooms in French departments, 1876–77 (in quintiles)

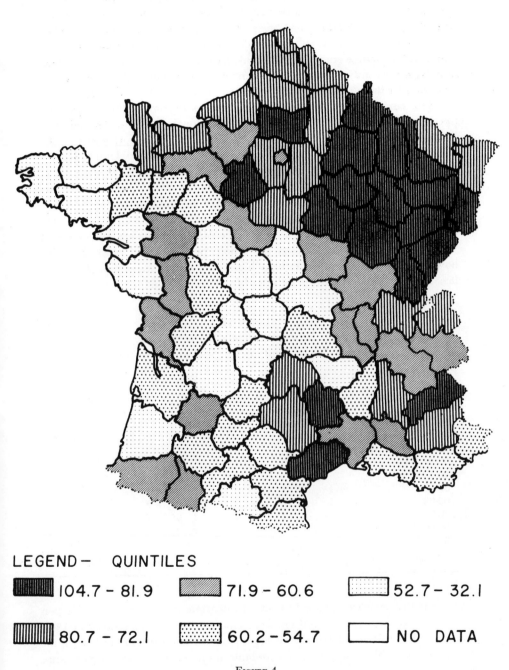

LEGEND— QUINTILES

▦ 104.7 - 81.9   ▨ 71.9 - 60.6   ▨ 52.7 - 32.1

▦ 80.7 - 72.1   ▨ 60.2 - 54.7   ☐ NO DATA

FIGURE 4
Primary school enrollment as percentage of 5- to 15-year-old children in French departments, 1863 (in quintiles)

men was now smaller, though departments were still disparate. With the passing of another third of a century the lagging departments for men had begun to pull up, and there had been some progress among women over most of the country. By the 1870's the mode for men was at the high end of the scale, and the range among departments had become much smaller; women now lagged by only about a quarter century, and a mode at the high end was emerging for them also. The focus-diffusion process had been at work.

The same data for France enable us to explore some of the evidence for persistence in the geographic patterns of educational advance and retardation. In Table 12 the literacy of grooms (signatures on marriage licenses) at the end of the seventeenth century is related to that one century later.[51] Broadly speaking, the departments retained their relative positions. Moving ahead three-quarters of a century, literacy in the middle of the nineteenth century was quite definitely related to that at the end of the eighteenth century. There had been more changes of relative position than during the preceding century and a definite clustering at higher levels; these data are not shown. A rough correlation persisted over the whole period of 170 years. By 1876, however, literacy was comparatively high in all departments, though the few laggard ones had been low from the earliest date.

TABLE 12

Relationship between Literacy Rates of Grooms in French Departments in 1686-90 and 1786-90

Percentage Literate in 1786-90	Percentage Literate in 1686-90							
	0-9	10-19	20-29	30-39	40-49	50-59	60-69	Total
0-9	1	1						2
10-19	3	7						10
20-29	4	11	4					19
30-39		6	5					11
40-49			4	3				7
50-59		1	1	3				5
60-69		1		1	5	1		8
70-79			1	1	1	2	2	7
80-89				2	2	1		5
90+				1		1		2
Total	8	27	15	11	8	5	2	76

Finally, one can relate literacy of departments in 1686-90 to the percentages of 5 to 15 year old children enrolled in primary schools in 1863. (See Table 13; the relationship is more clearcut in a scattergram than in the condensed table.) Despite a considerable number of aberrant departments,

51. The French editors of the source volume demonstrate that marriage-license data and recruit data agree quite well, allowing the proper lag in years, as do schooling data and recruit data.

TABLE 13

Relationship Between Literacy Rates of Grooms in French
Departments in 1686-90 and Percentage
of 5-15 Year Old Children Enrolled in Primary School in 1863

Percentage of School Enrollment in 1863	Percentage Literate in 1686-90							Total
	0-9	10-19	20-29	30-39	40-49	50-59	60-69	
30-39	1	5						6
40-49	2	3	1					6
50-59	1	11	4					16
60-69	3	4	3	1	2			13
70-79	1	3	5	2	3	1		15
80-89			1	3	2	2	1	9
90+		1	1	5	1	2	1	11
Total	8	27	15	11	8	5	2	76

the more literate departments at the earliest date tend to be those in which school attendance was relatively high 175 years later. This stability of educational interest or disinterest was emphasized by the editors of the source volume.

In the otherwise informative studies of economic historians, unfortunately little attention has been given to relating local educational developments to those in crafts, manufacturing, trade, and other economic affairs. The few data that have been located and summarized in this chapter promise a good reward for studies directed toward this important problem of how investment in human resources has been connected with broader economic events. Education, like production, tends to be localized in growing points and to diffuse in systematically observable patterns.

The need for growing points, Hirschman says, "means that international and interregional inequality of growth is an inevitable concomitant and condition of growth itself." A tendency to disperse investment funds widely may rest on a conception that economic progress is "a force that ought to affect equally all members and sections of the community. Wherever this idea prevails, governments are unprepared and unwilling to make the choices about priorities and sequences that are the essence of development programs."[52] Hanson sets forth this view at greater length.[53]

> The benefits of economic development are never, particularly in the earlier stages, evenly spread out over the whole population of a country. They tend to be concentrated in certain areas, in accordance with varying resource endowments, geographical and agronomical peculiarities, patterns of com-

52. A. O. Hirschman, *The Strategy of Economic Development* (New Haven: Yale University Press, 1958), p. 183.
53. A. H. Hanson, *Public Enterprise and Economic Development* (London: Routledge, 1959), p. 472.

munication, availabilities of ancillary services, and a large number of other factors. . . . Some types of benefit, admittedly, should be thinly and more or less evenly spread, even though they may thus be awkward and expensive to administer. But units of 'welfare' are not indefinitely subdivisible, and the conception of a many-sided and integrated service is quite rightly held in high regard by the social administrator, whose efforts need to be concentrated to a certain degree in order to produce any visible and measurable results. . . . [The pilot project] sets an example, firing people with ambition for better ways of life, and stimulating that discontent with the old and traditional which is one of the mainsprings of economic progress. The opportunity for making such an experiment in remoulding man should clearly not be missed, just because one person, thinking purely in terms of input-output figures, condemns it as 'uneconomic' and another has his sensitive conscience outraged by its 'inequity.'

How this problem has presented itself to several generations of colonial officials has been well summarized by Ward.[54] It happens commonly that "one people may develop an insatiable demand for education while some other peoples of the territory remain uninterested. Is the government in such cases to give the eager claimants all they want and thereby push them into a position of complete predominance, or is it in the name of fair shares for all to force schools on people who do not particularly want them?

At a later time (which may come quickly), when the desire for schools has spread more widely and most localities are able to express their demands politically, policy choices become even more difficult. In many developing countries, primary attendance is reaching high levels, with an ensuing demand for open doors into middle and secondary schools. Even when we set aside the problem of balancing school graduates with jobs, the scarcity of teachers and of other resources in the face of competing investment needs compels the adoption of one or another scheme for rationing education. Equal division of funds (per pupil) among areas irrespective of their level of present development may be the most equitable long-run policy, but development must take hold in the short-run or that equitable policy cannot be sustained. Shifting primary costs to local areas—apart from hardship cases—will relieve this pressure on resources, but it is inequitable. Even with uniform allocation of funds, as the previous pages indicate, localities and subpopulations will long differ in their effective utilization of educational opportunities.[55]

IV. EQUITY AND EFFICIENCY

Why Does the Question of Inequality Arise?

Though this question has already been answered by implication, we can be a bit more definite about the answer, particularly if we ask "how to get development" in the contemporary underdeveloped world. The reasons for

54. W. E. F. Ward, "Education in the Colonies," in A. C. Jones, *New Fabian Colonial Essays* (London: Hogarth, 1959), p. 194.

55. J. Lambert, "Croissance Demographique," *Population*, 15:661 (1960).

widespread concern about equality of educational opportunity will become clearer. One must face the test of efficiency, for to say that universal schooling is needed for democratic government, or that economic productivity presupposes heavy investment in training carries no definite implications about educational equality.

1) Equality of educational opportunity is widely propounded as a moral norm, exemplified by the UN declaration of universal human rights. This right is linked to welfare economic philosophy and to democracy in government—even in countries that have reversed the traditional meanings of those slogans.

2) It happens that many countries have been revived or become independent just as relative equality in education and many other goods is approaching realization in the "model" nations. These aims are adopted and inculcated in the citizens of new countries; they expect their governments to deliver.

3) Sophisticated notions of motivation and talent development have diffused similarly. From the necessity of widespread participation in modernized production, many conclude that equality of opportunity must play the same part it does today in advanced countries. Doubtless the proportion of a nation's children reaching a given high attainment will be larger if half rather than a tenth receive secondary education. But there is a wide gap between conclusions about motivation or the need for training and decisions about disposal of inadequate resources. Educational policy must be related to the stage of economic development. Modernization entails giving education a central place, to be sure. Many aspects of development will go forward only if education gets due attention. But just as absence of industrial conflict is no criterion of labor commitment,[56] so equality of educational opportunity is an equivocal criterion of prudent development policies. All the key items in these discussions turn out to be ambiguous unless they are dealt with in a context of sequential social change.

Equity

Parity of opportunity is the simplest definition of equity: If a group makes up 10 per cent of the population, it should receive 10 per cent of the school places. But even without dealing with discrimination, this seemingly simple notion has several variants with rather different implications for policy.

1) *An equal amount of education to everyone.* Examples of such a goal would be hard to find. Moreover, when an educational system approaches this condition (as in the United States for a large part of the population at secondary level), qualitative variations are emphasized more.

2) *Enough education to bring everyone to a given standard.* The spread

56. W. E. Moore and A. S. Feldman, *Labor Commitment and Social Change in Developing Areas* (New York: Social Science Research Council, 1960), p. 17.

of definite norms among a population (as, universal primary schooling) can achieve this goal as a "floor." Persistence beyond that level will then be brought under other norms and/or regarded as less important; meanwhile no one shall be allowed to lack the basic minimum. (In this situation, repeating and remedial teaching must be allowed for unless the standard is to be perfunctory.)

3) *Enough education to permit each person to reach his potential.* Only a wealthy society would try to meet this stipulation in anything like its full implications. It would entail schooling to the point of "school fatigue," for each individual's potentials are unlimited in some direction. Without compulsion this rule is often accepted, but with the qualification that potentials are defined in conventional terms. In practice, this goal encourages discrimination on the basis of some kind of invidious comparison of potentials.

4) *Continued education so long as gains in learning per input of teaching match an agreed norm.* In practice, however, learning will be viewed conventionally: "It just isn't worth our trouble to keep him in school any longer." Unfortunately, no definite measure of inputs is available. This criterion also raises questions of learning versus teaching, teaching versus training, and choice among kinds of training. Clearly, this is also an efficiency criterion.

Efficiency

1) *Give educational priority to those groups or areas where given inputs will evoke the largest response in attendance and in demand for further schooling.* This is perhaps the most practicable criterion. It relies upon demonstrated aspirations and willingness to sacrifice (at least leisure). It assumes that the populations assimilating the most formal education also consume or create the largest amount of extra-school training and self-teaching. It incorporates the demonstrated process of two-step communication by encouraging gradation of education with gradients of communication. However, except by insinuating a premise about group "merit," this rule violates most people's notions of equity. It favors the most developed areas and tribes.

2) *Maximize the ratio of gains in economic output to educational costs.* Presuming that absorption of education enhances productivity, resources can be invested in schools for different areas in relation to the output gains of the economy per unit of school cost. More often this criterion would be applied aggregatively, for the whole country. In a free-market system a crude approximation to this rule holds among individuals, as it does among countries. Literal application would be politically difficult in most countries, even apart from assembling the data to make the calculations. The policy is in effect adopted when higher schools and special training are assembled in key economic centers, when scholarships are apportioned between lines of study, or when secondary school places are restricted to equal estimated jobs at that level of schooling.

3) *Relying upon the rate of increase of per capita income (long or short-run).* Here costs are ignored; education pays so long as output is growing satisfactorily. This approach ignores the possibility that diverting part of present educational expenditures to non-educational investment would bring larger gains. If the long-run viewpoint is taken, a specific calculus is impractical.

Under colonial rule, the first efficiency criterion was often relied upon: demand determined supply of schooling. Newly independent governments tend to make broad assumptions about pay-off from schooling and to make vague promises of equity; their gamble in relying upon long-run hopes may or may not be wise. Usually the first efficiency test is the prudent norm, given economic development as the goal. Equity criteria would be applied within the constraints set by efficiency goals.

All conceptions of equity in schooling—except when used to counter transparent discrimination—are confounded by three problems: (1) their relation to conceptions of "ability to benefit"; (2) the fact that education is not a free good; and (3) compulsion versus the norm of "freedom of choice." Equity in practice is as hard to formulate as efficiency.

Except for the handicapped, not even the most affluent society pretends to cater to the potentials of all its children in other than "bookish" terms. Except by defining education in traditional terms, no defense of this view can be offered that does not turn into an efficiency norm. It is everywhere accepted that the supply of education should diminish as its level rises; some can learn more than others, and the higher skills need not be as plentiful as the lower. High-level people are needed, but few have the potentials, so we concentrate resources on the talented. In equity terms, though, "talent" has no more intrinsic merit than race, social class, or political or religious orthodoxy.

Education absorbs resources, and the societies today most sensitive to their shortfall in schooling have the least resources. Rough allocations to education are made; the problem is to elicit the maximum aggregate of learning for the available resources. In this context, populist demands for scattering schools everywhere will not seem reasonable to the harried official.

Balancing equity against efficiency is easier if one can work within given manpower specifications and shut his eyes to rationing qualified individuals out of their preferred training. However, restriction on free choice of career can have serious effects upon efficiency by damping motivation. It is only in advanced societies, perhaps, that equity can be regarded as essential to efficiency.

The new nations must build a resilient polity along with organizing their economy under the handicap of widespread democratic norms, backed up by universal suffrage and the pressures of locally oriented legislators. Leaders of western societies in the past could carry out their policies with little interference from those who suffered or nagging claims for equity on a broad base. Because of the consumption effects of primary education, wide and impartial distribution of schools throttles saving and inhibits the desired clustering of the factors of production. The public in new nations often quickly develop ambitious job aspirations that outrun the economy's capacity to generate jobs, and this disparity creates political unrest. Is "too much" education for the available jobs, then, really equitable? Since job opportunities are the main incentive for undergoing training, access to jobs should perhaps go with access to training for jobs if this education is to remain functional.

Status rigidities create obstacles to economic development, as well as being inequitable. A loose structure on the traditional Western pattern—or the peculiar "tight flexibility" of Meiji Japan—satisfies both criteria better. But to withstand the strains of development without throttling development, it is necessary to "appropriately" relate education to the imperatives of economic change.

PART IV
*Human-Factor
Preconditions,
The
Timing of
Emergence,
and the
Pace of Change*

In this section "the formation of human competencies" is reexamined in the light of historical evidence, complementing the more theoretical consideration, in Part II, of the factors in that formation. To be sure, the contributors of other chapters in this book have much to say on this aspect of the problem. But in Part IV we have two chapters presenting a broad range of historical data for many countries, and three historical case studies.

Literacy and schooling were more widespread in the pre-industrial period of the history of western nations that has been commonly appreciated, even by some of the conference participants. This is not to suggest that universal primary schooling or any fixed proportion of post-primary education is a precondition of development. The wastefulness of indiscriminate popular education was argued in several presentations. But there is convergent evidence that literacy of a large minority of males is a precondition for any significant transformation of an underdeveloped economy into one marked by sustained growth.

The evidence for continuity, and slowness, of development is impressive. Each author emphasizes the long period of educational preparation that preceded both the crystallization of mass schooling systems and the appearance of accelerating growth. Although Russia's economy apparently was retarded by ideologically determined resistance to the spread of education, Japan clearly had a more than sufficient fund of schooling ready to facilitate new economic patterns, once it had been decided to adopt a new technological system. In the pioneer country, England, economic events and educational programs responded to each other flexibly and cumulatively. Although education clearly seems to be a prerequisite to development, it alone will not assure development. Moreover, countries coming late on the scene probably must make a relatively heavier investment in education preparatory to development.

345

Of special interest is the all-too-scanty but impressive evidence set forth in several chapters that local foci of both education and economic development play a central part in development. Regional differentials in schooling and training as well as in economic activities are marked, and the two sets of differentials are congruent.

None of the authors succeeds in disentangling the role of formal schooling or literacy from that of practical and on-the-job training. Indeed, it is the coexistence of these complementary ways of forming human resources that is impressive. Most of the chapters make it clear that developing countries possess a rich texture of practical training programs, clusters of "projectors," industrialists, scientists, and learned men, reinforced by press and other media for exchange of experience and ideas. The mixture of men from various occupations and different social levels in those associations is no less impressive. Countries that do in fact develop are characterized by a rich context for technical and economic innovation and for schooling. This evidence should give pause to those who have faith that schools alone can create the human factors needed to undergird a new economic system.

None of the discussion went so far as to demonstrate how educational programs, of what kinds, can play what parts in arousing or sustaining innovative and productive behavior. How to create the ferment that was Petty's England or Tokugawa Japan remains to be elucidated. But chapters in this part do illuminate the importance of human attributes and interaction that are inevitably, and quite properly, set aside in aggregative input-output studies or calculations of rates of return to investment in schooling.

CHAPTER 18

LITERACY AND SCHOOLING ON THE DEVELOPMENT THRESHOLD: SOME HISTORICAL CASES

C. Arnold Anderson

There have been few investigations to ascertain the extent and distribution of formal schooling or of literacy—and these are not necessarily closely related—during the formative period of the western industrial economies. A superficial search has located no discussion in any book on economic history; scattered comments and an occasional chapter can be found in general histories, and a handful of historical articles deal explicitly with the topic. Few educational historians are interested in statistics, though their treatment of other topics often throws light on trends in popular education.

I. TRENDS IN LEVELS OF LITERACY

Very broadly, the data appear to support a generalization reached also by cross-sectional analysis of contemporary societies: about 40 per cent of adult literacy or of primary enrollment is a threshold for economic development. Needless to say, that level of education would not be a sufficient condition in societies lacking other supporting conditions. This brief historical survey also reveals some of the ways in which formal education shifts downward to successively lower socioeconomic strata (see Part III, Chapter 17).

England From the Fifteenth to the Nineteenth Centuries

Relying upon legal records for late medieval London around 1400, Thrupp concluded that the definitely lower-class men were mostly illiterate, but that large proportions of other classes were literate.[1]

> If 40 percent of the lay male Londoners of this period could read Latin, it is a fair guess that some 50 percent could read English. Latin having been taught in England since the second half of the fourteenth century, all successful grammar-school pupils would have been able to read both languages, and it was possible to study English alone. The goldsmiths had a rule, in force by 1478 and reissued in the 1490's, forbidding any member to take an apprentice "wtout he canne writte and Rede." .... To limit the picture to the merchant

1. S. L. Thrupp, *The Merchant Class of Medieval London* (Chicago: University of Chicago Press, 1948), pp. 157-71.

class, then, it is clear that all the men read English and that most of them had some training in Latin, and, as will be shown, there is reason to believe that most of the intelligent women had found ways of learning at least to read and write English.

From his examination of jury lists for two areas in England at about the same period, Adamson concluded that many workingmen were literate.[2]

> Anything of a statistical nature coming from fifteenth century Norfolk would be too favorable to be regarded as typical of England as a whole at that period. Not too much stress must therefore be laid on the descriptions of the twenty men who were called as witnesses respecting the will of Sir John Fastolf, 1466. . . . But the net result is that, ignoring the clerks, in a group of men drawn from widely separated social classes thirty-seven and a half percent are styled literate. Curiously, much the same proportion occurs in a document of 1373 relating to a suit between William of Wykeham and the Masters of St. Cross, Winchester.

Green points out that in fifteenth-century royal accounts for labor the workmen had signed their vouchers.[3] In the late Elizabethan period, according to Davies' survey of documents, literacy was widespread among yeomen, and it became even more extensive later.[4]

> How much education yeomen received, beyond this oral or semioral religious instruction of home and church, is not an altogether easy question to answer. The signatures of some 2,500 to 3,000 yeomen, attached to wills, leases, bonds, and the like, show that between 60 percent and 70 percent of those involved could write their own names. . . . Moreover it is probable that a fair proportion of the lower classes, both men and women, could read, and the majority of men, at any rate, could write. The prominent share women of the lower middle classes took in theological disputes and sectarian propaganda during 1640-60 would seem to prove that they were not ignorant, though it is possible that some of them were self-taught. . . . In several thousand petitions or receipts of Cromwell's army, usually signed by the men but sometimes their wives, the vast majority, even of the non-commissioned officers and men, could sign their names; and, in the relatively few documents containing the signatures of all the officers and men of regiments in Cromwell's army, perhaps four-fifths of the men signed their names.

Evidence for the eighteenth century is more complete. Sargant compiled voluminous data from signatures on marriage registers.[5]

> Comparing then, the middle of last century with a period thirty years ago, the most remarkable change is that in the relative position of town and country. On the accession of George III, 56 percent of the townspeople, and only 40 percent of the country people, signed their names: on the accession of Her Majesty, the towns people had scarcely improved, but the country people had risen from 40 signatures to 60. These results might have been

2. J. W. Adamson, "The Extent of Literacy in England," *The Library,* Ser. 4, 10: 166-8 (1929).
3. Mrs. J. R. Green, *Town Life in the Fifteenth Century* (New York: Macmillan, 1907), p. 15.
4. G. Davies, *The Early Stuarts* (Oxford: Clarendon Press, 2nd ed., 1959), p. 359.
5. W. L. Sargant, "On the Progress of Elementary Education," *Royal Statistical Society Journal,* 30:90-1 (1867).

anticipated: England, during those seventy-seven years, had become a great manufacturing country, and the towns had so far outgrown the means of instruction, that the educational efforts made had effected no improvement; but in the country, the conversion of the clergy to the cause of popular education, and the increased pastoral care arising from the gradual extinction of pluralities, had resulted in a great extension of instruction.

There has been much discussion about the validity of these sorts of data as a basis for inferences about literacy. Some English writers contend that ability to read was much more common than ability to write, and some of the data mentioned below support this inference. From an economic point of view, reading ability was no doubt the more important. However, there may have been national differences in this respect, for French statistics of the nineteenth century show few men able to read only; most who could read were able to write as well. One's confidence in the crude marriage-register indexes is increased by their congruence with other evidence, such as that summarized by Dobbs.[6]

It has been observed that the eighteenth century, a period during which the right of the poorer classes to education was seldom mentioned, was remarkable for the number of poor men who rose to high positions in Church and State and in the world of letters. Though examples may be drawn from all parts of the country, there is a mass of evidence ascribing to the northern counties, especially as they approach the Scottish border, a special pre-eminence, and revealing traces of a widespread belief in education, even in learning for its own sake, that had no parallel in the South. In Cumberland and Westmoreland at the close of the century there were few illiterates; and the superiority of the northern peasant in general knowledge was a common observation in diaries of travel. The writers allude, more precisely, to the 'superior arithmetical and literary knowledge' to be remarked 'in the middling and lower classes,' among whom were men tolerably acquainted with the classics and 'more than tolerable mathematicians.' At a much later date, well on into the second half of the nineteenth century, a government report refers to men of humble station who spoke with pride of their recollection of classical authors. Probably no single explanation is sufficient to account for a phenomenon so striking and so well attested. Special influences may be adduced in particular cases: an element of Presbyterian tradition on the Northumberland border, in Westmoreland a multiplicity of endowed schools. But undoubtedly the more general causes which gave freedom and stimulus to the native genius must be sought in the social environment: in the absence of conditions which elsewhere erected commercial standards, raised the cost of education, and discountenanced the poor, and in the survival of a social order led by the yeoman class—the class that had given to mediaeval universities their democratic character, and whose presence had once supplied the means of higher education. One way in which this influence reacted on educational opportunity was remarked as specially characteristic of the Lake District. The practice of recruiting the clergy from yeoman families made it necessary that the village school should combine, in some measure, the function of an academy with that of a place of elementary instruction for the poor; among

6. A. E. Dobbs, *Education and Social Movements 1700-1850* (London: Longmans, Green, 1919), pp. 67-8.

whom, in turn, some 'love of Greek and Latin' was found to diffuse itself after the disorderly fashion of that time and place.

The more plentiful data for the nineteenth century need only be referred to briefly since they are readily accessible. Estimates for workers in the 1830's range between two-thirds and three-fourths literate; rates in Scotland were slightly higher than in England, with towns regularly above rural areas. If these early nineteenth century levels are not so far above those for the eighteenth century as might have been expected, much of the explanation lies in the much-discussed halt to educational advance at the turn of the century. Another factor, implied in the previous quotation from Sargant, was the disorganization accompanying rapid urbanization and immigration from Ireland.

There were many kinds and qualities of school scattered around the country where reading, and less often writing, could be learned. The Sunday schools at that time devoted much attention to teaching reading. The slow rise in prosperity combined with philanthropic activities to multiply opportunities for simple instruction. Webb has brought together a mass of data for England from scattered sources, of which a few representative examples are quoted here.[7]

Agricultural Districts
    A much larger survey by the Herefordshire Auxiliary Bible Society showed that of 41,107 persons visited, 24,222 could read with ease, a figure just short of 60 percent. . . . A most striking record is to be found in three parishes in Rutland, almost entirely agricultural, where only 8 percent of nearly 500 adults could neither read nor write, while 31 percent could read only, and 61 percent could do both.

Mining and Metals
    Excellent figures are available in the reports of an educational inspector, the Reverend John Allen, writing on the mining districts of Durham and Northumberland in the early forties. The percentage figures for those unable to read or write vary from 16 percent to 25 percent, with an average of 21 percent. . . .
    At the Earsdon colliery, of 516 persons, 299 were above and 217 under fourteen. Of the older group, 154 could read and write (about 50 percent), 86 could read only, many very imperfectly, and 59 could do neither (about 20 percent or 30 percent should a third of the second group be added).

Handloom Weavers
    Of 195 adult shoploom weavers in Gloucestershire, an inspector reported that 108 could read and write, 72 could read but not write, and 15 could do neither. Of the heads of 176 families visited in Manchester, 102 of whom were handloom weavers, 130 claimed to be able to read, 15 to read imperfectly, while 23 could not read, and 8 made no statement.

7. R. K. Webb, *The British Working Class Reader* (London: Allen and Unwin, 1955), p. 22; "Working Class Readers in Early Victorian England," *English Historical Review*, 65:333-51 (1950).

Railway Labour

The resident director of the Chester and Holyhead Railway presented a return which showed that of the persons visited, both Welsh and English, there were 5379 above 25 years of age, 2024 below that age. Of those above 15 years of age, 1186 could not read. Although there is no basis here for precise calculation, it can be seen that the proportion does not differ much from that observed among the weavers.

Industrial Areas

The Central Society of Education undertook a study of a poor section of the metropolitan parish in Marylebone; their first publication showed that out of 1044 adults in the district investigated, 25 percent could neither read nor write, while 75 percent could read, or read and write. . . .

One investigation in Bristol lasted over 18 months and touched almost 6000 families, totaling more than 20,000 persons.

Heads of families who can read or write (more or less) ...	5122	51.9 per cent
Heads of families who can only read	2523	25.6 per cent
Total who can read	7645	77.5 per cent
Unable to read or write (including 12 not ascertained) ...	2216	22.5 per cent
	9861	100.0

The most extensive information comes from the area about Manchester.

	Total Population examined (working classes only)	Read and Write	Read only	Total readers
Bury	14,322	3909	4579	8588
Dunkinfield	8,146	2380	2112	4492
Stalybridge	15,799	4484	4188	8672
Ashton	17,937	4723	4334	9057
				Total read or write
Manchester	128,232			60,185
Salford	40,991			21,853

Insofar as one dare hazard a guess as to a single over-all estimate of reading ability, from the widely scattered and diverse figures given here, the commonest figure of literacy for the 'forties would seem to hover about two-thirds to three-quarters of the working classes, perhaps nearer the latter than the former.

The following summary and interpretation of Scottish data by Webb also underline the significant differences among occupations.[8]

There is, however, an interesting, if confessedly cursory, survey of the educational acquirements of hands in the works of the Grandholm Mills, Aberdeen, on 26 March 1833. Here it is very apparent that differentiation must be made between different types of factory workers:

8. R. K. Webb, "Literacy among the Working Classes in Nineteenth Century Scotland," *Scottish Historical Review*, 33:100-14 (1954).

	Readers Only	Per Cent	Readers and Writers	Per Cent	Cannot Read or Write	Per Cent	Total
Hackling	38	21.8	117	67.2	19	10.9	174
Spinning	349	55.6	77	12.3	202	32.2	628
Weaving	116	43.1	69	25.7	84	31.2	269
Mechanics	—	—	46	95.9	2	4.1	48
Total	503	44.9	309	27.6	307	27.5	1119

. . . Certainly the most significant and conclusive information which has turned up in this study is that indicating the variation in literacy among different occupational groups. The pattern is much more apparent in these few Scottish figures and comments than in the English surveys. It must indicate, for one thing, the persistence of the Scottish educational tradition where it was not beaten down by severe poverty and degradation; and it must mean as well that the illiterate groups were those most affected by immigration and by the depression of the lower levels of a fragmenting working class. But, most significantly, it can be taken to affirm the impression that the crucial elements of the working classes—the artisans, mechanics, and skilled labourers—were almost universally literate and of a fairly high degree of attainment.

One of the more revealing sidelights on educational changes in England lies in the long history of complaints from communities that teachers were in short supply, and the many controversies over the right to be a teacher. Irregular and uncertified schools appear to have been an object of official concern before 1200.[9] There are records of petitions from established teachers, at the end of the thirteenth and fourteenth centuries, that unauthorized grammar masters be barred.[10] In 1497 the City of London complained that the regular teachers could not take care of all the would-be pupils; the appointment of more was approved.[11] Exeter also, in 1612, demanded that the bishop designate more teachers.[12] That London usually had a relatively generous supply of school places, however, is indicated by the assertions that many youth migrated to London because of the "great alms" available there for schooling.[13] Official opinions sometimes upheld the monopoly of the duly-appointed teachers, but at other times they favored the volunteer (as in 1410 at Gloucester).[14] Even at a fairly early date the private-venture teacher responded to the growing demand for schooling.[15]

United States

There are indications that here, too, the late eighteenth century showed a decline in educational zeal, lasting for a couple of generations, even in New

9. J. E. C. De Montmorency, *State Intervention in English Education* (Cambridge: Cambridge University Press, 1902), p. 43.
10. *Ibid.*, p. 42
11. *Ibid.*, p. 46
12. W. T. MacCaffrey, *Exeter 1540-1640* (Cambridge: Harvard University Press, 1958), p. 120.
13. De Montmorency, *op. cit.*, p. 49.
14. *Ibid.*, p. 51.
15. For an American example, see R. L. McCaul, "Education in Georgia," *Georgia Historical Quarterly*, 40:248-59 (1956).

England. The American population was definitely more literate, however, than that of England and probably of most of Europe.

Kilpatrick studied document signatures in New York State for the late seventeenth and early eighteenth centuries; his figures for Flatbush, and his comments are summarized below.[16]

	Percentage of marks to total known ways of signing	*Percentage who made marks by place of training*	
		Holland	*America*
1675	37	29	67
1683	31	25	33
1698	13	17	13
1706	10	14	7
1738	5	—	6

The most interesting and gratifying result is seen in item 11 [the last item], showing the gradual improvement of the American-bred population as time went on. This improvement was probably due to the fact that the first generation of children to grow up after the principal immigration found little or no opportunity to attend school, whereas succeeding generations of children found well-established schools. Just why the Holland bred also should have made an increasingly better showing is not easy to explain. Possibly, the earlier immigrants were of a slightly lower grade of society than the later ones, so that the illiterates in 1675 were on the whole older and so died out earlier. The relatively better showing of the aggregate American bred (13 percent) as compared with the aggregate Holland bred (26 percent) is most striking. Evidently Flatbush presents an educational experience directly counter to that seen in some of the other American colonies where succeeding generations were less literate than the original stock.

Bruce's scrutiny of seventeenth-century document signatures by Virginia freemen revealed that over half the jurymen could sign their names (as could a quarter of the women on other documents). Among a group with somewhat higher status who signed land deeds, two-thirds were literate. Morison reports very extensive literacy in New England, even in interior towns.[17]

A careful compilation by Dr. Shipton of over twenty-seven hundred names from petitions, addresses, and other documents in the Massachusetts and Connecticut Archives yields the following result:

Date of Documents	*Per Cent Literate*
Massachusetts, 1640-1660	93
Massachusetts, 1661-1680	98
Massachusetts, 1681-1700	95
Connecticut, 1640-1679	94
Connecticut, 1680-1700	95
Total, 1640-1700	95

16. W. H. Kilpatrick, *The Dutch Schools of New Netherland and New York* (Washington: Government Printing Office, 1912), p. 197.

17. P. A. Bruce, *Institutional History of Virginia*, Vol. I (New York: Putnam, 1910), Ch. 18; S. E. Morison, *The Puritan Pronaos* (New York: New York University Press, 1936), pp. 67-82.

Geographical Groups	Per Cent Literate
Seaports and earliest settled towns	99
Connecticut valley towns of Massachusetts...............................	97
Interior and frontier towns, mostly Essex County........................	90
Connecticut Colony	94.5
Plymouth Colony (62 signatures)..	81

It must also be remembered that these literacy tests apply to writing as well as reading; and the compulsory school laws extend to reading only. It was the custom in the New England schools, following medieval and English practice, to teach children first to read, with a hornbook or primer. Writing and ciphering were begun only after they were able to read the primer or the Bible to satisfaction; and these subjects, as in Old England, were often taught by writing masters, or in special schools called writing schools, that paralleled the grammar schools up to a certain point. Consequently it is quite certain that very many, perhaps a major part, of the colonists, not only in New England, but in the Middle Colonies and Virginia, who were unable to write their names, could read the King James Bible and other simple English texts.

Grant's study of the frontier Connecticut town of Kent led him to conclude that in the eighteenth century all males and half the women were literate. On the more remote frontier, and later on in cities deluged with immigrants, these very high proportions dropped.

> Just as the records show that Kent possessed enough schools, teachers, and funds to provide a rudimentary education, they also show that the population was indeed literate. Practically all inhabitants affixed their signatures to land deeds at some time or other. No member of a Kent family who was raised in the town had to employ the "mark" device of an illiterate person. Kent education, then, was democratic in the sense that all acquired it. A groundwork was laid for democratic ideas if the pamphlets or books spreading such doctrine should ever reach the town.[18]

Other Countries

As Passin (Chapter 21) makes clear, literacy among Japanese men immediately after the opening of the Meiji period was about 40 per cent. In Russian cities at the end of the nineteenth century about 60 per cent of the urban male manual workers could read, 70 per cent of all city males and 40 per cent of all rural males; and in the age groups just entering the work force the figures were higher. (Additional information on trends in Russia is given by Kahan, Part III, Chapters 14 and 15.)

A summary of literacy data relating to the individual departments of France between the late seventeenth and late nineteenth centuries was given in Chapter 17 in Part III. The literacy rate for grooms rose from 29 to 81 per cent and that for brides from 14 to 71 per cent over the two-century span; but even more impressive was the vast disparity among the parts of the country. It appears that French literacy was slightly above that in England until the mid-nineteenth century, but that France lagged slightly thereafter.

18. C. S. Grant, *Democracy in the Connecticut Frontier Town of Kent* (New York: Columbia University Press, 1961), p. 200.

II. POPULARIZED LEARNING AND A POPULAR PRESS

In speaking of Burma, Furnivall remarks that "the postal system, introduced originally for the benefit of the foreign community, did more to promote literacy than all the lay schools; it fostered a latent demand for adult literacy, and the ability to read and write ceased to be merely an ornament that one discarded on leaving school.[19]

The religious reformers in Britain wrote in English for a recognized audience; otherwise the king would hardly have issued an edict (in 1543) forbidding laborers to read the English Bible.[20] In times of controversy, handbills in English were stuck up all over the towns.[21]

More than five thousand titles in English are known to have been published before 1557, including more than thirty editions of the Bible.[22] A large proportion of this output was religious, but there were also many "penny dreadfuls" (calculated to entice people to use their literacy) and innumerable practical volumes. Seven editions of a book on husbandry had come out by 1560, for example. Wright concludes that even before that date, "a large portion of the output of the printing presses had been designed for ordinary readers"; he also provides a lucid explanation of the broader social context for this expansion of effective literacy.[23]

> No phase of the middle-class background has greater cultural significance than the interest displayed by plain citizens in school learning from the mid-sixteenth to the mid-seventeenth century. . . . Since the premium put upon learning throughout the Renaissance enhanced the value of education as a means of rising from low to high estate, the sensitiveness of the ordinary layman to the importance of schools was greatly stimulated. With Protestantism came another incentive to education, in the firm belief (which the Reformed faith encouraged) that learning would open the kingdom of God to the faithful. With the rapid growth of an urban civilization there came also a more general realization of the prestige as well as the practical advantages that schooling bestowed, until there begins to be discernible the modern faith in education as a means to cure all social ills, to induce happiness, and to make mankind generally wiser, wealthier, and more godly. Elizabethan tradesmen, therefore, loosened their purse strings for the benefit of grammar schools and and university scholarships and earnestly strove to see that their sons received as much learning as the choice of the youths' careers permitted. . . . Since poverty and low degree were no barriers to learning, the schools thus early became associated in the popular consciousness with opportunity, for they provided training that was both academic and practical. With the commercial expansion of the fifteenth-century, the demand increased for apprentices and assistants who could read, write, and keep accounts – fundamentals

19. J. S. Furnivall, *Colonial Policy and Practice* (Cambridge: Cambridge University Press, 1948), p. 209.

20. H. S. Bennett, *English Books and Readers* (Cambridge: Cambridge University Press, 1952), p. 27.

21. N. Wood, *The Reformation and English Education* (London: Routledge, 1931), p. 4.

22. Bennett, *op. cit.*, pp. 20, 111.

23. L. B. Wright, *Middle-Class Culture in Elizabethan England* (Ithaca: Cornell University Press, 1958), pp. 81, 121.

which they might learn in petty schools maintained as a part of numerous religious foundations because teaching, as well as praying, was the duty of many chantry priests who undertook the instruction of the community children. Moreover, already in the fifteenth century wealthy tradesmen had begun to establish schools unattached to religious foundations, a habit which was to account for much of the later educational development.

Even if there had been no great expansion in the extent of literacy in the fifteenth and sixteenth centuries, it would have been more effective for economic and civic life, for the reasons set forth by Findlay.[24]

... The children who left school in 1440 learned Latin along with the mother tongue, but many of them ceased either to read or write after leaving school, since paper was scarce and manuscripts were still more costly. A century afterwards they were taught pretty much the same things at school, but on leaving school they had the means at their disposal to use the instruments of reading. For books were all around them; not only the Bible but books and pamphlets of many kinds were being spread abroad. . . .

But printers do not produce books except in response to demand, and the output of print is sufficient evidence that the generations who passed through the schools during Queen Elizabeth's reign made use of what they had acquired at the school bench. Letters are no longer a "mystery," they have become part and parcel of the common civilization: every child of sharp wits and ambitious disposition lays hold of the new tool, unless indeed he belongs to the lowest ranks of poverty. . . .

Schooling thus took on a new aspect; it had previously been an affair of status; in the Middle Ages it had been limited to those whose rank and calling justified the sacrifice of a child's time, identified in the public mind with the social group to which the child belonged, an affair of profession, class, or religious vocation. Henceforth this chain is broken; we recognize learning in its elementary forms as something which the individual may aspire to, whether he be rich or poor.

Now the beginnings of this alliance between practical and liberal curricula is to be witnessed in the seventeenth century as a direct result of the enhanced importance of trade. The first breach in the exclusiveness of the classical curriculum was effected when the trader induced the schoolmasters to introduce tare and tret, filderkins and firkins and other such measurements to the notice of school-boys.

Handbooks, "the Tudor and Stuart counterparts of the modern fifteen-easy-lessons," were becoming steadily more available.[25]

... For the Renaissance spirit was confined to no class, however different its manifestations might be in different groups. Since, however, the citizen had less time and means than the courtier for attaining his ends, he required speedy methods of instruction and usable compendiums of facts. The answer to his demands was the handbook, the printed guide, the Tudor and Stuart counterpart of the modern fifteen-easy-lessons which lead to bourgeois perfection. What the schools did not or could not accomplish, the citizen attempt-

24. J. J. Findlay, *The Children of England* (London: Methuen, 1923), pp. 79-80.
25. Wright, *op. cit.*, p. 121

ed to do for himself by private study of a convenient manual. The day of hand-book-learning for the generality of men had arrived. . . .

The handbook, ranging in its infinite variety from the treatise on a gentle-man's training to the lowly almanac, was firmly established in Elizabethan England as a powerful instrument of popular education. Although the schools exerted a tremendous influence upon the intellectual development of the middle class, the handbooks proved a worthy supplement and no doubt actually contributed more than did the schools to the guidance and informa-tion of the populace because they were the means of self-instruction used by purposeful citizens who could retain them for constant reference. Believing implicitly in the value of the information to be obtained therefrom, citizens applied themselves earnestly to the study of handbooks from which they might derive, not merely utilitarian facts, but also instruction in good manners, profitable learning, and true religion, which the middle class regarded as the essential elements leading to a successful life. Nor was the hope of social and material success the only reason for bourgeois application to short-cut methods of self-education, for some of the Renaissance zeal to learn and to know had stirred even tradesmen to seek out epitomes that would supply them with facts from all fields of knowledge. Thanks in part to convenient handbooks, infor-mation, of a sort, became common property. No longer was learning a monop-oly of clerk and aristocrat.

These interpretations are not merely suppositions by historians today; authors at the time often made it quite clear that they were writing useful manuals for actual workers, as shown in the following comment by Adamson:[26]

The character and method of a rudimentary instruction commonly acces-sible at the close of the sixteenth century and the standing of some of those who gave it may be gathered from a small book of less than one hundred pages which was first published in 1596. . . . 'The preface for direction to the reader' has this passage: 'I am now therefore to direct my speech to the 'un-skilfull, which desire to make use of it for their owne 'private benefit; and to such men and women of trade as 'Taylors, Weavers, Shoppe-keepers, Seam-sters and such others 'as have undertaken the charge of teaching others.' Study it diligently, and thou mayest sit on thy shop-board, at thy 'loomes or at thy needle and never hinder thy worke to heare 'thy Schollers, after thou hast once made the little book 'familiar to thee.' . . . .

This orientation of popularized learning to the active parts of the popula-tion continued into the eighteenth century. Thus both the *Lady's Diary* and the *Gentleman's Diary* magazines printed serious mathematical articles, and in 1737 a compendium *Bibliotheca Technologica* was published.[27]

III. TRENDS IN ELEMENTARY EDUCATION

Schooling in early industrial England was not restricted to the elite, either in principle or in reality, as the foregoing comments make clear. Those "plebeian" children who did receive schooling made up of course a much

26. Adamson, *op. cit.*, pp. 185-6.

27. N. Hans, *New Trends in Education in the Eighteenth Century* (London: Routledge, 1951), pp. 157, 152.

smaller proportion of their stratum than did those from higher levels. The clerkly flavor of the usual grammar schools no doubt failed to give the recipients the optimum preparation for participating in the furtherance of economic development. But development was not exclusively industrial, and this sort of schooling was more functional in the economy than might appear at first glance. One should not, moreover, underrate the stimulation gained from the religious atmosphere of those schools. In addition, they made a major contribution to building a viable polity that proved to be so essential when development accelerated later.

The separation of grammar (secondary) from elementary education appears to have occurred in England between 1550 and 1650. Since pupils were expected to be literate before they undertook grammar study, home preparation became increasingly inadequate as enrollments expanded. Watson contends that this differentiation had four stages: (1) grammar masters also gave elementary instruction; (2) this teaching was handed over to the advanced grammar pupils; (3) an elementary master was employed to teach the beginners; and (4) the elementary master and his pupils were moved into a separate school.[28] (Less respectable petty schools and dame schools already existed, and they continued to do so.) A similar two-level system of schools also flourished in New England until about 1830.

Whether the elementary schools flourished or lar.guished came to depend on diverse circumstances, often quite local in their incidence. The establishing of the Anglican church seems to have benefited mainly the grammar schools, though the broader currents of the Reformation stimulated a thirst for literacy. The ups and downs in literacy indicated by the meagre statistics that remain from earlier centuries sometimes reflected fluctuations in religious sentiment and in the fate of particular denominations. In the later medieval period, ecclesiastical ambition to bring more people under "benefit of clergy" (presupposing literacy) elicited rulings that even the unfree were eligible for schools. No doubt this canonical liberality stimulated priests in some parishes to take their pedagogical duties more seriously.[29] The rise in literacy in the fifteenth century at least partly reflected the spread of the Lollards; the suppression of this group seems to have checked the spread of schools for some decades, as did later attacks on other heresies.[30]

The unhappy fate of many grammar schools in the dissolution of monasteries, along with more self-seeking aims, motivated many merchants to revive and strengthen those schools.[31] Indeed, some writers, as Leach, contend that the supply of places in grammar schools was at a high point in the mid-sixteenth century.[32]

28. F. Watson, *The English Grammar Schools to 1660* (Cambridge: Cambridge University Press, 1908), pp. 150-4.

29. De Montmorency, *op. cit.*, p. 37.

30. *Ibid.*, p. 50.

31. W. K. Jordan, *Philanthropy in England 1480-1660* (New York: Russell Sage, 1959), p. 280.

32. A. F. Leach, *English Schools at the Reformation, 1546-8* (London: Constable, 1896), pp. 97-9.

The proportion of the population which had opportunity of access to Grammar Schools, and, as we can see, used their opportunites, was very much larger then than now. Certainly it was larger than the proportion at the time of the only authoritative statistics on the subject; viz., in 1865-6, as given in the Schools Inquiry Commission's Report. The Report gives some 830 Secondary Schools of all grades. This included a large number, little, if at all, above the merest Elementary Schools (and Elementary Schools were then for the most part very elementary), and many of those decrepit, and on the verge of extinction. That number was no more than one Secondary School for every 23,750 people, among the then population of 19 millions. "In at least two-thirds of the places in England named as towns in the census, there is no public School at all above the Primary School; and in the remaining third, the School is often insufficient in size and quality"....

It is commonly said that the population did not increase between the Black Death and the reign of Elizabeth.... Still, for the present purpose, we may accept the statement, and compare the Schools of 1546 with the population of 1377. Take, say, 300 Grammar Schools among 2-1/2 million people. This gives one for every 8,300 people instead of one for every 23,000, as in 1865.... To take a single county. The population of Herefordshire, as shown in the Poll-Tax return, was some 25,000; in addition to Hereford city, 3,568 and Ludlow then reckoned in Herefordshire, 2,198; or some 30,000 in round figures in all. Hereford had its primaeval Cathedral Grammar School, besides a lesser one, perhaps more or less elementary, in St. Owen's Church; Ludlow its Guild School, Ledbury its Chantry Grammar School in connection with its collegiate church, the flourishing state of which has already been commented on, sunk now to Elementary education. Besides these there were Leominster, unendowed, and the thirteen others mentioned in our records, of which nine alone were continued. That is, there were 17 Grammar Schools for a population of 30,000. Assume even that the population was not the same, in 1546, but doubled; cut off a fourth of the Schools as really Elementary; yet where should we find a population of 60,000 in 1860, or in 1896 for that matter, with 13 Grammar Schools at its command? ...

Yet a distinct and organized system of elementary education still awaited favoring conditions for its development; as a system it was not the offspring of the grammar schools.[33] Meanwhile, children from all social levels, in locally varying proportions, continued to attend the grammar schools; the "monopolization" of those schools by middle and upper classes came only in the nineteenth century in England, and never was predominant in the United States. The present American "ladder" system emerged fairly late and is only currently being generally adopted in Europe.[34] Grammar schools continued, though on a diminishing scale, to accept elementary pupils. In the nineteenth century, this same practice—accepting substandard applicants in order to insure a sufficient supply of students—was adopted by the zealous land-grant and other American colleges.[35]

Some indication of the strength of the demand for elementary schooling

33. E. H. Reisner, *The Evolution of the Common School* (New York: Macmillan, 1935), p. 2.
34. *Ibid.*, pp. 281, 361.
35. M. J. Bowman, "The Land-Grant Colleges in Human-Resource Development," *Journal of Economic History*, 22:523-46 (1962).

can be deduced from legal cases; for example, the one in 1700 that decided the church did not have the exclusive right to license elementary and vocational teachers.[36] Even in the previous century some English towns had openly challenged ecclesiastical control.[37] There seem to be no inventories of elementary schools at that period, but many indications of strong local interest exist.[38] Even in the sixteenth century some towns were raising taxes for common schools, at least sporadically.[39] Norfolk is reported to have begun in 1570 to use public money to pay a teacher for poor children in each ward; we do not know how long this practice continued.[40] We do know that the number of writing and ciphering schools multiplied, often on a private-venture basis.[41] In some communities at least, municipal concern for the manual training of orphan and pauper children was transformed into broader sorts of elementary schooling, no doubt stimulated by the poor law.[42]

The uneven local development of schools can be traced back into the middle ages in continental countries as well as England. As Potter says:[43]

> The part of Northern Europe in which the most marked educational progress was made during the later Middle Ages was the Low Countries. This area was more highly industrialized than any other, and populous towns were in relatively close proximity to one another. The social life of such a district was predominantly urban, the peasantry being kept in something like subjection to the weavers, while in the towns there was a steady demand for clerks who could write and calculate, and a leisured class existed which was not exclusively feudal. . . .

Additional light on the emergence of various sorts of "vocational" training for different artisans and business groups is summarized by Jarman.[44]

> . . . The fierce contentions which went on between the Church authorities and outsiders accused of keeping unlicensed schools, which took boys from the official ones, indicate that the keeping of a school was a profitable source of income. . . .

> Merchants, bankers, the higher craftsmen, and their clerks and accountants would need for their undertakings some elementary education, at least in reading, writing, and the operations of arithmetic. How did they get it? . . . .

> Certainly schools for this purpose existed on the Continent, at least in the fourteenth century. In 1338 the chronicler Villani when describing the

36. De Montmorency, *op. cit.,* p. 172.
37. Green, *op. cit.,* pp. 18ff.
38. A. L. Rowse, *The England of Elizabeth* (New York: Macmillan, 1951), pp. 494, 503.
39. J. H. Thomas, *Town Government in the Sixteenth Century* (London: Allen and Unwin, 1933), pp. 124-5.
40. W. K. Jordan, *The Charities of Rural England 1480-1660* (New York: Russell Sage, 1961), p. 154.
41. W. A. L. Vincent, *The State and School Education 1640-1660 in England and Wales* (London: S.P.C.K., 1950), p. 9.
42. J. Chambers, *Nottinghamshire in the Eighteenth Century* (London: King, 1932), p. 319.
43. G. R. Potter, "Education in the Fourteenth and Fifteenth Centuries," *Cambridge Medieval History* (Cambridge: Cambridge University Press, 1936), Vol. 8, Ch. 22.
44. T. L. Jarman, *Landmarks in the History of Education* (London: Cresset, 1951), pp. 84, 120.

city of Florence mentions boys and girls learning to read, and also boys who were learning calculation; these were mentioned as distinct from those learning grammar and logic. Popular schools, sometimes private concerns, sometimes run by a town council, existed in Germany in the fourteenth and fifteenth centuries, for the purpose of teaching reading and writing in German. The Lubeck scholasticus—the established ecclesiastical authority—complained that he lost income because of the new school of the town council. At Brunswick in 1420 we hear of a school curriculum limited, after a conflict with the Church, to 'writing and reading the alphabet and German books and letters', and in Hamburg such schools were found from the beginning of the fifteenth century and there were the same conflicts between Church and town council. At the same time the city schools were probably at first largely the result of a growing city life and not the result of any very clearly felt need for elementary or vernacular education. They were often Latin schools that sometimes gave a better Latin education than the older schools, and were not in the general sense anti-clerical. . . .

Parallel developments in Boston, with emphasis upon the strong position of the private-venture schools, have been explored by Seybolt.[45]

> In 1709, Owen Harris was giving instruction in "Writing, Arithmetick in all its parts; and also Geometry, Trigonometry, Plain and Sphaerical, Surveying, Dialling, Gauging, Navigation, Astronomy; The Projection of the Sphaere, and the use of the Mathematical Instruments." To this offering, John Green, in the same year, added reading and merchants accounts. . . .

> With the development of commerce and the trades, came the need for instruction in subjects not offered in the public schools maintained by the town. Competition and the changing techniques of the various occupations made their special demands on those who were preparing to engage in these pursuits. Certain vocations demanded a theoretical training which could not be provided satisfactorily by the apprenticeship system. This was particularly true of surveying, navigation, and business life. . . .

> The private schools were so varied in character that one hesitates to name or label them. During the colonial period the terms "elementary" and "secondary" were not used to designate schools. The public schools maintained by the town were called "Latin" or "grammar" schools, and "writing schools." For the private schools, there was no such simple, commonly accepted classification. A private school was usually advertised as a "School," and the designation, like "Day School" or "Evening School," was used without reference to the subjects taught. In private school usage a "Grammar School" was either an English grammar school or a Latin Grammar school.

> The public schools made no attempt to meet the educational needs of all. They continued in their old-accustomed ways. The private schools were free to originate, and to adapt their courses of instruction to the interests of the students. The masters sought always to keep strictly abreast of the time, for their livelihood depended on the success with which they met these needs. No such freedom or incentive was offered the masters of the public schools. It is quite evident that the private school was a flexible, growing

45. R. F. Seybolt, *The Private Schools of Colonial Boston* (Cambridge: Harvard University Press, 1935), pp. 83-4, 92.

institution which played an important part in the educational life of the town.

When the practice of apprenticeship (and the associated policies for dealing with pauper children) was transferred from England to New York and New England, one important innovation became common: schooling as well as training in a craft was stipulated. In Massachusetts, if masters could not themselves teach their apprentices to read, they were obliged to send them to school. In hardship cases the town paid fees, as they did erratically for poor children generally. Specially appointed inspectors were supposed to insure that these rules were carried out; as in other educational matters, conformity was no doubt fluctuating and uneven.[46]

A broader, and to us more familiar, pattern of elementary education emerged in eighteenth-century England. That century "established the idea of elementary education not, as in earlier ages, as a stage preliminary to the grammar schools, by which 'boys of parts' might climb to the universities, but as a system complete in itself."[47] The charity schools were a principal instrument for that program; apparently they proved inadequate to the task. In actuality, if not in intent, elementary education began again to lag in the late eighteenth century. Apart from obtuseness on the part of the complacent middle classes, three sets of circumstances help to explain this sluggishness.

1) The rapid growth of industrial centers unquestionably was accompanied by greater social isolation of the workers; there were fewer established groups to form a basis for organizing education. Many local and family traditions doubtless were ruptured by that disorganization. Nor did the activities of the established church in education ever keep up with the growing urban population.

2) As many local communities lost their economic base and a large part of their local leadership, educational traditions died out. The strong sense of community identity that had fostered local schools and at least tolerated attendance by children from all sections of the community often atrophied. The development of an urban industrial society seems to have attenuated the close articulation of status groups which had grown up over many generations in some sections of England.

3) The middle classes that had been the main support of so many educational movements became more self-sufficient. Elementary education had spread through their ranks, and their children absorbed a large proportion of the places in the better new elementary schools as well as in "public" schools and grammar schools, not to mention the workingmen's institutes.

46. *Ibid.*, passim.
47. M. G. Jones, *The Charity School Movement* (Cambridge: Cambridge University Press, 1938), p. 23.

CHAPTER 19

SOCIAL STRUCTURE, PUBLIC POLICY, AND THE DEVELOPMENT OF EDUCATION AND THE ECONOMY IN CZARIST RUSSIA

Arcadius Kahan

Research on the economic aspects of education and of training in pre-revolutionary Russia is terra incognita to most western students of economics. To deal exhaustively with the subject would require more time and other resources than the space given to it would warrant. Obviously some choice had to be made in terms of the source materials more readily available. It was with such limitations in mind that the selection of a few topics was made. Three of these are covered in discussions elsewhere in this volume (Part I, Chapter 1; Part III, Chapters 14–15). In this chapter I turn to a brief consideration of Russian social structure and public policy as they conditioned both opportunities and demands for schooling, and to an examination of the pace at which literacy and schooling diffused through the society as a whole before and after the Crimean War and the emancipation of the serfs. At the end I hazard a few remarks concerning the contrast between the actual as against the "optimal" pace of educational developments in Russia in relation to economic growth.

Despite the remarkable progressiveness of the Petrine period and the policies for development and recruitment of high-level manpower at that time, the progress of education over the following century was slow in relation to what was happening to the West. Indeed, far from catching up, Russia was lagging further behind. Educational facilities and access to educational opportunities were extremely limited and socially selective. It must be borne in mind that until 1861 serfdom existed over most of Russia, and that social and even territorial mobility were strictly regulated for the bulk of the population. Even after 1861 mobility of the peasants was impeded by the terms of emancipation. It is against such a background that both educational statistics and the history of government policy with respect to education must be understood.

Throughout this period the Russian government saw education almost exclusively as a pragmatic means to achieve certain utilitarian (from its own point of view, mostly political) ends.[1] Schools were established primarily

1. Examples of such a tradition can be found in the establishment of the Moscow Academy to support the position of the state and church against religious heresies and influences of other

to train officers for the army and navy or specialists for the mining and arma-
ment industries.[2] Special schools and instruction for the children of the
gentry and the top echelon of the bureaucracy furthered the "westernization"
of Russian society.[3] But elementary education for the lower classes made
little progress.[4]

Government action outside the areas of its immediate interest could be
influenced by public opinion, but during the pre-emancipation period this
was equivalent to vocal opinion of the gentry, perhaps including also the
upper strata of the merchants. Such opinion was not in favor of providing
educational outlets for the lower classes; and the lower classes themselves,
when faced with barriers to future advancement, obviously considered this
type of investment almost useless. Serf-peasant agriculture did not provide
any opportunities for getting a return even from elementary education.
Crafts and manufactures relied primarily on on-the-job training, internal
trade required only rudiments of education, and even the lowest ranks of
bureaucracy required bare literacy. Given the impediments to intergroup
mobility and the income restraint, the demand for education was not vigorous.
Although there were quite interesting cases of interclass mobility in which
education played a dominant role, in the eighteenth century, the economic
advantages of education had not yet been discovered or become attractive
to the mass of the population.[5]

Thus, given the nature of the Russian state and of the economy of Russia
in the eighteenth century, the achievements of government policies in the
field of education could be expected to be very modest indeed. The data in
Table 1 summarize the state of education in Russia by the end of the eighteenth
century.

Eighteenth-century governmental policies and social attitudes had
produced educational services for only 0.33 per cent of the total male popula-

---

denominations; in the Petrine school system to supply technicians and military officers; in the later
period the schools to train the gentry for the role of a ruling elite.

2. The following schools of the above mentioned type were established: Navigation school –
1701; Artillery school – 1701; Engineering school – 1709; Naval academy – 1715; mining schools
at state ironworks in Olonetsk (1716), and in Ekaterinburg in the Urals (1721).

3. Among the special schools for gentry the "Shliakhetskii Korpus" (established 1731) was the
best known. The Czar's decree of 1715 required that the children aged 10-15 of the gentry and
government officials living in the provinces, ought to study arithmetic and geometry. In a typical
Petrine fashion the decree provided that without proof that the above had been taught and con-
formed with the decree, no marriages could be concluded. The clergy was instructed to refuse the
performance of marriage rites for the ones disobeying the decree. *Polnde Sobranie Zakonov Ross-
iiskoi Imperii* (St. Petersburg, 1830), Vol. V, Nos. 2762, 2778.

4. In 1743 the previous *tsifirnye* schools were converted into schools for children of soldiers.
It was not until 1786 that an elementary secular school network with two- and four-year curricula
was set up.

5. A very interesting case is the one of the Baltic gentry of German origin. The rosters of
matriculation of Russian students in the political science departments at various German universities could be an almost perfect substitute for a "who's who?" of the Russian bureaucracy about
25 years afterwards. These were predominantly Baltic Germans of gentry origin, a group that during almost 200 years supplied the Russian government with efficient and highly influential civil
servants in the higher echelon.

TABLE 1

Educational Institutions and Their Enrollment
at the End of the Eighteenth Century°

Type of Institution	Number of Institutions	Number of Students
Universities and *gymnasiums*	3	1,338
Cadet Corps	5	11,980
Gentry boarding schools	8	1,360
Private boarding schools	48	1,125
Art Academy	1	348
Medical schools	3	270
Mining schools	2	167
Church seminaries and schools	66	20,393
Schools for soldiers' children	116	12,000
Elementary schools (4-year)	49	7,011
Elementary schools (2-year)	239	15,209
Other Schools	9	765
Total	549	61,966

°*Vestnik Moskovskogo Universiteta*, No. 2 (1959), pp. 110-119.

tion of the Russian empire. In addition, an approximate distribution of the total number of students between elementary education on one hand, and secondary, specialized, and higher education on the other, would indicate that about 53,000 received an elementary education only, while about 9,000 received an education above the primary level.[6]

The pace of providing educational facilities for various groups of the population quickened during the first third of the nineteenth century, although the total students relative to the population remained insignificant. The available data for 1834 illustrate the contention expressed above. The total number of students receiving instruction in all types of schools at all levels was 245,448, or .49 per cent of the total population; most students received only an elementary education.[7] It is also worth mentioning that in

6. The estimates are derived by assuming that only 10 per cent of the enrollment in the church schools were enrolled in the seminaries, while 90 per cent were receiving an elementary education. The 9,000 students estimated in educational institutions above elementary might be an overestimate. It would greatly depend upon the curriculum in the private boarding schools, for which information was not available.

7. The students in schools under the supervision of the Ministry of Education and the Greek Orthodox Church could be divided in the following categories:

Number of Schools and Students Under the Supervision
of the Ministry of Education, 1834

Institution	No. of schools	No. of students
Universities	6	1,899
Lyceums	6	915
Gimnazium	64	12,561
Boarding schools	209	6,870
Urban county schools	419	25,833

the schools under the supervision of the Ministry of Education, only 1,880 of 77,600 students were peasants, or about 2.4 per cent. The establishment of elementary schools for state peasants in 1842 increased the opportunities for a part of the peasantry and raised the total school attendance in the country as a whole.[8] Nevertheless, by 1856 only 450,000, or .7 per cent, of the total population were enrolled in schools. In 1856 more than 300,000 of these students were in urban schools (or 5.8 per cent of the urban population), so it would follow that the rural population had a much smaller school attendance than the average for the country. In addition, 38 per cent of all students attending schools were concentrated in a tenth of the administrative districts, thus manifesting a very uneven territorial distribution of schooling.

The literacy situation among the youth of 1850-1860 may be inferred from data for the age group 60 and over in the 1897 census, shown along with younger age categories in Table 2. Rates among urban males were approximating the 50 per cent mark, but they were lower for urban females; among the vast rural population which made up the bulk of the total, only 17 per cent of the male youth were literate around mid-century. This low proportion is

Institution	No. of schools	No. of students
Parish schools	574	23,041
Private schools	172	4,259
Other	12	2,241
Total	1,462	77,619

Institutions and Students Under the Supervision of the Greek Orthodox Church, 1834

Institution	No. of schools	No. of students
Theological academies	3	310
Theological seminaries	41	13,356
Urban county schools	155	} 43,706
Parish schools	186	
Total	377	57,372

In addition, about 19,000 soldiers were receiving elementary education in the schools of the War Ministry.

Source: A. G. Rashin, "Gramotnost' i Narodnoe Obrazovanie v Rossii v XIX i Nachale XX v," *Istoricheskie Zapiski*, 37, (1951).

8.   *Number of Schools and Pupils in the Villages of State Peasants, 1842-1859*

Years	No. of schools	No. of pupils (in 1,000)
1842	226	13.8
1843	1,235	28.5
1845	1,654	49.2
1847	1,819	61.5
1849	1,869	70.2
1851	1,892	75.1
1853	1,744	76.6
1855	1,805	79.4
1857	1,702	74.6
1859	1,799	76.8

Source: Istoricheskie Zapiski, No. 37 (Moscow, 1951), p. 55.

TABLE 2

Percentage of Literacy for the Total Population of Russia in 1897

| | Age Group | | | | | | | |
	10-19	20-29	30-39	40-49	50-59	60 & over	10-60	Total
Total Population								
Males	45	45	40	33	27	20		29
Females	22	20	16	13	11	10		13
Total	34	32	28	23	19	15		21
Urban Population								
Males	72	69	64	59	54	47	66	54
Females	56	49	40	32	32	26	44	36
Total	64	59	52	47	42	35	56	45
Rural Population								
Males	41	39	35	28	23	17		25
Females	17	15	12	9	8	7		10
Total	29	26	23	19	15	12		17

Source: *Obshchyi Svod po Imperii Rezul'tatov Razrabotki Dannykh Pervoi Vseobshchoi Perepisi Naselenia, Proizvedennoi 28 Yanvaria 1897 g* (St. Petersburg, 1905).

TABLE 3

Percentage of Literacy Among Males Taken into Military Service in the Russian Empire, 1880-1913

Year	% literate	Year	% literate	Year	% literate
1880	22	1891	32	1902	(52)
1881	23	1892	35	1903	53
1882	24	1893	36	1904	56
1883	25	1894	38	1905	56
1884	26	1895	(39)°	1906	58
1885	27	1896	40	1907	62
1886	28	1897	(42)	1908	64
1887	29	1898	45	1909	63
1888	30	1899	(47)	1910	65
1889	31	1900	49	1911	67
1890	32	1901	(50)	1912	68
				1913	68

°Figures in parentheses are estimated
Source: A. G. Rashin, *Formirovanie Rabochego Klassa Rossii* (Moscow, 1958), p. 582.

evidenced in the army recruitment figures for the 1870's as well (Table 3). It was not until the last quarter of the century that literacy showed a significant improvement.

In order to provide some indication of what happened between 1897 and 1917 with respect to literacy of the total population, the data of a census taken in 1920 for European Russia may be compared with the 1897 data for

TABLE 4

Literacy Rates for the Total Population of Russia and for
European Russia (1897 and 1920)

	Males	Females	Total
Russia, 1897	29.3	13.1	21.1
European Russia, 1897	32.6	13.6	22.9
European Russia, 1920	42.2	25.5	33.0

TABLE 5

Percentage Literacy of the Labor Force by Age:
RSFSR, All Manufacturing and Selected Industries, 1918,°
Vladimir District, Factory Labor, 1897

RSFSR, 1918

Age Group (Years)	Total	Metal Industry	Cotton Industry	Vladimir, 1897
Under 14	80.6	95.6	80.3	62.8
15 – 17	} 77.1	} 92.1	} 71.7	55.7
17 – 19				48.0
20 – 24	69.2	88.6	59.3	46.5
25 – 29	66.2	87.2	53.0	40.3
30 – 34	64.8	86.7	49.8	
35 – 39	59.2	81.1	43.8	} 36.7
40 – 44	58.2	79.7	43.3	
45 – 49	51.9	72.6	47.6	} 33.8
50 – 59	} 42.7	} 62.8	} 30.2	31.3
60 and over				29.2
All age groups	64.0	82.6	52.2	41.9

°The 1918 census of factory workers gives the breakdown of literacy and illiteracy for 973,600
workers.

Source: A. G. Rashin: *Formirovanie Rabochego Klassa Rossii* (Moscow, 1958), pp. 595, 602.

European Russia and for all Russia (Table 4). Literacy rates increased for the
total population by about 50 per cent, the largest gain being made by women.

Such a rise could certainly not exclude the industrial labor force. In fact
the 1918 RSFSR (Russian Socialist Federated Soviet Republic) census of
factory workers provided data for the total manufacturing labor force and for
a number of particular industries; these data are helpful in an appraisal of the
change that took place from one age group to the next (Table 5). This carries
us back to the cohort born in the 1860's and schooled around 1875-80.

A comparison between the factory labor force in Vladimir district in
1897 and that of the cotton industry in the census of 1918 is pertinent since
the Vladimir district labor force was largely employed in the cotton textile
industry (last column of Table 5); in the Vladimir factory labor force, however,
a higher percentage of males is represented than in the cotton industry.

Among the workers in manufacturing industries, as in the total population, the evidence points to a continuing increase of literacy from the mid-nineteenth century, when the 60-year-olds of 1897 were young, to the youth of 1918. Male literacy of the factory work force tended to run 30 to 40 per cent ahead of the female rates. Thus among the cotton mill workers for European Russia in 1897 male literacy was 54 per cent and female 20 per cent; for the RSFSR in 1918 the figures were respectively 77 per cent and 37 per cent.

Two factors were instrumental in accelerating the growth of educational facilities: (1) the emancipation of the serfs, and (2) the growth of modern industry. The emancipation of the serfs, although followed by institutional arrangements that impeded the peasants' mobility, not only provided more freedom of choice to the peasants, but made it imperative to raise the productivity of the agricultural labor force on both the peasant farms and the estates. This need met with the approval of the spokesmen of the gentry in the countryside and found its expression in the accelerated rate of school construction in rural areas and subsequent increases in enrollment. The demand for literacy among actual or prospective factory workers fostered the improvement of urban educational facilities in general, and in newly-developing industrial regions in particular. Thus students of elementary schools increased from 400,000 in 1856 to about 2,200,000 in 1885, an increase of 450 per cent. The largest part of the increase could, of course, be accounted for by the rural schools. One of the chief characteristics of the rise in enrollment was its uneven distribution by sex; in 1885, 147,300 out of 429,500 students in the urban elementary schools were girls, while girls were only 393,500 out of 1,754,500 in the rural schools. (This explains the literacy rate differential in industry at a later date.) Although much could probably be said about the quality of education in the one- or even two-grade elementary schools of that time, nevertheless it brought considerable progress in literacy of the population, as can be seen in the data on literacy of the military draft (Table 3).

While elementary education contributes to advancement on the job, it constitutes simultaneously a widening of opportunity to continue education on a higher level. It should also be considered as a vehicle of social advancement or as a substitute for the accumulation of wealth; in fact, probably more people have advanced into a "higher class" with the assistance of education but without wealth than vice versa. Although a modern society probably ought to welcome such a pattern of social advancement, as approaching a more rational utilization of human resources, this was not always true in nineteenth-century Russia. The available evidence points to a lagging utilization of education as a vehicle of social advancement, a process that was accelerated considerably in the twentieth century. This is reflected in the data provided in Table 6. The explanation for this phenomenon ought to be sought in the zigzags of government policies. During the reign of Alexander II (1855-81) the obstacles for enrollment in institutions of secondary and higher education were the "normal" ones (income, quota systems in various schools, favoritism, etc.), but during the reign of Alexander III (1881-94) a

TABLE 6

*Social Selectivity of the Student Body
in Secondary and Higher Education*

A. *Percentage Distribution of Secondary School Students
by Social Origin for Selected Years (1826/27 – 1914)*

Social Group	1826/27	1871	1881	1894	1904	1914
Gentry & officials	72.2	59.5	47.5	56.4	36.5	24.7
Clergy	3.1	4.6	5.2	3.4	4.0	4.7
Urban taxpaying groups	20.8	27.8	37.2	31.6	43.5	41.7
Rural taxpaying groups	3.9	5.7	8.0	6.0	14.1	25.5
Foreigners & others	n.a.	1.1	2.1	2.6	1.9	3.4

B. *Percentage Distribution of University Students
by Social Origin for Selected Years (1864/65 – 1913)*[*]

Social Group	1864/65	1880	1907	1913
Gentry and officials	67.2	46.7	45.1	36.0
Clergy	9.5	23.4	11.2	10.3
Urban tax-paying group	8.9	21.5	34.4	35.2
Rural tax-paying group	14.0	3.2	6.9	13.3
Foreign and others	.4	5.2	2.4	5.0

[*]Serious questions could be raised with regard to the representativeness of the university students; the universities in 1913 contained only about a third of all students enrolled in institutions of higher education.

Source: *Istoricheskie Zapiski* No. 37, Moscow 1951. pp. 72-75.

clear directive of governmental policy sought to prevent social advancement through education. This policy probably inflicted losses on the Russian economy at a later point.[9]

The Russian government oscillated between the Scylla of the demand for educated manpower in industry and business and the Charybdis of the preservation of a rigidly stratified society fortified by traditional (or archaic) criteria for stratification. The result was half-measures and inconsistency in educational policies. All the government claims of progressiveness in the area of education were outrun during the 1890's by the growing popular

9. The decree of June 18, 1887 which was referred to as "the decree about children of cooks" (*kukharkiny dieti*) proscribed that "*Gymnasiums* and *pro-gymnasiums* should prevent the entrance of children of coachmen, manservants, cooks, laundrywomen, small shopkeepers and the like; the children of whom, with the exception perhaps of unusually gifted ones, ought not to be allowed to escape from the environment to which they belong; because as an experience of many years has proven, it leads them to scorn their parents, to a dissatisfaction with their way of life and instills hatred against the existing, inescapable by the nature of things, inequality of property status. . . ."

demand for educational facilities, a demand that grew with the increasing number of the educated persons.[10] The dual nature of the educational policies can perhaps be illustrated by citing two positive attempts to meet the demands from various pressure groups. The first was the establishment of the so-called *real-schools,* which were secondary schools with less emphasis upon humanistic subjects than the *gymnasium,* and better preparation in mathematics and business- or industry-oriented subjects. It is clear from both the location of the schools and the social backgrounds of their pupils that this was a less "gentleman-like" education in terms of prestige, but could more successfully meet the needs of the business community for potential managerial or technical personnel.[11]

The second measure was even more successful in terms of growth. This was the establishment of *gymnasiums* and *pro-gymnasiums* for women. Previously, education for women had been available in very few institutions, mostly private boarding schools, and even girls of the gentry had had to rely upon private tutoring of questionable quality. In an attempt to raise the level of education of women in the higher classes in order to assure a particular "cultural atmosphere" in the homes of the well-to-do, a considerable effort went into the development of secondary schools for women. Between 1873 and 1914, or in a period of 40 years, the number of students increased more than 14 times.[12] Perhaps the fact that the expenditures per pupil were lower

10. The claim of Russian governments to being more progressive than society itself has deep historical roots, and the view to this effect is subscribed to by many scholars. Usually some government action is compared with some expression of public opinion in order to prove the point. It invariably assumes that the "opinions and attitudes" of the spokesmen for social groups coincided with the group's interests and real opinions, which ought to be difficult to prove. But even the apologists and proponents of state benevolence in Russian history would have to concede that in the area of education, whenever the government disregarded the backwardness of society and moved ahead, the means used were not conducive to society's cooperation or to the release of popular initiative.

11. The number of pupils in the *real-schools* grew very rapidly, as can be seen from the following figures.

Number of Students in the "Real Schools," Selected Years 1876-1914

Year	No. of students	Year	No. of students
1876	8,308	1904	46,425
1882	17,484	1907	55,500
1895	26,002	1914	80,800

According to the data on the students' social origin, the percentage of gentry and clergy was much smaller than in the *gymnasiums,* and the share of urban and rural taxpaying classes much larger, thus providing an avenue of social advance through education into business, with the expectation of potential opportunites that business could offer.

12. The number of students for selected years was as follows:

Students in Women's Gymnasiums and Pro-Gymnasiums for Selected Years 1873-1914 (In thousands)

Year	No. of Students	Year	No. of Students
1873	23.0	1883	55.1
1880	42.7	1893	65.1

in the women's schools facilitated the higher rate of growth of this type of school.[13]

Although the impact of women's education was very significant in terms of long-run growth, the immediate effect in the labor market was probably much less than the proportion of women in the total increase (in years of education) of the educational stock would indicate. Thus we are dealing here primarily with a long-run derived effect rather than with a calculable return to particular educational outlays (considered as investments).[14]

During the period 1860-1913 the number of employed industrial, construction, and railway workers increased about 4.3 times (from 1,960,000 to 8,415,000), while pupils in elementary and secondary schools increased 16 times (600,000 to 9,840,000). In 1860 there were three times as many workers as school attendants; by 1900 the number of students already exceeded the number of workers by about 40 per cent. However, during the years 1900-1913 workers increased relatively faster than pupils, and by 1913 students exceeded workers by only 12 per cent.

The average costs of education per student at the various levels of education cannot yet be calculated, since most of the available estimates that exist are given in terms of concepts (not always identical) of current net costs. It may, however, be useful just to present the data on relative costs per pupil at the different levels for comparison with costs in other countries. Strumilin's calculations yield for 1913 the amounts of 21 rubles per student in elementary schools, 116 rubles in secondary schools, and 261 rubles at the university. The elementary to secondary cost ratio was approximately 1:5, and the secondary to university ratio was 5:12.4. The striking feature of this relationship is the differential between the costs of elementary and secondary education. On the assumption that both items were computed using identical conventions they might reflect two important characteristics: first, the low salaries in elementary schools (particularly in the rural areas) against the relatively higher salaries in secondary and higher education;[15] second, costs of build-

Year	No. of Students	Year	No. of Students
1903	137.0	1907	200.8
1904	151.0	1913	303.7
1906	182.2	1914	323.6

In terms of social origin of the students the women's *gymnasium* occupied a middle position between the "aristocratic extreme" of the male *gymnasium* and the "democratic extreme" of the *real-school*.

13. According to Strumilin the expenditures per student in 1913 were 75.5 rubles per year in the women's secondary schools and 172.4 rubles in the *gymnasium* and *real-schools*. He explains the difference primarily by the relatively less expensive use of female teaching personnel. The explanation might be not entirely convincing but a cost differential unquestionably existed.

14. The data on women employed in occupations requiring secondary or higher education were not available at the time of preparation of this paper. To the extent that 1926 census data could serve as a guide for pre-revolutionary patterns, they indicate the concentration of educated women in the teaching profession and to a lesser extent in the lower ranks of the medical profession.

15. The average salary of an elementary school teacher in 1913 is estimated by Strumilin at 420 rubles per year while the salary of a full professor at the university was 3,000 rubles.

ings and equipment probably were vastly different, even more so per student, and account for a part of the differential.

Apart from cost factors, one could probably question the economic rational behind a policy that admitted so few into secondary schools and institutions of higher education. The distribution of enrollments among the three levels in the school year 1914/15 was 91.8 per cent for elementary (grades 1-4); 6.9 per cent for secondary (5-10); and 1.3 per cent for higher education.

Perhaps the scope of the educational effort in pre-revolutionary Russia on the eve of World War I and a reflection of the growth of school enrollment in the twentieth century could best be shown by the following data:

School Enrollment in Russia,° 1914/15 (in thousands)		
General education, grades 1-4		9,030.7
General education, grades 5-10		679.3
Formal education	625.0 ⎱	
Technical education	54.3 ⎰	
Higher education		127.4
Total		9,837.4

°Russia in the present political boundaries of the USSR.

These figures are cited to present the state of education at the end of the period of our primary interest. The productivity effects of the rapid growth of education in Russia during the decade preceding World War I could be realized only as the new youth became part of the labor force in the 1920's.

A problem often faced by economists studying the role of education in economic development is how to determine or rationalize the "optimal" proportion of various levels of education of particular cohorts, or the distribution of various skill levels in the labor force. The problems of returns to investment in education at various levels (or various "amounts"), as well as the question of the social contributions of various skills or occupations to the process of economic growth, are diligently studied. I will not attempt to provide answers to these fascinating problems in the Russian experience at various stages of its economic development. I would like only to indicate the scope of the problem of the rise of higher education in Russia and its relation to the economy.

Until the middle of the nineteenth century the government bureaucracy was the source of the chief demand for educated and more highly skilled manpower. For obvious reasons this demand increased very modestly over time and, more important, it did not provide for much upward social mobility. This situation was changed during the second half of the nineteenth century. Approximate data (based upon the 1897 population census) point to the fact that by the end of the century, the total employment of salaried white-collar workers in the nonagricultural sector of the economy exceeded the total employment in the government apparatus, and that employment in the

TABLE 7

Number of Students Enrolled in 55 Institutions
of Higher Learning and Specialized Secondary Education

Type of Institution	Higher Education		Secondary Specialized	
	Jan. 1, 1907	Jan. 1, 1914	Jan. 1, 1907	Jan. 1, 1914
Liberal education	28,672	41,161	——	——
Technical, engineering	8,162	12,947	42,975	53,665
Business	410	4,874	28,406	58,365
Medical	1,792	3,955	6,313	9,863
Teacher training	1,016	2,241	16,271	32,252
Law	852	854	——	——
Total	43,189	71,921	129,134	195,105

Source: L. K. Erman, *"Sostav Intelligentsii v Rossii v Kontse XIX i Nachale XX v,"* Istoria
SSSR No. 1 (1963), p. 172.

educational system exceeded the civilian government civil service. The
following very tentative data provide an approximate idea of the numbers
of employed educated white-collar workers in the few selected branches.

Number of Employed White-Collar Workers
Based Upon the 1897 Population Census (in thousands)

Branch		Employment
Government bureaucracy: Armed Forces	52,471 ⎱	203,816
Civilian bureaucracy	151,345 ⎰	
Education		172,842
Industry, railways, trade and banking		298,623
Medicine, law and other free professions		52,825

The significance of this development lies in the fact that an element of
dynamics was injected in the demand for secondary and higher education
and for training in higher specialized skills. This development brought about
a broadening of the market for educational services and led to much more
competitive market behavior. It also brought about an acceleration of the
process of growth of educated skilled professional manpower.

In the absence of detailed data on the growth of most of the separate
categories of professional manpower, these demands in the growing branches
of the economy and in the educational system itself can be indicated by the
supply response of students at the levels of higher and secondary specialized
education.

The following fragmentary data[16] in Table 7 indicate the general trend,
which, given the typical laggardness of Russian educational authorities, must
have been even stronger in reality. Obviously, the impact upon the economy

16. The data represent only 55 institutions of higher learning out of an existing 105, and for
the year 1914 approximately 72,000 students out of a total of 127,400. Nevertheless other evidence
supports the contention that the data are representative of all institutions of higher learning.

of training an increasing number of highly skilled specialists was uneven, depending upon the nature of the profession. Since in 1897 there was a total of 4,010 engineers employed in Russia, and by 1913 the yearly number of graduates of engineering schools was about 1,500,[17] the impact upon technology and the performance of Russian industry must have been visible and marked. On the other hand, an increase of the number of physicians in Russia (the present territory of the Soviet Union) from 13,344 in 1905 to 21,944 in 1913 could have had a long-run effect upon the volume and quality of medical services and health of the population, but the short-run effect was probably minimal.

Turning back to the nineteenth-century data on literacy and schooling of the Russian labor force, one might ask the legitimate question, "Was this much or little for the particular stage of industrial development of Russia?" My answer would be that it was too little; schooling dragged back on development. I suggest that there is a range within which the level of formal education is related to industrial performance in a particular historical context. In other words, a particular phase of industrial development presupposes (that is, requires), within some toleration range, a particular average level of formal education. It is basically an empirical problem to find out what the relationship has been in various countries in the past. It is also plausible to argue that a certain rule of thumb could be established for countries that are starting on the road of industrialization. Russian experience seems to indicate that the type and level of the technology borrowed might provide a clue to this rule of thumb.

One of the features of industrialization in the second half of the nineteenth century and in the twentieth century is the presence of certain discontinuites, particularly involving the borrowing of foreign technology; the discontinuities are not only technological but organizational. A program of rapid adaptation of foreign technology ought to set the requirements for particular types of labor, which implicitly involves a specific level of education. The level of borrowed technology therefore determines an "optimal" level of education higher than the one that was developed to satisfy the needs of the previously existing and less advanced level of techniques. Perhaps the level of formal education of the labor force in a country entering the stage of industrialization ought to be set, as a maximum, at the level of the country (countries) from which the basic technology was borrowed.[18] Since Russia's pre-revolutionary industrialization used a borrowed basic technology from German, a more nearly "optimal" level of education of the labor force would then have been one that corresponded somewhat more closely to that prevailing in Germany during this period, rather than to that which prevailed in England during the early stages of industrialization.

17. V. E. Komarov, *Ekonomicheskie Osnovy Podgotovki Spetsialistov Dla Narodnogo Khoziaistva* (Moscow, 1959), p. 43.
18. Adjustments obviously have to be made for differences between the structure and composition of industry in the model country and the desired composition in the developing country.

CHAPTER 20

EDUCATION AND INNOVATIVE
FERMENT IN ENGLAND, 1588–1805

W. H. G. Armytage

"I have often observed" wrote Boswell on March 28, 1772, "that Mr. Johnson is very fond of talking of manufactures, or giving any instruction as to the matters of utility."[1] The great lexicographer's life spanned the transcendence of the "oat barrier" in England,[2] and his fondness for "talking of manufactures" and "matters of utility" indicated the reasons why the legal wall inhibiting manufacture in favor of agriculture was breaking down. The design of this wall was embodied in the Statute of Apprentices (1563) and the Elizabethan poor law; its builders were the statesmen of the Elizabethan warfare-welfare state. But its sustainers were weak: paid "informers" and unpaid Justices of the Peace, with no police, only a small army, and a crown chronically short of money. All this led to a state of affairs best described by Charles Davenant in 1699: "Nowadays laws are not much observed which do not in a manner execute themselves."

In the generations between the Armada (1588) and Trafalgar (1805), war was for England a recurrent solvent and stimulus. These two naval engagements covered the preliminaries and the "take-off" into self-sustaining economic growth (as so brilliantly interpreted by W. W. Rostow). These two naval battles are selected as terminals for this inquiry because behind English maritime supremacy grew a number of private mathematical schools.[3] The skills they imparted were utilized also by surveyors, river improvers, and navigators.

1. Industrial Schools for the Poor

By the close of the sixteenth century, "technical" education was visible in towns like Chester, York, Lincoln, Hatfield, Plymouth, and Bury St. Edmunds. For example, at Lincoln in 1591, John Cheeseman the knitter was provided with spinning wheels and 40 stone of wool; and he agreed "to set on

1. W. K. Wimsatt and F. A. Pottle (ed.), *Boswell for the Defence, 1769-1774* (London: Heinemann, 1960), p. 74.

2. He was born when Thomas Newcomen was salvaging the mining industry of Cornwall, Staffordshire and Newcastle by the steam pump, and died in the year in which William Murdock first utilized this new energy slave as a means of traction.

3. Recently catalogued with painstaking scholarship by Professor E. G. R. Taylor in *The Mathematical Practitioners of Tudor and Stuart England* (Cambridge, 1954).

376

work in his science all such as are willing to come to him or are sent by the aldermen, and to hide nothing from them that belongeth to the knowledge of the said service."[4] Such schools were fostered by charitable bequests. In 1628 Sir William Borlase founded a Free School at St. Martins to teach 24 boys and girls to knit, spin and make bone lace. Another was founded in 1642 at Lydbury North, Shropshire, in an outhouse; there girls were to be instructed in the art of spinning wool and flax.[5] One was set up in 1670 by William Bower, a merchant of Bridlington, for "the art of carding, knitting or spinning of wool."

Mercantile writers fanned this passion for productive efficiency. Andrew Yarenton, author of *England's Improvement by Land and Sea* (1677, 1681), commended the spinning schools of Germany. Thomas Firmin published *Some Proposals for the Employment of the Poor* (1681) and followed it up by trying to run a self-supporting technical school. Four years later, in *Good Order Established in Pennsylvania and New Jersey,* Thomas Budd suggested a seven-year school where "Boys could be taught and instructed in some Mystery or Trade as the making of Mathematical Instruments, Joynery, Turnery, the Making of Clocks and Watches, Weaving, Shoemaking or any other useful Trade or Mystery that the school is capable of teaching; and the Girls to be taught and instructed in the spinning of Flax and Wool, and Knitting of Gloves and Stockings, Sewing, and making of all sorts of useful Needle-Work, and the making of Straw Work, as Hats, Baskets, etc., or any other useful Art or Mystery that the school is capable of teaching." A few years later, John Bellers, the Quaker, issued *Proposals for raising a College of Industry* (1696).

Such ideas circulated at governmental level. The Board of Trade received in 1697 a report from John Locke urging the establishment of working schools in every parish to which all children between the ages of 3 and 14 were to be sent. At local level, too, such ideas found favor, and in 1698 a Workhouse School was founded in London where children were set to spin wool, knit stockings, and cobble before being apprenticed at 12 or 14. The General Act for the Relief of the Poor (9 Geo. 1. c.7) in 1723 resulted in a number of workhouses appearing, along with charity schools,[6] like the spinning schools at Findon and Artleborough in Northamptonshire.[7] So impressed was the S.P.C.K. that its secretary, Henry Newman, recommended them as models. The idea haunted legislators up to the time of William Pitt the Younger, who in 1795 envisaged the establishment of industrial schools for poor children. Though this did not materialize, the Society for the Betterment of the Poor did, and Sarah Trimmer succeeded in reviving a number of industrial schools. By 1803, 20,336 out of 188,794 children between the ages of

---

4. E. Lipson, *Economic History* (London: Macmillan, 1941), iii, pp. 430-33.
5. Foster Watson, *The Beginnings of the Teaching of Modern Subjects in England* (London, 1909), xliv.
6. M. Marryott, *Account of the Workhouses in Great Britain* (London, 1725).
7. M. G. Jones, *The Charity School Movement in the XVIII Century* (Cambridge, 1938).

5 and 14 receiving parish relief had been, or were, pupils in schools of industry.[8] By 1844 less than 1 per cent of the schools of the country were non-industrial.

On a higher plane were schools of navigation, dating back in a non-institutional form to the Elizabethan era. Jonas Hanway, in his *Proposal for Country Naval Free Schools . . . giving such effectual instruction to Poor Boys as may nurse them for the Sea Service* (1783), urged that each county should levy a tax to sustain them. His scheme was adopted by, among other places, Hull Trinity House, which built a school in 1787 to "promote the advancement and improvement of navigation and the good breeding of seamen."[9]

2. The Royal Society of London: Forum of Discovery

The marriage of science and social amelioration eloquently advocated by Francis Bacon[10] was symbolized by the founding of the Royal Society of London in 1660.[11] Starting with a hundred "virtuosi," or fellows, in 1660, it doubled in size in ten years and then remained fairly' stationary, rising slowly to two hundred by 1800. Some of the fellows, like William Petty, were active researchers in compiling histories of trades. According to the proposed statutes drawn up by the first Curator of Experiments, Robert Hooke, the "business and design" of the Royal Society was "to improve the knowledge of natural things, and all useful arts, mechanic practises, Engynes, and Inventions by Experiments." To record a "rational account of the causes of things" the Society issued *Philosophical Transactions;* it was edited by one of the first joint secretaries, Henry Oldenburg, whose frequent correspondence with the continental scientists was to provide one of the main communicating links between the society and other academies.

Indeed, it was by correspondence with Robert Hooke that Thomas Newcomen, the Darthmouth blacksmith, obtained information about Papin's proposals to obtain motive power by exhausting air from a cylinder furnished with a piston. And from the *Philosophical Transactions* many country gentlemen obtained ideas to benefit their estates. Thus, for instance, Sir Godfrey Copley found useful information about fountains and canals, and in return gave the Copley Medal.[12]

8. M. G. Jones, *op. cit.,* p. 158.
9. K. J. R. Robson found that the Trinity House Marine School still possesses a copy of Hanway's proposals together with an opal ring of his, presented by a member of the original committee. See "Schools of Industry—their part in the Development of Technical Education in Hull," *The Vocational Aspect,* v (1953), pp. 32-36.
10. For which see B. Farrington, *Francis Bacon, Philosopher of Industrial Science* (London, Schuman, 1951).
11. For which see Martha Ornstein, *The Role of Scientific Societies in the Seventeenth Century* (Chicago: University of Chicago Press, 1938).
    Dorothy Stimson, *Scientists and Amateurs* (London: Schuman, 1949) and various articles in *Notes and Records of the Royal Society.*
12. W. H. G. Armytage, "Sir Godfrey Copley and his Friends," *Notes and Records of the Royal Society* (London, 1954), Vol. X, pp. 54-74.

Newton's dominance in the Royal Society led it to diverge from the closed pattern of the French Academy and become a forum of discovery. Many of these discoveries were to be made in smaller groups springing up in Britain at this time. English industrial growth depended on these informal groups; just as the Royal Society itself owed much to coffee houses, for the "virtuosi" (as Fellows of the Royal Society were called) also disseminated their knowledge in more informal ways.

3. *Spawning and Diffusion of Ideas in the Coffee Houses*
"Eavesdropping" on the virtuosi enabled all sorts and conditions of men to acquire a rudimentary knowledge of their work. Nowhere was this eavesdropping more pleasant and palatable than in a coffee house. The pioneer of these, in 1655, was one run by Arthur Tillyard near All Saints, Oxford, where Millington and Peter Pett, together with early members of the Royal Society, used to meet. Peter Staehl taught chemistry there until 1662, when he migrated to Robert Boyle's laboratory in London.[13]

The ephemeral character of these coffee houses should not blind us to the positive instruction that took place in them. At Garaway's, where tea was first sold, Robert Hooke, F.R.S., "taught quaker to make cantilever," discussed clockmaking with Tompion or experiments with Shortgrave, his assistant. On December 11, 1675, he and John Hoskins, F.R.S., were at Joe's Coffee House where, said Hooke, "we began New Club Society" — this time with Robert Boyle F.R.S., Christopher Wren, F.R.S., Nehemiah Grew, F.R.S., Theodore Haak, F.R.S., and others. This society discussed on July 15, 1676, "Logarithmotechnia," "an Aritmetick Engine," and music. A third venture, which Hooke launched with Aubrey in this year, was a "Rosicrucian Club" to study alchemy, but it came to nothing.[14] And Hooke, as we know from his *Diary*, visited 154 coffee houses.[15]

In the coffee houses, men from the provinces could hear what was afoot, doctors could meet their patients, and apothecaries could consult specialists. Thoresby, F.R.S., the Yorkshire scientist, used to meet Newton and Halley at the Grecian in Devereux Court.[16] Sir William Petty, for instance, who invented the catamaran, or double-hulled boat, attended a club at the Turk's Head, Westminster, where an amateur parliament was sustained. It was from the Grecian that Steele proposed to date his articles in *The Tatler*.

Aware of this universal thirst, John Salter, the servant of Sir Hans Sloane (the secretary of the Royal Society), set up a coffee house at 18 Cheyne Walk, Chelsea. Stocked as a parody of a virtuoso's collections, it attracted the attention of Steele, who described it in *The Tatler* (June 28, 1709) as having "Ten

13. G. H. Turnbull, "Peter Staehl, the First Public Teacher of Chemistry at Oxford," *Annals of Science* Vol. 9, (1953), pp. 265-70.

14. M. D'Espinasse, *Robert Hooke* (Berkeley: University of California Press, 1956), pp. 190ff.

15. Henry W. Robinson and Walter Adams, *The Diary of Robert Hooke* (London: Taylor, 1935), pp. 463-470.

16. *Ibid.*, pp. 11, 111.

thousand gimcracks, round the room and on the ceiling." ("Gimcrack" was humorously associated in Steele's day with the interest of the Royal Society.)

Insurance companies and lotteries (like the South Sea Bubble) that flourished in coffee houses provided a great stimulus to mathematics. At the Marine Coffee House in Birchin Lane, (where the London Assurance Company did business till 1748), John Harris, F.R.S., (1667-1719) was lecturing on mathematics in 1698; he continued there till 1704 when his *Lexicon Technicum, or a Universal English Dictionary of the Arts and Sciences* was published — the first of a long line of English encyclopedias. Another such teacher, Abraham de Moivre, a French exile, published his *Doctrine of Chances* in 1716.

The Rainbow coffee house cradled two societies. A Botanical Society was formed in 1721 by Johann Jacob Dillen (or Dillenius), the Sherardian professor of botany at Oxford, and John Martyn, (1699-1768) an amateur entomologist. The second, formed in 1735, was a Society for the Encouragement of Learning, established with the general aim of "promoting the Arts and Sciences." An Aurelian Society similarly took shape in the Swan Tavern in the Cornhill in 1745, though a fire three years later destroyed it. In its resurrected form it used to meet at the York coffee house in St. James Street; from this was formed, at the Marlborough coffee house in 1788, the Linnaean Society.[17]

Perhaps the best symbol of the way in which scientific societies, encyclopaedias, newsletters, insurance companies, and town libraries were incubated in coffee houses was to be seen at Button's in Russell Street, Covent Garden (of which Martin Foulkes was a member). There stood, on its western side, a postbox fashioned in the shape of a lion's head, "holding its paws under the chin, on a box which contains everything that he swallows." Addison, who used it to collect material for his paper *The Guardian*, remarked that it was "a proper emblem of knowledge and actions, being all head and paws." This "lion postbox" was later removed to the Bedford, a coffee house even more directly concerned with science; for there John Stirling, F.R.S., and later J. Theophilus Desaguliers, F.R.S., lectured on experimental philosophy. Stirling was a friend of Isaac Newton and of the Swiss mathematician Nicholas Bernouilli; he later went on to become a mine manager in Lanarkshire. Desaguliers also discoursed at large over the great piazza at Covent Garden to, among others, the Fieldings, Hogarth and Goldsmith, Woodward and Lloyd.

The Bedford took its name from the landlord of the area, the Duke of Bedford, who, like many eighteenth-century noblemen, did not hesitate to employ empirical scientists and engineers like John Stirling for the improvement and exploitation of his estates. Well might John Houghton (d.1705)

17. A. T. Gage, *History of the Linnaean Society of London* (London, The Society, 1-10, 1938). Martyn translated Tournefort's works, practised as an apothecary and lectured in London before becoming a professor of botany at Cambridge in 1732.

comment that they had "improved useful knowledge" as much as the universities.

Joshua Ward (1685-1761), who was aptly caught by Hogarth in the *Harlot's Progress,* made such good use of the scraps of gossip and information he picked up at the Bedford that in 1736 he was able to manufacture sulphuric acid by the bell process. He reduced the price of this valuable commodity some sixteenfold. The local inhabitants at Twickenham were so offended by the smell of burning brimstone and nitre that they forced Ward to remove his distillery to Richmond. By 1749 he had patented his process; and by 1758, when the French metallurgist and "industrial spy" Gabriel Jars began visiting England, he noticed that Ward was employing Welsh-speaking women, probably so that the secret of his work would not be divulged.

Ward was not the only chemist who frequented coffee houses for professional reasons. Dr. Morris had an elaboratory at Roberts coffee house in the great piazza at Covent Garden, where a number of crucibles were tested in 1757.[18] By 1782 a chemical Society was meeting in the Chapter coffee house in London.[19]

At Jack's coffee house in Dean Street and later at young Slaughter's coffee house in St. Martin's Lane, a "scientific club" existed in the 1780's under John Hunter, the surgeon. Among its members were Sir Joseph Banks and his protegés George Fordyce and D. C. Solander. Here Captain Cook and the naturalist J. C. Fabricius used to be seen on their visits to London.[20]

We know from Boswell that at the London coffee house, in 1772, a club consisting of physicians, dissenting clergy, and masters of academics used to meet and exchange ideas.[21] There Boswell was to have met Benjamin Franklin on March 26, 1772, and did meet Dr. Joseph Priestley.

In the provinces, too, the coffee houses incubated local groups. At Liverpool the Conversation Club, which discussed among other things the reasons for the decline of the potter's art in Liverpool,[22] used to meet in St. George's coffee house.

The famous Literary and Philosophical Society met during its first year at the Assembly coffee house (probably near the Exchange)[23] before getting premises of its own. A new religion, based on "revelations" to a scientist, was founded in the London coffee house at Ludgate Hill on December 5, 1783. This was the "New Jerusalem," or Swedenborgian, church, of which William Blake was a member.[24]

18. F. W. Gibbs, "Peter Shaw and the Revival of Chemistry," *Annals of Science,* VII (1951), p. 234.

19. "Some Eighteenth-Century Chemical Societies," *Endeavour* (1942), p. 106.

20. A. Armitage, "A Naturalist's Vacation. The London Letters of J. C. Fabricius," *Annals of Science,* XIV (1958), p. 124.

21. *Boswell for the Defence, 1769-1774, op. cit.,* p. 68.

22. G. Chandler, *Liverpool* (London: Batsford, 1957), p. 334.

23. W. H. Brindley, The Manchester Literary and Philosophic Society, *Journal of the Royal Institute of Chemistry,* LXXIX (1955), p. 63.

24. J. D. Davies, *The Theology of William Blake* (Oxford: Oxford University Press, 1948), p. 34.

4. The Royal Society of Arts

Perhaps the best known of the coffee houses was Rawthmell's in Henrietta Street, Covent Garden. Haunted nightly by Martin Folkes (1690-1754), president of the Royal Society in 1741, it was a magnet for eavesdroppers. According to one fellow, Folkes chose the council and officers out of "his junto of sycophants" that used to meet him there. On March 22, 1754, a group of Fellows of the Royal Society at Rawthmell's listened to a Northampton drawing master's proposals to subsidize inventions by prizes, in much the same way as horsebreeding was fostered by competition at the Northampton horse fair. This drawing master, Shipley, was anxious to find substitutes for cobalt and madder, both dyes used in the cloth trade, both imported and both difficult to obtain. Meeting again at Rawthmell's a week later, they decided to make their meetings more formal and arranged to gather regularly at a circulating library in Crane Court, Fleet Street. From this grew the Society for the Encouragement of Arts, Manufactures, and Commerce, perhaps better known today as the Royal Society of Arts.[25]

The Royal Society of Arts attracted support from a number of chemists: Stephen Hales, Peter Woulfe, Morris Fordyce and Robert Dossie among them. Robert Dossie's *Elaboratory laid open* had so impressed Dr. Johnson that he proposed him for the Society. Dossie's frank admiration of French practice led him to envisage the Society of Arts becoming a center of experimental research, as well as a collector and transmitter of information.[26] It was apt that the Royal Society of Arts should later help incubate the Chemical Society (in 1841) and the Institute of Chemistry (in 1877).

5. Growth of Chemical Research Societies and Laboratories

Since chemistry was becoming fashionable and profitable, other private laboratories grew. From about 1736 William Lewis sustained a teaching laboratory off Fetter Lane; from 1747, at Kingston, he planned to issue a periodical and also proposed to use laboratory experiments to find new materials and investigate uses for by-products, with the help of Alexander Chisholm. Lewis' contributions, wrote Dr. Gibbs, "showed for the first time that great benefits could arise from the systematic application of scientific knowledge and method to industrial problems." By differentiating between physics and chemistry, Lewis showed how both were important to industrial development. The laboratory he described (and used) at Kingston was classed by Gibbs as "unique in that it was the first designed specifically for research in applied chemistry and physics."[27] Lewis also went on journeys to see iron works in Rotherham, Staveley, Kitley, and Coalbrookdale, and to in-

25. Derek Hudson and K. W. Luckhurst, *The Royal Society of Arts* (London: Murray, 1954).
26. F. W. Gibbs, "Robert Dossie and the Society of Arts," *Annals of Science*, VII (1952), p. 149.
27. F. W. Gibbs, "William Lewis, M.B., F.R.S. (1708-1781)," and "A Notebook of William Lewis and Alexander Chesholm," *Annals of Science*, VIII (1952), pp. 122 and 202.

vestigate the use of coal and coke for the production of iron. So did Henry Cavendish, the wealthy private chemist.[28]

Other societies also took shape, especially in Lincolnshire, where Maurice Johnson (1688-1755) founded the Gentleman's Society at Spalding in 1709-10, acting as its secretary for thirty-five years. His son-in-law, Dr. Green, made his botanical enthusiasms public, and spread the discoveries of continental correspondents like Boerhaave and Linnaeus.

A second society was founded in 1734 at Peterborough, where the engineer William Elstob carried on a vigorous program of mathematics and mapping.[29] A third was at Boston (founded in 1750), in an area where "Nature is rack'd and improved ten thousand ways and made to submit to the powerful Laws of Mechanism"; there modern archaeology took shape from the efforts of William Stukeley (1687-1765), a medical practitioner of Boston, and from 1729 to 1747 vicar of All Saints, Stamford. Stukeley was a pupil of the great Dr. Mead, another disciple of Boerhaave; his field work on Avebury and Stonehenge was of such quality that a modern archaelolgist has described him as "almost a corporate sum of his contemporaries, with all their achievement, and their intellectual crochets concentrated and magnified in one man."[30] (Stukeley, a friend and biographer of Isaac Newton, gave us the authentic version of the story of the fallen apple and the discovery of the law of gravitation.) Stukeley was a friend of Stephen Gray (1666-1736) and regarded him as "the first eminent propagator of electricity"; as a student at Cambridge in 1706, Stukeley, with Gray's nephew, used to watch him produce sparks from his "cylindric glass tube."[31]

Gray was sustained by Desaguliers, whose own thoughts and experiments upon electricity (published in the *Philosophical Transactions,* July-October 1739) revealed that he had held back from pursuing the subject "because I was unwilling to interfere with the late Mr. Stephen Gray, who had wholly turn'd his Thoughts that way; but was of a Temper to give it entirely over, if he imagin'd, that anything was done in Opposition to him."[32] Gray's wholehearted absorption in research probably had led him to approach Hans Sloane in 1711 for admission to the Charterhouse as a pensioner, where "those many and great interruptions I now meet with would be removed so that I should then have time enough to make a farther Progress than I have yet done in . . . Astronomy and navigation and might happily find out something that might be of use."[33] Desaguliers was a French Huguenot refugee who had become curator and demonstrator of the Royal Society,

28. See, for instance, his papers at Chatsworth, Derbyshire, which contain accounts of a tour he made with Charles Blagdon, F.R.S.

29. H. J. J. Winter, "Scientific notes from early minutes of the Peterborough Society," *Isis,* XXXI (1939-1940), pp. 51-59.

30. Stuart Piggott, *William Stukeley* (Oxford: Oxford University Press, 1950), p. xi.

31. B. Cohen, "Neglected Sources for the Life of Stephen Gray, *Isis,* XLV (1944), pp. 41-49.

32. *Ibid.*

33. *Ibid.*

Chaplain of the Duke of Chandos, military strategist, Hanoverian publicist, an authority on water engineering and ventilation, and, above all, a popularizer of science. In 1719 he became Grand Master of the Grand Lodge of London, formed two years earlier.[34]

Freemasonary was the ethic behind the encyclopedism of the time, which sought to diffuse the light of knowledge. John Harris' *Lexicon Technicum or Universal English Dictionary of the Arts and Sciences* (1704) went to a second edition in four years, and forty years later Dr. John Campbell published a revision. Ephraim Chambers (1680-1740) published *Cyclopaedia or General Dictionary of Arts and Sciences* (1728), which ran to at least six editions. Encyclopedists kept a weather eye on the Royal Society too; John Barrow dedicated to the president his *New Universal Dictionary of the Arts and Sciences* (1753). From there on they multiply. A *New and Complete Dictionary of Arts and Sciences comprehending all the branches of Useful Knowledge* was issued by a "Society of Gentlemen" in 1754. Such societies were another common feature of the time, as we have seen.

6. *Popularization of Science Through Lectures,*
Essays and Handbooks

Popularizers of science flourished in eighteenth-century England. Peter Shaw (1694-1763) retailed public lectures on its applications; and with Francis Hawksbee he issued schemes for portable laboratories.[35] When Henry Pemberton returned from Leyden and began to lecture at Gresham College in 1730, a new spirit was abroad. Francis Peck (1692-1743) advocated during the years 1731-39 a kind of scientific sustentation fund; not the first, however, for plans to found a "Chamber of Arts" had been put forward in 1721-22.[36] Peck spoke from a county that had been vastly improved by "art," for Lincolnshire waterways and agricultural land owed much to successive generations of skilled engineers. His own researches led him to resurrect the story of the University of Stamford, a vanished fourteenth-century foundation.

Another Lincolnshire surveyor, John Landen, F.R.S., was stimulated to contribute mathematical papers to the *Ladies' Diary*, a remarkable publication which was edited by Henry Beighton, F.R.S., another surveyor and engineer, from 1713 to 1744. This made mathematics acceptable and popular for the public. Beighton was a friend and collaborator of Desaguliers (es-

---

34. N. Hans, *New Trends in Education in the Eighteenth Century* (London: Routledge, 1951), pp. 136ff.

35. F. W. Gibbs, "Peter Shaw and the Revival of Chemistry" *Annals of Science*, VII (1951), p. 211.

36. F. W. Gibbs, "Chemistry in Industry," *Annals of Science*, VIII (1952), p. 275. In the following year, 1723, certain noblemen, depressed by the low state of manufactures in Scotland and the neglect of husbandry, determined to raise the standard of skill "in those who make a profession thereby," and formed the Honourable Society of Improvers in the knowledge of Agriculture in Scotland. They met at the house of Thomas Hope of Rankeilar, for twenty-three years; unfortunately most of their members were implicated in the 1745 Rebellion so it came to an end.

pecially in the second volume of the latter's *Course in Experimental Philosophy*) and also a notable technologist; a steam engine erected by him[37] had an improved valve that, in the words of a popular lecturer of the day, "divested it of nearly all the complicated machinery which has previously been employed for that purpose."[38]

This popular lecturer was James Ferguson, F.R.S., who from 1749 began to rhapsodize over the possibilities of mechanical energy slaves. His lectures on hydraulic engines (illustrated by plates of an engine at Blenheim), mechanical powers, pile drivers, wheel carriages, air pumps, and the like were given to select audiences of from twenty to sixty people in places as widely dispersed as Bath, Norwich, Cambridge, Bristol, Liverpool, Scotland, and New-castle-on-Tyne. Ferguson was also intoxicated with the possibilities of electricity; his *Introduction* to the subject reached a third edition by 1779. He looked on an electrical machine as a challenge to experiment. His Experiment XVI was a model of a triple-pump mill (for raising the water by the force of wind) put into motion by electricity. Both Birkbeck and Brewster regarded him as the first "popular" or "elementary" writer. Brewster went further:

> . . . To his labours we must attribute that general diffusion of scientific knowledge among the practical mechanics of this country, which has in great measure banished those antiquated prejudices and erroneous means of construction that perpetually mislead the unlettered artist.[39]

7. *The Lunar Society and its Kin: Provincial Industrialists, Doctors and Amateurs of Science*

By 1764, the need for institutionalizing the exchange of technical information was being discussed outside London. In that year Richard Watson, newly appointed professor of chemistry at Cambridge, was convinced that "the improvement of metallurgy and the other metallic arts might best be made by the public establishment of an Academy." He took heart from the establishment of such institutions in Saxony and urged that "in time of peace and tranquility" such an academy should "become an object not unworthy of the attention of the King or the Legislature."[40] But his advice fell on deaf ears.

37. R. H. Thurston, *History of the Steam Engine* (London, 1878), pp. 61-63, has a portrait of it.
38. J. Ferguson, *Lectures of Select Subjects in mechanics, hydro-statics, etc.* (London, 1825), p. 166. He wrote that Henry Beighton materially improved the engine by making it self-acting.
39. Preface to an edition of Ferguson's lectures. Ferguson's lectures went to a phenomenal number of editions. Those on *Astronomy* went to 12; and *Select Subjects* to 9 and were translated into German. They were reissued by C. F. Partington, a mechanics institute lecturer in 1825. In 1760, John Wesley, issuing another edition of his *Primitive Physic*, first published in 1747 and revised in 1755, wrote "In this course of time I have likewise had occasion to collect several other Remedies . . . and one, I must aver, from personal knowledge, grounded on a thousand experiments, to be far superior to all the other medicines I have known; I mean *Electricity*. I cannot but entreat all those who are well-wishers of mankind, to make full proof of this. Certainly it comes the nearest a universal medicine, of any yet known in the world."
40. L. J. Coleby, "Richard Watson, Professor of Chemistry in the University of Cambridge," *Annals of Science*, IX (1953), p. 101.

Also in 1764, an American professor, William Small, came to England (with a letter of introduction from Benjamin Franklin) to buy instruments for the College of William and Mary in Virginia. Settling in Birmingham, he became physician to Matthew Boulton. In his quest for instruments, Small got into touch with James Watt, once an instrument maker at the University Glasgow, then working with John Roebuck (a graduate of Leyden) on a steam engine. Small introduced Boulton to Watt. He also knew others whose interests marched with his own: Erasmus Darwin (1731-1802), a physician and ancestor of Charles Darwin, whose own ideas anticipated the theory of evolution; Josiah Wedgwood (1730-1795), a potter-chemist; James Keir (1748-1820), translator of Macquer and compiler of the first chemical dictionary in England; John Whitehurst (1713-1788); William Withering (1741-1799); Thomas Day (1748-1789); and Richard Lovell Edgeworth (1744-1817).

After Small's death this group became a kind of dining club, calling themselves the Lunar Society. Reinforced by Joseph Priestley (1733-1804), the unitarian chemist; Samuel Galton (1753-1832), gun manufacturer, ornithologist and grandfather of Thomas Galton; Jonathan Stokes (1755-1831), physician and chemist; and R. A. Johnson (?-1799), they developed a kind of corporate stimulus. They were interested in most mechanical and engineering toys like clocks, balances, micrometers and dividing engines. The nearby factory of Boulton and Watt was building engines and sending mechanics out to service them, who carried their skills all over the world. Boulton himself had a chemical laboratory and knew a number of clockworkers, and in his factory entertained eminent foreigners. Of the Lunar Society itself, Dr. Schofield remarks, "it is not unreasonable to claim [it] as an informal technological research organisation. Transport, roads, wheels, steam engines, geology, chemistry: all fell within the scope of their inquiries."[41]

Other provincial societies, composed of a similar mixture of industrialists, doctors, and amateurs of science, sprang up in the last quarter of the century. At Derby a society was founded by Erasmus Darwin in 1784. "Perhaps," he wrote to a friend at Birmingham, "like the free mason societies, we may sometime make your society a visit." Though no visit is recorded, the dispatch of an air balloon was arranged. Among the members of the Derby Society was William Strutt, F.R.S., whose firm built one of the earliest iron-framed buildings in the world; the society's library included books from France and America.[42]

A third society, to which Erasmus Darwin and the sons of both Priestley and Watt were elected, was formed at Manchester in 1781. Here the moving spirit was Thomas Percival, M.D., a former student at Warrington, Edinburgh,

41. R. E. Schofield, "Membership of the Lunar Society of Birmingham," *Annals of Science* XII (1956), p. 118; and "The Industrial Orientation of Science in the Lunar Society of Birmingham," *Isis,* LXVIII (1957), p. 408.

    See also Eric Robinson, "The Lunar Society and the Improvement of Scientific Instruments," *Annals of Science* Vol. 12, 296-304 (1956) and Vol. 13, 1-8 (1957).

42. Eric Robinson, "The Derby Philosophical Society," *Annals of Science,* IX (1953), pp. 359-367.

and Leyden. It incubated in 1783 a college of science applied to the trades of the town.[43]

A fourth society was founded in 1783 at Leeds, the original home of Joseph Priestley.[44] A fifth took root at Newcastle under William Turner, a unitarian minister, and George Chalmers, the mayor, who wrote to Boulton enclosing the plans.[45]

A sixth, but short-lived, version of the Lunar Society started at Sheffield in 1805 through Samuel Lucas, who had moved from Birmingham to Sheffield in 1787 to become a partner in a refining and smelting works. Just as he was the first to import foreign smelting materials from the continent, so he seems to have brought the Birmingham spirit with him, for in 1791 he had taken out the first of a series of patents for making cast steel and malleable iron. He acted in 1805 as president of the Sheffield Society for the Promotion of Useful Knowledge. Lucas also corresponded with John Dalton, a member of the Manchester Literary and Philosophical Society.[46]

8. Experimental Farm and Pneumatic Institute

Both Priestley and Wedgwood were also interested in establishing research institutes: Priestley[47] for the investigation of electricity, Wedgwood[48] for the pottery industry. Neither got beyond the project stage but two others did, both in the west country.

The first was an experimental farm at Weston; the first of its kind in England, it was established in 1779 on the farm of a Mr. Bethell by Edmund Rack and the Bath and West Society. This farm was praised by the great agricultural publicist Arthur Young. The Bath and West Society had been formed by Edmund Rack two years earlier as a society to reward "the diligent and ingenious who have excelled in the departments of husbandry, in useful manufactures, and in the most famous specimens of art." It had been formed at a meeting on September 8, 1777, at York House, Bath, attended by representatives from Bath, Bristol, and the counties of Somerset, Wiltshire, Gloucestershire and Dorset. Rack as secretary was greatly assisted by Dr. Falconer, F.R.S., an ardent believer that the society "should diffuse the knowledge it rewards."[49]

The second was the Pneumatic Institute established by Thomas Lovell Beddoes (1760-1808) at Bristol. This deserves more attention than it has hitherto received, for it owed much to the Lunar Society as well as to con-

43. W. H. Brindley, "The Manchester Literary and Philosophical Society," *Journal of the Royal Institute of Chemistry*, LXXIX (1955), p. 62.

44. A. N. Clow, *The Chemical Revolution* (London: Batchworth, 1952), p. 614.

45. *Ibid.*, p. 304.

46. R. E. Wilson, *Two Hundred Precious Metal Years: A History of the Sheffield Smelting Company* (London, 1950).

47. Rollo Appleyard, *The Institution of Electrical Engineers* (London: The Institution, 1939).

48. R. E. Schofield, "Josiah Wedgwood and a Proposed Eighteenth Century Industrial Research Organisation" *Isis*, XLVII (1956), p. 16ff.

49. J. A. Scott-Watson and M. A. Hobbs, *Great Farmers* (London: Faber, 1951), pp. 273-280.

tinental advances. Thomas Beddoes, Edgeworth's son-in-law, was an able linguist. Born in Staffordshire, then a cradle of industrial innovation, he derived constant stimulus from the exploitation of Nature's pantry. Beddoes became a reader in chemistry at Oxford, and his lectures (according to his later associate and biographer J. E. Stock) attracted a greater audience for chemistry than had been known before. Here he was assisted by John Sadler, a well-known aeronaut. The connection between balloons and chemistry was close at that time, and the lifting power of hydrogen trapped in a glazed envelope had been suggested by Joseph Black of Edinburgh, who taught Beddoes his chemistry.

With gas-producing machines supplied by James Watt of Birmingham, £1000 from Josiah Wedgwood of Etruria, and technical assistance from James Sadler, Beddoes opened the Pneumatic Institute in 1798, intending to expose hypochondriacs, opium addicts, the scrofulous, the asthmatic, and the catarrhal to his "factitious airs" and so cure them.

George Watt, then employed as a representative of the firm of Boulton and Watt in Cornwall, recommended to Beddoes the son of a lady with whom he was lodging. When to Watt's recommendation was added that of Beddoes' friend Davies Giddy (later Sir Davies Gilbert, F.R.S.), the young man was taken on as an assistant. This young man, who showed his worth by an essay in Beddoes' *Contributions to Medical and Physical Knowledge from the West of England* (1799), was Humphrey Davy (1778-1829). It was at the Pneumatic Institute in 1799 that Davy discovered the properties of nitrous oxide. Davy also got to know James Keir (F.R.S.), who had originally wanted Beddoes to work with him.[50]

9. Noble Patrons of Research

The real research institutes of those days were the noble patrons. Perhaps the most distinguished of these was the millionaire Henry Cavendish (1731-1810), who for a time had as his private secretary an army physician, Charles Blagden (1748-1820), later secretary of the Royal Society, who Dr. Johnson thought was "a delightful fellow." Cavendish sustained a large library at Clapham, allowing his friends free access to it.[51]

Affluent men of science like Sir Joseph Banks and William Hunter also supported other scientists. In Soho Square the magnificent herbarium and library of Sir Joseph Banks was tended successively by D. C. Solander (1736-1782), J. Drysander (1748-1810), and Robert Brown (1773-1858); the first was a pioneer with Captain Cook, the second a notable cataloguer, and the third probably the greatest of British botanists. Similarly the museum of the great anatomist William Hunter in Great Windmill Street, probably the

50. J. E. Stock, *Thomas Lovell Beddoes* (London, 1871).
51. A. J. Berry, *Henry Cavendish* (London: Hutchinson, 1960).

finest in Europe, offered a haven to T. P. Yates, who looked after the insects; G. Fordyce, who looked after the minerals; and Charles Combe, who catalogued the coins.[52]

Another nobleman, the Earl of Shelburne, engaged Joseph Priestley as his librarian or literary companion in 1772, giving him a house at Calne in Wiltshire and an income of £250 a year plus £40 more for scientific experiments. After five years his friends, through the Quaker doctor John Fothergill, contributed another £40 to sustain him. By 1780 the Earl wanted to transfer Priestley to Ireland, but he preferred to go to Birmingham where others, including Samuel Galton, made themselves responsible for his welfare.[53]

Priestley was accused in 1775 by Bryan Higgins, a medical doctor of Lyden, of plagiarizing his experiments. Priestley replied by accusing Higgins of being "an empiric." Higgins went on to promote a cement of his own invention, which was noticed in Italy by C. Amoretti and P. Soave, and also in Russia, where the Empress invited him to lecture. On his return he plunged into a scheme for improving the manufacture of sugar and rum. Convinced of the importance of applying chemistry to life, Higgins then (1793) formed a Society for Philosophical Experiments and Conversations. It met weekly and comprised some fifty people, including Earl Stanhope and Dr. Pitcairn. The "didactic experimenter" was Higgins himself, helped by three "assistant experimenters." They studied Kier's edition of Lavoisier.

To Priestley himself a number of other science lecturers were indebted. Adam Walker (1731?-1821) a self-taught mechanical engineer who built an "eidouranion," or transparent orrery, was persuaded by Priestley to take a house in George Street, Hanover Square, where in the wintertime he lectured to audiences; in the summer he constructed water-raising engines, wind and steam carriages, ploughs, and rotating lights to be used in lighthouses off the Scilly Isles. Walker's practical genius, displayed also in ventilating houses and improving harpsichords, coupled with his gifts of exposition, led to his being invited by the provost of Eton and the headmasters of Westminster and Winchester to lecture at their schools. In this role he was succeeded by his son Deane Franklin Walker (1778-1865). Walker, when he saw the Paris military school, remarked, "The young men are dressed much like those in our Military Academy, but seem more numerous . . . ours are brought up amid cannon, mortars and bullets . . . the French in a superb mansion surrounded by fine walks, even military matters smell of frankincense and Popery here."[54]

Many of these lecturers, such as Henry Moyes, had transatlantic as well as provincial contacts. He was a friend of Benjamin Rush, knew of Volta's work on electricity, and moved easily in the various provincial groups which

52. H. C. Cameron, *Sir Joseph Banks* (London, 1952).

53. A. Holt, *A Life of Joseph Priestley* (Oxford: Oxford University Press, 1931).

54. A. Walker, *Travelling Remarks Written on the Spot in an Excursion to Páris* (London, 1785).

sprang up in the midlands and north of England.[55] Priestley's migration there indicates how powerful such provincial organizations were becoming.

10. Patronage and University-Supported Research in Scotland

In Scotland patronage and university-sustained science went together. While a student in Edinburgh, Thomas Percival, M.D., of Manchester, attended, a weekly *conversazione* at James Hope's Linlithgow home. On his return to Manchester in 1767, he instituted weekly meetings at his King Street home—the probable origin of the Literary and Philosophical Society. Edinburgh was the center of a brilliant group—geologists, chemists, economists, and engineers, like Hutton, Joseph Black, Adam Smith, and John Robinson. The spirit of those men was caught up in the work of Joseph Black, professor of anatomy and lecturer in chemistry first at Glasgow, then at Edinburgh. His establishment of the doctrine of latent and specific heat was materially to assist James Watt in the improvement of the steam engine. After Black's migration to Edinburgh in 1766 (when he left his post in anatomy), he created a school of chemistry that affected not only England but America as well. One of his earliest pupils there was Benjamin Rush (1745-1813), who later held the first American chair of chemistry, established at the University of Pennsylvania in 1769. It was through the influence of Rush that James Woodhouse founded the first chemical society in America, at Philadelphia in 1792.

Black caught up not only the "English" chemistry of Shaw, Lewis and Thompson, but also that of Macquer, Lavoisier and the French school. This heady brew was in turn retransmitted into the English nonconformist academies. (*Brew* is certainly an uncomfortable and uncomplimentary term for Black's lectures, which were never fossilized in print, but always renovated and reinvigorated by whatever current advances were made in chemical theory.) So attractive and authoritative were the lectures given during Black's thirty-three years in the chair in Edinburgh that the students took them down in delight.[56]

11. Dissenters' Academies and the Marriage of Science and Industry

Scottish universities profited from the presence of English dissenters who were excluded from the universities of Oxford and Cambridge in 1661 by the Act of Uniformity. When these dissenters returned to England they often taught in academies of their own. The obscure academy at Carmarthen (Wales), founded in 1668 by the Congregationalists, was studying in 1764,

55. J. A. Harrison, "Blind Henry Moyes, An Excellent Lecturer in Philosophy," *Annals of Science*, XIII (1957), p. 109.

56. T. Kent (ed.), *An Eighteenth Century Lectureship in Chemistry* (London: Jackson, 1950)

among other works, those of Keil, Musschenbroeck, and Fergusson.[57] It possessed an orrery, mathematical instruments, an electrical machine, and a set of artificial magnets. It lasted till 1820, as did the Bristol Baptist Academy founded some twelve years later. This also had "an Electrifying Machine," a horseshoe magnet, Fergusson's optical cards, a microscope, and "a square tin vessel for electrical experiments."[58] Perhaps the best known of all was Warrington Academy (1757-1786) where Joseph Priestley was a tutor from 1762-1767, writing his *History of Electricity* and conducting the experiments that led to his election to the Royal Society. Here experiments were performed, lectures in chemistry and medicine were given, and one of the tutors invented and made apparatus for the most notable academy of all, Hackney.[59]

From these academies came many of those who were to marry science and industry; men like John Roebuck, whose activities as a gun founder and chemical engineer were strengthened by training at an academy at Northampton before his university course at Edinburgh and Leyden.

Other dissenting teachers were busy popularizing the *Philosophical Transactions;* John Eames (F.R.S.), a tutor in the Moorfields Academy, with John Martyn (F.R.S.), published an abridged version of them in 1732. The Rev. Abraham Rees (F.R.S.), who taught Hebrew and mathematics at Hoxton and Hackney Dissenting Academies, not only re-edited *Chamber's Encyclopaedia* (1786), but between 1802 and 1820 produced a 45-volume *New Cyclopaedia,* a magnificently illustrated synthesis of science and technology up to that time.

It was the dissenters who in 1808 began to move for a university in London. This was to find its most redoubtable promoter in Henry Brougham, in whom Scottish zest and English nonconformity found a political mouthpiece. His *Objects, Advantages and Pleasures of Science* (1826) heralded a new age.[60]

By this time the British economy had reached "take-off." Education was appreciated not only as a means of boosting economic growth, but also as a way of alleviating the miseries brought in its train.[61]

CONCLUSION

The vigor of noninstitutional educational life was stimulated by the price rise, which drove many curates to teach in order to augment an income

57. H. MacLachlan, *English Education Under the Test Acts* (Manchester: Manchester University Press, 1931), p. 54.

58. *Ibid.,* p. 101.

59. *Ibid.,* p. 54.

60. The establishment of a University of London in 1826 provided an umbrella under which a number of institutions could shelter. The story of the increasing involvement of these Universities with the Government and of their contribution to industrial growth can be seen in *Civic Universities,* Some Aspects of a British Tradition by W. H. G. Armytage (London: Benn, 1955).

61. Chester New, *Life of Lord Brougham to 1830* (Oxford: Oxford University Press, 1961).

that would barely keep them single, much less married, and also prevented many grammar schools tied to founders' statutes from expanding their facilities to include modern subjects. But the great stimulus to noninstitutional, easy two-way flow between education and society was the general attitude, best expressed perhaps by John Locke's statement that man has "a title to perfect freedom and uncontrolled enjoyment of all the rights and privileges of the law of nature." As one recent writer has put it, "Eighteenth-century authors . . . along with their readers, were able to accept the idea of natural rights all the more readily because of the generous faith in human nature which they on the whole and for most of the time possessed. This faith, in the writings of Priestley and Godwin, was ultimately to reach the highest pitch of human optimism that modern non-Marxist thought has known."[62]

The structure of society favored this too. Politics was for gentlemen; the government was disinclined to intervene in any matter. When they did, it was in wartime, and then only to lop off restrictions on teaching in schools by nonconformists (as in 1779) or Roman Catholics (as in 1791).

Above all, there was an experimental attitude about the whole of eighteenth-century life that led its great ideologist Dr. Johnson to exclaim: "The age is running mad after innovation; all the business of the world is to be done in a new way; men are to be hanged in a new way; Tyburn itself is not safe from the fury of innovation."[63]

And innovation was what characterized the "take-off," especially after 1760. Agriculture and industrial innovations reacted on each other and multiplied. Enclosures, improved communications, and the rise of factories all sprang from the increasing use of coal; and all demanded a certain amount of skill. The problem was not so much to diffuse this skill as to get the workers in the factories to conform to routine; and it is noticeable that the first schools in the industrial England of the nineteenth century utilized the factory technique in their teaching, through the monitorial system. As Sir Thomas Bernard, one of the founders of the Society for Bettering the Condition of the Poor, described the monitorial system: "As the division of labour applied to intellectual purposes . . . the principle in schools and manufactories is the same."

Consequently, while England was involved in the war with France that, with few intermissions, lasted from 1792 to 1817, she was able to learn still further from a country which, in the Ecole Polytechnique, had established the first state hatchery for scientists. By then the first industrial change had reached the point of take-off. Exports had increased from 8.5 million in 1730 to 40.8 million in 1800; iron output had increased from 25,000 tons in 1730 to more than 100,000 tons by 1800.

There were two psychological drives: the drive for luxury, which began

62. A. J. Youngson, *Possibilities of Economic Progress* (Cambridge: Cambridge University Press, 1959), pp. 107-108.
63. T. S. Ashton, *The Industrial Revolution* (Oxford: Oxford University Press, 1948), p. 11.

to be increasingly justified by writers from Mandeville to Hume,[64] and the almost fanatical drive for mastery of the sea—"a strange phrenzy," wrote a contemporary, "which has infected the whole English nation."[65] As Professor Youngson has wisely observed, this "strange phrenzy" had a decidedly useful aspect, in providing the country with new ideas, extensive prospects and the hope as well as the real possibility of ambitious undertakings.[66]

64. A. W. Coats, "Changing Attitudes to Labour in the Mid-Eighteenth Century," *Economic History Review*, XI (1948-9), pp. 35-51.
65. Josiah Tucker, *Reflections on the Present Matters on Dispute Between Great Britain and Ireland* (London, 1785), pp. 2-3.
66. Youngson, *op. cit.*, p. 140.

CHAPTER 21

PORTENTS OF MODERNITY AND THE MEIJI EMERGENCE

Herbert Passin

I. INTRODUCTION

Educational Growth

One of the difficulties of cross-cultural study is knowing just what to compare with what. Are we comparing two total cultural-historical entities in their entire trajectory, or are we comparing selected time points? If we want to see what Japanese experience can tell us about the problems of contemporary underdeveloped countries, then we must obviously compare them at roughly comparable points of development. Japan of 1964 is as different from Africa of 1964 as the United States and Western Europe are. She can provide models, techniques, expert help, and educational materials, but her experience is too different to provide a direct model. In 1964 she had universal literacy, a fully-developed modern school system, and almost 7 college students per 1,000 population. By contrast, a new African state would be struggling to establish an elementary school system and perhaps a specialized high-level university for the training of technicians and administrators, in the face of near-universal illiteracy and economic stagnation.

How Japan reached her present point may be relevant, but to see how this is so, we must look to the Japan of a similar stage of development. This would be approximately the period from 1855 to 1912, that is, from thirteen years preceding the "opening" of the country until the end of the Meiji period (1868-1912). In these fifty-odd years, Japan does what the contemporary underdeveloped countries are hoping to do: she moves from her pre-industrial, agrarian, feudal past to modern industrial nationhood. By the end of the Meiji period, all the principal institutions of modern society are well established, virtually the entire population has attained functional literacy, and compulsory school attendance is as close to 100 per cent as it can be.

The record is a remarkable one. Effective universal compulsory attendance was achieved within about thirty years of the beginning of the modern school system, and near-universal literacy (with the exception of oldsters) within another twenty. But what was spectacular by the standards of the late nineteenth and early twentieth century may appear plodding by those of the

TABLE 1

Elementary School Attendance Rates for Selected Years°

Year	Percentage (Boys and Girls Together)
1873	28.13
1878	41.26
1880	41.06
1883	51.03
1887	45.00
1891	50.31
1892	55.14

° Calculated from Mombusho, *Gakusei 80-nen-shi (80 Years of the School System)*, (Tokyo, 1954), Table 1, pp. 36-37.

more exigent mid-twentieth. Our contemporary nation-builders·may not be content, perhaps rightly, to settle for a pace of development that takes thirty to fifty years for fruition, that is, from one to two generations. Seen macroscopically, the smoothed-out long-range curves seem to advance relentlessly in an unbroken sweep. But the ant's-eye view, toiling laboriously up and down the short-term curves, may be closer to present realities. Thirty years after the Meiji Restoration, Japan still had only one university; and even by 1904, when there were two, together they had produced only some 5,000 graduates.[1] For a nation that then numbered about 45,000,000, the figure is somewhat less impressive. The rate of production of higher school graduates did go up rapidly. In the period from 1912 to 1925, there were 42,654 university graduates and 240,357 college graduates (total, 283,011); and from 1926 to 1939 there were 159,839 university graduates and 470,271 college graduates (total, 630,110).[2] But the first thirty years, indeed the first fifty years, which constitute the effective life of any "present" generation, must have seemed slow indeed.

In the same way, although the smoothed curve of elementary school attendance is a dramatic upward one, the raw curve shows some serious dips, which were as wrenching to the spirits of the Meiji nation-builders as present difficulties are to contemporary ones (see Table 1). As Table 1 shows, it was only twenty years after the promulgation of the modern school system in 1872 that the curve of elementary school attendance took an unwaveringly upward bearing. Whether 50 per cent school attendance after twenty years of effort is a good record or not is perhaps the old question of the half-filled jug—for some, it is half full; for others, it is half empty.

1. Alfred Stead (ed.), *Japanese by the Japanese. A Survey by Its Highest Authorities* (London: William Heinemann, 1904), p. 238.
2. Calculated from materials in Ministry of Education (Research Section, Research Bureau), *Demand and Supply for University Graduates—Japan* (Tokyo, August 1958), Appendix, pp. 64-69.

Japan as a Model

Another possible limitation on the pedagogical usefulness of Japan's experience is that her modern career started from a remarkably high point. Japan of 1850 was already a society showing every disposition and readiness for a modern transformation. In Bertrand Russell's apt definition, she was an "economically but not culturally backward" country.[3] She was a highly centralized national state, with most of her "national" problems well behind her. Her population was ethically homogeneous, acknowledging the same systems of authority, sharing a common religious and ethical outlook. She had the incalculable advantage of a unified national language (in spite of dialectical variations) that proved capable of modern development. By contrast with many other underdeveloped countries, she was therefore very quickly able to carry on her educational system in her own language. Japan in the middle of the nineteenth century was a country with a long tradition of secular literature and speculative philosophy, a well-developed script, and a differentiated intellectual class. The considerable literacy, particularly of her upper classes and urban population, provided substantial audiences for writers and artists.

By the Genroku period (1688-1704) a surprisingly "modern" publishing industry had developed, characterized by large commercial publishing houses and professional writers and book illustrators. Books were often published in editions of 10,000 copies to satisfy the audiences created by the spread of literacy and the cultural efflorescence of the cities. There were even commercial lending libraries to distribute books to larger audiences.

All of this reflects a relatively high literacy rate for a pre-modern nation and some institutional arrangement whereby this literacy was produced. In 1868, from which date we usually count the art of Japan's "modernization," there were already something on the order of 17,000 schools of all kinds, ranging from Confucian "colleges" (the iron frame of Tokugawa orthodoxy) to "parishioners' schools" (*terakoya*) for the commoners. When the modern school system began to be put into effect, from 1872, much of this had to be scrapped. But what is equally important is that much of it proved to be salvageable. Hundreds, if not thousands of the older schools served as component units of the new school system, particularly during the transition period. Before the new normal schools started to turn out enough teachers with modern training, the *terakoya* teachers filled much of the gap.

Japan did not therefore begain a modern school system entirely from scratch. The concept of formal education, if not of a school system itself, was already part of the intellectual climate of late pre-modern Japan, and millions of people had experienced some kind of schooling.

It will be useful, therefore, for understanding the early developments in modern education, to look briefly at the system of education that prevailed toward the end of the Tokugawa period.

3. Bertrand Russell, *The Problem of China* (London, 1922).

II. TOKUGAWA EDUCATION

School Attendance

Unfortunately there are no definitive data available on school attendance before the Meiji period. By the end of the Tokugawa period, it would be fair to say that practically all of the children of the samurai class (and of the traditional court nobility, which was very small in number) attended some kind of school for some period of time. Private tutoring at home was also fairly common. For commoner attendance, ingenious calculations by Ototake[4] suggest that an average figure of 40 to 50 per cent would not be far wrong. However, the variation by urban-rural residence, relative affluence, and rank appears to have been considerable. All-in-all it appears that attendance actually dropped between 1867 and 1873, the first year of the "modern school system."

In the city of Edo (Tokyo), for example, common school attendance in the period 1848-1860 was about 86 per cent.[5] "It would not be wrong to think that above the level of petty shopkeepers, practically all children in Edo went to the *terakoya*."[6] Similar high figures seem likely in the other great metropolitan centers, Kyoto and Osaka. While we have no exact indications for Osaka, it is quite clear that this center of merchant culture valued education highly. It was at least sufficiently widespread among commoners that toward the end of the Tokugawa period, it spilled over into schools for outcastes both in Osaka and in Edo.[7] Ototake found that virtually all reports of "practically complete attendance" were from the great metropolitan centers, the castle towns (which were the headquarters of the domain lords [*daimyō*], post towns on the great administrative circuits, and port towns.[8] In other words, it was in the more "advanced" urban aggregates, the centers of administration, culture, commerce, and publishing, that school attendance achieved its highest ratios before 1868.

As against these impressive urban rates, however, there were many isolated rural areas where practically no children attended school. If the advanced centers of the *Kantō* (Tokyo area) and *Kinki* (the area including Kyoto and Osaka) could boast of a majority of children attending some kind of school, the backward Northeast (the *Tōhoku*, which remains relatively "backward" even today), and the southern island of Kyūshū probably had, at

4. Ototake Iwazō, *Nihon Shomin Kyoiku-shi (A History of the Education of the Common People in Japan)*, (Tokyo, 1929), Vol. 6, Ch. 2, pp. 926-946. Between 1915 and 1917, Ototake held detailed interviews with somewhat over 3,000 "oldsters," whose schooling age had come before the Meiji period, mainly in the years 1848-1867. On this basis he was able to reconstruct statistically many aspects of pre-Meiji schooling. Although the method raises many questions, Ototake himself was not unaware of them, and he handled his materials with great circumspection.

5. Kaigō Tokiomi and Hiro'oka Torazō (ed.), *Kindai Kyōiku-shi (History of Modern Education)*, (Tokyo, 1951), p. 317. Ototake's estimate is slightly lower—70 to 80 per cent (*op. cit.*, V. 4, Ch. 5, Section 2; also V. 6, Ch. 2, p. 935.).

6. Kaigō and Hiro'oka, *op. cit.*, p. 318.

7. Ototake, *op. cit.*, V. 6, Ch. 2, p. 944.

8. *Ibid.*, p. 935.

best, about 25 per cent of their children in schools.[9] In Okinawa, apart from two or three areas, there was virtually no education available for commoners.[10] However, rural villages in the advanced areas of the country often showed urban rates of attendance. An analysis of school records in a mountain village near Kyoto yielded an attendance ratio of 56 per cent for boys and 15 per cent for girls.[11]

The rural-urban difference was perhaps even more striking in the case of female attendance. The Confucian conception of the role of women tended to keep them out of the schools and in the homes. "It is well," said Matsudaira Sadanobu, the Shogunal Chancellor from 1786 to 1793, "that women should be unlettered. To cultivate women's skills would be harmful. They have no need of learning. It is enough if they can read books in *kana* [the Japanese syllabary as distinct from the more difficult Chinese characters]. Let it be that way."[12] Among the samurai, therefore, the girls were usually tutored at home. Although we do not have the details, it is quite clear from the literature of the period that samurai women were not only literate but often cultivated. But among the commoners we find only small proportions of girls actually attending school in the more conservative areas of the country. In the great metropolitan centers, however, female attendance in the immediate pre-Meiji period was very little below that of boys. During 1860-1864 in Edo, they may very well have outnumbered the boys.[13] But this applied only to the great cities. When we descend to the next urban level, of castle and post towns, girls are a very small minority. If we accept K. Ishikawa's estimate that average attendance for girls during this period was about 39 per cent of that of boys, the range would appear to be from 42 per cent in the *Kantō* area to 5 per cent in the backward *Tōhoku*.[14] In Okinawa, neither samurai nor commoner women attended school.[15]

It is equally clear, if perhaps more difficult to document statistically, that relative affluence was an important differentiating element in school attendance. In the rural areas, affluence and rank were very closely associated. The villages of the late Tokugawa period were relatively autonomous; as long as they performed their public obligations, paid their taxes, and maintained law and order, they were free to organize their internal affairs under their traditional leaders. But village administration required a high degree of literacy — records had to be kept, taxes and assessments made, and instructions from higher authorities properly understood, interpreted to the people,

9. *Ibid.*, pp. 930, 932.

10. *Ibid.*, p. 938.

11. Kaigō and Hiro'oka, *op. cit.*, pp. 317-321.

12. Quoted from Karasawa Tomitarō, *Kyōshi no Rekishi (History of Teachers)*, Tokyo, 1956), p. 105.

13. Uchiyama, Kumaya, Masuda, *Kinsei Nihon Kyōiku Bunka-shi (History of Early Modern Education in Japan)*, (Tokyo, 1961), Table 9, p. 79.

14. Ishikawa Ken. *Nihon Shomin Kyōiku-shi (History of the Education of the Common People in Japan)*, (Tokyo, 1929).

15. Ototake, *op. cit.*, p. 938.

and carried out. Literacy was therefore very common among the upper rural classes from whom these traditional leaders—*shōya, toshiyori, kumigashira,* etc.—were drawn. Not only was their own motivation sufficiently high to impel them to organize education for their children, but many of the more enlightened lords and shogunal authorities encouraged it. We find, therefore, that children of upper-class rural families constituted the majority of those attending the various kinds of village schools.

Literacy

If we can assume that schooling equals literacy, then we have here the basis for some estimate of the extent of literacy in pre-modern Japan. Again, between 40 and 50 per cent male literacy would not appear unreasonable. Even if we cannot assume a straight-line correlation, we do know that the need for literacy was very widespread, and that this need was increasingly fulfilled in some manner or other. The samurai, as the administrative class, required a high level of literacy and education for the work of governing. For the merchant and higher artisan classes of the city, the need was equally great, even if it was not for the same kind of education. Merchants might not need Chinese poetry and Confucian classics—"Learning was the ruination of the family . . .", the young man is told in an eighteenth-century novel, "put away your reading and pick up your account book.[16] But they did need arithmetic, accounting, and letter-writing. "The art of poetry," according to the *Treasure House of Japan,* "is for the nobles; the way of the bow and the horse for the samurai. But for the merchants, there is the way of arithmetic and the account-book."[17] But the account-book, too, requires education and literacy, and this kind, at least, the urban merchant classes had in ample measure.

In the rural areas, it was not only the village official class that required literacy. Ordinary villagers, down to a rather low level, had some need of it. A peasant who could read the document he was required to seal, or the order he was called upon to obey, had an obvious advantage. Tokugawa local administration placed a premium on literacy in other ways. Its lowest unit was the *gonin-gumi,* or five-household group, which was collectively responsible for obedience to orders from above. Each group had its leader, who was required to see that every householder under his charge was fully aware of instructions and information passed down from above. This he achieved by circulating a notice-board, which assumed literacy on the part of the subordinate households, or by personally reading them the contents. The tradition of encouraging the ability to read the *gonin-gumi* Register had already been started by the Shogun Yoshimune in 1723. Thus, at the very least, the head of one of the five households in the *gonin-gumi* had to be literate.

16. Ejima Kiseki, *Seken Musuko Kishitsu (Characters of Worldly Young Men),* V. 5, Story 5. First published in 1715.
17. Ibara Saikaku, *Nihon Eitaiqura* (Tokyo: Iwanami Bunko), V. 5, p. 90. First published in 1688.

All of this, however, is a development of the latter half of the Tokugawa era, from, let us say, about the beginning of the eighteenth century. The need, as well as the response to it, was cumulative, resulting from the increasing complexity of administration, the growth of bureaucracy, and the development of commerce and industry. At the beginning of the seventeenth century, it is very unlikely that the majority of even the samurai class was literate. But in the peaceful society that developed after the victory of the Tokugawa, the word and the document became more important instruments of rule than the sword.

Official Encouragement of Learning

In 1615, as part of the settlement that ended the civil wars that had wracked Japan for almost a century, Tokugawa Ieyasu, the founder of the Tokugawa regime, issued a set of instructions for the regulation of the military houses (Buke Shohatto). Article 1 called upon the samurai to devote themselves both to learning, which he placed in the first position, and to the military arts. The injunction was piously repeated over the succeeding centuries by later shoguns, and then echoed on down by leading daimyō to their own retainers. In 1629, Shogun Iemitsu reiterated the injunction in his own revised instructions to the warrior class: "learning on the left, and arms on the right." In 1622, Shogun Ietsuna ordered that samurai "always be concerned with learning and arms." Shoguns Ienobu in 1710 and Yoshimune in 1716 again repeated the same sentiments. "The bushi [samurai]," said the Budō Shoshin-shū,[18] "stands above the three classes [of commoners]. In order to fulfill his vocation of managing affairs, he pursues Learning and he discriminates the Reason of things. . . ." It is therefore "impermissible that a bushi, whose duty it is to govern, should be unlettered and ignorant."

If Ieyasu meant by "learning" little more than the acquisition of the Confucian virtues needed for proper governance of the state, the consequences in the long run far exceeded anything he could have imagined in 1615. As an earnest of their intentions, the Tokugawa supported the establishment in 1630 of a Confucian academy, the Shōheikō, under the hereditary direction of the Hayashi family.[19] This was followed by other Shogunal institutions, and quickly became the model for Confucian schools for the samurai in the feudal domains.

Educational institutions, and with them literacy, expanded slowly throughout the seventeenth century. But from the end of the eighteenth century, growth was rapid in all types of schools, as shown in Table 2.[20] Be-

18. A compilation of moral instructions on the "way of the warrior," published in 1834.

19. For an account of the development of Confucian education, see John W. Hall, "The Confucian Teacher in Japan.," in D. S. Niveson and A. F. Wright (eds.), Confucianism in Action (Stanford: Stanford University Press, 1959).

20. These figures are used for narrative consistency. However, I estimate higher values. See the appendix on Tokugawa educational statistics in my Society and Education in Japan (New York: Columbia University, Teachers' College, 1964). In his later work, Kinsei no Gakkō (The School in the Early Modern Period), published in 1958, Ishikawa also gives a somewhat different

TABLE 2
Number of New Schools of Various Types,
by Period of Establishment

| Period | Domain Schools° | Local Schools (Gōgaku) | | | Terakoya‡ |
		For Commoners†	Samurai and Commoners†	Total†	
1661-1687	6				
1688-1715	8				
1716-1750	17				
1751-1788	49	7	47	54	558
1789-1829	89	26	42	68	3,050
1830-1867	50	78	44	122	6,691
1868-1872	32	304	18	322	1,003
Date unknown	3	1	1	2	
Evidence not conclusive	23				
Total	277	416	152	568	11,302

° From Ishikawa Ken, Kinsei no Gakkō (The School of the Early Modern Period), (Tokyo: Kōriku-sha, 1957), p. 264.

† Ibid., pp. 267-268.

‡ From Ishikawa Ken:[20] Nihon Shomin Kyōiku-shi (History of the Education of the Common People in Japan), (Tokyo, 1929), pp. 121-122. The years covered in this column are slightly different from the others: from top to bottom, in order: Before 1803; 1804-1843; 1844-1867; after 1868.

tween 1781 and 1871, some 200 of the 277 domain schools were established. Commoner education started later, but snowballed even more spectacularly. Of the 416 gogaku (local schools) for commoners in 1872, 7 had been established before 1789, 104 between 1789 and 1867, and 305 in the five years before the establishment of the modern school system. Of the lower-level commoners' schools, the terakoya, 558 were established before 1803; then another 3,050 between 1803 and 1843; and 6,691 more between 1844 and 1867.

III. THE SCHOOL SYSTEM

It will be useful to keep three considerations in mind as we pursue our account of the Tokugawa educational system. First, Tokugawa Japan (1603-1867) was neither a fully national state nor a completely decentralized feudalism, but rather a combination. Over time the balance gradually shifted in the direction of greater centralized control. The feudal wars of the sixteenth century had ended with the Tokugawa House in substantial overlordship of the country. They ruled as Shogun (or "generalissimo") in the name of the Emperor. The Shogun's government, called the Bakufu, or "tent government"

set of figures: 254 domain schools, and 23 domains about which no information was available. (See table on p. 264).

(referring to its military origin), was both the national government, to the extent that there was one, and the administrator of the domains under the direct rule of the Tokugawa House. These domains accounted for about 40 per cent of the land area of the country. The remaining 60 per cent were under the authority of their own feudal lords, the *daimyō*, subject, however, to the overriding authority of the Shogun.[21] These relatively autonomous provinces, of which there were on the average about 280 during the Tokugawa period, were called *han* (referred to here as "domain," "province," or "fief").

Second, the situation of the later part of the era, the *Bakumatsu* (to use the Japanese term), was very different from that of the earlier period. From the end of the eighteenth century, Japan was becoming increasingly aware of the West, and increasingly restive about it. Disastrous economic problems that led to a series of reforms in the 1840's were soon followed by the new problems of Western pressure brought on by the arrival of Commodore Perry. The 14 years between Perry's arrival and the overthrow of the Shogunate were years of constant political turmoil and intellectual ferment, as Japan sought some mode of accommodation to the Western presence. The rapid final spurt of educational development came in this period.

Third, the underlying conception of Tokugawa education was essentially a class one. Higher education was required by the samurai to maintain their position and efficiency as the governing class. It was therefore officially supported and carefully watched. For the common people, however, an education suitable to rulers was inappropriate. Although commoner education was not prohibited, neither did it receive much patronage or official interest. Only towards the end of the era did it become an important subject of concern to the higher authorities. Yet although the class separation was very strict, it was not absolute. By the end of the era, there was a very considerable mixing.

1. Education for the Nobility

Before the Tokugawa period, when the military classes rose to dominance, learning and the genteel arts had been virtually a monopoly of the court nobility and the priesthood. With the new regime, however, the traditional nobility fell on rather hard times. Few in number, and with practically no political influence, their life was an anachronistic echo of their Heian period heyday (794-1192). In the 1840's, an officially sponsored school for the children of the court nobility, the *Gakūshuin*, was established in Kyoto. Here Confucian studies were taught to members of the court nobility between the ages of 15 and 40. They developed a momentary importance in the Bakumatsu period because "Imperial Restoration" had become one of the main slogans of the movement to overthrow the Shogunate. The *Gakū-*

---

21. The Shogun held as direct lands (*chokkatsuchi*) 30 per cent; branch families of the Tokugawa House another 10 per cent; hereditarily allied lords (*fudai*), 20 per cent; and non-allied, or "outer," lords (*tozama*) 40 per cent.

shuin was the first institution of higher education reopened by the Meiji
government (March, 1868) during the confusion of the Restoration.

2. *Education for the Samurai*

Shogunal Schools. The establishment of the Shōheikō in 1630
may be taken as a convenient date for the start of officially sponsored education for the governing classes. This became the supreme institution of
Confucian orthodoxy and was extremely influential in both the domain and
the private Confucian academies that grew up later. At one time, for example,
of 657 chairs in domain schools, 242 were held by Shōheikō graduates.[22]
The Shōheikō was founded on the Chu Hsi version of Confucianism, which
became official Tokugawa doctrine; in 1790, it was formally forbidden to
teach other doctrines. Although established only for samurai retainers of
the Shogunate, eventually it was allowed to register commoners, on a low
priority basis, who intended to enter scholarly professions.

By the end of the era, there were some 27 Shogunal schools for samurai,
many of them among the most important in the country. Children of the
Shogun's bannermen *(hatamoto)* and of the Tokugawa domain samurai were
required to attend school between the ages of 8 and 15; beyond that, further
education depended on their status and personal aspirations. They had,
however, a wide range of Shogunal institutions to choose from. Nor were all
of them orthodox Confucian in character; the Shogunate took the leadership in the development of certain kinds of Western studies. Some Japanese
scholars argue that the Shogunate's purpose was to defang these potentially
subversive fields of learning by bringing them under official control and to
monopolize their practical benefits. As long as they confined themselves to
practical matters — medicine, gunnery, industry, cartography — and did not
stray onto the fields reserved for orthodoxy, they were acceptable. In any
event, whatever the complex of motives may have been, in 1740 Shogun
Yoshimune ordered two of his retainers to study the Dutch language under
Dutch teachers, and this set the official seal of approval on what had until
then been the preserve of medical men or of philosophical dissidents.

In 1756 a Western medical college that later formed the nucleus of the
Tokyo University Medical School was established. As early as 1811 the
Bansho Wage Goyō (Office for the Translation of Barbarian [Western]
Writings) was established; it was a forerunner of the later and far more important *Bansho Torishirabedokoro* (Institute for the Investigation of Barbarian Writings) of 1856, where Western learning, or *yōgaku*, was supported.
The *Kōbusho*, or Western-style military school, was started in 1854; a naval
school in 1857; and the Meirindō in the city of Nagasaki, where foreign
languages, particularly Dutch, were taught. Even the "national learning,"

22. Ishikawa Ken, *Nihon Gakkōshi no Kenkyū (Studies in the History of Schools in Japan)*,
(Tokyo, 1960), pp. 251-260.

TABLE 3

*Special Subjects Supported by Domains**

Subject	No. of Schools
Chinese medicine	45
Western medicine	12
Western medicine and studies in general	1
Western studies	29
Dutch studies	3
English†	6
National studies	16

* From Ishikawa, *Kinsei no Gakkō, op. cit.*, pp. 265-66.

† "English" included not only language, but military science, ordnance, geography, astronomy, etc.

which is often considered by later historians to have, at least implicitly, challenged the legitimacy of the Shogunate, was supported in the *Wagaku Kōdansho*, established in 1790.

The Domain Schools. Tokugawa Japan was divided into approximately 280 feudal domains *(han)*, both large and small, under the overlordship of their own feudal lords, or *daimyō*. Almost every one of them, except possibly the very smallest, had at least one school *(hankō)*, generally modeled on the Shogunal schools. In the course of time, about one-half became involved in extending education among commoners. The *gōgaku* (local schools), which developed rapidly after the middle of the 19th century, very often started out as, or soon turned into, almost a "branch" of the main domain school; which meant that they came to some extent under official patronage as well as supervision, and that the domain authorities paid careful attention to their curricula, text materials, and general conduct. Towards the end of the era, some of them had mixed samurai-commoner student bodies.

It would not be unreasonable, therefore, to assume that there were upwards of 300 of these domain schools maintained for the education of the domain samurai. Although there was much diversity, in general they were based on a classical Confucian curriculum, to which was added, in differing proportions, such subjects as "national learning," history (both Japanese and Chinese), calligraphy, composition, and etiquette. Towards the end of the era, many of the domain schools made further additions to this core curriculum: Dutch studies, English language, navigation, Western ordnance, military drill, Western mathematics, etc. (see Table 3). These schools were usually set up in their own buildings, separate from the main domain school quarters. For more advanced study of these subjects, promising students were often sent to Shogunal or private schools in Edo, Osaka, and Nagasaki.

The domain schools, no less than the Shogunal ones, maintained strict class divisions. Separate education was provided for the different ranks of the samurai. In the Mito domain school for example, the attendance requirements varied by family rank: for the older sons of families of 300 *koku* income or above, 15 days attendance per month was required; for the junior sons of 300-*koku* families and the older sons of 150-300 *koku* families, 12 days; for the junior sons of 150-300 *koku* families and the older sons of below-150 *koku* families, 10 days; and for junior sons of below-150 *koku* families, 8 days.[23] Differences in dress, number of attendants permitted to accompany the student to and from school, seating position, and even classrooms were often carefully specified.

Many of the domain schools insisted upon separate curricula for the various ranks. The higher samurai looked down upon arithmetic as fit only for merchants. Fukuzawa Yukichi tells a revealing story about this in his autobiography. His father, who had the traditional samurai contempt for money, ". . . once sent [his children] to a teacher for calligraphy and general education. The teacher lived in the compound of the lord's storage office, but having some merchants' children among his pupils, he naturally began to train them in numerals: 'Two times two is four, three times two is six, etc.' . . . when my father heard this, he took his children away in a fury. 'It is abominable,' he exclaimed, 'that innocent children should be taught to use numbers — the instruments of merchants. There is no telling what the teacher may do next.'"[24] But for the lower samurai, arithmetic was often compulsory (for the middle ranks, it was optional).[25] It is only fair to note, however, that in some of the schools, mathematics was treated as one of the "six Confucian arts," and therefore as entirely suitable to persons of high status. Even in the strictly military arts a division was made. Swordsmanship, riding, and archery were taught to the upper-class samurai as a form of spiritual training, but lower-class samurai were taught *jujutsu*, lancemanship, group tactics, and rifle.[26]

Samurai education was in general considered to be education for character rather than specialized training. The specialist was usually looked down upon as being a mere technician rather than a person of general culture. Therefore, although Western subjects were gradually introduced into the domain schools, characteristically they were provided only for the lower samurai ranks, rather than for the higher; and it was Western military science that attracted most attention. The orthodox views were that Western learning was quite appropriate to practical matters, perhaps, but that it was entirely unsuitable for the realm of wisdom and virtue, and therefore not for

23. Kasai Sukeji, *Kinsei Hankō no Kenkyū* (*Studies on the Domain Schools of the Early Modern Period*), (Tokyo, 1960), p. 202. A *koku* is a measure of approximately 5 bushels. The size of a domain was described by its estimated taxable yield expressed in *koku*. To say that a family had X-*koku* income meant that it derived revenues from ricelands capable of producing that amount of rice, not that it received that amount of rice.

24. *The Autobiography of Fukuzawa Yukichi* (Tokyo: Hokuseido, 1948), pp. 2-3.

25. Karasawa Tomitarō, *Nihon Kyōiku-shi* (*History of Japanese Education*), (Tokyo, 1962), pp. 171-172.

26. Kasai, *op. cit.*, p. 229.

the governing classes. Sakuma Shozan had summed it up in the famous phrase: "Western science, Oriental morality." As long, therefore, as Western studies were confined to technical matters, many domains were willing to allow them. The regulations of the Meishinkan school in Echizen province specified that Western studies were to be taught but that they must not contravene what was permitted by the Shogunate. By 1871, 28 of the domains had established schools of Western studies, 35 medical schools, and 18 schools of Japanese studies, entirely apart from the regular domain schools.[27]

Whether all of the qualified samurai children went to their domain schools is not entirely clear. If they did not, then it was very likely because there were so many other types of school available to them, often private or only partly official. Moreover, the domain schools varied considerably in the level of education they provided. Some provided only elementary education, obliging ambitious students to go elsewhere for advanced work; while others provided only intermediate or advanced work, so that students had first to acquire the rudiments of education either through a private tutor or in a private school. A survey of 238 such schools found that 48 took students only after the age of 11, so that they must have had their primary schooling privately; and 55 ended schooling before the age of 15, which means that students had to carry on their advanced work elsewhere.[28] It is at any rate quite clear that a good part of the elementary military training was provided first in private academies and that only later did the students go on to the domain school. By the end of the Tokugawa era, there were some 236 of these in existence.[29]

Under the *sankin kōtai* (alternate attendance) system, *daimyō* were required to maintain a residence in the Shogun's capital city of Edo. Around these residences, very considerable retinues of servants, family members, and administrators grew up. Many of the domains began to provide schools and academies in their Edo headquarters for children and young people in their retinue, and some of these went far beyond primary education. Ambitious youth could advance their studies while living in Edo by utilizing the facilities and libraries of the great Shogunal academies, such as the Shōheikō.

Towards the end of the era, commoners were increasingly permitted to attend the domain schools. Ototake estimated that of the 234 domain schools he studied, 120 "did not forbid" the entry of commoners (see Table 4).

One of the earliest examples was the Meirindō of Kanazawa, which carried on what might be called "adult education" among the merchant classes. Once a month commoners were permitted to sit among the two-sword-bearing samurai students and listen to the lectures. But even the domain schools that refused the entrance of commoners, such as the Meirinkan of Hagi, for example, did feel increasingly impelled to provide special

27. Ishikawa Ken, *Gakkō no Hattatsu (The Development of the Schools),* (Tokyo, 1951), p. 262.
28. Ishikawa Ken, *Nihon Gakkō-shi no Kenkyū (Studies in the History of Schools in Japan),* (Tokyo, 1960), p. 265.
29. *Ibid.,* p. 261.

Restrictions on Entry of
Commoners to Domain Schools

Restrictions Imposed	Number of Schools	
(1) Did not forbid the entry of commoners	120	
No commoner students		(27)
Small number of commoner students		(10)
Number of commoners unknown		(83)
(2) Forbade entry of commoners	89	
(3) Unclear	25	
Total	234	

° From Ototake, *op. cit.*, p. 902.

facilities for them. When commoners were permitted to attend domain schools, they were usually required to wear clothing suitable to the samurai class.

Shijuku. Alongside the officially supported schools a wide variety of private schools, or *shijuku,* grew up. Although most of them can be fairly characterized as institutions of higher education largely for the samurai, they ran the full range from elementary schools offering the bare rudiments of literacy all the way to advanced institutions of learning that functioned much on the order of colleges and research institutes. Many of these also opened their doors to commoners. In the later Tokugawa period there were at least 1,500, ranging from tiny schools with 20 or 30 students all the way to huge academies rivalling the Shogunal and domain colleges, with thousands of students. According to a recent estimate,[30] there were 437 *shijuku* in 1829; 1,066 in 1853; 1,529 in 1867; 1,374 in 1870; and 1,182 in 1871. Where the student body was large, senior students were often called on to help out in the teaching. The more important *shijuku* offered specialized curricula such as medicine, Dutch studies, Western learning, military subjects, and navigation. Because they were private they were freer than the official schools to teach unorthodox doctrines, such as the "national learning" or one of the Confucian doctrines forbidden in the Shogunal schools. Some of them therefore became centers of unorthodoxy and opposition to the regime. In the Choshu domain that played such a leading role in the overthrow of the Shogunate, for example, Albert Craig has described for us how important it was that most of the radical young rebels had come under the influence of Yoshida Shoin and his academy.[31]

Usually these schools centered around some distinguished teacher, who

30. From unpublished materials in a report by Sano Yohko and Hasegawa Tsuneo. "The Estimated Number of Pupils in All Japan — 1854-67 and 1868-70."

31. Albert Craig, *Choshu in the Meiji Restoration* (Cambridge, Harvard University Press, 1961).

had strong views, whether political, philosophical, or educational, that he wished to propound. It was his personal qualities that attracted students, and a great teacher would draw his students from many parts of the country. The most important of the *shijuku* were essentially institutions of advanced education. The teachers were dedicated scholars, usually of samurai or *rōnin* origin. Often they were men who had taught in domain schools and then later resigned to establish their own schools. In Tokugawa Japan, as John Hall has observed, "it was possible for an independent Confucian teacher to make a living by writing and taking in pupils."[32] But not all teachers were of samurai origin. In a study of the background of 118 *Shijuku* teachers in the single province of Echigo—one of the less advanced provinces—the following distribution was found: 65 commoners, 33 doctors (or priests), 14 samurai, and 6 others.[33]

Originally the *shijuku* were conceived as schools for the education of people who wanted to enter the scholarly professions. Therefore, although samurai were normally in the majority, from the start many of them took commoner students as well, and even, as we have seen in the preceding paragraph, employed commoner teachers. Characteristically, it was in these schools that the principles of merit and achievement began to come into conflict with class ranking. In the formal Confucian lecture halls, it was perhaps possible to maintain the official fiction that students of upper-class origin were inherently superior to commoners. But when students lived together in dormitories, as was often the case in the private academies, and were stimulated to competitive individual performance, the fiction began to wear thin. Examinations, grades, and individual recitations emphasized the individual rather than his class. The fiction was further eroded by the growing interest, on the part of both the Shogunal and domain authorities, in the "cultivation of talent" and "human resources." Although these principles were never carried to their logical conclusion during the Tokugawa era, they were sufficiently widespread to be an important part of the amalgam of ideas that formed the ideology of the Restoration, and they explain much about the ease of transition to a merit system in the early Meiji period.

It was also important that most of these schools, and certainly the famous ones, were located in the metropolitan centers and domain capitals, where their political influence could be felt. Until the end of the eighteenth century, Kyoto was the great center of the *shijuku*. But by the nineteenth century, Osaka and particularly Edo took the lead. Not only was it the Shogunal center and the home of the Shōheikō, but its increasing population and commercial importance gave it the greater weight. Nevertheless, the *shijuku* in rural areas and small towns should not be underestimated. They produced many

32. Hall, *op. cit.*, p. 272.
33. From Itō Tasaburo, *Kokumin Seikatsu-shi (History of the People's Life)*. Vol. 3; *Seikatsu to Gakumon Kyōiku (Life and Academic Education)*, (Tokyo, 1958), p. 367.

TABLE 5°
Social Origins of Terakoya Teachers

Origin	Per Cent
Commoners	38
Samurai	23
Buddhist Priests	20
Doctors	9
Shinto Priests	7
Others	3
	100

° Quoted in Ototake, *op. cit.*, p. 883, from *Nihon Kyōiku-shi Shiryo-jo; Terakoya-kyō.*

local leaders and helped spread Western ideas as well as knowledge of the political controversies going on during the late Tokugawa period.[34]

If at the higher levels, the *shijuku* were institutions for advanced education, at their lower they were scarcely distinguishable from the *terakoya,* which might be characterized as primary schools for commoners.

3. *Education for the Commoners*

The Terakoya. The most important and widespread institution for commoners' education was the *terakoya*.[35] Although the term suggests that they were schools run by Buddhist temples, somewhat on the order of the "pagoda schools" of Burma, this is misleading. The *terakoya* derives from a pre-Tokugawa institution that had in fact been organized and run by Buddhist priests. But by Tokugawa times it was a purely secular institution for the common people, having no particular connection with the temple. A survey of the social origin of *terakoya* teachers in the Bakumatsu period gives the distribution shown in Table 5.

Throughout most of the Tokugawa era, officials were mainly interested in samurai education, and commoners were left to their own devices. All the more remarkable, therefore, was the rapid growth of popular education. Schools were started by public-spirited citizens either as an expression of their own conviction of the need for public education or in response to the growing demand from the urban and rural commoner classes. Shrines, temples, vacant buildings, or private homes were used. As often as not, the teacher simply gathered pupils into his own home for instruction.

34. See Marius Jansen's account of the political importance of the fencing academies in Tosa Province as the Meiji Restoration drew near, in his *Sakamoto Ryoma and the Meiji Restoration* (Princeton: Princeton University Press, 1961).
35. Usually translated as "temple school." More accurately, however, the term refers to the "children of the temple," and therefore might perhaps be rendered as "parishioners' school."

The most rapid development of the *terakoya* came in the nineteenth century. By the year 1850, there were certainly 6,000 or more, and in another twenty years the numbers doubled (see Table 2). In the last twenty years of the Shogunate there must have been few areas of the country hopelessly beyond their reach. "Distance from a school" ranked very low among the reasons for nonattendance offered by Ototake's respondents.[36] The distribution of schools, however, was very uneven. The greatest concentration was in the urban areas. In Edo, for example, it is estimated that there were about 1,200 at the end of the Tokugawa period.[37] As against this relative density, many rural areas were extremely deficient.

The demand for education in the cities and towns was very high, and it is a fair presumption that a majority of the children, at least the boys, attended school for some period or other. Among the more affluent merchants and city people, many children went on to private schools for a much higher level of education than that provided in the *terakoya*.

The demand for education in the rural areas came primarily from the upper strata, who needed literacy and basic educational skills in their administrative work. This need prevailed not only among the top village leaders, but penetrated right down to the level of heads of neighborhood associations. Bare literacy was not enough. As a governing group, the village leader class shared much of the outlook of the samurai, and in many areas they came increasingly to resemble them in their styles of life. Very often the only private collection of books in a village would belong to the *shōya* (village head). And in many villages there were great landowners who carried on a life of considerable cultivation, guided by Confucian standards essentially similar to those of the samurai, and as deeply imbued with a sense of political responsibility. As the "representative of the people" they often had an even more immediate feeling of responsibility than the remote and bureaucratic samurai. It is not surprising, therefore, that it was usually the village heads who took the initiative in the establishment of schools. In many areas, it was only their children who attended the schools, but as time went on, attendance from lower strata continued to increase.

This rise of the commoner class, which was one of the most important developments of the late Tokugawa, is reflected in the distribution of *terakoya* management and teaching staff. If before 1623, priests (both Shinto and Buddhist) constituted 45 per cent of the operators of *terakoya*, by 1867 they had fallen to about 25 per cent. Commoner management went up from 27 per cent in the earlier period to 41 per cent by 1867.[38] More significant than the over-all figures was the regional distribution. Priests and doctors were predominant among teachers in isolated rural areas. In the castle and post towns, samurai were in a majority. But in the large cities and commercial

36. Ototake, *op. cit.*, pp. 939-940.
37. Ogata Hiroyasu, *Nihon Kyōiku Tsūshi (Simple History of Japanese Education)*, (Tokyo, 1960), p. 151.
38. Uchiyama, Kumaya, Masuda, *op. cit.*, p. 76.

ports, where the commoner culture was most advanced, it was the commoners who were predominant.[39]

What was *terakoya* education like? In many cases it must have been not too unattractive. Later, after the modern school system begins, we find many people looking back on their *terakoya* days with the utmost nostalgia. In fact, when in the 1870's and 1880's the Meiji government was having great difficulties maintaining regular school attendance, one common complaint was that the new schools lacked the warmth and practicality of the old *terakoya*. An 1875 report from Aichi prefecture officials, analyzing public resistance to compulsory education, listed, among other causes, that the people "miss the old *terakoya*."[40]

Among the more than 14,000 *terakoya* (with more than 17,000 teachers), conditions were obviously very diverse. Some of the schools were outstanding, others extremely poor. In general, however, they averaged between thirty and sixty pupils per school, usually under a single teacher, or the teacher and immediate members of his family. Although coeducation was the norm, there were usually far fewer girls than boys, and the two groups were rigidly separated in seating. Boys usually entered between the ages of 6 and 8, leaving between 11 and 13, that is, in time to begin work or apprenticeship. For girls, the leaving age was usually one year later. At a rough guess, boys averaged about four years of schooling and girls perhaps as much as five. Attendance requirements were casual, and easily adjusted to the work routines of shop or farm. During the busy agricultural season, village schools were recessed. Children were given plenty of time to keep up with their household chores.

The children were not divided into classes. If there was any separation, it was on the basis of the teacher's intuition. The usual daily stint was between three and four hours. The teacher would instruct each student in turn, and between individual drill or recitation the students practiced their writing or reading. Reading and writing were the heart of the curriculum, followed in order of importance by the third R. To this basic core curriculum, different schools added subjects they felt were of vocational or moral importance to the lives of the children, such as etiquette, morals, and accounting. Some of the *terakoya* added more academic subjects, such as Chinese *(kambun)*, history, geography, and composition, and later even Western subjects, such as science, military arts, and, in a few, even English. More advanced students might be assigned the simpler Confucian classics, such as the *Four Books;* and girls given some suitable Confucian work or Kaibara Ekken's improving tract for samurai women, the *Greater Learning for Women (Onna Daigaku)*. But these were the minority. For the overwhelming majority, the curriculum was basically the three R's plus some instruction in morals and manners.

39. Ototake, *op. cit.*, pp. 885-892.
40. Tamaki Hajime, *Nihon Kyōiku Hattatsu-shi (History of the Development of Japanese Education)*, (Tokyo, 1954), p. 31.

Methods were completely unstandardized. Pupils studied and made their recitations individually rather than as a group. In most schools, the basic subjects were taught either from teachers' prepared texts or from simple primers, the *Oraimono*. Arithmetic texts were rare, except in Osaka, Edo, and two or three of the other larger cities, where the standards of the merchants were somewhat more exigent. Normally there were neither examinations nor grades.

Most of the teaching was a voluntary labor of love, particularly in the rural areas. Part-time teaching by public-spirited samurai, *rōnin*, village officials, and educated commoners was not unusual, and retired village officials often devoted their final years to teaching. But even when, as in some of the large cities, the teachers were professional—in the sense that they earned their living from their work—there was no uniformity in their preparation or methods. Unlike the domain school teachers, *terakoya* teachers were neither licensed nor inspected. Anyone with the will was free to become a teacher.

Regular fees were not levied, and the schools were usually supported by the patronage of wealthy individuals and by contributions. These "donations" were usually paid in kind, proportionate to the capacity and status of the individual family. More affluent families gave presents of dried sardines, sweets, lengths of cloth, or even occasionally money; farmers might pay in agricultural produce; others perhaps in personal service, such as repairing the teacher's house mats. Many of the schools took in a small number of boarders who acted, in effect, as servants in the teacher's household.

But from the eighteenth and, especially, the nineteenth centuries, officials began to pay more attention to the *terakoya*. In Edo, several close retainers of the Shogunate opened schools for commoners that were run on high standards. Otatake estimates that 31 of the domains he inquired into were positively encouraging commoner education towards the end of the Shogunate.[41] Although the figure must be taken with some reserve, it does suggest the approximate extent of domain interest. Some of the domains not only encouraged the commoner schools, but even gave financial support. Prizes were sometimes awarded to meritorious teachers, and in a few cases the prescribed textbooks of the domain schools were assigned for use.

If many of the *terakoya* did little more than provide the bare rudiments of literacy, others, particularly those in the cities, attained rather high standards of primary education. In some of them, what might be called "prevocational" training was very thorough. Many were sufficiently effective in their general cultural training to awaken their pupils to a high degree of awareness of the political problems of their times. Thomas Smith writes:

> Education was apparently widely used to indoctrinate local youth. Take, for example, the activities of Sugita Senjuro. . . . The elder Sugita . . . was

41. Ototake, *op. cit.*, p. 903.

a fervent supporter of the imperial cause and his home was a regular stopping place for pro-Emperor samurai. . . . In 1857 Sugita established a school at his own expense, we may believe for a political purpose, since the Fukui *han* (domain) stripped him of his offices of Oshoya, a kind of super village headmanship, and put him under house arrest. . . .[42]

It is also significant that popular literature was able to count on such extensive readership that many publishing houses became commercial successes.

Gōgaku. But the official authorities placed greater emphasis in their promotion of commoner education on a different kind of institution, the *gōgaku*, or, translated literally, the "local school."[43] The first of this type was established in Okayama province in 1670 by Lord Ikeda Mitsumasa. As the feeling of responsibility for commoner education developed, public authorities began to encourage special schools that emphasized not only the usual rudimentary and vocational training, but Confucian moral training as well. In spite of official interest and support, a good part of the financial burden was left to the local people. In the case of an Okayama province school established in 1671, for example, the domain provided the initial capital cost plus the first five years of operation. After that, it was expected that the local people would have developed enough interest and understanding to take over the operation themselves.[44]

What these schools aimed at was the improvement of the level of the ruling elements of the commoner class: village heads in the rural areas and town chiefs in the urban areas. An instruction of the year 1671 on the establishment of a *tenaraisho* (writing school, a variety of the *gōgaku*) in Okayama province says that the children of village masters, elders, and solid farmers *(hirabyakushō)*—that is, children who can be expected upon maturity to take over village affairs—are to be placed in a school *(tenaraisho)* to study writing and calculation, in order to be able to carry on public business, and morals, in order to be able to hold the community together.[45]

By contrast with the *terakoya*, it was not uncommon, particularly in the later period, for both commoners and samurai children to attend the *gōgaku*. The Shogunate itself supported three, and perhaps another fifty were maintained in direct Tokugawa fiefs. Throughout the first half ot the nineteenth century, the number of *gōgaku* slowly increased, as one after another of the

42. Thomas C. Smith: *Political Change and Industrial Development in Japan; Government Enterprise, 1868-1880* (Stanford: Stanford University Press, 1955), pp. 19-20.
43. Also called *gōkō.* Varieties of this type of school went by many different names, some of them of purely local use, others signifying some variation in their main emphasis. Among them are: *tenaraisho* (writing school); *kyōyūsho* (hall of precepts); *shōgakusho* (elementary school); *shūgakusho* (writing school); *kyōdōsho* (educational leadership school); *jogakkō* (girls' school). K. Ishikawa classified the *shingaku*, a type of religious school we discuss later, among the *gōgaku* type. (See his *Kinsei no Gakkō, op. cit.*, p. 268.)
44. K. Ishikawa, *op. cit.*, p. 189.
45. *Okayama-ken Kyōiku-shi (History of Education in Okayama Prefecture)*, v. 1, p. 188. (from K. Ishikawa, *op. cit.*, p. 190)

more enlightened domains established them. Their official character was so strong that for all practical purposes the best of them were treated as branches of the domain schools,[46] and they were subjected to similar supervision in textual materials, programs, and teachers. In level they lay somewhere between the *terakoya* and the domain school *(shijuku);* that is, they formed a kind of secondary educational level. Their greatest thrust forward, however, came in the few short years between the overthrow of the Shogunate and the promulgation of the modern school system.

Popular Religious Schools. We may conclude our description of formal education for the commoners with a brief mention of two other developments essentially of religious origin. *Shingaku* was a movement started by one of the great religious figures of the early eighteenth century, Ishida Baigan. It would take us too far afield to discuss his views, but suffice it to say that his insistence that people could improve themselves by their own efforts had revolutionary implications for a society in which the prevailing conception had been that people were completely at the mercy of destiny. His doctrines appealed primarily to commoners, particularly the merchants. The chief objective of the movement was to elevate the moral standards of the common people by teaching them true morality, which for *Shingaku* was largely Confucian with some Buddhist overtones. However, to many orthodox Confucians these doctrines smacked of subversion because they implied that commoners were as capable of virtue and higher learning as the samurai. This is the burden of Sakuma Shōzan's attack on *Shingaku*, delivered in his *Memorandum on the School System (Gakusei Ikenshō)* in 1837.[47] Nevertheless, *Shingaku* had a modest efflorescence, attracting some support even in official quarters since it was believed to have a civilizing effect on the lower orders.

Shingaku schools first opened in Kyoto and Osaka and then gradually spread to Edo and to a number of rural areas. By the end of the era there were almost 200 of all types — *terakoya, gogaku,* and private academies — claiming to base their curricula and training on *Shingaku* concepts.[48] Since *Shingaku* believed firmly in the necessity of training in the higher virtues for the common people, its schools taught morals along with the usual useful and practical subjects. They were noted for their special pedagogical methods, which made extensive use of such devices as moral tales and pictures rather than simply the laborious repetition of difficult and uninteresting texts. One of Shōzan's complaints about *Shingaku* was that although its moral tales did not fail to make some distinction between commoners and samurai, they violated the Confucian principle that "the people must not be informed; they must be made to follow."

Another important movement that had some educational repercussions,

46. K. Ishikawa, *op. cit.,* p. 154.
47. See K. Ishikawa, *op. cit.,* pp. 96-97.
48. See Robert Bellah, *Tokugawa Religion* (New York: Free Press, 1957), pp. 170-172.

particularly in rural areas, was Sontoku's *Hōtoku-kyō.* This movement, which also had religious overtones, reached its greatest extension in the period following the disasters and famines of the early nineteenth century. It preached an association of ethics, economic ideas, and the virtues of work.

Vocational Training. Apart from formal schooling, a highly developed apprenticeship system provided direct vocational training. Young boys, usually at the age of 10, were articled to large commercial houses for long periods of service and training. Junior sons were preferred because of the danger that a senior son might leave to take over his family's occupation. For the first period of his apprenticeship, the young man was kept at chores around the home and shop. At a later stage, he would be assigned occasional errands and tasks outside. By the age of 15 or 16, he was given a new name that symbolized his relation to the master's house, along with enlarged responsibilities. Absolute obedience was required of him, and his personal life was regulated down to the smallest details. Discipline and punishment were severe. Perhaps as heavy a burden as any were the constant admonitions to which he was subject: ". . . do not speak unnecessarily to the Master; do not be resentful; do not talk back . . ." Evenings were usually spent in "improving" occupations, including academic study, particularly the three R's.

If he managed to survive the discipline, by the age of 18 or 19 he became a *tedai,* which signified a kind of half-maturity. Upon attaining his majority, perhaps a year or two later, he was suddenly taken into the warm bosom of the family. A great party would be held for him, presided over by the master and the head clerk *(bantō),* where he was overwhelmed with presents. Freshly ordered clothing suitable to his new status was provided, and he was treated for the first time as if he were a full member of the family. The next stage in his progress would be to take entire charge of some operation in a shop. If all went extremely well for him, he might reasonably look forward to becoming a formal "branch family" of his master's house and be set up in business, perhaps as a branch of the main firm, as a subcontractor, or as a retailer in the main firm's trade.

Artisanal apprenticeship was also widespread, particularly in the skilled crafts. By contrast with the great commercial houses, however, this training was usually more narrowly vocational. In the case of carpenters, for example, the youth would be taken at the age of 12 or 13, when he had presumably completed his *terakoya* education, and kept on until the age of 21 or 22. During those years he lived in his master's home, and in return for his room, board, and clothing, he was constantly at his master's beck and call.

PORTENTS OF MODERNITY

It is obvious that Tokugawa education was far from stagnant, even in its purely formal development. Were we to look at the intellectual developments, the picture would be even more impressive. Nineteenth-century

Japan was stirring with new life, buzzing with new ideas and with political and philosophical debates. The open arrival of the West, in the figure of Commodore Perry, raised the already simmering cauldron to boiling point.

It is equally apparent that during the last thirty or so years of the Tokugawa era, many of the conceptions that went into the making of the post-Restoration educational system had already been thought of by one person or another, and some of them had even been tried out experimentally. The need for commoner education, for example, was not only recognized, but there were many voices advocating an end to the separate class education. The *gōgaku*, officially supported schools where commoner and samurai children attended together, anticipated the modern type of school. The domain schools which hesitantly, and the *shijuku* which more willingly accepted commoners; the *terakoya* which took in samurai; and the *gōgaku*, where the mixing of commoners and samurai was more explicitly recognized, were all exemplifications of this concept. Some of these schools became the forerunners of the modern type of school, and the gradual drawing together of the extremes and the blurring of sharp lines foreshadowed the possibility of the emergence of a unified system.

The importance of practical education is another example. In spite of a certain resistance by conservative Confucianists, domain schools increasingly adopted "practical" subjects, or made some provision for them in the establishment of separate institutions. Among the common people, vocational education was certainly widespread. Practical education was supported not only by the *yōgakusha*, the Western scholars, but also by Baigan's *Shingaku* and Sontoku's *Hōtoku-kyō*, and by the merchant and artisan classes of the cities. In the final years of the era, the Shogunate and some of the important domains made major efforts in the development of technical training. When the Shogunate brought in French technicians to build the Yokosuka shipyards in 1864, it organized a language and technical training program so that Japanese might eventually replace the foreigners.

> The training program was conducted on two levels. Samurai were selected for training as "engineers" and were instructed in French by the chief interpreter and in technical subjects by the various department heads. Young workers at the foundry were selected by the French engineers for training as "technicians"; they were given instruction in their respective jobs in the morning and attended school in the afternoon for instruction in "drafting and other essential studies." The instruction at Yokohama was on a lower level: one hundred Japanese artisans were trained in Western techniques by French instructors. In addition, a language school was opened in Yokohama in April 1865, with fifty-seven students and five French teachers, to provide interpreters for the foundries, and six of the students were shortly afterward sent to France for study.[49]

The cry for *jinzai*—the cultivation of human resources—which was such an important underlying element in the ideology of early Meiji education,

49. Smith, *op. cit.*, p. 9.

had already started in the 1840's. By the end of the Tokugawa era, it was a commonplace. Similarly, the recognition that ability and class did not necessarily coincide was already implicit in the grading and examination systems of the *shijuku*.[50]

Nor was the notion of universal compulsory education completely new. As early as the eighteenth century, such orthodox scholars as Nakai Chikusan were already proposing a kind of national education system.[51] By the middle of the nineteenth century, such proposals were legion.

The beginnings of the modern conception of three levels of schooling —primary, secondary, and higher—was already visible in the three grades of Tokugawa schools—the *terakoya,* the *gōgaku,* and the higher academies of the domain and the Shogunate. Although he proposed a two-grade system— primary school up to 15 years of age, and higher education between 15 and 25—in his 1825 memorial to the Lord of Matsushiro province, Sakuma Shōzan urged the development of clear criteria to distinguish the various levels of schooling.[52]

In early Tokugawa, Western subjects had been strictly forbidden, and throughout most of the era they suffered under many disabilities. But by the end of the 18th century the Shogunate had given its blessing, even if occasionally with hesitation, and a number of schools had been started. Some of the domains, following the Shogunate lead, began to introduce Western subjects, and by the beginning of the Meiji period there were almost 80 that supported Western studies in one form or another. If to this we add the large Shogunal institutions plus perhaps several hundred of the private academies *(shijuku)* and remember that *yōgaku* was even percolating down to the lower school levels of *terakoya* and *gōgaku,* then we will realize that the penetration of Western studies was rather more extensive than is usually assumed.

Continuities

We shall not be surprised, therefore, that many Japanese scholars feel that the continuities in Japanese education across the gap of modernity are at least as important as the discontinuities. From one point of view the gap appears absolute between the Tokugawa system of samurai schools and *terakoya,* based on the class system of a late-feudal society, and the modern system of primary, middle, and higher schools, based on the concept of equality of educational opportunity. But Meiji education can also be looked upon as an extension of the trend lines already forming themselves in the Tokugawa period. School attendance in the year 1873, for example, the first year of the modern school system, was probably no different from what it was in the closing years of the Tokugawa era—40 per cent for boys, and 15

50. See Ronald Dore, "Talent and the Social Order in Tokugawa Japan," *Past and Present,* No. 21 (April, 1962).

51. In his *Sōbo Kigen,* a memorandum to Matsudaira Sadanobu, written in 1789-91.

52. K. Ishikawa, *op. cit.,* pp. 101-102.

per cent for girls. The modern primary schools were in a large proportion of cases simply converted, and sometimes unconverted, *terakoya*. Until the new normal-school system began to produce enough graduates, most of the teachers were *terakoya* teachers using their familiar methods and their familiar textual materials. The modern university emerged from an amalgamation of the higher educational institutions – the Confucian Academy, the Medical School, and the Institute for the Investigation of Barbarian Writings (later renamed the *Kaisei-jō*) – of the Tokugawa period.

There is a profound sense, therefore, in which the Bakumatsu schools prepared the way, and perhaps even laid the groundwork, for the rapid growth of a modern system of education. The sheer presence of education as an element in the environment to which people must respond is important, no matter what the content of the education may be. Japan was prepared for a modern school system because by the end of the Tokugawa period millions of families had assimilated the routines it required into their mode of life. The notions of spending several hours a day for part of the year away from home, associating with non-kin agemates, entering relations with a special kind of adult, and following a sequence of study, were already familiar ones to a good part of the population. The distance between the Meiji school and the Tokugawa school was therefore not as great as that between school and no school.

It also meant that large numbers of people were already familiar with the idea of education as sequence and growth, of starting with the rudiments and then advancing to higher levels in regular order. Graded textbooks and graded content were also familiar ideas. That there was some relation between physical and mental maturity, amount of time spent in study, and educational progress was also known in a general way. In other words, the Japanese population was ready for the routines and disciplines of modern education because it had already had a long experience of learning in a setting of formal routines and disciplines.

People were also familiar with the conception of formally organized levels of education. The sequence *terakoya-gōgaku-shijuku* (or any of its variants) was already an embryonic three-level system essentially similar to the modern Meiji system. In Tokugawa society the main issue was not the discrimination of levels of education but whether a particular level corresponded to a particular class. The official doctrine supported this view, but within a few decades of the nineteenth century the pendulum swung over to an increasingly bold conception of the equal educational opportunity. The recognition that the country (or more accurately, the domains) needed "men of talent," that they had to make use of their "human resources" – "without regard for high and low," in the usual phrasing – mediated the two extreme positions. The modern philosophy of the Preamble of the 1872 Code of Education, that education is for *all* the classes, was widely known, even if it continued to encounter some resistance right into the modern period. Some of the early modern plans envisioned higher education only for the samurai, and universal compulsory education, but at an elementary level, for the common people. These were, however, given short shrift as the modernizers gathered momentum.

The very awareness that the higher learning and high status went together may, paradoxically, have hastened the end of class education by showing the way to upward mobility. Even in the heyday of the Tokugawa era, it had always been possible for commoners to improve their status by entering a life of scholarship or one of the liberal professions, and specific provision for this possibility had always been made in official schools, even if on a very small scale. Commoners who became scholars, or doctors, might acquire the "assimilated rank" of samurai. Or if they became priests, they were considered to be "outside" the system, which to a commoner meant relative improvement of status. The steady increase throughout the nineteenth century of commoner leadership in the organization and operation of schools, in spite of the absence of official interest, was an expression of the rapid rise of the curve of popular demand for education. In the end, as we have seen, the official classes had to take cognizance of this trend, which they did by cautiously opening some of their institutions to commoners, increasing their support for *terakoya* and *gōgaku,* and in general taking more interest in the affairs of the lower level schools. In some of the provinces, the end of the Tokugawa era saw something approaching the beginnings of a genuine integrated province-wide system of education based on the notions of public responsibility and equalization of opportunity. It was in these few provinces that the transition to the modern system was easiest.

When feudal Japan first blinked her eyes open on the modern world, there is reason to believe that she could count on something like 40 per cent male literacy. Much of it was certainly of a very low order—perhaps the bare ability to write one's name or to read simple materials with effort. But a surprising amount, rising continuously with each successive decade of the nineteenth century, was of a very advanced level. We shall probably never be able to explore fully the ramifications of literacy in Japanese life, but that its relatively high level at the "take off" point—particularly by comparison with other non-Western underdeveloped countries—facilitated rapid development appears indisputable. At the very least, literacy made it possible for people to be aware of things outside of their own immediate experience. It also made it possible for them to conceive of arrangements that differed from those with which they were familiar. They were therefore much more accessible to new ideas and new techniques than they would otherwise have been.

Less tangible, but equally important, literacy brings people into a communication network that increases their self-awareness and their awareness of others, so that the sense of being part of a larger community than one's immediate kin or neighborhood group is enhanced. The lower classes were therefore much more able to feel themselves part of a national entity than would have been the case had literacy not spread so far among them. It was also possible for many commoners, and certainly their leaders through whom this understanding could also have been diffused, to be aware of many of the important political issues and disputes taking place. If the structure of Tokugawa society did not allow them to take much part, they were at least not completely in the dark. Literacy helped to narrow the gap between the Two Nations to proportions at least more manageable than those we often find in most non-Western countries.

Among the upper classes, Tokugawa education helped to create a common universe of discourse. In spite of the great diversity and decentralization of schools, the area of common content was surprisingly large. Many people read the same books, shared the same preconceptions, and pointed themselves, even if from different angles, towards the same issues of debate. That it was possible to have real debate and disagreement—that is, that people could argue to the same points—was probably as important as that they shared so much intellectual content in common.

Orthodox Confucianism has been often, and perhaps rightly, criticized for its narrowness and inflexibility. And yet it may have served Tokugawa Japan better than most people are prepared to believe. For one thing, the neo-Confucianism that came to Japan in the seventeenth century was strongly committed to rationalism. If it was given to logic-chopping and system-building, it also came equipped with usable categories for natural philosophy and even experimentation and positivism. Kyūri—the investigation of things—could be interpreted to allow some forms of natural inquiry. Moreover, since Japan was an island country, perhaps more cut off from contact with the outside world than any other major country in the world, Confucianism, which was of foreign origin, helped to keep in the forefront a perspective and an awareness that might otherwise have been absent. The study of Chinese classics, of Chinese systems of administration, law, and thought, and of Chinese history, introduced a tension between what was Chinese and what was Japanese that made up for some of the insularity of Japan's isolated position. Within the framework of Confucianism itself, even had the Japanese been limited to it, there was ample room for debate and conflict among the different schools and theories. Despite the official endorsement of the Chu Hsi school, and the occasional denunciation of other schools as heretical, the Wang Yang-ming and other tendencies found their supporters and institutional base in particular schools.

The debates of late Tokugawa times were therefore very broad. Not only did they involve the various schools of Confucianism, but also the so-called "national learning" (kokugaku), which was strongly supported in the Mito domain school, the new religious ideologies, and, increasingly as time went on, the "Western learning" as well. All of them, it might be noted, implied particular theories of education, and these came to form much of the staple of debates over education in the early years of Meiji.

It is not surprising therefore that true nationhood was attained before the modern period, in spite of the decentralization of feudal administration. There were no secession movements and no minority nationalities struggling for their rights. And the schools and widespread literacy promoted the diffusion of a true national language.

Japan's modern school system was therefore in no sense a pure import from the West. It emerged from the intricate dialectic between Western ideas and the Japanese situation in the last decades of the *ancien régime*. But much of this dialectic unfolded itself within the framework of the Tokugawa school and the system of thought that it produced. The outlines of the new system of education were already taking shape within the womb of the old.

CHAPTER 22

A NOTE ON THE EVIDENCE OF HISTORY

*Richard A. Easterlin**

I wish merely to suggest the need for fuller research based on historical experience. Before elaborating, I should like briefly to indicate the potential availability of data and its relevance to some of the issues debated at the Conference.

Some Historical Data

Tables 1 and 2 in the Appendix bring together figures on school enrollment as a percentage of total population for a number of countries. These figures, which I hastily assembled some time ago, can scarcely be dignified by the term *research,* for reasons abundantly clear from the introductory note to the tables. They are perhaps adequate for forming some rough impressions of "low" versus "high" enrollment ratios at different times and places (I would use around 10 per cent as a rough dividing line), but should not be taken as reliably indicating the change for a given country between any two successive dates. Of immediate interest, however, is the indication they provide of the potential range in time and space of quantitative data on education, a situation hardly surprising in view of the widespread participation of government in the provision of schooling. The figures for some of the European countries and their overseas descendants extend back to the early nineteenth century, and even for the less developed areas a surprising amount of information seems available.

Even these crude figures appear to have bearing on some of the arguments advanced at the conference on the role of formal education in the transfer of the knowledge underlying modern economic growth. For example, Professor North asserted that there is little evidence of a relationship between formal education and the transfer of technology.[1] He emphasized

Editor's note: The editors and the Committee on Economic Growth of the Social Science Research Council decided to omit comments on individual papers from the publication of these proceedings of the April 1963 conference. However, in addition to his discussion of Rottenberg's paper, Professor Easterlin contributed some interesting data and a running commentary on selected aspects of the discussions. We know no better way of concluding this volume than to reproduce Easterlin's terse comments and challenge to future historical research on the problems with which the conference was concerned.

1. Elsewhere, however, he does treat education as important in economic growth. Cf. *The Economic Growth of the United States, 1790-1860* (Englewood Cliffs, N.J.: Prentice Hall, 1961).

instead the causal importance in this transfer of factor price differences among countries which led to a modification of British technology. But the evidence provided by the tables, to the extent to which it can be accepted, is not unfavorable regarding the importance of formal education in the spread of the new knowledge. For example, the first and (to me) quite unanticipated finding is that in the nineteenth century the countries to which modern technology spread most rapidly – the U.S., Germany, Switzerland, the Low Countries, Scandinavia, and perhaps France – almost uniformly had relatively high school enrollment ratios as early as 1830. For some of these countries this was doubtless true for some time prior to this date. There is at least a suggestion here that some minimum exposure to formal schooling was widespread among these populations, very likely for older cohorts as well as younger.

To my mind it is unlikely that relative factor prices in these countries differed from Great Britain in a way uniformly encouraging the *modification* of British technology. The really important question is how did the people in these countries *learn* the new technique, whether or not they had to be modified? The present figures are at least consistent with the hypothesis that, given the pressure of economic competition, formal education had equipped a sufficient number in the population at various age levels for successful mastery of the new knowledge.

Professor Smelser, in discussing Kahan's paper, expressed skepticism about the suggested rule of thumb that "the level of formal education of the labor force in a country which enters the stage of industrialization ought to be set, as a maximum, at the level of the country (countries) from which the basic technology was borrowed." Smelser suggested instead that populations are perhaps being overeducated in underdeveloped countries. While the figures in the present tables can not be taken as a definitive test of Kahan's rule or Smelser's criticism of it, two seemingly relevant points are suggested. (1) The very countries which successfully acquired British technology first in the nineteenth century *all* had a higher level of formal schooling than Great Britain at that time. (Indeed, the apparent intermediate level of the pioneer country's own enrollment rate itself suggests an interesting subject for inquiry.) (2) In *all* countries which have achieved substantial and sustained economic growth, formal education was either already at a high level or was raised to a high level in fairly short order.

Even if these inferences are correct, this does not mean, of course, that raising education levels will in itself cause modern economic growth. One must distinguish between education as *a* cause of growth and education as *the* cause, and also between the *ability* and the *incentive* to adopt new technology. In the past, market forces provided the incentive for adoption to those who felt the direct impact of new competition arising from technical progress; in many areas, however, without the ability to master the new knowledge, producers went under. On the other hand, education might provide the ability, but institutional conditions stifle the incentive. Education may be one essential element for economic growth; it does not of course assure development.

Needs for Research

I should like to emphasize that I consider these tentative generalizations about historical experience as far from well established. Indeed, though they seem more consistent with this fragment of (untested) data than do remarks to the contrary, I put them forward with considerable reluctance, for they suffer from other defects common to such propositions. Specifically, "knowledge," or "technology," is left in its usual amorphous state, "education" is far too aggregative, and geographic differences within countries are obliterated. In concluding, therefore, I wish to argue for research that, while following from the comment to this point, may enable one to observe in more concrete terms the relation between education and the movement of technological knowledge. This type of research has also been put forward by Mr. Mosher, namely, an investigation of the *specific* types of education which have been associated with the adoption of *specific* techniques.

I would suggest first that such investigation should be in terms of small, sub-national geographic units over time, such as are employed in Professor Hägerstrand's paper. It is disturbing that except for the session devoted to historical experience most of the discussion in the Conference views the world as divided into two parts—developed and underdeveloped (or to use the current euphemism, "developing"). This view ignores the heterogeneity within the two areas—some parts of developed countries are still underdeveloped; some parts of underdeveloped countries are developed. Why not widen the range of experience under study by recognizing subdivisions of as many countries as possible, both underdeveloped *and* developed, adopters *and* non-adopters of modern technology? Furthermore, this dichotomy ignores history: some (perhaps all) of the areas now in the developed category were once in the underdeveloped. How did *they* acquire the new knowledge? As Kuznets has implied, the problem of underdeveloped areas today— viewed in historical perspective—is essentially the same problem of mastering new knowledge that at an earlier time faced today's developed areas. In discussing the problem of transferring knowledge to less developed areas today, we are discussing only the latest phase of a process stretching back into history.

Secondly, I would suggest that "education" be disaggregated much further—the Conference discussion tended to distinguish technical from general, formal from informal, and that is about all. But as Eckaus pointed out, this does not really tell us much about what is involved in education. What subjects were taught? What materials used? How much time was devoted to each? How were they taught? We need to know much more about the content of education in time and space than is provided by simple aggregative concepts and figures.

Finally, the content of the new knowledge or technology needs to be identified. Instead of general references to modern or industrial technology — which cannot to my knowledge be quantified — we should examine the introduction and spread of specific techniques. Here I would like especially to include agricultural improvement, which is so often ignored in the broad references to "technology." On this issue, Professor Hägerstrand's fascinating paper points a way toward measurement of the growth and diffusion of specific innovations.

In sum, I am arguing for historical studies (including current experience) of the relation between specific forms of formal and informal education and the spread of specific innovations. In such studies, small local areas would be the unit of association; national boundaries, as well as the great one between developed and underdeveloped, would be subordinated. In this way, we might perhaps be able to establish with some confidence the connection between the acquisition of new techniques and educational attainment of the population.

Appendix

SOME UNREFINED DATA ON SCHOOL ENROLLMENT

Author's Note:

The attached tables were compiled from the secondary sources indicated in the table notes. With few exceptions figures were transcribed as published without attempting to identify or adjust for variations in time and space in coverage or concept. Though generally restricted to primary, secondary, higher, and technical schools, occasionally data for nursery and adult schools are included. The 1954 figures omit entirely enrollments in higher education, but the downward bias is less than six-tenths of a percentage point for all countries except the United States and Canada. Among other comparability problems are the occasional inclusion of attendance rather than enrollment data (the former tend to be somewhat lower); variations in the time of year for which enrollment data are reported; differences in the length of the school day and school year; and differences in the proportion of school age to total population. The last doubtless results in a downward bias in the twentieth-century data for a number of developed countries where a decline in the ratio of school age to total population followed with a lag the decline in the birth rate.

Table 1

*Estimated Percentage of Total Population Enrolled in School,
Selected Countries in Europe, Northern America,
and Oceania, 1830–1954*

	(1) 1830	(2) 1850	(3) 1878	(4) 1887	(5) 1928	(6) 1954
England and Wales°	⎫	12	⎫	16	16	15
Scotland	⎬ 9	—	⎬ 15	16	17	17
Ireland	⎭	7	⎭	14	18	20
USA	15	18	19	22	24	22
Canada	⎫ 6	—	⎫ 21	20	—	20
Australia	⎭	—	⎭	14	16#	17
Germany	17	16†	17	18	17	13‡‡
Switzerland	13	—	15	18	13°°	13
Netherlands	⎫ 12	13	⎫ 16	14	19	20
Belgium	⎭	12	⎭	11	15††	15
Denmark	⎫	14‡	⎫	12	16	16
Norway	⎬ 14	14	⎬ 14	13	17	14
Sweden	⎭	13	⎭	15	13	15
Finland	—	—	—	17	13	17
France	7	10	13	15	11	15
Austria	⎫ 5	⎫ 7	⎫ 9	13	14	13
Hungary	⎭	⎭	⎭	12	16	14
Italy	3	—	7	11	11	13
Poland	—	—	—	—	14	13
Czechoslovakia	—	—	—	—	16	16
Spain	4	—	8	11	11	11§§
Portugal	—	1	—	5	6	11
Yugoslavia	—	—	—	3″	10	13
Bulgaria	—	—	—	9	12	15″″
Rumania	—	—	—	2	12	13
Greece	—	5	—	6	12	15
Russia/USSR	—	2§	2	3	12	15

SOURCES:

Cols. 1,3: Michael G. Mullhall, *The Progress of the World* (London, 1880), p. 89.

Col. 2: J.D.B. DeBow, *Statistical View of the United States* (Washington, 1854), pp. 42, 147-8. Estimates shown here are based primarily on data on students given in text discussion, pp. 147-8, rather than Table CLI, since latter appeared to be in error for several countries, notably for Sweden, Denmark, and Holland. Also "England and Wales" is incorrectly labeled "Great Britain" in the table.

Col. 4: U.S. Bureau of Education, *Report of the Commissioner of Education 1888-89* (Washington, 1891), pp. 76-7, except for Australia, from Michael G. Mullhall, *Dictionary of Statistics*, 4th ed. (London, 1899), p. 231.

Col. 5: Bureau International d'Education, *L'Organisation de L'instruction publique dans 53 Pays* (Geneva, 1932), pp. 6-370, except Belgium and Switzerland, from United Nations, Department of Social Affairs, *Preliminary Report on the World Social Situation* (New York, 1952), pp. 91-2.

Col. 6: United Nations, Bureau of Social Affairs, *Report on the World Social Situation* (New York, 1957), pp. 82, 84-86.

GENERAL NOTE: For each country, estimate is for date for which data are available closest to that shown at head of column. Deviations rarely exceed two years. Unless otherwise specified, national boundaries are for date shown.

°Estimate for England and Wales in 1818, 6 per cent: DeBow, *Statistical View. . . ., op. cit.*, p. 148.

†Based on data for Prussia, Bavaria, Saxony, and Würtemburg, covering about two-thirds of the German population.

‡Primary schools only.

§"Russia in Europe."

"Estimate for Servia.

#Based on data for about 60 per cent of Australian population.

°°1938 estimate of primary school enrollment as per cent of total population plus 1949 estimate of post-primary enrollment (excluding technical schools) as per cent of total population.

††1937 estimate of primary school enrollment as per cent of total population plus 1948 estimate of post-primary enrollment as per cent of total population.

‡‡Federal Republic of Germany (including West Berlin).

§§Public schools only.

""Includes enrollment in evening courses.

TABLE 2

Estimated Percentage of Total Population Enrolled in School,
Selected Countries in Latin America, Asia,
and Africa, 1887–1954

	(1) 1887	(2) 1928	(3) 1938	(4) 1954
Latin America°				
Argentina	7	14	16§	16
Chile	4	—	15	18
Cuba	3	—	14	13
Mexico	5	9	11	12
Peru	–	—	8″	12
Venezuela	5	—	8	12
Colombia	2	—	9#	10
Brazil	3	—	9°°	9
Asia				
Japan	7‡	13	17††	23
Philippines	–	—	12	19
Thailand	–	—	9	16
South Korea	–	—	4‡‡	17
India	2	4	4§§	7
Burma	–	—	3	7
China (Mainland)	–	2	3″″	10
Indonesia	–	—	4	9
Pakistan	–	—	—	7
Iran	–	—	1	5
Turkey †	3	4	5	9
Africa				
Egypt	3	6	8##	10
Algeria	3	—	3	6
Morocco	–	—	1	5
Nigeria	–	—	1	5
Belgian Congo	–	—	2	9°°°
Un. South Africa	4	9	10	11°°°,22†††

Col. 1: U.S. Bureau of Education source cited for Table 1, column 4, except Japan, India, Egypt, Algeria, and Union of South Africa, from Mulhall source cited in same place.

Col. 2: Bureau International d'Education source cited for Table 1, column 5.

Col. 3: United Nations, Department of Social Affairs, *Preliminary Report on the World Social Situation* (New York, 1952), pp. 86-90, 94-6. Since 1938 data were given only for primary school enrollment as percentage of total population, these were increased by adding data for earliest postwar year (around 1947-50) on post-primary school enrollment as percentage of total population as given in same source table.

Col. 4: Same source as for Table 1, column 6 (pp. 79-84).

GENERAL NOTE: For each country, estimate is for date for which data are available closest to that shown at head of column. Deviations rarely exceed two years. Unless otherwise specified, national boundaries are for date shown.

°Estimate for "Spanish America" in 1830, 2 per cent; in 1878, 4 per cent: (Mulhall, *Progress of the World, op. cit.*, p. 89).

†Estimate for Turkey in 1830, 2 per cent; in 1878, 2 per cent: *Ibid.*, p. 89.

‡Estimate for Japan in 1901-2, 11 per cent: U.S. Bureau of Education, *Report of the Commissioner of Education 1902* (Washington, 1903), II, p. 2400.

§Excluding technical and agricultural schools.

"Public schools only.

#Excludes 270 secondary schools (out of 713) not reporting.

°°Including kindergartens.

††Estimate for primary school enrollment only.

‡‡Includes North Korea.

§§Includes Pakistan.

""Excludes Manchuria.

##Including elementary, kindergarten, and preparatory schools.

°°°Non-European population.

†††European population.

INDEX

QUEEN MARY
COLLEGE
LIBRARY

WITHDRAWN
FROM STOCK
QMUL LIBRARY

TF 093830

Dumfries and Galloway Libraries, Information and Archives

This item is to be returned on or before the last date shown below.

ST

29 OCT 03 ST   E 8 NOV 2005 ST

-5 DEC 2003

□2 DEC 03 ST   [1 7 FEB 2006] ST
-3 DEC nz ST   E 5 JAN 2007 ST

27 DEC 03 ST   [2 4 JAN 2009 ST

=7 JAN 04 ST
                1 APR 2010 ST
29 JAN 04 ST
[1 2 FEB 04 sy 2 0 JAN 2011 ST
[19 FEB 04 ST
E 6 MAR 04 ST [1 6 FEB 2011 ST
                [1 7 SEP 2011 ST

E 5 MAY 04   1 0 DEC 2012 ST
28 MAY 04 ST
                2 2 MAY 2013 ST
                2 8 FEB 2014 ST
[1 6 DEC 2004 ST
                0 7 APR 2014 ST
                2 6 APR 2014 ST
1 6 JUL 2005 ST
[1 7 OCT 2005 ST   2 7 AUG 2018

F

Awarded for excellence in public service
Dumfries and Galloway
Libraries, Information and Archives

Dumfries and Galloway
L I B R A R I E S
Information and Archives

Central Support Unit: Catherine Street Dumfries DG1 1JB
tel: 01387 253820   fax: 01387 260294   e-mail: libs&i@dumgal.gov.uk

24 HOUR LOAN RENEWAL BY PHONE AT LO-CALL RATE - 0845 2748080
OR ON OUR WEBSITE - WWW.DUMGAL.GOV.UK/LIA